Bentley, Gerald Eades

THE PROFESSIONS OF DRAMATIST AND PLAYER
IN SHAKESPEARE'S TIME, 1590–1642

One-volume paperback edition

The Profession of Dramatist in Shakespeare's Time 1590-1642

GERALD EADES BENTLEY

Published by Princeton University Press,
41 William Street, Princeton, New Jersey 08540
In the United Kingdom:
Princeton University Press, Guildford, Surrey
Copyright © 1971, 1984 by Gerald Eades Bentley

First Princeton Paperback printing, 1986
LCC 85-43372
ISBN 0-691-01426-4 (pbk.)

To Ellen

This paperback edition combines in one volume Gerald
Eades Bentley's *The Profession of Dramatist in Shakespeare's
Time* (1971) and *The Profession of Player in Shakespeare's
Time* (1984). A few corrections have been made to *The
Profession of Dramatist in Shakespeare's Time*. The pagination
remains the same for both books. Clothbound editions of
Princeton University Press books are printed on acid-free
paper, and binding materials are chosen for strength and
durability. Paperbacks, while satisfactory for personal col-
lections, are not usually suitable for library rebinding.

Printed in the United States of America by
Princeton University Press, Princeton, New Jersey

To Ellen

Preface

FOR MORE than two centuries there has been much speculation about the circumstances of the composition of individual plays by the best-known Elizabethan dramatists—especially Shakespeare. Many of these studies have been illuminating, but not infrequently they have postulated circumstances which would have been highly abnormal, if not impossible, in the usual situation of a professional dramatist in the reigns of Elizabeth, James, and Charles. But what were the ordinary working conditions during the years of the greatest flowering of the English drama? This book is an explication of the normal working environment circumscribing the activities of those literary artists who were making their living by writing for the London theatres.

A good many of the facts I have marshaled in this explication are to be found, usually in other contexts, in the fourteen volumes of *The Elizabethan Stage, The Jacobean and Caroline Stage*, Greg's edition of *Hens-*

lowe's Diary, and J. Q. Adams's edition of *The Dramatic Records of Sir Henry Herbert*. Others come from contemporary lawsuits, contracts, and agreements, the front matter of seventeenth-century editions of plays, miscellaneous publications of the time, and a few from remarks of dramatic characters making obvious allusions to customs or attitudes familiar to their audiences.

Perhaps I ought to explain the chronological limits which have been set. The terminal date is obvious enough. On 2 September 1642 the Puritan-dominated Parliament issued "An Order of the Lords and Commons Concerning Stage-Plays," directing "that while these sad Causes and set times of Humiliation doe continue, publike Stage-Playes shall cease, and bee forborne." For eighteen years thereafter only the most sporadic and profitless dramatic performances were staged in England, and no professional playwright could carry on his old vocation. The earlier date is less obvious, for some argument could be made for beginning at 1558 or at 1576. I have selected 1590 because by that date the organization of acting companies and theatres was well developed, many men were writing plays, and it was becoming possible for the steadiest of them to make a living preparing scripts for the regular London acting companies. Before 1590, moreover, records are so scanty, and such a large proportion apply to amateur or semiprofessional theatrical activities, that conclusions about working conditions must be very shaky. One cannot even be sure that a profession of play-writing had yet developed.

The Elizabethan spelling, capitalization, and punctuation of the longer quotations has been reluctantly modernized, but for one- or two-line passages, such as extracts from title pages or pithy remarks from legal testimony, I have succumbed to long habit and retained the form of the original.

viii

Most of the material used here I collected while I was engaged in research for *The Jacobean and Caroline Stage*, often with only the vaguest idea of what use I could ever make of it. Accordingly my indebtedness to the research institutions which have fostered my work extends over a long period. I am grateful for the hospitality and help of the Public Record Office, the Guildhall Library, Somerset House, the British Museum, the Bodleian, Cambridge University Library, the Huntington, the Folger, the Houghton, and the Newberry Libraries. They provide not only precious collections of books and manuscripts but also that atmosphere of devotion to learning which is a comfort and a stimulus to their readers.

This book has been improved by the generous advice of Alfred Harbage and Miriam Brokaw, who saw problems and suggested solutions which had eluded me. Patrick O'Donnell checked hundreds of quotations and references and pointed out a number of faulty inferences. Joanna Hitchcock has been the most meticulous and helpful editor I have ever had. To all of them I am grateful.

G.E.B.
Princeton
May 1971

Contents

THE PROFESSION OF DRAMATIST
IN SHAKESPEARE'S TIME, 1590–1642

CHAPTER I

Introduction

IN THE GREAT DAYS of the "Elizabethan" drama the production of plays for the London populace was largely in the hands of professionals. Indeed, the rise of professionalism in dramatic affairs in the last quarter of the sixteenth century is one of the distinguishing marks of the emergence of "the Age of the Drama." Before the accession of Elizabeth and even halfway through her reign, English drama was almost wholly amateur.

The episodes of the great medieval English cycles were staged and acted by men who were earning their living as glovers, shipwrights, bakers, cordwainers, bowyers, fletchers, mercers, and butchers, not by professional actors and producers. The plays they performed are nearly all anonymous, but there is no evidence whatever that they were written by men supporting themselves by dramatic writing, and there is much evidence to the contrary. Even the moralities and interludes of the sixteenth century, though they were often performed by groups of strolling professional players, were written by men whose time was principally devoted to nondramatic activities, as a glance at the most important writers of plays before the reign of Elizabeth will show. Henry Medwall and John Bale and Nicholas Grimald were clergymen; Nicholas Udall and George Buchanan were schoolmasters and scholars; John Rastell was a lawyer and printer; John Heywood was a musician and entertainer. The dramatic entertainment of the Middle Ages and early sixteenth century in England was produced in buildings or at sites used only occasionally for acting: there were no permanent theatres. Thus the enterprise of writing and presenting plays was largely an amateur one before 1558: part-time playwrights, part-time playhouses, part-time managers and producers, and, until the time of the strollers and the court troupe, part-time actors.

A little of this amateur dramatic activity extended into the later years of Elizabeth and the reigns of James and Charles, for plays continued to be performed by students at schools and at the colleges in Oxford and Cambridge; by lawyers for their entertainments at the Inns of Court; occasionally by apprentices in London; sometimes by guests and the household at great houses such as Draiton and Chartley, where the servants and family of the Earl of Essex produced plays and masques, or at Apthorpe, where the plays and shows of the Earl of Westmorland were performed by his children and servants. But these amateur enterprises were the exceptions. The overwhelming majority of the plays witnessed by the subjects of Elizabeth in her later days and by those of her two successors were performed in buildings planned and built for the presentation of plays, and acted by men and boys whose profession was acting. This much professionalism in the drama of the days of the greatest English achievement has been generally acknowledged for a long time.[1]

1. Professionalism was recognized as early as 1699 in the first account of the English drama of the earlier seventeenth century,

Since professionalism in the presentation of plays during the reigns of Elizabeth, James, and Charles has been so commonly observed for nearly three centuries, and since the development of such professionalism has often been accounted one of the significant stages in the development

---

Historia Histrionica . . . A Dialogue of Plays and Players. The first ten pages of this pamphlet, dealing with personal reminiscences of drama in the reigns of James and Charles, discuss professional actors and professional playing places and the existence of amateur productions is scarcely noticed, though a good deal is said about them in the second half, which is concerned mostly with secondhand information about medieval and sixteenth-century dramatic activities. Edmund Malone, in his *Account of our Ancient Theatres* and *Historical Account of the Rise and Progress of the English Stage,* both published in 1790, concentrates on playing by professional actors in buildings to be used as theatres. The same is true of the standard nineteenth-century histories of the "Elizabethan" dramatic achievement. J. P. Collier's three-volume *History of English Dramatic Poetry to the Time of Shakespeare and Annals of the Stage to the Restoration,* 1831, includes much discussion of amateurs in the long section dealing with English plays from the twelfth century to 1575, but the following 360 pages of his *Annals* are devoted almost wholly to productions of professional actors. Similarly Frederick Gard Fleay's *Chronicle History of the London Stage, 1559–1642,* published in 1890, deviates from the professional theatre only in its discussion of the masques at court; each of his seven discursive chapters has a separate section retailing the actions of each professional company, and another summarizing the history and occupancy of each professional theatre.

In the twentieth century the same realization that professional actors and professional theatres dominated the presentation of plays to Londoners is basic for the writers of the major studies. In his standard four-volume work, *The Elizabethan Stage,* 1923, Sir Edmund Chambers devotes his second volume to actors and theatres. In his section on "The Play-Houses" about 95 percent of the space is given to professional theatres; in the section on performing groups about 75 of the 294 pages are given to boy companies, a few of which were amateur or only semiprofessional; nearly all the names in his dictionary of actors are those of professionals like Edward Alleyn, Christopher Beeston, Richard Burbage, Henry Condell, Nathan Field, John Heminges, William Sly, and Richard Tarlton.

In more specialized studies, the same proportions reflect the same

of mature English drama, it is somewhat surprising that the development of professionalism in the *writing* of plays has not been observed as frequently as the development of professionalism in the *presenting* of them. In fact, none of the standard histories cited in note one develops the distinction between amateur or occasional writers for the stage and fully professional playwrights; indeed, most of them show little awareness that there was a difference.

This unawareness seems, at first glance, to be very curious indeed. Nearly all those dramatic historians who have considered "Elizabethan drama" have noted that, with

---

judgment of the comparative importance of professionalism. Joseph Quincy Adams published his *Shakespearean Playhouses: A History of English Theatres from the Beginning to the Restoration* in 1917. Adams begins with the fifteenth century, and his initial discussions concern innyards which were occasionally used for the presentation of plays. But he devotes only 17 pages to these part-time playing places, and more than 400 pages to the permanent theatre buildings, like the Globe, the Fortune, the Red Bull, the Swan, the Rose, the Blackfriars, the Phoenix, and Salisbury Court. Even these proportions underrate the professional dominance, for at least one of his innyards, that of the Boar's Head in Whitechapel, had a permanent stage and permanent seats for a paying audience, and in 1604 the Boar's Head was a principal theatre for Queen Anne's men and had been for at least two years (see G. E. Bentley, *The Jacobean and Caroline Stage*, Oxford, 1941–1968, VI, 121–31).

The same dominance of the professionals is apparent in John Tucker Murray's *English Dramatic Companies, 1558–1642*, 2 vols., 1910. The first volume devotes 322 pages to the adult professionals and only 45 to all the boy companies, some of which—like Beeston's Boys—were highly professional. The second volume is given over to acting troupes in the provinces, and these records are often too laconic to be revealing about the identity of the visiting players. The most numerous records concern the provincial tours of the professional companies of London, but a number of the names of other troupes are not mentioned in any other documents, and they may have been almost anything, even amateurs. But in any case, there is no evidence that these purely provincial troupes—professional or amateur—had any perceptible influence on the development of the "Elizabethan" drama.

occasional exceptions—like the halls of great houses or of royal palaces or of the Inns of Court—the buildings for which Shakespeare, Jonson, Webster, and Fletcher prepared their masterpieces were structures designed and built for the performance of plays and seldom used for anything else; i.e., they were *professional* buildings. And they have noted that the men who acted in these performances were, with scattered exceptions, such as the officers of an English ship at sea, or the children of the Earl of Westmorland, or students at Oxford and Cambridge, supporting themselves and their families by acting plays, when not prevented by plague or bankruptcy; i.e., they were *professional* actors. Why has there been so little discussion of the fact that professional playwrights developed in this period as did professional actors and professional playing places? Even the violent theatre-haters of the time, like William Prynne, recognized that there were professional dramatists as well as professional actors. On the long and intemperate title page of his notorious *Histriomastix, The Players' Scourge, or Actors' Tragedy*, published in 1633, he proclaims

. . . that the Profession of Play-poets, of Stage-Players; together with the penning, acting, and frequenting of Stage-playes are unlawful, infamous, and misbeseeming Christians. . . .

The reason that professionalism among the "Elizabethan" dramatists has been so seldom discussed or even recognized by critics and historians in the nineteenth and twentieth centuries is not far to seek. In spite of the fact that a large part of the drama which William Prynne so hated and feared was written by professional playwrights (i.e., men who, for long periods, were writing plays for profit), the greatest of these writers have usually been thought of in the category of poets, not of dramatists. Their professionalism has received comparatively little attention because their productions have commonly been examined as literary phenomena rather than as working scripts for professional actors in a professional theatre. Most often the plays have been analyzed and evaluated as poetry or as philosophy; sometimes as psychology, or (more recently) as sociology. This common antiprofessional attitude towards the masterpieces of the professional dramatists can be seen in hundreds of examples. The attitude is neatly summarized in a couple of sentences from a review published in February 1970 of a book which had first appeared in 1956: "——reads Shakespeare's plays as though they were difficult poems. Readers like myself, who think that's the right way to do it, place this book among the permanent modern contributions of Shakespeare criticism."

In fields such as nondramatic poetry, philosophy, psychology, or sociology the experience and maturity of the writer studied is certainly of importance, but his professionalism is of little consequence. The poet and the philosopher work alone; the cooperation of most nondramatic writers with their colleagues in presentation—copyists, printers, editors, booksellers—is often of biographical interest, but only occasionally is it a prime consideration in the impact made by his creation upon its intended audience.

In the world of the theatre, on the other hand, the impact of the author's creation is in good part determined by the playwright's cooperation with his colleagues in presentation. The tailoring of the literary product to the qualities of the actors, the design of the theatre, and the current conventions of production is of vital importance in achieving the effects which the author planned. The production of plays, in whatever era, is always a cooperative art. Though the Renaissance poet or writer of romances could compose as many songs as he liked in the parts of as many characters as he chose, the playwright could not. If he was a professional working for a repertory group (as all "Elizabethan" professionals were) he knew that songs could be written into the parts of only those actors who sang well; he knew that the roles of women and children must be limited to the number which could be handled by the boys presently in his company; he knew that if he wanted more adult male characters than the number of sharers and hired men in his troupe (as he generally did) he must plan the structure of his play to allow for doubling;[2] he knew that he must take into consideration the character of the audience for which he was writing: at the Red Bull it was notoriously vulgar, at the Blackfriars it was notoriously sophisticated.

Because of such inescapable realities of the theatre, professionalism in the playwright is of far greater significance than in the nondramatic poet, the novelist, or the essayist. The relations of Spenser or of Francis Bacon with their printers are always of biographical interest and sometimes of textual importance, but they did not normally require any alteration of the author's conception of *The Faerie Queene* or of *Novum Organum* to allow for the number of compositors in the printing house, or the size of the edition proposed, or the format of the volume to be sold.

Since professionalism is important in the theatre, and since it has been so frequently noted in the development of acting organizations and of playhouses, one ought to profit from a study of professionalism among writers for the theatres in the years of the finest florescence of the English drama, 1590–1642. How many truly professional playwrights were there? Who were they? What proportion of the plays of the time did they write? What were the normal conditions of their working situations? What was their usual output? Who paid them, and how much? How often and in what way did they collaborate? How often and by whom were their plays revised? Who cen-

2. See David Bevington, *From Mankind to Marlowe*, Cambridge, Mass., 1962, and William A. Ringler, Jr., "The Number of Actors in Shakespeare's Early Plays," in G. E. Bentley, *The Seventeenth-Century Stage*, Chicago, 1968, pp. 110–34.

sored their manuscripts, and for what? What was expected of them besides the preparation of the original scripts for their theatres? What did they have to do with the publication of their plays?

The ensuing chapters of this book are designed to organize and present a representative portion of what has survived of the once copious theatrical materials which can help to answer these questions. Such questions cannot, of course, be resolved in complete detail for each dramatist because of the destruction of the vast majority of all theatre records. But enough remain to enable us to trace the general outlines of the normal professional life of a writer of plays in these years.

CHAPTER II

Amateur Dramatists and Professional Dramatists

A THOUGHTFUL CONSIDERATION of all plays and playwrights in England during the period 1590–1642 underscores the fact that the plays of the time were provided by writers who varied widely in motive and in theatrical experience. Most clearly defined are the amateurs who were not writing primarily for profit, who generally showed a certain disdain for the commercial theatres, who usually hurried their plays into print, who, with a few exceptions, wrote only one or two plays, and whose productions were usually prepared for amateur actors.

At the opposite end of the scale were the regular professional playwrights who supported themselves and their families by providing plays for the London theatres, whose production of play scripts was copious and generally regular, and whose attitude toward publication was much more reserved than that of the amateurs. When I call these men professionals, I am implying nothing about their excellence. The terms "professional" and "professionalism" are used here and throughout this book in sense II: 4b of the *Oxford English Dictionary*,

> Undertaken or engaged in for money or as a means of subsistence; engaged in by professionals as distinct from amateurs.

Although the plays of the professionals are generally better plays than those of the amateurs, professionals sometimes wrote bad plays and amateurs occasionally wrote good ones. Such distinctions, while interesting and important in many contexts, are not relevant here.

Between these two extremes of the amateur and the regular professional are twenty or thirty experienced writers who show some but never all the characteristics of one or another of these two classes. They wrote plays for the commercial theatres, and they generally wrote for profit. They wrote a good many more plays than the amateurs, but their associations with the London acting companies were less close and exclusive than those of the regular professionals. Like the amateurs they generally had significant sources of income (often nondramatic writing or patronage) other than the London theatres, but they did not disdain the financial rewards of play-writing as most of the amateurs did, or at least pretended to do.

Thus the most essential differentiating characteristic of the regular professional dramatist was his primary dependence on the commercial theatres for his livelihood. In a time when the social status of the playwright was low, the biographical data concerning the writers of plays is inevitably scanty, and our knowledge of the sources of a dramatist's income is therefore largely inferential; but it is not so very difficult to classify roughly into amateurs or professionals most of the 250 or so men who are known to have written plays in England between about 1590 and 1642. Indeed, the low social status of people regularly concerned with commercial theatres, a status which inhibited the writing of biographies of even such successful and comparatively respected playwrights as the "great triumvirate" (Ben Jonson, William Shakespeare, and John Fletcher),[1] is in some respects a help. Those men who were anxious to be considered gentlemanly amateurs, in spite of the fact that they had written one or more plays which may have been acted in the London theatres, often arranged (unlike the majority of the regular professionals) to secure a fairly prompt publication of their plays. And in dedications, or addresses to the readers, or prefaces, or prologues they shrilly proclaimed their nonprofessional status.

A fairly characteristic example of the attitude of the amateur dramatist toward professionalism is to be seen in the front matter of the 1639 edition of Jasper Mayne's *The City Match*, acted at court and later in the Blackfriars theatre. The address to the reader says:

> The Author of this Poem, knowing how hardly the best things protect themselves from censure, had no ambition to make it this way public, holding works of this light nature to be things which need an apology for being written at all, nor esteeming otherwise of them, whose abilities in this kind are most passable, than of masquers who spangle and glitter for the time, but 'tis thorough tinsel. As it was merely out of obedience that he first wrote it, so when it was made, had it not been commanded from him, it had died upon the place where it took life. . . .

And the same attitude is reiterated in Mayne's court prologue for his play:

Prologue to the King and Queen

. . . . . .

1. The designation is a seventeenth-century, not a modern, one. See G. E. Bentley, *Shakespeare and Jonson: Their Seventeenth Century Reputations Compared*, rev. ed., Chicago, 1969, pt. 1, pp. 67–68, and pt. 2, pp. 8–9, 12, 232.

Such works, he thinks, are but condemn'd to live

.   .   .   .   .   .

For he is not o' th' trade, nor would excel
In this kind, where 'tis lightness to do well.

Jasper Mayne's concern to clear his amateur skirts of any soil "o' th' trade" is repeated by other men who were anxious lest anyone might think that they would demean themselves to provide plays regularly for the commercial theatres.

A further means of differentiating between the professionals and the other writers of plays is the notably larger number of scripts known to have been prepared by those men at least partially dependent upon the commercial theatres for their livelihood. Not only are the known canons far larger for the professionals than for the others, but the difference in output between them was certainly even greater than we can now discover: their involvement with plays of presently unknown authorship, with lost plays, and with plays not even known by title was extensive. The number of these anonymous, lost, and wholly disappeared plays is great, and it is salutary to pause for a moment to consider them.

About 350 anonymous plays are known at least by title from the period 1590–1642.[2] And we are forced to conclude from the evidence of Henslowe's diary that a good proportion of the plays performed in the London theatres have vanished without leaving any evidence that they ever existed—not even an anonymous title.

The theatrical accounts of Philip Henslowe for the period 1592–1602 are spotty, but they are many times as full as any other diurnal theatrical records before the Restoration. Henslowe set down his receipts from the performances of named plays for seven scattered periods between

2. Most of them are listed in E. K. Chambers, *The Elizabethan Stage*, Oxford, 1923, IV, 1–55, and in *Jacobean and Caroline Stage*, V, 1281–1456.

February 1591/92 and November 1597, a total of 40-odd months of recorded performances in a period of 69 months. On other pages of the same ledger he set down his payments to writers for furnishing his companies with named plays during the latter half of this decade, that is, 1597–1602. The total number of different plays mentioned in these two independent sets of incomplete records of the activities of this single manager is about 280.

Of these 280 named plays, only about 40 are still extant, and at least 170 would now be totally unknown—even by title—had Henslowe's accounts been destroyed as were the vast majority of all other theatre records of the period 1590–1642. Even in the diary years of 1591/92 to 1602, how many plays from Henslowe's numerous rival and less well-documented theatres have disappeared without leaving a trace? Plays from the repertories of the Theatre, the Curtain, the Blackfriars, St. Paul's, the Swan, and the Globe—170 more?[3]

I doubt that the number of vanished plays is as great as, say, 340, or even 170, for each decade of the later period, 1612–1642. In those later years managers needed fewer new plays because they had available a far greater number of acceptable old plays suitable for revival (especially printed plays) than Philip Henslowe ever enjoyed, and because play publishing was more common than it had been

3. Fynes Moryson remarked on the extraordinary multiplicity of plays in London. After the publication of his *Itinerary* in 1617 he prepared further papers on his observation of European countries in his ten years of travel, papers which remained in manuscript until 1903. In the section on England, probably written about 1617–1620, Moryson says: "The City of London alone hath four or five companies of players with their peculiar theatres capable of many thousands, wherein they all play every day in the week except Sunday . . . as there be in my opinion more plays in London than in all the world I have seen" (Charles Hughes, *Shakespeare's Europe. Unpublished Chapters of Fynes Moryson's Itinerary. Being a Survey of the Condition of Europe at the End of the 16th Century.* London, 1903, p. 476).

from 1592 to 1602. Probably we now know at least the titles of a majority of the plays in the Jacobean and Caroline repertories of the second Blackfriars, the Phoenix, the Salisbury Court, and the Globe. But from the repertories of the less esteemed theatres—the Fortune, the Red Bull, the Hope, and the Curtain—we know the names of far fewer plays, even though performances were taking place at the Red Bull and the Fortune for 37 and 42 years respectively, and for only 25 years at the Phoenix and 13 at the Salisbury Court.[4]

From such evidence it seems conservative and reasonable to conclude that between 1590 and 1642 there probably were written as many as 500 plays of which we know not even the titles. Many of them are likely to have been prepared by dramatists already known to us from their extant plays,[5] and thus the canon of the professional dramatists is likely to have been even larger than it now appears. But ignoring the number of their plays which are probably

4. Compare the number of titles in the known repertories of the King's Men at the Blackfriars and the Globe, 1616–1642 (*Jacobean and Caroline Stage*, 1, 108–34) and those of the Lady Elizabeth's Company, Queen Henrietta's Company, and Beeston's Boys at the Phoenix and the Salisbury Court (ibid., 1, 194–97, 250–59, and 337–42) with the much smaller number assignable to companies acting at the four less esteemed theatres (ibid., 1, 156–57, 214–17, 282, 300–301, and 322–23).

5. Examples of plays unknown until the twentieth century though they were written by well-known dramatists are George Chapman's *The Old Joiner of Aldgate* (C. J. Sisson, *Lost Plays of Shakespeare's Age*, Cambridge, 1936, pp. 12–79), and Thomas Middleton's *The Viper and Her Brood* (*Modern Language Notes*, XLII [January 1927], 35–38). Even such a publication-conscious dramatist as Ben Jonson told William Drummond in 1619 "that the half of his comedies were not in print." If Jonson and Drummond were both reliable, this statement means that more than three of his plays are wholly unknown to us now, for in 1619 eleven of his acknowledged plays were in print, and we know of only eight of his other plays written before 1619, including collaborations, which had not been published by that year.

still unknown to us, the presently ascertainable output of the professional playwrights is large, notably larger than that of the semi-professionals and the amateurs.

Keeping in mind these general facts about the production and preservation of plays in England during the years 1590–1642, we can turn to the more particular characteristics of the different classes of playwrights in the period. It is not vital that there should be complete agreement on the category to which every single name is assigned, but it seems to me that the groups of professionals and amateurs were pretty much as outlined in the following sections.

The Amateurs

The amateurs who wrote plays for production in England between 1590 and 1642 are fairly easy to distinguish as a class. There were, of course, many more of them than of the dramatists who wrote for pay, but even with their larger numbers they were concerned with far fewer plays. There are approximately 1,200 plays written by known authors in the period, but of this number only about 265 were written by just over 200 amateur dramatists.

As these figures indicate, most of the amateurs wrote a single play, not infrequently for some special occasion. Such were many of the Latin plays composed for some university event and ordinarily acted in one of the college halls. Examples are Walter Hawkesworth's play called *Labyrinthus*, prepared for the Bachelor's Commencement and acted at Trinity College, Cambridge, in February or March 1602/1603; or John Chappell's *Susenbrotus, or Fortunia*, performed at Royston during a visit of King James and Prince Charles in March 1615/16; or Thomas Vincent's *Paria*, acted at Trinity, Cambridge, on the occasion of a visit of King Charles to the University on 3 March 1627/28.

But the occasional play by an amateur was not always in Latin, even at one of the universities. It might have been in English, like Peter Hausted's *The Rival Friends*, performed before the King and Queen at Trinity, Cambridge, in March 1631/32. Even the commercial theatres in London sometimes performed an amateur's only play. Such was John Clavell's single dramatic composition, *The Soddered Citizen* of about 1630. The play was performed by the King's company at their Blackfriars theatre, and the players had probably cajoled the piece out of Clavell, the author of *The Recantation for an ill led Life*, in order to exploit the sensation of the sentencing and later pardoning of this gentleman-turned-highwayman.

Similarly occasional was *The Launching of the Mary, or the Seaman's Honest Wife*, written during a voyage home from India by Walter Mountfort, an employee of the East India Company, to defend the company from certain charges and no doubt also to bolster his own shaky reputation with his employers.

The Hog hath Lost his Pearl was another such amateur single play, prepared by Robert Tailor for performance by a group of London apprentices in the Whitefriars theatre in February 1612/13. Unfortunately the apprentices' performance—allegedly critical of their betters—was suppressed by the sheriffs, and, so far as is known, Robert Tailor's dramatic career came to an end.

Occasional in a rather different environment was the comedy called *Apollo Shroving*, which William Hawkins, a schoolmaster at Hadleigh in Sussex, prepared for performance by his pupils on Shrove Tuesday 1626/27.

Another one-play amateur was Thomas Rawlins, whose tragedy called *The Rebellion* was acted with great success by the King's Revels company—presumably at the Red Bull. Rawlins was an engraver who later became chief engraver at the Royal Mint; like so many amateur writers of plays he was insistent that he was not a professional dramatist. Though he was himself an artist, Rawlins wrote for the 1640 quarto of his play an address which displays the usual gentlemanly attitude toward professional play-wrights. Condescendingly he warns his readers: "Take no note of my name, for a second work of this nature shall hardly bear it. I have no desire to be known by a thread-bare Cloak, having a Calling that will maintain it woolly."

This attitude toward the profession of play-writing is usual among the amateur dramatists. Indeed, one who reads through the front matter of all the plays of the period comes to see it as one of the hallmarks of the amateur.

But though the usual canon of the amateur dramatist in this period was one play, not all amateurs stopped after a single experience. An example of an amateur who wrote as many known plays as some of the writers for profit was Lodowick Carlell, Huntsman to Charles I, and later Keeper of the Royal Park at Richmond, who said in the prologue to one of his plays that hunting and gamekeep-ing and feeding his deer occupied his time, "Not some, but most fair days throughout the year."

Lodowick Carlell wrote eight plays—if each five-act part of his two-part plays is counted—four or five of which were performed by the King's company at Blackfriars. Yet he was an amateur and not a professional, or even a semi-professional, and he and his publishers were anxious to keep his status clear. The dedication to two courtiers of his *Deserving Favorite*, whose title page says "As it was lately Acted first before the Kings Maiestie, and since publikely at the Black-Friers" shows his attitude toward professional dramatists: "Approved Friends, this Play, which know at first was not design'd to travel so far as the common stage, is now pressed for a greater journey, almost without my knowledge."

An amateur playwright much more aristocratic than Lodowick Carlell was William Cavendish, then Earl and later Duke of Newcastle. Cavendish, who was also a patron of the drama, during his long lifetime rewarded at least half a dozen dramatists, one of whom, James Shirley, is said to have been an assistant in, if not the principal author of, his lordship's two pre-Commonwealth plays, *The Country Captain* and *The Variety*, both performed at Blackfriars in the last three years of the Caroline theatre.

Another noble playwright was Fulke Greville, Lord Brooke, in his early life a friend of Sir Philip Sidney and later a patron of dramatists, notably William Davenant.[6] Between 1594 and 1601 Greville wrote three tragedies, *Antonie and Cleopatra*, *Mustapha*, and *Alaham*. The first he himself destroyed; the other two are extant in both manuscript and print. Clearly, as Greville himself said, none was intended for the stage, and Greville's amateur standing can scarcely be doubted, but his lines seem to have had a great appeal to his contemporaries.[7]

Somewhat like Greville was William Percy, third son of the Earl of Northumberland, who left in autograph manuscript six plays apparently written between 1600 and 1603. Some of them he evidently intended to be acted by Paul's Boys before the end of the reign of Elizabeth, but there is no evidence that they ever were—or should have been.

Even the aristocratic ladies were sometimes tempted to dabble in the drama. Lady Elizabeth Cary, later Viscountess Falkland, wrote a lost play set in Syracuse, and another, published anonymously in 1613, called *The Tragedie of Miriam the Faire Queene of Jewry*.

These fourteen occasional writers are sample types of the more than 200 amateurs, men and women, who are known to have written plays in England between 1590

6. Nothing has ever been made of the statement by David Lloyd that Greville wanted to be known to posterity as the master of Shakespeare and Jonson, the patron of Chancellor Egerton, Bishop Overall's Lord, and Sir Philip Sidney's friend. See E. K. Chambers, *William Shakespeare*, Oxford, 1930, ii, 250.

7. See *Studies in Philology*, xl (April 1943), 200–201.

and 1642. Although about half those I have so far mentioned produced pieces which were performed in the London theatres, this is not true of the majority of amateurs; most of them prepared their plays for performance in Oxford or Cambridge colleges, at schools, at the Inns of Court, or at private houses. A number of these amateurs wrote closet drama which was not intended for performance anywhere.

The largest group of plays by amateurs was made up of those performed in Oxford and Cambridge colleges, a group which includes 30 to 40 percent of all the amateur plays known in the period. There are records of college play-acting in almost every year of the period, sometimes five or six or even eight in a single year.

Very occasionally a college play, written to be performed by the undergraduates and fellows of a college, such as Christ Church, Oxford, or Trinity, Cambridge, was later performed by the professional actors of the London companies. Such was the fortune of Jasper Mayne's *The City Match* and Thomas Goffe's *The Careless Shepherdess*. More notorious was William Cartwright's *The Royal Slave*, which was such a great success when performed by the students of Christ Church before the King and Queen at Oxford that it was staged again at Hampton Court by the King's players, but so far as is known they never acted it at Blackfriars or the Globe.

But these professional London revivals of Oxford and Cambridge plays were most unusual; many of the college plays were written in Latin, and as for the others, the London players no doubt agreed with the comment assigned to the veteran comedian, Will Kempe, by the university authors of the second part of *The Return from Parnassus*, produced in St. John's College, Cambridge, in 1601/1602: "Few of the university [men] pen plays well. They smell too much of that writer *Ovid*, and that writer *Metamorphoses*, and talk too much of *Proserpina* and

Jupiter. Why here's our fellow *Shakespeare* puts them all down, aye and *Ben Jonson* too."[8]

The same suspicions of university plays by the London professional theatre is seen 35 years later in the prologue written to still the misgivings of the Salisbury Court audience at the performance of Richard Lovelace's lost comedy, *The Scholars*: [9]

> A Gentleman to give us somewhat new,
> Hath brought up *Oxford* with him to show you;
> Pray be not frightened—Tho the Scæne and Gown's
> The *Universities*, the Wit's the Town's;
> The lines, each honest *Englishman* may speake;
> Yet not mistake his Mother-tongue for *Greeke*,
> For still 'twas part of his vow'd Liturgy,
> From learned Comedies *deliver me*!
> Wishing all those that lov'd 'em here asleep,
> Promising *Scholars*, but no *Scholarship*.

Another large group of amateur plays—about 40—was made up of closet drama, a type with which the writers for the commercial theatres were concerned only rarely. The plays of Fulke Greville and Lady Elizabeth Cary fall into this class, as do *Imperiale*, by Sir Ralph Freeman, Master of Requests, Thomas Neale's autobiographical *The Warde*, and the four *Monarchick Tragedies* written by Sir William Alexander, Earl of Stirling and tutor to Prince Henry. Late in the period satiric political tracts in the form of closet drama, like *Canterbury his Change of Diet*, begin to appear, and they become fairly common after the closing of the theatres.

Of the dramatic scripts written for private performance, many were entertainments, shows, satires, or little masques rather than plays, but complete plays were sometimes written by amateurs for only slightly known private

8. J. B. Leishman, ed., *The Three Parnassus Plays*, London, 1949, lines 1766–70.

9. See *Jacobean and Caroline Stage*, IV, 722–24.

occasions. Such was William Cartwright's *The Lady Errant* and Francis Quarles's *The Virgin Widow* and, most interesting of all, the series written by Mildmay Fane, Earl of Westmorland, for performance at his house at Apthorpe—*Candy Restored, The Change,* and *Time's Trick upon the Cards.*

Probably a good many more plays than we know now were written by amateurs like Mildmay Fane for productions in great houses like Apthorpe. The autobiography of Arthur Wilson, called *Observations of God's Providence in the Tract of my Life,* implies that such household theatricals were common. Wilson, a retainer of the Earl of Essex, says:

> The winters we spent in England [i.e. not campaigning in the Palatinate]. Either at Drayton, my Lord's grandmother's; Chartley, his own house; or some of his brother, the Earle of Hartford's houses. Our private sports abroad, hunting; at home, chess or catastrophe. Our public sports (and sometimes with great charge and expense) were masks or plays. Wherein I was a contriver both of words and matter. For as long as the good old Countess of Leicester lived (the grandmother to these noble families,) her hospitable entertainment was garnisht with such, then harmless, recreations.[10]

Wilson's own plays, extant in manuscript but not published until the nineteenth century, *The Corporal, The Inconstant Lady, or Better Late than Never,* and *The Swisser,* were presumably originally written for these great house performances, though all of them were later acted at Blackfriars.

In a time of great dramatic activity, more plays than we now know were probably written by totally untalented amateurs. No doubt the great majority of them have mercifully disappeared, but a few are extant in manuscript, or

10. Philip Bliss, ed., *The Inconstant Lady,* London, 1814, p. 119.

23

known by chance references. One such is the anonymous play of the reign of Charles I called *The Cyprian Conqueror, or the Faithless Relict*, extant only in a manuscript in the Sloane collection.[11] The plotting, stage directions, characterization, and lines are so immature that it is difficult to imagine that anyone anywhere in England would ever have listened to it; but the prologue and epilogue give evidence that the naïve author certainly hoped that they would.

More sensational, at least in its results, was the lost, unnamed play which brought the author, Jasper Garnett, and others before the Star Chamber in 1621. Garnett's play, acted at Kendal Castle in Westmorland, "was intended to present the case of the tenants of the barony" against the encroachments of the landlords. According to the Star Chamber records:

> One of the scenes showed an ingeniously constructed *hell* placed a little to the side and below the stage wherein ravens were supposedly feeding on poor sheep. Henry Ward and Thomas Ducket, two of the tenants, in their character of clown or fool inquired of a boy who stood looking into this hell what he saw there. The boy replied that he "did see Landlords and puritanes and Sheriffs bailiffs and other sorts of people," whereupon the one clown said to the other: "Ravens quotha, no, thou art far by the square, its false landlords makes all that croakings there, and those sheep we poor men, whose right these by their skill, would take away, and make us tenants at will, and when our ancient liberties are gone they'll puke and pool, & peel us to the bare bone."[12]

These amateur dramatists, though numerous and diverse, and indicative of the strong appeal of the drama in these years, were never people who looked to the commer-

11. See *Jacobean and Caroline Stage*, v, 1316–17.

12. Mildred Campbell, *The English Yeoman under Elizabeth and the Early Stuarts*, New Haven, 1942, p. 152.

cial theatres for a living. Though a very small percentage of the amateur plays did get to the London theatres, they were very seldom intended for them. When they did come to town they generally came to the Blackfriars because of royal enthusiasm for them in some other place, as did *The Royal Slave*, *The City Match*, and Carlell's plays.

Those amateur dramatists who expressed themselves on the subject normally looked down upon the commercial theatres and the professional dramatists. They tended to speak of plays, including their own, as trifles or baubles.

Playwrights for Profit

Though the count of about 265 dramatic pieces composed by about 200 amateur playwrights may seem large, it is a small part of the 1,200 plays written by assignable authors (i.e., eliminating anonymous compositions) during the years 1590–1642. Clearly amateurs were only minor participants in the great "Elizabethan" dramatic outburst; it was dominated by the writers who were selling their services to the Elizabethan, Jacobean, and Caroline professional acting companies.

These 900-odd plays which provided most of the entertainment in the London theatres over a period of 52 years offer several notable contrasts to the group of about 265 amateur dramatic compositions and their 200 authors. Most striking of course is the larger number of professional than amateur plays. Equally notable is the much smaller number of playwrights who were concerned with them. Except for a few authors of single plays, the more than 900 scripts for the commercial theatres were provided by some 50-odd writers. A few of them composed or collaborated in only two or three plays, often apparently in special circumstances, such as an emergency in which an actor or manager was persuaded to help out. Thus William Bird, alias Borne, a very active member of the Lord Admiral's–Prince Henry's–Palsgrave's companies and a friend and agent of Henslowe and Alleyn, helped out with *Judas* and with the revision of *Doctor Faustus*; and Charles Massey, a long-time member of the same groups, appears to have contributed to *The Siege of Dunkirk* and *Malcolm, King of Scots*. In 1623 and 1624 Richard Gunnell, the prominent actor and manager, supplied three plays to the struggling company at the Fortune, which he appears to have been managing.[13]

The great bulk of the theatrical fare in these years, something over 850 plays, was provided by 44 playwrights who clearly were not amateurs, though the number of plays they wrote and the time-span over which they worked for the theatres varied widely. Greene, Lyly, Marlowe, Peele, and Nashe wrote a good portion of their plays before 1590 and were dead or had deserted the commercial theatres before the end of the century. Thomas Jordan and John Tatham wrote a few plays for the Caroline companies, but the bulk of their work was done after the closing of the theatres. There are some 22 writers who wrote or collaborated in a dozen or more plays[14] for the commercial theatres in the period 1590–1642, who were clearly being paid for their literary efforts, and who in a general sense may be considered more or less professional, at least for a certain period of years. The list is comprised of the following men:

13. See R. A. Foakes and R. T. Rickert ed., *Henslowe's Diary*, Cambridge, 1961, pp. 185 and 206, and *Jacobean and Caroline Stage*, IV, 749 and 516–19.

14. There will not be universal acceptance of the exact number of plays written by each of these dramatists because scholars disagree on the exclusion or inclusion of a few plays—usually collaborations—in the canon of dramatists like Beaumont, Fletcher, Marston, Massinger, Middleton, and Rowley. On the whole I have been conservative, and I think few would vary from my count by more than two or three plays even in the canon of so uncertain a dramatist as Francis Beaumont. The elimination of masques, entertainments, and pageants reduces the numbers for men like Jonson, Middleton, and Anthony Munday.

Thomas Heywood	Richard Brome
John Fletcher	William Haughton
Thomas Dekker	George Chapman
Philip Massinger	Michael Drayton
Henry Chettle	Robert Wilson
Thomas Middleton	William Hathaway
William Shakespeare	Anthony Munday
James Shirley	John Ford
Ben Jonson	Wentworth Smith
William Rowley	John Webster
John Day	Francis Beaumont

It is useful to note how prolific these men were, especially in comparison with the amateurs, and to consider the concentration of their work for the theatres. Very little biographical information has been unearthed on several of the Henslowe playwrights, like Henry Chettle, John Day, William Hathaway, William Haughton, Wentworth Smith, and Robert Wilson; most of their plays are lost and we are dependent upon the diary for nearly all our information about them. But for at least fourteen of the others there is enough extant information about their company associations, their beginnings, their retirement from active work for the theatres, and the character of their plays to justify some tentative conclusions about their professional careers.

The professional who served the theatre for the longest period, Thomas Heywood, wrote an address to the reader for the 1633 quarto of his play *The English Traveller* some eight years before his death. In his address Heywood said that he had already written or at least "had a maine finger in" 220 plays.[15] John Fletcher wrote or col-

15. This figure provides another basic fact for any consideration of the number of plays written in this time which have vanished without leaving a trace. It is notable that of the 220 plays Heywood says he wrote before 1633, only 56—including collaborations and lost plays known by title—can now be identified, leaving 164 plays which are presently unknown or at least unassignable.

laborated in 69, nearly all of them prepared for the King's company. Thomas Dekker wrote at least 64 plays in a total period of 34 years, but for six years of this time he was in jail, and in the later part of his life his play-writing was only sporadic. In the years 1598 to 1602 alone he is known to have written all or parts of 44 different plays for Henslowe. Philip Massinger wrote all or parts of at least 55, the majority of them also for the King's men. Henry Chettle wrote or collaborated on 50 plays in about five years, according to Henslowe's records of his payments to dramatists. Shakespeare wrote 38, nearly all of them for the Lord Chamberlain–King's players. James Shirley also wrote at least 38, first for Queen Henrietta's company, and then, after his return from Ireland, for the King's men. Thomas Middleton wrote 31, excluding about a score of masques and pageants.

These numbers are large for the major dramatists of any time; when we remember that for each of them the number is almost certainly too small, we cannot fail to be impressed by the industry of these professionals. Even Heywood's monstrous 220 is too small a number for him, for he wrote at least two plays and four Lord Mayor's pageants after he had made his statement in 1633.

So far as presently available records show, these eight men were the most prolific playwrights of their day. But there were 14 others who wrote a large number of plays for profit and had many of the characteristics of the regular professionals for at least part of their careers. In some instances I suspect that the smaller number of their recognized plays is due to the fact that a larger portion of their output is lost or is still unrecognized; Anthony Munday is an example. In other cases the smaller number is due to the short period of time for which we have any records about the work of the man; William Haughton is known from Henslowe's diary to have contributed to 25 plays in five years; Richard Hathaway, 18 in five; and Wentworth Smith, 15 in two.

The fourteen additional playwrights who wrote a dozen or more plays for pay and had periods of attachment to London companies were Ben Jonson, who wrote 28 plays in 41 years; John Day, with 25 plays in ten years; William Rowley, 24 plays in 18 years; Richard Brome, 23 in 13 years, or 24 in 18; William Haughton, 23 in five years; Michael Drayton, 23 in five years; George Chapman, about 21 in 15 years; Robert Wilson, 20 in 20 years, but 16 of them for Henslowe in three years; Richard Hathaway, 18 plays in five years; Anthony Munday, 17 in nine years besides his entertainments; John Ford, 17 in 17 years; Wentworth Smith, 15 in two years and apparently one for amateurs about 12 years later; John Webster, 14 in about 24 years; and Francis Beaumont, about 14 in eight years.

These 22 men were the most prolific of more than 250 who are known to have written plays in the years between 1590 and 1642. They were all professionals in the limited sense that they were paid for writing a significant number of plays for acting companies at the commercial theatres. The most obvious characteristic of the group as a whole is that they were prolific; among them they provided perhaps half the 1,200 plays known from the period.[16] Nearly all of them wrote the major part of their literary work for actors, though several, like Ben Jonson, Thomas Middleton, and Anthony Munday prepared a number of scripts for actors at Court or in the City pag-

16. A simple addition of the number of plays in which each man is known to have participated gives an exaggerated total because of the number of collaborations involved. Most of Fletcher and Beaumont's compositions were collaborations, and so are counted at least twice in the list; and it is the same with Chettle, Haughton, Wilson, Hathaway, and Smith.

eants, in addition to the larger number designated for the commercial theatre in London. They were paid, of course, by all three groups.

The Attached or Regular Professionals

Within this group of 22 authors who served the commercial theatres there was a smaller group which I shall call attached or regular professionals. These men had a closer and more continuous association with the London theatres than the others. Their production of plays was more regular and consistent. They were, so far as our information goes, primarily dependent upon the theatres for their livelihood. They did not easily or frequently shift their company associations, but tended to work regularly for one troupe for long periods. I suspect that they had oral or written contracts with their companies. They had more reservations about publishing their own plays than Jonson or Chapman or Middleton had.

Perhaps the clearest way to indicate their differences from the other professionals is to point out the reasons why more than two-thirds of the 22 cannot be classified as regular professionals or attached professionals.

The first to be eliminated, and no doubt the one whose elimination may be most questioned, is Ben Jonson. His achievement as a playwright was great, and other writers of the seventeenth century praise him more frequently and more fulsomely than any other dramatist of their time.[17] He wrote a large number of plays, and he certainly had more to say in print about the standards and functions of dramatic composition than any of his contemporaries. Indeed, I should say that for the first period of his writing career Jonson may have been an attached professional or a regular professional, but these years were few. In the

17. See Bentley, *Shakespeare and Jonson*, I, 63–70; II, 52–53, 54–56, 58–59, 169–70, 206. See also the anonymous *Jonsonus Virbius*, London, 1638, passim.

period 1597–1602 he wrote at least eleven plays, six or seven for Philip Henslowe's companies and five for other companies, and there is evidence that for at least part of this period he was himself an actor. Before about 1600 he is not known to have had any significant means of support besides the theatre.

But this is not the pattern for most of Jonson's career, nor for his most distinguished years. From no later than 1602 he was not primarily dependent upon the commercial theatres for his livelihood. He is known to have had patrons for long periods.[18]

From 1604 to 1634 the production of Jonson's magnificent series of 41 court masques and entertainments must have absorbed a large proportion of that fabulous energy which had once gone into plays for the commercial theatres, for instead of producing about two plays a year as he had in his early days, in the later years, from 1604 to 1634, when he was much better known, plays appeared at the rate of only about one every two years. In 1619 Jonson told Drummond that "of all his Playes he had never Gained 2 hundred pounds." This is less than £10 per year, certainly too little to maintain Jonson in the circles he frequented in Jacobean times. From at least as early as 1602 a share of Jonson's creative energy was devoted to particu-

18. In February 1601/1602, John Manningham wrote in his diary, "Ben Jonson, the poet, now lives upon one Townshend and scornes the world," and for the following five years he seems to have lived with Lord Aubigny. In 1606, 1607, 1608, and 1609 the Earl of Salisbury paid him as much for each of four slight entertainments as other dramatists were getting for full-length plays (see Scott McMillan, "Jonson's Early Entertainments: New Information from Hatfield House," *Renaissance Drama*, n.s. [1968], pp. 153–66). In 1619 Jonson told William Drummond of Hawthornden that "every first day of the new year" the Earl of Pembroke sent him £20 to buy books. In these years between 1602 and 1619 more than twenty of his masques and entertainments—including most of the great ones—were produced under the patronage of the sovereign or of great nobles.

lar patrons who, in the mores of the time, were expected to be financially responsive.

These facts make it clear enough that after 1602 Jonson could not have been dependent on the commercial theatres for the major part of his support. But perhaps even more significant is the evidence to be found in his own repeated statements about himself and his work that in these years Jonson did not think of himself as a professional dramatist in the way that Heywood, Fletcher, Massinger, Shakespeare, Shirley, and Brome did.

Rather like Jonson in a number of ways was George Chapman, though his canon is more uncertain than Jonson's because of several dubiously ascribed plays and the very unreliable dating of a number of them. He wrote approximately 21 plays between about 1595 and about 1613, but there are several years in this period when he appears to have written no plays at all; he was not consistent in giving his allegiance to one company for long periods; and the publications of his nondramatic works, especially his translations from Homer, are scattered throughout this period. Chapman may have been an attached professional playwright for about 14 months in 1598 and 1599 when he wrote all or parts of what appear to be seven plays for the Lord Admiral's men. He appears again to have been writing plays fairly consistently during about the last year or so of Elizabeth's reign and the first and second years of James's. These plays were all prepared for boy companies, but Chapman does not appear to have been working regularly for any one of them: he wrote for the Children of the Chapel, for Paul's Boys, and for the Queen's Revels boys. Sometime in this second period of dramatic productivity or just after it Chapman received the patronage of Prince Henry. A later group of plays, mostly produced by boy companies, are too uncertain in date to give any assurance that Chapman was devoting himself wholly to work for the theatres. Furthermore, he was under the patronage of Prince Henry during part of these years, and these were the years of the principal *Iliad* publications.

Though Chapman wrote a number of excellent comedies and tragedies, there is no reason to think that he was an attached professional playwright except for the short period of a year or two when he was preparing scripts for the Lord Admiral's company. In two later periods he was preparing plays for boy companies with some regularity, but the number of these plays is not great and in neither period does he seem to have been wholly dependent upon the theatres for his living. Thus he seems, like Ben Jonson, to have been an author who wrote many plays for profit but was not an attached or regular professional.

After Chapman and Jonson, John Ford and John Webster are probably the dramatists whose literary achievement might suggest to many readers that they may have been attached to London acting companies. Both of them wrote a good many plays for the commercial theatres; both wrote two or three masterpieces; both, for limited periods, produced with some regularity for the playhouses.

But neither Ford nor Webster had the protracted period of steady writing for the theatres which characterizes the attached or regular professional playwrights like Heywood, Fletcher, Massinger, Shakespeare, Brome, and Shirley. Ford apparently wrote 17 plays, but four of the lost ones are undatable and assigned to Ford on rather scanty evidence. Most of the others fall into two periods, 1621–1624, when he collaborated with Thomas Dekker on five plays, and 1628–1638, when he wrote three plays for Blackfriars and five for the Phoenix. From the extant records it appears that Ford probably wrote no plays before the age of 35 and none between the ages of 38 and 42. This is not the pattern of work of the attached professional dramatist, though it does show frequent dealings with the regular acting companies.

33

Furthermore, the attitude which Ford displays toward his plays in prefaces and dedications resembles that of the amateurs. In his dedication of the 1629 quarto of *The Lovers' Melancholy* to four lawyer friends of Gray's Inn he says: "The account of some leisure hours is here summed up, and offered to examination . . . I care not to please many." And in his dedication to John Wyrly and his wife of the 1639 quarto of *The Lady's Trial* he tells them: "In presenting this issue of some less serious hours to your tuition, I appeal from the severity of censure to to the mercy of your judgments."

Brilliant as he was in some of the tragedies of his later career, 1628–1638, Ford did not then think of himself as a professional playwright, and the pattern of his production is not that of the attached professional.

John Webster, whose canon is somewhat more uncertain than Ford's, was similarly sporadic in his composition. He was writing plays fairly steadily between 1602 and 1605 when he participated in seven collaborations for various companies. None of his dramatic work is clearly assignable to the years 1606 to 1609, but his best plays, *The Devil's Law Case*, *The White Devil*, and *The Duchess of Malfi*, were prepared—two for Queen Anne's company and one for the King's men—during the period 1609–1614. Then there is a long break to the time of his later plays written between 1624 and his death. To me these facts indicate that Webster may have been an attached professional from 1602 to 1605, but that later he wrote plays only occasionally and had no settled company affiliation.

Francis Beaumont is probably thought of by his most ardent admirers as an amateur and by those most interested in his successful collaborations for the King's company as a professional. There is some evidence for each classification. His career before 1608 was that of an amateur. He was born into a family of landed gentry; in February 1596/97 he was matriculated at Broadgates Hall,

Oxford; on 3 November 1600 he was entered at the Inner Temple, where his father had been a Bencher; in 1602 his metrical tale, *Salmacis and Hermaphroditus*, was published; in or before 1607 the Children of Paul's acted his *Woman Hater*, and in 1607 the Children of the Queen's Revels company performed his *Knight of the Burning Pestle*. This is the life pattern of an amateur dramatist, but between 1608 and 1613 Beaumont wrote in collaboration with John Fletcher and others about twelve plays for the King's men and one, *Cupid's Revenge*, for the Queen's Revels boys. In 1613 he married an heiress and presumably retired to her estates in Kent, where he died in March 1615/16.

This summary suggests that for most of his rather short life Beaumont's career corresponded to that of many amateur dramatists, but from 1608 to 1613 he seems to have fallen into the pattern of the attached professionals, writing about two plays a year with John Fletcher and preparing them all for the King's men—with the exception of *Cupid's Revenge*, which may indeed have preceded the collaborators' attachment to King James's company.[19] Because of this sharply divided career Beaumont does not quite belong to the category of the regular attached professionals.

Thomas Middleton was another of the rather prolific professionals who appears never to have had any long sustained company attachment, but to have sold his plays here and there. Early in the century he did two or three plays for the Admiral's men, then half a dozen for Paul's Boys in a period of three or four years, apparently interspersing them with a play or two for the Queen's Revels company and one for Prince Henry's company. From 1608 or 1609 until his death he wrote alone or in collaboration at least three plays for Prince Charles's men, four for the Lady

19. See James Savage, "The Date of Beaumont and Fletcher's *Cupid's Revenge*," *ELH*, xv (December 1948), 286–94.

Elizabeth's men, six or seven for the King's men, and three or four, including two lost plays, which cannot confidently be assigned. This is not the activity of an attached playwright; even the series for the King's men is broken by plays for the Lady Elizabeth's company and for Prince Charles's company. Furthermore Middleton, for a good part of his career, was not solely dependent upon the commercial theatres. In the last fourteen years of his life he did about a score of city shows and pageants, and for the last seven years he was the salaried City Chronologer. Middleton was a talented and successful writer for the theatres, but he was not an attached playwright.

Drayton and Munday were Henslowe playwrights whose dramatic work, except for three or four plays, has disappeared. In the few years they were working for Henslowe they were prolific, but neither had a long-term attachment to the theatre, and neither appears to have had anything to do with commercial theatres for the last 28 or 30 years of his life.

We have too little information on six other playwrights in this list of the 22 most prolific to call them attached or regular professionals. About Henry Chettle, John Day, William Hathaway, William Haughton, Wentworth Smith, and Robert Wilson we know very little apart from some details of Henslowe's payments and loans to them. The overwhelming majority of all their known plays have disappeared; for none of the six do we have certain birth dates and death dates, and for several we have neither; it is their obscurity and not their nontheatrical interests or eclectic placing of their plays which prevents their consideration as attached professionals. Actually there is one fact which suggests that Henry Chettle, the most prolific of the group, was attached. On Lady Day in 1602 he signed a bond to write for the Admiral's men, but nevertheless he wrote or contributed to several plays for the

Earl of Worcester's company in the following thirteen or fourteen months.

THE ELIMINATION of these 14 experienced playwrights, who certainly wrote for profit and had short or scattered periods of more or less close association with the London commercial theatres but not long-term exclusive attachments, leaves eight of the more prolific dramatists in our list of 22 who profited from furnishing plays for the theatres. These eight men I have called the regular professionals, or the attached professionals. In the order of their known dramatic productivity they are:

> Thomas Heywood
> John Fletcher
> Thomas Dekker
> Philip Massinger
> William Shakespeare
> James Shirley
> William Rowley
> Richard Brome

It is from their careers and their plays that I shall draw a large part of the evidence in the ensuing discussions of the profession of the dramatist in Shakespeare's time.

CHAPTER III

The Status of Dramatists, Plays, Actors, and Theatres

IN THE PRECEDING CONSIDERATION of the classes of playwright during the years 1590 to 1642 there have appeared occasional statements about the normal degree of esteem which literate men of the time accorded to plays and the men who wrote them. Jasper Mayne's publisher said that the author of *The City Match* had no ambition to publish his play, ". . . holding works of this light nature to be things which need an apology for being written at all, not esteeming otherwise of them, whose abilities in this kind are most passable, than of masquers who spangle and glitter for the time, but 'tis thorough tinsel."

Even Ben Jonson, who is never accused of being unaware of the value of his own compositions, was familiar with the Jacobean status of plays, and he expressed the common attitude clearly when he wrote from prison to the Earl of Salisbury in 1605, when he and Chapman had been committed to jail for the affair of *Eastward Ho*. Jonson said:

> . . . I am here (my most honored Lord) unexamined or unheard, committed to a vile prison, and (with me) a gentleman (whose name may perhaps have come to your Lordship) one Mr. George Chapman, a learned and honest man. The cause (would I could name some worthier) though I wish we had known none worthy our imprisonment, is, a (the word irks me that our Fortunes hath necessitated us to so despised a course) a play, my Lord.[1]

In the same year Samuel Daniel, whose literary reputation at that time was at least as great as Jonson's, wrote to Viscount Cranbourne expressing the same low opinion of acted plays in comparison with other literary work. At the time Daniel was in difficulties over alleged parallels to the trial and execution of the Earl of Essex in his tragedy *Philotas*, which had been acted by the Children of the Queen's Revels. None of his earlier or later plays and masques are known to have been acted in the commercial theatres, and the reasons can be seen in the opening lines of Daniel's letter:

> Right honorable, my good Lord:
> My necessity, I confess, hath driven me to do a thing unworthy of me, and much against my heart, in making the stage the speaker of my lines, which never, heretofore, had any other theatre than the universal dominions of England, which so long as it shall keep the tongue it hath will keep my name and travails from perishing. . . .[2]

These assumptions about commercially acted plays made by Leonard Lichfield in 1639 and by Ben Jonson and

1. C. H. Herford and Percy and Evelyn Simpson, *Ben Jonson*, Oxford, 1925–1953, I, 194–95.
2. Laurence Michel, ed., *The Tragedy of Philotas by Samuel Daniel*, New Haven, 1949, p. 37.

Samuel Daniel in 1605 are characteristic of the period. They are much less contemptuous than those reflected in most writings of the 1570s or in the fulminations of the professed Puritans from 1570 to 1660. Lichfield and Jonson and Daniel speak as reasonable men of their time.

It is one of the most familiar observations of the student of literature that the popular and admired writing of one generation is the soporific or the scandal of another. The reaction of most twentieth-century readers to the many hundreds of Elizabethan and Jacobean published sermons is a fully documented example of the former reaction; an amusing speculative example of the latter is the reaction of the chastity-preaching Elizabethans to the popular novel of sexual promiscuity widely read and frequently praised in the reign of Elizabeth II.

But a knowledge of these changing standards and the application of such knowledge in the assessment of the motives, customs, expectations, and compromises of Elizabethan dramatists, especially of Shakespeare, has been painfully rare in the criticism of the last two hundred years. Too often the assumption of the critic—generally tacit— has been that Elizabethan standards and values were those of his own time, and on these assumptions the critic posits the reputation or the response of Shakespeare or Marlowe or Heywood and of the audiences for which they wrote.

An instructive example of the power of this almost irresistible anachronism is afforded by a comment of F. J. Furnivall, who had been looking through the interesting diary and account books of Sir Humphrey Mildmay, preserved in the Harleian collection at the British Museum. In the records of Sir Humphrey's 57 visits to London theatres during the last decade before the Civil Wars there is a mention of one Shakespearean play which he saw, *Othello*, an allusion which Furnivall duly reported to the editor of the *Shakespeare Allusion Book*.[3] Naturally Fur-

3. John Munro, 1932 ed., Oxford, 1932, I, 397.

nivall was disappointed not to find more Shakespeare allusions in these accounts, which are the fullest extant records of the theatre attendance of any playgoer in the three reigns. He continued his comment on the records: "And on turning back to the Diary, leaf 10, back, I find under April 28 'this after Noone, I spente att a play wth good Company'—and so forgot to say what the play was: probably not one of Shakespeare's or it would have overpowered the recollection of the 'good company.' " Now Furnivall was very widely read in English literature of the sixteenth and seventeenth centuries, and he was a careful scholar. Yet when it came to critical assumptions, his Edwardian values easily overpowered his own scholarly observations. A careful reading of Mildmay's diary would by itself have demonstrated to him that he was foisting Edwardian tastes onto a Caroline spectator. Mildmay's London residence was near the Blackfriars, the most distinguished theatre of his time, and his diary shows that he went there more often than to any other playhouse. At this theatre Shakespeare's plays were then in the active repertory, and there are still extant records of the company's performance of ten of them in the decade of Mildmay's accounts. Sir Humphrey must have seen several in his 57 recorded visits to theatres; yet he names only one, *Othello*, whereas he names four of Fletcher's plays, three of Jonson's, and two of Davenant's.[4] Mildmay's typical Caroline tastes are implicit in his own records, yet, where Shakespeare was concerned, a man so informed and so careful as Furnivall could not resist the assumption that Sir Humphrey must have had Furnivall's own Edwardian tastes and not those of an aristocratic patron of the theatres in the reign of Charles I.

Even so astute and careful a scholar as Sir Walter Greg, who knew a good deal more about the theatre and the drama than Furnivall did, could be led into a foolish state-

---

4. See *Jacobean and Caroline Stage*, II, 673–81.

ment by attributing twentieth-century conceptions of the status and importance of poetry to an Elizabethan theatre magnate. After he had spent several years editing and analyzing the extensive and illuminating theatre records of Philip Henslowe, Greg prepared several appendices generalizing from Henslowe's records of play purchases and performances. Concluding his discussion of the scale of payments to authors, Greg wrote: "A decade later [i.e., in 1612 and 1613] prices had greatly risen. A third-rate poet like Daborne, evidently deep in Henslowe's toils, gets £10 to £20 a play. . . ."[5] The facts are accurate, as usual, but the assumptions underlying that phrase "a third-rate poet" are twentieth-century and nontheatrical assumptions, exquisitely inappropriate to a hard-driving theatre man like Henslowe. They seem intended to suggest that if a third-rate poet like Daborne got £10 to £20, first-rate poets in these years, like Shakespeare and Webster, must have received a good deal more. But certainly Henslowe and his rival theatre managers were not competing for the praise of twentieth-century poetry lovers; they were trying to buy plays which would bring pennies into the box at the Fortune and the Globe and the Red Bull. In buying plays Henslowe could scarcely have ignored the performance records at his own theatres where, so far as his accounts show, *The Jew of Malta* and *Doctor Faustus* had indeed been popular, but *The Wise Man of West Chester*, *Jeronimo*, *Bellendon*, and *A Knack to Know an Honest Man* had outdrawn any of the plays of Chapman, Greene, or Dekker. Poetic distinction may be a criterion for the selection of plays for twentieth-century anthologies, but not for building repertories in Jacobean theatres.

Such misleading aberrations on the part of scholars as experienced and distinguished as F. J. Furnivall and Sir Walter Greg demonstrate the almost irresistible distorting

5. W. W. Greg, ed., *Henslowe's Diary*, London, 1904–1908, II, 127.

power of one's own cultivated standards in assessing the facts of the professional environment of Shakespeare and his contemporaries. The mistakes of Furnivall and Greg underscore the importance of maintaining a clear understanding of the status which their London contemporaries assumed for professional playwrights in the reigns of Elizabeth, James I, and Charles I.

This status changed somewhat in the course of the period 1590–1642, but it was always closely related to the status of actors, theatres, and plays. Because of greater financial success, increasing royal and aristocratic patronage, and the accumulation of printed texts, all four were thought less insignificant by writers in 1640 than they had been thought fifty years before, but even after this half century of rising respectability, the playwright and his professional environment were less esteemed than most readers of Shakespeare, Jonson, Ford, and Webster are likely to assume.

At the beginning of the period we are considering, the condemnation of public plays and of the people concerned with them was fairly general. Still current were the violent diatribes against all phases of the drama—especially the drama in the public theatres—which had followed the opening of the Theatre. The writings of men like John Rainolds, John Northbrooke, Phillip Stubbes, and Stephen Gosson were not forgotten, but many more cool and responsible people expressed their disapproval of plays and theatres in emphatic and unambiguous terms. The Corporation of the City of London and several of the great City companies which it represented were consistent and vocal opponents of the commercial theatre almost throughout the period. In 1592—as in several later years—they were involved in a plan for the suppression of all the theatres in town.

On 25 February 1591/92 Sir William Roe, the Lord Mayor, wrote an official letter to the Archbishop of Canterbury:

Our most humble duties to Your Grace remembered. Whereas by the daily and disorderly exercise of a number of players and playing houses erected within this City, the youth thereof is greatly corrupted and their manners infected with many evil and ungodly qualities by reason of the wanton and prophane devises represented on the stages by the said players, the apprentices and servants withdrawn from their works, and all sorts in general from the daily resort unto sermons and other Christian exercises to the great hindrance of the trades and traders of this City and profanation of the good and godly religion established amongst us. To which places also do usually resort great numbers of light and lewd-disposed persons as harlots, cutpurses, cozeners, pilferers, and such like and there under the colour of resort to those places to hear the plays devise divers evil and ungodly matches, confederacies and conspiracies, which by means of the opportunity of the place cannot be prevented nor discovered, as otherwise they might be. In consideration whereof we most humbly beseech Your Grace . . . to vouchsafe us your good favor and help for the reforming and banishing of so great evil out of this City, which ourselves of long time though to small purpose have so earnestly desired and endeavored by all means that possibly we could. . . . Whereof Your Grace shall not only benefit, and bind unto you the politic state and government of this City which by no one thing is so greatly annoyed and disquieted as by players and plays and the disorders which follow thereupon, but also take away a great offence from the church of God and hinderance to his gospel. . . .

The reply of the Archbishop of Canterbury to this plea from the City government to help drive the players and their plays from London has not been preserved, but its contents are implied in the reply of the Lord Mayor ten days after his first letter:

My humble duty to your Grace. I read your Grace's letter wherein I understood the contents of the same and imparted the same to my brethren the Aldermen in our common Assembly, who together with myself yield unto your Grace our most humble thanks for your good favor and Godly care over us in vouchsafing us your health for the removing of this great inconvenience which groweth to this City by plays and players. As touching the consideration to be made to Master Tilney [Master of the Revels] and other capitulations that are to pass betwixt us for the better effecting and continuance of this restraint of the said plays in and about this City, we have appointed certain of our brethren the aldermen to confer with him forthwith, purposing to acquaint your Grace with our agreement and whole proceeding herein as occasion shall require. . . .[6]

The proposal which the Archbishop had made in his lost letter was evidently that the corporation of the City of London arrange to pay the Master of the Revels an annuity to gain his cooperation in driving the players and theatres and their plays out of London. This inference of the contents of the Archbishop's letter is easily derived from a minute in the court books of the Merchant Taylors' Company recording their reaction to the proposal two weeks later on 22 March. Though the Merchant Taylors did not agree with the method proposed, this great City company which often had private plays in its own hall was entirely in agreement with the attempt to rid the City of the commercial theatre. The entry in their court books reads:

A precept directed from the Lord Mayor to this company showing to the company the great enormity that this City sustaineth by the practice and profane exercise of players and playing houses in this City and the corruption of youth that groweth thereupon [and] inviting the company by the consideration of this mischief to yield to the payment of one annuity to one Mr. Tilney, Master of the Revels of the Queen's house, in whose

6. *Malone Society Collections*, Oxford, 1907, I, pt. I, 68–70.

hands the redress of this inconvenience doth rest and that those plays might be abandoned out of this City. Upon consideration of which precept, albeit the company thinks it a very good service to be performed, yet weighing the damage of the precedent and invocation of annuities upon the companies of London [and weighing] what further occasions it may be drawn into, together with their great charge otherwise which this troublesome time hath brought and is likely to bring, they think this no fit course to remedy this mischief but wish some other ways were taken in hand to expel out of our City so general a contagion of manners and other inconveniences wherein if any endeavors or travail of this company might further the matter they would be ready to use their service therein. . . .[7]

These were the opinions of metropolitan officials and business leaders of London concerning plays and theatres. But gentry in the country, who usually considered their station well above that of the men of commerce in London, did not have a very much higher opinion of the theatres and their activities. Lady Bacon, the mother of Sir Anthony and Sir Francis, would have been in essential agreement with the Lord Mayor, the Archbishop of Canterbury, and the court of the Merchant Taylors' Company. The writer in Thomas Birch's collection reports that

About the latter end of April, or in the beginning of May, 1594, Mr. Bacon removed from Recburne in Hertfordshire, which was too remote from the capital for the carrying on his numerous correspondences; and he settled himself in London, in a house in Bishopsgate street; tho' the situation of it was highly disliked by his mother, not only on account of its neighborhood to the Bull-inn, where plays and interludes were continually acted, and would she imagined, corrupt his servants, but likewise out of zeal for his religious improvement. . . .[8]

7. *Malone Society Collections*, III, 166–67.
8. Thomas Birch, *Memoirs of the Court of Queen Elizabeth* . . . , London, 1754, I, 173.

Lady Bacon's attitude toward plays was colored by her moral, or perhaps we should say economic, apprehensions. But she was by no means unusual in her fears; it was not only the provincial mothers of youthful sons in London who assumed that plays and theatres were instruments of seduction and the disruption of households.

The general idea of plays and theatres which lay behind Lady Bacon's fears is expressed by John Stow in his *Survey of London* published in 1598. Speaking of the development of plays, Stowe says that they began with amateurs,

> But in process of time it became an Occupation; and many there were that followed it for a Livelihood. And which was worse it became the Occasion of much Sin and Evil. Playhouses thronged. And great Disorders and Inconvenience were found to ensue to the City thereby. It occasioned Frays and evil Practices of Incontinency. Great Inns were used for this Purpose, which had secret Chambers and Places, as well as open Stages and Galleries. Here maids, especially Orphans and good Citizens' Children under Age, were inveigled and allured to privy and unmeet Contracts.[9]

A couple of years later another solid Englishman used language in a petition which revealed the common estimate of plays and players. In the year 1600 the son of Henry Clifton, Esquire, of Toftrees in Norfolk was impressed by Nathaniel Giles, Master of the Children of the Chapel Royal—ostensibly to sing in the royal choir. Henry Clifton complained to the Star Chamber that the boy was not really taken to sing, for he had no talent as a singer, but that he had been taken

> unto the said playhouse in the Blackfriars aforesaid and there to sort him with mercenary players and . . . there to detain and compel to exercise the base trade of a mercenary interlude player to his utter loss of time ruin and disparagement. . . . [The boy was] committed to the

9. 1720 ed., London, 1598, book 1, p. 247.

said playhouse amongst a company of lewd and dissolute mercenary players . . . [to be trained] in acting of
parts in base plays and interludes. [The boy's father
was assured] that his said son should be employed in
that vile and base manner of a mercenary player in that
place. . . .[10]

These are opinions of theatres, actors, and theatre audiences, but the playwrights were, of course, simply the employees of the actors and theatre managers and provided
for them the means of producing these "great disorders
and inconveniences . . . frays and evil practices of incon-
tinency." Though one could not expect Elizabethans with
the prejudices of the Lord Mayor, the Archbishop, the
Merchant Taylors, Lady Bacon, John Stowe, and Henry
Clifton to have had a very high opinion of playwrights,
others who were far more interested in the drama did not
think very highly of the regular dramatists either.

The man who probably contributed larger sums to the
income of poets than any other individual in his time—
Philip Henslowe—showed no undue respect for his playwrights. Most revealing of his true estimate of dramatists
is his account, in a letter to his son-in-law, the great actor
Edward Alleyn, of the death of one of the actors of the
Lord Admiral's company, Gabriel Spencer, in a duel with
Ben Jonson. The letter was written on 26 September 1598,
at a time when Jonson had already written two or three
plays, at least one of which Henslowe had paid for.

> Now to let you understand news, I will tell you some,
> but it is for me hard and heavy. Since you were with
> me I have lost one of my company, which hurteth me
> greatly, that is Gabriel, for he is slain in Hogsden Fields
> by the hand of Benjamin Jonson, bricklayer. Therefore
> I would fain have a little of your counsel if I could. . . .[11]

10. F. G. Fleay, *A Chronicle History of the London Stage, 1559–
1642*, London, 1898, pp. 127–32.

11. W. W. Greg, ed., *Henslowe Papers*, London, 1907, pp. 47–
48.

48

No doubt Henslowe was exasperated when he wrote, but often people's true opinions come out at such a time. Jonson had indeed been apprenticed to a bricklayer, but he was 26 years old when Henslowe wrote, and he had been a soldier, an actor, and a playwright since his bricklaying days.

Philip Henslowe naturally thought of playwrights as hirelings of actors and managers, as the hundreds of transactions with them recorded in his accounts attest. But other Elizabethans with no connections with the London professional theatre thought similarly. What university students thought is sometimes recorded in college plays. In 1602 or 1603 the undergraduates at St. John's College, Cambridge, performed a play they had written called *The Return from Parnassus*, part 2. The chief characters in the play are Cambridge students who—like many of their successors—are troubled as to how they will make a living after they leave the university. They consider writing plays, and in act IV, scene 4, they even call in Richard Burbage and Will Kempe, Shakespeare's fellows in the Lord Chamberlain's company, to consult about employment. The more susceptible students are somewhat romantic admirers of the poetry of Shakespeare, and one, in his audition before the two actors, recites the opening of *Richard III*. Yet the students have no respect for the theatrical enterprise and less for the position of the playwright, exploited by the actors. In the following scene the two students have become wandering musicians, and *Studioso* justifies their choice of the one profession over the other:

Better it is amongst fiddlers to be chief,
Than at a player's trencher beg relief.
But is't not strange these mimic apes should prize
Unhappy scholars at a hireling rate?
Vile world, that lifts them up to high degree,
And treads us downe in groveling misery.
England affords these glorious vagabonds,

That carried erst their fardels on their backs,
Coursers to ride on through the gazing streets,
Sooping[12] it in their glaring satin suits,
And pages to attend their masterships:
With mouthing words that better wits have framed
They purchase lands, and now Esquires are named.[13]

A much more cultivated man, and one who had more respect for poetry than Philip Henslowe or even the Cambridge undergraduates, expressed by implication his acceptance of the inferior status of plays a few years later. When John Donne wrote his *Catalogus Librorum Aulicorum* he was about thirty years old with a good deal of London experience. Sir Richard Baker, under the heading *Of Men of Note in His* [James I] *Time* says: "And here I desire the reader leave to remember two of my own old acquaintance. The one was Mr. *John Donne*, who leaving *Oxford*, lived at the Inns of Court, not dissolute, but very neat; a great visitor of ladies, a great frequenter of plays, a great writer of conceited verses. . . ."[14] Yet "great frequenter of plays" though he was when he lived at Lincoln's Inn in the 1590s, Donne shows that he did not consider plays in the category of significant literature. His *Catalogus Librorum Aulicorum* was first written, Evelyn Simpson thinks, about 1604 or 1605 and revised in 1611, in the decade of the greatest achievements of Shakespeare, Jonson, Chapman, Marston, Heywood, and Middleton, and well after the deaths of Christopher Marlowe and Robert Greene. The *Catalogus* is a satiric piece in the manner of Rabelais which presents a mock catalogue of 34 works by 30 different authors. Among the contemporary, or near-contemporary, writers whom Donne names and satirizes

12. Sooping = sweeping.
13. J. B. Leishman, ed., *The Three Parnassus Plays*, London, 1949, p. 350 (modernized).
14. *A Chronicle of the Kings of England*, London, 1643, section IV, p. 156, Vvvv₂ᵛ.

are Sir John Harrington, Sir Francis Bacon, Sir John Davies, John Florio, Thomas Campion, Nicholas Hill, John Foxe, Sir Hugh Platt, Hugh Broughton, and Matthew Sutcliffe. But he lists no dramatists and no play titles. Mrs. Simpson points out that,

> The name of no dramatist appears in [this] list which was drawn up in the decade which produced the greatest English drama of all time. . . . But in truth the *Catalogue* is one more proof that in Shakespeare's lifetime the drama was not thought of as literature. Plays were to be acted, not read. They were the property of the company of actors rather than of the playwright.[15]

In any event, John Donne evidently did not think that the writers of the plays he had seen in his many visits to the theatres sufficiently well known in literary circles to be worthy of mention in 1604 when *Hamlet* and *Othello* were being performed at the Globe, or even when he made his revisions in 1611 as *The Winter's Tale*, *The Alchemist*, *The Tempest*, and *Catiline* were in the active repertory at Blackfriars.

A much more sweeping and explicit denigration of plays is Sir Thomas Bodley's. About 1598 Sir Thomas began making plans for what has become one of the chief libraries of the world. He bought books in great quantities and shipped them to Oxford; he wrote constantly to his librarian; he persuaded the King to visit his foundation in 1605; he got for his library grants of lands for its endowment; he gave his own lands. Most significant of all for the formation of a great library, in December of 1609 he concluded an agreement with the Stationers' Company of London that they should send to his library in perpetuity a perfect copy of every book printed by a member of the Stationers' Company. Since the members of this guild printed

15. Evelyn M. Simpson, ed., *The Courtier's Library or Catalogus Librorum Aulicorum. . .* , by John Donne, London, 1930, pp. 23–24.

nearly every book published in England, a greater bibliographical benevolence can scarcely be imagined.

Obviously the wholesale preservation of English literature at Oxford was one of the far-sighted aims of the founder of the Bodleian Library. Much of his correspondence with Thomas James, the keeper of his library, is still extant, and some of it throws light on the status of plays and playwrights in the middle of the reign of James I. On the first of January 1611/12 Sir Thomas wrote:

> Sir, I would you had forborne to catalogue our London books, until I had been privy to your purpose. There are many idle books, and riff-raffs among them, which shall never come to the library, and I fear me that little, which you have done already, will raise a scandal upon it, when it shall be given out by such as would disgrace it, that I have made up a number with almanacs, plays, and proclamations: of which I will have none, but such as are singular.

In his next letter, written three days later on 4 January 1611/12, Sir Thomas takes up the matter with his librarian again:

> . . . I can see no good reason to alter my opinion for excluding such books as almanacs, plays, and an infinite number, that are daily printed, of very unworthy matters and handling, such as, me thinks, both the keeper and underkeeper should disdain to seek out, to deliver unto any man. Haply some plays may be worth the keeping: *but hardly one in forty.* For it is not alike in English plays, and others of other nations; for they are most esteemed for learning the languages, and many of them compiled by men of great fame for wisdom and learning, *which is seldom or never seen among us.* Were it so again, that some little profit might be reaped (which God knows is very little) out of some of our playbooks, the benefit thereof will nothing near countervail the harm that the scandal will bring unto the library, when

it shall be given out, that we stuff it full of baggage books. . . . This is my opinion, wherein if I err, I think I shall err with infinite others: and the more I think upon it, the more it doth distaste me, that such kind of books, should be vouchsafed a room, in so noble a library. . . .[16]

Though the Bodleian Library today has the largest or the second largest collection of Elizabethan and Jacobean plays in the world, the playbooks came through the efforts of eighteenth- nineteenth- and twentieth-century librarians and collectors and not by the design of its founder. Sir Thomas was a true Jacobean, and to him, as to so many of his contemporaries, these precious play quartos of Shakespeare, Jonson, Tourneur, and Webster were "riff-raffs" or "baggage books."

Even a dramatist who had written a number of plays himself, though he cannot be considered a regular professional, tended to distinguish between professional dramatists and men who had written plays but were not dependent upon the theatres for a living. The well-known list of dramatists in the epistle which John Webster wrote for the 1612 edition of his *White Devil* has been frequently discussed, partly because it is a Shakespeare allusion, partly because it is one of the very few documents of the time noting the accomplishments of writers of plays, and partly because of the odd order in which Webster lists the writers. He expresses his appreciation

of other men's worthy labours; especially of that full and heightened style of Master *Chapman*, the labor'd and understanding works of Master *Johnson*, the no less worthy composures of the both worthily excellent Master *Beaumont*, and Master *Fletcher*, and lastly (without wrong last to be named) the right happy and copi-

16. G. W. Wheeler, ed., *Letters of Sir Thomas Bodley to Thomas James, Keeper of the Bodleian Library*, Oxford, 1926, pp. 219–22. Italics mine.

ous industry of M. *Shakespeare*, M. *Dekker*, and M. *Heywood*.

Discussions of Webster's order have usually turned on modern literary values, but Webster's order is a Jacobean hierarchical order. The last three dramatists, of "right happy and copious industry" were regular professional playwrights, and in the year 1612 had been so for fifteen to twenty years. In the normal Jacobean ordering they were placed in a group at the end without individual characterization. Though George Chapman may have been a regular professional for several years around the turn of the century in 1610, 1611, and 1612 he was not writing plays and was better known as the translator of Homer than as a playwright. Jonson had probably been a regular professional from 1597 to 1602, but for the last decade before Webster wrote he was not regularly attached to an acting company. In this decade he had written three times as many court masques and royal entertainments as he had plays, and his reputation as a nondramatic poet was growing. "Master *Beaumont*" and "Master *Fletcher*" were gentlemen who had only recently fallen into the status of professionals.

On the other hand, Shakespeare, Dekker, and Heywood grouped together at the end of the list were all attached professionals. Each had written 30 or more plays at this time; each had been regularly attached to an acting company; each was dependent on the theatre for his living; and two of the three were or had been actors. If one thinks of the social milieu of Jacobean London and not of modern literary values, Webster's ordering of the dramatists he appreciates is what one would expect.

The status of the dramatist was closely related, as we have seen, to the status of players and theatres, both of which improved under the notably increasing patronage of King James I and the members of his court. But there were other factors in this slowly rising status, as noted by the historian Sir Richard Baker, who lived much in London from 1587 to 1645. On 13 September 1619 Edward Alleyn's deed of foundation of his College of God's Gift at Dulwich was read before a gathering of notables in London. Baker pointed to one result in his *Chronicle of the Kings of England*. Under the heading "Works of Piety Done by this King [James I] or By Others in His Time" he says:

> About this time also *Edward Alleyn* of *Dulwich* in *Surrey*, founded a fair hospital at *Dulwich*. . . . This man may be an example, who having gotten his wealth by stage playing converted it to this pious use, not without a kind of reputation to the Society of Players.[17]

Of course players and theatres and the writers who worked for them did not immediately become highly respected, but popular references to actors as rogues and vagabonds did not come quite so easily to people who knew something of the famous actor Edward Alleyn's College of God's Gift at Dulwich.

Bracketing Edward Alleyn's foundation of Dulwich College were two other events which in the next few years also tended to rehabilitate somewhat the reputation of plays and playwrights. These two events were the appearance of the Jonson folio in 1616 and the Shakespeare folio in 1623. *The Workes of Beniamin Jonson* is a landmark. No collection of plays by an English author had ever appeared before, and it was years before Jonson ceased to be derided for his presumption in using the term "Workes" for anything so trivial as plays. With the seven comedies and two tragedies in the folio were published the masques and entertainments prepared for the King, epigrams, and occasional poems, a number of them addressed to persons of great social distinction. Probably no other publication

17. *Chronicles of the Kings of England*, London, 1684, p. 423, Mmm₄.

55

before the Restoration did so much to raise the contemporary estimate of the generally belittled form of plays.

The Shakespeare folio of 1623, though so much the more important volume to us now, was only the second such collection, and it did not include such items of social prestige as the masques and entertainments prepared for King James nor the epigrams and poems with noble sponsors. But the two volumes were alike in making a mute claim to dignity which had an irrational effect not visible to modern readers. Before 1616 nearly all plays which got printed had appeared on the bookstalls as unbound cheap quartos looking like almanacs, joke books, coney-catching pamphlets, and other ephemera. The degrading association is neatly expressed by two characters in Shakerley Marmion's play *Holland's Leaguer*, first acted at the Salisbury Court theatre in December 1631.

> *Fidelio.* Then know that I have boasted of your beauty;
>   Nay more, exposed thy virtues to the trial.
> *Faustina.* You have not prostituted them on stalls, To
>   have the vulgar fingers sweat upon them, As they do
>   use your plays and pamphlets?
>
> [act 2, scene 2]

On the other hand the large folio format was generally reserved for sermons, geographies, the classics, royal books like *The Works of King James*, and other such literature thought to be of permanent significance. The fact that two collections of plays were to be seen on the bookstalls in the dignified and ponderous format of *The Works of King James* had its effect, during the later twenties and thirties, in diminishing the literary contempt for plays. This changing situation is clearly pointed up by the bitter comment of the fanatical Puritan, William Prynne, in his *Histriomastix, the Players' Scourge, or Actors' Tragedy* in 1633. In his preface Prynne says:

Some playbooks,[1] since I first undertook this subject, are grown from *Quarto* into *Folio*; which yet bear so good a price and sale that I cannot but with grief relate it, they are now[2] new printed in far better paper than most Octavo or Quarto *Bibles,* which hardly find such vent as they.

[1] Ben Jonson's, Shakespeare's, and others.

[2] Shakespeare's plays are printed in the best Crown paper, far better than most Bibles.[18]

But the increased dignity which the appearance of the Jonson and Shakespeare folios brought to plays and playwrights must be seen only as a rise from an exceedingly low status to a moderately low one. Plays and their writers were still far from the respect shown for other writings published in folio. Their usual status, improved but not exalted, is illustrated in the dialogue of a Caroline writer, a dialogue which makes use of the very publications we have noticed.

The illustrative lines are an exchange between two Inns of Court students in Thomas Nabbes' play, *Tottenham Court,* a play acted at the Salisbury Court theatre in 1633. Since this theatre was within a few hundred yards of the Inner Temple and the Middle Temple it seems likely that the actors could have expected students from the Inns of Court, notorious play-haunters, to be in the audience at most of their performances.

Sam. Let's home to our studies and put cases.
James. Hang cases and bookes that are spoyl'd with them! Give me *Johnson* and *Shakespeare*; there's learning for a gentleman. I tell thee *Sam*, were it not for the dancing-schoole and Play-houses, I would not stay at the Innes of Court for the hopes of a chiefe Justice-ship. [act 3, scene 1]

The satiric intent of James's preference for Jonson and Shakespeare, the only two dramatists whose plays had ap-

18. Preface, **6ᵛ.

peared in collected editions before 1633, may not be immediately apparent to readers unfamiliar with Caroline estimates of dramatists, but the intent of his coupling theatres and the dancing-school is unmistakable.

Plays and their authors were not particularly cherished even by those who had reason to have great interest in the drama and the production of plays. We have heard so much in our time of the value of first editions and of unique manuscripts that we tend to transfer some of our values. One of the Caroline holders of unique play manuscripts left a record of her estimate of them. Susan Baskervile was concerned with plays and players and theatres most of her life. She was the wife of a well-known actor and company manager, Thomas Greene, from whom she inherited theatrical properties, and she was the mother of another actor, William Browne. She was involved in a series of suits concerning theatrical affairs and on 25 May 1635 she signed an affadavit concerning her inheritance from her son. She said that she "hath had and received no part of the goods and chattels that William Browne, deceased, died possessed of, save only one cloth cloak, one old horseman's coat, two pair of laced cuffs, and a house clock, a silver tobacco box, and four play books, things of small value."[19] These "four play books" were probably prompt books for plays acted at the Red Bull theatre or the Salisbury Court. They may well have been autograph, but to Susan Greene, alias Baskervile, they were "things of small value."

The status of the professional playwright in the late 1630s is clearly indicated in the praeludium for a revival of Thomas Goffe's *Careless Shepherdess* about 1638 at the Salisbury Court theatre after Goffe's death. This induction, quite different in tone from the play which follows, was

19. Public Record Office, Req. Misc. Books, Affadavit Book, Hilary to Trinity 10 and 11 V Charles I, vol. 138.

evidently written by some theatrically knowledgeable writer connected with the theatre.[20] It is a little scene in which several spectators question the doorkeeper about the play which is to follow, and then discuss theatrical matters among themselves.

> *Thri[ft]*. Sir, was't a Poet, or a Gentleman
> That writ this play? The Court, and Inns of Court,
> Of late bring forth more wit, than all the Tavernes,
> Which makes me pity Playwrights; they were poor
> Before, even to a Proverb; Now their trade
> Must needs go down, when so many set up
> I do not think but I shall shortly see
> One Poet sue to keep the door, another
> To be prompter, a third to snuff candles.
> Pray Sir, has any Gentleman of late
> Beg'd the Monopoly of Comedies?

Thrift implies the inferior social status of playwrights by his use of words like "trade" and his suggestion that they may even descend to the status of the company's lower hired men, such as doorkeepers, prompters, and candle-snuffers. Thrift's ranking is mostly an economic one, but an anonymous writer of an epigram about the same time makes his distinction wholly on the basis of more respectable and less respectable writing.

The subject of the epigram is the prolific professional dramatist, Thomas Heywood. In the decade of the thirties, Heywood, still prolific in his sixties, had written—in addition to at least three or four plays and seven Lord Mayor's shows—a number of prose pamphlets and more extended nondramatic works, like *England's Elizabeth*, *The Hierarchie of the Blessed Angels*, *Pleasant Dialogues and Dramas*, and *The Exemplary Lives . . . of Nine the Most Worthy Women of the World*. To the writer of the epi-

20. See *Jacobean and Caroline Stage*, IV, 501–505, and V, 973–74.

gram, published in *Wits Recreations*, 1640, these works, especially *The Hierarchie*, seemed a much more respectable and appropriate activity than play-writing.

> 5. *To Mr. Thomas Heywood*
> Thou hast writ much and art admir'd by those,
> Who love the easie ambling of thy prose;
> But yet thy pleasingst flight, was somewhat high,
> When thou did'st touch the angels Hyerarchie:
> Fly that way still it will become thy age,
> And better please then groveling on the stage.

This epigram has often mistakenly been interpreted as advice to Heywood to cease acting. It is true that Heywood had long been an actor, but the last clear record that he was still a player had appeared twenty-one years before in 1619; he is in none of the numerous records of actors in the twenties or thirties. Moreover the anonymous writer of the epigram is clearly speaking of literary activities, and the appropriate contrast to *The Hierarchie* is plays, not acting.

Finally there is a comment of John Dryden at the end of the seventeenth century which brings into sharp relief the comparative insignificance of writers of plays in the minds of audiences and managers. On 4 March 1698/99 in a letter to Mrs. Steward, Dryden wrote:

> This day was played a revived comedy of Mr. Congreve's called *The Double Dealer*, which was never very taking. In the playbill was printed,—'Written by Mr. Congreve; with several expressions omitted.' What kind of expressions those were you may easily guess, if you have seen the Monday's Gazette, wherein is the King's order for the reformation of the stage; but the printing an author's name in a play-bill is a new manner of proceeding, at least in England.[21]

21. Charles E. Ward, *The Letters of John Dryden With Letters Addressed to Him*, Durham, N.C., 1942, letter 59, pp. 112–13.

The ephemeral nature of playbills makes it impossible to check the accuracy of Dryden's statement, for none is extant for the first half of the century, but the theatre is always highly conservative, and Dryden's experience with it had been long and active; at least one can be sure that his own name had not appeared in the bills for the performances of the more than thirty plays he had prepared for London theatres. If it was thought irrelevant to print the laureate's name on the bills for the performance of his plays during the Restoration period, it is unlikely that the names of the playwrights had been so dignified in the theatrical advertising of the reigns of the first James and Charles.

CHAPTER IV

The Dramatist
and the Acting Company

In this period of the highest development of the English drama, the basic fact in the situation of the professional dramatists is that they were the employees of the acting companies. The relationship could take various forms, but it was always the acting company which the dramatist had to please first; it was the acting company which paid him eventually; and it was the acting company, which, under normal circumstances, controlled what we should call the copyright of his play.

There were certain exceptions to this normal situation. The boy companies, for instance, in whose direction the boy actors had no voice, were controlled by a group of managers of whom one or more might be playwrights, like John Lyly in the 1580s or Samuel Daniel in 1604 or Robert Daborne in 1610. There were cases of royal interference, when an amateur play which had pleased the King was handed over by His Majesty to his London company with orders to perform it—without payment to the author of course. Examples of such interference are William Cartwright's Oxford play, *The Royal Slave*, which so pleased the court at Oxford that Charles ordered his own company to perform it at Hampton Court. Another is Jasper Mayne's *The City Match*, intended for Oxford performance but actually performed at the King's request by the King's men in London.[1] Another exception was created by the playwright of strong and belligerent personality, who, though he had to please the actors before he achieved production in the first place, managed to exercise more control than most dramatists did in the publication of his play. Ben Jonson is the most notable and familiar example—so familiar, in fact, that his highly exceptional conduct and reputation are all too often taken to be normal.

Often, perhaps usually, there were middle men who facilitated the dealings between a company of actors and their writers. The intermediary best known to us now—because his records are the only ones which have been preserved—is Philip Henslowe. His function as play-purchasing agent for the company has often been misinterpreted by modern critics, who are incensed by his commercial attitude toward art and confused by accounting practices which inadequately distinguished his actions as financial agent for Worcester's men or the Lord Admiral's men from his related but independent transactions as pawnbroker, theatre owner, and personal loan agent. In his usual transactions with playwrights preparing manuscripts for the companies, Henslowe merely paid the dramatists, acting on orders from responsible members of the acting troupe and charging the payment against the company. Only rarely did he buy a play without authorization from a company he was financing. There is some evidence that Thomas Woodford acted in a similar capacity at different

1. See *Jacobean and Caroline Stage*, III, 134–40, and IV, 847–50.

times for companies performing at Paul's, Whitefriars, and the Red Bull. There is rather more evidence that Christopher Beeston, a player and leader of Queen Anne's company, was acting in a similar capacity for them from about 1609 to 1617, and still more likelihood that he was doing the same for Queen Henrietta's company and for the King and Queen's Young Company or Beeston's Boys from 1625 to 1638. Apparently Richard Gunnell was fulfilling this function at the Fortune in the 1620s and at the Salisbury Court in the early 1630s. Richard Heton was probably doing the same at the Salisbury Court theatre in 1639 and 1640. Nothing is known of William Davenant's activities as manager of the King and Queen's Young Company in the brief period 1639–1640, but considering his practices as manager twenty years later during the Restoration it might be guessed that he too had dealt with playwrights for the company in his short period of management before the wars. Unlike the heirs of Philip Henslowe, alas, the families of Woodford, Beeston, Gunnell, Heton, and Davenant allowed the ledgers of these entrepreneurs to be destroyed. We have only scattered allusions, law suits, and occasional memoranda to suggest that they fulfilled Henslowe's function for other companies.

But whether there was some financial agent or manager to act as intermediary or not, it was normally the acting company which decided to buy the play or to commission the dramatist to write it. A direct statement showing this sequence is found in a letter from the actor-dramatist Samuel Rowley, a patented member of the Lord Admiral's company, to Philip Henslowe, the financial agent for the company, authorizing an initial payment to John Day, William Haughton, and Wentworth Smith for a play which, we learn from other records, was called *The Conquest of the West Indies.*

Mr. Henslowe, I have heard five sheets of a play of the Conquest of the Indies and I do not doubt but it will be a very good play. Therefore I pray you deliver them forty shillings in earnest of it and take the papers into your own hands and on Easter eve they promise to make an end of all the rest.

Samuel Rowley

The request was carried out by Henslowe, and in his ledger he made the entry: "Lent unto John Day and William Haughton the 4 of April 1601 in earnest of play called The Conquest of the West Indies at the appointment of Samuel Rowley the sum of . . . 40s."[2]

This sequence of the transactions between the acting companies and the dramatists is fully demonstrable only in the records of Philip Henslowe. Of the fifteen or twenty companies operating in London at one time or another in the period 1590–1642, extensive records of this sort have been preserved for only the Lord Admiral's men and the Earl of Worcester's men acting at Henslowe's theatres 1597–1604. In spite of repeated statements to the contrary, however, there is no evidence that the King's company, or Queen Henrietta's company, or the Palsgrave's company, or the Lady Elizabeth's company, or any of the others handled their play purchases very differently unless the dramatist was himself a patented member of the troupe. It seems easy for many critics to forget that all the London acting companies were commercial organizations trying, however unsuccessfully, to make a living for actors, playhouse owners, playwrights, musicians, and theatre attendants. The general organization of the adult companies was much the same whether the actors were the Lady Elizabeth's men or the King's men, whether the dramatists were Richard Hathaway or Robert Daborne or William Shakespeare or James Shirley, whether the theatre was the Rose or the Hope or the Globe or the Phoenix.

Henslowe's system can be seen from the full form, often

2. R. A. Foakes and R. T. Rickert ed., *Henslowe's Diary*, Cambridge, 1961, pp. 294 and 167.

abbreviated, of his records of a transaction about payment to a dramatist for a play to be acted by one of the companies he financed.

> Lent [i.e. paid out in cash to be charged against the company] unto _____ [an actor, a patented member of the company] to pay to _____ [the author, or authors of the play] in earnest of _____ [the play, usually unfinished at the time of the first payment] . . . 10s.

These are the essentials of the transaction between the playwright and the producers of his play as usually set down in the only surviving full theatrical records of the period. The actual entry in Henslowe's ledger may be stated in a variety of ways, but the vital information is usually there, however the form of the record may vary.

> Lent unto Thomas Downton the 20 of February 1598 [/99] to lend unto Anthony Munday upon his second part of The Downfall of Earl Huntington Surnamed Robin Hood, I say lent the sum of . . . 20s.

> Lent unto Harry Chettle the 9 of September 1598 in earnest of a book called Brute. At the appointment of John Singer the sum of . . . 20s.

> Received by me William Haughton for the use of Thomas Dekker on the 30th of January the sum of . . . 20s. In part of payment for the book of Truth's Supplication to Candle Light.[3]

Sometimes Henslowe's records have misled modern readers as to the essential nature of his play-buying transactions because some of the men we think of as dramatists were also actors and patented members of companies. As such they could act as company representatives, without any reference at all to their literary capacities, as Shakespeare did when he received payment, along with William Kempe and Richard Burbage, for two performances be-

3. Ibid., pp. 87, 98, 64.

fore the Queen by the Lord Chamberlain's men in December 1594. In Henslowe's records actor-dramatists like Thomas Heywood or Charles Massey or Samuel Rowley sometimes act as representatives of the company in authorizing Henslowe's purchase of another man's play for their fellows, as indicated in Henslowe's payment in May 1603: "Lent at the appointment of Thomas Heywood and John Duke unto Harry Chettle and John Day in earnest of a play wherein Shore's wife is written the sum of . . . 40s."[4] Here the coupling of the names of the two patented members of the Earl of Worcester's company, Heywood and Duke, makes it clear that Heywood was acting as a member of the company authorizing payment to the playwrights Henry Chettle and John Day, and not as a dramatist himself. Sometimes Henslowe does not name the agent but simply records that his payment for the manuscript was authorized by the real purchasers of the play for whom he acted:

> Paid at the appointment of the company the 12 of February 1602 [/03] unto Thomas Heywood in part of payment for his play called A Woman Killed with Kindness . . . £3.
>
> Lent unto the company the 12 of October 1598 to pay unto Mr. Chapman in full payment for his play called the Fountain of New Fashions . . . 20s.[5]

In all these various and sometimes confusing forms of entry the essential fact is always the same—the dramatists were the employees of the company, and Henslowe was not buying the play for himself, but simply acting as agent for the Lord Admiral's company or the Earl of Worcester's men.

All the evidence we have suggests that this system was not peculiar to Henslowe or to the last decade of Queen

4. Ibid., p. 226.
5. Ibid., pp. 224, 99.

Elizabeth's reign. The Star Chamber case concerning the writing and acting of George Chapman's lost play *The Old Joiner of Aldgate* by Paul's Boys in February 1602/1603 indicates that Thomas Woodford (later one of the lessors of the Whitefriars theatre) was acting in a capacity not unlike Henslowe's for that theatre. Woodford, who was one of the defendants in the libel suit about the play, admitted in his deposition that:

> ... he did buy a stage play of George Chapmen ... and paid for the same twenty marks [£13 6s 8d] which play was called *The Old Joiner of Aldgate* and was played at some several times the last Hilary term by the Children of Pauls by this defendant's means and appointment, but before the playing thereof the same was licensed to be played by the Master of the Revels. ...[6]

George Chapman, another of the defendants in the Star Chamber case, deposed that:

> before Christmas last past ... Woodford coming to me and being then acquainted that I was about a play called *The Old Joiner of Aldgate*, I then told ... Woodford that he should have the same play of me when it was finished. And so I then sold the same to Woodford but did not finish it until after Christmas last and then I delivered the same out of my hands.[7]

In this case, as in the similar one 21 or 22 years later concerning *Keep the Widow Waking*, all the defendants and many of the witnesses were concerned to avoid charges of conspiracy and defamation, and much of the testimony—including earlier parts of Chapman's—is evasive. Probably Chapman was admitting as little involvement as he could, and he may even have suppressed facts; surely his relation-

6. C. J. Sisson, *Lost Plays of Shakespeare's Age*, Cambridge, 1936, p. 70.
7. Ibid., p. 66.

ship with Woodford was not quite so casual as he implies, since he wrote several plays for the rival boy company and at least one other one for Paul's Boys. Indeed the pointedly contemporary if not libelous play of *The Old Joiner of Aldgate* might almost be taken as an attempt to meet the complaint about the company made by a character in *Jack Drum's Entertainment* a couple of years before.

> *Fortune.* I saw the Children of Paul's last night,
> And troth they pleased me pretty, pretty well:
> The apes in time will do it handsomely.
> *Planet.* I'faith, I like the audience that frequenteth there
> With much applause: A man shall not be choked
> With the stench of garlic; nor be pasted
> To the barmy jacket of a beer-brewer.
> *Brabant Jr.* 'Tis a good, gentle audience, and I hope the boys
> Will come one day into the Court of Requests.
> *Brabant Sr.* Aye, and they had good plays. But they produce
> Such musty fopperies of antiquity,
> And do not suit the humourous age's backs
> With clothes in fashion.   [act 5, scene 1]

However much George Chapman may have omitted or evaded in his testimony, what he does admit clearly shows Woodford advancing the money to pay him for a play which all the testimony in the case shows to have been shortly acted by the boys.

Essentially the same system was operating ten or twelve years later in the affairs of the Lady Elizabeth's company, as shown in correspondence, contracts, and complaints left by Edward Alleyn and now preserved among the muniments of Alleyn's College of God's Gift at Dulwich.

Most explicit is the statement in the articles drawn up between Nathan Field, the leader of Lady Elizabeth's company, on the one part and Philip Henslowe and Jacob Meade, owners of the Bear Garden and later of the Hope theatre on the other. One of the articles of the agreement reads:

> And further the said Philip Henslowe and Jacob Meade do for them their executors and administrators covenant and grant to and with the said Nathan Field by these presents in manner and form following, that is to say that they the said Philip Henslowe and Jacob Meade or one of them shall and will from time to time during the said term disburse and lay out such sum or sums of money as shall be thought fitting by four or five of the sharers of the said company to be chosen by the said Philip and Jacob, or one of them, to be paid for any play which they shall buy or condition or agree for. So always as the said company do and shall truly repay unto the said Philip and Jacob, their executors or assigns all such sum and sums of money as they shall disburse for any play upon the second or third day whereon the same play shall be played by the said company without fraud or longer delay. . . .[8]

The vellum of this document has decayed, and the lower part, which would have carried the date and the signatures of the principals and the witnesses, has been torn away, but it is likely that it was completed and signed about the end of June 1613. The document nonetheless shows what the pattern was and how the principals in the handling of the affairs of the Lady Elizabeth's company assumed that dramatists and their manuscripts would be handled.

The operation of this process as agreed between the leader of Lady Elizabeth's company and Henslowe is shown in some of their correspondence preserved in the same muniment room. About the end of June 1613, Field wrote for the company to Henslowe:

Mr. Henslowe:
    Mr. Daborne and I have spent a great deal of time in conference about this plot which will make as bene-

8. W. W. Greg, ed., *Henslowe Papers*, London, 1907, p. 24.

ficial a play as has come these seven years. It is out of his love he detains it for us. Only £10 is desired in hand, for which we will be bound to bring you in the play finished upon the first day of August. We would not lose it, we have so assured a hope of it, and, on my knowledge, Mr. Daborne may have his request of another company. Pray let us have speedy answer, and effectual. You know the last money you disbursed was justly paid in, and we are now in a way to pay you all. So, unless you yourself for want of small supply will put us out of it again, pray let us know when we shall speak with you. Till when and ever, I rest

Your loving and obedient son
Nat: Field[9]

In spite of some confusion about the antecedents of his pronouns whereby "we" sometimes refers to Daborne and Field, as dramatist and company leader, but more often to the sharers of the Lady Elizabeth's company, Field makes it clear enough that as representative of his troupe he is urging their financial agent to make a large down-payment for them to Robert Daborne, who is at work on a most promising play.

However successful Robert Daborne may have been as a playwright, he was none too reliable a character, as his correspondence shows, and it would appear that he was capable of playing Henslowe off against the players. This game is suggested in a letter of his dated 14 October 1613, but it nonetheless shows the agreement of Henslowe, Meade, and Field at work. It also shows some of the troubles which the financial agent for a Jacobean acting company had to go through. Daborne writes:

Mr. Henslowe, I builded upon your promise to my wife, neither did I acquaint the company with any money I had of you because they should seek to you as I know they will and give you any terms you can desire. If they

9. Ibid., p. 84.

do not, I will bring you your money for the papers, and many thanks. Neither will I fail to bring in the whole play next week. Wherefore I pray sir of all friendship disburse one forty shillings, and this note shall suffice to acknowledge myself indebted to you with my quarter's rent £8 for which you shall either have the whole company's bonds to pay you the first day of my play being played, or the King's men shall pay it you and take my papers. Sir, my credit is as dear to me now as ever, and I will be as careful of it as heretofore, or may I never prosper nor mine. So desiring this may satisfy you till you appoint a time when I shall bring you the company's bond, I rest, expecting your no more deferring me.

14 October   Ever at your command,
1613   Rob: Daborne[10]

Daborne's threat that the King's company, playing at the Globe and Blackfriars, were eager to take his play may or may not be true, but he thought it might influence Henslowe, and such competition for manuscripts was not unusual.

This playing off of Henslowe against the company was a very reckless procedure. It was sure to make difficulties at this time when the Lady Elizabeth's company was not very successful and was having internal troubles of its own, as various other documents show. One such document consists of a series of articles of grievance against Henslowe drawn up by the Lady Elizabeth's players in 1615. The company was heavily in Henslowe's debt, and most of the articles charge that Henslowe confused the debts of individual actors in the company with the indebtedness of the company as a whole, or that he withheld from the company articles that were rightfully theirs. It should be remembered, however, that these are the complaints of actors in financial straits, and that no copy of Henslowe's defense has survived. Anyone who has read the bills of the plain-

10. Ibid., p. 76.

tiffs and the answers of the defendants in Elizabethan and Jacobean lawsuits is familiar with the vastly different assertions about the same series of events always made by the two antagonistic parties. At any rate, one of the charges, however exaggerated or unfounded, concerned Henslowe's buying, as their agent, of plays for the repertory of the company. "Also we have paid him for play books £200 or thereabouts, and yet he denies to give us the copies of any one of them."[11] The players here assumed as normal Henslowe's purchase of plays for them; the disagreement concerned possession of the manuscripts. Henslowe would probably have claimed that he kept the manuscripts as security for the company's general debt to him, but the Lady Elizabeth's men wanted to keep them in their own archives, since they said they had repaid the sums he advanced for plays and the manuscripts were legally theirs.

The records of Philip Henslowe preserved by his son-in-law in the muniment room at Dulwich College are so uniquely numerous and varied that one tends to forget that other managers or enterpreneurs surely had nearly as many, but lacked a son-in-law who was at once in the same profession, devoted to it, rich, and the founder of a permanent institution. Casual destruction has been the fate of most Elizabethan and Jacobean records of all kinds, including those theatrical archives of James Burbage, Philip Rosseter, Aaron Holland, John Heminges, Thomas Woodford, Richard Gunnell, Christopher and William Beeston, and Richard Heton. All these men must have kept records which would have paralleled Henslowe's at many points, but all have disappeared and we can glimpse their similar activities only when they are revealed indirectly in the archives of some governmental or ecclesiastical body—in Treasury payments, the Lord Chamberlain's accounts, or the wills preserved at Somerset House, or in

11. Ibid., p. 89.

the documents of lawsuits in Chancery, the Court of Requests, the King's Bench, and the Star Chamber.

One such revealing legal action is set out in a bill of information in the Star Chamber against John Audley and several dramatists and other theatre people to recover damages for the alleged victimization of Anne Elsden. One action complained against was the writing and acting at the Red Bull of a defamatory play in 1624. Thomas Dekker was called as a witness and testified

> . . . that John Webster . . . William Rowley, John Ford, and this defendant were privy consenting and acquainted with the making and contriving of the said play called Keep the Widow Waking and did make and contrive the same upon the instructions given them by one Ralph Savage. And this defendant sayeth that he this defendant did often see the said play or part thereof acted, but how often he cannot depose. . . .[12]

Dekker's testimony suggests that in 1624 Ralph Savage, who Professor Sisson thought was the successor of Aaron Holland, builder and owner of the Red Bull, was acting as financial backer and intermediary with dramatists in a capacity not unlike that of Philip Henslowe for the actors at the Rose, Fortune, and Hope.

This relationship of dramatist and acting company as employee and employer appears to have been standard. It was still in effect in the 1630s at the Red Bull, the most vulgar of the public theatres,[13] and at the Salisbury Court, one of the exclusive private theatres. It was taken as normal in the suit of *Heton* versus *Brome*, brought in 1640 in the Court of Requests but citing events and conditions going back as far as 1633. In his answer to the bill of complaint, the dramatist Richard Brome, a protégé of Ben

---

12. *Library*, 4th series, VIII (September 1927), 258.
13. See *Jacobean and Caroline Stage*, VI, 238–247.

Jonson, says that eighteen months before July 1635 the company at Salisbury Court

> did entice and enveigle this defendant to depart and leave the company of the Red Bull players being the Prince's highness servants [i.e., Prince Charles (II) company which had been formed in 1631] and where this defendant was then very well entertained and truly paid without murmuring or wrangling and to come and write and compose and make plays for the said complainants and their said company. . . .[14]

Brome does not give the particular conditions under which he was writing plays for the Red Bull company in the early 1630s, but he does say that he was "very well entertained and truly paid" and evidently considered himself a servant of the troupe at the Red Bull then—Prince Charles's [II] company.

The suit from which this statement comes primarily involved Richard Brome's relations with another company as a dramatist under contract to them. The full details of this contract can be more appropriately discussed later, but it is relevant to note here that on 20 July 1635 Brome contracted with the troupe acting at the Salisbury Court theatre and with the owners of that theatre

> Anthony Berry, William Cartwright, the elder, Christopher Goad, George Stutville . . . Curtis Greville, John Young, Edward May, Timothy Reade, William Wilbraham and William Cartwright the younger the then owners and actors of the said house [Salisbury Court theatre] . . . that he the said Brome should for the term of three years then next ensuing with his best art and

14. Answer of Richard Brome, 6 March 1639/40, to the bill of Richard Heton and the Salisbury Court Players, 12 February 1639/40 in the Court of Requests, as transcribed by Ann Haaker in "The Plague, the Theatre and the Poet," *Renaissance Drama*, n.s. (1968), pp. 296–306.

industry write every year three plays and deliver them to the company of players. . . .[15]

A normal part of the dramatist's preparation of his play for the acting troupe was the reading of his manuscript to them for their approval. Since, as is well known, all the companies of the time were repertory companies, the dramatist knew in advance a good deal about the kind of production his play might get, and a skillful writer of experience could go far in adapting the requirements of at least the major roles to the leading members listening to his reading. In this situation a great advantage lay with the actor-dramatists like Samuel and William Rowley, William Shakespeare, Thomas Heywood, and Nathan Field, whose daily familiarity with the styles and talents of their fellows made it easier for them to exploit special gifts and to anticipate difficulties.

There are various allusions to this usual step of the reading to the company. In March of 1598/99 Henslowe paid Drayton, Dekker, and Chettle £6 5s in two installments for a play called *The Famous Wars of Henry I and the Prince of Wales*. It is indicative of a common attitude of the players and their agents toward the plays the dramatists were preparing for them that when Henslowe made his first payment in behalf of the company for this piece he did not know the title, but he *did* know about a leading role which the playwrights were writing into it. He called the piece "A book wherein is a part of a Welshman written which they have promised to deliver by the twentieth day next following." After his entry recording the payment in full, he notes: "Lent at that time to the company for to spend at the reading of that book at the Sun in New Fish Street . . . 5s."[16] About a year and a half later Robert Shaw reported another play-reading to Henslowe, in this case,

15. Ibid., p. 297.
16. Foakes and Rickert, p. 88.

apparently, of a manuscript which had been completed without any installment payments:

Mr. Henslowe:

We have heard their book and like it. Their price is eight pounds, which I pray pay now to Mr. Wilson, according to our promise. I would have come myself, but that I am troubled with a sciatica,

Yours,

Robert Shaa.[17]

In May and June of 1602 Henslowe financed for the Lord Admiral's men the writing and production of a play probably entitled *Jephtha Judge of Israel* but which Henslowe persistently calls "Jeffa." It was written by Anthony Munday and Thomas Dekker who were paid £5 for their work on 5 May 1602. Evidently the company expected a good deal of the new play, for in the next two months expenditures of £13 17s are recorded for costumes and properties for "Jeffa." The play had its reading before the company, for in the ledger is recorded an expenditure of two shillings "Laid out for the company when they read the play of Jeffa for wine at the tavern. Delivered unto Thomas Downton."[18]

Ten years later the correspondence between the dramatist Robert Daborne and Henslowe shows that Daborne took for granted the reading of his manuscript to the company as the final step in his composition. On 16 May 1613 Daborne wrote asking for further advances and reassuring Henslowe that his manuscript was almost finished, though he was not yet quite ready to read it to the assembled members of the Lady Elizabeth's players. ". . . I doubt not on Tuesday night if you will appoint I will meet you and Mr. Alleyn and read some, for I am unwilling to read to the general company till all be finished, which upon my

17. Ibid., p. 288.
18. Ibid., p. 201.

credit shall be to play it this next term with the first."[19] But Daborne's promises were never reliable and nearly a month later he had not yet finished the play but was still taking for granted his reading before the company.

> . . . Before God they shall not stay one hour for me, for I can this week deliver in the last word and will that night they play their new play read this, whereof I have sent you a sheet and more fair written. You may easily know there is not much behind and I intend no other thing, God is my judge, till this be finished . . . wherefore I pray send me the other twenty shillings I desired and then when I read next week I will. . . .[20]

At the end of the year Daborne was working on two other plays for the Lady Elizabeth's company, one the revision of an old play, and the other a new one called *The Owl*. At the end of a letter dated 31 December 1613 asking for more money in advance, this time ten shillings, Daborne adds a postscript: "On Monday I will come to you and appoint for the reading the old book and bringing in the new."[21] At the foot of the letter Henslowe has added a note, "Paid upon this bill toward *The Owl* 10s."

Though the dramatist's reading of his completed manuscript to the assembled company seems to have been customary, as these items show, preliminary readings to the actors of portions of an unfinished manuscript were not unknown. In his ledger Henslowe made the entry: "Lent unto Benjamin Jonson the 3 of December 1597 upon a book which he showed the plot unto the company which he promised to deliver unto the company at Christmas next the sum of . . . 20s."[22]

Sixteen years later Robert Daborne was prepared for a similar reading of an uncompleted manuscript which, as usual, was behind schedule.

19. Greg, *Henslowe Papers*, p. 70.
20. Ibid., pp. 72–73.
21. Ibid., p. 81. 22. Foakes and Rickert, p. 85.

Some papers I have sent you, though not so fair written all as I could wish; I will now wholly intend to finish my promise which though it come not within compass of this term shall come upon the neck of this new play they are now studying. My request is the £10 might be made up whereof I have had £9. If you please to appoint any hour to read to Mr. Alleyn, I will not fail, nor after this day lose any time till it be concluded.[23]

Henslowe was again accommodating, and a signed receipt for £1, dated 8 May 1613 is written at the foot of the letter.

Rejections

Even in a time of such constant demand for plays as the days of Elizabeth, James, and Charles, a number must have been rejected by the acting companies. Of course the great majority of the plays of whose preparation we have any knowledge were performed; nevertheless a few records of rejections by the players have been preserved.

One would guess that even in a time when the social status of the playwright was low, a fair number of amateur plays would have been boldly or surreptitiously offered to the London acting companies and rejected by them. For though many extant plays of the period were written by dilettantes and often given amateur performance, it is surprising how few of them reached the boards of the metropolitan theatres—at least before the reign of Charles I. Of more than 500 plays known to have been given professional performance in London between 1590 and 1625, less than half a dozen (aside from a group of four or five acted by the King's Revels Boys in 1607–1608) are known to have been written by amateurs. For the most part the presumed rejections of amateur offerings are unrecorded, but one is mentioned in print.

In 1635 the printer Richard Royston brought out John

23. Greg, *Henslowe Papers*, p. 69.

Jones's play *Adrasta, or the Woman's Spleen and Love's Conquest.* John Jones wrote a dedication to his friends in which he said:

> Having long since (honored Gentlemen, and friends) finished this play and fitted it for the stage, I intended to have had there the Promethean fire of action infused into it: being thereto encouraged by the general good liking and content which many of you had vouchsafed to receive in the hearings of it. . . . This I say was encouragement enough for me to prefer this little glowworm . . . to the stage, and to bring it to that noble nursery of action. . . . But the players, upon a slight and half view of it, refused to do it that right. . . .

The modern reader of this play, even "upon a slight and half view of it," is likely to think that the judgment of the players was quite sound.

Of course plays by professionals or semiprofessionals were also rejected on occasion, and a few records of such rejections have been preserved. After Henslowe had paid installments amounting to £1 19s to Richard Hathaway and William Rankin for a play eventually to be called *The Conquest of Spain by John of Gaunt,* he received a letter in April 1601 from Samuel Rowley, a leading member of the Lord Admiral's company, saying: "Mr. Henslowe, I pray you to let Mr. Hathaway have his papers again of the play of John of Gaunt and for the repayment of the money back again he is content to give you a bill of his hand to be paid at some certain time as in your discretion you shall think good."[24] Of course there is no indication of what the company thought was wrong with the play, but their rejection occasioned no serious break with Hathaway, for he wrote at least three more plays for the Admiral's men in the next year and a half.

Nearly forty years later a semiprofessional, Thomas

24. Greg, *Henslowe Papers,* p. 56.

Nabbes, left a record that one of the plays he offered an acting company had been refused. Nabbes was fairly experienced, and at the time of his rejection at least four of his plays had had professional London productions at the Phoenix or the Salisbury Court theatres. But his piece called *The Unfortunate Mother* was rejected by the actors, to his considerable annoyance. On the title page it is designated "A Tragedie. Never acted," and in the dedication to Richard Brathwait the author says:

> I have (though boldly being a stranger) elected you to countenance a piece that (undeservedly I hope) hath been denied the credit which it might have gained from the stage; though I can accuse myself of no error in it, more than a nice curiosity (which notwithstanding I must boast to be without precedent) in the method: where I have denied myself much liberty, that may be allowed a Poet from old example, and new established custom.

The method by which he denied himself "much liberty" was probably his careful maintenance of a unity of place within each act, but evidently his scrupulosity did not appeal to the actors.

A more experienced and successful playwright than Jones or Nabbes has also indicated that he had plays rejected by a London acting company. In the suit of *Heton* versus *Brome*, Richard Brome states in his answer to the bill of complaint that in the autumn of 1638 he had signed a new contract to write plays and do other dramatic chores for Queen Henrietta's players at the Salisbury Court theatre.

> And this defendant upon the last agreement in the bill mentioned for twenty shillings a week . . . composed another new play for the said complainants, and before Easter term 1639 this defendant brought them another new play written all but part of the last

scene. But this defendant found that divers of the company did so slight the last-mentioned plays and used such scornful and reproachful speeches concerning this defendant divers of them did advise the rest of them to stop all weekly payments towards this defendant, so as this defendant understood that they took occasion daily to weary the defendant from and out of their employment. . . .[25]

At the time he prepared this answer to Heton's bill Brome was being sued for breach of contract by the players and proprietors of the Salisbury Court theatre for whom he had written a number of plays; it was therefore to his advantage in the suit to emphasize the "scornful and reproachful speeches" of the actors. Nevertheless it can scarcely be doubted that the plays mentioned were refused by the players, though not necessarily with so much scorn as it was to Brome's advantage to assert.

Plays Bought without Reference to the Authors

Though the usual way for an acting company to secure a manuscript for production was to deal with the dramatist who wrote it, there were others. A good many records have been preserved showing that companies sometimes secured the manuscripts of plays and then acted them without any dealings with the author at all, and in most instances evidently without his knowledge. This custom, which so offends the modern concept of literary property, was not illegal, and there are few if any records of protests by the playwrights. The dramatist sold his manuscript to the acting company for which it had been prepared; after that it was no more his than the cloak that he might have sold to the actors at the same time.

In the spring of 1598 Henslowe bought for the company a collection of old plays offered to him by Martin

25. Answer of Richard Brome, as transcribed by Haaker in "The Plague, the Theatre, and the Poet," p. 304.

Slater, a leading actor and later a company manager. Slater had, until recently, been a member of the Lord Admiral's company which had in the past three years produced all these plays; how he got the manuscripts is not known, but the fact that he was later a company manager and a member of the Ironmongers' Company suggests that he probably had some capital, and there are other records of actors who acquired play manuscripts as personal property. Henslowe records that he: "Lent unto the company the 16 of May to buy 5 books of Martin Slater called 2 parts of Hercules, and Phocas, and Pythagoras, and Alexander and Lodowick, which last book he hath not yet delivered, the sum of . . . £7."[26] Evidently this payment did not completely cover *Alexander and Lodowick*, which Slater for some reason did not deliver with the others, but two months later he brought it in and was paid separately: "Paid unto Martin Slater the 18 of July for a book called Alexander and Lodowick, the sum of . . . 20s."[27]

In September 1601 Henslowe bought for the Lord Admiral's company, from Edward Alleyn, the manuscript of *The Wise Man of West Chester*, almost certainly the same play as *John a Kent and John a Cumber*, the manuscript of which is still extant. He recorded in his ledger: "Paid at the appointment of [the name of some member of the Lord Admiral's company is omitted] the 19 of September 1601 for the play of the Wise Man of West Chester unto my son E. Alleyn the sum of . . . 40s."[28] Since this play had previously been one of the most popular in the repertory of the company, this manuscript bought from Alleyn was probably a revision which had come into his possession. In any case, Anthony Munday, the author, was not a party to the transaction.

Four months later the company again authorized Henslowe to buy plays from Alleyn, again plays which had

26. Foakes and Rickert, p. 89.
27. Ibid., pp. 89 and 93.   28. Ibid., p. 181.

been in the repertory five to eight years before. "Paid at the appointment of the company the 18 of January 1601 [/1602] unto E. Alleyn for three books which were played called The French Doctor, The Massacre of France, and The Nut, the sum of . . . £6."[29]

It is notable that Henslowe was buying these secondhand plays at the rate of £2 per manuscript. The rate was the same for Alleyn and for Slater, if one considers the two parts of *Hercules* as one play and notes that Henslowe withheld half the price for *Alexander and Lodowick* until he had the manuscript in hand. The rate was also the same in August following when Henslowe paid Alleyn £4 for two more old manuscripts, one of *Philip of Spain* and another of *Longshanks*, and again the same in October when he paid Alleyn £2 for "his Booke of tambercam."[30] It appears that in the last five or six years of the reign of Elizabeth the going rate for secondhand plays was approximately one-third that for new plays—at least with the Henslowe companies.

This traffic in old play manuscripts was still current thirty years later when the Master of the Revels noted in his office book: "Received of Beeston [Christopher Beeston, manager of Queen Henrietta's company at the Phoenix or Cockpit in Drury Lane] for an old play called *Hymen's Holiday*, newly revived at their house, being a play given unto him for my use, this 15 August, £3. Received of him for some alterations in it £1."[31] The play, which is lost, had been written by William Rowley for his company, the Duke of York's men, sometime before February 1611/12 when it was performed at court. Since at the time of Herbert's entry Rowley had been dead for seven or eight years, it is not likely that the play was given to Beeston

29. Ibid., p. 187.
30. Ibid., pp. 204 and 205.
31. J. Q. Adams, ed., *The Dramatic Records of Sir Henry Herbert*, New Haven, 1917, p. 35.

by the author but by someone who had come by the manuscript. Probably it had been long unacted, since Beeston considered it necessary to pay for having it revised.

Though in particular cases we seldom know how the vendor of a play manuscript by some other man came by his commodity, we do have repeated examples of one method.

Among Henslowe's papers is a deed of sale made by the actor Richard Jones to Edward Alleyn and dated 3 January 1588/89.

> Be it known unto all men by these presents that I Richard Jones of London yeoman for and in consideration of the sum of £37-10/- . . . to me by Edward Alleyn of London gentleman well and truly paid have bargained and sold and . . . have delivered to the same Edward Alleyn all and singular such share, part, and portion of playing apparel, play books, instruments and other commodities whatsoever belonging to the same as I the said Richard Jones now have or of right ought to have jointly with the same Edward Alleyn, John Allen, Citizen and Innholder of London and Robert Browne yeoman to have, hold, and enjoy all the singular my said share of playing apparel, play books, instruments and other commodities whatsoever. . . .[82]

By this deed Richard Jones is making over to Alleyn those properties, including play books, which he held jointly with Edward Alleyn, John Allen, and Robert Browne as the sharing members of some acting company, perhaps the Earl of Worcester's men. We have here one of the possible sources from which Alleyn secured some of the costumes and play manuscripts which were later bought by Henslowe on behalf of one or another of the companies he financed.

But Alleyn and Slater were not peculiar. Twenty to thirty years later there is still evidence of this same phe-

32. Foakes and Rickert, pp. 273–74.

nomenon of play manuscripts from the repertory of a hard-pressed or breaking company getting into the hands of a solvent or unscrupulous actor. About 1618 or 1619 five of the patented members of Queen Anne's London company, Richard Perkins, John Cumber, William Robbins, James Holt, and Thomas Heywood, brought suit in the Court of Chancery against their former fellow in the company, Robert Lee. They say that Lee had left the troupe two years before and had agreed, for a consideration, to give up playing and to restore to the company "all such clothes, books of plays, and other goods belonging thereunto as he had then or were trusted in his hands or custody. . . ." They say he had returned nothing but had set up another acting company by enticing away seven of their young men and "also detaineth from your orators divers books, apparel, and other goods of theirs to the value of £100. . . ."[33] Lee's answer has not been found, but his defense would probably have been that his former fellows had defaulted on their bonds. In any case Lee had in his possession the manuscripts of plays which had been written for Queen Anne's men. Perhaps he used them in performances by his new company, but there was nothing to prevent him selling them to some other acting company or to a manager like Beeston or an entrepreneur like Edward Alleyn.

Another player and sharer in an acting company is known to have been in possession of play manuscripts. William Browne, a fellow of Prince Charles [II] company acting at the Red Bull made his will on 23 October 1634 and was buried at St. James's, Clerkenwell, on 6 November following. In his will he left to his mother Susan Greene, alias Baskervile, whom he made his executrix,

> All such sum and sums of money, debts, duties, claims challenges, and demands whatsoever as either is ought, or shall be due, owing, or belonging unto me forth, out

33. Public Record Office, Chancery Proceedings, James I, P 16/14.

of, and from the Red Bull playhouse . . . whereof I am a member and a fellow sharer, or of or by any of the shares or other persons players there or owners thereof and of in or to any house or houses to the said playhouse adjoining. . . .[34]

Later, suit was brought in the Court of Requests against Susan Greene, alias Baskervile, concerning financial relations with the company at the Red Bull. As part of the proceedings she made an affidavit on 29 May 1635 saying that she "hath had and received no part of the goods and chattels that William Browne deceased died possessed of save only one cloth cloak, one old horseman's coat, two pair of laced cuffs, and a house clock, a silver tobacco box, and four play books, things of small value."[35] There is no known record of what Susan Baskervile did with the play manuscripts her son had retained from the archives of Prince Charles's [II] company, but she had long experience of the London theatre world since the time of her first actor-husband, Thomas Greene, and it is not unlikely that she found some manager who would pay her for her manuscripts.

These various records of the ownership and sale of play manuscripts without reference to the author not only suggest one of the ways in which London acting companies came to act plays known to have been written for some other company, but they further emphasize the playwright's lack of control over his own compositions. Far from being a sacred holograph, a dramatist's manuscript was often treated simply as another theatrical commodity, like a cloth cloak or laced cuffs, "things of small value."

34. *Jacobean and Caroline Stage*, ii, 391–92 and 636–37.
35. Public Record Office, Req. Misc. Books, Affidavit, Hilary to Trinity, 10 and 11 Charles I, vol. 138.

CHAPTER V

Dramatists' Pay

THOUGH PLAYWRIGHTS were the servants of the acting companies and theatres, and though actors, theatres, and dramatists stood rather low in social esteem in these times, a little consideration of contemporary remunerations shows that professional playwrights were not ill paid.

The financial rewards of the dramatist in the reigns of Elizabeth, James, and Charles have too often been lamented in the romantic context of golden words poured out for posterity by the starving drudge in the frigid garret, or, for example, in a scandalized comparison of the £6 Thomas Heywood received for the composition of *A Woman Killed with Kindness* with the £6 13*s* paid for a single costume to be used in the performance of his tragedy.[1] As a matter of fact, the scattered evidence of

1. This discrepancy between the sum paid for a play and the sum paid for a fine costume is simply sound economy on the part of the Earl of Worcester's men. Every new play was a gamble; it might fail dismally and the sum paid its author would constitute a total

payment records, compensation correspondence, contracts, and the comments of contemporaries suggests that professional playwrights like Chettle, Dekker, Heywood, Middleton, Shakespeare, Shirley, and Brome took in more cash from their professional activities than was usual for writers or for those in some related professions. We can look at a few comparative figures of payments in the time.

Precise information about any payments to nondramatic writers in the three reigns is scanty; anything like a record of consecutive payments or annual incomes of nondramatic writers is almost unheard of. Of course they commonly cry poor, but so do most men in most times; the literary man is simply better equipped to carry his cry to posterity.

In the sixteenth and seventeenth centuries the ancient system of patronage was still in vogue, though writers who mention it generally call it inadequate—often insulting. But printing and publishing became a profitable trade during the reign of Elizabeth, and writers were supplementing or often substituting the publishers' payments in cash or in kind for patronage from the noble or wealthy. Thus many writers drew their incomes from two sources.

There is only one known detailed account of such income from a writer of the time. Richard Robinson, who published from 1576 to 1600, left an account of his literary receipts, called *Eupolemia,* which forms part of a manuscript now preserved in the British Museum.[2] In these accounts Robinson set down his receipts for a number of his publications from *A Record of Ancient Histories,* 1577, to *A Fourth Proceeding in the Harmony of King David's*

---

loss for the company. A fine costume, on the other hand, could be used for years and for many different plays, whether the production for which it had been originally purchased was a long-running success or a complete failure.

2. *Royal 18 A* LXVI, fols. 5–13. A transcript was published in 1924 by George McGill Vogt in *Studies in Philology,* XXI (October 1924), 629–48.

Harp, 1596. Apparently he tried for a gift from a patron in connection with each publication, but he was only intermittently successful. When he presented *Part of the Harmony of King David's Harp* to the Earl of Warwick, he received nothing; when he dedicated *The Laudable Society, Order and Unity of Prince Arthur and his Knights of the Round Table* to Thomas Smith, president of the London Archery Society, he was rewarded with a present of five shillings; Alexander Nowell, Dean of St. Paul's, the dedicatee of *The Dial of Daily Contemplation for Sinners*, gave him ten shillings; he fared better when he dedicated a book of prayers to Sir Philip Sidney, who gave him £2, to which his father, Sir Henry, added 10 shillings more. He did best with the Earl of Rutland and Sir Christopher Hatton, both of whom gave him £3, the former as a reward for the dedication of a translation of Melancthon, and the latter for a dedication in 1583.

Robinson often supplemented these gifts from dedicatees by selling copies of his book which the publisher had given to him as payment. By such peddling he sold 25 copies of the volume he had dedicated to the Dean of St. Paul's and added 25 shillings to the ten which the dean had given him. In the same way he sold 25 copies of a translation he had dedicated to a judge of the Admiralty and added 25 shillings to the 12 he had received from the judge. When the Earl of Warwick gave him nothing for his dedication, Robinson took 100 copies from the publisher, which he succeeded in selling for £10—but he notes that it took him two years to sell them. These peddling activities were clearly intended to supplement inadequate rewards from dedicatees, for Robinson notes in reference to the book for which Sir Christopher Hatton gave him £3: "I bestowed very few of these books abroad by reason of his liberality which kept me from troubling my friends abroad for one whole year's space afterwards."[3]

3. Vogt transcription, *Studies in Philology*, XXI (October 1924), 636.

Robinson's total receipts from his writing in this period of nearly twenty years have been analyzed by Edward Haviland Miller.[4] In three instances Robinson's accounts are incomplete and Miller has supplemented them with receipts estimated from those recorded for the other books. During the period of these accounts Robinson's gifts from patrons to whom he had made dedications amounted to £23 6s 4d; his receipts from peddling the copies of his books which the publisher had given him came to £29 11s 1d; so that his total recorded remuneration from writing between 1577 and 1596 reached the grand total of £52 17s 5d for an average of less than £3 per year.

We have similar records of payments made to writers for the theatres, but these are the only detailed accounts of payments made in the period to writers for patrons and publishers. How far from the average receipts of nondramatic writers were Robinson's? The very few casual records of rewards and payments suggest that Robinson's literary income was not so very far short of those of some other nondramatic writers.

A few scattered allusions to payments or gifts to poets were collected by David Nichol Smith for his account of "Authors and Patrons" in *Shakespeare's England*, 1916. There are several assertions that the publishers' usual rate for a pamphlet was 40 shillings. In the Cambridge University play of about 1600, *The Return from Parnassus*, part 1, act 1, scene 3 opens with the entrance of *Ingenioso* (probably a caricature of Thomas Nashe) and "Danter the Printer":[5]

> *Ingenioso.* Danter thou art deceived, wit is dearer than thou takest it to be. I tell thee this libel of Cambridge has much salt and pepper in the nose; it will sell

4. *The Professional Writer in Elizabethan England*, Cambridge, Mass., 1959, pp. 160–63.

5. John Danter published in London from 1589 to 1599. He printed a number of pamphlets and more than a dozen plays, including two of Shakespeare's, and is known to have sometimes been involved in surreptitious printing.

sheerly underhand [i.e. sell well by stealth] whereas these books of exhortations and catechisms be moulding on thy shop board.

Danter. It's true; but good faith, Master Ingenioso, I lost by your last book, and you know there is many a one that pays me largely for the printing of their inventions; but for all this you shall have 40 shillings and an odd pottle of wine.[6]

The same fee was mentioned by John Stephens in "The Author's Epistle Popular" which he prefixed to his anonymously published closet drama, *Cynthia's Revenge or Menander's Ecstasy*, in 1613. Stephens sneers at the front-matter appeals of popular writers of the time, who

> . . . assure the hood winked buzzards of this age that every syllable savors of milk sops, doth require an easy stomach, slight concoction, simple and weak judgment &c *ad infinitum*. Thus do our piebald naturalists depend upon poor wages, gape after the drunken harvest of forty shillings, and shame the worthy benefactors of Helicon. . . .

Whatever the reader may think of the comparative literary merits of Stephens's interminable play and the hackwork of the poetasters whom he castigates, his statement of the usual fee paid by the publishers is clear enough.

About a decade later George Wither, who had done a good deal of publishing of various kinds, indicated near the end of his pamphlet, *The Scholars' Purgatory*, that the usual fee was still the same as it had been in 1600.

> For what need the stationer be at the charge of printing the labors of him that is Master of his Art, and will require that respect which his pain deserveth? Seeing he can hire for a matter of 40 shillings some needy Ignoramus to scribble upon the same subject, and by a large

6. J. B. Leishman, ed., *The Three Parnassus Plays*, London, 1949, pp. 247–48.

promising title make it as vendible for an impression or two as though it had the quintessence of all art?[7]

And as late as the 1640s the standard payment for pamphlets appears to have remained unchanged. When John Aubry put together his notes on Sir John Birkenhead, editor of the famous Royalist newsbook *Mercurius Aulicus* and later a fellow of the Royal Society, he noted Birkenhead's activities after the fall of Oxford and his expulsion from his fellowship at All Souls. Aubry says that Birkenhead "got many a forty shillings (I believe) by pamphlets, such as that of *Colonel Pride*, and *The Last Will and Testament of Philip Earl of Pembroke*, &c."[8]

Publishers sometimes appear to have done better by their writers than they did by Robinson and the pamphleteers, but the circumstances are so ambiguous that one cannot tell how much work by the writer the payments represent. A case in point is the payment to John Stow in 1602.

John Stow was a best-selling English popular historian. His *Summary of English Chronicles* first appeared in 1565 and had gone through ten new editions with revisions before 1602; *A Survey of London* had been first printed in 1598. Both copyrights appear to have passed from the original publishing firms into the hands of the Stationers' Company itself. In 1602, and perhaps for some time before, Stow was making additions and revisions to both histories, which were to be reissued with additions, the former in 1604 and the latter in 1603. In these circumstances the court of the Stationers' Company, at its meeting of 2 August 1602, issued an order: "It is ordered that Mr. Stow shall have £3.0.0 and 40 copies for his pains in the book called *The Survey of London*. And £1.0.0. and 50 copies for his pains in *The Brief Chronicle* [i.e. *A Summary of*

7. *The Scholar's Purgatory*, London, n.d. (1625?), I₁ᵛ, p. 130.
8. Oliver Lawson Dick, ed., *Aubry's Brief Lives*, London, 1949, p. 23.

English Chronicles]."⁹ This order seems to authorize payment to Stow for his revisions and additions—which were extensive—in anticipation of good profits. The circumstances are obviously unusual because the high court, representing the entire membership of the guild of printers and publishers and not an individual printer, was involved. Nevertheless the remuneration is very little more than Richard Robinson was receiving, and the popular John Stow, like the less well-known Robinson, was required to peddle his own books.

The account that Richard Robinson left in his *Eupolemia* shows the average rewards from patronage for an ordinary writer in the last two decades of the sixteenth century. Other payments from patrons which are known are very scattered, and one can never tell—as one can with Robinson—to what extent they are representative of the writer's experience. Spenser's reward was a pension which he received only after years of work on *The Faerie Queene*; Prince Henry's individual gifts to writers were numerous, but the greatest one, to Chapman, was *promised*, but apparently never delivered before the death of the Prince; Drayton had from him an annuity of £10 per year, and Sylvester £20; Jonson said in 1619 that the Earl of Pembroke gave him £20 a year to buy books. But these records of patronage seem unusual. Nichol Smith concludes his survey of the patronage situation:

> In the absence of further evidence about the reward for the dedication of minor works, what Peele was given by the Earl of Northumberland for *The Honour of the Garter* may be taken as typical. Peele celebrated in this poem the earl's installation as a knight of the Garter in 1593, and he received for it £3.¹⁰

9. W. W. Greg and Eleanor Boswell, *Records of the Court of the Stationers' Company, 1576-1602*, London, 1930, pp. 90 and lxx–lxxi.

10. *Shakespeare's England*, Oxford, 1916, II, 210–11.

Before comparing these records of payments made to non-dramatic writers with those that professional playwrights received, it is worth recalling that the scale of pay for most intellectual activities during these three reigns also seems very low. University education was certainly no road to riches in the sixteenth and seventeenth centuries.

A calling somewhat comparable to that of the writer—at least in its requirements of literacy and training, though certainly not in respectability—was that of the schoolmaster. The profession was not unassociated with the drama: much of the development of English drama before the period of professionalism was in the hands of schoolmasters and teachers like Nicholas Udall, Thomas Ashton, John Redford, Richard Edwards, and John Ritwise; and even after the complete dominance of professionalism in the seventeenth century, plays were written by schoolmasters like John Mason, Samuel Bernard, Robert White, William Hawkins, and Thomas Singleton. Some of the professional dramatists had—or are said to have had—experience as schoolmasters. William Beeston, the son of Shakespeare's colleague Christopher Beeston, told John Aubrey that Shakespeare "had been in his younger years a schoolmaster in the country."[11] James Shirley was certainly a schoolmaster at St. Albans in the early 1620s before he came to London and became the regular dramatist for Queen Henrietta's company in the reign of Charles I.[12]

Various extant records give the pay of schoolmasters. According to the town charter of 1553 the salary of Shakespeare's schoolmaster at Stratford was fixed at £20 per annum. Sir Edmund Chambers comments on this rate of pay: "This was much more than the £12.5 paid at Warwick or than the amounts usual in grammar schools outside Westminster, Eton, Winchester and Shrewsbury. It

11. E. K. Chambers, *William Shakespeare: A Study of the Facts and Problems*, Oxford, 1930, II, 254.
12. *Jacobean and Caroline Stage*, V, 1065–72.

was better than the emoluments of an Oxford or Cambridge fellowship."[13]

Chambers's observation that the Stratford schoolmaster's salary was abnormally high is confirmed by Robert Burton, who lumps schoolmasters with the comparable curates and lecturers. In *The Anatomy of Melancholy*, part 1, section 2, member 3, subsection 15, where he speaks of the hard fate of the university man, Burton says:

> . . . he is as far to seek [preferment] as he was (after twenty years standing) at the first day of his coming to the *University*. For what course shall he take, being now capable and ready? The most parable and easy, and about which most are employed, is to teach a School, turn Lecturer or Curat, and for that he shall have falconers wages, ten [pounds] *per annum* and his diet, or some small stipend, so long as he can please his Patron or the Parish; if they like him not, as usually they do above a year or two, serving-man-like, he must go look a new Master. . . .

This is the way Burton estimated the graduate's wage in his first edition of 1621. It is significant that though he revised, clarified, and slightly expanded this passage in the editions of 1624, 1628, 1633, 1638, and 1651, he never saw need to alter the sum of £10 as the usual expected wage for a university graduate in a schoolmastership, a curacy, or a lectureship.

Somewhat higher was the rate of pay received by James Shirley after he had received his B.A. from Cambridge and before he became the regular professional for the actors of Queen Henrietta's company. Of course Shirley's teaching days came half a century and more after the years for which we know the schoolmasters' salaries at Stratford-

---

13. *William Shakespeare*, I, 10. It is true, however, that about the same time as £20 was set up as the stipend for Stratford, Sir Andrew Judd is said to have bequeathed land to Tunbridge to pay a salary of £20 to the schoolmaster and £8 to his usher (John Stow, *Survey of London*, London, 1603, p. 114).

upon-Avon and Warwick, and these were years of rising prices. Yet his salary in the years 1621–1623 was not significantly greater than the Stratford master's had been in 1553. The several payments recorded to him in the account books of the borough of St. Albans are somewhat irregular, but after going through them all Albert Baugh concluded that the normal rate of pay for the schoolmaster was £6 3s 4d per quarter for four quarters, and for his usher £2.[14] The schoolmaster's salary was supposed to be supplemented by a payment of 2d per quarter from the parents of each pupil, but there is no record of how many pupils there were or how regularly this fee was paid. Thus in the early 1620s Shirley took in £24 13s 4d plus probably not more than £2 or £3 in twopenny fees.

Against this background of customary rewards for their services made to nondramatic writers and to schoolmasters and curates we can see more clearly what the true economic situation of the dramatist was. Fortunately there are a good many records of the financial rewards of the playwright.

The most extensive and detailed evidence about payments to theatre writers comes, of course, from the records —diary and correspondence—of Philip Henslowe. From late 1597 to early in 1603 he entered hundreds of payments made to dramatists in behalf of the companies he financed. It is interesting to note that the prices do not vary much, and since we have the amounts paid for well over

14. Albert C. Baugh, "Some New Facts about Shirley," *Modern Language Review*, XVII (July 1922), 228–35.

Shirley's salary as schoolmaster was better than the one Edward Alleyn, the actor-manager-philanthropist, was paying four or five years earlier at the College of God's Gift at Dulwich. On 24 March 1617/18, Alleyn noted in his diary that he had paid to "M[r] Young my chapline and Schoolm[r]" £5 as his quarterly wages. But Mr. Young's usher was better paid than Shirley's; Alleyn records his quarterly wages as £3 6s 8d (J. P. Collier, *Memoirs of Edward Alleyn, Founder of Dulwich College*, London, 1841, p. 147).

one hundred plays, we can be fairly sure of the going rates.

Sir Walter Greg summarized these rates in the commentary volume of his superb edition of the diary:

> From the end of 1597 onwards, we have, on the contrary, very full evidence which shows that the sums paid to authors were gradually rising. This was only part of the general rise in prices. . . . The earliest play for which we have complete records [22 December 1597–5 January 1597/98] is *Mother Redcap* for which Drayton and Munday received £6 in full. This appears to have been the usual sum, though it is probable that in some cases not more than £5 was given, as for each part of *Robin Hood* [Munday, Part I; Munday and Chettle Part II, 15 February–8 March 1597/98]. The first part of *Black Ba[teman of the North*, by Chettle, Dekker, Drayton and Wilson, 2-22 May, 1598] was bought for £7, but for Part II [Chettle, Porter and Wilson paid 26 June–14 July] the authors only got the usual sum of £6. This continued the standard for a long time with occasional variations of £5 on the one hand and £7 on the other. . . . The prices paid by Worcester's men are exactly the same and it may be said that throughout the standard price remains £6, but that while in the earlier period £5 is not uncommon, toward the end payments of £7 and even £8 become comparatively frequent. . . .[15]

In addition to these payments for their contributions to new plays, the professional dramatists of the diary earned additions to their incomes by revising old plays, writing prologues and epilogues, preparing special material for court performances, and occasionally by writing a play so successful that the writers were awarded a special bonus by the company. All these activities together produced an income for a professional dramatist in the years 1597–1603 which surpassed the cash receipts of many other literary

15. W. W. Greg, ed., *Henslowe's Diary*, London, 1904–1908, II, 126–27.

men and notably exceeded the recorded remunerations of some other trained professional men like schoolmasters and curates.

It may be helpful in putting the professional dramatist in a somewhat more accurate economic perspective to make a rough tally of the cash payments known to have been made to a few of them. Of course these figures must be incomplete; even in the diary Henslowe sometimes makes payments for plays or parts of plays and does not name the recipient, who may well have been one of the dramatists whose receipts I have totaled. And there were usually other payments. Normally playwrights had a benefit, a percentage of the receipts at the second or third performance of their new play, and since such payments were made directly by the company, Henslowe had no reason to enter them, as they were not part of his accounts. Sometimes playwrights were given gratuities, as when Edward Alleyn recorded in his own diary on 19 November 1621 "Given to Charles Massey at his play . . . 5 shillings."[16]

It is also true that Henslowe's regular professionals are known to have written occasional plays for other troupes while working mostly for his companies. Thus Dekker wrote *Satiromastix* for the Children of Paul's and the Lord Chamberlain's men, but this seems to have been quite rare. We can be reasonably sure that the totals I have assembled for a few of the professional dramatists from Henslowe's accounts fall short of the total incomes of these men for the periods specified.[17]

16. William Young, *The History of Dulwich College*, London, 1889, II, 224. How common such gifts at first performances were is not known. Henslowe records another such to Munday, Drayton, Wilson, and Hathaway at the opening of *Sir John Oldcastle* in November 1597, and one of 10*s* to John Day after the playing of the *Second Part of Tom Strode*, and another to Thomas Dekker "over and above his price for his book, *A Medicine for a Curst Wife*."

17. These figures are conservative. In general I have credited a playwright with a payment only when Henslowe names him. There

The most faithful playwright and the largest earner to be revealed by Henslowe's accounts is Henry Chettle. In the diary he is recorded as having a hand in 52 plays, mostly collaborations and several probably unfinished, in the five years between his first payment entered 25 February 1597/98 and his last recorded one on 9 May 1603. Total payments of £123 17s 8d are entered to him—an average of about £25 a year. But his output was sporadic, due at least in part to irregularities in the theatrical seasons. In the ten and one-half months from 25 February 1597/98 to 28 November 1598 he was paid £36 12s 4d for his contributions to 17 plays, only three of which were unaided compositions. No payments to him are recorded in December 1598 or January 1598/99, but in the ten months between 16 February 1598/99 and 17 December 1599 he was paid £24 5s for his part in nine plays. He was paid

---

are some payments for which no dramatist is named but he is known from other sources; such payments I have omitted. Sometimes Henslowe's listing of authors suggests omissions. The first payment for *Christmas Comes But Once a Year* was £3 to Heywood and Webster; the second was £2 to Chettle and Dekker; the third was £2 to Chettle only "in fulle paymente." I have my doubts about the accuracy of these indications of distribution, but I have credited them as Henslowe does. Once he credits a payment to "An: Munday & the rest."

There is a further source of error in the division of a lump sum among the dramatists named. Though the majority of the plays bought are collaborations, Henslowe generally records simply a total of £4 to four men or £3 to three men. In such cases I have credited the money evenly among the collaborators. I suspect that is often wrong, for two or three times Henslowe does break down his lump payment, as when he noted that he had divided £4 5s into 30s, 30s, and 25s to Wilson, Chettle, and Munday for *Chance Medley*; or when he divided 50s for *The Second Part of Godwin*: Drayton, 30s; Wilson, 10s; and Chettle, 10s.

Henslowe left too much room for choice in his bookkeeping, and some other amateur accountant might get totals different from mine, but I doubt that we would vary much. I am confident that these playwrights received somewhat more from the Lord Admiral's men and from Worcester's men than I have credited them with.

nothing between 17 December 1599 and 16 February 1599/1600, but in the following four months up to 19 June 1600 he received £14 15s for his part in six plays. In 1601 he was paid £16 15s for contributions to four plays in nine months; in 1602, £27 10s 4d for contributions to eleven plays in twelve months; in 1603, £4 for contributions to three plays in four months.

In these last years Chettle may have had some supplementary unrecorded dramatic income from the Lord Admiral's men, for on 25 March 1602 Henslowe recorded that at the appointment of representatives of the company he paid out £3 "at the sealing of h Chettells band to writte for them."[18] The stipulations of the bond are not given, but it is notable that Chettle agreed to write for the company, not for Henslowe. In the only such dramatist's contract to write for a company which is known in detail (Richard Brome's in 1635–1639) the poet is guaranteed weekly wages.

Thomas Dekker wrote almost as many plays for the companies financed by Henslowe, and he was paid almost as much, but his annual totals fluctuated even more. He had a hand in 45 plays prepared for these companies and was paid a total of £110 9s 2d in six years. But in two of the six years he contributed only single plays—a collaboration with Chettle in late April and early May of 1601 and *The Honest Whore* with Middleton in March 1603/1604. Clearly in these two years he was concerned mostly with nondramatic work or plays for other companies. In the four years during which he received regular payments from Henslowe he contributed 43 plays for a total of £103 9s 2d, or an average of about £25 per annum. In 1598 he worked on 16 plays between 8 January and 30 December and was paid £37 1s 8d. In 1599 he worked on eleven plays in nine months and received £28 7s 6d. In 1600 he worked on seven plays in eleven months for £14 11s; and in 1602

18. Foakes and Rickert, p. 199.

Henslowe paid him £27 19s for contributions to nine plays in ten and one-half months.

These two playwrights, Henry Chettle and Thomas Dekker, were, so far as Henslowe's surviving records show, the most reliable providers of plays for the Lord Admiral's and the Earl of Worcester's men in the last five years of Elizabeth's reign. But there were eight others in the diary who are each shown to have contributed ten or more plays for the Henslowe companies in these years, though none was so prolific or so regular as Chettle and Dekker.

William Haughton was concerned with 24 plays in a period of five years from 5 November 1597 to 8 September 1602 for which he was paid £56 15s. But in three of these years he was paid for only a single play; he was contributing steadily to the companies only in the last half of 1599, in 1600, and in 1601. In the four months from 20 August to 17 December 1599 he worked on five plays; in the eleven months from 13 February 1599/1600 to 1 January 1600/1601 he worked on seven; and in the eight and one-half months from 29 January 1600/1601 to 8 November 1601 he worked on nine. In these years he was paid £10 12s 6d, £15 5s, and £21 2s 6d. Thus in a period of 23½ consecutive months Henslowe paid Haughton in behalf of the companies £47, or about £24 per year.

Michael Drayton participated in a similar number of plays for a similar sum, 23 plays for £50 16s 3d in a period of four and one-half years, between 22 December 1597 and 29 May 1602. But only one was written in 1597, one in 1601, one in 1602, and two in 1600. Drayton's steady work for the Henslowe companies was done between 13 March 1597/98 and 20 January 1598/99, though he did contribute to two more plays in the last two months of 1599. In that period of ten months of steady work he contributed to 16 plays for which he was paid £32 6s 8d. He also received income from boy companies, but the fullest records we have for any period of his life show that when he was producing plays steadily for the Henslowe companies in 1598 he was paid £32 6s 8d in ten months.

The other playwrights who were paid for numerous contributions to the repertories of the Lord Admiral's and the Earl of Worcester's companies, John Day, Richard Hathaway, Anthony Munday, William Smith, Robert Wilson, and Thomas Heywood, wrote less and earned less. The number of plays they contributed varies from 11 to 22.

Considering the very large number of plays Thomas Heywood "had a hand or at least a main finger in" during his long life, it is at first glance surprising that Henslowe paid him for only eleven in the period 6 December 1598 to 6 March 1602/1603. I would infer that in 1598 when he was paid for one play, in 1599 one, and in 1600 none, he was devoting most of his time to acting, for on 25 March 1598 he contracted to act at Henslowe's theatres exclusively for a period of two years or to forfeit £40. In the last four months of 1602 he contributed to seven plays and was paid £20 2s. Probably by 1602 he was a sharer in the Earl of Worcester's company and was expected to devote more time to writing; certainly he had become a sharer before the time of the company's draft patent of 1603–1604.[19]

The earnings of one of the other dramatists for the companies financed by Henslowe are worth noting. George Chapman was not a long-term Henslowe playwright, but he did write for the companies from 16 May 1598 to 17 July 1599. In these fourteen months he was paid £28 10s for contributing to seven plays. These were very good earnings at the end of the sixteenth century.

Unhappily there are no comparable records of the payments to their regular playwrights by competing companies like the Lord Chamberlain's men, but in a period of such intense theatrical competition as these years it is not likely that the Lord Chamberlain's company paid Shakespeare less than Henslowe was authorized to pay Chettle,

19. Chambers, *Elizabethan Stage*, II, 229–30.

Dekker, or Chapman. Indeed, there is a little evidence that during these years of Henslowe's dealings with Chettle, Dekker, Haughton, Heywood, and the others the managers of the *boy* companies were paying *more* for individual plays than he was, though it is unlikely that the boys were purchasing so many new plays. In the suit brought on by the performance of Chapman's *The Old Joiner of Aldgate* by Paul's boys, plaintiffs and defendants agreed that in February 1602/1603 Chapman was paid twenty marks (£13 6*s* 8*d*) for his play, about double Henslowe's rate at the time. Some dramatists had directorial functions in the boy companies and shared in the profits. At one time or another in the years 1594–1610 the managing syndicate of the Revels companies or the Chapel companies included the dramatists John Marston, Michael Drayton, Lording Barry, John Mason, and Robert Daborne. When the boys were doing well, the managerial functions were a source of profit for these playwrights, but the various lawsuits and suppressions in which the boys were involved suggest that Chettle and Dekker probably did better for themselves by writing steadily for the Lord Admiral's, and the Earl of Worcester's companies.

These earnings of professional dramatists writing for the Henslowe companies form an interesting contrast to the earnings of Richard Robinson, a nondramatic writer in the immediately preceding years. Over a period of nineteen years Robinson records his total earnings from literature as £52 17*s* 5*d*. In five and one-half years the acting companies paid Henry Chettle a total of £123 17*s* 6*d*; over a period of six years they paid Thomas Dekker £110 9*s* 2*d*; in a single year they paid George Chapman £28 10*s*. The average yearly earnings of Richard Robinson from publishers and patrons combined was a little less than £2 17*s*. From the acting companies Chettle averaged about £25; Dekker averaged £19.

Robinson's best years are almost impossible to isolate,

since he lists his books under the year of publication, and in the same entry lumps in receipts for later editions in subsequent years; moreover he usually does not say how long it took him to sell the copies paid him by his publisher, though in one instance he notes that it took two years. I can find no indication that in his best year his receipts can have exceeded £7 or £8, whereas Henslowe's records show that the actors paid Chettle £36 12s 4d in one period of ten and one-half months, Dekker £37 1s 8d in one year, and Chapman £28 10s in one year.

No other records of the earnings of dramatists remotely comparable in fullness to Henslowe's diary exist in the period. Scattered correspondence and comments make it clear enough that the price of plays was increasing, apparently faster than the general price rise in the reign of James. In 1613 and 1614 Robert Daborne was involved with Henslowe in a correspondence which has been preserved in the archives of Dulwich College.[20] On 17 April 1613 Daborne signed a memorandum agreeing with Henslowe to deliver to him "before ye end of this Easter Term" a tragedy called *Machiavel and the Devil* for which he was to receive £20, of which he had already had £6. On 25 June 1613 Daborne wrote offering another play, *The Arraignment*, and asserting that if Henslowe did not take the play "Before God I can have £25 for it as some of the company know." In August Daborne wrote in some financial straits about a collaboration, *The Bellman*: ". . . we will have but £12 and the overplus of the second day . . . and from £20 a play am come to £12, therefore in my extremity forsake me not." On 28 March 1613/14 Daborne wrote about *The She Saint* and seemed to settle on £12 as his expected initial payment, though he seemed to imply additional later payments. "I desire you should disburse but £12 a play till they be played."

These letters written by Robert Daborne indicate that—

20. Gregg, *Henslowe Papers*, arts. 70, 71, 72, 81, 84, 97.

at least as far as this playwright and Philip Henslowe were concerned—the going rate for plays in 1613–1614 was double to triple Henslowe's rate in 1598–1601. It may be only a coincidence that a college dramatist, Thomas Tomkis, was rewarded at a similar rate for his play, *Albumazar*, in the following year. In the bursar's account books for Trinity College, Cambridge, for 1615 is the entry, "Item, given Mr. Tomkis for his pains in penning and ordering the English Comedy at our Master's appointment, £20."[21]

The most explicit surviving figures about a dramatist's rate of pay are those revealed in the suit of *Heton* versus *Brome* about Richard Brome's contract as regular dramatist for the Salisbury Court theatre in the years 1635 to 1639. The various provisions of the two contracts may be discussed more conveniently later, but here the money Brome was to receive as regular company playwright is relevant. According to his contract of 20 July 1635, to run for three years, Brome was to receive 15 shillings a week plus a benefit performance for each new play he wrote for the company. If Brome was to be paid for 52 weeks, his earnings were expected to be £39 plus benefits.

Of course the dramatist's return from these benefit performances could be expected to vary a good deal with the weather, the competing attractions, the political situation, and the appeal of the particular play, but Brome himself makes an estimate of what it would be. He says that because the plague restrained playing just after the presentation of his second play he was not paid his benefit, "And this defendant's said clear day's profit of the said second new play was never allowed unto him to the damage of five pounds and upwards." Brome also says that one of the plays he wrote for the Salisbury Court theatre "styled and called *The Sparagus Garden* was worth to them by general conjecture and estimation and as by their own

21. *Notes and Queries*, 3rd ser., XII (August 1867), 155.

books and writings being produced this defendant verily believeth may appear the sum of one thousand pounds and upwards."[22] No doubt his estimate of £1,000 profit on *The Sparagus Garden* is exaggerated, as was common in suits, but it does suggest that his expectation of £5 or more from his benefits is not unreasonable. Thus Brome's yearly income on the contract of 20 July 1635 might well have been expected to be £54 for 52 weeks.

Evidently the company did not think the terms of this contract excessive, for in August 1638 a new agreement was made, according to which Brome was to be given a 33 percent increase and paid 20 shillings a week, the contract to run for seven years.[23]

These terms indicate what the company thought a playwright might be paid, 1635–1639. The fact that the suit *Heton* versus *Brome* shows that because of the bad plague of 1636–1637 and for other reasons the contract stipulations seem to have been violated by both parties does not alter the estimation of what reasonable pay for the Salisbury Court playwright was thought to be.

It is probable that these contractual payments to Richard Brome amounted to a good deal less than certain other professional dramatists were receiving from their companies in these years, for the Salisbury Court theatre was one of the less distinguished and less profitable in the 1630s. The two most distinguished London theatres in the reign of Charles I were clearly the Blackfriars and the Cockpit

22. Ann Haaker, "The Plague, the Theatre, and the Poet," *Renaissance Drama*, n.s. (1968), pp. 302 and 301.

23. Ibid., 298, 299, 304. These terms of 20*s* a week are confirmed by another source, generally called Heton's Papers. These are notes for an agreement which the manager of the Salisbury Court theatre, Richard Heton, drew up for the company, setting out their respective charges. According to one item the company is to pay "half the poet's wages, which is 10 shillings a week" (*Jacobean and Caroline Stage*, II, 686).

or Phoenix in Drury Lane.[24] Their regular dramatists in
1635 were Philip Massinger and James Shirley, and it is
probable that these two were paid more by the King's men
and Queen Henrietta's men than the Salisbury Court company could afford to give Brome.

There is a certain amount of specific evidence—beyond
their popular reputations—that the Blackfriars at least was
a good deal more profitable than the Salisbury Court. It
will be recalled that Brome expected his benefit to bring
him "five pounds and upwards" on a *new* play after the
expenses of the house had been deducted. Now from 1628
to 1633 Sir Henry Herbert had a similar benefit arrangement with the Blackfriars, namely the take minus the expenses of the house. The difference was that his benefit was
on the *second* day of a *revived* play, notoriously less popular than a *new* play. For five years Sir Henry recorded his
receipts from this benefit at the Blackfriars. The benefit
paid on the different plays recorded were £17 10s, £9 16s,
£12 4s, £13, and £15.[25] These sums which Sir Henry Herbert was paid are from two to three times as much for the
second performance of a *revived* play as Brome expected to
receive from his benefit performance of a *new* play at the
Salisbury Court theatre. Philip Massinger's arrangements
at Blackfriars are likely to have been similar to Brome's at
the Salisbury Court, i.e., wages and benefits. If so, they are
likely to have yielded a good deal more than Brome's
estimated £54.

THESE ACCUMULATED FIGURES indicate, it seems to
me, that the professional playwrights made more money
than other literary men of their time, and more than they
could have made as schoolmasters or curates—professions
which might have been open to many of them. Not only

24. See *Jacobean and Caroline Stage*, VI, 12–15, 33–35, 47,
59–61.
25. See ibid., I, 23–24.

do the extant accounts of payments show very respectable incomes for the time, but unrecorded payments for special gifts, occasional plays sold to other companies, benefit performances (except for Richard Brome), and occasional non-dramatic writings (such as the pamphlets of Heywood, Dekker, Middleton, and Rowley) certainly added to the income of most professional playwrights.

It is also notable that these extant figures, though they represent fees from four or five different companies, in no case represent the payments made to those dramatists regularly attached to the most stable and the richest acting organization of the time, the Lord Chamberlain–King's men. This company had more and better theatres than any other; it held its actors longer, it seems to have had no difficulty in hiring actors away from other troupes, its receipts from court performances were always greater than those paid to any other performing group, its plays were more often preserved and praised than those of any other, and it hired and held the best dramatists of the time. It seems almost certain therefore that the regular dramatists of this company with the greatest prestige and the greatest wealth of the time would have been paid more than the regular dramatists of lesser companies. If Chettle, Dekker, Haughton, Drayton, Chapman, and Brome were paid well, clearly the King's men's sequence of William Shakespeare, Nathan Field, John Fletcher, Philip Massinger, and James Shirley would have been paid better.

The widespread impression of the ill-paid Elizabethan dramatist derives in part, of course, from romantic predispositions about the artist, predispositions which (for the anti-Stratfordians) make the unmistakable evidence of Shakespeare's substantial estate seem such an unanswerable argument against the identification of the man of Stratford with the poet of *A Midsummer Night's Dream*. And selected evidence from documents of the time—evidence like the rate of composition for the dramatists of the Lord

Admiral's and the Earl of Worcester's companies and their
repeated borrowings recorded in Henslowe's diary, like the
begging and borrowing letters of Robert Daborne, Nathan
Field, and Philip Massinger, like the poverty poems and
prefaces of Massinger, Jonson, Randolph, and Greene, like
the imprisonment of Dekker and Field and Massinger—
such evidence can be made to suggest that the sufferings
of these playwrights demonstrate their low payment.

But debts and borrowings and financial straits do not
necessarily indicate abnormally low incomes, as any court of
bankruptcy could demonstrate. If the poverty complaints
of Massinger, Jonson, Randolph, and Greene are to be
quoted, they ought to be balanced against the evidence of
property bequeathed in the wills of theatre people like
Edward Alleyn, Samuel Rowley, Thomas Greene, Philip
Henslowe, William Shakespeare, John Heminges, John
and Elizabeth Condell, James Shirley, and John Shank.

Dekker, Daborne, Massinger, and Brome may have complained about their poverty, but they were not ill-paid for
the plays they wrote.

CHAPTER VI

Dramatists' Contractual Obligations

CLOSE AND CONTINUED ASSOCIATION of certain playwrights with certain companies has been implied in several contexts in preceding chapters—"Amateur Dramatists and Professional Dramatists," "The Dramatists and the Acting Company," and "Dramatists' Pay." So many scholars have noted such an association of William Shakespeare with the Lord Chamberlain–King's company that the observation has become a commonplace. How conventional was such an association? What did it entail? And was it formalized or simply a free selection by an independent artist of his favorite among several competing companies?

It is likely enough that arrangements between dramatists and acting companies were not completely uniform among all the fifteen or so companies of the period. And it is further likely that there was some development in the relationships—probably in the direction of greater formalization—during the 52 years under consideration. But the organized presentation of plays tends to become conventionalized in any era; it has many times been shown that the theatre is usually conservative.

One would expect, therefore, that different as the companies were, the adult companies at least would tend to conform to a pattern in their relations with their principal dramatists as they did in admission prices, length of plays, plan of theatre buildings, use of boys, and the size and character of actors' organizations. And one would expect that these playwright–company relationships would sooner or later be formalized in a contract.

The only contract between dramatist and acting company which is known in detail is that entered into by Richard Brome and the actors and proprietors of the Salisbury Court theatre on 20 July 1635 and renewed with minor alterations in August 1638. Since the theatre was so conventional in its arrangements, it is probable that Richard Brome's two contracts in 1635 and 1638 were traditional and similar in their basic provisions to those of "ordinary"[1]

---

1. The term "ordinary poet," which is used in this period in connection with the theatres is evidently used according to definition 3b under the entry for the adjective "ordinary" in the *OED*: "Of officials, persons employed, etc.: Belonging to the regular staff or to the fully recognized staff of such. . . . Now mostly represented by *in-ordinary*."

The theatrical usage is well illustrated by one of the complaints about the hardships caused by the closing of the theatres. It occurs toward the end of the pamphlet, *The Actors' Remonstrance, or Complaint. . . . As it was presented in the names and behalf of all our London Comedians. . . .* January 24, 1643[/44]. "For some of our ablest ordinary poets, instead of their annual stipends and beneficial second days, being for mere necessity compelled to get a living by writing contemptible penny pamphlets. . . ." (Reprinted by William Carew Hazlitt in *English Drama and Stage*, London, 1869, pp. 259–65.)

playwrights for other major companies, at least in the reigns of James and Charles. It ought to be useful, therefore, to review the explicit provisions of Brome's contracts and then to note evidence of the responses to such presumptive requirements in the activities of other attached professional dramatists.

The details of these two contracts are known from a suit brought against Richard Brome in the Court of Requests by the "owners of the playhouse in Salisbury Court, London" and the members of Queen Henrietta's company, the acting troupe at that theatre.[2] As usual in lawsuits, plaintiffs and defendant disagreed on the charges of the plaintiffs. Fortunately for us however, the disagreement was wholly concerned with the acts of the two parties in carrying out their agreements; there was no disagreement about what the contracts provided. The troubles seem to have arisen largely from the sufferings of both parties under the long closing for the plague from 12 May 1636 to 2 October 1637,[3] and each seems to have had some justification for its violations. But since our concern here is with what a company customarily asked its regular dramatist to do, and with what the dramatist expected to do, the points of agreement of the two parties provide what we

2. The bill and the answer in the suit were discovered by C. W. Wallace at the Public Record Office early in this century. He never published them or revealed their location, but he inserted two or three sentences about the contract in a popular article in *The Century Magazine* in 1910. In response to a letter from Clarence Edward Andrews he revealed a few more facts, which Andrews published in *Richard Brome: A Study of his Life and Works*, New York, 1913.

A few years ago the Henry E. Huntington Library acquired the Wallace Papers with transcripts of the bill and answer. Ann Haaker checked these transcripts in the Public Record Office and published them with an introduction under the title "The Plague, the Theater, and the Poet," *Renaissance Drama*, n.s. 1 (1968), pp. 283–306.

3. See *Jacobean and Caroline Stage*, II, 661–65.

need. It might be interesting if we could tell the extent to which each was irresponsible, or arbitrary, or dishonest, but that is not material here.

Perhaps it will be most helpful to consider the various provisions of the contracts separately and to note under each heading such evidence as comes to hand that other attached professional dramatists working for other companies tended to meet the same requirements.

Exclusiveness

Both Brome's contracts specify that he would do no writing for any other company during the terms of the agreements. The plaintiffs assert that according to the terms of the contract of 1635 "the said Richard Brome should not nor would write any play or any part of a play to any other players or playhouse, but apply all his study and endeavors therein for the benefit of the said company of the said playhouse." And they further assert that this clause was simply restated in the second contract of July 1638, "And that he should not write, invent or compose any play tragedy or comedy or any part thereof for any other playhouse."

Now the violation of these clauses in both contracts was one of the principal issues in the suit. Therefore Brome's admission that he had agreed to such a stipulation and his attempts to excuse himself for violating it strongly imply that such clauses were so common that everyone would have assumed their existence. Brome in his answer to the bill of complaint admits that he "did agree . . . that he would write for no other company but apply his labors totally unto them as aforesaid. . . ." He further recognizes the company's legitimate contractual expectations when he excuses himself for composing fewer than three plays a year by asserting that

some of the complainants on behalf of the residue of them did undertake and assuredly affirm to this defendant . . . that their main purpose in expressing such a number of plays was but only to oblige this defendant to dedicate all his labor and plays totally unto their sole profits.[4]

In excuse for his violation of this exclusive clause Brome explains that as the plague continued his salary was not paid—at least in full—and that in his poverty and desperation he went to William Beeston who lent him £6 on his agreement to write a play for Beeston's company at the Cockpit. But the Salisbury Court players got the play back from Beeston and persuaded Brome to come back to them.

Obviously Brome accepted his obligation to write exclusively for the company at the Salisbury Court—hence his excuses for his deviation. Moreover, there is a suggestion that William Beeston, the old theatre-hand who had possession of Brome's manuscript, recognized the irregularity of Brome's conduct; otherwise it is difficult to understand why he was willing to turn over the manuscript of a profitable play to a rival company. The plaintiffs in their bill of complaint say that Brome "did sell and deliver one of the plays which he made for your subjects in the said time unto Christopher Beeston, gentleman, and William Beeston." And Brome admits that because of his financial straits he did violate the exclusive clause in his contract:

> And as to the new play which the complainants suppose this defendant to have sold unto the said Christopher or William Beeston, this defendant confesseth it to be true that the stoppage of his weekly means and unkind carriage aforesaid forced this defendant to contract and bargain for the said new play with the said William Beeston, but yet the said complainants and their company had it and acted it and by common estimation got a thousand pounds and upwards by it.[5]

4. Bill of complaint, Haaker transcript, pp. 297 and 298; Brome's answer, ibid., pp. 301–302.

5. Bill, Haaker transcript, p. 298; answer, ibid., p. 305.

Though no contract has yet been found for any other professional playwright, several of the well-known attached professionals can be shown to have followed this practice of exclusive composition, presumably under the terms of an agreement, like Brome's, with the companies to which they were attached.

In the case of Brome's contemporary, James Shirley, there are enough license records and title-page statements to demonstrate that he wrote exclusively for King Charles's company after he returned from Ireland, regularly furnishing them with an autumn play and a spring play in 1640, 1641, and 1642. No play written for any other company can be found in his canon during this period. In his earlier career in London, 1625–1637, before he left for Ireland, Shirley wrote regularly for Queen Henrietta's men at the Phoenix, producing plays at about the same rate as he later did for the King's men. This pattern of exclusive attachment to the Queen's men was broken once, as Brome's was broken later. For unknown reasons *The Changes, or Love in a Maze,* licensed in January 1631/ 32, was performed by a rival company at the Salisbury Court theatre, and both the prologue and the epilogue for the play emphasize Shirley's transferred allegiance and the company's hopes for their new and struggling troupe. Could the reason have been the expiration of a seven-year contract and disagreement about its renewal? Whatever the reason, the breach in Shirley's allegiance to Queen Henrietta's men was soon healed, and all his subsequent plays in this period of his life were demonstrably the property of the Phoenix company.

Philip Massinger was the "ordinary poet" for King Charles's company between the incumbencies of John Fletcher and James Shirley, i.e., 1626–1639 inclusive. Before 1626 Massinger frequently wrote for the company, usually in collaboration with Fletcher, but he also wrote several other plays in those years for the Lady Elizabeth's company. After Fletcher's death he apparently wrote exclusively for the King's men—with one probable exception. The evidence is not complete because a number of Massinger's plays, though known by title, are lost and furnish no evidence of date or ownership, and Malone and Chalmers were not so consistent in copying the licenses for his plays from the office book as they were for Fletcher's and Shirley's. But at least half his plays after 1625 were demonstrably written for the King's men, and none of them—with the possible exception of *The Great Duke of Florence*—is known to have been written for any other company. That play, apparently written in 1627, was published in 1636 as acted by Queen Henrietta's men. There is some confusion about it, and the piece may be one of Massinger's earlier productions for the Phoenix, but the weight of the evidence now available seems to indicate a single aberration, like Shirley's composition of *The Changes* for the Salisbury Court.

John Fletcher's attachment to King James's company at the Blackfriars and the Globe appears to have been similarly exclusive. Since most of his plays were licensed before the period of Sir Henry Herbert's office book, and since their popularity was so great that the company withheld most of them from publication until 1647, the evidence for date of production and original ownership is less complete than for Shirley or Brome. It is complete enough, however, to suggest and almost to demonstrate that he was attached exclusively to the King's company from Shakespeare's retirement to Fletcher's death in the plague of 1625. None of his own plays or his collaborations in this period can be shown to have been written for any other company, and the great majority are in the King's repertory of unprinted plays submitted to the Lord Chamberlain in 1641.[6]

Shakespeare's exclusive attachment to the same company

6. See *Jacobean and Caroline Stage*, 1, 65–66 and 108–15.

is well known. After the organization and establishment of the Lord Chamberlain's men late in 1594, no Shakespearean play can be shown to have been composed for any other company, and for most of them the evidence of composition for the Lord Chamberlain–King's company is complete. Shakespeare's exclusive attachment was probably a part of his involvement as a patented member and leading sharer in the organization, but exclusive it certainly was.

The regular dramatists for the other leading adult companies in the reigns of James and Charles probably worked with similar exclusiveness, but the dates and ownership of their plays are confused or totally unknown, and the histories of such troupes as Queen Anne's men, the Prince Henry–Palsgrave's company, and the Lady Elizabeth's company are so meager and their continuity so broken that their policies cannot be demonstrated.

There is evidence, however, that the custom of guaranteeing the exclusiveness of a successful playwright's services came into being fairly early. Not only is there the example of Shakespeare's preparing all his plays for the Lord Chamberlain's men, but there are entries in Henslowe's accounts which suggest that the system was developing at the time he was writing.

At the beginning of the new year 1598 (old style) Thomas Heywood signed an agreement with Henslowe. The principle was exclusiveness, and the seven witnesses to the contract were six of the leading members of the Lord Admiral's company and the dramatist who was writing plays for them; but the services specified, though exclusive, were not literary, and the attachment was not to the company but to Henslowe:

> Memorandum that this 25 of March 1598 Thomas Heywood came and hired himself with me as a covenant servant for two years by the receiving of two single pence according to the statute of Winchester and to begin at the day above written and not to play anywhere

public about London, not while these two years be expired but in my house. If he do then he doth forfeit unto me the receiving of these two pence, forty pounds and witness to this

Anthony Munday	William Borne
Gabriel Spencer	Thomas Downton
Robert Shaw	Richard Jones[7]
Richard Allen	

On the face of it this seems to be an ordinary agreement with a hired man of the company. But six leading members of the company and their dramatist are not likely to have been present simply by chance when Heywood signed, and why should they have been called in for a mere hired man? Again, the hired man is attached to Henslowe and not to the company as was usual. This agreement does not constitute a dramatist's contract, but there are enough odd features about the entry to spur speculation.

The entry Henslowe made about a year later on 28 February 1598/99 is still not quite a contract for the exclusive services of a dramatist to a company.

Lent unto Harry Porter at the request of the company in earnest of his book called *Two Merry Women of Abington* the sum of forty shillings and for the receipt of that money he gave me his faithful promise that I should have all the books which he writes either himself or with any other; which sum was delivered upon the 28 of February.
I say . . . 40 shillings.

Thomas Downton   Robert Shaw[8]

Here again the agreement was witnessed by two members of the Lord Admiral's company, and not by all the principal sharers, but Henslowe did note that his payment was made "at the request of the company." Moreover, this

7. Foakes and Rickert, p. 241.
8. Ibid., p. 105.

agreement did specify plays, though the dramatist was bound to Henslowe, not the company.

The third entry in Henslowe's accounts represents an agreement which has the essentials of the exclusive clause in Brome's contract thirty-three years later. Only the month date is given, but the position of the entry shows that the year was 1602. "Lent unto Harry Chettle March 25 at the appointment [of] Thomas Downton and my son E. Alleyn at the sealing of H. Chettle's bond to write for them the sum of . . . £3."[9] Downton and Alleyn were both leading members of the Admiral's company, and both frequently authorized Henslowe to make payments in behalf of the company. Here the sealing of a bond is mentioned, not simply the signing of an agreement, and the payment of £3 is not related to payment for a play—as Porter's £2 was connected with *The Two Merry Women of Abington*—but seems to have been related to the contract only. This entry would appear to record something very close to, though not necessarily so detailed as, Richard Brome's contract with the Salisbury Court organization.

All in all, then, the clause in each of Brome's contracts stipulating that he should give all his plays to the Salisbury Court players and write nothing for any other company would seem to represent a traditional arrangement between a settled company and its principal dramatist. Although there is not enough evidence to prove finally that every major troupe had such an understanding with its "ordinary poet," there is enough to make it apparent that such an arrangement had become a convention in the reigns of James and Charles.

Annual Quota of Plays

The two contesting parties agree that the contract of 20 July 1635 required Brome to write for the company three plays a year for three years. Brome says that he gave

9. Ibid., p. 199.

a total of six plays to the company in the three years of the first contract (the plaintiffs say five) though some were very late because of the confusion at the time of the plague when the company was taking in little or no money and the playwright's salary was either stopped or only partly paid. Brome says that at the signing of the first contract he objected to the quota of three plays a year "as being more than he could well perform." And he comments that several members of the company, on behalf of others,

> did undertake and assuredly affirm unto this defendant that howsoever they had desired to have three plays yearly for three years continuance together to be undertaken and promised by this defendant yet upon trust and confidence and by the true and fair intent and plain meaning of all parties, the plaintiffs neither should nor would exact nor expect from this defendant the performance or composition of any more plays than so many only as this defendant could or should be able well and conveniently to do or perform and that their main purpose in expressing such a number of plays was but only to oblige this defendant to dedicate all his labor and plays totally unto their sole profits.[10]

The plaintiffs say that the second contract of August 1638 also stipulated three plays a year, but Brome does not mention the quota, though he does mention the contract and the increased rate of pay to 20 shillings a week.

The parties agree that Brome did write two plays a year (or the plaintiffs say about one and two-thirds) for the company, and Brome seems to indicate that at the beginning he thought this was about his capacity, or at least that three a year was too much.

Those other professional dramatists whose company attachments were steady and whose plays can be dated with some precision seem to have come quite close to this rate of two plays a year. James Shirley, whom Brome succeeded

10. Answer, Haaker transcript, pp. 301–302.

as dramatist at Beeston's Phoenix theatre, had written for Queen Henrietta's company at this rate. Sir Henry Herbert's licenses for most of Shirley's plays were copied from the office book by Malone and Chalmers. Beginning with *Love Tricks with Compliments*, licensed 11 February 1624/25, shortly after he came to London from St. Albans, and ending with *The Duke's Mistress*, licensed 18 January 1635/36, a few months before the plague closing during which Shirley went to Ireland and wrote for the St. Werburgh Street theatre in Dublin, we have the Master of the Revels' licenses for 20 plays. In addition *The Arcadia* and *The Wedding* certainly belonged to the Phoenix company and were evidently written in this period, though Malone and Chalmers did not copy their allowances from the office book. Thus Shirley's output as regular dramatist for Queen Henrietta's company was 22 plays in 11 years—about the same annual production as Brome's.

When Shirley returned to London after his three years of absence in Ireland, he became regular dramatist for King Charles's company in succession to Philip Massinger, who had died in March 1639/40. His work for this company shows a sequence even more regular, a spring and an autumn play each year. Herbert licensed *Rosania* (June 1640), *The Imposter* (November 1640), *The Politic Father* (May 1641), *The Cardinal* (November 1641), and *The Sisters* (April 1642). Apparently the autumn play for 1642 was *The Court Secret*, but it was not licensed by Herbert because, as he wrote in his office book, "Here ended my allowance of plays, for the war began in Aug. 1642." This inference is supported by the statement on the 1652 title page of *The Court Secret*: "Never Acted, But prepared for the Scene at Black-Friers."

Shirley's predecessor as regular dramatist for the King's company was apparently working to a similar schedule, but for him the evidence is less complete. Some time after the death of Fletcher, probably in 1626, Massinger seems to have become the regular playwright for the company, but Malone and Chalmers were evidently not so interested in his plays as in Shirley's and failed to copy the license entry of the Master of the Revels for many of them. A number of Massinger's plays which we know at least by title have no preserved license, and several of them are extremely uncertain in date.

There are seventeen or eighteen plays by Massinger definitely recorded as the property of the King's men, most of them precisely dated by the licenses of the Master of the Revels, and produced between 1626 and 1639 inclusive, beginning with *The Roman Actor*, which Sir Henry licensed for the company on 11 October 1626, and ending with the lost play *The Fair Anchoress*, which was allowed for them on 26 January 1639/40. Two others, *The Forced Lady* and *The Italian Night-Piece*, though lost, are known to have been acted by the King's men in the twenties or thirties. Seven other lost plays known by title and attributed to Massinger in the Stationers' Register would make up the total to 26 or 27, quite close to two plays a year for fourteen years, especially considering that in this period the theatres were closed for seven months in 1630 and in 1636–1637 for nearly seventeen. These figures for the quota and regularity of Massinger's work as contracted dramatist for the King's men fall short of a conclusive demonstration that he produced for the King's company at the same rate as Brome for the Salisbury Court theatre and James Shirley for Queen Henrietta's men and the King's men, but they show that his rate must have been similar to theirs.

Massinger's predecessor as regular dramatist for the King's company was John Fletcher. The evidence for his rate of production for the company is more involved than that for Massinger: first, because most of his plays were produced before Sir Henry Herbert began to keep his office book, much the most complete production record

123

extant for the Jacobean and Caroline theatre; secondly, because his popularity in the theatre persuaded the King's men to withhold most of his works from publication until after the closing of the theatres, thus depriving us of more evidence of production date; thirdly, because so many of his plays were collaborations which obscure the total work of the author more than the generally unaided plays of Massinger, Shirley, and Brome; and finally, because the dates of his exclusive attachment to the King's company are less clear than those for the other three. Certainly he was principal dramatist for the company from Shakespeare's death to his own, but how long before? Shakespeare's compositions for the company were greatly reduced from 1608 or 1609 to 1612 or 1613, and they ceased entirely from 1613 to 1616. It seems to me likely that Fletcher's regular association probably began about 1609 or 1610, for at least ten of his plays in the company's repertory appear, on the rather shaky evidence we have, to date from the period 1609–1615. From the period 1616 to 1625 we have 32 plays, including lost pieces like *The Devil of Dowgate, The Jeweller of Amsterdam*, and *A Right Woman*, and excluding plays in the Caroline repertory of the King's company but known to have been composed originally for other troupes—plays such as *The Scornful Lady, The Honest Man's Fortune*, and *Monsieur Thomas*.

Thus we know that Fletcher participated in about 42 plays written for the King's company in the years 1609–1625. But at least 21 of them have been shown to be collaborations including work of Beaumont, Field, Shakespeare, Rowley, and especially Massinger. If we assume that Fletcher's lines in these collaborations would have been, on the average, approximately half the play, then his contribution to the repertory of the King's men in the period from 1609 to his death in August 1625 would have been about 32½ plays in a period of 16½ years. This is reasonably close to the norm of two plays a year found in the contracted work of Brome, Shirley, and Massinger.

Fletcher's predecessor as principal dramatist for the Lord Chamberlain–King's company was, of course, William Shakespeare. Though the problem of dating the plays is more complex for Shakespeare because of the scantiness of the external evidence before the death of Queen Elizabeth, many times more scholars have devoted their efforts to Shakespearean dating problems than to Fletcherian ones. As a consequence there is fair general agreement on the approximate dating of most of the 38 plays. Most scholars have recognized a falling-off in the frequency of composition after *Timon of Athens*, about 1608. Probably the most generally accepted chronology is set out by Sir Edmund Chambers. This list shows an average of two plays per year from the season of 1590–1591 to that of 1607–1608, and after that, six plays (including two collaborations) in the next five years. While a number of scholars might quibble with the precise seasons in which many of these first 32 plays fall, the average of two a year is clear enough.[11]

11. See *William Shakespeare*, I, 270–71. The statement of John Ward is of interest here. Ward was vicar of Shakespeare's parish, Holy Trinity, Stratford-upon-Avon, from 1662 to 1681. He kept extensive notebooks and included several remarks about the poet who had been buried in his church 45 years before Ward came to the parish. He could never have known the playwright and probably never knew any of the members of the company of the King's men, but the stories he collected in Stratford are worth consideration. Ward wrote:

. . . he frequented the plays all his younger time, but in his elder days lived at Stratford and supplied the stage with two plays a year, and for that had an allowance so large that he spent at the rate of £1,000 a year, as I have heard (ibid., II, 249–50).

Allowing for the exaggerations of most local gossip and the haziness about time-spans 50 to 75 years in the past, Ward's remarks do no violence to our other information if we assume that "two plays a year" applies to the period *before* and not after retirement.

For the other professional dramatists the evidence is too obscure or too incomplete to allow any conclusions. The great majority of the 220 plays in which Thomas Heywood says that he "had either an entire hand or at least a main finger" are not even known by title, much less by date. Nor can one tell how many of the plays in this huge total were two-, three-, four-, or even five-man collaborations. Rowley and Field, though clearly attached professionals, were important actors and were evidently not expected to devote full time to writing as Brome, Shirley, Massinger, and Fletcher were. Dekker's company affiliations—after his Henslowe career—are too unsettled to suggest any contractual production, and so are Middleton's, except for his early years with boy companies. The chief Henslowe dramatists certainly *participated* in more than an average of two plays a year for the companies whose accounts are preserved in the diary, but the great majority of their plays were collaborations, often three, four, five, or even six writers participating in a single composition. Often it is impossible to tell whether the plays for which Henslowe recorded serial payments were ever completed, though in a number of instances it is clear that they were not. In these circumstances it seems folly to attempt to work out any pattern of composition for Haughton, Munday, Hathaway, Wilson, or Wentworth Smith. For what it is worth, I am inclined to doubt that the Lord Admiral's company or Worcester's men had any set agreed quotas with these men during the years of Henslowe's payment records, 1597–1604.

Salary

According to the contract of 20 July 1635 the salary was to be 15 shillings per week plus a benefit. Both parties quote this figure, and Brome even names the pay day: "In consideration whereof the said complainants or some of them or some of their company did agree to pay fifteen shillings weekly upon every Saturday unto this defendant. . . ."

In the 1638 contract this weekly salary was increased to £1 and the benefit stipulation continued as in the first contract. Both parties to the suit agree on these figures. Apparently the pound-a-week salary was not considered excessive at the time, for in February 1639/40 the plaintiffs claimed that Brome had left them for a higher salary:

> And upon the said [William] Beeston's promise to be his good friend and to give him more salary than your subjects by the agreement aforesaid, he, the said Richard Brome did voluntarily fail to present unto your subjects any more of the said plays for which he was in arrears with your subjects. . . . But the said Brome being tampered withall by the said Beeston as aforesaid hath and doth refuse and deny to compose make or present unto your said subjects the said three plays which by the first article he is in arrears in and behindhand with your subjects as aforesaid, but wholly applies himself unto the said Beeston and the company of players acting at the playhouse of the Phoenix in Drury Lane. . . .[12]

I know of no other direct references to the payment of a weekly salary to a dramatist by a company, though I have little doubt that at certain times other companies operated in the same way as this suit indicates Queen Henrietta's company acted in the 1630s. It is notable that the King's Revels company made the original contract with Brome, which was taken over by Queen Henrietta's men when they replaced the King's Revels at the Salisbury Court, and it must therefore have been their custom to pay a dramatist a weekly salary too. Brome says in his answer in the suit that the original company in the contract, the King's Revels, had enticed him away from Prince Charles [II] company at the Red Bull:

12. Haaker transcript, pp. 302 and 299–300.

> And upon their [i.e., the King's Revels company's] spe-
> cious pretense and promises of reward and bountiful
> retribution and love did entice and inveigle this defend-
> ant to depart and leave the company of the Red Bull
> players being the Prince's highness servants, and where
> this defendant was then very well entertained and truly
> paid without murmuring or wrangling. . . .[13]

From this statement of the dramatist one might assume
that he had been paid a weekly wage by Prince Charles's
company as he was by the others, but he does not explicitly
say so.

Benefit Performances

Both plaintiffs and defendant in the suit agree that under
the first contract Brome was to receive the profits from a
benefit performance of each new play in addition to his
weekly wage. (The plaintiffs say that the same provision
was written into the second contract, but Brome neither
affirms nor denies this.) In their complaint Queen Henrietta's men say it was stipulated in the first contract that:

> . . . the said covenantees should pay unto the said Rich-
> ard Brome the sum of fifteen shillings per week during
> the said term of three years and permit the said Brome
> to have the benefit of one day's profit of playing such
> new play as he should make according to the true intent
> and meaning of the said articles (the ordinary charges
> of the house only deducted). . . .

And they say that the same benefit provision was set out
in the new contract of August 1638:

> that they should pay unto or for the said Richard Brome
> the sum of twenty shillings per week and permit and
> suffer him to have one day's profit of the said several
> new plays (except as before excepted) in manner as in

13. Answer, ibid., p. 301.

the said first recited articles of agreement is mentioned and expressed. . . .[14]

And in his answer Brome verifies this benefit provision with a little more detail. He says that in the first contract the company agreed:

> to pay fifteen shillings weekly upon every Saturday unto this defendant to have the clear benefit of any one day's playing unto himself within the space of ten days after the first playing of any such play at this defendant's election (the common charge deducted as by the said articles). . . .

And Brome confirms that the company allowed him the profits of his benefit upon at least one occasion. He says that he gave them the manuscripts of two new plays within the first three-quarters of the year after the contract was drawn up on 20 July 1635: "And true it is that this defendant for the first of the said two plays had one day's clear profit as they affirmed by their account deducting as aforesaid according to the said articles." However, the second play was delivered just before the plague closing of 12 May 1636 and the "said clear day's profit of the said second new play was never allowed unto him to the damage of five pounds and upwards. . . ."[15]

There is complete agreement between the two parties that Brome was to receive the take minus the regular house charges at one benefit performance of each play he wrote. Benefit performances for dramatists are many times referred to; the only odd feature of the Brome–Salisbury Court agreement is Brome's statement that he was to select the day of his benefit: "The clear benefit of any one day's playing unto himself within the space of ten days after the first playing of any such play at this defendant's election. . . ." Most references to the custom state that the

14. Bill, ibid., pp. 297 and 299.
15. Ibid., p. 302.

benefit was the second or the third day of performance. Ordinarily in the repertory system of the time a new play would not have been performed more than three or possibly four times in the first ten days of its stage life; perhaps this odd clause was intended to give Brome the option of taking receipts on the second, third, or fourth performance. The only advantage I can see of the third or fourth performance over the second is a gamble on better weather.

The fact that most dramatists had benefit performances of their new plays seems to have been common knowledge in seventeenth-century London. It is not clear just when it began, but William Davenant implies very early. Toward the end of the first act of his *The Playhouse to be Let*, there is a conversation between Player and Poet concerning the proposed play. Player says

> There is an old tradition
> That in the times of mighty Tamberlane
> Of conjuring Faustus, and the Beauchamps bold,
> You poets used to have the second day.
> This shall be ours, sir, and tomorrow yours.

Though the play was written to be acted in 1663, Davenant had had plenty of experience of the Caroline theatre: he had written ten or more plays to be acted by the King's company at Blackfriars or the Globe; for almost a year he managed the company at the Phoenix theatre; and in 1638 and 1639 he was developing plans for a huge new theatre of his own. Certainly he knew a good deal about theatre customs before the war, but these lines imply benefits for Marlowe and Heywood[16] in the last ten or fifteen years of Elizabeth's reign. There is no other evidence of benefit performances at such an early date, unless two entries in the accounts of Philip Henslowe are to be so interpreted.

16. *The Bold Beauchamps* is lost, and though there are half a dozen or more references to it as a popular piece, only one, in the 1660s, attributes it to Heywood. See Arthur Melville Clark, *Thomas Heywood, Playwright and Miscellanist*, Oxford, 1931, pp. 13–15.

In April or May 1601 Henslowe noted that he had "paid unto John Day at the appointment of the company 1601 after the playing of the second part of Strowd the sum of . . . 10s." And in September 1602 there is another suggestive entry: "Paid unto Thomas Dekker the 27 of September 1602 over and above his price of his book called *A Medicine for a Curst Wife* the sum of . . . 10s."[17]

The first payment, that to John Day, is recorded as a payment from the company, but the round sum suggests a reward rather than the more usual share of receipts due on a benefit performance. In the case of *A Medicine for a Curst Wife*, previous payments in the months of July, August, and early September show that Dekker had already received a total of £10 for this play. The 10 shillings paid on 27 September was thus evidently not a part of the regular payment for the play, but the round sum again suggests a reward and not a benefit.

But the custom appears to have been well established, and Thomas Dekker evidently assumed that his audience was familiar with it when in 1611 he wrote the prologue for his play *If This Be Not Good the Devil Is in It*, acted by Queen Anne's men at the Red Bull and published in 1612. After some rather cynical remarks about the reception of plays, the prologue continues,

> It is not praise is sought for now, but pence,
> Though dropped from greasy-aproned audience.
> Clapped may he be with thunder that plucks bays
> With such foul hands, and with squint-eyes does
>   gaze
> On Pallas shield, not caring (so he gains
> A crammed third day) what filth drops from his
>   brains.

A benefit performance on the second day, not the third, seems to be referred to in a letter of Robert Daborne to

17. Foakes and Rickert, pp. 168 and 216.

Philip Henslowe about payment for the play he was writing: ". . . I pray sir go forward with that reasonable bargain for the Bellman. We will have but twelve pounds and the overplus of the second day. . . ."[18]

Edmund Malone, who had the original manuscript of Sir Henry Herbert's office book for some time but published only such extracts as seemed pertinent for his discussions of the theatre of Shakespeare's time, did make a few generalizations about what he found in these allowance records. He says, ". . . I have learned from Sir Henry Herbert's office-book, that between the years 1625 and 1641 [dramatists'] benefits were on the second day of representation."[19] Malone seems to imply that these benefits were the custom in all companies in Caroline London, but it would be comfortable to have his evidence.

The epilogue to Richard Brome's play *The Novella*, whose title page says that it was "Acted at the Black-friars by his Majesties Servants, Anno 1632," suggests a benefit performance some time after the opening, though it is none too precise:

> Cause 'tis the custom, by the Poet, sirs,
> I'm sent to crave a plaudit; and the spurs
> That prick him on to 't is, his promised pay
> May chance to fail if you dislike the play.

More explicit is the prologue to Jasper Mayne's play *The City Match*, which was acted by the King's company at Blackfriars in 1637 or 1638 after a previous performance at court. The arrogance of the amateur, and his contempt for the professional playwright, are also apparent in this prologue.

> Whether their sold scenes be disliked or hit
> Are cares for them who eat by the stage and wit.

18. Greg, *Henslowe Papers*, p. 75.
19. James Boswell, ed., *The Plays and Poems of William Shakespeare. . . Comprehending . . . an Enlarged History of the Stage, by the late Edmund Malone*, 21 vols., London, 1821, III, 158.

He's [the author is] one whose unbought
  muse did never fear
An empty second day or a thin share;
But can make th' actors, though you come
  not twice,
No losers, since we act now at the King's price,
Who hath made this play public, and the same
Power that makes laws, redeemed this from the
  flames.

At about the same time that *The City Match* was acted
at Blackfriars, a lost play by Richard Lovelace was performed at Salisbury Court. The prologue and epilogue
were published in the collection of Lovelace's verse,
Lucasta, in 1649. Both prologue and epilogue express the
same amateur fear of commercial contamination as Mayne's
verses do. The last four lines of the epilogue refer to the
usual author's benefit on the second day:

Profit he knows none
Unless that of your approbation,
Which, if your thoughts at going out will pay,
He'll not look farther for a second day.

More explicit reference to the exact procedure in the
theatre after the dramatist's benefit performance is set out
at the end of the epilogue of William Davenant's *The
Unfortunate Lovers*, which was licensed for performance
on 16 April 1638 and acted before the Queen by the King's
men at Blackfriars a week later.[20]

And though he never had the confidence
To tax your judgment in his own defence,
Yet, the next night when we your money share
He'll shrewdly guess what your opinions are.

This allusion at the first performance of the play to "the
next night when we your money share" not only indicates
the second performance as the dramatist's benefit night,

20. See *Jacobean and Caroline Stage*, III, 220–22, and VI, 34–
35.

but implies that the actual cash of the receipts was shared after the performance.

An authoritative allusion to the common practice occurs in the anonymous pamphlet, *The Actors' Remonstrance*, which purports to represent the actors at Blackfriars, the Phoenix, and the Salisbury Court. The piece was published on 24 January 1643/44, about a year and a half after the closing of the theatres, and laments the hard lot of the theatre people who have been deprived of their livelihood. After mentioning the trials of the housekeepers, the actor-sharers, the hired men, the comedians, the boy actors, the doorkeepers, the musicians, the tire-men, and the tobacco-men, the authors of the pamphlet come to the dramatists: "For some of our ablest ordinary poets, instead of their annual stipends and beneficial second days, being for mere necessity compelled to get a living by writing contemptible penny pamphlets."[21]

Finally Henry Harington alludes to the custom in the verses he wrote for the Beaumont and Fletcher folio of 1647.

> You wits o' th' age
> You that both furnished have, and judged the stage,
> You, who the Poet and the Actors fright,
> Lest that your censure thin the second night.[22]

Additional Chores

Besides plays, Brome wrote other dramatic material for the company at the Salisbury Court theatre. In the plain-

21. Reprinted by William Carew Hazlitt in *The English Drama and Stage*, London, 1869, pp. 259–65.

22. Beaumont and Fletcher folio f4^v. There are other allusions to the custom of the dramatists' benefit night in the verses signed "Thy Friend C. G." before John Tatham's *Fancies Theatre*, 1640; the prologue to John Denham's *The Sophy*, 1642; the epilogue scene to Thomas Killigrew's *The Parson's Wedding*, 1663, but performed in 1639 or 1640; "Dr. Smith's Ballet," in *Musarum Deliciae, or The Muses' Recreation*, 1656; and the induction scene 1, 2, of the anonymous *Lady Alimony*, 1659.

tiffs' account of the contract they say nothing of these extra chores, and Brome himself does not state specifically that they were required by the contract. But he does enumerate several other contributions necessary to a repertory theatre which he says he furnished. In defending himself against the plaintiffs' accusation that in the plague period he did not contribute as many plays as his contract called for, Brome asserts:

> . . . In lieu of which he hath made divers scenes in old revived plays for them and many prologues and epilogues to such plays of theirs, songs, and one Introduction at their first playing after the ceasing of the plague, all which he verily believeth amounted to as much time and study as two ordinary plays might take up in writing. . . .[23]

Brome's statement that new scenes, prologues, epilogues, songs, and the induction involved as much writing as two new plays ought to be taken with a grain of salt because two new plays was exactly the amount the plaintiffs charged that he had agreed to bring to them before Michaelmas 1638 to make up for his alleged arrears. On the other hand I see no reason to doubt that he did do such necessary repertory chores for them, since there is evidence that other dramatists did such work.

Prologues and Epilogues

There is a good deal of evidence that prologues and epilogues were often written separately from the play to which they were attached and frequently by the dramatist attached to the company, and not by the author. Probably the clearest evidence of this custom is found in *Poems &c By James Shirley*, 1646. The book is a miscellaneous collection of his shorter works brought together by the author after the closing of the theatres. One section of the volume is entitled "Prologues and Epilogues; Written to several plays presented in this Kingdom and elsewhere."

23. Answer, Haaker transcript, p. 305.

"Elsewhere" is Dublin, where Shirley worked as dramatist for the Saint Werburgh Street theatre between the periods of his regular service to Queen Henrietta's company at the Phoenix and to the King's company at Blackfriars and the Globe. In this section of the book Shirley prints six of the prologues and epilogues to his own plays, but he also prints "A Prologue to Mr. Fletcher's play in Ireland," "A Prologue to *The Alchemist* acted there," "A Prologue to a play there called *No Wit to a Woman's*," "A Prologue to a play there called *The Toy*," "To another there," and "To a play there called *The General*."

Obviously these prologues which Shirley indicates that he had written as part of his duties to the Irish theatre were chores of the same sort that Brome says he carried out for the Salisbury Court; Shirley is not even able to remember the name of one of these plays by other men, though he evidently still had the manuscript for his prologue among his papers in 1646.

New prologues and epilogues for revived plays and for court performances were already commonplace in Henslowe's time. There is no convincing evidence that the Henslowe dramatists had contracts with their companies, but the companies did authorize Henslowe to make payments for special prologues and epilogues. In January 1601/1602 the diarist noted that he had "paid unto Thomas Dekker at the appointment of the company for a prologue and an epilogue for the play of Pontius Pilate the 12 of January 1601 [/1602] the sum of . . . 10*s*." There is no other record of a play called *Pontius Pilate* and no good reason to think Dekker had written it himself. Later in the same year the Lord Admiral's company authorized Henslowe, through its usual representative, Thomas Downton, to pay for writing special prologues and epilogues for court performances of Greene's old play, *Friar Bacon and Friar Bungay*, and for another unnamed play.

Lent unto Thomas Downton the 14 of December 1602 to pay unto Mr. Middleton for a prologue and an epilogue for the play of Bacon for the court the sum of . . . 5s.

Lent unto Thomas Downton the 29 of December 1602 to pay unto Harry Chettle for a prologue and an epilogue for the court the sum of . . . 5s.[24]

Numerous prologues and epilogues mention that they were written for a revival or refer to the author of the play as dead, and must therefore have been written by another, probably as a rule the regular dramatist of the company staging the revival. There are several in the Beaumont and Fletcher canon, most of them probably written by Massinger or Shirley.[25]

Evidently the company dramatist sometimes saved time by using an old prologue or epilogue for a different play. The same prologue is printed with *Thierry and Theodoret* and *The Noble Gentleman*; Dekker's *Wonder of a Kingdom* and Rowley's *All's Lost by Lust* have the same prologue; the prologue printed in the 1613 edition of Beaumont and Fletcher's *Knight of the Burning Pestle* is almost the same as that printed in the 1584 edition of John Lyly's *Sapho and Phao*, a play which had been acted 25 years before, but also at the Blackfriars theatre.

These examples indicate that Brome's chore of writing prologues and epilogues for the plays of other men was not peculiar to the Salisbury Court theatre, and suggest that the task was probably a customary one for the "ordinary poet" of a well-established theatre.

24. Foakes and Rickert, pp. 187 and 207.

25. See, e.g., the prologues or epilogues in the 1637 quarto of *The Elder Brother*, and those for *The Loyal Subject*, *The Nice Valour*, *The Lovers' Progress*, *The Custom of the Country*, and *The Noble Gentleman* in the 1647 folio. See also those in the 1633 *Jew of Malta* and the prologue in the 1656 quarto of Goffe's *Careless Shepherdess*, referring to events long after Goffe's death.

New Scenes in Old Plays

Brome says that among his other chores for the Salisbury Court company he had "made divers scenes in old revived plays for them." This method of giving new life to old plays in the repertory was not peculiar to the Salisbury Court, and probably most such scenes were written by the company dramatist, but in most instances there is no external evidence of the authorship of the added scene. Precisely what Brome was talking about is illustrated in a license granted by Sir Henry Herbert to the Salisbury Court company about a year before Brome signed his contract and while he was still working for the Red Bull. Herbert allowed, "An old play with some new scenes, *Doctor Lamb and the Witches* to Salisbury Court the 16th August, 1634 . . . £1." In this instance it is possible to make a good guess at the occasion and circumstances of the additions to the old play.[26]

The same routine additions to old plays were being made at the Fortune theatre a couple of years later. Again the evidence is found in Herbert's office book. "Received of old Cartwright for allowing the [Fortune] company to add scenes to an old play, and to give it out for a new one this 12th of May 1636 . . . £1."

Such additions to old plays were by no means peculiar to the inferior theatres. The same thing was done by the King's men and the results presented at court, as shown by the title page of the third edition of *Mucedorus* in 1610, which says that the play was "amplified with new additions, as it was acted before the King's majesty at Whitehall on Shrove Sunday night. By his highness servants usually playing at the Globe."[27]

26. See below, chap. IX, pp. 253–55.
27. See "*Mucedorus,* Most Popular Elizabethan Play?" *Studies in the English Renaissance Drama,* ed. J. W. Bennett, Oscar Cargill, and Vernon Hall, Jr., New York, 1959, pp. 248–68.

In 1602 when Dekker and Heywood were working regularly for the Earl of Worcester's men and the Lord Admiral's men they performed this chore on plays they had not written originally, as indicated by Henslowe's payments:

> Lent unto John Thare the 7 of September 1602 to give unto Thomas Dekker for his additions in Oldcastle, the sum of . . . 10s.

> Paid unto Thomas Heywood the 20 of September [1602] for the new additions of Cutting Dick, sum of . . . 20s.

Probably best known of all is the payment made at the company's order to two of the leading members of the Lord Admiral's troupe for their additions to a very famous play: "Lent unto the company the 22 of November 1602 to pay unto William Bird and Samuel Rowley for their additions in Doctor Faustus the sum of . . . £4."[28]

There are many examples of plays on which other playwrights had carried out Brome's chore for his company of making "divers scenes in old revived plays for them"; a number of others are cited below in the chapter on revisions. All Brome's statement adds to our knowledge of revisions is (as might have been guessed) that such addition of new scenes was normally one of the duties of the regular dramatist for the company owning the play.

Added Songs

The addition of songs—sometimes just more songs—to old plays is also a phenomenon confirmed by other sources. The 1638 edition (fifth) of Heywood's *Rape of Lucrece*, originally written thirty or more years before for his company (Queen Anne's men) at the Red Bull, carries a statement on the title page: "The Copy revised, and sundry Songs before omitted, now inserted in their right places."

28. Foakes and Rickert, pp. 216 and 206.

In this edition five additional songs are printed. Just when these new songs had been written is not apparent, but they are not in earlier editions of the play, which, in 1639, was still in repertory.

Somewhat similar to the statement in *The Rape of Lucrece* is the announcement on the title page of the second issue of *A Fair Quarrel* in 1617: "With new additions of Mr. *Chaugh's* and *Tristram's* Roaring, and the Bawd's song. *Never before printed. As it was acted before the King, by the Prince* his Highness Servants." The new songs are inserted after act 4 in four leaves which were added to this edition. Since William Rowley was both a collaborator in the original composition of the play and a patented member of Prince Charles's company, it seems likely that he wrote the new songs for the company.

Another well-known play to which songs were added is Shakespeare's *Macbeth*. Many scholars have observed that before the play was first printed, in the 1623 folio, material had been interpolated into it, and most agree that the Hecate material, including two songs in the third and fourth acts, were such interpolations. The songs also occur in Middleton's play *The Witch*, almost certainly later in composition than *Macbeth*. But the man who added the songs to *Macbeth* was not necessarily Middleton, since the manuscript of *The Witch* belonged to the King's men and any reviser with access to the Blackfriars archives could have transferred the songs from *The Witch* to *Macbeth*. In any event, the addition of these songs to *Macbeth*, however ill advised it may seem to Shakespeareans, is the sort of chore Brome said he performed for Queen Henrietta's company twenty-five or thirty years later.

Introductions or Inductions

The chore which Brome indicates in his list as "one Introduction at their first playing after the ceasing of the plague" is probably the least familiar one, since most occasional inductions of this type were of such ephemeral interest that they were never printed. But such inductions or introductions are a natural development in a repertory theatre where the friendly relations of audience and actors were a greater source of continued profit than enthusiasm for a particular play or dramatist. This is, of course, also the reason for the popularity of prologues and epilogues in repertory theatres—witness the number which say so little about the play to be performed that they have sometimes been attached to other plays.[29]

The type of induction which Brome and probably all other regular company playwrights wrote might be called the occasional induction; it is not like the more familiar ones that Jonson wrote for a half a dozen of his plays and Shakespeare for *The Taming of the Shrew*. These familiar inductions are essentially a part of the play; they could not be used for another play on a similar occasion. The only Jonson induction which approaches the occasional type is that for *Bartholomew Fair*, which is partly occasional in that it has much on the players and the particular playhouse and may indeed have been written for the opening of the new Hope theatre, but has mostly to do with the fair and Jonson's depiction of it, and could not have been used for any other play.

Precisely like the "Introduction at their first playing after the ceasing of the plague" which Brome says he wrote for the Salisbury Court theatre in 1637 is one which Thomas Randolph wrote when he was probably regular dramatist for the same theatre seven years earlier, after the plague of 1630. This one also failed to achieve print, but it is extant in a British Museum manuscript (Add. MS 37

29. Readers of Elizabethan plays are often confused about prologues and epilogues, partly because they tend to think about plays as pieces for the study, and partly because the most familiar prologues—those for *Romeo and Juliet*, *Henry V*, *Every Man in His Humour*, *The Alchemist*—are those least characteristic of the form.

425 fols. 54-55). The manuscript is headed simply "Prae-ludium," but it is endorsed "T. Randall after the last Plague." It consists of about two hundred lines of dialogue between Histrio and Gentlemen, mostly concerned with the trials of the players during the plague closing; it could have been used before any play.[30]

A similar introduction, induction, or praeludium was probably the lost piece which the King's company pre-sented at court on 5 November 1630. It is known only from the bill the King's men presented for their perform-ances at court in 1630 and 1630/31. The item reads, "The 5 of November, an Induction for the House and The Mad Lover." Apparently this forepiece for Fletcher's popular play was a celebration of the opening of the new Cockpit playhouse designed by Inigo Jones for the court.[31]

Similar occasional pieces concerned with the actors and the theatre, not with the play, were written by John Tatham when he appears to have been attached to the Red Bull players in and about 1640. Tatham called his pieces prologues, and they are not dialogue, but the occasions are as nonliterary as Brome's and Randolph's. One was printed in his *Fancies Theatre*, 1640, and the other in his *Ostella*, 1650, and neither was given any connection with any play. They are entitled *A Prologue spoken upon the removing of the late Fortune players to the Bull* and *A Prologue spoken at the Cock-pit at the coming of the Red Bull play-ers thither*. It is significant that Tatham's titles for these pieces make mention of the occasion and not of the play they preceded. When he printed the prologue for an ordi-nary occasion, he named the play, as Shirley did for the

30. See "Randolph's *Praeludium* and the Salisbury Court Thea-tre," *Joseph Quincy Adams Memorial Studies*, ed. James G. Mc-McManaway, Giles E. Dawson, and Edwin E. Willoughby, Washing-ton, D.C., 1948, pp. 775–83.

31. See *Jacobean and Caroline Stage*, I, 28–29; III, 373–76; and VI, 267–84.

prologues he printed in *Poems &c.* One other prologue printed in *Ostella* is called *A Prologue spoken at the Red-Bull to a Play called the Whisperer, or what you please.*

Of the many printed inductions[32] the great majority are really a part of the play with which they were published, though not always essential to it. Less occasional than the pieces written by Brome and Randolph and the unknown author of "An Induction for the House" or John Tatham's two prologues, but partially divorced from their plays and essentially theatrical in character, are the inductions for Goffe's *Careless Shepherdess*, Marston's *Malcontent*, and the anonymous *Lady Alimony*. In the last what is really an induction has been printed as act 1 in the text of 1659. Obviously none was written by the author of the play, and all make much of theatrical affairs.

Irregular pieces like these would normally have been productions of the theatre's ordinary poet, for they were much concerned with the affairs of the theatre and the company.

Publication

The plaintiffs in their complaint of 12 February 1639/40 say that one of the clauses in the second contract of August 1638 prohibited publication:

> And that he should not suffer any play made or to be made or composed by him for your subjects or their successors in the said company in Salisbury Court to be printed by his consent or knowledge, privity, or direction without the license from the said company or the major part of them.[33]

This clause too appears to have been conventional. Brome does not mention it, but his publication record shows that he observed it; the printing of his plays is not an issue

32. There is a convenient list of 56 of them published by Stephen C. Young in *Philological Quarterly*, XLVIII (January 1969), 131–34.
33. Haaker transcript, p. 298.

in the suit. This subject of the publication of plays, 1590–1642, has involved so much heated controversy over the last century, and it is so complex, that it requires an independent discussion. The subject will be considered at length in Chapter X.

CHAPTER VII

Regulation and Censorship

ALL PLAYS presented in the London theatres throughout the period required approval by the Master of the Revels, whose censorship seldom admitted of any appeal. Every dramatist knew this, every manager, every player, and every factotem of the company. One important stage in the intricate progression of every play from an idea in the playwright's head to first performance was the submission of the manuscript to the Master of the Revels for his official permission to proceed. Normally his permission was set down in his own autograph at the end of the manuscript. Several of these autograph official statements have been preserved. The manuscript of *The Second Maiden's Tragedy* (British Museum MS Lansdowne 807) carries on the verso of the last leaf the autograph statement

This second Maydens tragedy (for it hath no name inscribed) may wth the reformations bee acted publikely, 31 octob^r 1611   By me G. Buc

Sir Henry Herbert, successor to George Buc's successor as Master of the Revels, was using approximately the same form 22 years later. Another British Museum play manuscript (Egerton 1994) carries his license on the last page:

> This play, called the Seaman's Honest wife, all the oaths left out in the action as they are crossed in the book, and all other reformations strictly observed may be acted, not otherwise. This 27 June 1633. Henry Herbert. I command your bookkeeper to present me with a fair copy hereafter and to leave out all oaths, profaneness, and public ribaldry, as he will answer it at his peril. Herbert.[1]

A third play in the same manuscript volume at the British Museum (Egerton 1994) bears an autograph license at the end. This time the Master has evidently assigned the censorship of the play to his deputy.

> This play called the Lady-mother (the Reformations observed) may be acted. October 15. 1635 Will. Blagrave deputy to the master of the Revels.

Even the printed texts of plays in one or two instances bear testimony to the customary form and position of the Master of the Revels's license for acting. The quarto of Thomas Jordan's very popular *Walks of Islington and Hogsdon*, said to have been "Acted 19 days together," is an example. Evidently the compositor set the play from the theatre's prompt copy, for when he came to the end he set up Herbert's acting license from the manuscript before him. On H₄, after the epilogue, he set up

> This Comedy, called, *The Walks of Islington and Hogsdon, With the Humours of Woodstreet-Compter*, may be Acted: This 2 August, 1641.
> *Henry Herbert.*

Even in extant play manuscripts which no longer bear the license statement of the Master of the Revels there is

---

1. J. Q. Adams, ed., *The Dramatic Records of Sir Henry Herbert*, New Haven, 1917, pp. 34–35.

sometimes evidence that it once was there. Massinger's *Parliament of Love* was licensed, according to the office book, for the Cockpit company on 3 November 1624, though it was never printed in the seventeenth century. The manuscript of the play, now in the Victoria and Albert Museum, is rather badly mutilated by damp and carelessness, but there has also been deliberate vandalism, as Edmond Malone and successive editors have noted. At the end of the manuscript, where the Master normally wrote his allowance, a strip of paper 5⅞ by 1⅝ has been neatly cut out of the page.[2]

These licenses to act are Jacobean and Caroline examples of the workings of a system gradually developed in the entertainment world. Edmund Tilney, George Buc, John Astley, and Henry Herbert were the successive Elizabethan, Jacobean, and Caroline Masters of an office set up in the reign of Henry VIII to regularize the supervision of court entertainment, which had previously had *ad hoc* direction.

The Office of the Revels was originally established to select, organize, and supervise all entertainment of the sovereign, wherever the court might be. Such supervision would cover masques, shows, plays, exhibitions, contests, and all the equipment they required, so that costumes, properties, sets, and weapons accumulated in great store in the London Office of the Revels. At first the Masters of the Revels and their subordinates confined their activities to the selection of entertainment for the sovereign and the complex supervision of its presentation. But gradually the power of general dramatic censorship came into the hands of the Master of the Revels. After a good deal of jockeying for position between the authorities of the City of London (generally hostile to the theatre) and the representatives of the generally sympathetic royal authority, usually exercised through the Privy Council of the sovereign, a

2. See K. M. Lea's edition for the Malone Society, Oxford, 1928, pp. v–xiii.

new patent was issued to the Master of the Revels, Edmund Tilney, in 1581. This patent was intended to centralize the regulation of "all and every player or players, with their playmakers," and it was reissued to Sir George Buc in 1603 and to Sir John Astley in 1622.

> . . . we have and do by these presents authorize and command our said servant, Edmund Tilney, Master of our said Revels, by himself, or his sufficient deputy or deputies, to warn, command, and appoint, in all places within this our realm of England, as well within franchises and liberties as without, all and every player or players, with their playmakers, either belonging to any nobleman, or otherwise bearing the name or names of using the faculty of playmakers or players of comedies, tragedies, interludes, or what other shows soever, from time to time, and at all times, to appear before him with all such plays, tragedies, comedies, or shows as they shall have in readiness, or mean to set forth; and them to present and recite before our said servant, or his sufficient deputy, whom we ordain, appoint, and authorize by these presents, of all shows, plays, players, and playmakers, together with their playing places, to order and reform, authorize and put down, as shall be thought meet or unmeet unto himself, or his said deputy in that behalf.
>
> And also likewise we have by these presents authorized and commanded the said Edmund Tilney that in case if any of them, whatsoever they be, will obstinately refuse upon warning unto them given by the said Edmund, or his sufficient deputy, to accomplish and obey our commandment in this behalf, then it shall be lawful to the said Edmund, or his sufficient deputy, to attach the party or parties so offending, and him or them to commit to ward, to remain without bail or mainprise until such time as the said Edmund Tilney, or his sufficient deputy, shall think the time of his or their imprisonment to be punishment sufficient for his or their said offences in that behalf; and that done, to enlarge

him or them so being imprisoned at their plain liberty, without any loss, penalty, or forfeiture, or other danger in this behalf to be sustained or borne by the said Edmund Tilney, or his deputy, any act, statute, ordinance, or provision heretofore had or made to the contrary hereof in any wise notwithstanding.[3]

Though there was uncertainty for several years in the application of these powers, and though the Lord Mayor and Corporation never ceased to express their hostility, generally through letters and petitions to the Privy Council, nevertheless these are the powers which had to be recognized and accommodated by Shakespeare, Henslowe, Heywood, Heminges, Webster, Alleyn, Chapman, Burbage, Brome, Beeston, and all other dramatists, actors, and managers from 1581 to 1642. The hypotheses so often and so solemnly advanced by many critics and readers of Tudor and Stuart plays about the dramatist's "advice to the Queen" or "protests against the law" or "assertions of his religious dissent" must be made either in ignorance of the powers of the Master of the Revels or in assumption of his incompetence or his venality.

By 1590 the procedures in the Revels office were pretty well established, though Sir Henry Herbert later made them more explicit and rigorous. As theatres, companies, and dramatists became more numerous in the 1580s and 1590s, the demands upon the initiative of the Master became too great for him to "warn, command, and appoint" the players "to appear before him with all such plays, tragedies, comedies, or shows as they shall have in readiness, or mean to set forth; and them to present and recite before our said servant." Instead, all companies were required voluntarily to bring in for inspection all play manuscripts before the plays were acted. This system of individual licenses for individual plays before performance was

3. Albert Feuillerat, *Documents Relating to the Office of the Revels in the Time of Queen Elizabeth,* Louvain, 1908, p. 52.

already in effect in 1574. On 10 May 1574 Queen Elizabeth issued a royal patent to James Burbage and the other members of the Earl of Leicester's men. They were allowed to act in London and the provinces, and provincial officials in towns and boroughs throughout the realm were ordered to permit their performances, "provided that the said comedies, tragedies, interludes and stage plays be by the Master of our Revels for the time being before seen and allowed."[4] The same provision stated in another form is found in the license of another company nearly ten years later. In March 1583/84 a company of players visited the town of Leicester and requested permission to act. In proof of their legitimacy they showed their credentials, dated 6 February 1582/83, and the warrant was copied into the town records at Leicester. One sentence in this warrant for the players reads: "No play is to be played, but such as is allowed by the said Edmund Tilney and his hand at the latter end of the said book they do play."[5]

Ten years later Henslowe's diary shows that he was making regular payments to the Master of the Revels in behalf of the companies he financed for the allowance of their new plays; he was also making payments on his own behalf for the licensing of his theatres while acting was in progress. In early 1592 he was paying the Master five shillings a week for permission to operate his theatre, and later in the year he was paying 6s 8d; in the later nineties and the first two years of the seventeenth century he was paying 40s and later £3 a month.

A Note what I have laid out about the house . . .

. . . .

Item paid unto Mr. Tilney's man 26 of February 1591
5s

4. *Elizabethan Stage*, II, 87–88.
5. William Kelly, *Notices Illustrative of the Drama and Other Popular Amusements*, Leicester, 1865, p. 212.

Item paid unto Mr. Tilney's man 4 of March 1591
5s

Item paid unto Mr. Tilney's man 10 of March 1591
5s

.   .   .   .

Item paid unto Mr. Tilney's man the 20 of May 1592
6s 8d

Item paid unto Mr. Tilney's man the 9 of June 1592
6s 8d

Item paid unto Mr. Tilney's man the 14 of June 1592
6s 8d[6]

Later, in the year 1601, increased fees for the operation of the theatres were shown in a different form of record.

Received of Mr. Henslowe the 9 of June £3 which he is to pay for the month's pay for the Fortune, and due unto the Master of Revels

Robte Hassard

Received from Mr. Henslowe by me William Plaistowe to the use of my master, Master Edmond Tilney Master of Her Majesty's Revels for one month's pay due unto him the day and year above written [31 July 1601] the sum of £3, I say . . . £3.[7]

Such payments for licenses for their theatres were ordinarily made by the theatre owners, and not by the players, except in those rare cases where the actors also owned the theatres—as Shakespeare, Burbage, Heminges, Condell, Phillips, and Kempe owned the Globe, and later Shakespeare, Burbage, Heminges, Condell, and Sly the Blackfriars.

Of greater significance for most dramatists were the activities of the Master of the Revels in licensing their plays for performance in those theatres which he had already allowed. Again, Henslowe's records show the sys-

6. Foakes and Rickert, pp. 14–15.
7. Ibid., 194, 164.

tem. These payments to the Master of the Revels for inspecting and allowing their plays Henslowe, as financial agent, charged against the acting companies, whereas the payments for the Fortune and his other theatres were Henslowe's own expense as owner of the theatres.

> Laid out for my Lord Admiral's men as followeth, 1597
> Lent unto Thomas Downton for the company to pay to the Master of the Revels for licensing of 2 books 14 shillings, abated to Downton 5 shillings and so rest . . . 9s.
> Paid unto the Master of the Revels's man for the licensing of a book called the Four Kings . . . 7s.
> Paid unto the Master of the Revels's man for licensing of a book called Beech's Tragedy the sum of . . . 7s.
> Paid unto the Master of the Revels's man for licensing of a book called Damon and Pithias the 16 of May, 1600, the sum of . . . 7s.[8]

These records show clearly enough that Henslowe had to pay a fee in behalf of his companies for the allowance of each of the plays they acted at his theatres, and they show what he paid the Master for his trouble. Such records do not show, however, very much about what the Master did. Such knowledge comes mostly from the records of a later successor of Edmund Tilney, Sir Henry Herbert.

Tilney was succeeded in his office by Sir George Buc, who served from 1597 as his deputy, taking over many of his duties; after 1607 he seems to have performed all the duties of the office. In May 1622 Sir John Astley took over, but he functioned in the office for only a little over a year and in July 1623 turned over to Henry Herbert. Herbert served until the closing of the theatres and tried, with only partial success, to reestablish his right to the office after the Restoration of Charles II.

8. Ibid., 86, 106, 130, 134.

Scattered bits from the records of all these Masters are extant, but the only one whose office book is known to have been preserved well beyond his own time is Henry Herbert. Until the end of the eighteenth century it was extant and was examined by Edmund Malone and George Chalmers and by an unidentified transcriber, perhaps Craven Ord. Since then the manuscript has disappeared, and we must rely on the transcriptions of these scholars. Fortunately their notes are extensive enough to illustrate the Master's customary treatment of dramatists' manuscripts, though it must always be remembered that these three scholars did not copy everything, but tended to concentrate on well-known plays and dramatists. Insofar as we can tell from these extant notes, Sir Henry followed the pattern of his predecessors, though one gets the impression that he was more efficient than Buc or Astley.

The simplest and commonest action of the Master when he was brought a manuscript, usually by the manager of the theatre in which it was to be acted, was to read the script, find nothing objectionable, and write his allowance at the end, like the one at the end of the British Museum manuscript (Egerton 2828) of *Believe as You List* which Philip Massinger had prepared for performance by the King's company: "This Play, called Believe as you list may be acted this 6 of May 1631 Henry Herbert."

These official licenses were recorded by the Master or his clerk in the lost office book whence they were transcribed by the eighteenth- and nineteenth-century scholars mentioned. The form of entry in the office book varies a little with the passage of time—or possibly only with the degree of interest of Chalmers or Malone.

1622, 10 May A new Play, called *The Black Lady* was allowed to be acted by the Lady Elizabeth's Servants.

1623, 30 July For the Prince's Players, A French Tragedy of *the Bellman of Paris*, written by Thomas Dekker and John Day, for the company of the Red Bull.

1623, 29 October For the Palsgrave's Players; a new Comedy, called, *Hardshift for Husbands, or Bilboes the best blade*. Written by Samuel Rowley.

1624, 17 April For the Fortune; *The way to content all women, or how a Man may please his Wife*: Written by Mr. Gunnel.[9]

23 June 1641. Recd for the licensing a book for the Fortune comp. called the Doge and the Dragon . . . £2.[10]

It will be noted that the fee for allowance of a new play had risen from the 7 shillings Henslowe's companies paid in the 1590s to £1, which seems to have been the standard fee for the Master in the 1620s; sometime in the 1630s the fee was doubled to £2.

These licenses are all perfectly straightforward allowances for the company to act plays in which the Master of the Revels found nothing objectionable. But in a number of instances the Herbert memorandum of allowance shows that some alteration in the dramatist's manuscript was required of the company, and that the Master had indicated on the manuscript what was to be changed.

1624/25, 25 January For the Prince's Company; A new Play called, *The Widow's Prize*; which containing much abusive matter, was allowed of by me, on condition, that my reformations were observed.

And more specific objections were noted a few years later when Queen Henrietta's company sent in a better-known play by a famous dramatist.

R. for allowing of *The Tale of the Tub*, Vitru Hoop's part wholly struck out, and the motion of the tub, by command from my Lord Chamberlain; exceptions being taken against it by Inigo Jones surveyor of the king's

9. Adams, Herbert, pp. 23, 24, 26, 28.
10. *Jacobean and Caroline Stage*, v, 1321.

works, as a personal injury unto him. May 7, 1633 . . .
£2.[11]

Not only did the Master require that the dramatist or
the company bookkeeper make alterations in manuscripts,
but he sometimes refused to allow the play at all. This he
did when a representative of the King's company brought
him a play written for them by Philip Massinger: "This
day being the 11 of Janu. 1630, I did refuse to allow of a
play of Massinger's because it did contain dangerous
matter. . . ."[12] On another occasion he sent a messenger to
stop the performance of a play after the bills had been
posted and the actors were ready to begin. The play was
at least twenty years old, and there must have been con-
sternation at the Blackfriars when Sir Henry's warrant was
delivered.

On Friday the nineteenth [actually eighteenth] of October, 1633, I sent a warrant by a messenger of the
chamber to suppress *The Tamer Tamed*, to the King's
players, for that afternoon, and it was obeyed; upon complaints of foul and offensive matters contained therein.
They acted *The Scornful Lady* instead of it; I have
entered the warrant here:
These are to will and require you to forbear the acting of your play called *The Tamer Tamed, or the Taming of the Tamer* this afternoon, or any more till you
have leave from me: and this at your peril. On Friday
morning the 18 October 1633.
To Mr. Taylor, Mr. Lowins, or any of the King's
players at the Blackfryers.
On Saturday morning following the book was brought
me, and at my Lord of Hollands request I returned it
to the players the Monday morning after, purged of
oaths, profaneness, and ribaldry, being the 21 of October
1633.[13]

11. Adams, *Herbert*, pp. 30, 34.
12. Ibid., p. 19.   13. Ibid., p. 20.

When Herbert returned the manuscript of their play to the King's men he added a note to the company bookkeeper which throws a little more light on the vicissitudes of a dramatist's manuscript in the playhouse before the first performance. Fortunately he copied this note into his office book.

> Mr. Knight,
> In many things you have saved me labor; yet where your judgment or pen failed you, I have made bold to use mine. Purge their parts, as I have the book. And I hope every hearer and player will think that I have done God good service, and the quality no wrong; who hath no greater enemies than oaths, profaneness, and public ribaldry, which for the future I do absolutely forbid to be presented to me in any playbook, as you will answer it at your peril. 21 October 1633.
> This was subscribed to their play of *The Tamer Tamed*, and directed to Knight, their bookkeeper.[14]

One must sympathize with the harassed bookkeeper, who was only an employee of the company, hired to take care of the manuscripts, prepare parts, and adjust the texts for prompt use. Now the Master of the Revels was expecting part of the censoring to be done for him by the poor bookkeeper before the manuscript was submitted for official approval. How would his bosses, the sharers of the company, take to this presumption? Or even the regular dramatist, Philip Massinger? Backstage life is never serene, but Herbert's demands in 1633 seem calculated to produce even more friction. Altogether, there must have been a series of crises within the company over *The Tamer Tamed* business. The indignation of the actors does not need to be imagined; the Master himself attests to it. Not only did he comment in his note of 21 October that his action "hath raised some discourse in the players, though no disobedience," but at the end of the whole affair, nearly a week

14. Ibid., p. 21.

156

after his sudden cancellation of the Blackfriars performance, he recorded a final step in the imbroglio: "The 24
October 1633, Lowins and Swanston were sorry for their
ill manners, and craved my pardon, which I gave them in
the presence of Mr. Taylor and Mr. Benfeilde."[15] These
four men were the top brass in the King's company in
1633; no other record in the office book reveals the presence of such a large company representation. One would
guess that John Lowin and Eyllaerdt Swanston had lost
their tempers with the Master over his proscription of an
already advertised and rehearsed play, and that Benfield
and Taylor, horrified at the contemplation of the endless
trouble that an estranged Master of the Revels could cause
them, had prevailed upon their hot-tempered fellows to
make a formal apology to the Master. Since it took nearly
a week to persuade them, one must suspect that the original outburst was rather more than "some discourse in the
players," which Herbert admitted.

This example of the sudden proscription of a once allowed play may appear to set the limits of the arbitrary
power which the Master of the Revels could exercise over
the affairs of players and playwrights. But the King's men
were more fortunate than most; they had powerful friends
throughout the reigns of James and Charles, and what the
Earl of Holland (Henry Rich) did for them on this occasion other noblemen did earlier and later. At any rate they
got their manuscript back, and they presented the "purged"
play at court a little over a month later.

Herbert's disapproval of play manuscripts could be more
arbitrary and final than it was in the case of *The Tamer
Tamed*. On 8 June 1642 a manuscript was brought into
the Revels office by Mr. Kirke, who was probably the
manager of the Red Bull theatre. It did not please Sir
Henry: "Received of Mr. Kirke for a new play which I

15. Ibid., pp. 20, 21.

burnt for the ribaldry and offense that was in it . . . £2."[16]
Though the Master of the Revels often marked parts of a
manuscript for alteration or deletion, this is the most drastic reaction to a script that is known. The Red Bull theatre
had the lowest reputation of any in London at this time,
and it may be that Herbert thought they needed a lesson,
but his action evidently did not reflect a permanent disapproval of Kirke, for the last extant record from the office
book, made apparently on the same day, is, "Received of
Mr. Kirke for another new play called *The Irish Rebellion*, the 8 June, 1642 . . . £2."[17]

As Master of the Revels, Sir Henry Herbert took his
responsibility very seriously and he exercised some control
over revivals at the theatres as well as over new plays being performed for the first time. Not long after he had
come into office, he made the entry:

> For the king's players, An old play called *Winter's Tale*,
> formerly allowed of by Sir George Bucke, and likewise
> by me on Mr. Hemmings his word that there was noth-
> ing profane added or reformed, though the allowed
> book was missing; and therefore I returned it without
> a fee, this 19 of August, 1623.[18]

Evidently John Heminges, who was the active and trusted
manager of the King's company at this time, was sufficiently aware of Sir Henry's meticulousness to take precautions because the manuscript of Shakespeare's play which
the company was using was not the one with Buc's holograph allowance at the end. Since the dramatist was Shakespeare, there has been much speculation about what happened to the allowed manuscript and which one was used
as copy for the first folio. Nobody knows, but the revival
for which Heminges was preparing was obviously successful, for the company presented the play at court five
months later.

16. Ibid., p. 39.   17. Ibid., p. 39.   18. Ibid., p. 25.

On the same day that John Heminges brought in a manuscript of Shakespeare's *Winter's Tale*, a representative of Prince Charles's company appeared with the manuscript of an old play in their repertory. This transcription of the allowances is the one made by Craven Ord, and is somewhat more complete than the one made by George Chalmers.

> For the Prince's servants of the Rede Bull; an oulde playe called the Peacable King or the lord Mendall formerly allowed of by Sir George Bucke (likewise by mee) because itt was free from addition or reformation I tooke no fee this 19th August, 1623.[19]

However favored the King's company was at this time, their manuscript of *The Winter's Tale* received from the Master of the Revels the same treatment as the Red Bull manuscript of *The Peaceable King or The Lord Mendall*.

The manuscript of *The Winter's Tale* bearing the official allowance of Sir George Buc was not the only one that the King's company lost, and the same situation which Heminges had handled with the Master of the Revels was managed some eighteen months later by another leading actor of the royal company, Joseph Taylor. At this time Taylor, in conjunction with John Lowin, was gradually taking over the company representative's chores which had been handled so long and so ably by the now aging Heminges and Condell. Herbert recorded Taylor's visit and also noted one of the ways in which the company representatives were accustomed to facilitate their constant dealings with the Master of the Revels. "For the King's company. An old play called *The Honest Man's Fortune*, the original being lost, was reallowed by me at Mr. Taylor's intreaty, and on condition to give me a book this 8 February 1624[/25]."[20]

19. *Jacobean and Caroline Stage*, v, 1393, from the Folger manuscript.
20. Adams, *Herbert*, p. 30.

Herbert's most explicit statement about the regulation of revived plays is made in connection with the affair of *The Tamer Tamed*, which has already been noted. By 1633, when he handled that case, he was settled in his office and his procedures were clearly worked out in his own mind. He made some precise statements about policy, far more explicit than one usually finds from Stuart officials—at least as far as plays are concerned. To the statements already quoted Herbert added these remarks:

> Because the stopping of the acting of this play for that afternoon, it being an old play hath raised some discourse in the players, though no disobedience, I have thought fit to insert here their submission upon a former disobedience, and to declare that it concerns the Master of the Revels to be careful of their old revived plays, as of their new, since they may contain offensive matter, which ought not to be allowed in any time.
>
> The Master ought to have copies of their new plays left with him, that he may be able to show what he hath allowed or disallowed.
>
> All old plays ought to be brought to the Master of the Revels, and have his allowance to them, for which he should have his fee, since they may be full of offensive things against church and state; the rather that in former time the poets took greater liberty than is allowed them by me.
>
> The players ought not to study their parts till I have allowed of the book.[21]

Herbert was a conscientious Master, probably more conscientious, or at least better organized, than his predecessors, as he implies in his statement "rather that in former time the poets took greater liberty than is allowed them by me," but what he was looking for in old plays was generally the same as what Buc and Tilney had sought:

21. Ibid., pp. 20–21.

"offensive things against church and state." All the Masters occasionally dozed, as Herbert himself sometimes did, but no matter how alert Tilney and Buc may have been they could not have been expected to anticipate political change. The Statute of Oaths did not become law until 1606, and expressions of simple realistic vigor to Tilney were censorable to Herbert. In the same way international relations changed, and statements about Spain which could be applauded in 1595 offended the government in 1623. And of course the sensitivity of the Privy Council and the Master of the Revels to comments on church government was much greater in 1633 than it had been in 1605.

The policy which the Master had been at such pains to set down in the case of *The Tamer Tamed* was accepted and followed by the King's men, and no doubt by the other London companies. Their conformity, and Herbert's care to remove lines which had once been acceptable, is shown in the record of the submission of another old play by the company at Blackfriars a month later.

> The King's players sent me an old book of Fletchers called *The Loyal Subject*, formerly allowed of by Sir George Bucke, 16 November 1618, which according to their desire and agreement I did peruse, and with some reformations allowed, the 23 November of 1633, for which they sent me according to their promise . . . £1.[22]

But however uneasy Herbert may have been about the possibility of offensive matter in revived plays, he not only sanctioned revivals, but licensed revisions made in preparation for the revivals, as various of his office book entries show.

Often Sir Henry is vague about what the dramatist has done in his preparation of the old play for revival, but

22. Ibid., p. 22.

several times he is more particular. In January 1631/32 his statement about the revived play is quite vague: "For allowing of an old play, new written or furbished by Mr. Biston, the 12th of January, 1631 . . . £1."[23] "Mr. Biston" was Christopher Beeston, manager of Queen Henrietta's company and principal owner of their playhouse, the Phoenix or Cockpit in Drury Lane. The fee charged implies that the revisions must have been considerable. Beeston, though a very well-known theatre figure, is not otherwise known as a dramatist, and the fact that he "furbished" this play suggests that the function of "play doctor" may sometimes have been performed by an experienced man of the theatre who was not the company dramatist.

In an entry two years earlier Herbert was more specific about what had been done in revising the play, though less specific concerning by whom and for whom the additions were made: "For allowing of a new act in an old play, this 13th of May 1629 . . . 10s."[24] At this time his fees had not yet been increased and the charge of 10 shillings indicates the earlier rate, not that the new act was only half as extensive as Christopher Beeston's refurbishings.

The powers of the Master of the Revels over players, playwrights, and theatres were so great that one tends to think of him as omnipotent in theatrical matters, but this was not the case: the Master had a master. And on occasion Sir Henry Herbert and Sir John Astley are known to have been overruled. Their superior was the Lord Chamberlain, and now and then he interfered in the licensing of plays. Before Herbert took over the office, Sir John Astley wrote in the office book:

> Item 6 Sept. 1622, for perusing and allowing of a new play called *Osmond the Great Turk*, which Mr. Hemmings and Mr. Rice affirmed to me that the Lord Chamberlain gave order to allow of it because I refused to

23. *Jacobean and Caroline Stage*, III, 17.
24. Adams, *Herbert*, p. 32.

allow at first, containing 22 leaves and a page. Acted by the King's players . . . 20s.[25]

And even the Lord Chamberlain had a superior who sometimes intervened to get approval for the manuscript of a playwright with influential friends. The affair of Davenant's comedy, *The Wits*, discussed later, gives an amusing picture of such intervention.

These numerous records of the control exercised by Tilney, Buc, Astley, and Herbert over the play manuscripts which the dramatists had sold to the players leave no room for uncertainty about the extent of their powers. But most players in any time are by temperament a reckless lot, otherwise they would not be in such an always risky profession. In spite of all the checks and regulations, the London companies did sometimes stage plays or parts of plays which were not acceptable. Two examples from Sir Henry Herbert's accounts will illustrate.

In December of 1624 the King's company actually staged a play which the Master of the Revels had never licensed at all. This folly is known from the letter of apology which they wrote, and which Sir Henry copied into his office book nine years later at the time of *The Tamer Tamed* affair for the reason which he noted in the margin: " 'Tis entered here for a remembrance against their disorders." The letter reads:

To Sir Henry Herbert, Kt. master of his Majesty's Revels. After our humble service remembered unto your good worship, whereas not long since we acted a play called *The Spanish Viceroy*, not being licensed under your worship's hand, nor allowed of: we do confess and hereby acknowledge that we have offended, and that it is in your power to punish this offence, and are very sorry for it; and do likewise promise hereby that we will not act any play without your hand or substitute's hereafter,

25. *Jacobean and Caroline Stage*, III, 119.

nor do anything that may prejudice the authority of your office. So hoping that this humble submission of ours may be accepted, we have thereunto set our hands. This twentieth of December, 1624.

Joseph Taylor	John Lowin
Richard Robinson	John Shancke
Elyard Swanston	John Rice
Thomas Pollard	Will. Rowley
Robert Benfeilde	Richard Sharpe
George Burght[26]	

Most interesting is the fact that this letter is an official document, for it is signed by every one of the patented members of the company except John Heminges and Henry Condell. They were the oldest and most experienced of the sharers—though by no means the most distinguished actors. One wonders if they had had the foresight somehow to dissociate themselves from the company's folly.

Another device which indiscreet actors sometimes used to circumvent the Master of the Revels is recorded in the accounts of Jonson's comedy *The Magnetic Lady*. The play had been licensed regularly enough, as the office book allowance shows: "Received of Knight, for allowing of Ben Jonson's play called *Humours Reconciled, or the Magnetic Lady* to be acted this 12 October, 1632 . . . £2."[27] But after the play was performed, troubles arose. There was offensive matter in the lines spoken by the players, who were evidently hauled up before the Court of High Commission. This fact, and the device the players had used to get their lines past the censor, is revealed in another memorandum which Sir Henry set down in the official records of his office:

Upon a second petition of the players to the High Commission court, wherein they did me right in my care to

26. Adams, *Herbert*, p. 21.   27. Ibid., p. 34.

purge their plays of all offense, my lords Grace of Canterbury bestowed many words upon me, and discharged
me of any blame and laid the whole fault of their play,
called *The Magnetic Lady*, upon the players. This happened the 24 of October, 1633, at Lambeth. In their
first petition they would have excused themselves on me
and the poet.[28]

Herbert's statement that in their first petition to the court
the players of the King's company "would have excused
themselves on me and the poet" means that they told the
court they had acted only what Jonson had written and
Herbert had licensed for performance. Evidently Herbert
somehow proved that he had not licensed objectionable
lines, and in their second petition the players admitted that
Jonson and Herbert were not at fault, and the Archbishop,
as spokesman for the court, "laid the whole fault ... upon
the players." That is, the players in their performances
had added offensive lines not to be found in Jonson's manuscript which Herbert had read. Now and again dramatists in jeopardy had accused actors of such enlivening of
their texts, but I can recall no other instance in which the
players are known to have admitted the charge.

Before passing on to an attempt to classify the grounds
on which plays were censored in these years, it is relevant
to note one period of what appears to have been excessive
violation. Anyone conversant with the history of the Jacobean stage has probably observed that the infringement of
the standards and regulations of the Master of the Revels
and the Privy Council appear to have been violated with
excessive frequency by the boy companies in the first decade
of the reign of James I. Of course we may be misled by
the comparative paucity of direct theatre records in the
absence of Henslowe's diary and Herbert's office book in
these years, but Heywood's statement in his *An Apology
for Actors*, published in 1612, suggests that the impression

28. Ibid., pp. 21–22.

is not false. He wrote at the end of his defense of his profession:

> Now to speak of some abuse lately crept into the quality, as an inveighing against the State, the Court, the Law, the City and their governments, with the particularizing of private men's humors (yet alive) Noblemen and others. I know it distastes many; neither do I anyway approve it, nor dare I by any means excuse it. The liberty which some arrogate to themselves, committing their bitterness and liberal invectives against all estates to the mouths of children, supposing their juniority to be a privilege for any railing, be it never so violent. I could advise all such to curb and limit this presumed liberty within the bands of discretion and government. But wise and judicial censurers, before whom such complaints shall at any time hereafter come, will not (I hope) impute these abuses to any transgression in us, who have ever been careful and provident to shun the like. I surcease to prosecute this any further, lest my good meaning be (by some) misconstrued; and fearing likewise lest with tediousness I tire the patience of the favorable reader, here, though abruptly, I conclude my third and last treatise.

It should be borne in mind that Heywood wrote as both an attached professional playwright and a patented member of Queen Anne's company. He clearly intends to distinguish between "children" like the company of the Queen's Revels at Blackfriars, the Children of the King's Revels at Whitefriars, and Paul's Boys, on the one hand, and the adult companies like the King's men, Prince Henry's company, the Duke of York's company, and his own troupe of Queen Anne's men on the other. He refers to the former as "the mouths of children" and to the latter as "us, who have ever been careful and provident to shun the like." He appears to impute these distasteful violations to the irresponsibility of the managers and playwrights of the boy companies. It is notable that he tries to disassociate them from the responsible members of the profession.

Grounds for the Censorship of Plays

These quoted records of their activities show clearly enough that the Masters of the Revels regularly examined the dramatists' manuscripts in the hands of the London companies and frequently ordered deletions from them. But most of the examples so far quoted do not make very clear just what the Masters sought to suppress, or what was found objectionable by superior authorities though the Master had missed it when he first censored the manuscript.

An analysis of the scattered surviving records of censorship, reprimand, and punishment of the players for offenses in their plays shows that most of the censoring activities were intended to eliminate from the stage five general types of lines or scenes.

1. Critical comments on the policies or conduct of the government
2. Unfavorable presentations of *friendly* foreign powers or their sovereigns, great nobles, or subjects
3. Comment on religious controversy
4. Profanity (after 1606)
5. Personal satire of *influential* people

Some of these classes are, of course, overlapping. The unfavorable presentations of foreign powers or their leaders is obviously entangled with criticism of the government; it could get the King and his ministers into difficulties with the ambassadors of the friendly powers, as in the cases of Chapman's *Byron* and Middleton's *A Game at Chess*. Similarly, the influential person satirized might also be an official of a friendly foreign power, like Count Gondomar. Of course the Masters of the Revels did not have before them such a list of offenses as I have made, but most of their known repressive actions can be classified under these heads.

The most seriously objectionable lines in plays were those making political comments which were critical (or implied criticism) of the government. Such criticism was very seldom direct: more often it was the dramatization of a scene which might be thought analogous to some current political situation, or lines, which, though spoken by a foreigner about a foreign government, might be thought applicable to policies of Elizabeth or James or Charles; or it was an attack on a foreign power or foreign sovereign at the moment friendly to England or whose friendship the government was trying to cultivate.

The best-known example of the analogous scene is the deposition scene in Shakespeare's *Richard II*. Elizabeth and some of her ministers saw an analogy—or rather thought many people fancied an analogy—between Elizabeth and Richard II. Therefore the staging of a scene showing the deposition of Richard might be thought to hint at similar actions against Elizabeth. The Essex conspirators evidently thought so when they bribed the Lord Chamberlain's company to revive the play on the eve of the Essex rebellion. That the deposition scene was thought censorable by someone is demonstrated by its deletion from the first three quarto editions of the play in 1597, 1598, and again in 1598; it does not appear in print until the fourth quarto of 1608, five years after Elizabeth's death. Whether the scene was cut before the play was ever staged or only deleted from later performances and from the early printed texts is not material at the moment. The significant fact is that the deposition scene is the sort of material which someone in authority found censorable in 1597 and 1598.

For similar reasons Samuel Daniel's play *Philotas* made trouble for the author and the actors in 1605. There had been a good deal of murmuring after the trial and execu-

tion of the popular Earl of Essex in February 1600/1601,
and for several years thereafter the Privy Council was
acutely aware of disaffection among the former partisans
of Essex. Daniel's play, which was acted by the Children
of the Queen's Revels, dramatized the classic story of
Alexander and Philotas; in acts 4 and 5 he handled the
trial and punishment of Philotas, which seemed to the
Privy Council too much like the affairs of the Earl of
Essex. In protesting his innocence to the Earl of Devon-
shire, whom he seems to have implicated, Daniel wrote:

> And therefore I beseech you to understand all this
> great error I have committed. First I told the Lords I
> had written three acts of this tragedy the Christmas be-
> fore my Lord of Essex's troubles, as divers in the city
> could witness. I said the Master of the Revels had
> perused it. I said I had read parts of it to your honor,
> and this I said having none else of power to grace me
> now in Court and hoping that you out of your knowl-
> edge of books and favor of letters and me might answer
> that there was nothing in it disagreeing nor anything as
> I protest there is not but out of universal notions of
> ambition and envy, the perpetual arguments of books
> and tragedies. I did not say you encouraged me to the
> presenting of it, if I should I had been a villain, for
> that when I showed it to your honor I was not resolved
> to have had it acted, nor should it have been had not
> my necessities overmastered me. . . .[29]

Whether Daniel was as innocent of perception of the
analogy between the affairs of Philotas and of Essex as he
protested is not significant here. The significant fact for
understanding the principles of Jacobean censorship is that
there *was* an analogy whether the author had had it in
mind when he wrote or not, and therefore the play was
dangerous and required suppression by authority.

29. Laurence Michel, ed., *The Tragedy of Philotas by Samuel
Daniel*, New Haven, 1949, p. 38.

Almost as well known as the affair of *Richard II* is that of *A Game at Chess*, which Thomas Middleton wrote for the King's company in 1624. The censorable matter in this play is clear enough, and its allowance by Sir Henry Herbert on 12 June 1624 was probably a matter of collusion between the Master of the Revels and certain members of the Privy Council. The political situation the play exploited was most unusual. For several years King James had been cultivating Spain and deferring to the skillful Spanish Ambassador, Count Gondomar, in spite of the increasingly violent anti-Catholic and anti-Spanish feeling in the nation. In 1623 the King had gone so far as to try to arrange a marriage between his heir, Prince Charles, and the Spanish Infanta, and when the Prince and the Duke of Buckingham returned, foiled and angered from Madrid, the general popular rejoicing was so great that their return had been celebrated with bonfires in the streets. In this instance popular sentiment was overwhelmingly against the King and the pro-Spanish faction at court, and Middleton and the King's players seized the opportunity to capitalize.

The topical play was *A Game at Chess*, produced (by design?) when the King and most of the Privy Council were out of town, at the Globe in August 1624. It ran for nine days, the greatest hit of the first quarter of the century, before the Privy Council intervened, closed down the theatre entirely, arrested the players, and tried to jail Middleton. The collusion which was necessary to get the play licensed in the first place and to run so long without suppression is not relevant here, but the material which made the play so objectionable to those not on the popular side is. The play was partly an allegory of recent affairs, partly a dissemination of scandals against the Catholics, and especially the Jesuits. The characters—all chessmen—are the White King (James I), the White Knight (Prince Charles), the Black King (Philip IV of Spain), the Black Bishop (the Father General of the Jesuits), the Black

Knight (Gondomar), and so on. Obviously this was political comment with a vengeance, and Middleton and the fellows of the King's company must have thought either that it was past history and all national policy was now reversed, or that they had friends powerful enough to protect them. In the latter assumption they appear to have been correct, for though they had to post a bond of £300 and were restrained from acting at all for about ten days, the sums they were reputed by contemporaries to have made out of the play more than compensated. For a time the Master of the Revels was in serious trouble for having allowed *A Game at Chess*, but he was functioning regularly in his office in the next month. However the licensing and performance of *A Game at Chess* are accounted for, the play is clearly an example of the sort of dramatic work the Master of Revels was expected to suppress.[30]

Sometimes the writer of the offending lines could be more innocent in his intentions than Middleton was in *A Game at Chess*. The manuscript of Walter Mountfort's play, *The Launching of the Mary, or the Seaman's Honest Wife*, bears on the last page the allowance of the Master of the Revels with the qualification that all oaths "as they are crossed in the book and all other reformations strictly observed." Herbert has crossed out all references to the Amboyna massacres, a total of seventy-five or eighty lines at different places in the play.

Now Walter Mountfort, an employee of the East India Company for at least twenty years, had written his play, as he notes on his manuscript, during a long voyage from India to England. The Amboyna massacre had taken place in 1623 on the island of that name in the Southern Moluccas, when the Dutch garrison tried, tortured, and executed about eighteen Englishmen, agents of the East India Company. There was a good deal of excitement when the news

30. See *Jacobean and Caroline Stage*, IV, 870–79.

reached England, but for political reasons and in spite of popular indignation, no significant retaliatory action was ever taken, and the massacre rankled in the popular mind in England. It was inflammatory, therefore, when Mountfort had a shipbuilder describe the tortures and name several of the Dutchmen involved. Clearly Mountfort hated the Dutch as did many Englishmen, especially in the East India Company. He probably did not know as he wrote during his long voyage home that he was writing during a time of complex maneuvering with the French, the Dutch, and the Spanish about affairs in the Low Countries, and that in such a time the English government was anxious that no overt public hostility toward the Dutch should be reported back to the States by the Dutch ambassador. Whether Mountfort was aware of anything more than the hatred of his company and his friends for the Dutch or not, it is clear that Herbert suppressed the inflammatory Amboyna material in the play because it might have embarrassed the government in its dealings with supposedly friendly foreign powers.

Another play written by Philip Massinger for the King's company shows the kind of lines which seemed, by analogy, to be comments on current English political controversy. In 1638 when the country was becoming more incensed by King Charles's desperate taxation measures, Sir Henry not only quoted some of the lines he had censored in a play, but proudly indicated that King Charles concurred in his judgment:

> Received of Mr. Lowin for my pains about Massinger's play called *The King and the Subject*, 2 June, 1638 . . . £1.

> The name of *The King and the Subject* is altered, and I allowed the play to be acted, the reformations most strictly observed, and not otherwise, the 5th June, 1638.

At Greenwich the 4 of June, Mr. W. Murray gave me power from the King to allow of the play, and told me that he would warrant it.

Moneys? We'll raise supplies what ways we please
And force you to subscribe to blanks, in which
We'll mulct you as we shall think fit. The Caesars
In Rome were wise, acknowledging no laws
But what their swords did ratify, the wives
And daughters of the senators bowing to
Their wills as deities, . . .

This is a piece taken out of Philip Massinger's play called *The King and the Subject*, and entered here forever to be remembered by my son and those that cast their eyes upon it, in honor of King Charles my master, who reading over the play at Newmarket, set his mark on the place with his own hand, and in these words: "This is too insolent, and to be changed." Note, that the poet makes it the speech of a king, Don Pedro, King of Spain, and spoken to his subjects.[31]

In the light of the fact that these lines were written in the time of the protests about ship money and corporate monopolies and other forms of alleged royal tyranny, Massinger must have been naïve to think that they would be approved by the Master of the Revels. Such lines, which could easily be thought to express criticism of current actions or policies of the government, are just what the Master of the Revels was appointed to eliminate from plays performed in the London theatres.

The second type of officially offensive material was the unfavorable presentation of friendly foreign powers or their sovereigns, great nobles, or subjects. As has been suggested, this second type of material was very closely related to the first, for the friendly foreign powers attacked were friendly because of the current policy of the govern-

31. Adams, *Herbert*, pp. 22–23.

ment. An example of censorship for this reason is to be found in Sir Edmund Tilney's deletions in *Sir Thomas More* at some unascertained date in the 1590s. It was the play's sympathetic treatment of English riots against arrogant foreign merchants and artisans in London that was the source of Sir Edmund's severe treatment. This play is extant in a mutilated and much revised manuscript in the British Museum (Harley 7368). One of the several revisers of the manuscript is often thought to have been William Shakespeare, hence the numerous studies of the play. But the names of the collaborators and revisers—three of whom were Anthony Munday, Henry Chettle, and Thomas Dekker—are not so relevant here as the objections of the Master of the Revels. On the first page of the manuscript he has written:

> Leave out the insurrection wholly and the cause thereof and begin with Sir Thomas More at the Mayor's sessions, with a report afterwards of his good service done being sheriff of London upon a mutiny against the Lombards only by a short report and not otherwise at your own perils.
>
> E. Tilney[32]

These objections would eliminate a good part of the play, and it is not clear that the manuscript was ever thoroughly rewritten as suggested or that the play ever reached performance. In any case the fears of the Master of the Revels that the objectionable scenes might stimulate new attacks on the foreigners whom the government allowed to work in London is clearly implied in his signed statement.

Also offensive to a friendly power was Chapman's two-part play, *The Conspiracy and Tragedy of Charles, Duke of Byron, Marshall of France*, published in 1608 after having been acted at Blackfriars earlier in the same year. The published text shows heavy cuts: the fourth act of

32. Chambers, *William Shakespeare*, I, 503.

The Conspiracy has been drastically cut, leaving it only about half as long as the other four acts; in *The Tragedy* at the end of act 1 and the beginning of act 2 one or more episodes have been expurgated. Chapman himself alluded to the expurgations when he spoke of "these poor dismembered poems" in his dedication of the 1608 quarto to Sir Thomas Walsingham and his son. Though the official records of the censorship of this play are lost—as are most of the records from the incumbency of Sir George Buc—a letter preserved in the Bibliothèque nationale shows what happened. The letter was written by the French Ambassador in London to the Marquis de Sillery. A translation of the relevant part reads:

> April 8, 1608, I caused certain players to be forbid from acting the history of the Duke of Byron; when, however, they saw that the whole Court had left the town, they persisted in acting it; nay, they brought upon the stage the Queen of France and Mademoiselle de Verneuil. The former, having accosted the latter with very hard words, gave her a box on the ear. At my suit three of them [i.e., the players] were arrested, but the principal person, the author, escaped.[33]

The scene mentioned does not appear in the printed play and is clearly one of the long passages cut out; this scene was offensive to a friendly power and the players suffered for staging it. Possibly the French ambassador slightly exaggerated his power and influence in his letter to his friend in France, but there is no need to doubt the essential facts he records. The Queen of France was unfavorably presented in a play and the objections of the French Ambassador led to censorship, and, in this case, contributed to the suppression of the guilty company.

The dramatists' awareness of the stern opposition of

33. Thomas Marc Parrott, *The Plays and Poems of George Chapman: The Tragedies*, New York, 1910, p. 591.

authority to the presentation in the theatres of critical por-
traits of friendly foreign powers or their nobles is evi-
denced in the prologue printed in the 1615 quarto of *The
Hector of Germany, or the Palsgrave, Prime Elector*. The
author wants to make sure that everyone understands that
the Palsgrave of his play is *not* Frederick IV, Count Pala-
tine of the Rhine, who had married James's daughter,
Elizabeth, with many royal and national celebrations on
14 February 1612/13. The speaker of the prologue an-
nounces to the audience:

> Our author, for himself, this bade me say,
> Although the *Palsgrave* be the name of th' Play,
> 'Tis not that Prince which in this kingdom late
> Married the maiden-glory of our state:
> What pen dares be so bold in this strict age
> To bring him while he lives upon the stage?
> And though he would, Authority's stern brow
> Such a presumptuous deed will not allow:
> And he must not offend Authority. . . .

A couple of years later an unknown author of an unknown play was not so careful. At their regular sitting on
22 June 1617, the Privy Council sent an order to the official in charge of the regulation of plays, players, and
playwrights:

> A letter to Sir George Buck, Knight
> Master of the Revels.

> We are informed that there are certain players or come-
> dians, we know not of what company, that go about to
> play some interlude concerning the late Marquesse d'
> Ancre, which for many respects we think not fit to be
> suffered. We do therefore require you upon your peril
> to take order that the same be not represented or played
> in any place about this city or elsewhere where you have
> authority. And hereof have you a special care.[34]

34. *Malone Society Collections*, Oxford, 1911, 1, parts 4 and 5,
376.

The Marquesse d'Ancre, the favorite of the French Queen, had been murdered in Paris less than two months before, and some company was evidently trying to capitalize on a current sensation, as the King's company did with Fletcher and Massinger's play, *Sir John van Olden Barnavelt*, two years later. Since the councillors say "go about to play," they apparently had advance notice from some interested party—possibly the French Ambassador.

In 1630/31 the Master of the Revels refused to license a play for the King's company because it came into this same class of objection. In this case the Master was gratifyingly explicit:

> This day being the 11 of January, 1630, I did refuse to allow of a play of Massinger's because it did contain dangerous matter, as the deposing of Sebastian King of Portugal, by Philip the Second and there being a peace sworn betwixt the Kings of England and Spain. I had my fee notwithstanding which belongs to me for reading it over, and ought to be brought always with the book.[35]

The third type of material which the Master was alert to expunge from the dramatists' manuscripts was that bearing on religious controversy. Essentially such material was political too, since it concerned the state church and the attempts of the government to suppress dissent, one phase of which was ridicule of persons or practices in the established church. Obviously such instances of conflict were tempting to players and playwrights, and they could assume a good deal of public interest if they could succeed in getting a dramatization of them past the censor. There are various records of their occasional success in the first stage—a performance license—but suppression after the play was on the stage.

---

35. Adams, *Herbert*, p. 19. Massinger's revisions to make this suppressed play acceptable will be discussed in Chapter IX.

In 1619 there was a good deal of London interest in political affairs in the Netherlands involving the conflict which was echoed in English church–state difficulties of the time. One climax in the Dutch struggle was the downfall, trial, and execution of the Dutch patriot, Sir John van Olden Barnavelt, in the spring and early summer of 1619. The King's company saw an opportunity to exploit the London interest in these events, and their regular dramatist, John Fletcher, probably with the assistance of Philip Massinger, prepared for them a play on the subject. They must have worked with great dispatch, since their play was rehearsed and ready for the stage on 14 August 1619, though it included an event not known in London until 14 July. The manuscript was allowed by Sir George Buc, whose initials are signed to one correction on the prompt manuscript. But at the last moment religious authority stepped in. A letter written from London on 14 August 1619 to Sir Dudley Carleton, King James's Ambassador at The Hague, reports that, "The players here were bringing of Barnavelt upon the stage, and had bestowed a great deal of money to prepare all things for the purpose, but at the instant were prohibited by my Lord of London." The Bishop of London was not normally directly concerned with the performance of plays, but he was the director of censorship of printed matter and a member of the Privy Council, and his authority was great. What alterations he required in the performance are not known, but his objections were satisfied, for Sir Dudley received another letter from the same correspondent dated 27 August 1619, in which he said, "Our players have found the means to go through with the play of Barnavelt and it hath had many spectators and received applause."

One suspects that players and printers may have been uneasy about this play: there are no records of its performance after those original Globe afternoons; it did not appear in the company's list of unprinted plays in their repertory in 1641; though its later interest to the company must have been slight, it was never printed in quarto; it was omitted from both the first and the second Beaumont and Fletcher folios in 1647 and 1679; indeed, it was never published at all until A. H. Bullen printed it from the British Museum manuscript in his *Collection of Old English Plays* in 1883. The ever-increasing virulence of the religious conflict from 1619 to 1642 certainly did nothing to make the religious implications of *Sir John van Olden Barnavelt* less dangerous.[36]

One of the problems of the Master of the Revels in his endeavors to keep controversial religious implications out of performances in the London theatres lay in the very nature of the theatre: impressions on audiences are made visually as well as orally. The normal meanings or implications of words can be changed by the action and spectacle which accompanies them. Something of the sort must have happened on the stage of the Salisbury Court theatre when the King's Revels company produced an unnamed play in February 1634/35. In his office book Sir Henry records only his stern action on the occasion.

> I committed Cromes, a broker in Long Lane, the 16 of February, 1634, to the Marshalsea for lending a church robe with the name of JESUS upon it to the players in Salisbury Court to present a Flamen, a priest of the heathens. Upon his petition of submission, and acknowledgment of his fault, I released him the 17 February, 1634.[37]

If Herbert said anything about his punishment of the players who performed this play, Malone and Chalmers failed to copy it. The employment of such a robe for "a priest of the heathens" cannot have been innocent in intent.

A clearer example of the defiance of religious censor-

36. See Wilhelmina Frijlinck, *The Tragedy of Sir John van Olden Barnavelt*, Amsterdam, 1922, pp. i–clviii.
37. Adams, *Herbert*, p. 64.

ship by the players occurred four years later. By this time
the controversy over religious ceremonial was in its later
stages of violence, and the approach of civil war was apparent to many. Our knowledge of this event comes not
from Herbert—though his lost office book must have carried some reference to it—but from correspondence printed
in the *Calendar of State Papers, Domestic*. In a letter of
8 May 1639 Edmund Rossingham wrote to Viscount
Conway:

> Thursday last [2 May] the players of the Fortune were
> fined £1,000 for setting up an altar, a bason, and two
> candlesticks, and bowing down before it upon the stage,
> and although they allege it was an old play revived,
> and an altar to the heathen gods, yet it was apparent that
> this play was revived on purpose in contempt of the cere-
> monies of the Church; if my paper were not at an end
> I should enlarge myself upon this subject, to show what
> was said of altars.

There is another account of this affair over a year later. It
appears in an antiepiscopal propaganda pamphlet, and its
details are therefore suspect. Certainly it dishonestly implies a date much nearer the end of 1640 than the facts warrant, and I suspect the propagandist patness of some of the
details, such as the name of the play and other insinuations
of the common Puritan charge that Archbishop Laud expected to be made Roman Catholic cardinal of England.
Nevertheless this account in *Vox Borealis*, though not trustworthy in all its details, shows why the authorities had
good reason to fear such plays as the one produced at the
Fortune.

> In the meantime let me tell ye a lamentable Tragedy,
> acted by the Prelacy against the poor players of the For-
> tune Playhouse which made them sing
> > *Fortune my foe, why dost thou*
> > *frown on me? &c*

for they having gotten a new old play, called *The Cardinal's Conspiracy*, whom they brought upon the *stage* in as great *state* as they could, with *Altars, Images, Crosses, Crucifixes*, and the like, to set forth his pomp and pride. But woeful was the sight to see how in the midst of all their *mirth*, the Pursuivants came and seized upon the poor cardinal, and all his consorts, and carried them away. And when they were questioned for it in the High Commission Court, they pleaded *Ignorance*, and told the Archbishop *that they took those* examples of their *Altars, Images*, and the like from *Heathen Authors*. This did somewhat assuage his anger, that they did not bring him on the stage. But yet they were fined for it, and after a little imprisonment got their liberty. And having nothing left them but a few old swords and bucklers, they fell to act *The Valiant Scot*, which they played five days with great applause, which vexed the bishops worse than the other, insomuch as they were forbidden playing it any more, and some of them prohibited ever playing again.[38]

Vox Borealis is much too gleeful in his account of the discomfiture of the hated bishops to be fully trusted, especially in his selection of the title *The Valiant Scot* so as to bring slyly to the minds of his nonconformist readers the salutary drubbing which the noble Scottish Presbyterians had given to the Episcopalians in the Bishops' Wars, actually much later than the players' fine of 4 May 1639.

Such bringing of religious controversy onto the stage as these examples have illustrated was one of the major offenses which the Master of the Revels was trying to detect and eliminate as he read over play manuscripts. Of course he had not been appointed to read without prejudice; it is noteworthy that all these punished offenses involved attacks on the established church, not on the dissenters. Sneers at Puritans and Brownists and Presbyterians are

38. See *Jacobean and Caroline Stage*, VI, 167–68.

common enough in the allowed plays, as all readers of Jonson, Middleton, and Shirley know.

The fourth of the principal offenses which the censor was looking for was profanity. Unlike the previously discussed offenses this one was defined during the period. Also different was the fact that enforcement was more dependent upon the personal ideas of the Master, as some of the examples will show. From 1590 to 1606 there is very little evidence as to what was thought profane or what was done in the way of restricting it. But in 1606 Parliament passed an act which was intended to purify the language in plays.

An Act to Restrain Abuses of Players

For the preventing and avoiding of the great abuse of the holy name of God in stage plays, interludes, May-games, shows, and such like; be it enacted by our sovereign Lord the King's majesty and by the Lords spiritual and temporal, and Commons in this present Parliament assembled and by the authority of the same, that if at any time or times, after the end of this present session of Parliament, any person or persons do or shall in any stage play, interlude, show, May-game or pageant jestingly or profanely speak or use the name of God or of Christ Jesus, or of the Holy Ghost or of the Trinity, which are not to be spoken but with fear and reverence, shall forfeit for every such offense by him or them committed ten pounds, the one moiety thereof to the King's majesty, his heirs and successors, the other moiety thereof to him or them that will sue for the same in any court of record at Westminster, wherein no essoigne, protection, or wager of law shall be allowed.[39]

This statute, with its legal provision for rewards to informers, set up the possibility that any member of a theatre audience might make himself £5 by tattling in a court of law about what he had heard. A careful bookkeeper in the theatre might be well advised to regularize any casual

39. Chambers, *Elizabethan Stage*, IV, 338–39. Transcribed from *Statutes of the Realm*, *1101–1713*.

exclamations he found in a play manuscript even before he sent it to the Master of the Revels. Probably this often happened, for certain texts are extant which show more meticulous expurgation than it is easy to imagine the Master performing. An eloquent example is the folio text of *Othello*. A collation of this 1623 edition with the first quarto of 1622 shows scores of petty revisions. Since the play is known to have been performed at court by the King's company eighteen months before the profanity statute was passed, the folio revisions may be assumed to be due in part to fear of the penalties of the law. A few examples of these changes show what was involved.

	1622	1623
1.2.35	And I, God blesse the marke	And I (blesse the marke)
1.1.94	Zounds [God's wounds] sir you are robd.	Sir, y'are rob'd
2.2.91	Fore God an excellent song	Fore Heaven: an excellent song
2.2.167	Zouns, you rogue, you rascal	You rogue; you rascal
3.3.180	Zouns	What dost thou mean?
3.3.203	Good God, the souls of all	Good Heaven, the souls of all
3.4.92	Then would to God	Then would to Heaven
4.3.114	God me such usage send	Heaven me such uses send
5.2.105	O Lord, Lord, Lord.	[Line omitted]
5.2.148	O Lord, what cry is that?	Alas! what cry is that?
5.2.270	O God, O heavenly God. Zouns, hold your peace.	Oh Heaven! O heavenly Powers! Come, hold your peace.

The manuscript of Walter Mountford's play, *The Launching of the Mary, or the Seaman's Honest Wife*, which is preserved in the British Museum (Egerton 1994), carries on the last page the autograph allowance of Sir Henry Herbert, and the text of the play shows the Master's marks of disapproval at several points. Some, as we have observed, require the deletion of politically offensive material, but others indicate offensive oaths, as the Master explicitly states in his license "all the oaths left out in the action as they are crossed in the book. . . ." Sir Henry most frequently required the omission of the comparatively inoffensive "faith," which he marked for deletion at least nineteen times. He also marked "Troth" and " 'Slife" and "by the lord."

On the same grounds he marked for omission in act 2, scene 1, the third line of Captain Fitz John's exclamation:

> O happy above many happy man
> Born and brought up in Time's full happiness
> Next to the sole redeemer of my soul
> How I am bound, obliged, engaged, devoted
> to my much honored masters.

Evidently Sir Henry Herbert found the profanity still used in Fletcher's *The Tamer Tamed* offensive in 1633, though the play had been duly licensed by his predecessor long before. After he had stopped the revival performance of the play, he returned the manuscript to the King's men, as he says, "I returned it to the players the Monday morning after purged of oaths, profaneness, and ribaldry."

In January 1633/34 Sir Henry recorded an unusual series of events which illuminate the problem of defining censorable profanity. William Davenant, who had previously prepared two or three plays for the King's company, had another manuscript ready late in 1633. We first hear of it after Herbert had recently rejected or perhaps only heavily censored it, and Davenant's friend and patron,

Endymion Porter, had interfered on behalf of the play-wright. Sir Henry says:

> This morning, being the 9th of January, 1633[/34] the King was pleased to call me into his withdrawing chamber to the window, where he went over all that I had crossed in Davenant's playbook and allowing of *faith* and *slight* to be asseverations only and no oaths, marked them to stand and some other few things, but in the greater part allowed of my reformations. This was done upon a complaint of Mr. Endymion Porters in December.
>
> The King is pleased to take *faith, death, slight,* for asseverations and no oaths, to which I do humbly sub-mit as my master's judgment; but, under favor, conceive them to be oaths, and enter them here to declare my opinion and submission.
>
> The 10 of January, 1633[/34], I returned unto Mr. Davenant his play-book of *The Wits* corrected by the King.
>
> The King would not take the book at Mr. Porter's hands, but commanded him to bring it unto me, which he did, and likewise commanded Davenant to come to me for it, as I believe; otherwise he would not have been so civil.[40]

Either this manuscript was not the final one produced by the company at Blackfriars (possibly because Davenant wanted to treasure it as a royal memento) or else more time than usual was spent in incorporating the corrections, for the final official license which Malone noted in the Revels manuscript but did not copy was dated 19 January. At any rate the company went into immediate production at Blackfriars, for Sir Humphry Mildmay saw the play there on the 22nd.

This affair was a most unusual one on several counts, most notably because of the overriding of the Master of

40. Adams, *Herbert*, p. 22.

the Revels by King Charles, who was not accustomed to concern himself with such petty details of Revels office business. But Endymion Porter was a favorite, and Davenant was his protégé. Secondly it was unusual for anyone but the producing company to have the manuscript. How Davenant got his manuscript back from the bookkeeper at Blackfriars can only be guessed, but somehow this was all a personal matter—witness the fact that Herbert gave the manuscript back to Davenant and not to the representative of the King's company.

Finally it is unusual for a Master to be so specific about his objections and to record significant differences of opinion. Herbert thought of *faith*, *death*, and *slight* as being obvious corruptions of "God's faith," "God's death," and "God's light" and therefore forbidden by the statute which set punishments for players who "jestingly or profanely speak or use the name of God. . . ." The King thought the old corruptions had passed into common usage and lost their original denotations. Herbert was not convinced.

It is easy to think of the Master of the Revels as an enemy to dramatic genius and the stern foe of the players, for most of his recorded activities are inhibitive. But he did not think of himself this way, and some understanding of his position between the Puritan bitter enemies of players and playwrights and the overindulgent Cavalier audiences can be seen in the compliments he paid to a play James Shirley wrote for Queen Henrietta's men. These comments were written in July 1633, six months before Davenant's troubles with *The Wits* and just at the time when William Prynne's virulent *Histriomastix, The Players' Scourge and the Actors' Tragedy* was rallying the antitheatrical forces in London. When he licensed the play on 3 July 1633, Herbert wrote this most unusual comment:

> The comedy called *The Young Admiral*, being free from oaths, profaneness, or obsceneness, hath given me much delight and satisfaction in the reading, and may

serve for a pattern to other poets, not only for the better-
ing of manners and language, but for the improvement
of the quality, which hath received some brushings of
late.

When Mr. Shirley hath read this approbation, I know
it will encourage him to pursue this beneficial and clean-
ly way of poetry, and when other poets hear and see his
good success, I am confident they will imitate the original for their own credit, and make such copies in this
harmless way, as shall speak them masters in their art,
at the first sight, to all judicious spectators. It may be
acted this 3 July, 1633.

I have entered this allowance for direction to my successor, and for example to all poets that shall write after
the date hereof.[41]

These comments on *The Young Admiral*, a rather foolish
tragicomedy, may not place Sir Henry very high in the
ranks of dramatic critics—especially modern ones—but
they do demonstrate that in his own mind he was not
simply the watchdog for the King's prerogative, the bishops' hegemony, and the tender sensibilities of the ambassadors of friendly foreign powers, but the promoter of the
best interests of the national theatrical enterprise. Though
he could not foresee that in nine years the enemies of the
theatre would triumph and abolish the enterprise, he could
see the strength of Prynne and his sympathizers in the London of 1633, and he could appreciate some of the theatrical
customs which gained them adherents. When he says that
plays free from oaths, profaneness, and obsceneness like
The Young Admiral will serve "for the improvement of
the quality [i.e., the profession of players and playwrights]
which hath received some brushings of late" he is not
thinking of the freedom of the artist—actor and dramatist—to observe and to comment, but of the preservation
of their joint enterprise. However narrow-minded he may

41. Adams, *Herbert*, pp. 19–20.

have been in his censorship, he had clearly before him those antitheatrical sentiments so frequently expressed in the city parishes, the London corporation, and in parliamentary debates, to say nothing of the 1,100 pages of *Histriomastix*. The quality had indeed received some brushings of late.

The final classification of the censoring activities of the Master of the Revels was the suppression of personal satire on the stages in London. This was a very tricky chore. The Master had, essentially, two problems: first, was there satire in the performance which had not been apparent in the text? and second, was the person or persons ridiculed sufficiently influential to count? Because of the first difficulty, the records we have of suppression for personal satire come mostly from actions taken after performance: most of the plays had scraped past the Master. Because of the second, the Master had to make nice estimates of prominence and influence, and modern critics are sometimes fooled into imagining satire of the King or members of the Privy Council because they have seen allowed satire of nonentities like Thomas Dekker and Captain Hannam and Ben Jonson in 1601, or Agnes Howe or Ann Elsdon, or enemies of the establishment like William Prynne. It was the favored and the influential whom the Master of the Revels and the Privy Council tried to protect, not just anyone whom the players chose to ridicule.

This distinction between impersonation of ordinary Londoners and impersonation of gentlemen of good desert and quality is exemplified in the minute of a letter sent to certain Justices of the Peace in Middlesex by the Privy Council on 10 May 1601:

> We do understand that certain players that use to recite their plays at the Curtain in Moorfields do represent upon the stage in their interludes the persons of gentlemen of good desert and quality that are yet alive under obscure manner, but yet in such sort as all the hearers may take notice both of the matter and the per-

sons that are meant thereby. This being a thing very unfit, offensive, and contrary to such direction as have been
heretofore taken that no plays should be openly showed
but such as first were perused and allowed and that
might minister no occasion of offense or scandal we do
hereby require you that you do forthwith forbid those
players to whomsoever they appertain, that do play at
the Curtain in Moorfields to represent any such play and
that you will examine them who made that play and
to show the same unto you, and as you in your discretion shall think the same unfit to be publicly showed to
forbid them from henceforth to play the same either
privately or publicly, and if upon view of the said play
you shall find the subject so odious and inconvenient as
is informed, we require you to take bond of the chiefest
of them to answer their rash and indiscreet behavior
before us.[42]

Even the favored and influential might be impersonated,
it would appear, if the impersonation were complimentary.
An instance of such a presentation is recorded in a letter
of 1599. On 26 October of that year Rowland Whyte
wrote from the Strand in London to Sir Robert Sydney:

> Two days ago, the overthrow of *Turnholt* [Turnhout]
> was acted upon a stage, and all your names used that
> were at it; especially Sir *Fra.Veres*, and he that played
> that part got a beard resembling his, and a watchet Satin
> Doublet, with Hose trimmed with silver lace. You was
> also introduced, killing, slaying, and overthrowing the
> *Spaniards*, and honorable mention made of your service,
> in seconding Sir *Francis Vere*, being engaged."[43]

42. Chambers, *Elizabethan Stage*, IV, 332, from *The Acts of the
Privy Council of England.*
43. Arthur Collins, *Letters and Memorials of State*, London,
1746, II, 136. Rowland Whyte's interest in the actor's attempt to
suggest the person of Sir Francis Vere was probably characteristic of
the gossip of London audiences about plays. Twenty-five years later
John Chamberlain reported the gossip about a less innocent play, *A
Game at Chess* (which he had not seen himself). He reports the

But innocent or admiring impersonation was not the concern of the Master of the Revels as he read the play manuscript, nor of the other officials who took action later after a libelous piece had been performed.

In Herbert's time, it was probably personal satire which the Master had in mind when he cut the anonymous lost play called *The Widow's Prize* on 25 January, 1624/25. "For the Prince's company, a new play called *The Widow's Prize*, which containing much abusive matter was allowed of by me on condition that my reformations were observed."[44]

He was more explicit and more severe in the case of the comedy called *The Ball* written by James Shirley, regular playwright for Queen Henrietta's company, and he expressed his disapproval to Christopher Beeston, manager of the company and owner of their theatre, the Phoenix.

> 18 November 1632. In the play of *The Ball*, written by Shirley and acted by the Queen's players, there were divers personated so naturally, both of lords and others of the court, that I took it ill, and would have forbidden the play, but that Beeston promised many things which I found fault withall should be left out and that he would not suffer it to be done by the poet any more, who deserves to be punished; and the first that offends in this kind of poets or players shall be sure of public punishment.[45]

Edmund Malone, in his notes from the original manuscript of the office book, recorded that this play had been

---

talk about the impersonation of Count Gondomer, the hated Spanish ambassador, "They counterfeited his person to the life, with all his graces and faces, and had gotten (they say) a cast suit of his apparel for the purpose, and his litter, wherein the world says lacked nothing but a couple of asses to carry it, and Sir G. Peter or Sir T. Mathew to bear him company" (N. E. McClure, ed., *The Letters of John Chamberlain*, Philadelphia, 1939, II, 578).

44. Adams, *Herbert*, pp. 18–19.

45. Ibid., p. 19.

licensed to be acted two days earlier, on the 16th. Both the dates and the phrase "personated so naturally" suggest that Herbert had not recognized the personal satire in the manuscript, but it was brought out by the actors, and this interpretation is also consonant with his threat of future punishment of "poets or players." In these notes on his action Herbert makes it clear when he says that those who were so naturally personated were "both of lords and others of the court" that it was the rank and influence of those impersonated which made the satire of poet and players culpable.

The importance to the Master of considering the standing and influence of the individual satirized is illustrated in his allowance of another play for Queen Henrietta's company six months later. He wrote,

> Received for allowing of *The Tale of the Tub*, Vitru Hoop's part wholly struck out, and the motion of the tub, by command from my lord chamberlain; exceptions being taken against it by Inigo Jones, Surveyor of the King's Works as a personal injury unto him. May 7, 1633 . . . £2.[46]

The Lord Chamberlain, Sir Henry's superior, did not intercede for just anyone; Inigo Jones stood high at this time as architect of the principal Whitehall buildings, including the Banqueting Hall, designer of Court masques, and one of the authorities in art matters for the art-loving King Charles. He was in the category of "lords and others of the court" in *The Ball*, not of William Prynne and Henry Burton.

Sometimes the weight of authority came down on players and playwrights for their mixture of individual satire and political satire of projects favored by the government in which those individuals were involved. Such a mixture was found in the lost anonymous play called *The Whore*

---

46. Ibid., *Herbert*, p. 19.

New Vamped, which must have evaded the vigilance of Sir Henry, though neither Malone nor Chalmers copied his license. At any rate Prince Charles's [II] company was already performing the play in the troubled autumn of 1639 when the Privy Council heard about it and took steps against all concerned. Their action is recorded in the minutes of the meeting of 29 September 1639. The "Cain" mentioned in the account of the performance was Andrew Cane, the leader of the company, and at the time the most talked about comedian in London.

> Order of the King in Council. Complaint was this day made that the stage-players of the Red Bull [have for] many days together acted a scandalous and libelous [play in which] they have audaciously reproached and in a libel [represented] and personated not only some of the aldermen of the [city of London] and some other persons of quality, but also scandalized and libeled the whole profession of proctors belonging to the Court of [Probate], and reflected upon the present Government. Ordered that the Attorney-General be hereby prayed forthwith to call before him, not only the poet who made the play and the actors that played the same, but also the person that licensed it, and having diligently examined the truth of the said complaint, to proceed roundly against such of them as he shall find have been faulty, and to use such effectual ex[pedition] to bring them to sentence, as that their exemplary punishment may [check] such insolencies betimes.
>
> Exceptions taken to the play above referred to. In the play called "The Whore New Vamped" where there was mention of the new duty on wines, one personating a justice of the peace says to Cain, "Sirrah, I'll have you before the alderman"; whereto Cain replies, "The alderman, the alderman is a base, drunken, sottish knave, I care not for the alderman, I say the alderman is a base, drunken, sottish knave." Another says, "How now Sirrah, what alderman do you speak of?" Then Cain says, "I mean alderman [William Abell], the blacksmith in

Holborn"; says the other, "Was not he a Vintner?" Cain answers, "I know no other." In another part of the play one speaking of projects and patents that he had got, mentions among others "a patent of 12d a piece upon every proctor and proctor's man who was not a knave." Said another, "Was there ever known any proctor but he was an arrant knave?"[47]

The Privy Council is refreshingly explicit in stating the grounds for objecting to the popular play at the Red Bull. *The Whore New Vamped* was offensive not because *somebody* was impersonated, but because it had "personated . . . some of the aldermen of the city of London and some other *persons of quality.*" It was doubly censorable because it had also "scandalized and libeled the whole profession of proctors belonging to the Court of Probate, and *reflected upon the present government.*" If it had been regularly licensed, the Master of the Revels ("the person that licensed it") was also culpable.

The character of the quotations from *The Whore New Vamped*, naming no characters but using the name of the best-known actor in the company, strongly suggests that the Privy Council did not have the manuscript but were taking testimony from a member of the audience at the Red Bull, perhaps an informer of the type authorized by the 1606 Statute of Oaths. The offense seems serious, and certainly the prompt and sweeping action of the Privy Council indicates that they thought so, but there is no further record of the play. The company was not disgraced, for a few weeks later, in the month of November, they performed three plays at court, for which the accused Andrew Cane received payment in the following May. But even supposing that the report was exaggerated or that the informer was a liar, the reaction of the Council and the

47. William Douglas Hamilton, ed., *Calendar of State Papers, Domestic, Series of the Reign of Charles I, 1639*, London, 1873, pp. 529–30.

nature of the report on which they acted show clearly what this high authority considered to be "scandalous and libelous."

All these examples of the activities and the power of the Master of the Revels were well known to the dramatists preparing plays for the London companies. They were themselves in personal danger if their plays violated the standard restrictions, as shown in the cases of Nashe and *The Isle of Dogs*, Jonson, Chapman, and Marston in *Eastward Ho*, and Middleton in *A Game at Chess*. But the threat of inconvenience, financial loss, and actual imprisonment to the managers and players was even more constant. As we have seen, there were various degrees of severity in the actions taken against offenders in the theatres. Least severe were the inconvenient required alterations in the text of the play which the company had bought. This requirement is seen in the cited examples of *The Seaman's Honest Wife*, *The Widow's Prize*, *The Tamer Tamed*, *The King and the Subject*, and *The Tale of the Tub*. More severe and inconvenient for the players were the Master's orders that the performance of the play be stopped, as in the instances of *The Loyal Subject* and *The Tamer Tamed*. Still more severe was the requirement that the play be stopped and the theatre closed, as in the case of *The Isle of Dogs* and *A Game at Chess*. And in extreme cases the Master went so far as to stop the play, confiscate the manuscript, close the theatre, send actors or dramatist or both to prison, and appoint a new manager for the company. The clearest example of such extreme punishment is the case of William Beeston and the actors of the King and Queen's Young company at the Cockpit in Drury Lane in the spring of 1640.

William Beeston had succeeded his father, Christopher, as manager of the company at the Phoenix in October 1638, and in the spring of 1640 his company had produced a play commenting on current political affairs and not licensed by the Master of the Revels. At this time many people were deeply disturbed by the King's military expedition to Berwick to suppress the Scottish revolt against the Prayer Book and the bishops, and by the failure of the expedition. This was the situation very foolishly dealt with in the play William Beeston had staged at the Phoenix. Herbert recorded his actions in his office book.

> On Monday the 4 May 1640 William Beeston was taken by a messenger and committed to the Marshalsea by my Lord Chamberlain's warrant for playing a play without license. The same day the company at the Cockpit was commanded by my Lord Chamberlain's warrant to forbear playing, for playing when they were forbidden by me and for other disobedience, and lay still Monday, Tuesday, and Wednesday. On Thursday, at my Lord Chamberlain's entreaty I gave them their liberty and upon their petition of submission subscribed by the players I restored them to their liberty on Thursday.
>
> The play I called for and, forbidding the playing of it, keep the book because it had relation to the passages of the King's journey into the North and was complained of by his Majesty to me with command to punish the offenders.[48]

The two warrants from the Lord Chamberlain mentioned by Herbert are recorded in the warrant books of the Lord Chamberlain's office, the first ordering the suppression of this play and all other plays at the Cockpit, and the second ordering the imprisonment of the leaders of the company: "A warrant of apprehension and commitment to the Marshalsea of William Beeston, George Estotville, and [Michael] Moon [or Mohun] upon the above specified occasion."[49] Severe as this punishment sounds, there was more for William Beeston, who was probably the principal culprit. It is not known how long he was allowed to pine

48. Adams, *Herbert*, p. 66.
49. *Malone Society Collection*, II, part 3, 394.

in the Marshalsea, but he was ousted from his position as manager of the King and Queen's Young company, and before the end of the next month William Davenant was officially appointed by the Lord Chamberlain to take his place, and the members of the company were ordered "that they obey the said Mr. Davenant and follow his orders and directions as they will answer the contrary."[50]

Probably only a few managers and dramatists suffered punishments as severe as William Beeston's, but they all knew that such punishments were within the Master's powers. The inhibitions which such knowledge produced are not difficult to imagine. They affected what the professional dramatists wrote for the companies; they affected what the managers and the sharing members of the company were willing to accept; and they affected what the bookkeeper did to the manuscript as he worked on the prompt copy and the players' sides. The number of recorded plays which nevertheless dared to transgress the standards of the Master of the Revels may seem to be large. But when the number is considered in the light of the two thousand or so plays which were probably written in England between 1590 and 1642, it is evident that players and playwrights ordinarily took pains to avoid those words, subjects, and attitudes proscribed by the Master of the Revels.

50. Ibid., 395.

CHAPTER VIII

Collaboration

COLLABORATION AND REVISION were related activities of the professional dramatists since each required one author to accommodate his writing to that of another. But since the analysis of each activity must be complicated, it is expedient to consider them in consecutive chapters rather than in a single discussion.

The two assignments are frequently entangled in the printed texts which have come down to us. This entanglement is most familiar in the plays of the Beaumont and Fletcher folios of 1647 and 1679 in which Massinger evidently had a hand. The evidence is overwhelming that Beaumont had nothing to do with most of the plays in these two collections; there is no doubt that Massinger and Fletcher several times collaborated, and no doubt that Massinger sometimes revised the work of Fletcher. But for several plays it is doubtful whether Philip Massinger collaborated or revised or did both.

Collaboration is inevitably a common expedient in such

a cooperative enterprise as the production of a play. Every performance in the commercial theatres from 1590 to 1642 was itself essentially a collaboration: it was the joint accomplishment of dramatists, actors, musicians, costumers, prompters (who made alterations in the original manuscript) and—at least in the later theatres—of managers.

To the professional dramatist all this cooperation was very familiar; he had it in mind when he began to write. Even amateurs like Lodowick Carlell and Thomas Goffe knew a good deal about it. In an enterprise which could get nowhere without the give and take of joint efforts, collaboration between two or more writers on the original script was to be expected. Long before 1590 it had begun.

Even before the appearance of the regular commercial theatres in London collaboration was a well-known phenomenon in the drama, and all students know of the joint work of Norton and Sackville on *Gorboduc*, of Gascoigne and Kinwelmershe on *Jocasta*, and of Wilmot, Stafford, Hatton, Noel, and "G. Al." on *Gismond of Salerne*. A similar collaboration just before the beginning of our period was that of Hughes, Bacon, Trotte, Fulbeck, Lancaster, Yelverton, Penroodock, and Flower on *The Misfortunes of Arthur*.

All these compositions were prepared for amateur production, but before 1590 comparatively little is known of the men who wrote plays for the professional companies: the large majority of all English plays before the reign of Elizabeth are anonymous, and even from 1558 to 1590 the authors of most plays are unknown. In such circumstances it is not surprising that most of the early Elizabethan plays by named writers—extant or lost—were prepared for production at an Oxford or Cambridge college, at a public school, at one of the inns of court, at some company hall, or in some private house.

When we come to the period of the professional theatre

in the reigns of Elizabeth and James, collaboration has become one of the notable features of the activities of the professional dramatists; in the days of Charles I it falls off somewhat.

Since records of authorship are so sparse for the period as a whole, we can only guess at the precise amount of collaboration involved in the plays, but the evidence still extant shows that it must have been large. We know the titles (often no more) of about 1,500 plays from 1590 to 1642. For about 370 we know nothing at all about authorship. For the remaining 1,100 or so, we have evidence that between 1/5 and 1/6 contained the work of more than one man as either collaborator, reviser, or provider of additional matter. If we consider the professional dramatists only, this proportion is much too low, for the total includes over 200 amateur plays, which after 1590 were seldom collaborated, and it includes many plays about whose authorship we have only a title-page statement, which tended, as a number of known examples show, to simplify the actual circumstances of composition. Altogether the evidence suggests that it would be reasonable to guess that as many as half of the plays by professional dramatists in the period incorporated the writing at some date of more than one man. In the case of the 282 plays mentioned in Henslowe's diary (far and away the most detailed record of authorship that has come down to us) nearly two-thirds are the work of more than one man.

The first recorded collaboration in our period was *A Looking Glass for London and England,* the joint work of Robert Greene and Thomas Lodge, acted in or about 1590 probably for the Queen's company. The play was published in 1594 and a number of times thereafter, and both the title pages and the entry in the Stationers' Register assert that it was the work of Greene and Lodge. This collaboration evidently remained viable for a long time:

not only are there five editions extant, but the play was still in repertory from twenty to thirty years after it was written.[1]

Probably acted about the same time as *A Looking Glass for London and England,* and certainly first published in the same year as that play, was *Dido, Queen of Carthage,* whose 1594 title page says, "Played by the Children of Her Majesty's Chapel. Written by Christopher Marlowe and Thomas Nash. Gent." The play had nothing like the extended stage life of *A Looking Glass,* and there have been suggestions by Marlowe enthusiasts that Nashe's contribution may have been that of continuator or editor rather than collaborator. In the present state of style-identification studies the extent or timing of Nashe's work cannot be determined.

But these collaborations are known only from chance recordings on title pages (many title pages in this decade name no author at all) and the chance preservation of a theatre manuscript. It is not until we get to Henslowe's detailed records of his payments for plays that the full evidence of the extent of joint authorship is revealed. The change is striking: for 1597 *The Annals of English Drama* lists 23 plays, six with single authors, one collaboration, and 16 of unknown authorship; for 1598 the full details of Henslowe's accounts are available in addition to the publication and allusion testimony, and together they give a much more complete account of what was actually going on in the London theatres. For 1598 the same *Annals* lists 46 plays, 16 by single named playwrights, 20 collaborations by two or more, and only ten whose author or authors are unknown. Theatres and writers did not change in 1598; the proportion of records preserved changed. There is no reason to think that the true situation in 1597 was different from that in 1598.

1. See *Modern Philology,* xxx (August 1932), 29–51, and the Malone Society reprint of the play.

A few of Henslowe's many payments for collaborations will illustrate the prevalence of this method of play-writing; they also illustrate the frequency with which these records reveal the existence of plays not known from any other sources and the activities of dramatists inadequately known from printed texts and occasional allusions.

In August 1598 Henslowe bought a finished play for the Lord Admiral's company: "Lent unto the company the 18 of August 1598 to buy a book called Hot Anger Soon Cold of Mr. Porter, Mr. Chettle, and Benjamin Jonson in full payment the sum of . . . £6."[2] Ben Jonson, who has more to say about himself and who published his plays with greater care than any other dramatist of his time, carefully avoided all mention of this play, and it would be unknown without this record.

The very next day Henslowe was making payments on another otherwise unknown play for the Lord Admiral's men.

> Lent unto the company the 19 of August 1598 to pay unto Mr. Wilson, Munday, and Dekker in part of payment of a book called Chance Medley the sum of £4 5s in this manner Wilson 30 shillings, Chettle 30 shillings, Munday 25 shillings. I say . . . £4 5s.

But there was still another collaborator involved in *Chance Medley*, for five days later a further payment was entered: "Paid unto Mr. Drayton the 24 of August 1598 in full payment of a book called Chance Medley the sum of . . . 35s."[3] A somewhat more common method of payment to the company's dramatists is illustrated in the accounts for the lost and otherwise unknown play called *Robert II, or the Scot's Tragedy*.

> Lent unto Thomas Downton the 3 of September 1599 to lend unto Thomas Dekker, Benjamin Jonson, Harry

2. Foakes and Rickert, p. 96.
3. Ibid., pp. 96 and 97.

Chettle and other gentleman in earnest of a play called Robert the second King of Scot's Tragedy, the sum of . . . 40s.

Lent unto Samuel Rowley and Robert Shaw the 15 of September 1599 to lend in earnest of a book called The Scot's Tragedy unto Thomas Dekker and Harry Chettle, the sum of . . . 20s.

Lent Harry Chettle the 16 of September 1599 in earnest of a book called The Scot's Tragedy, the sum of . . . 10s.

Lent unto William Borne the 27 of September 1599 to lend unto Benjamin Jonson in earnest of a book called The Scot's Tragedy, the sum of . . . 20s.[4]

Robert II, or the Scot's Tragedy, like *Hot Anger Soon Cold*, is a dramatic effort of which the redoubtable Ben did not choose to inform posterity, and these payments are the only records of its existence.

Seven months later in March 1599/1600 another cooperating group of dramatists were paid for their work on a play, but the entry forms are somewhat different. The first entry is written not in Henslowe's hand, but in that of William Birde, one of the leading members of the Lord Admiral's company, who signed the acknowledgment. The second is the usual form of entry in Henslowe's hand; the third is also in Henslowe's hand, but it is signed by the actor-dramatist Samuel Rowley, another leading sharer in the company, who authorized the payment and apparently took charge of the money.

Received of Mr. Henslowe the one of March to pay to Henry Chettle, Thomas Dekker, William Haughton, and John Day for a book called The Seven Wise Masters the sum of . . . 40s.

W. Birde

Lent unto Samuel Rowley the 8 of March 1599 to pay unto Harry Chettle and John Day in full payment for

4. Ibid., p. 124.

a book called The Seven Wise Masters the sum of . . . 50*s.*

Samuel Rowley

Lent unto Harry Chettle the 2 of March 1599 in earnest of a book called The Seven Wise Masters the sum of . . . 30*s.*[5]

Other collaborations for which Henslowe paid involved plays which made their way into print and are now available in various editions. But the diary sometimes gives information which significantly alters the statements on the original title pages. In 1607 *The Famous History of Sir Thomas Wyatt* was published. The play concerns the development of the Lady Jane Gray faction, the Wyatt Rebellion, and the suppression and punishment of those concerned, and the title page of the 1607 quarto gives the information, "As it was played by the Queen's Majesty's Servants. Written by Thomas Dekker and John Webster." But Henslowe's payments show that the title page gives only part of the truth. Henslowe did make his payments in behalf of the Earl of Worcester's company (the troupe whose name was changed on the accession of James to Queen Anne's company or Her Majesty's Servants) and Dekker and Webster were indeed concerned with the composition, but there were others unnamed on the title page:

Lent unto John Thare the 15 of October 1602 to give unto Harry Chettle, Thomas Dekker, Thomas Heywood, and Mr. Smith and Mr. Webster in earnest of a play called Lady Jane the sum of . . . 50*s.*

Lent unto Thomas Heywood the 21 of October 1602 to pay unto Mr. Dekker, Chettle, Smith, Webster, and Heywood in full payment of their play of Lady Jane the sum of . . . £5 10*s.*

5. Ibid., p. 131.

> Lent unto John Duke the 27 of October 1602 to give unto Thomas Dekker in earnest of the second part of Lady Jane the sum of ... 5s.

> Lent unto John Duke the 6 of November 1602 for to make a suit of satin of _____ for the play of the Over Throw of Rebels, the sum of ... £5.[6]

The payment of five poets for collaborating on the same play is not unusual in the diary, nor is the use of two different titles for the same piece. Six months earlier in the same year a group of five playwrights, including two of the authors of *Lady Jane*, were paid on behalf of another company, the Lord Admiral's men, for another collaboration.

> Lent unto the company the 22 of May 1602 to give unto Anthony Munday and Michaell Drayton, Webster and the rest, Middleton, in earnest of a book called Caesar's Fall the sum of ... £5.

> Lent unto Thomas Downton the 29 of May 1602 to pay Thomas Dekker, Drayton, Middleton, and Webster and Munday in full payment for their play called Two Shapes, the sum of ... £3.[7]

In a modern impresario's books the two different titles would strongly suggest two plays, but in Shakespeare's time this variation in names was not unusual before the play had been acted—or sometimes (as in the cases of *Othello*, *Henry IV*, *Twelfth Night* and *Much Ado*) even after. The proximity of the two dates, the identity of the five names, and the fact that the first payment was "in earnest" and the second "in full payment" demonstrate that *Caesar's Fall* and *The Two Shapes* were one play.

Most of the plays of joint authorship so far noted are no longer extant, and several would have been totally unknown without Henslowe's diary. But collaboration was a common phenomenon of the period, and well-known plays

6. Ibid., pp. 218 and 219.
7. Ibid., pp. 201 and 202.

were also collaborations, though sometimes this would never have been known from their title pages alone.

Dekker's play, *The Honest Whore*, was rather popular, at least with readers, for it went through five early quarto editions—more than most of the plays of Shakespeare. The title page of the 1604 quarto reads:

> The Honest Whore, With the Humours of the Patient Man and the Longing Wife.
> Tho: Dekker.

The later editions of 1605, 1615, 1616, and the undated one all display the same statement of authorship on their title pages, but a diary payment shows that Dekker did not work alone.

> Lent unto the company to give unto Thomas Dekker and Middleton in earnest of their play called The Patient Man and The Honest Whore the sum of . . . £5.[8]

The number of collaborations attested by Henslowe's records is very great. Indeed they show that the majority of the plays he bought for both the Lord Admiral's company and for the Earl of Worcester's men were not individual compositions but collaborations. This troublesome fact has inclined a number of critics to assert that collaboration was a peculiar feature of Henslowe's policy and imposed by him upon the companies he financed. Such a distinction is highly improbable; the significant difference among the companies is rather that for the other London troupes there are almost no records at all, outside government and legal documents, literary allusions, and play publications. If the theatrical archives now preserved at Dulwich College had been destroyed, as the financial records of all *non*-Henslowe companies have been, then we would know as little of the repertories and purchasing policies of the Lord Admiral's men and the Earl of Worcester's company as we do of those of the Lord Chamberlain's.

8. Ibid., p. 209.

But joint composition was common in the repertories of the other London troupes of actors, though the surviving evidence is scanty in the total absence of their own financial records.

Shortly after Henslowe advanced money for Prince Henry's company (the new Jacobean name for the old Lord Admiral's troupe) to pay for Dekker and Middleton's collaboration on *The Honest Whore*, Ben Jonson was working with George Chapman and John Marston on a play for the Queen's Revels company at Blackfriars. Jonson's arrogance and belligerence would appear to have made him one of the most unlikely collaborators among the Elizabethan dramatists, but he had been involved in joint authorship for Henslowe in *Hot Anger Soon Cold*, *Robert II, or The Scot's Tragedy*, and *The Page of Plymouth*, and he had worked on another man's play when he wrote additions to *The Spanish Tragedy* for the Admiral's men in 1602.

The play he created with Chapman and Marston was *Eastward Ho!* whose production got the company and the authors into trouble. Jonson himself spoke of this collaboration and of the consequent dangers to the authors. In his conversations with William Drummond years later, he told his host that

> He was delated by Sir James Murray to the King for writing something against the Scots in a play, Eastward Ho, and voluntarily imprisoned himself with Chapman and Marston, who had written it amongst them. The report was that they should then [have] had their ears cut and noses.[9]

Jonson evidently took collaboration for granted as a common method of composition in his time and felt no shame or hesitancy in acknowledging his participation to

9. C. H. Herford and Percy and Evelyn Simpson, *Ben Jonson*, Oxford, 1925–1953, I, 140.

Drummond. In his address "To the Readers," prepared for the first quarto of *Sejanus* a couple of years after its performance by the King's company at the Globe with William Shakespeare in the cast, he wrote:

> Lastly I would inform you that this book, in all its numbers, is not the same with that which was acted on the public stage, wherein a second pen had good show: in place of which I have rather chosen to put weaker (and no doubt less pleasing) of mine own, than to defraud so happy a genius of his own right by my loathed usurpation.

Perhaps only Jonson, with his growing preoccupation with posterity, would have gone so far as painstakingly to weed out of his text all the words of his collaborator, whoever he was, and to replace them with his own. This meticulous effort is quite like that which he expended on the 1601 text of *Every Man in his Humour* to transform it into the version published in 1616. These examples are widely known, but it is often not observed that in textual concern with his plays Jonson was unique. He is the only active dramatist among Shakespeare's contemporaries who expended anything remotely approaching this effort on his play texts.

But though Jonson was not typical in his concern for his text, he was normal enough in his familiarity with collaboration. Not only had he himself been involved in five or more collaborations, but he took the prevalence of collaboration sufficiently for granted to make him think it worthwhile to point out specifically that *Volpone*, which the King's men had acted in 1606, was *not* a collaboration. In the prologue to this play he wrote:

> 'Tis known, five weeks fully penned it
> From his own hand, without a coadjutor,
> Novice, journeyman, or tutor.

It is tempting to speculate on the varieties of collaboration which a meticulous writer like Jonson intended to imply in the words "coadjutor," "novice," "journeyman," "tutor." But it is safer to be content to note Jonson's obvious assumption that the Globe audience would think it likely enough that more than one dramatist had been involved in the writing of *Volpone.*

By the time Jonson published his prologue for *Volpone,* the mostly widely advertised collaborators in Elizabethan drama had begun writing plays for the London theatres. Whether Fletcher had a hand in the preparation of *The Woman Hater* for the Children of Paul's or *The Knight of the Burning Pestle* for the Queen's Revels at Blackfriars may be doubted by some, as is Beaumont's participation in *The Woman's Prize.* But by 1608 or 1609, when the King's company performed *Philaster,* this writing partnership was established and these collaborating dramatists were producing for the King's men in the last years of Shakespeare's active participation in the affairs of the company *The Captain, The Coxcomb, Cupid's Revenge, Philaster, A King and No King,* and *The Maid's Tragedy,* and others.

This most famous collaboration must have come to an end in 1613 or 1614 when Beaumont married an heiress and apparently retired to her estates in Kent, but Fletcher wrote regularly for the King's company until his death in August 1625. The title of the 1647 folio *Comedies and Tragedies Written by Francis Beaumont and John Fletcher, Gentlemen* has long been recognized as grossly misleading, since at least thirty of the plays were written after Beaumont's death. About the time of the publication of the 1647 folio, Sir Aston Cokayne wrote a verse letter to his cousin Charles Cotton protesting that

> Had *Beaumont* lived when this edition came
> Forth, and beheld his ever living name
> Before plays that he never writ, how he

Had frown'd and blushed at such impiety!

. . . . .

And my good friend old *Philip Massinger*
With *Fletcher* writ in some that we see there.[10]

In the same volume Cokayne printed another set of protesting verses to the publishers of the folio, Moseley and
Robinson, and finally a third set making even greater
claims for the collaboration of Massinger with Fletcher.

> An Epitaph on Mr. John Fletcher, and Mr. Philip Mas-
> singer, who lie buried both in one Grave in St. Mary
> Overies Church in Southwark.
>
> In the same grave Fletcher was buried here
> Lies the stage-poet Philip Massinger:
> Plays they did write together, were great friends
> And now one grave includes them at their ends:
> So whom on earth nothing did part, beneath
> Here (in their fames) they lie, in spight of death.

All Fletcher's plays written after 1616 were, so far as
we can tell now, the property of the King's men, and this
powerful company succeeded in withholding all but one of
them from publication until after the closing of the theatres in 1642. For these plays there are no quartos which
might have acknowledged Massinger's work on their title
pages, only the blanket and false attribution of the folio
of 1647. Many analyses of these folio plays have been
made in the last century, and though they by no means
show unanimity in their findings, the best of them presents
reasonable evidence that Massinger's work is to be found
in 19 plays of the folios.

Even more suggestive of the importance of collaboration for the leading Jacobean company is the fact that *most*
of the plays published at one time or another under
Fletcher's name show evidence of the writing of another
man, whether Massinger, Beaumont, Field, Rowley, or

10. *A Chair of Golden Poems*, London, 1658, pp. 91–93.

Shirley.[11] Such evidence is much too extensive and complex for consideration here, but it gives overwhelming support to the view that joint authorship was a commonplace in the repertory of the King's company, at least from 1616 to 1642. In this period, 46 plays of the Beaumont and Fletcher folios can be shown to have been performed by the King's men (compared with 16 from the Shakespeare folio).[12]

The vogue of these collaborated plays at court was equally great. The majority of the records of the performances of selected plays before members of the royal family and the court do not give the name of the play acted, but there remain a number of records of such performances by the King's company between 1616 and 1642 that do give play titles. Of the performances at court of plays listed by name, 42 performances (including repetitions) are of plays from the Beaumont and Fletcher folios, compared to 18 performances of plays written by Shakespeare, and 7 performances of plays written by Jonson. The not uncommon notion that collaborated plays were inferior and probably notable only in the Henslowe companies is thoroughly exploded by these records of the productions of the most distinguished and powerful company in London in the reigns of James I and Charles I.

At the same time other less familiar collaborations were being offered in various London theatres. In most instances the fact that the plays were collaborations is known only from the title pages, and the examples of *Sir Thomas Wyatt*, *The Honest Whore*, and *Sejanus* have shown that the information on single-author title pages is often incomplete. Nevertheless on the title pages or in the printed

11. See Cyrus Hoy, "The Shares of Fletcher and His Collaborators in the Beaumont and Fletcher Canon," *Studies in Bibliography, Papers of the Bibliographical Society of the University of Virginia*, vols. VIII–XV, Charlottesville, Va., 1956–1962.

12. See *Jacobean and Caroline Stage*, I, 108–34.

epistles the publishers indicate that in the first decade of King James's reign John Day, William Rowley, and George Wilkins were collaborating on *The Travels of the Three English Brothers* for Queen Anne's company; Dekker and Middleton on *The Roaring Girl* for Prince Henry's men at the Fortune; Beaumont and Fletcher on *Cupid's Revenge* for the Children of the Queen's Revels; Heywood and William Rowley on *Fortune by Land and Sea* for Queen Anne's men at the Red Bull; and Beaumont and Fletcher on *The Scornful Lady* for the Queen's Revels company.

One of the most active collaborators in this decade and a little later was a man whose dramatic compositions have not yet been noticed, the actor-dramatist Nathan Field. Because of their intimate association with the company and its needs, such men who were both players and playwrights had special contributions to make in joint compositions, and there is a notably high proportion of collaboration in the known work of Samuel Rowley, William Rowley, Heywood, and Field.

Nathan Field, the son of a Puritan and the brother of a bishop, began his stage career at the age of twelve or thirteen when he became one of the boy actors in the Queen's Revels troupe at Blackfriars, and until his early death at the age of thirty-three or thereabouts he was conspicuous on the London stage; Ben Jonson and several later writers pair him with Richard Burbage as one of the great actors of his time. His plays published as by Field alone are *Woman is a Weathercock* and *Amends for Ladies*, the first for his boy company and the second for the Lady Elizabeth's company, of which Field became one of the principals. In this company he was both a leading actor and a dramatist, as he was later in the King's company. Some of his correspondence with Philip Henslowe in both capacities has been preserved. At the end of June 1613, Field was writing a play with Robert Daborne for his com-

pany. The name of the play is unknown. Field wrote to
Henslowe:

> Mr. Daborne and I have spent a great deal of time in
> conference about this plot which will make as beneficial
> a play as hath come these seven years. It is out of his
> love he detains it for us, only £10 is desired in hand,
> for which we will be bound to bring you in the play
> finished upon the first day of August. . . .

The collaborated play about which Robert Daborne later
wrote to Henslowe on 30 July 1613 was probably this same
lost work with Field. Daborne was, as usual, trying to get
another advance from Henslowe on an unfinished play. He
said, in part: ". . . I pray, sir, of your much friendship
do me one courtesy more till Thursday when we deliver
in our play to you as to lend me twenty shillings. . . ."[13]

About the same year Field was involved in another collaboration for the Lady Elizabeth's company. The letter
is undated, and the play, as usual, unnamed; it may have
been a totally unknown play, and it may have been—as
the name of Fletcher suggests—one of the pieces (possibly
The Honest Man's Fortune) published together in the
1647 Beaumont and Fletcher folio. The vaguely allusive
letter to Henslowe is written from jail by Field, with post-
scripts by Philip Massinger and Robert Daborne. At the
moment of writing, the need for bail was more important
to these dramatists than the name of their play.

> Mr. Henslowe:
> You understand our unfortunate extremity, and I do
> not think you so void of Christianity but that you would
> throw so much money into the Thames as we request
> now of you rather than endanger so many innocent lives.
> You know there is £10 more at least to be received of

13. W. W. Greg, ed., *Henslowe Papers*, London, 1907, pp. 84
and 74–75.

you for the play. We desire you to lend us £5 of that, which shall be allowed to you, without which we cannot be bailed, nor I play any more till this be dispatched. It will lose you £20 ere the end of next week besides the hinderance of the next new play. Pray, sir, consider our cases with humanity, and now give us cause to acknowledge you our true friend in time of need. We have intreated Mr. Davison to deliver this note, as well to witness your love as our promises and always acknowledgment to be ever

Your most thankful and loving friends,
Nat: Field

The money shall be abated out of the money remains for the play of Mr. Fletcher and ours.

Rob: Daborne

I have ever found you a true loving friend to me and in so small a suit it being honest I hope you will not fail us.

Philip Massinger

The letter was effective, for at the end appears the receipt, written in another hand:

Received by me Robert Davison of Mr. Henslowe for the use of Mr. Daborne, Mr. Field, Mr. Massinger the sum of £5.

Robert Davison.[14]

It is likely that during the years of his membership in the Lady Elizabeth's company Field was engaged in joint work on several plays with other writers for the company such as Massinger, Fletcher, Beaumont, Daborne, Tourneur, or Middleton.

In or about 1616 Field was taken into the premier London company, King James's men, in which he was prominent for the four or five remaining years of his life. T. W. Baldwin thinks that he succeeded to Shakespeare's shares

14. Ibid., pp. 65–67.

in the company,[15] and he certainly became a leading actor, several plays of this period showing that they were composed for dual male leads, a young man and an older man—almost certainly Nathan Field and Richard Burbage.

There is no doubt that he collaborated on certain of the company's plays and a very strong probability that he made some contribution to others. He certainly worked with Massinger on *The Fatal Dowry*, which was acted by the King's men at court in February 1631/32 and published later in the year, "As it hath been often Acted at the private house in Blackfriars, by His Majesty's servants. Written by P. M. and N. F."

Another collaboration for his company was the play about the notorious murder of the Dutch jeweler, John de Wely, in the household of Prince Maurice in 1616. It was probably written soon after the event, as was the similar timely play about Dutch affairs, *Sir John van Olden Barnavelt*, composed by Fletcher and Massinger and acted by the King's men at the Globe in August 1619. Nathan Field's similarly topical play for the company is lost—as was *Sir John van Olden Barnavelt* until the manuscript was discovered in the late nineteenth century. The manuscript of Field's collaboration was still extant in 1654, when it was entered by Humphrey Moseley in the Stationers' Register: "A play called The Jeweler of Amsterdam or The Hague. By Mr. John Fletcher. Nathan Field, and Philip Massinger."

Other plays in which the collaborating hand of Nathan Field has been seen with some show of evidence by various scholars are *Four Plays in One*, *The Knight of Malta*, *The Laws of Candy*, *The Queen of Corinth*. Final demonstration of Field's contribution to these plays in the Beaumont and Fletcher folio is not yet possible, and it is unlikely that he would have made *major* contributions to all

15. T. W. Baldwin, *The Organization and Personnel of the Shakespearean Company*, Princeton, 1927, p. 51.

of them in the years when he was involved in his *known* collaborations and in developing his reputation as a leading London actor. There is no doubt, however, that he was a steady collaborator while he was a leading player in one or the other of his companies.

Another actor-dramatist-collaborator whose career was similar to Field's was William Rowley. They were writing in much the same years, but Rowley published a good deal more because his first known play appeared two years before Field's, and he lived five or six years longer. Both were more famous as actors than Shakespeare, Heywood, or Samuel Rowley. Field was known as a "juvenile" lead and Rowley as a comedian who specialized in the part of the fat clown. Indeed Rowley sometimes recorded his type roles himself, signing the address to the reader "Simplicitie," the name of the clown in the piece, in his collaboration *The World Tossed at Tennis*, and listing in the dramatis personnae of *All's Lost by Lust* "Jaques, a simple clownish Gentleman, his sonne, personated by the Poet." Rowley also represented his company several times at court when he signed the receipt for payment for their performances before royalty.

Both Field and Rowley are known to have worked mostly in collaboration; both wrote nearly always for the companies in which they acted; both spent the last few years of their lives as patented members of the leading London company, King James's men; and finally both were collaborators with John Fletcher, the principal dramatist of the royal company.

For most of his acting career, however, Rowley was a member of Prince Charles's company, which had been known as the Duke of York's men before its patron became the heir apparent on the death of his elder brother, Henry, in November 1612. Rowley was one of the leaders of this company from before March 1610, when his name appeared second in the royal charter of the company, until about 1623, when he became a patented member of the King's company. It is not unlikely that he had had some early attachment to Queen Anne's troupe, for inexperienced actors were not normally made chartered members of prominent companies, as Rowley was in 1610. His two earliest compositions, both collaborations, were *The Travels of Three English Brothers*, acted by Queen Anne's men in 1607, and *Fortune by Land and Sea*, written with a patented member of the Queen's company, Thomas Heywood, and acted by that group a year or so later. One of his three unassisted plays, *A Shoemaker a Gentleman*, was probably also written for this same troupe about this time, but the evidence is not conclusive.

The largest group of plays by this actor-dramatist consists of those he wrote for the company he belonged to for the longest time, Prince Charles's men, who performed variously at the Curtain, the Phoenix, and the Red Bull. Rowley's earliest known work for them was his unassisted comedy, *Hymen's Holiday or Cupid's Vagaries*, which he and his fellows performed at court on 24 February 1611/12 and which was revived in another court performance 22 years later before the King and Queen, a performance which Sir Henry Herbert says was "Likte."

A few years later Rowley worked with Thomas Middleton on another play for his company, *A Fair Quarrell*, which was also acted before the King. The second issue of the play has three additional pages of comic material which are probably Rowley's. In his next collaboration Rowley brought in Philip Massinger as well as Middleton. The piece was called *The Old Law, or a New Way to Please You*, and though there is no clear indication of the company for which it was prepared, it may have been the Prince's men again.

In 1621 Rowley collaborated with John Ford and Thomas Dekker on a topical play for Prince Charles's company called *The Witch of Edmonton*. In fact there may have been other collaborators, for the title page of the only edition says "A known true story. Composed into a Tragi-Comedy by divers well-esteemed Poets; *William Rowley, Thomas Dekker, John Ford &c.*" This play too attained a performance before royalty in December 1621.

There are three plays by Rowley in the early twenties which were eventually acted by the Lady Elizabeth's company at the Phoenix. It is not entirely clear for which company Rowley originally wrote them, but since Lady Elizabeth's company succeeded Prince Charles's men at the Phoenix, since Christopher Beeston financed both companies in the early twenties, and since, for a short time at least, there seems to have been some sort of cooperation between them, it may have been that Rowley's break from his acting company in these three compositions was only apparent and not real. The three plays are his unaided composition, *All's Lost by Lust*, and the two collaborations with Thomas Middleton, *The Changeling* and *The Spanish Gypsy*. The first, though later acted by Lady Elizabeth's men, was written before that company was reorganized for its London career at the Phoenix, and in the dramatis personnae of the play Rowley identifies himself as the actor who created the role of Jaques. *The Changeling* is probably Rowley's best-known play, and the serious parts of the tragedy have impressed many critics, but it was the comic parts—probably Rowley's portion—which seemed most memorable to contemporaries. It was the comic material that gave the play its title, and the actors mentioned especially in seventeenth-century performances, William Robbins, Timothy Reade, and Thomas Sheppy, were all comedians.

The Spanish Gypsy, the latest of Rowley's six known collaborations with Thomas Middleton, was another successful play which was kept in the repertory of the Phoenix for at least sixteen years and was revived more than once after the Restoration.

In the late summer of 1624 Rowley was working with
John Ford, Thomas Dekker, and John Webster, preparing for the stage a dramatization of two recent scandalous
events in London, a matricide and a seduction. The play
is unfortunately lost, but a good deal is known about it
from the lawsuit brought by the son-in-law of the slan-
dered woman. The piece was called *The Late Murder of
the Son upon the Mother, or Keep the Widow Waking*,
and it was acted at the Red Bull, probably by Prince
Charles's company. If so, this was Rowley's last composition for his old company, with which he appears to have
retained some sort of ambiguous connection.[16]

He became a member of the King's company and in the
summer of 1623 collaborated with the company's principal dramatist, John Fletcher, on *The Maid in the Mill*,
a play in which Rowley again acted one of the chief roles.
He is also known to have created the role of the Archbishop of Spolato in Middleton's sensational hit, *A Game
at Chess*, which ran for an unprecedented nine days at the
Globe in August 1624.

It is likely that Rowley was involved in other compositions for his new company in 1624 and 1625, but the evidence is very confused. *A New Wonder, A Woman Never
Vexed* was published six years after his death, in 1632, with
a title page saying "Written by William Rowley, one of
his Maiesties Servants," but with no indication of company
and little of date. There are several other plays, mostly
lost, which have been dubiously attributed to him in the
Stationers' Register after the closing of the theatres or on
Restoration title pages.

In the years in which Rowley was working with Middleton on plays for the Phoenix and then with Fletcher on
plays for the King's men at Blackfriars and the Globe,
other London theatres were commissioning plays for joint

16. See *Jacobean and Caroline Stage*, ii, 556.

authorship. For the company playing at the Fortune, Sir Henry Herbert, Master of the Revels, licensed on 22 October 1624 "For the Palsgrave's Company, a new play called *The Bristow Merchant*, written by Ford and Dekker." The play is lost, and nothing beyond this official license to be acted is known of it.

Probably also at the Red Bull, in addition to the sensational *Late Murder of the Son upon the Mother, or Keep the Widow Waking* by Dekker, Ford, Rowley, and Webster there was the collaboration of John Ford and Thomas Dekker on the lost play called *The Fairy Knight*. It was licensed for performance by Sir Henry Herbert on 11 June 1624, and though he did not mention the theatre, it is likely to have been the Red Bull.

Another Red Bull collaboration was a lost play written by Thomas Dekker and John Day. The entry in Sir Henry Herbert's office book in a version somewhat fuller than the one usually printed reads: "The Princes Players—A French tragedy of *The Bellman of Paris*, containing 40 sheets written by Thomas Dekker and John Day for the company of the Red Bull this 30 July 1623 . . . £1."[17] Of the five plays whose manuscript length is noted by Sir Henry, this is so much the longest that one wonders why. Is it caused by extra songs? Extra prologues or epilogues or an induction? Extensive revisions? General sprawl?

Also at the Red Bull they performed the joint composition of William Sampson and Gervase Markham called *Herod and Antipater*. Though Sampson wrote two other plays and Gervase Markham one, these two men were not professional dramatists, and *Herod and Antipater*, an otherwise unremarkable production, is one of the few collaborations known to have been written by amateurs for the professional acting companies in London.

17. From an independent transcript, probably made by Craven Ord, and now pasted into Halliwell-Phillipps's scrapbooks at the Folger Shakespeare Library.

At the Phoenix or Cockpit in Drury Lane, several collaborations are known to have been acted during these four or five years. Middleton and Rowley's *Changeling* in 1622, their *Spanish Gypsy* in 1623, and Rowley's further collaboration for his company with Dekker and Ford on *The Witch of Edmonton* have already been noticed. In addition the company had licensed on 2 October 1623 "A new comedy called *A Fault in Friendship* Written by Young Johnson and Brome." The play is lost, and Herbert's odd designation "Young Johnson" has given rise in the writings of the impressionable to a mythical play-writing son for Ben Jonson. The laureate had no son who survived to manhood; Herbert's designation makes an implication about the age of Richard Brome's collaborator, but not about his parentage.

A fifth joint composition known to have been prepared for a Phoenix production in these years was a curious piece called *The Sun's Darling*. When the Master of the Revels licensed it on 3 March 1623/24, he wrote: "For the Cockpit company *The Sun's Darling* in the nature of a masque by Dekker and Ford." And when a revision was published in 1656 the title page read *The Sun's Darling: A Moral Masque*. It is not a regular court masque, though the same title page adds the statement: "As it hath often been presented at Whitehall by their Majestys' Servants; and after at the Cock-pit in Drury Lane with great Applause." And it is not a simple moral allegory, though it has many of the features ordinarily found in such writings. Some of the planned stage effects would surely have overtaxed the resources of the Phoenix. However puzzling Dekker and Ford's composition may be, the Master of the Revels's license makes it clear enough that it was planned for regular production in Drury Lane.

After the death of Fletcher and the accession of Charles I, there appears to have been a decline in the number of collaborated plays prepared for the London stage. One must always be chary of such generalizations, for one can be perfectly certain that most of the evidence of theatrical activities has disappeared. Nevertheless it is clear enough that certain changed conditions in the London theatre world made collaboration less necessary.

Most obvious is the existence of large repertories of actable old plays. We know the titles of approximately 835 plays written between 1590 and 1625 inclusive; and at least 400 of them were presumably available to Caroline companies, since they are still available in print or in manuscript in the twentieth century.[18] Of the now well-known "Elizabethan" plays the great majority were written before 1626.

A rather striking piece of evidence that in the reign of Charles I the better London companies not only could have but actually did live in large part on their old repertories and did not commission new plays at anything like the old rate is to be found in the records of performances at court of the King's company, the troupe whose prestige in the time of Charles I was unrivaled. From the year 1625 to 6 January 1641/42 (the last recorded appearance of the company at court before the wars) there are records of 256 performances of the King's men before royalty. Usually these command affairs are known only from payment for blocks of performances without the names of the individual plays, but on 88 occasions the play is named. Now the Caroline court was certainly avid for new thrills in the theatre—as elsewhere—and one would expect most of the plays selected for the court in these 17 years to have been the newest acquisitions of the company. But they were not. Sixty-four of the 88 named plays were old ones, and only 24 were plays first produced within a year of the court performances. Not only were the majority of the plays not new, but many were twenty or more years old;

18. See Alfred Harbage and S. Schoenbaum, *Annals of English Drama, 975–1700*, London, 1964, pp. 54–122.

plays such as *A Midsummer Night's Dream, Volpone, The Maid's Tragedy, A King and No King, Philaster, Henry IV, The Duchess of Malfi, Everyman in his Humour, Richard III, The Taming of the Shrew, The Faithful Shepherdess, Cymbeline, Bussy D'Ambois, Catiline, Epicoene, The Beggar's Bush, The Loyal Subject, Othello, Hamlet, Julius Caesar, The Merry Wives of Windsor, The Chances, The Coxcomb, Rollo, Duke of Normandy.*

This tendency to rely on a classic repertory accumulated through the longest period of successful operation (1594 to 1625–1642) of any known company is a suggestive feature of the operation of the King's men at the Blackfriars and the Globe in the reign of Charles I. Edmund Malone, who examined at length and made random excerpts from the now lost records of the Master of the Revels, 1622–1642, said that in these years the King's men licensed only about four new plays a year. The company's reliance in Charles's time on a classic repertory is also made apparent by the terms in which James Shirley, regular dramatist for the company between 1640 and 1642, complained, in the prologue to his comedy, *The Sisters*, about the slim attendance at Blackfriars in the ominous spring of 1642.

> Does this look like a Term? I cannot tell,
> Our Poet thinks the whole town is not well,
> . . . . .
> What audience we have, what company
> "To Shakespeare comes, whose mirth did once beguile
> Dull hours, and buskined made even sorrow smile,
> So lovely were the wounds that men would say
> They could endure the bleeding a whole day":
> He has but few friends lately, think o' that,
> He'll come no more, and others have his fate.
> "Fletcher, the Muses' darling, and choice love
> Of Phoebus, the delight of every grove;
> Upon whose head the laurel grew, whose wit
> Was the time's wonder and example yet,"

'Tis within memory, trees did not throng
As once the story said to Orpheus' song.
"Jonson t' whose name wise art did bow, and wit
Is only justified by honoring it:
To hear whose touch, how would the learned choir
With silence stoop? And when he took his lyre,
Apollo dropped his lute, ashamed to see
A rival to the God of Harmony."
You do forsake him too, we must deplore
This fate, for we do know it by our door.

Their selection of a repertory for court performances
and Shirley's complaint of the sparce attendance in 1642
at performances of the customary favorites both show how
the Caroline King's company was relying on its glorious
past. But this was not the pattern for other times in this
company, nor necessarily for this time in all London companies. Not even the Phoenix had such a repertory, to say
nothing of the Red Bull, the Fortune, and Salisbury Court.

In the 1590s and the first decade of the seventeenth century new plays, especially collaborations, had been required
at a great rate because no acceptable inherited repertory
was available. The expedients necessary in this situation are
made clear from Henslowe's records of payments for new
play manuscripts in the years 1598 to 1602. Suppose Henslowe and the Burbages and Alleyn had tried to rely on
plays twenty to thirty years old, as their heirs did in the
1630s? What was available to them? Those still extant
from the accession of Queen Elizabeth to 1580 are Wager's
Life and Repentance of Mary Magdalene, *The Longer
Thou Livest the More Fool Thou Art*, and *Trial of Treasure*; Philip's *Patient and Meek Grisel*; Heywood's *Thy-
estes*; Sackville and Norton's *Gorboduc*; Bower's *Appius
and Virginia*; Edwards's *Damon and Pithias*; Gascoigne's
Supposes, *Jocasta*, and *Glass of Government*; Wilmot's
Gismund of Salerne; Pickering's *Horestes*; Fulwell's *Like
Will to Like*; Garter's *Most Virtuous and Godly Queen*

Hester; Woodes's *Conflict of Conscience*; Walpull's *Tide Tarrieth No Man*; Lupton's *All for Money*; and Merbury's *Marriage between Wit and Wisdom*. However interesting these plays may be to historians of the drama, the Burbages and Henslowe needed no prescience to guess that they would never draw spectators to the Curtain, the Globe, the Rose, the Fortune, or Blackfriars.

But however much the production of new plays and especially of collaborations fell off in the reign of Charles I, joint authorship did not entirely cease to be practiced. Thomas Randolph alluded to the situation in his play *The Jealous Lovers*, produced in the spring of 1632 after he had spent a period as regular playwright for the King's Revels company at the Salisbury Court.[19] Randolph makes his character Asotus, who has just crowned Charylus and Bromolochus poets laureate, say to them:

> I will not have you henceforth . . .
>
> .   .   .   .   .
>
> . . . nor work journey work
> Under some playhouse poet, that deals in
> Wit by retail.

Two other plays, one of which was acted in the same year as Randolph's *Jealous Lovers*, were later published as collaborations, but they were not. In 1639 Andrew Crooke and William Cooke published *The Ball* and *Chabot, Admiral of France* with the same statement on both title pages:

> As it was presented by her Majesty's Servants at the private house in Drury Lane
>
> | | George Chapman |
> | Written by | and |
> | | James Shirley |

Neither is a collaboration. *Chabot* is an old play of Chapman's written about 1621 but apparently never acted for political reasons. Shirley revised it for the production at

19. See *Jacobean and Caroline Stage*, v, 966–67.

his theatre, the Phoenix or Cockpit in Drury Lane, in 1635 when Chapman was dead. There is reason for confusion here, for the play clearly contains work by both men, though there is no likelihood that they worked together. *The Ball* was wholly by Shirley, as the license of the Master of the Revels and his severe comment in censoring the play shows. The publishers simply used the same setting of type for the performance and authorship statements about each play. Probably they were simply confused.

Even the King's company, with a repertory as large and distinguished as we have seen, still sometimes commissioned collaborations. In the summer of 1634 Richard Brome and Thomas Heywood worked together to produce *The Late Lancashire Witches* for the Globe. This was a timely play, rushed through to capitalize the popular interest in the Lancashire women accused of witchcraft and brought to London for trial in 1634. Other London companies were interested in exploiting this sensation and the urgency of the need felt by the King's men to get their play on the Globe stage is documented in a petition they made to the Master of the Revels, a petition which was recorded in the warrant books of the Lord Chamberlain's office:

> A petition of the King's players complaining of intermingling some passages of witches in old plays to the prejudices of their designed comedy of the Lancashire Witches and desiring a prohibition of any other till theirs be allowed and acted. Answered per reference to Blagrave in the absence of Sir Henry Herbert. July 20, 1634.[20]

There were two other collaborations by Brome and Heywood which are now lost and known only from an entry of the manuscripts in the Stationers' Register by the great

20. See *Malone Society Collections*, ii, part 3, p. 410, and *Jacobean and Caroline Stage*, iii, 73.

dramatic publisher Humphrey Moseley. The entry, on 8 April 1654, reads: "Mr. Moseley. Entered for his copies two plays called The Life and Death of Sir Martin Skink, with the wars of the Low Countries, by Richard Brome and Thomas Heywood. And the Apprentice's Prize &." The entry gives no hint as to the date at which the plays were written nor of the company for which they were prepared. The collaboration of the same two men on *The Late Lancashire Witches* might suggest that they too were prepared for the King's company about 1634, but this is by no means certain. Indeed, the form of the entry would not necessarily mean that *The Apprentice's Prize* had the same authorship as *Sir Martin Skink*.

A couple of plays acted at Blackfriars in the last three years before the outbreak of the wars are often asserted (probably with reason) to have been joint compositions. The two are *The Country Captain* and *The Variety*, published together in 1649 as "Written by a person of honor. Lately presented by his Majesty's Servants at the Blackfriars." The person of honor was the famous Duke of Newcastle, then Earl of Newcastle and Baron Ogle. After he had become a Royalist general, his Puritan enemies frequently sneered at him as a playwright, "one that in time of peace tired the stage in Blackfriars with his comedies," "A great pretender of wit, a member of the Blackfriars College, a stage player," "At best but a playwright, one of Apollo's whirligigs, one that when he should be fighting would be fornicating with the Nine Muses or the Dean of York's daughters."

When it is remembered that the noble lord, who was a patron of many literary men, was engaged in numerous activities in the last three years before the wars, that during most of this time James Shirley was the regular dramatist, probably under contract, for the company at Blackfriars, and that later Newcastle was a patron of Shirley, who followed him to the wars, some association seems not unlikely. Anthony à Wood in his *Athenæ Oxoniensis* is very specific about it: "Our author Shirley did also much assist his generous patron, William, Duke of Newcastle, in the composition of certain plays which the Duke afterwards published."[21]

Methods of Collaborating

These records of plays of joint authorship should have made it abundantly clear that a good proportion of the pieces prepared for performance in the London theatres between 1590 and 1642 were the work of more than one author. Since collaboration was so common there is likely to have been a normal method of procedure when more than one man was assigned to prepare a new piece for the stage of the Rose or the Fortune, the Red Bull or the Globe.

Methods of cooperation are much more difficult to discover than the mere fact of joint authorship: printed title pages and Henslowe payments and occasional nondramatic statements have furnished copious evidence that dramatists *did* work together, but very few of them give hints as to *how* they worked together. In the modern theatre where joint authorship (at least acknowledged joint authorship) is not so common, most accounts indicate a sort of blending of the writing of two or more men who often spend time working in the same room jointly developing scenes or even lines. Such a method seems natural enough.

Considering how incomplete, scattered, and contradictory is our evidence of the ways in which Elizabethan, Jacobean, and Caroline dramatists worked together, no one can be dogmatic about their methods. An analysis of collaborated manuscripts like *Sir Thomas More* and a comparison with results of examinations of the various styles in the collaborated plays in the Beaumont and Fletcher

21. 1721 edition, London, II, 378.

folios would reveal a good deal of variety in the apparent division of the work. Moreover, a few playwrights—notably William Rowley—appear to have specialized in certain types of scenes or characters. A complete consideration of types of joint effort displayed in the extant plays of the time would require hundreds of pages.

But there is one method of collaboration used by the playwrights in these years which is most frequently referred to and which was evidently so much more generally practiced then than now that it deserves discussion. Separate composition of individual acts is a division of labor which was quite common from 1590 to 1642.

Very early in the period Robert Wilmot testified that this method of collaboration by separate acts was old. When he revised *Tancred and Gismund* for publication in 1591, he stated on the title page that the play was "Compiled by the Gentlemen of the Inner Temple, and by them presented before her Majesty." And at the end of each act he indicated the name of the author: *"Rod. Staff."* (Stafford?), *"Hen. No."* (Henry Noel), "G. Al."(?), *"Chr. Hat."* (Christopher Hatton). The epilogue he signs *"R. W."* (Robert Wilmot, the editor) and presumably he means that he was the author of the preceding act 5, as well. Since the original play had been acted before Queen Elizabeth in 1566 or 1567, composition by acts was not new in 1591.

The many entries about payment for plays in Henslowe's diary are never explicit in assigning individual acts to the different collaborators, but most of his serial payments are compatible with such composition, especially in the several instances where he pays one or two writers for a play in his early payments and adds others in his final payments.

The composition of the notorious lost play, *The Isle of Dogs*, for which dramatists and players were imprisoned, bringing all acting temporarily to a halt, was by acts, if the statement of Thomas Nashe, one of the authors, is to be trusted. A couple of years after the sensational suppression of July 1597, Thomas Nashe, who had fled at the time of the difficulties about his play, wrote in his pamphlet, *Nashe's Lenten Stuffe*, that the play was:

An imperfect Embrion I may well call it, for I having begun but the induction and first act of it, the other four acts without my consent, or the least guess of my drift or scope, by the players were supplied, which bred both their trouble and mine too.[22]

Nashe seems to say that the last four acts were composed "by the players," which is at best something of a quibble, for one of them was Ben Jonson, who was imprisoned for his share. Perhaps by "supplied" he meant arranged for by the players.

Three entries concerning the work of Ben Jonson and George Chapman certainly show composition by acts, but it is not clear that only one play is involved or that Jonson and Chapman worked together. The first entry simply shows a payment to Jonson for initiating the work on a play: "Lent unto Benjamin Jonson the 3 of December 1597 upon a book which he was to write for us before Christmas next after the date hereof which he showed the plot unto the company. I say lent in ready money unto him . . . 20 shillings."[23] Presumably the second entry refers to this plot which Chapman had taken up, but there is no specific notation of Jonson's collaboration beyond the plot, and the delay seems rather long for compositions for Henslowe: "Lent unto Robert Shaw and Juby the 23 of October 1598 to lend unto Mr. Chapman on his play book and two acts of a tragedy of Benjamin's plot the sum of . . . £3." It is not clear whether the third entry belongs with these two, but it seems likely, for the acts correspond, though Jonson is not mentioned. "Lent unto Mr. Chapman the 4 of Janu-

22. R. B. McKerrow, ed., *The Works of Thomas Nashe*, Oxford, 1958, iii, 153–54.
23. Foakes and Rickert, p. 73.

ary 1598/99 upon three acts of a tragedy which Thomas Downton bade me deliver him the sum of . . . £3."[24] In any event, whether these three entries represent one, two, or possibly even three different plays, the wording shows that composition was proceeding by acts.

In 1613 Daborne's correspondence with Henslowe shows that he was writing by acts and in at least one instance collaborating by acts. On 17 April 1613 Daborne signed an agreement about completing a play for Henslowe:

> Memorandum 'tis agreed between Philip Henslowe, Esquire, and Robert Daborne, gentleman, that the said Robert shall before the end of this Easter term deliver in his tragedy called *Machiavelli and the Devil* into the hands of the said Philip for the sum of £20, £6 whereof the said Robert acknowledgeth to have received in earnest of the said play this 17th of April and must have other £4 upon delivery in of three acts, and other £10 upon delivery in of the last scene, perfected. In witness hereof the said Robert Daborne hereunto hath set his hand this 17th of April, 1613
>
> per me Rob: Daborne[25]

A fortnight later Daborne needed more money before it was due, but he still spoke in terms of composition by acts when he wrote a letter to his creditor.

> Mr. Henslowe:
>
> I am inforced to make bold with you for one 20 shillings more of the £10, and on Friday night I will deliver in the three acts fair written and then receive the other 40 shillings, and if you please to have some papers now you shall, but my promise shall be as good as bond to you. . . . At your command
>
> Rob: Daborne[26]

24. Ibid., pp. 100 and 103.
25. Greg, *Henslowe Papers*, p. 67.
26. Ibid., p. 69.

On another play, *The Owl*, Daborne was again working by acts, as a letter written about the end of December 1613 or the beginning of January 1614 indicates:

> Mr. Henslowe I acquainted you with my necessity which I know you did in part supply, but if you do not help me to 10 shillings by this bearer, by the living God I am utterly disgraced. On Friday night I will bring you papers to the value of three acts. Sir, my occasion is not ordinary that this suddenly I write to you. Wherefore I beseech you do this for me as ever you wished me well, which if I requite not, heaven forget me
> Yours at command,
> Rob: Daborne[27]

In most of the correspondence of Robert Daborne making allusion to joint compositions in which he was engaged with Massinger, Field, or Fletcher he makes no mention of the method by which they collaborated. But in a letter concerning his work with Cyril Tourneur he does say how they were working. The statement implies that Henslowe did not know that Daborne had a collaborator, and it also implies that Henslowe would have no objections; indeed Daborne seems to feel that Henslowe ought to be pleased that he was taking intelligent steps to make haste.

> Mr. Henslowe:
> The company told me you were expected there yesterday to conclude about their coming over or going to Oxford. I have not only labored my own play [*Machiavelli and the Devil*] which shall be ready before they come over, but given Cyril Tourneur an act of *The Arraignment of London* to write that we may have that likewise ready for them. I wish you had spoken with them to know their resolution, for they depend upon your purpose. I have sent you two sheets more fair written. . . . 5 June 1613   At your command,
> Rob: Daborne[28]

27. Ibid., p. 81.   28. Ibid., p. 72.

Such evidence as we have, then, indicates that composition and collaboration on plays written for Henslowe companies was by acts. But the method was not confined to these troupes. The numerous scholars who have tried to disentangle the respective work of Beaumont, Fletcher, Field, Massinger, Rowley, and Middleton as printed in the Beaumont and Fletcher folios have generally found that joint composition was basically by acts—and this regardless of which playwrights were involved, and regardless of whether the play was prepared originally for the Queen's Revel's company, the Lady Elizabeth's company, or, in the case of the majority, for the King's men.[29]

The most explicit statement about collaboration methods comes from a lawsuit involving a play written for still another theatre, the Red Bull. In September 1624 the Master of the Revels licensed "A new tragedy called *A Late Murder of the Son upon the Mother*: Written by Ford and Webster." Like so many licenses, this one is incom-

29. The most satisfactory of the many attempts to break down the authorship of the plays in the two Beaumont and Fletcher folios is, of course, that of Cyrus Hoy. (*Studies in Bibliography, Papers of the Bibliographical Society of the University of Virginia*, vols. VIII–XV, 1956–1962.) Hoy simply identifies styles of two or more different dramatists in the plays and seldom tries to distinguish whether the writers other than Fletcher were collaborating or revising. In numerous instances there is external evidence of revision. As a consequence his stylistic analysis must inevitably show more multiple authorship within the acts of revised plays than was present in the version of a given play at first performance. Even so the plays on which both Fletcher and Massinger worked are highly suggestive. Massinger was not only Fletcher's most frequent collaborator, but the one whose linguistic habits are most sharply distinguished from Fletcher's. In these circumstances it is notable that in at least a dozen of the plays in which they worked together they obviously divided the first two acts between them, and the style of neither appears in the other's act. That this should still be apparent in the texts after many have been revised suggests that Fletcher and Massinger, the most productive collaborating partnership of the time, normally began their work by dividing up at least the two opening acts.

plete; the play was written for the company at the Red
Bull theatre and it was a collaboration not of two playwrights, but of four. And the play had a subtitle, *Keep the
Widow Waking.* The additional information comes from
the testimony in a suit brought by Benjamin Garfield ac-
cusing a number of people of slandering his mother-in-law,
the principal character in the subplot called *Keep the
Widow Waking.* As one of the admitted authors of the
play at the Red Bull, Thomas Dekker was called upon to
testify. In his deposition he says:

> that John Webster . . . William Rowley, John Ford,
> and this defendant were privy consenting and acquainted
> with the making and contriving of the said play called
> Keep the Widow Waking and did make and contrive
> the same upon the instructions given them by one Ralph
> Savage. And this defendant sayeth that he this defend-
> ant did often see the said play or part thereof acted but
> how often he cannot depose. . . .[30]

More particular testimony as to how the four dramatists
worked together on their play is given by Dekker in his
answer as one of the defendants.

> . . . . and whereas in the said information mention is
> made of a play called by the name of Keep the Widow
> Waking, this defendant saith that true it is he wrote two
> sheets of paper containing the first act of a play called
> The Late Murder in Whitechapel, or Keep the Widow
> Waking and a speech in the last scene of the last act of
> the boy who had killed his mother. Which play (as all
> others are) was licensed by Sir Henry Herbert Master
> of His Majesty's Revels authorizing thereby both the
> writing and acting of the said play.[31]

Dekker testifies to the same kind of collaboration by acts
which is implied in the other contemporary statements

30. *Library*, 4th series, VIII (1927), 258.
31. Ibid., p. 257.

noted. He does not testify as to the parts written by his three collaborators, and the only other one of the authors cited in the suit was William Rowley, who died before his testimony could be taken. An equable division would have been the division of acts two, three, and four among Ford, Webster, and Rowley, with each man writing a scene or a long speech in the last act.

COLLABORATION between two or more dramatists, especially professional dramatists, was a common method of composition in the greatest days of the English drama. It was more common in the reigns of Elizabeth and James, but it was not unusual in the time of Charles I. Well-known collaborations like those of Beaumont and Fletcher or Middleton and Rowley or Shakespeare and Fletcher should not be looked upon as oddities, but as common occurrences in the careers of professional dramatists of the time. Indeed, it is probable that a number of plays actually contain the work of more men than the first known records indicate. *The Honest Whore*, *Sir John Oldcastle*, *Sir Thomas Wyatt*, and *The Late Murder of the Son upon the Mother* are clear examples of a simplification of authorship on title pages and in official records which is likely to have occurred more frequently than we yet know.

CHAPTER IX

Revision

REVISION IS ASSOCIATED with collaboration both in the problems it presents to the modern scholar and in the activities of the professional playwright. For the scholar the two are often entangled: in a given text which appears to present the work of more than one man, is the second (or third or fourth) hand that of a collaborator, or of a reviser who may never have known the principal author? Several playwrights, like Philip Massinger, are known to have performed both functions on the work of one principal dramatist; in *The Little French Lawyer* he was almost certainly a collaborator; in *The Lovers' Progress or Cleander* he was the reviser. In fifteen or sixteen plays of the Beaumont and Fletcher folios, though it is almost certain that he was either collaborator or reviser, it is usually not clear which; in a few it seems likely that he was both. But Massinger's revising activities are only those best known; they are by no means peculiar.

There were two exceedingly common kinds of occasions

for revisions of a dramatist's completed manuscript, revisions which occurred regularly in the theatres of the time. The first must have affected almost all manuscripts for pieces which were accepted for performance; the other probably affected nearly all plays which attained *success* in performance.

The first kind of revisions consisted of those which the prompter or book-holder made in the manuscript his company had bought in order to prepare it for use by prompters in the playhouse. There are not many literary allusions to these practices, but the thirty or so extant play manuscripts which show alterations or additions written in the theatre make it abundantly clear that such work on the playwright's manuscript was apparently invariable.[1]

The few literary allusions to the treatment of a dramatist's manuscript in the playhouse are mostly printed complaints about cuts. John Webster, who certainly authorized the publication in 1623 of the ten-year-old *Duchess of Malfi*, since he wrote a dedication to Baron Barkeley and collected commendatory verses from Middleton, Ford, and Rowley, presumably authorized the statement on the title page, "The perfect and exact copy, with diverse things printed that the length of the play would not bear in the presentment."

This record of the cutting of the dramatist's original text is duplicated by Richard Brome nearly twenty years later. At the end of the 1640 edition of his popular play *The Antipodes*, Brome appended a curious note:

> Courteous Reader, you shall find in this book more than was presented upon the stage, and left out of presentation for superfluous length (as some of the players pretended). I thought good all should be inserted according to the allowed original and as it was, at first,

1. See W. W. Greg, *Dramatic Documents from the Elizabethan Playhouses*, passim, but esp. 1, 189–221. See also C. J. Sisson's edition of Massinger's *Believe as You List* in the Malone Society series.

intended for the Cockpit stage in the right of my most deserving friend, Mr. William Beeston, unto whom it properly appertained. And so I leave it to thy perusal, as it was generally applauded and well acted at Salisbury Court.

Farewell, Ri. Brome.

The confusion about companies in this note derives from Brome's troubles over his playwright's contract with the Salisbury Court players,[2] and the slight animosity in the phrase "as some of the players pretended" reflects his irritation at what he thought was his ill-usage. Nevertheless he records the fact that *The Antipodes*, like *The Duchess of Malfi*, was cut for performance in the theatre.

Rather more animosity about the players' treatment of his text is shown by Thomas Nabbes in his dedication of *The Bride* to the gentlemen of the Inns of Court. The play had been acted by Queen Henrietta's company at the Phoenix two years before Nabbes published it in 1640 with the dedication. He says that *The Bride* "is here dressed according to mine own desire and intention; without ought taken from her that myself thought ornament, nor supplied with anything which I valued but as rags." These allusions to the prompter's alterations made by Webster, Brome, and Nabbes are simply records of a few occasions in which the usual theatrical cuts seemed excessive to the dramatists.

The other type of revision of dramatists' manuscripts in the theatres occurred when the actors prepared the play for a revival. There are a great many records of one sort or another of this common practice; even the general public seems to have taken it for granted.

When Thomas Campion published his *Fourth Book of Ayres* about 1612, he said in his Address to the Reader:

> You may find here some three or four songs that have been published before, but for them I refer you to the

2. The contract is discussed above, pp. 112–44.

players' bill that is styled, "Newly Revived with Additions" for you shall find all of them reformed either in words or notes.

And even the players took it for granted that their audiences were familiar with the custom of revision, whether it was admitted or not. The actor in the King's company who delivered the prologue at the opening of *The False One* about 1620 said:

> New titles warrant not a play for new,
> The subject being old; and 'tis as true,
> Fresh and neat matter may with ease be fram'd
> Out of their stories that have oft been nam'd
> With glory on the stage
>
> .   .   .   .   .   .
>
> What we present and offer to your view
> Upon their faith, the stage yet never knew.

Of course the prime consideration of the King's company here was that their audience should not think that this new play of Fletcher and Massinger about Cleopatra was a revision of Daniel's *Tragedy of Cleopatra*, or Brandon's *The Virtuous Octavia*, or Shakespeare's *Antony and Cleopatra*. Thomas May's *Tragedy of Cleopatra, Queen of Egypt* was not acted until five or six years later. Evidently they could assume that a Blackfriars or Globe audience would suspect a revised play when a familiar subject was dramatized. As Lupton said in his Character 20, entitled "Playhouses," in *London and the Country Carbonadoed and Quartered into Several Characters*, 1632, "They [the actors] are as crafty with an old play as bawds with old faces: the one puts on a new fresh color, the other a new face and name."

Shakerley Marmion, who had a good deal more experience with actors and theatres than Lupton ever had, develops the same figure and expands it with more detail. In act 2, scene 4 of *A Fine Companion*, acted by the Prince's company at Salisbury Court in 1632 or 1633, he makes his character Littlegood say:

Look you, here comes the old lecher! He looks as fresh as an old play new vampt. Pray see how trim he is, and how the authors have corrected him; how his tailor and his barber have set him forth; sure he has received another impression.

Thorough revision was sometimes frankly admitted rather than concealed. In 1634 Philip Massinger completely revised Fletcher's play, *The Lovers' Progress*, which had first been acted by the King's men in the winter of 1623. Massinger called the complete revision *Cleander*, but the prologue for the new version acted by the same company makes no attempt to conceal the fact that the play was an old one made over. The prologue actor says for Massinger:

A story, and a known one, long since writ,
Truth must take place, and by an able wit,
Foul mouth'd detraction daring not deny
To give so much to *Fletcher's* memory;
If so, some may object, why then do you
Present an old piece to us for a new?
Or wherefore will your professed writer be
(Not taxed of theft before) a plagiary?
To this he answers in his just defence,
And to maintain to all our innocence,
Thus much, though he hath traveled the same way,
Demanding, and receiving too the pay
For a new poem, you may find it due,
He having cheated neither us nor you;
He vows, and deeply, that he did not spare
The utmost of his strength and his best care
In the reviving it, and though his powers
Could not as he desired, in three short hours
Contract the subject, and much less express
The changes, and the various passages

> That will be looked for, you may hear this day
> Some scenes that will confirm it as a play,
> He being ambitious that it should be known
> What's good was *Fletcher's*, and what ill his own.

In the epilogue of this piece, along with the customary plea for applause, Massinger returns to the same undisguised discussion of aspects of the thorough revision of a Fletcher play and the presentation of it under a new title.

> Still doubtful, and perplexed too, whether he
> Hath done *Fletcher* right in this history,
> The Poet sits within, since he must know it,
> He with respect desires that you would show it
> By some accustomed sign, if from our action,
> Or his endeavors you meet satisfaction,
> With ours he hath his ends, we hope the best
> To make that certainty in you doth rest.

Such a prologue and epilogue show how misleading was Humphrey Moseley's publisher's blurb in the front matter of the 1647 Beaumont and Fletcher folio. Like so many publishers he claims a good deal more for the full and unaltered character of his texts than the facts warrant. Probably very few of the plays in the folio appear just as Beaumont and/or Fletcher wrote them. Revisions can be demonstrated in many of them, and Moseley himself had printed this revealing prologue and epilogue for *The Lovers' Progress*. Yet he said in his preface to "The Stationer":

> One thing I must answer before it be objected; 'tis this: when these *Comedies* and *Tragedies* were presented on the stage, the actors omitted some scenes and passages (with the authors' consent) as occasions led them; and when private friends desired a copy, they then (and justly too) transcribed what they acted. But now you have both all that was acted and all that was not; even the perfect and full originals without the least mutilation.

Moseley was trying to clear himself of the objections which some of his aristocratic readers who had manuscript copies of Beaumont and Fletcher plays might have made because of the differences between their copies and his printed texts. Fletcher plays were so popular that a number of such copies must have been in existence then, and several still are. Besides the two or three remaining playhouse manuscripts of these plays one can still examine private transcripts of just the sort Moseley mentioned: the Folger manuscript of *The Beggars' Bush*, Lord Harlech's manuscript of *The Humorous Lieutenant* entitled *Demetrius and Enanthe*, the Egerton manuscript of *The Elder Brother*, and the British Museum manuscript of *Sir John van Olden Barnavelt*.

Moseley covered himself against the protests of these owners of private transcripts, but his final statement about "the perfect and full originals without the least mutilations" is certainly untrue. It is doubtful that even the ten still living sharers of the King's company who signed the dedication to the Beaumont and Fletcher folio and who probably furnished Moseley with most of his texts had themselves ever seen "perfect full originals without the least mutilation" after the plays had been in active repertory for seventeen to thirty years.

In the reigns of Elizabeth, James, and Charles, only unacted or unsuccessful plays were likely to get into print in "the perfect full originals without the least mutilation." Probably we have one such—barring the usual printer's errors—in Samuel Harding's *Sicily and Naples, or the Fatal Union*. One of the writers of commendatory verses for this unacted play shows by his sneers not only his bias against theatres but what would have been expected had the text come from a playhouse. Nicholas Downey, after the usual comparison of his friend's work with that of the great Ben Jonson, says:

> Thine is exposed to the world's large eye,
> In its unchang'd and native infancy
> Before some Players brain new drenched in sack
> Does clap each term new fancies on its back.

Though Downey's phrase "unchang'd and native infancy" is apt in more ways than he intended, his notion of what happened to texts in the London theatres is not inaccurate except in its implied frequency. "Does clap each term new fancies on its back" alleges that for each of the three terms of the law courts (seasons important in theatrical economy) revisions of a popular play were made. This is surely an exaggeration, but it does reveal the popular assumption that plays regularly performed would be regularly revised.

Even the title pages of printed plays frequently give evidence that the following text certainly does not appear in "its unchang'd and native infancy." On the title page of the 1602 quarto of *The Spanish Tragedy* appears the statement, "Newly corrected, amended, and enlarged with new additions of the Painters part, and others, as it hath of late been divers times acted." Another revision of a popular play is announced on the title page of the third edition of *Mucedorus* in 1610. William Jones "dwelling near Holborn Conduit at the sign of the Gun," who had also published the first two editions, has added to this title page the statement "Amplified with new additions, as it was acted before the King's Majesty at Whitehall on Shrove Sunday night. By His Highness Servants usually playing at the Globe." A rough collation of the texts shows that this advertising statement is honest—there *are* additions and alterations.

The third edition of *The Malcontent*, printed like the first two editions in 1604, bears the title page statement, "Augmented by Marston. With the additions played by the King's Majesty's servants. Written by John Webster." Again a little examination of the text shows that an induction as well as other less conspicuous additions have been made to the text which had appeared in the two previous editions.

The frequently discussed additions to Marlowe's *Doctor Faustus* which were first printed in 1616 are not advertised in the edition of that year, but by the time he brought out his edition of 1619 John Wright had evidently concluded that the new material was worth advertising, and he added to the title page of that edition the statement, set off between rules, "With new Additions."

For the second edition of Chapman's *Bussy D'Ambois* in 1641, the publisher, Robert Lunne, had a title page printed with an unusually explicit statement: "Bussy D'Ambois: A Tragedy: As it hath been often acted with great applause. Being much corrected and amended by the Author before his death." The corrections and amendments do indeed appear in the text which Lunne had printed; whether the revisions had been made by Chapman, as asserted, is not quite so certain.

Early in the reign of James I, Thomas Heywood wrote for his company, Queen Anne's men, at the Red Bull, a successful play called *The Rape of Lucrece*. The play was printed five times, and evidently the songs were one of its popular features, for even the first edition carried an address to the reader which spoke of songs, "which were added by the stranger that lately acted Valerius his part." The fourth edition of 1630 contained various additions, including new songs, and the fifth edition of 1638 still more songs and more additions. This time Nathaniel Butter advertised the revisions on the title page, "The Rape of Lucrece. A True Roman Tragedy. With the several songs in their apt places, by Valerius the merry Lord among the Roman Peers. The Copy revised, and sundry songs before omitted, now inserted in their right places." One of the most explicit statements made by a Jacobean publisher about the revisions he found in his copy is that which John Trundle printed on the title page of the second issue of Middleton and Rowley's collaboration, *A Fair Quarrel*: "A Fair Quarrel. With new additions of Mr. Chaugh's and Tristram's Roaring, and the Bawd's song. Never before Printed. As it was acted by the Prince his Highness Servants." And he prints the new material as he has evidently received it, on additional pages bound in at the end and not distributed through the play, as it would have been when acted by Prince Charles's men before the King and on the public stage.

The majority of the plays of Beaumont and/or Fletcher were withheld from publication by the King's company which owned most of them until after the closing of the theatres, but a few were published in quarto, and two of the quartos advertise their revision. The second edition of *The Maid's Tragedy*, 1622, carried the title-page advertisement: "Newly perused, augmented, and enlarged. This second impression." A collation of this text with the previous one of 1619 shows a number of additions and alterations, as advertised.

A similar statement is found on the title page of the 1622 quarto of *Philaster*: "As it hath been diverse times acted at the Globe and Blackfriars by His Majesty's Servants. . . . The second impression, corrected and amended." And again collation verifies the advertisement, for the 1622 text shows a number of changes, including thorough revisions of the opening and the ending of the tragicomedy.

These sample statements of publishers on their title pages show the common knowledge that plays on the stage were regularly revised. And they show publishers frequently assuming that the reading public would be interested in buying the latest revisions which company dramatists had made for revivals of plays already in print. In those examples cited the advertisement of the publisher was honest, as a comparison of his text with the previous one shows. But the assumption of the publishers that readers with dramatic interests offered a better market for revised than for unrevised plays is equally demonstrated by the false advertisement of revisions. On the title page of the 1602 edition of Shakespeare's *Richard III*, Andrew Wise printed the claim, "Newly augmented." But he was lying in the hope of attracting new readers, for the edition was set up from his own 1598 text of the play. This dishonest tactic seems to have been successful, for Andrew Wise was only repeating what he had done before. In 1599 he had printed a third edition of *Henry IV*, part 1, with the title-page assertion, "Newly corrected by W. Shake-speare." Again there is no truth in his claim, for the text was set up from his own edition of the previous year.

Even after the closing of the theatres false claims about new texts were thought to be effective. In 1650 Francis Leake published another edition of *The Maid's Tragedy* with the statement on the title page, "The Sixth impression, Revised and Corrected exactly by the original." Though it is true, as we have seen, that *The Maid's Tragedy* had had a good deal of revision, as shown by a collation of the 1622 with the 1619 edition, Leake's text of 1650 does not differ from the two preceding editions.

As all readers of Shakespeare know, there are a good many plays which have come down to us in two or more editions, some of which, when collated, show extensive revisions. Yet the publisher either has not known about the revisions or has not chosen to advertise them. Examples can be seen in the 1633 (fourth) edition of Heywood's *The Second Part of If you know not me, You know nobody* and the 1616 edition of *Doctor Faustus*, which incorporated, but did not advertise, those revisions advertised on the 1619 title page.

Of course the great majority of plays acted in the London theatres between 1590 and 1642 were either not printed at all or appeared in only one edition, and we have no clue to the specific deletions, alterations, and additions they underwent during their years in repertory; but for a number some records of revision other than printed texts do exist. Generally the records clearly indicate that something was done to the play, but do not specify what it was. Henslowe several times speaks of "mending." On 15 February 1597/98 Anthony Munday had been paid £5 for his play *The First Part of Robinhood*, and the Master of the Revels had licensed both parts on 28 March following. Yet seven or eight months later the company decided that the play needed revision and Henslowe noted, "Lent unto Robert Shaw the 18 of November 1598 to lend unto Mr. Chettle upon the mending of the First part of Robinhood, the sum of . . . 10s."[3] Another play was handled similarly three years later. From July to November in 1601 William Haughton and John Day were paid £5 in four installments to write a play called *Friar Rush and the Proud Woman of Antwerp* for the Lord Admiral's company. After only two months, revisions were in order, and again Henry Chettle was paid for doing the work: "Lent unto Robert Shaw the 21 of January 1601/1602 to give to Henry Chettle for mending of the book called The Proud Woman, the sum of . . . 10s."[4] Sometimes we have evidence of more than one revision of a play. One of Henslowe's greatest outlays was on the two parts of *Cardinal Wolsey*, which he alternately called *The Rise of Cardinal Wolsey* and *The Life of Cardinal Wolsey*. The accounts for these plays seem to be confused in two or three instances, but from June to the middle of November 1601 Henslowe made at least 25 entries of payments for one or the other part of *Cardinal Wolsey*, and he laid out more than £60, mostly for new costumes. Two of these entries concern revisions; even such an expensive property as *Cardinal Wolsey* was expected to profit from further expenditures for revisions before it was a year old, and the Admiral's company authorized payments.

3. Foakes and Rickert, p. 101.
4. Ibid., p. 198.

Laid out at the appointment of my son and the company unto Harry Chettle for the altering of the book of Cardinal Wolsey the 28 of June 1601, the sum . . . 20*s*.

Lent unto Thomas Downton the 15 of May 1602 to pay Harry Chettle for the mending of the first part of Cardinal Wolsey, the sum of . . . 20*s*.[5]

The revisions of the anonymous *Tasso's Melancholy* come later in the play's existence than those Chettle made in *Cardinal Wolsey*. *Tasso* had been rather successful in the last half of 1594 and the first half of 1595 when Henslowe entered his part of the receipts at twelve performances. Evidently the leaders of the Admiral's company thought that the play might draw custom to the Fortune in 1602, and they authorized Henslowe to pay Dekker for two sets of alterations. It is suggestive that they were willing to invest in alterations about half what the play probably cost them in the first place.

Lent unto Thomas Dekker at the appointment of the company the 16 of January 1601[/1602] toward the altering of Tasso, the sum of . . . 20*s*.

Lent unto my son E. Alleyn the 3 of November 1602 to give unto Thomas Dekker for mending of the play of Tasso, the sum of . . . 40*s*.[6]

These four plays are lost and are now obscure, but a well-known and popular play like *Sir John Oldcastle*, which a publisher once tried to pass off as Shakespeare's, went through the same revisions. Philip Henslowe had paid Anthony Munday, Michael Drayton, Robert Wilson, and Richard Hathway the high price of £14 for the two parts of this play in October and December 1599. It started off so well in the theatre that the poets were presented with 10 shillings at the first performance. Yet within three years *Sir John Oldcastle* was being revised, as shown by

5. Ibid., pp. 175 and 200.   6. Ibid., pp. 187 and 206.

the entry: "Lent unto John Thare the 7 of September 1602 to give unto Thomas Dekker for his additions in Oldcastle, the sum of . . . 10s."[7]

Few plays have a record of greater success in the theatre than Marlowe's *Doctor Faustus*. Not only are there many allusions to it, but Henslowe's very incomplete performance records alone show that it was one of the best drawing pieces in the repertory. Yet, as is generally known, the play underwent extensive revisions. The diary has the entry: "Lent unto the company the 22 of November 1602 to pay unto William Bird and Samuel Rowley for additions in Doctor Faustus the sum of . . . £4."[8] When one recalls that many payments for "mending" or "additions" in these records were 10 shillings or 20 shillings and that at this time new plays brought £6 to £8, it is evident that Bird and Rowley must have revised rather extensively.

At least as popular as *Doctor Faustus* was *The Spanish Tragedy*, often called *Jeronimo*, yet it too underwent revisions probably more than once. Two entries in the accounts seem to indicate more than one stage in the alterations: "Lent unto Mr. Allen the 25 of September 1601 to lend unto Benjamin Jonson upon his writing of his additions in Jeronimo, the sum of . . . 40s." Nine months later there is a composite payment involving more changes in Kyd's play: "Lent unto Benjamin Jonson at the appointment of E. Alleyn and Wm. Bird the 22 of June 1602 in earnest of a book called Richard Crookback, and for new additions for Jeronimo, the sum of . . . £10."[9]

Even Jonson's own masterpieces, written after he had attained a great reputation and already in print, underwent the usual revisions in the theatre. *The Alchemist* had been part of the repertory of the King's company for nearly thirty years when Mrs. Ann Merricke wrote to her friend Mrs. Lydall: "I could wish myself with you, to ease you

7. Ibid., p. 216.   8. Ibid., p. 206.
9. Ibid., pp. 182 and 203.

of this trouble, and withall to see *The Alchemist*, which I hear this term is revised, and the new play a friend of mine sent to Mr. John Suckling and Tom. Carew (the best wits of the time) to correct. . . ."[10]

IN THESE QUOTED PAYMENTS to dramatists for alterations one cannot tell precisely what the revisers did to the plays in the repertories, but the word "additions" is the one which is most frequently used in reference to their activities. In the payments for *Doctor Faustus, The Spanish Tragedy*, and *Sir John Oldcastle* their work is called "additions," and elsewhere the term is common. "Paid unto Thomas Heywood the 20 of September [1602] for the new additions of Cutting Dick, sum of . . . 20*s*."[11]

In November and December 1602 and January and February 1602/1603 Henslowe had paid John Day, Richard Hathaway, Wentworth Smith "and the other poet," on behalf of the Earl of Worcester's men, for writing the two parts of *The Black Dog of Newgate*. A few months later, in February 1602/1603, part 2 was thought to need revisions. In this instance, contrary to the usual practice, the additions were made by the original authors of the play.

> Lent unto Thomas Blackwood the 21 of February 1602 [/1603] to give unto the four poets in earnest of their additions for the second part of The Black Dog, the sum of . . . 10*s*.

> Lent unto Thomas Blackwood the 24 of February 1602 [/1603] to give unto the four poets in part of payment for the additions in the second part of The Black Dog . . . 10*s*.

> Lent unto John Duke the 26 of February 1602 [/1603] to pay the poets in full payment for their additions for the second part of The Black Dog, the sum of . . . 20*s*.[12]

10. John Munro, ed., *The Shakespeare Allusion Book*, Oxford, 1932, 1, 443.

11. Foakes and Rickert, p. 216.   12. Ibid., p. 224.

Even in the texts of their plays the dramatists sometimes alluded to this common practice of supplementing plays well known in the repertory. In the first scene of the fifth act of Middleton's *Hengist King of Kent, or the Mayor of Quinborough* a group of confidence men or cheaters are passing themselves off as strolling players, and they discuss with the mayor the plays they might perform for him:

> *1 Cheat. The Cheater and the Clown.*
> *Symon.* Is that come up again?
>   That was a play when I was prentice first.
> *2 Cheat.* Aye, but the cheater has learned more tricks since, sir
>   And gulls the clown with new additions.

Plays could, of course, have even more extensive revisions than these examples indicate, and they could have been made by the original author for theatrical rather than literary reasons. On 11 January 1630/31 the Master of Revels recorded that "I did refuse to allow a play of Massinger's because it did contain dangerous matter, as the deposing of Sebastian King of Portugal by Philip the Second and there being a peace sworn twixt the Kings of England and Spain. . . ."[13] Massinger was at this time the regular dramatist for the King's company, and he completely revised and reset his play, as his extant manuscript shows. The original manuscript play concerned Sebastian, King of Portugal, who was supposed to have been killed in Africa in 1578, and whose throne was annexed by Philip II. Almost all evidences of this original setting and the names of the original characters have been excised by the dramatist for the King's company and the piece has been reset in Roman times and made to concern Antiochus the Great who was eventually defeated by the Romans in 191 B.C. The completely revised play was called *Believe as You*

13. J. Q. Adams, ed., *The Dramatic Records of Sir Henry Herbert*, New Haven, 1917, p. 19.

List; it was licensed for performance by the Master of the Revels on 6 May 1631 and was performed by the King's company. Like most plays of the time, it failed to attain print, and it is known from Massinger's most illuminating manuscript preserved in the British Museum.[14]

In the extant records of the Masters of the Revels there are also many accounts of the revisions of plays. But the interests of Henslowe and of the Masters in this constant play-doctoring were different. Henslowe needed to remember, primarily, how much money he had paid out in behalf of the company for the revisions. It was also helpful to him—though less important—to remember who had authorized the payments and who had done the revising. The Master of the Revels needed to remember first that he had passed on the revisions, and second how much he had been paid. Thus Henslowe always recorded the amount paid, usually the name of the reviser, though seldom what the reviser has done; whereas the Master of the Revels often set down what the revisions were, usually the fee paid him, but seldom the name of dramatists who had done the work for the acting company. As in all official or financial records, the bookkeeper was setting down the facts which might be useful for his own future reference, not, alas, those which would be most illuminating for posterity.

In 1624 Sir Henry entered his fee for allowing a revision of *The Virgin Martyr*. The play had been written four years before by Thomas Dekker and Philip Massinger for the company of the King's Revels acting at the Red Bull theatre. At that time there had been some trouble about censorable matter in the play, and Sir George Buc, Herbert's predecessor as Master of the Revels, had charged a double fee "for new reforming *The Virgin Martyr*." What Herbert allowed in 1624 was not the modification of censorable material, but an addition. "For the adding of

14. See the excellent edition of C. J. Sisson in the Malone Society Reprints, 1927.

a scene to *The Virgin Martyr*, this 7th July, 1624 . . .
10*s*."[15] This play had got into print two years before, probably because of the difficulties of the Queen Anne's–King's
Revels company, which was in a decline, and three plays
from its repertory were published in 1622. In 1624 the
company had declined to a provincial status, and it is not
known what organization paid the unknown dramatist—
and Sir Henry—for the additions to the play.

Five years later another extract from the office book of
the Masters of the Revels attests the addition of a full act
to an old play. Probably the Master had made a number
of such allowances in the five years, for it is difficult to
remember that we have only scattered extracts from Sir
Henry's accounts. The manuscript of his official records,
which was seen by Edmund Malone and George Chalmers
at the end of the eighteenth and the beginning of the nineteenth century, has since been lost, and we have only the
extracts these two scholars chose to make for illustrative
purposes; they were understandably interested mostly in
entries naming well-known plays or well-known dramatists. The following extract from the office book is not
characteristic of the usual interests Malone and Chalmers
displayed in the notes they published; in the original manuscript, however, it was probably more common. In this
entry Herbert mentions neither company nor dramatist,
but only the extent of the revision and the fee paid: "For
allowing of a new act in an old play this 13th of May
1629 . . . 10*s*."[16]

In another license for a revision four years later Sir
Henry is rather more informative. The play is Fletcher's
The Night Walker, whose date of original composition is
uncertain, perhaps about 1611. By 1633 it was in the hands
of Queen Henrietta's company, the owners of at least three
of Fletcher's plays, all first written for other Jacobean

15. Adams, *Herbert*, p. 29.
16. Ibid., p. 32.

companies before John Fletcher became the regular dramatist for the King's men. In 1633 *The Night Walker* was
revised, and the Master of the Revels in this instance
named the reviser as well as the allowance fee: "For a play
of Fletcher's corrected by Shirley called The Night Walk-
ers, the 11 May, 1633, £2. For the Queen's players."[17]
This revision must have been an extensive one, for Herbert's usual fee at this time for licensing alterations was
£1, and it was only for new plays that he was accustomed
to charge £2. Shirley had been for eight years the regular
dramatist for Queen Henrietta's company, and his revisions were very recent at the time of the license, for the
text of the play contains, in the third act, an allusion to
"the late Histriomastix," that is, William Prynne's sensational *Histriomastix, The Players' Scourge, or Actors'
Tragedy*, which was not published until 1633.

Three months later Christopher Beeston, the manager
of Queen Henrietta's company, was again in Herbert's
office on a double errand about another of the company's
old plays. This one was more than twenty years old, William Rowley's *Hymen's Holiday*. Herbert notes: "Received of Beeston for an old play called *Hymen's Holiday*,
newly revived at their house, being a play given unto him
for my use, this 15 August, 1633, £3. Received of him for
some alterations to it . . . £1."[18] In all likelihood the alterations were the work of the regular poet at the Phoenix in
Drury Lane, though Herbert does not name him as he had
done in *The Night Walker* entry three months before.
This revision was evidently a good job, for not only did
Sir Henry receive £3 as his share of the receipts, but the
company selected the play for a performance at court four
months later on 15 December, when it is said to have been
"Likte."

More informative than the records of the revision of
these plays in the 1630s are those for another one; this

17. Ibid., p. 34.   18. Ibid., p. 35.

time a play which was revised not *for* the King's company but for competition with them, "An old play with some new scenes, *Doctor Lambe and the Witches*, to Salisbury Court the 16th August, 1634 . . . £1."[19] Though the play is lost, this transaction is one which can be supplemented with other information. Doctor Lambe was a notorious London character, alleged to have been a conjurer, and widely hated and feared because he was an agent of the hated Duke of Buckingham. In June 1628 he had been attacked by a mob as he was leaving the Fortune theatre and stoned so mercilessly that he died of his injuries the next day. Because of his great notoriety (there are several accounts of his death, including a ballad on the subject) and because his patron and protector, the Duke of Buckingham, was assassinated two months later, Doctor Lambe was a prime subject for a topical play, like *Keep the Widow Waking*, or *The Old Joiner of Aldgate*, or *A Game at Chess*, or *The Whore New Vampt*. But the obvious time for such a play was late 1628 or 1629, not 1634. By 1634 Doctor Lambe was a stale subject, but there was a new popular scandal in the summer of that year which could be made to appear related to Doctor Lambe. This new scandal was that of the witches in Lancashire, who were brought to trial in London in the summer of 1634. The King's company at the Globe exploited this scandal in their play, *The Late Lancashire Witches*, written for them by Richard Brome and Thomas Heywood. The company at Salisbury Court had the same idea, but they were forestalled, as a petition in the Lord Chamberlain's warrant books makes clear.

> A petition of the King's players complaining of intermingling of some passages of witches in old plays to the prejudice of their designed comedy of the Lancashire witches, and desiring a prohibition of any others till

19. Ibid., p. 36.

theirs be allowed and acted. Answered per reference to Blagrave in absence of Sir H. Herbert. July 20, 1634.[20]

It seems very likely that the play the King's men complained of was *Doctor Lambe and the Witches*, revised from an old play about Doctor Lambe by an unknown dramatist at the order of the players of the Salisbury Court theatre. And Herbert's date, 16 August 1634, is near enough to one month after the petition of 20 July to show that the King's men's request of a month's delay had been granted.

It would be interesting to have the two versions of the Doctor Lambe play to compare as an example of revision techniques, but the extant evidence is enough to show one of the causes for revising plays, and the petition phrase "intermingling of some passages of witches" and Herbert's phrase "some new scenes" are enough to suggest something of the method of the unknown revising playwright.

Another allowance by Sir Henry in 1636 gives official confirmation of a charge often leveled against the actors: "bawds with old faces." This time Sir Henry gives the name of the man who brought in the manuscript, "old Cartwright." He is called "old" to distinguish him from his son and namesake, William Cartwright, who was also an actor at the Fortune. William Cartwright, senior, who had been a friend and associate of Edward Alleyn, was at this time a leading actor and probably the manager at the Fortune theatre in Golding Lane, in the parish of St. Giles-without-Cripplegate. Sir Henry's entry reads: "Received of old Cartwright for allowing the [Fortune] company to add scenes to an old play, and to give it out for a new one this 12th of May, 1636 . . . £1."[21] Unfortunately there is nothing in the entry to show what the Master of the Revels meant by "give it out for a new one"; he is not known

20. *Malone Society Collections*, II, part 3, 410.
21. Adams, *Herbert*, p. 37.

to have had any control over the playbill advertising of the company, nor over the admission prices charged at the theatres—generally double for a new play.

Sometimes the new additions or deletions in an old play are conspicuous in the text. A familiar example is the 1641 edition of Chapman's *Bussy D'Ambois*, published seven years after Chapman's death and thirty-three years after the last previous issue of 1608. Though the title page puffs the edition as "Being much corrected and amended by the Author before his death," there is some disagreement as to whether the 250-odd changes were made by Chapman or by another.[22] In any event there are extensive changes, and the prologue refers to at least three different productions, in one of which the lead was played by Nathan Field and in another probably by Eyllaerdt Swanston—at least he is known to have excelled in the role.

A better example of a quarto showing revisions of a text long after the original composition is the 1656 quarto of Thomas Goffe's pastoral comedy, *The Careless Shepherdess*, as produced at the Salisbury Court theatre about 1638. Though there are some obvious disturbances in its lines, the play proper reads like an academic production, perhaps for Christ Church, Oxford, where other of Goffe's plays were acted, but the long and interesting induction and the prologue were certainly not written by Goffe, for they are full of explicit and detailed references to conditions and practices at the Salisbury Court theatre. Goffe is not known to have had any experience of the London theatre, and the Salisbury Court, explicitly named as the setting for the induction, which refers to its actors, customs, rooms, and charges, was not yet built at the time of Goffe's death. In this case internal evidence in the play shows clearly enough that an old play by Thomas Goffe was revised for the

22. See Berta Sturman, *Huntington Library Quarterly*, XIV (February 1951), pp. 171–201, and Peter Ure, *Modern Language Review*, XLVIII (July 1953), pp. 257–69.

Salisbury Court theatre about 1638 by the addition of an induction and a prologue, and probably by other changes in the body of the play which are less obvious now.

In the case of *The Careless Shepherdess* we have a strong suggestion, though not final proof, as to who the revising dramatist was. In July 1635 Richard Brome had signed a contract with the acting company at the Salisbury Court theatre to be the company dramatist. The contract was for three years and it was renewed in August 1638. In the suit which was brought against Brome in February 1639/40, alleging breach of contract, Brome replied by reciting some of his regular activities as contracted dramatist for the company during the previous four years. He says that in addition to the new plays which he had written for the company at Salisbury Court "he hath made divers scenes in old revived plays for them and many prologues and epilogues to such plays of theirs, songs, and one Introduction at their first playing after the ceasing of the plague."[23] This statement of Richard Brome's shows clearly that alterations of and additions to the revived plays in the repertory of a company were the usual work of the regular dramatist at the theatre. Consequently when the name of the attached dramatist for a company is known, we have a strong suggestion of the identity of the author of the revisions made in that company's plays during his incumbency. It would be a neat dovetailing of records if one could believe that the induction for *The Careless Shepherdess* was the very "Introduction at their first playing after the ceasing of the plague" to which Brome refers. Probably, however, it was not. There is nothing about the plague in the induction to *The Careless Shepherdess* as there is in Thomas Randolph's *Praeludium* for this theatre at its reopening after a previous plague in 1630. Moreover, the reopening Brome refers to was on 2 October 1637, and several allusions in

23. Ann Haaker, "The Plague, the Theater, and the Poet," *Renaissance Drama*, n.s. 1 (1968), p. 305.

the induction to *The Careless Shepherdess* seem to refer to events a few months after that. Nonetheless, that induction is one of those company dramatist's chores which Brome specifically says that he was carrying out for the Salisbury Court theatre from 1635 through 1638.

Another of the chores of the company dramatist mentioned by Richard Brome is to be seen in many texts and references. This is the writing of new prologues and epilogues for revivals and for special occasions. Several of Henslowe's payments are for such special new material in a play already acted. After he had paid Henry Chettle on 18 November 1598 for "mending of the first part of Robinhood," another payment one week later shows further additions to prepare the play for a special occasion: "Lent unto Harry Chettle at the request of Robert Shaw the 25 of November 1598 in earnest of his comedy called 'Tis No Deceipt to Deceive the Deceiver [and] for mending of Robinhood for the court . . . 10s."[24] And the next year just before the court season Henslowe again recorded part of the company's preparation for a command performance, this time on their popular play *Fortunatus*, which had already been revised once a couple of weeks before: "Paid unto Mr. Dekker the 12 of December 1599 for the end of Fortunatus for the court at the appointment of Robert Shaw, the sum of . . . 40s."[25] And the same situation came up again in preparation for the court season of 1600–1601, when *Phaeton* seems to have required more work than *Robinhood* and *Fortunatus* did.

> Lent unto Samuel Rowley the 14 of December 1600 to give unto Thomas Dekker for his pains in Phaeton, the sum of . . . 10s.
>
> for the court

24. Foakes and Rickert, p. 102.
25. Ibid., p. 128.

Lent unto Samuel Rowley the 22 of December 1600 to give unto Thomas Dekker for altering Phaeton for the court . . . 30s.

Lent unto William Bird the 2 of January 1600[/1601] for divers things about the play of Phaeton for the court, the sum of . . . 20s.[26]

Even in the printed texts of plays there is much evidence of prologues and epilogues prepared not by the original dramatist for an opening performance, but by some other writer for a revival. Sometimes the new material is called "Prologue at the Reviving of this Play" or some such; sometimes there is only one prologue or epilogue printed, but that one refers to "some twenty years ago" or contains the lines

This Comedy, long forgot, some thought dead,
By us preserved, once more doth rise her head.

Now and then there is an even more explicit statement about the occasion of the revival for which the new prologue or epilogue has been written. A good example is the one for Fletcher's *Faithful Shepherdess*, which was first published in an undated quarto of about 1610. Various commendatory verses indicated that the play was a failure in its first production, but it had an elaborate revival twenty-three or -four years later when the Master of the Revels remarked that there "was presented at Denmark house, before the King and Queen Fletcher's pastoral called *The Faithful Shepherdess*, in the clothes the Queen had given Taylor the year before of her own pastoral."[27] And the new quarto of 1634 itself calls attention to some of the new material for the revival: "This Dialogue, newly added, was spoken by way of Prologue to both their Majes-

26. Ibid., pp. 137 and 138.
27. Adams, *Herbert*, p. 53.

259

ties at the first acting of this pastoral at Somersethouse on Twelfth Night, 1633."

There are other printed revival prologues and epilogues in the 1600 *Old Fortunatus*, the 1641 *Bussy D'Ambois*, the 1653 edition of Brome's *The City Wit*, as well as in the folio editions of *The Custom of the Country*, *The Elder Brother*, *The Noble Gentleman*, *The Coxcomb*, *Wit at Several Weapons*, *The Woman Hater*, *The Chances*, *Love's Cure*, and *The Nice Valor, or the Passionate Madman*. In his postscript for the 1647 folio, the publisher, Humphrey Moseley, who had been so insistent on the purity of his texts, even admits that "We forgot to tell the *Reader*, that some *Prologues* and *Epilogues* (here inserted) were not written by the *Authors* of this *Volume*; but made by others on the *Revival* of several *Plays*."

By far the most numerous and detailed studies of play revisions in the Elizabethan and Jacobean theatres are those of the texts of the plays of the principal dramatist of the Lord Chamberlain–King's company, William Shakespeare. Unfortunately for an understanding of the normal practices of professional dramatists in the time, these studies have an orientation not very helpful for the historian of the theatre. Dazzled by the genius of Shakespeare, scholars have inevitably concentrated on explications of his poetic achievements or on the misadventures of his creations in the printing houses. Both are rewarding and necessary; but, except for the often brash and generally discredited analyses of the disintegrators, most studies tend to take Shakespeare's plays out of the theatres for which they were created and to analyze them in the milieu of the lyric and philosophical poet and not in the milieu of the hard-working professional playwright devoted to the enterprise of the most successful and profitable London acting company of the time—or perhaps of any time.

Any detailed analysis of the demonstrable revisions of Shakespeare's plays before the closing of the theatres in

1642 would throw completely out of balance such a survey as this one, but the collations of his texts which have now gone on for more than two centuries are sufficiently familiar to make summarizing references intelligible.

Half the plays are known in one text only, since the King's men withheld them from publication until 1623, and they can furnish evidence of revision only through exacting and often not wholly satisfying analysis. The familiar fact of this single text, post-mortem publication of half Shakespeare's plays—a fact so mysterious to the anti-Stratfordians and to anachronistic critics—should be regarded as normal in the context of the Jacobean theatre with which Shakespeare was so intricately involved. The unusual event is the appearance of the first folio at all.

During Shakespeare's lifetime, under normal conditions —that is when the company was solvent, as the Lord Chamberlain–King's company always was, and the dramatist honest and modest—the acting company kept the manuscript which the playwright had sold to them in their own archives and out of the hands of the printers. Unsuccessful plays and plays too antiquated to revise were another matter; they could be sold to publishers as dead wood cleared out of the repertory. Publishers, of course, not infrequently secured play manuscripts in spite of the objections of the legal owners, through theft, dishonest dramatists, or private transcripts which the company had sanctioned in order to please important patrons. The fact, therefore, that half Shakespeare's known plays were first published in 1623 is evidence that these plays were successful at the Blackfriars and the Globe and therefore worth keeping exclusive in their repertories and also that they belonged to an acting company solvent enough to sell only what they did not want and powerful enough to discourage unfriendly publishers and unscrupulous rival theatres. It is illuminating to note in this context how the publication of Shakespeare's plays divides at about 1599. Before this date the company was pressed by competitors, especially the Lord Admiral's men. In 1599 the building of the new and handsome Globe signalized the new dominance of the company, which was seldom seriously challenged thereafter. And this new dominance was illustrated by their ability to withhold their plays from publication. By 1600 the King's men had influence enough to keep other companies from performing their plays even if they were in print, and the King's men themselves helped to arrange the publication of the first folio not for profit, but "onely to keepe the memory of so worthy a Friend & Fellow aliue, as was our SHAKESPEARE," as the leaders of the company, John Heminges and Henry Condell, say in their dedicatory epistle to the Earls of Pembroke and Montgomery.

But even in these limiting circumstances we have fairly clear evidence of revisions in the texts of the majority of Shakespeare's plays. The fact has been somewhat obscured because most Shakespearean scholars have been less interested in the clear evidence that the play has been revised at some time or other than in the much more difficult problem of who wrote what lines and when. For 25 of the plays in the canon we have some evidence that the text has undergone a revision. In eight or nine the evidence for revision is rather slight, as is the evidence for cutting in *All's Well* and *Measure for Measure* and for interpolation in the vision scene in *Cymbeline*—but in 16 of the plays there are clear differences in texts which go beyond printing-house variants, as in the added scene in *Titus*, the added lines in *Henry IV*, part 2, and *King Lear*, and the differences between the second quarto and the folio versions of *Hamlet*. The normal revision of plays kept in the repertory of a successful company is generally, though not invariably, exemplified in the extant texts of the plays of Shakespeare.

ALL THIS SCATTERED EVIDENCE makes it clear that if a play had sufficient theatrical appeal to be kept in the repertory of an Elizabethan, Jacobean, or Caroline acting company, it was normal for the text to be revised for at least one of the revivals. This revision would usually have been made—at least in the more settled Jacobean and Caroline days—by the regular dramatist for the company. In the only specific references to the contract of such a dramatist, he was required by the terms of his contract to doctor the old plays for revivals. Such a dramatist's knowledge of the personnel of the company made him the best-qualified writer for such a service, since a common change would have been the adjustment of lines or songs or scenes to any actors who may have succeeded those for whom the originals had been designed. Further changes to adjust to altered tastes or to exploit current scandals, as in *Doctor Lambe and the Witches*, or to delete political allusions which had become dangerous since the original appearance of the play, must have been frequent, but less invariable than adjustments to the company of actors.

On the basis of the extant evidence one can safely say that all the attached professional dramatists must have been involved in the revision of plays—their own as well as other men's—for the refurbishing of old plays in the repertory seems to have been the universal practice in the London theatres from 1590 to 1642. As a rough rule of thumb one might say that almost any play first printed more than ten years after composition and known to have been kept in active repertory by the company which owned it is most likely to contain later revisions by the author or, in many cases, by another playwright working for the same company.

CHAPTER X

Publication

SINCE THE PLAYS of the Elizabethan dramatists have customarily been read and analyzed as literary documents for the study rather than as working scripts for the theatres, the normal practices of those writers of plays who were the regular employees of the theatres—the group of attached professional dramatists—have been obscured by the publishing habits of unattached professionals like Ben Jonson, John Marston, John Ford, and William Davenant, or even amateurs like Lodowick Carlell or Jasper Mayne.

In general the attached professionals refrained from publication without the consent of the acting troupe for which the play had been written and whose property it was. Many circumstances could elicit the consent of the company, and others could frustrate its objections. Disbanded companies or bankrupt companies, or even financially hard-pressed companies either were in no position to object to the dramatist's sale of his script to a publisher or in their desperation sold it themselves. John Charlewood recorded one such occasion in the address to the reader which he printed with his edition of Lyly's *Endymion* in 1591:

> Since the plays in Paul's were dissolved, there are certain comedies come to my hands by chance, which were presented before her majesty at several times by the Children of Paul's. This is the first, and if in any place it shall displease, I will take more pains to perfect the next. I refer it to thy indifferent judgment to peruse, whom I would willingly please. And if this may pass with thy good liking, I will then go forward to publish the rest. . . .

Even more eloquent of a situation in which the company had to give up control of its plays is the publication in 1647, after all hope of the revival of the theatres had been abandoned, of 34 of the carefully guarded, twenty- to forty-year-old, unpublished manuscripts of Beaumont and Fletcher. This publication is most explicit in its evidence of official company consent, since the dedication of the collection is signed by all ten of the surviving actor-sharers of the King's company, which had so long and so successfully withheld them from publication, and the "Address to the Reader" was written by the last regular dramatist for the company, James Shirley.

Similarly indicative of the relaxation of company restraints in times of distress is the appearance in print of an unparalleled number of plays by professional dramatists during and immediately after the disastrous plague of 1636–1637, when the theatres were closed and the companies in distress for all but one week of 17 months. In the four years 1637, 1638, 1639, and 1640, 60 plays by the professional dramatists appeared on the London bookstalls, whereas in many of the previous years not a single one had been printed; and in no previous period of four years had so many as half this number of plays by professional dramatists come into print.

Even the attached professional dramatists themselves several times ushered into print the plays they had written for a particular company *after* their relations with that company had been broken. This phenomenon is apparent in the patterns of publication of Richard Brome and James Shirley, as will be noted presently. And in the canons of the regular professional playwrights there are several examples where company consent to publication appears to have been given for the printing of plays which had failed in the theatre or which had outlived their audience appeal. A consideration of the publication records of a few dramatists will support these generalizations.

The only contract so far discovered between an attached professional dramatist and the acting company and theatre owners who employed him is, as we have seen, the one which Richard Brome signed on 20 July 1635 and renewed for seven years in August 1638. In the suit against Brome the entire contract is not quoted, but both parties cite certain portions of it, including the section on publication. The company says that this part of the contract stipulated that Richard Brome

> should not suffer any play made or to be made or composed by him for your subjects or their successors in the said company in Salisbury Court to be printed by his consent or knowledge, privity, or direction without the license from the said company or the major part of them.[1]

1. Haaker transcript, p. 298. Explicit indications of the objections of other companies to the publication of the plays which had been written for them are to be seen in Henslowe's payment in March 1599/1600 of the large sum of 40 shillings to "staye the printinge" of *Patient Grissell*, which had been written for the company by Dekker, Chettle, and Haughton three or four months before.

The sharers in the Whitefriars theatre had the same attitude toward publication a few years later when they made their agreement of 10 March 1607/1608, in which Item 8 stipulates:

> Item, it is also covenanted, granted, concluded and fully agreed between the said parties . . . that no man of the said company

In his reply to his employers Brome made no protest about this section of his contract; the company, which accused him of a number of other violations, never accused him of failure to observe this stipulation, and the records of his rather numerous publications show that he never did violate it. That is, during the period the contracts were in force, 1635–1639, he published no plays and no piece of his was entered in the Stationers' Register.

Brome's abstention is notable in the publishing records, for this period was a very active one for the printers of plays. During the full five years of his contracts, the London publishers entered nearly one hundred plays in the Stationers' Register, and well over forty written by professional dramatists appeared in print. And it is not that Brome was averse to publication, for in the three years *before* his contracts he had published two plays, and in the twenty years *after* his contracts, twenty of his plays were either entered in the Stationers' Register or printed or both. Not only this, but immediately after the abrogation of his contract Brome had three plays in the hands of the printer, Francis Constable, who entered them together in the Stationers' Register on 19 March 1639/40. Two of them, *The Antipodes* and *The Sparagus Garden*, were plays which had been written for the Salisbury Court under his contract,

---

shall at any time hereafter put into print . . . any manner of play book now in use, or that hereafter shall be sold unto them upon the penalty and forfeiture of £40 sterling or the loss of his place and share of all things amongst them, except the book of *Torrismount*, and that play not to be printed by any before twelve months be fully expired (*Transactions of the New Shakespeare Society*, 1887–1892, p. 276).

In later years the better companies themselves persuaded the Lord Chamberlain to forbid the publication of their plays without their consent, and that official wrote such letters for the King's men in 1619, and for the King's men and for the King and Queen's Young company in June 1637 (see *Malone Society Collections*, II, part 3, 384–85).

and they were published with Brome's consent and supervision, as signed dedications, commendatory verses, and an address to the reader show. The third play, *Wit in a Madness*, probably had the same history, but one cannot be certain, since it was never published and the only references to it are in the Stationers' Register.

These various facts add up to the conclusion that Richard Brome, an attached professional playwright not averse to publication when not under contract to the contrary, carefully refrained from giving the printers any of his plays written under his contract to the Salisbury Court theatre so long as that contract was in force, but that as soon as the agreement was abrogated, he immediately gave the manuscripts of two or three of those plays to Francis Constable for publication.

Finally, there is evidence that when Brome left the Salisbury Court for William Beeston's company at the Phoenix or Cockpit in Drury Lane—the lawsuit says at a higher salary than his previous pound a week—he similarly refrained from publication of the plays he wrote for his new employers. Though Brome had seven plays in the hands of the printers in 1640–1642 (the years he presumably continued to write for Beeston) none of them was a Cockpit play. But after the closing of the theatres when all contracts of players and playwrights were in abeyance, at least three of the plays he wrote for his new employers appeared in print, *The Court Beggar*, *The Jovial Crew*, and *A Mad Couple Well Matched*.[2]

Though Brome's contract is the only extant written record of an attached professional dramatist's agreement to refrain from publishing those plays he wrote for them without the company's consent, there is a good deal of evidence that other regular professionals were working under like restrictions. James Shirley's writing and publication show a similar pattern.

2. *Jacobean and Caroline Stage*, III, 61–65, 70–73, 80–81.

In 1640, 1641, and 1642 Shirley regularly delivered an autumn play and a spring play to King Charles's company, presumably under contract. The plays were *Rosania or the Doubtful Heir*, *The Impostor*, *The Politic Father or the Brothers*, *The Cardinal*, *The Sisters*, and *The Court Secret*.[3] Now during the three years that Shirley wrote for the King's company at the Blackfriars and the Globe he certainly did not refrain from *any* publication. In the year 1640 alone, six of his own plays and one of Fletcher's, which Sir Henry Herbert had allowed with Shirley's revisions in 1633, were published, but all of them were plays he had written for his *former* companies, either Queen Henrietta's men at the Phoenix or the St. Werburgh Street theatre in Dublin. But none of the six plays he wrote for the King's men did he give to the printers while he was regular dramatist for the company.

All six plays did achieve print, but not until long after the King's men as a London troupe were no more. In 1653 Humphrey Robinson and Humphrey Moseley brought out *Six New Plays. . . . The First five were acted at the Private House in Black Fryers with great Applause. The last was never Acted. All Written by James Shirley*. Robinson and Moseley certainly printed with Shirley's cooperation, for each play has a separate address or dedication signed by the author. These are all the plays he wrote for the King's company, carefully withheld from publication until eleven years of suppression had killed all hope for a revival of the old days.

Before he left for Ireland during the long plague closing of 1636–1637, Shirley had been the ordinary poet for Queen Henrietta's company at the Phoenix since 1626. His writing and publication pattern in those years is similar, but not quite so clear.

During the eleven years he was attached to the Phoenix

3. Ibid., v, 1105–7, 1123–25, 1082–84, 1084–88, 1147–49, and 1100–2.

theatre, Shirley wrote 20 or 22 plays for them—20 were eventually published as performed by Queen Henrietta's men at this theatre, and two others, *Look to the Lady* and *The Tragedy of St. Albans*, were entered in the Stationers' Register in February and March 1639/40 but are now lost and may or may not have been written for Beeston's company. These plays constitute about half of all the new plays—i.e., not revivals inherited from previous companies—in the repertory of this prominent troupe in the years 1625–1636, and the spring and autumn regularity with which they were produced make Shirley's attachment to the company, probably contractual, quite clear.[4]

It is also clear that Shirley, a dramatist who saw to it that nearly all his plays eventually got into print, was exercising restraint during the years he was writing regularly for the Phoenix. The restraint was not total as it was during the three years he was attached to the King's men, but at least thirteen of Queen Henrietta's plays were kept out of the hands of the publishers until he had left the company and gone to Ireland, and then all thirteen were issued between 1637 and 1640, a clear indication of self-restraint during his term as ordinary poet for Queen Henrietta's company.

During these eleven years, seven of Shirley's plays did appear in print, but one of them, *The School of Compliment*, though later acted by Queen Henrietta's men, was originally licensed by the Master of the Revels in February 1624/25, before the company was formed, and was therefore evidently not subject to their agreement with Shirley. Another, *The Changes*, was written for a different troupe, His Majesty's Revels's company, and licensed in January 1631/32. This was Shirley's only play written for a company other than his own during the term of his attachment. I can only guess that there was some irregularity

4. See the company repertory, *Jacobean and Caroline Stage*, I, 250–59 and 226–27, n. 7.

(possibly the expiration of one seven-year contract and disagreement about the terms of a new one). At any rate, his
regular sequence of plays for the Queen's company was
only briefly broken, for his *Love's Cruelty* was licensed to
be performed by them two months before *The Changes*,
and *Hyde Park* three months after.

This leaves five of the 20 or 22 plays written for the
Phoenix which were nevertheless published during Shirley's incumbency. They were *The Wedding*, published
1629, *The Grateful Servant*, 1630, *The Witty Fair One*,
1633, *The Bird in a Cage*, 1633, and *The Traitor*, 1635.
None was surreptitiously printed, for each carries a dedication signed by the author; one, *The Wedding*, gives the
cast of Queen Henrietta's men, and three contain sets of
verses commending Shirley. Evidently the company allowed the publication of these five, though not of the other
fifteen. One can only speculate as to what the reasons may
have been.

Philip Massinger's attachment to the King's company
from sometime after Fletcher's death in August 1625 to
his own death in March 1639/40 shows a pattern of composition and publication similar to Shirley's, except that
Massinger, thirteen years the elder, had been writing plays
for at least thirteen years before he achieved his regular
attachment to the King's men, whereas Shirley was ordinary poet at the Phoenix almost from the beginning of his
play-writing career. Before Fletcher's death, Massinger
had written plays for the Lady Elizabeth's company (*The
Honest Man's Fortune*, *The Renegado*, *The Bondman*,
The Parliament of Love) and for the companies at the Red
Bull (*The Virgin Martyr*, *The Maid of Honor*) as well
as a number of collaborations, generally with Fletcher, for
the King's company.

Indeed, Massinger's contribution to the Beaumont and
Fletcher plays are so numerous—he contributed to perhaps
as many as twenty plays—that one might suspect that his

contractual relationship with the King's men had begun before Fletcher's death. But there are several facts which make such a relationship in the early years doubtful. Since the great majority of the Fletcher plays in question were never published during the lifetimes of either Fletcher or Massinger, and since most of them offer only stylistic and not *external* evidence of Massinger's participation, there is the greatest uncertainty as to how much of Massinger's work in these plays was collaboration, and how much revision which may have been done as one of his normal chores after he became regular dramatist in succession to Fletcher. Indeed, several of these plays showing work of both Fletcher and Massinger have prologues or epilogues in the 1647 folio which explicitly call attention to the fact that they are revisions. In the second place, during the years 1615–1625 Massinger wrote several plays for other companies—*The Old Law* and *A New Way to Pay Old Debts*, as well as the six already mentioned for the Lady Elizabeth's men and the Red Bull companies. The powerful King's company would scarcely have allowed a contracted dramatist to write eight plays or more for rival, if inferior, London troupes.

On the whole, therefore, it seems likely that though in the years 1615 to 1625 Massinger did a good deal of work for the King's company—collaborations not only with Fletcher but with Nathan Field as well—he did not have a contract to work exclusively for them as Fletcher did, but only replaced Fletcher, probably in 1626.

From 1626 to 1639 the evidence that Massinger was the "ordinary poet" for the King's company is fairly clear. In these fourteen years he certainly wrote seventeen or eighteen unaided plays for them at fairly regular intervals; he revised at least three of Fletcher's late, perhaps unfinished, plays, *The Elder Brother*, *Love's Cure*, and *Cleander*, as well as others less certain; and some of his lost and unassignable plays, *The Tyrant*, *The Honor of Women*, *Fast* and *Welcome, The City Honest Man, The Painter,* and *The Prisoners,* are likely to have been part of his regular work for King Charles's company in these years.

None of his numerous plays at this time can be assigned to any other company, with the single exception of *The Great Duke of Florence,* which was licensed to be performed by Queen Henrietta's men at the Phoenix in July 1627. This manuscript may originally have been prepared earlier for performance at this same theatre by the predecessors of the Queen's men, for whom Massinger had written three plays in 1623 and 1624,[5] but in the current state of our knowledge we must allow it as the single exception to the exclusiveness of Massinger's work for the King's men.

The evidence of his publication in these years suggests that Massinger, like Brome and Shirley, had an agreement not to publish without their consent any of the plays he wrote for the company. At first glance he seems to have published too many plays between 1626 and 1639 to allow any such belief, but a little analysis of the Massinger publications of these years suggests the contrary. Nine of his plays appeared on the bookstalls in this period. But three of them, *The Renegado, A New Way to Pay Old Debts,* and *The Maid of Honor,* had been written for other companies before 1626, and a fourth, *The Great Duke of Florence,* was certainly written for another company, though the date may be later. A fifth, *The Elder Brother,* is really a Fletcher play in which Massinger probably collaborated, though only Fletcher's name appears on the title page of the 1637 edition. This is the only play of the nine which was printed without a dedication signed by the author or reviser. I doubt that Massinger had anything to do with the publishing of this play.

The Unnatural Combat was published by John Waterson in 1639 with a dedication by Massinger in which he

5. *Jacobean and Caroline Stage,* iv, 786–88.

calls it "this old Tragedy," and makes play with old and
new fashions. Such evidence as can be collected suggests
that it was probably a play of the early 1620s written before Massinger became regular dramatist for the company
or had any agreement with them about withholding his
plays from the printers.[6]

The remaining three plays, *The Roman Actor*, published
1629, *The Picture*, 1630, and *The Emperor of the East*,
1632, were all published with Massinger's cooperation, for
they all carry dedications signed by the author and all have
commendatory verses which one may assume that the
author collected. Since Massinger certainly wrote at least
seventeen or eighteen plays for the company in these years,
and very likely several of the undatable and lost ones as
well, the publication of only three out of the twenty to
twenty-five indicates some restraint on the part of a playwright as interested in publication as Massinger's numerous
dedications show that he was. I suspect that these three
plays were all published with the consent of the King's
men.

The Roman Actor certainly was, for one of the sets of
commendatory verses printed in the 1629 quarto was
signed by Joseph Taylor, who was a leading sharer in the
company and the principal manager of their affairs in 1629
with John Lowin and who had played the lead in the company's production of *The Roman Actor*.[7]

The Emperor of the East, published in 1632, was ill received in the theatre, as two of the three sets of commendatory verses in the quarto explicitly point out. It is therefore not at all surprising that, since the play had been
shown to be unpopular in the theatre, Lowin and Taylor
should have agreed to its publication soon after performance, as the Stationers' Register entry eight months after
Herbert's acting license suggests.

6. Ibid., IV, 821–24.
7. Ibid., II, 590–98.

274

The Picture, 1630, like *The Emperor of the East*, was printed about a year after Sir Henry Herbert had allowed it to be acted. There are no records of its performance, as there are for many of Massinger's plays, and it was never reprinted, though Waterson, its publisher, assigned it over to Thomas Walkley. I suspect that it too was a failure in the theatre and that the company was willing to see it published.

In sum, then, the records of Massinger's play production strongly suggest that, like Brome and Shirley, he was working under a contract which restrained him from publishing without their consent any of the plays he wrote for the King's men in the years 1626–1639.

Massinger's predecessor as regular dramatist for this company was the extremely popular John Fletcher, as has already been mentioned. Though Fletcher was a prolific dramatist, he was clearly not a publishing dramatist: he is known to have had a hand in about 69 plays, but only nine of them were published in his lifetime. This withholding of 87 percent of his compositions from the printers reveals something of his professionalism as a dramatist: he was writing for the theatre audience, not for readers. A little analysis of the publishing circumstances of those nine plays which did appear in print throws into even stronger relief his attitude as the chief dramatist of King James's company toward publication of the plays he had written for them.

Fletcher's dramatic compositions which the Jacobean public was allowed to read during his lifetime were *The Woman Hater*, *The Knight of the Burning Pestle*, *Cupid's Revenge*, *The Scornful Lady*, *The Faithful Shepherdess*, *Philaster*, *A King and No King*, *The Maid's Tragedy*, and *Thierry and Theodoret*. Only one of the nine offers evidence that Fletcher had anything to do with its publication. Four of them were printed with no author's name on the title page; five were printed with no front matter at all—dedications, addresses to readers, commendatory poems, epistles—though such front matter was used in these years by Jonson, Middleton, Marston, and Webster, and later (for plays published outside their contracts) by Shirley, Brome, and Massinger. The front matter in the other three (excepting *The Faithful Shepherdess*) comes from the publisher, not from the author.

When we look at these plays one at a time, Fletcher's care in withholding from publication without their consent those plays he wrote under his exclusive arrangements with the King's company becomes quite evident.

The Woman Hater was not written for the King's men, but for the Children of Paul's: the anonymous title page of the 1607 quarto records, *"As it hath been lately Acted by the Children of Paules."*

The Knight of the Burning Pestle, though it may have been the work of Francis Beaumont alone, is also a play for a boy company, and the dedication to Robert Keysar signed by the publisher, Walter Burre, shows one route by which plays came into print without any cooperation from the author. Robert Keysar was the lessor of the Blackfriars theatre for the last three years before the King's men took it over, and for three or four years he had been manager of the company of the Children of the Queen's Revels. Burre says that Keysar preserved the play after it had failed in the theatre and "you afterwards sent it to me"; Burre had kept it for two years and then printed it. No author is involved in the transaction.

Cupid's Revenge was also performed by a boy company: the title page of the 1615 quarto notes, "As it hath beene diuers times Acted by the Children of her Maiesties Reuels." The play is printed with Fletcher's name on the title page, but he had nothing to do with the publication. Though the publisher, Thomas Harrison, is not, like Walter Burre, considerate enough to tell us exactly how he got his manuscript, he is kind enough to say in his signed address to the reader:

'Tis the custom used by some writers in this age to dedicate their plays to worthy persons, as well as their other works. . . . But not having any such epistle from the author (in regard I am not acquainted with him) I have made bold myself, without his consent, to dedicate this play to the judicious in general.

The Scornful Lady is a fourth play from the series which Fletcher wrote for boys, "As it was Acted (with great applause) by *the Children of Her Maiesties* Reuels." Though Beaumont and Fletcher are named as authors on the 1616 title page, there is no front matter and no indication of their involvement in the publication. Like several other plays originally written for boys (e.g., *The Silent Woman, The Conspiracy and Tragedy of Charles Duke of Byron, The Faithful Shepherdess*), this one eventually came into the hands of the King's men, and their name is substituted on the title page of the 1625 quarto, but the text is simply the old one reprinted.

The Faithful Shepherdess, published in 1609 or 1610, is the only play of nearly seventy in the Fletcher canon which shows clearly that the author himself was concerned in its publication. He wrote and signed three separate dedications; he wrote and signed an address to the readers; and he collected commendatory verses from his friends Francis Beaumont, Ben Jonson, Nathan Field, and George Chapman. The familiarity of this interesting front matter for *The Faithful Shepherdess* has obscured the fact that such care in presenting a play to readers is unique in the prolific career of John Fletcher. The piece was written for a boy company, and it attained early publication because it was a failure in the theatre, and because Fletcher and his friends, smarting over the failure, were eager to point out its misunderstood character as a pastoral tragicomedy. All the verse writers and Fletcher himself point to the failure of the play on the stage. Evidently the company which owned the piece was not eager to keep it exclusive in their repertory. Unhappily Fletcher had long been dead when his pastoral tragicomedy was presented at court, nearly thirty years later, before King Charles and Queen Henrietta Maria, in costumes which the Queen herself had given to the King's men for the production.

In addition to these five plays never composed for the King's men and therefore not subject to any publication agreement with them, four of the plays which Fletcher *did* write for the royal troupe came into print before he died, *A King and No King*, 1619, *The Maid's Tragedy*, 1619, *Philaster*, 1620, and *Thierry and Theodoret*, 1621. Since he is known to have written alone or collaborated in at least forty-two plays for the company, this small number in itself bears witness to some publication restriction, but an examination of the four texts themselves demonstrates even more. None of the four shows any evidence of the cooperation of the author—no author's dedication, address to the readers, epistle, or commendatory verses. Three of the four do not even have any dramatis personnae, the simplest aid an author, or even a publisher, can provide for a printed play.

The one piece which does have any front matter is *A King and No King*, published in 1619 with a title page asserting that it was "Acted at the Globe, by his Maies*ties* Se*ruants.* Written by *Francis Beaumont* and *Iohn Fletcher*" and "Printed for Thomas Walkley." The only front matter printed with this quarto, which does not have even a list of characters, is an epistle written and signed by the publisher Thomas Walkley. He wrote to Sir Thomas Neville: "I present, or rather return unto your view, that which formerly hath been received from you, hereby effecting what you did desire. . . ." Thus we have explicit testimony that the manuscript of *A King and No King* was not conveyed to the printer by the author or by the acting company, but that Sir Thomas Neville gave Walkley for publication a manuscript which had presumably been made for his private library, since the text shows no sign that it had been set up from a prompt copy.

This analysis of the publication of John Fletcher's plays shows that though his compositions were among the most highly reputed of the productions at Blackfriars, he did not, during the course of his fifteen or eighteen years of exclusive work for the King's company, himself put a single one of them into the hands of the printers. Furthermore, the sharers of the King's company were successful in keeping more than 90 percent of his compositions for them from reaching the hands of the printers by any means—legitimate or illegitimate—during the reign of James I. These facts reflect some nonpublishing arrangement between an ordinary poet and his dramatic company at least as clearly as do the similar ones in the careers of Richard Brome, James Shirley, and Philip Massinger.

John Fletcher's predecessor as regular playwright for the King's company was William Shakespeare. The publishing history of the plays he wrote for the company, though more complex and though studied in infinitely greater detail than the others, is basically the same as the others we have surveyed in its conformity to the patterns of the professional dramatist. In some ways it is even more straightforward: from the formation of the Lord Chamberlain's company in 1594[8] to Shakespeare's death in 1616 there is no evidence that he ever wrote any play for any other company—a longer period of fidelity than that known for any other dramatist, and one which was never interrupted, as Massinger's, Shirley's, and Brome's appear to have been.

Shakespeare's pattern is again like that of the other at-

8. It is possible that the plays written *before* 1594 were also prepared for this company in its earlier form. But the precise antecedents from which the Lord Chamberlain's men were derived are so obscure and confused that it is safer and simpler to begin with 1594. See Chambers, *William Shakespeare,* I, 57–64.

tached professionals in that he did not himself take to the printers any of the plays he wrote for the Lord Chamberlain–King's company. When his plays were published they appeared without any indication of the author's sponsorship—no dedications, no epistles, no addresses to the readers, no commendatory verses from friends, not even a list of characters, and for most of them neither prologue nor epilogue. Moreover, the multitudes of textual studies of his plays during the last two hundred years have accumulated so many scores of obvious errors in all the quartos that one can be sure no author proofread the sheets at the printing house. Nor can it be hypothesized that the numerous errors may derive from an author who really *was* interested in the publication of his plays, but who was temperamentally careless about the dull chore of proofreading. This cannot have been the temperament of William Shakespeare, for he did take great pains with his text when he published his poems. In *Venus and Adonis*, 1593, and *The Rape of Lucrece*, 1594, he not only provided dedications but gave his readers excellent texts, far cleaner than those displayed in any of his play quartos. In whatever manner Shakespeare's several plays may have come into the hands of the printers before 1616 (and the possible methods are various) it is reasonably clear that he himself refrained from ushering them into print in the fashion of so many of his contemporaries in these years—Ben Jonson, John Marston, Samuel Daniel, Barnabe Barnes, John Day, Lewis Machin, Thomas Middleton, Nathan Field, Thomas Heywood, John Webster, John Stephens, Wentworth Smith, Thomas Dekker.

Shakespeare's conformity to the regular professional's pattern of refraining from publishing the plays he had prepared for his company is shown not only by the character of the texts of the plays which did get into print during his lifetime, but equally by the number of those which had never appeared on the bookstalls by 1616. At the time of his death slightly more than half his plays remained in manuscript in the archives of the company for which he had prepared them.

THE DRAMATISTS whose publications have so far been discussed had fairly settled careers with well-established companies. But in any activity so precarious as the commercial presentation of plays, it is not usual for organizations to have such long periods of success and prosperity as did the Lord Chamberlain–King's company and Queen Henrietta's men. Much more characteristic of theatrical annals are the obscure histories of such troupes as the Earl of Leicester's men, the Earl of Pembroke's men, the Palsgrave's men, the Lady Elizabeth's men, the Red Bull–King's company, the King's Revels company, and the troupe of Prince Charles [II]. A number of plays are known to have been written for these organizations, but the facts of their histories are so obscure and confused that little can safely be deduced about their relations to the composition and publication of the plays written for them.

But something of the customary pattern of relationship to his regular company, the Earl of Worcester–Queen Anne's men, can be seen in the publications of Thomas Heywood. Most eloquent of his restraint is the fact that in his long life Heywood could have seen in print fewer than twenty plays with his name on the title page. Since Heywood himself said eight years before his death that he "had either an entire hand or at least a main finger" in 220 plays, these figures alone make quite clear his attitude toward the publication of the plays he wrote for his regular company. But twenty-five years before he recorded the number of plays he had written or contributed to, Heywood made an explicit statement about a regular professional playwright's publication of his plays.

In 1608 John Busby and Nathaniel Butter brought out *The Rape of Lucrece* with a title page bearing Heywood's name and the production statement, "Acted by her Maiesties Seruants at the Red Bull." For this edition the author wrote an address to the reader:

It hath been no custom in me of all other men (courteous readers) to commit my plays to the press: the reason, though some may attribute it to my own insufficiency, I had rather subscribe in that to their severe censure, than by seeking to avoid the imputation of weakness, to incur a greater suspicion of honesty: for though some have used a double sale of their labors, first to the stage and after to the press, for my own part I here proclaim myself ever faithful to the first [i.e., Queen Anne's company] and never guilty of the last. Yet since some of my plays [i.e., *If You Know Not Me You Know Nobody*, part 1, 1605, part 2, 1606, *A Woman Killed with Kindness*, 1607, and perhaps others not attributed to Heywood on their title pages] have (unknown to me, and without any of my direction) accidentally come into the printer's hands and therefore so corrupt and mangled (copied only by the ear) that I have been as unable to know them as ashamed to challenge them. This therefore, I was willinger to furnish out in his native habit: first being by consent [i.e., with the permission of the rightful owners, Queen Anne's company] next because the rest have been so wronged in being published in such savage and ragged ornaments. Accept it courteous gentlemen, and prove as favorable readers as we [i.e., Heywood himself and the other members of Queen Anne's company] have found you gracious auditors.

Yours, T. H.

One of these plays printed without any cooperation by the author, or, presumably by Queen Anne's men who owned it, was *If You Know Not Me You Know Nobody, or the Troubles of Queen Elizabeth*. The play had first been published in 1605, and it was reprinted in 1606, 1608, 1610, 1613, 1623, 1632, and 1639. Sometime before 1637

this old, frequently reissued piece was revived at the Phoenix by Queen Henrietta's men, a company which had inherited several plays of the repertory of the long defunct
Queen Anne's men. For this revival of his old play Heywood wrote a prologue making explicit application of the
charge about unauthorized publication which he had made
in his address to the reader in the 1608 quarto of *The
Rape of Lucrece*. He published this prologue in 1637 in
his collection of miscellaneous verse, translations, and play-
lets called *Pleasant Dialogues and Dramas*.

> Plays have a fate in their conception lent,
> Some so short liv'd, no sooner showed than spent:
> But born today, tomorrow buried, and
> Though taught to speak, neither to go nor stand.
> This (by what fate I know not) sure no merit,
> That it disclaims, may for the age inherit,
> Writing 'bove one and twenty; but ill nurst.
> And yet received as well performed at first,
> Graced and frequented, for the cradle age,
> Did throng the seats, the boxes, and the stage
> So much that some by Stenography drew
> The plot, put it in print (scarce one word true)
> And in that lameness it hath limped so long,
> The Author now to vindicate that wrong
> Hath took the paines, upright upon its feet
> To teach it walk, so please you sit and see't.

Heywood's own statements in 1608 that he refrained
from publishing his plays because such conduct would bring
on him "a greater suspicion of honesty" and that such publication by other dramatists constituted "a double sale of
their labors, first to the stage and after to the press" show
his acceptance of an obligation of restraint. And he further
proclaims himself "ever faithful to the first," that is, the
acting company for which he wrote, Queen Anne's men. In
spite of these explicit declarations, he was concerned with
the publication of four other plays, *The Golden Age*, pub-

lished in 1611, *The Silver Age*, 1613, *The Brazen Age*, 1613, and *The Four Prentices*, 1615, before the final blow to his company, the death of its patron in 1619. The last play was not given to the printer by Heywood, for he says in a dedication that it was fifteen or sixteen years old and

> written many years since, in my infancy of judgment in this kind of poetry, and my first practice; yet understanding (by what means I know not) it was in these more exquisite and refined times to come to the press, in such a forwardness ere it came to my knowledge that it was past prevention, and knowing withall that it comes short of that accurateness both in plot and style that these more censorious days with greater curiosity require, I must thus excuse.

The Golden Age also came to the printer without the knowledge of the author, who says in his address to the reader in the 1611 quarto, "This play coming accidentally to the press, and at length having notice thereof, I was loathe (finding it my own) to see it thrust naked into the world, to abide the fury of all weathers, without either title for acknowledgement, or the formality of an Epistle for ornament."

The other two plays, *The Silver Age* and *The Brazen Age*, were both printed by Nicholas Oakes in 1613. Both were printed with addresses to the reader by Heywood, and neither address indicates that they had come to the press without the knowledge of the playwright. They were probably old plays, and they may have been published with the consent (and perhaps to the profit) of the other sharers of Queen Anne's company, who were beginning to experience those financial difficulties which plagued them for years and led to a series of lawsuits.[9]

Though Heywood was attached to a company more

9. See *Elizabethan Stage*, II, 237–40, and *Jacobean and Caroline Stage*, I, 158–70.

obscure and less successful than the companies of King James and King Charles and that of Queen Henrietta Maria, and though his own canon contains far more lost plays than those of Brome, Shirley, Massinger, Fletcher, and Shakespeare, the evidence which is extant suggests that his observation of restraints on publication of those plays he wrote for his regular company was similar to that of those better-known attached professional playwrights. No one knows how many of his 220 plays had been written for the Worcester–Queen Anne's men, but surely well over half, for he was a leading member of the organization for more than half (and the most active half) of his writing life. After the final disappearance of this struggling troupe, Heywood cannot be shown to have been regular dramatist for any company. He did write several plays for the companies of his former colleague Christopher Beeston at the Phoenix, two or three for the King's men, and a number of Lord Mayor's pageants, and he published seven or eight plays in the 1630s, but there is no evidence of a later contractual attachment.

LEST IT BE SUPPOSED that such attitudes toward publication as these of the attached professional dramatists may well have been characteristic of most playwrights of the period, it may be helpful to give a little attention to the very different publication patterns of a few well-known dramatists who evidently were *not* attached to major acting companies. John Marston is a good example.

For six or seven years at the beginning of the seventeenth century Marston was producing plays fairly regularly; indeed, his output of about two a year was not unlike that of Brome, Shirley, Massinger, Fletcher, and Shakespeare; but he soon gave up play-writing, and for twenty-five years or more appears to have had nothing to do with the stage. But though his output for a time was rather like that of these professionals, his publication pattern was entirely different, as a little attention to dates and quartos will show.

The Marston canon offers fewer problems than the canons of a number of his contemporaries. Eliminating two or three dubious attributions which have been made on stylistic grounds, we find that Marston had a hand in twelve plays, if we include *Jack Drum's Entertainment*, *Histriomastix*, and *Satiromastix*. None has been lost; all twelve were printed during Marston's lifetime, indeed, twenty years or more before his death; all but one or two were published within three years of composition. All but the three doubtful ones were printed with Marston's name or initials on the title page. One-third of them were printed with addresses or dedications signed by Marston; three others have arguments or Latin mottoes or inductions or dramatis personnae which strongly suggest, though they do not prove, the participation of an author. The contrast here with the publishing records of those attached professionals who were Marston's contemporaries—Heywood and Shakespeare—is rather striking.

Similar to Marston in the pattern of his theatrical activities was William Davenant, though he wrote during the reign of Charles instead of at the end of the reign of Elizabeth. Between 1626 and 1639/40, before the closing of the theatres, Davenant wrote eleven plays and five masques. Though he produced plays at a slower rate than the regular professionals, he was like them in staying with one acting company, King Charles's men, who performed nearly everything he wrote. Davenant's publication pattern, however, is different from those of the regular dramatists for this company, Shakespeare, Fletcher, Massinger, and Shirley. None of his plays escaped publication, as did many of those of Fletcher and Massinger, and at least two of Shirley's. About half of them were in print within two or three years of their first performance. Davenant himself was certainly concerned with the publication of at least five of them, for he furnished dedications which he signed, and for three of them he collected commendatory verses. In spite of the fact that his plays were regularly produced by the King's men, Davenant probably had no contract with them; he shows no resolve, as Fletcher and Shirley did, to keep them out of the hands of the printers.

Another Caroline dramatist who produced a good number of plays but did not exercise the attached professional's publication restraint was John Ford, who wrote about sixteen plays (excluding *An Ill Beginning* but including *The London Merchant* and *The Royal Combat*) between 1621 and 1638. Six of them are lost. Of the remaining ten, two of which were collaborations whose manuscripts Ford may not have possessed, three did not achieve print until a decade or two after the author's death. The remaining seven plays were all printed with Ford's cooperation. For all of them he prepared dedications which he signed, and for four of them he collected commendatory verses. Again there is no evidence of publication restraint. Though in the early 1630s Ford wrote five plays for Christopher Beeston's companies at the Phoenix theatre, all five were published with signed dedications within a very few years of performance.

Another writer of plays who showed no hesitation in offering them to the printers shortly after performance was Thomas Nabbes. He wrote seven plays and a masque during the thirties, when Massinger, Shirley, and Brome were functioning as ordinary poets for the principal London companies and restricting their publication of the plays they wrote for their companies. All Nabbes's plays were printed in the years 1637 to 1640; and in 1639, two years before his death, there was even a sort of collected edition, an odd assembly which Sir Walter Greg called a "nonce collection." This consists of copies of the eight dramatic compositions, some with cancel title pages, bound together with a joint title page reading *Plays, Maskes, Epigrams, Ele-*

gies, and Epithalamiums. Collected into One Volume.[10]
Nabbes was not a closet dramatist, for five of his plays have
statements on their title pages informing readers that they
had been performed by Queen Henrietta's company or by
Beeston's Boys. All the plays, including the two apparently
unacted ones, were published with the cooperation of the
playwright, who wrote and signed dedications for seven of
them. The eighth, *Hannibal and Scipio*, was printed two
years after performance with a cast of Queen Henrietta's
men and two sets of verses about the play, one of which,
"To the Ghosts of Hannibal and Scipio," is signed by the
playwright.

Though Nabbes furnished plays for Queen Henrietta's
company fairly regularly during a short period, he seems
to have had no contractual obligation to them as James
Shirley did, and he certainly showed none of Shirley's restraint in taking to the London printers the pieces he had
prepared for the stage at the Phoenix.

By far the most distinguished of the unattached dramatists of the period was Ben Jonson, and his eclectic attitude
toward the London acting companies, as well as his publication patterns, are in sharp contrast with those of Shakespeare, Heywood, Fletcher, Massinger, Shirley, and
Brome.

The most obvious reflection of this eclecticism is the variety of companies which produced his plays: the Lord Admiral's company, the Queen's Revels boys, the Lord Chamberlain's company, the Children of the Chapel, King James's
company, the Lady Elizabeth's company, King Charles's
company, and Queen Henrietta's men. And finally there
are two unfinished plays, *The Sad Shepherd* and *Morti-
mer His Fall*, which were never acted at all. The only
long period when all his plays were acted by the same

10. W. W. Greg, *A Bibliography of the English Printed Drama
to the Restoration*, 4 vols., London, 1939–1959, III, 1098–99.

troupe was 1616 to 1632, when there is no record of any Jonsonian play being given to any company except the King's men. But this record reflects the obvious choice of the most distinguished company by the most distinguished playwright, certainly not an attachment as an ordinary poet, for there are only four certain plays (with the possible addition of contributions to *The Widow* and *The Bloody Brother*) in a period of seventeen years. And for nine years in the middle, 1617 to 1625, there are no plays at all.

Furthermore, Jonson did not think of himself as a servant of the commercial theatres. Fortunately he was so highly articulate, so self-conscious, and so aware of posterity that he left in print an unparalleled number of statements about his conception of himself and of his art.[11] No one who reads through these numerous statements—often arrogant in their independence—can fail to be struck, or even amused, by the violent contrast with the attitude of the attached professional, as expressed by Thomas Heywood:

> . . . I had rather subscribe in that to their severe censure, than by seeking to avoid the imputation of weakness to incur a greater suspicion of honesty; for though some have used a double sale of their labors, first to the stage and after to the press, for my own part I here proclaim myself ever faithful to the first and never guilty of the last.

Unfortunately Jonson's unique statements about himself and his work are so much more widely known and discussed than this one, more characteristic of the regular professionals, that many erroneous deductions about the unstated attitudes of other professionals have been derived from them.

Finally, Jonson's publication patterns are quite unlike those of Heywood, Shakespeare, Fletcher, Massinger,

11. See James D. Redwine, Jr., *Ben Jonson's Literary Criticism*, Lincoln, Neb., 1970.

Shirley, and Brome. Most conspicuously abnormal was his collection and publication of his own plays in *The Workes of Beniamin Jonson*, 1616. Never before had plays from the commercial theatres been collected in a single volume, much less published under the aspiring title "Workes." The pretentiousness of the volume, the elaborate engraved title page with its theatrical and symbolic figures, the Latin motto, the numerous sets of commendatory verses, several of them in the language of learning, the formal table of contents, the inclusion of eighteen masques and entertainments prepared for nobility and royalty with plays from the commercial theatres—all this constituted a direct claim to status and permanence unprecedented in the English theatre world and quite foreign to the practices of the attached professional dramatists.

But even before his careful preparation of the folio of 1616 Jonson had himself seen to the publication of most of his plays. Four of the early ones written for Henslowe, mostly collaborations, *Hot Anger Soon Cold*, *Robert II*, *King of Scots*, *The Page of Plymouth*, and *Richard Crookback*, he chose to suppress and never mentioned in his numerous discussions of his work. But the other plays were all published, usually soon after performance, and with clear evidence of the author's participation in the publication project: *Every Man Out of His Humor*, printed in 1600, with a Latin title-page motto and elaborate characters for the dramatis personnae; *Cynthia's Revels*, 1601, with Latin mottoes; *Every Man in His Humor*, 1601, with Jonson's Latin motto as well as his name on the title page; *Poetaster*, 1602, with a Latin motto and a Latin address to the reader; *Sejanus*, 1605, with a signed dedication and commendatory verses; *Volpone*, 1607, with dedication and commendatory verses; *Catiline*, 1611, with a signed epistle and commendatory verses; and *The Alchemist*, 1612, also with a signed epistle and commendatory verses. The only

ones appearing before the folio without clear evidence of
Jonson's participation are *The Case is Altered*, 1609, and
Jonson's collaboration with George Chapman and John
Marston, *Eastward Ho!* 1605. A presumed edition of *Epi-
coene* of 1612 has been lost.

The publication of Jonson's plays written after the appearance of the 1616 folio is less regular, but the pattern
of his production and publication shows no more of the
attitude of the regular professionals than does the earlier
pattern. From 1616 to 1625 he produced no new play,
though he does say that in his fire in 1623 "parcels of a
Play" were destroyed. In the twenty-five years between the
performance of the last play in the 1616 folio, *Catiline*,
and his death in 1637, only six new plays by Jonson
reached the London stage, four performed by the King's
men in 1616, 1626, 1629, and 1632, *Bartholomew Fair* by
the Lady Elizabeth's company in 1614, and *A Tale of a
Tub* by Queen Henrietta's men in 1633. Three were prepared for publication by the bedridden Jonson, apparently
in a project for a second folio,[12] and were printed in 1631.
Two others, *The Magnetic Lady* and *A Tale of a Tub*, did
not appear until the second folio, four years after Jonson's
death, but again the text appears to have been prepared by
the author.[13]

Jonson's independence of the commercial theatres and
his deep involvement with the preservation of his plays
and his ideas for posterity sets him apart not only from all
the attached professional dramatists, but from nearly all
the other writers of his time. In his attitude toward his
text and toward the significance of the drama he is more
Edwardian than Jacobean.

12. See Jonson's correspondence, Herford and Simpson, *Ben Jonson*, I, 211, and discussions of texts of the three plays, VI, 3–8, 145–
54, 273–76.
13. Ibid., VI, 501–504 and III, 3–6.

THIS ANALYSIS of the publication patterns of eleven dramatists seems to me to show fairly clearly that there was a distinct difference between the attitudes toward publication displayed by the attached professional dramatists on the one hand, and by those professional writers for the commercial theatres who evidently had no contractual relation with the acting companies for which they wrote on the other. Only in the case of Richard Brome is there extant evidence of a written contract forbidding the dramatist to publish without the company's consent. Yet a study of the timing and sponsorship of the publication of their plays by Shirley, Massinger, Fletcher, Shakespeare, and Heywood seems to me to show that they must have had understandings with the companies to which they were attached that were not unlike Brome's written contract with the players at the Phoenix. It is equally evident that John Marston, William Davenant, John Ford, Thomas Nabbes, and Ben Jonson, who were certainly paid for their plays, observed no such restraint.

Index

293

328

THE PROFESSION OF PLAYER
IN SHAKESPEARE'S TIME, 1590-1642

PRINCETON UNIVERSITY PRESS

The Profession
of Player in
Shakespeare's Time
1590-1642

GERALD EADES BENTLEY

All Rights Reserved
Library of Congress Cataloging in Publication Data
will be found on the last printed page of this book
ISBN 0-691-06596-9

Publication of this book has been aided by the
Whitney Darrow Fund of Princeton University Press

This book has been composed in Linotron Janson
Clothbound editions of Princeton University Press books are
printed on acid-free paper, and binding materials are
chosen for strength and durability

Printed in the United States of America by
Princeton University Press, Princeton, New Jersey

For G.B.E., Jr.

Contents

Preface

THIS BOOK is planned as a companion to *The Profession of Dramatist in Shakespeare's Time*. Its purpose, like that of its predecessor, is to set forth, as fully as I can, what was normal in the conduct of one of the two major components in that phenomenal creative outburst we call the "Elizabethan Drama." Most of the great flood of modern studies concerning that astounding florescence are confined to single dramatists or single plays or single themes in a limited group of writings for the theater during the reigns of Elizabeth, James, and Charles. Too many such studies simply assume conditions of composition or performance for their plays that would have been highly abnormal, if not impossible, in the theatrical milieu of late sixteenth- and early seventeenth-century London. If these two studies can help to indicate the *usual* conduct of the Elizabethan playwrights and their employers, they will have accomplished their purpose.

My use of the word "player" instead of "actor" may seem eccentric to some readers; indeed, I had at first injudiciously intended to use the title "The Profession of Actor in Shakespeare's Time." But the more I went over my notes and pored over contemporary documents, especially lawsuits and parish records, the more it was borne in upon me that such a choice would be somewhat anachronistic as well as inaccurate. Since the word "actor" has been the term in most common usage for a theatrical performer for more than three centuries now, it is understandable that we should assume that the usage was the regular Elizabethan, Jacobean, and Caroline one. It was not. "Player" and "playing" are the standard usages in these three reigns. Though "actor" is sometimes used by the printers and occasionally in the texts of plays, in the profession itself "player" was the normal term. The evidence for this seems to me overwhelming, and I set it forth here.

The most extensive single document concerning theatrical dealings of the time is the so-called Diary of Philip Henslowe. Since the majority of Henslowe's diversified dealings were with theater people, he seldom found it necessary to record their occupations; even so, he—or his witnesses—use the term "player" or "players" more than a score of times, never "actor."

Probably our best index to common usage is the London parish registers. Most of the theatrical performers in London during the reigns of Elizabeth, James, and Charles appeared in these registers sooner or later, and the entries were set down by a variety of parish clerks during the fifty-two-year period 1590-1642. Usually the extant registers are mere lists of names under the headings "Marriages," "Christenings," and "Burials," but in at least three parishes the clerks normally gave the occupations of male parishioners. In the registers of the populous parish of St. Giles Cripplegate, where so many of the performers at the Fortune theater lived, the different parish clerks used the term "player" to designate the occupation of a parishioner over 150 times, but I did not encounter "actor" at all. At St. Saviour's Southwark, home of so many of the performers at the Globe, the Hope, the Swan, and the Rose, the registers call them "players" more than 80 times, but never "actors." At St. Botolph's Aldgate, different clerks used "player" about 30 times, sometimes varied to "stage-player," but never "actor."[1] Since these records were set down by a variety of parish clerks over a period of more than half a century in different parts of London, "player" was evidently the standard professional designation in the parishes.

The government official most constantly engaged with all professional players and their performances was the Master of the Revels. Few records of the Masters before 1622 are extant, but for 1622 to 1642 there are copious extracts from the Office Book of Sir Henry Herbert. In his accounts, though, he usually calls the acting troupes "The King's Men" or "The Queen's Servants"; he calls them "players" over 50 times, "actors" never.

Even in papers written after 1660 when he was trying to reestablish himself in his old office and when the word "actor" was in more general use, Sir Henry writes "player" five or six times as often as he writes "actor." Thus Sir Henry Herbert, the man in most constant contact with all affairs theatrical during the latter part of our period, uses, like all the parish clerks noted, the standard popular term "player" and not "actor."

The common use of the term "player" was by no means confined to the metropolis. Giles Dawson studied the local records of thirteen towns in the County of Kent and found many hundreds of payments to entertainers of one sort or another.[2] In these various records the term "player" is used between 700 and 800 times; "actor" not at all.

---

[1] "Records of Players in the Parish of St. Giles Cripplegate," *PMLA* 44 (1929), 789-826; "Shakespeare's Fellows," *Times Literary Supplement*, 15 November 1928, p. 856; "Actors' Names in the Registers of St. Botolph's Aldgate," *PMLA* 41 (1926), 91-109.

[2] "Records of Plays and Players in Kent, 1450-1642," *Malone Society Collections* 7 (1965).

This invariable usage in the thirteen towns of Kent was not peculiar to the South. The practice in Yorkshire and in the great houses of the North was the same as in the borough records of Kent. Professor Lawrence Stone published "Companies of Players Entertained by the Earl of Cumberland and Lord Clifford, 1607-39."[3] These thirty-one records were set down by different stewards in three northern castles of the family. In 29 of the accounts the stewards used the designation "player" for the visiting entertainers; "actor" does not appear in these records at all.

Professor Bernard Beckerman has called my attention to the fact that the few casts or lists in the quartos and folios before 1642 all use the word "actor" except Ben Jonson's early editions, which use either "Tragœdians" or "Comœdians." Of course these examples are very few compared with the many hundreds of uses of the term "players." I can only guess that "actor" seemed less tainted with the contemporary commercial theater and that it was perhaps preferred by some printers. Nevertheless, the accumulated evidence seems to me to be clear that "player" was the word in normal use by the profession and by the general public from 1590 to 1642.

In my consideration of the profession of player I have considered the apprentices of the major London troupes, but not the children of the boy companies who were so prominent around the turn of the century. Good as these boys may have been for short periods, they were not true professional players, they were not paid for their acting. Most of them were singers who were pressed to act by certain masters. Or they were schoolboys whose performance of plays was not their primary activity. There is no evidence that these boys ever had anything to do with the administration of their activities, the selection of their plays, or any profit which might accrue from their endeavors. The boy companies were an astonishing activity of their time, and they certainly had an influence on the adult professional companies for a period, as the famous

---

[3] *Malone Society Collections* 5 (1960), 17-28.

passage in the Folio edition of *Hamlet* shows; however, they were not really professionals, though a few of them, like Nathan Field, later became professionals.

This book is not designed as a collection of contemporary records concerning players, but as an organization and interpretation of these documents, though there are a fair number of previously unpublished contemporary records transcribed. In order to make these records as clear as possible, I have generally modernized the spelling, capitalization, punctuation, and abbreviations in the transcriptions of lawsuits, financial records, letters, contracts, charters, court reports and such. For literary work of major writers there may be some risk in modernization, but I see few hazards, and I hope it will be a boon for many readers for me to regularize Philip Henslowe's play title "The Jeylle of dooges" to "The Isle of Dogs" or "the sute of Tho: Woodford compl^t againste Aaron Holland def^t vpon the mocon . . ." as copied by the clerk of the Jacobean Court of Requests, into "the suit of Thomas Woodford, complainant, against Aaron Holland, defendant, upon the motion. . . ."

There is an exception to this modernization rule in the appendix. In the extant early casts (especially in the Plots and prompt manuscripts), abbreviations, nicknames, and eccentric spellings are common, and sometimes mutilation leaves names incomplete. In view of the resulting uncertainties it has seemed less misleading to reproduce the original than to rely on my own solution to a puzzle.

My principle of organization has been to consider first the relations between the player and his company; then the three components of all adult companies—sharers, hired men, and apprentices; then three aspects of the players' activities—managing, touring, and casting; and then an attempt to draw some of the material together in a summarizing statement.

For hospitality during the pleasant task of accumulating evidence I am grateful to the Public Record Office, the Guildhall Library, the Bodleian Library, the Huntington Library, the Folger Library, and to the Clark Library, which made me a Fellow.

For help in the more onerous chore of selecting and organizing this evidence I have received suggestions and advice from Bernard Beckerman, Mary Ann Jensen, William.A. Ringler, Jr., and especially from David Bevington, whose unstinted help has gone far beyond scholarly obligations.

In the many stages of book-making from manuscript revision to proofreading under difficult conditions I have enjoyed the shrewd and patient help of my wife.

G.E.B.

Princeton
13 December 1983

THE PROFESSION OF PLAYER
IN SHAKESPEARE'S TIME, 1590-1642

CHAPTER I

Introduction

T HE PHENOMENAL popularity of English theatrical entertainment in the half century from 1590 to 1642 is vaguely
known to many, though perhaps not fully realized even by
many writers on dramatic subjects. During these years there
were professional performances of English plays *in English* not
only all over Britain, from Folkstone and St. Ives to Aberdeen
and Edinburgh, but in Germany, Holland, Belgium, Denmark, Poland, and even in France.

This unusual popularity of the London theater was recognized at the time by travellers. Fynes Moryson wrote in the
second part of his *Itinerary*, licensed for printing on 14 June
1626:

The City of London alone hath four or five companies of
players with their peculiar theatres capable of many thou-

sands, wherein they all play every day in the week but Sunday, with most strange concourse of people. . . . as there be, in my opinion, more plays in London than in all the parts of the world I have seen, so do these players or comedians excel all others in the world.[1]

Though there were many amateur performances, especially in the schools, at local fetes, at noblemen's houses, and in nearly all the thirty or forty colleges at Oxford and Cambridge, the vast majority of the performances were in the hands of professionals. During this half century more than a thousand players are known by name.[2] And it is likely that there were many others, for more than one hundred of these thousand named players are identified as such from the chance survival of only a single record. That record, usually a citation in a lawsuit or a parish register, sets down the profession of the man as "player" or "stage-player." New names keep turning up, and they are often those of men of some achievement in their profession. Simon Jewell, a sharer in Queen Elizabeth's company, was unheard of until Mary Edmonds published his will in 1974.[3] Two sharers in Queen Anne's company were totally unknown until references to them were discovered in the testimony of the dramatist Thomas Heywood and of the distinguished player Richard Perkins in the 1623 Chancery suit of *Ellis Worth and Thomas Blaney v. Susan Baskervile and William Browne.* (See Chapter III, "Sharers.")

An enterprise so popular and so allegedly profitable as this inevitably developed certain standards or customs of organization, of procedure, of remuneration, of division of labor, of conduct, of hierarchy, of the acquisition of property, and even

---

[1] Charles Hughes, ed., *Shakespeare's Europe: A Survey of the Condition of Europe at the End of the 16th Century, Being Unpublished Chapters of Fynes Moryson's Itinerary (1617)*, 2nd ed., New York, 1967, p. 476.

[2] See Edwin Nungezer, *A Dictionary of Actors and of Other Persons Associated with the Public Representation of Plays in England before 1642*, New Haven, 1929; supplemented by G. E. Bentley, *The Jacobean and Caroline Stage*, 7 vols., Oxford, 1941-1968, II.

[3] *Review of English Studies* 25 (1974), 129-36.

of providing for the widows of deceased members. These customs and the evidence for them are the subject of this book.

Generally speaking, the London professional players in the time of Elizabeth, James, and Charles were poor men, as they have been in almost all ages of the theater. This basic fact, reflected in the constant breaking up of companies and in the flight to provincial or foreign fields, has been somewhat obscured because a few widely celebrated players—perhaps twenty out of approximately one thousand performing in the time—are known to have accumulated respectable estates. One who amassed a proper fortune was Edward Alleyn, a very famous player.[4] He retired from the stage before he was forty and spent the next twenty years or so building and renting theaters; buying and selling costumes, play scripts, houses, and land; running the Bear Garden as Master of the Royal Game of Bears, Bulls, and Mastiff Dogs; and administering Philip Henslowe's estate, most of which he inherited. He bought the manor of Dulwich and established Alleyn's College of God's Gift at Dulwich, furnishing it with an endowment that still supports it. Alleyn, however, was unique.

No other player is known to have amassed such a fortune in these years, though wills and various property transactions show that several players managed their investments well: John Heminges, Henry Condell, William Shakespeare, Christopher Beeston, Michael Bowyer, John Shank, Augustine Phillips, Thomas Greene.[5] These men who are known to have

[4] John Payne Collier, *The Alleyn Papers*, London, 1843, pp. xxi-xxvi.
[5] For evidence of the estates accumulated by these players, see their wills. John Heminges: James Boswell, ed., *The Plays and Poems of William Shakespeare . . . By the Late Edmund Malone*, London, 1821, III, 191-96; Henry Condell: John Payne Collier, *Memoirs of the Principal Actors in the Plays of Shakespeare*, London, 1846, pp. 145-49; William Shakespeare: S. Schoenbaum, *William Shakespeare: A Documentary Life*, Oxford, 1975, pp. 243-48; Christopher Beeston: Leslie Hotson, *The Commonwealth and Restoration Stage*, Cambridge, Mass., 1928, pp. 398-400; Michael Bowyer: Bentley, *The Jacobean and Caroline Stage*, II, 635-36; John Shank: Bentley, *The Jacobean and Caroline Stage*, II, 646-48; Augustine Phillips: George Chalmers, *An Apology for Believers in the Shakespeare Papers*, London, 1797, pp. 431-35; Thomas Greene: F. G. Fleay, *A Chronicle History of the London Stage, 1559-1642*, London, 1890, pp. 192-94.

accumulated respectable estates, it must be noted, were all sharers, not hired men. At least six of the eight were house-keepers, i.e., owners of shares in theater buildings, as well as sharers; it is not unlikely that Thomas Greene also owned shares in the Red Bull, but no such direct evidence has sur-vived. Furthermore, they had all belonged to major London companies: the Lord Admiral's men, the Lord Chamberlain-King's men, or the Queen's men. They did not come from the score or more minor London companies, nor from the many struggling provincial troupes.

The few "Elizabethan" players who became prosperous were not only members of the superior companies and usually housekeepers in theaters, but none of them is known to have been a hired man for any length of time. Hired men of all companies, members of minor troupes, and provincial players made up the bulk of actors in this period, and most of them were poor.

Though there was no London guild of players like those of the Cordwainers or Drapers or Stationers, the players used the general principles of guild organization common to the time. The organized acting companies of London did not em-ploy the same names for their ranks as the Grocers, Station-ers, or Merchant Tailors did. They divided themselves into apprentices, hired men, and sharers; the basic hierarchy was nevertheless similar to that of the guilds.

The players also differed from the older London guilds in that they had no central organization of all troupes in the profession, like that of the Lord Mayor and Council, and nothing like the tight organization of the regular guilds such as the Ironmongers or Stationers with their own system of Master and Court and set regulations for all units of the same trade. Of course they had nothing like the prestige of the Goldsmiths or Grocers and no Hall of their own.

One of the consequences of this lack of professional organ-ization and structure is that material concerning players of the time is not to be found in one place but is exasperatingly scattered through lawsuits, parish registers, licenses, plays, contracts, correspondence, financial accounts, letters, court orders, joke books, pamphlets, wills, prefaces, commendatory verses, prompt manuscripts, and sessions of the peace records.

WHERE THE PLAYERS LIVED

In London there were certain neighborhoods that were popular with players. A few are easy to identify because the clerks of those parishes frequently wrote the occupations of parishioners into their registers. As one would expect, the parishes favored by the players were close to theaters, and this proximity must have made rehearsals, special summonses, play readings, and new member consultations convenient.

The most certain of such districts was the Bankside, especially Paris Garden and the Clink, convenient to the Globe, the Hope, the Rose, the Swan, and rather less so to Newington Butts. The parish church was St. Saviour's, sometimes still called St. Mary Overies. The registers contain the names of many players, scores of them with their occupations named. This parish still preserves its old token books, so that for many players it is possible to ascertain the exact houses in which they lived.

Another popular players' neighborhood was St. Giles without Cripplegate, a very populous parish just outside the city walls, which included the Fortune theater. In the registers of this church the clerks also frequently mentioned the occupations of players, members of whose families were christened, married, or buried there. And so in St. Botolph's Aldgate. This parish was popular with players in the early period rather than the later because its nearby playing places fell into disuse early—the Bull Inn, the Bell Inn, the Cross Keys, The Theatre, and the Curtain.

Later a fairly popular area was the parish of St. Giles in the Fields, where in 1616 Christopher Beeston built the Phoenix, a playhouse which struggled on into the Restoration. A number of players lived near this theater, tenanted at different times by the Lady Elizabeth's men, Prince Charles's (I) company, Queen Henrietta's men, and for the last few years of the period by the King and Queen's Young company. Since the parish clerks at St. Giles in the Fields did not record occupations, the players can be identified with less certainty than in three of the other parishes, but several of the names of actors at the Phoenix or Cockpit are distinctive, and a number of others with less distinctive names probably represent players who are known to have performed at Beeston's house.[6] Other parishers in which several players have been found to reside are St. James's Clerkenwell, St. Leonard's Shoreditch, St. Mary's Aldermanbury, and St. Anne's Blackfriars.

THE STATUS OF PLAYERS

A great deal has been written about the low status of the players' profession in Shakespeare's time, mostly bolstered by quotations from the moralists and some of the preachers of the sixteenth century. Of course the opposition to plays and playing cannot be doubted, but not quite so familiar is the fact that the status of players rose notably before the closing act of 1642; the general attitude toward the profession was not the same in 1635 as it had been in 1580.

In the late years of the reign of Elizabeth and throughout those of her two successors most of the players were no longer "masterless men," "rogues," and "vagabonds," though their enemies often called them so. All the London companies and a great many of the provincial ones held licenses or patents or charters which established their connections with some noble or royal household and assigned to them rights and privileges

---

[6] "Shakespeare's Fellows," *Times Literary Supplement*, 15 November 1928, p. 856; William Ingram, *A London Life in the Brazen Age: Francis Langley, 1548-1602*, Cambridge, Mass., 1978, p. 301 n. 24; Emma Marshall Denkinger, "Actors' Names in the Registers of St. Botolph's Aldgate," *PMLA* 41 (1926), 91-109; "Players in the Parish of St. Giles in the Fields," *Review of English Studies* 6 (1930), 2-18; "Records of Players in the Parish of St. Giles Cripplegate," *PMLA* 44 (1929), 789-826.

that could not have been claimed by the wanderers of the early sixteenth century.[7] Opposition to the players had always been heard from certain elements in the city as well as in the country. But performers who carried a document with the seal of a great nobleman, like the Lord Chamberlain or (after 1603) that of the King or Queen or Prince, were not generally treated with the contempt some of the Puritan preachers or William Prynne would have liked.

Not without influence in the somewhat improved status of the players was the great increase in the number of times they were called to perform before royalty and the assembled court. While Elizabeth in the last decade of her reign summoned the companies to play before her four to eight times a year, twenty or more performances in a season were not exceptional in the time of James and Charles.[8] Such displays at Whitehall and St. James's and Hampton Court were not unknown to the London populace, and the status of the performers was not lowered thereby.

Perhaps the most tangible impetus to the slowly altering status of the players was the publication of the Jonson folio in 1616. For many years the normal form of publication for those plays that did achieve print was cheap pamphlets looking like joke books, almanacs, coney-catching pamphlets, and other such ephemera, frequently with no author's name on the title page. In contrast this handsome Jonson folio volume was set up like a collection of sermons or *The Works of King James*, printed in the same year. Furthermore the individual plays were dedicated to persons of standing, like the great historian Camden and Lord Aubigny, Lady Wroth and the

[7] The procedure of obtaining a patent is set out and fourteen examples of such document for dramatic companies are transcribed by E. K. Chambers and W. W. Greg in "Dramatic Records from the Patent Rolls: Company Licenses," *Malone Society Collections* 1, pt. 3 (1909) 260-84.

[8] See E. K. Chambers, *The Elizabethan Stage*, 4 vols., Oxford, 1967, IV, 104-130; and Bentley, *The Jacobean and Caroline Stage*, I, 94-100 and VII, 16-128.

Earl of Pembroke. Never before had English plays been treated with such dignity.[9]

But even more significant for the players was another innovation in the Jonson folio. Each of the nine tragedies and comedies in the volume was accompanied by a list of the names of the players who had created the principal roles; they are called either "Comœdians" or "Tragœdians." Such formal recognition for the lowly players had never been shown in an English book before. It was followed in a different form in the Shakespeare folio of 1623 and in the second Beaumont and Fletcher folio of 1679.

Possibly of some influence in the gradual improvement of the status of the players was Thomas Heywood's *An Apology for Actors* in 1612 and Nathan Field's "Field the player's letter to Mr. Sutton, preacher at St. Mary Overs, 1616." Both works of these player-dramatists were reasonable and informed. Heywood's is bolstered with a good deal of classical evidence. Field's letter, first printed separately by Halliwell-Phillips in an issue of twenty-five copies in 1865, is pious with a good display of Biblical knowledge.

Another event that tended to enhance the status of the players in these years was Edward Alleyn's deed of foundation of his College of God's Gift at Dulwich in 1619. This deed was read before a gathering of notables in London. The influence of such an event was recognized by the contemporary histo-

---

[9] It should be noted, however, that to some writers the Jonson volume seemed pretentious, especially the use of the designation "Works." George Fitz-Geoffry, Thomas Heywood, John Suckling, John Boys, and an anonymous writer in *Wits Recreation* all twit Jonson, generally by the easy quibble on "play" and "work." See Jesse Franklin Bradley and Joseph Quincy Adams, *The Jonson Allusion Book*, New Haven, 1922, pp. 119, 167, 175, 196, 271, and G. E. Bentley, *Shakespeare and Jonson: Their Reputations in the Seventeenth Century Compared*, 2 vols. in 1, Chicago, 1969, II, 35.

Of course in the milieu of London publishing in 1616 the Jonson volume *was* rather ostentatious. But there it was, displayed on the bookstalls for all to see, and there were the names of the noble dedicatees for individual plays and the conspicuous list of players for each comedy or tragedy.

rian, Sir Richard Baker. In his *Chronicle of the Kings of England* he wrote:

> About this time also *Edward Allen* of *Dulwich* in *Surrey* founded a fair hospital at *Dulwich*. . . . This man may be an example, who having gotten his wealth by stage playing converted it to this pious use, not without a kind of reputation to the Society of Players.[10]

The rising status of the players—especially the King's men—is reflected about this same time in Ralph Crane's *The Works of Mercy*, 1621, in which the scrivener says:

> And some employment hath my useful pen
> Had 'mongst those civil, well-deserving men,
> That grace the stage with honor and delight,
> Of whose true honesties I much could write,
> But will compress 't (as in a cask of gold)
> Under the Kingly service they do hold.
>
> $$[A_6]$$

It should be remembered, of course, that these remarks apply primarily, if not exclusively, to a few superior companies and their leading sharers, like Heminges and Condell who were longtime churchwardens at St. Mary's Aldermanbury. Though the whole profession of players was less vilified in the later days of James and the reign of Charles I, the hundreds of hired men and most of the provincial players were far from enjoying positions of dignity.

[10] *A Chronicle of the Kings of England*, London, 1684, p. 423.

CHAPTER II

The Player and His Company

FOR THE PROFESSIONAL player in London during the years
1590-1642, the primary focus of his life was usually the theatrical troupe to which he was attached at the moment. One
must say "at the moment," for life in the theater is always
precarious. Only one troupe, the Lord Chamberlain's-King's
company, had a continuous existence throughout the period;
other troupes came and went, usually overwhelmed by their
debts but sometimes dispersed because a theater landlord like
Henslowe or Beeston or Meade or Langley had reason to expel them from the playhouse he owned. Since about twenty
different commercial companies performed in London during
this period at one time or another, the failure rate is striking.
Even so, not nearly all the commercial companies were primarily metropolitan ones. Well over a hundred troupes are

known to have been touring in the provinces at some time during these years, and the majority of them are never heard of in London.[1]

All normal London commercial companies of adult players in these years were made up of the same three groups: sharers, hired men, and boys or apprentices. Of course there were many changes as the years passed and prosperity and inflation increased. Since all troupes were repertory companies whose principal assets were their costumes and their exclusive library of dramatic scripts, most of the plays were kept out of print—at least until they were obsolete or the failing company was forced to sell its most precious assets in order to eat. The Red Bull and the Blackfriars theaters in the Caroline period tended to draw the preponderance of their audiences from different social classes, so there were differences in the play

[1] In the first decade of this century Professor John Tucker Murray made a somewhat superficial survey of the records of provincial towns in England from 1558 to 1642. (J. T. Murray, *English Dramatic Companies 1558-1642*, 2 vols., London, 1910, II, *passim*.) He found well over a hundred named dramatic companies which visited provincial towns in his period.

Recently a much more thorough survey of provincial records has been undertaken by a Canadian group. In a preliminary report on the records of the town of Leicester, Alice B. Hamilton notes:

I have counted over fifty different companies of actors that came to Leicester in the sixteenth and seventeenth centuries, who were rewarded for playing or for not playing at the Town Hall. They came sporatically between 1531 and 1547, but not all borough records exist for these years and visits by actors may have occurred more frequently than appears from the surviving fiscal rolls. The hosts of companies come after 1569. (*Records of Early English Drama*, Toronto, 1979, I, 18)

Even these astonishing numbers are too small, for the records of many provincial towns have not yet been thoroughly examined, and many of the records that have been examined neglect to give the name of the company that was paid, but simply say "to the players." The clerk was interested in the money spent, not in the identity of the company—unless there had been trouble. Nor do these numbers include the many troupes of English players touring the continent, especially Germany and the Low Countries, and playing in English. Truly the rage for theatrical entertainment was astounding, though most of these companies could never have been very profitable.

requirements of different theaters and in the requisites of their performers. Jig dancers were long in demand at the Fortune, seldom if ever at the Blackfriars.[2]

In spite of these differences, however, there was a norm—witness the fact that there are scores of examples of players who transferred from one troupe to another during these years,[3] and the fact that in several instances the same play is known to have been performed at different times by different companies, Kyd's *Spanish Tragedy* and Marston's *Malcontent*, for instance. It is possible, therefore, to outline what was usual in a London professional adult acting troupe during the period.

It was normal for a company to be attached to a single theater owned by a landlord or a group of landlords—speculators, not players. The company's rent was not a fixed sum but a percentage of the take at each performance.

To this normal arrangement there were one or two exceptions, most conspicuously, as usual, the Lord Chamberlain-King's company. In the early nineties they were playing at The Theatre, a playhouse built by the father of their great actor Richard Burbage and inherited by Richard and his brother Cuthbert. In 1598 they transported The Theatre, timber by timber, across the river, embellished and enlarged it, named it the Globe, and vested the ownership of the house in the Burbage brothers and several leading fellows or sharers of the company: William Shakespeare, Augustine Phillips, Thomas Pope, John Heminges, and William Kempe. These men were the "housekeepers," and they received the rent that other companies paid to their real estate landlords.

In 1608 this company took over the Blackfriars, a private

---

[2] For the reputations of audiences at the Fortune and Red Bull theaters, see Edmund Gayton's *Pleasant Notes upon Don Quixote* (1654); relevant passages are quoted in my *Jacobean and Caroline Stage*, 7 vols., Oxford, 1941-1968, II, 690-91. See also the section on "The Reputation of the Red Bull Theatre," ibid., VI, 238-47.

[3] See E. K. Chambers, *The Elizabethan Stage*, 4 vols., Oxford, 1967, II, 295-350; and Bentley, *The Jacobean and Caroline Stage*, II, 343-628.

theater (small and expensive), which they owned and operated by the same sort of combination: the Burbage brothers, four sharers, John Heminges, William Shakespeare, Henry Condell, William Sly, and a former lessee, Thomas Evans. The Lord Chamberlain-King's theatrical troupe was the only company operating two theaters and maintaining over a long period of time the same system of ownership.

There is some evidence that Edward Alleyn was trying to work out a similar system of cooperative ownership for the Palsgrave's men at the Fortune in the early twenties; but it did not last long and the company disintegrated in a few years.[4]

None of the other score or more of London theatrical troupes in the period is known to have enjoyed the control of its own playhouse. Troubles with owners were common. A long list of the grievances of the Lady Elizabeth's company in 1615 against their landlord and financial agent Philip Henslowe is still extant among Edward Alleyn's papers.[5] The list of grievances, mostly financial, is long and complex, and few of them can be checked now, but it is clear that at the time there was bad blood between theater owner and company. The Lady Elizabeth's men conclude their list, "Also within 3 years he hath broken and dismembered five companies." It is not surprising that the Lady Elizabeth's company shortly disappears from London records for the next several years and is found in provincial accounts only.[6]

Such troubles as these were one of the conditions leading to another feature in the lives of all players except the Lord Chamberlain-King's men, namely the moving about from theater to theater or from London to the provinces as conditions became intolerable at one house or a better bargain was offered at another. Thus Thomas Heywood's company, the Earl of Worcester-Queen Anne's men, moved from the Rose to the Curtain to the Boar's Head to the Red Bull and to

---

[4] See Bentley, *The Jacobean and Caroline Stage*, I, 141ff.
[5] W. W. Greg, ed., *Henslowe Papers*, London, 1907, pp. 86-90.
[6] See Bentley, *The Jacobean and Caroline Stage*, I, 176-80.

Beeston's new Phoenix, all between 1603 and 1617. At the latter end of our period Prince Charles's (II) company moved from the Salisbury Court to the Red Bull to the Fortune in a period of ten years. Probably neither series of flittings is a record, but they do illustrate again the rather precarious life of most London players and the unique stability and profitability of the premier troupe of the time.

This constantly threatening departure or disintegration of the London theatrical companies was a hazard to most of the London theater owners and managers as well as to the players. Not only were desertions or transfers frequent, but several records of attempts to forestall such withdrawals survive.

According to a suit brought in the Court of Requests in November 1597, Francis Langley persuaded five leading members of the Earl of Pembroke's company to sign bonds forfeiting £100 if they left his Swan theater to play elsewhere. There are other charges in the complaint and answer, but both parties agree that such bonds were signed.[7] For a variety of reasons the bonds did not accomplish their purpose, and the players involved went to Henslowe's nearby Rose theater.

But Henslowe too was worried about retaining his players. From 1597 to 1600 he persuaded a dozen or more of the leading sharers and hired men of the Admiral's company to sign bonds according to which they forfeited from 100 marks to £40 if they left Henslowe's theater in the course of the next three, or in some instances two years.[8]

Two or three decades later, in 1624, Richard Gunnell, manager of the Fortune, tried to hold together the faltering Palsgrave's company by persuading six of the sharers to sign a bond to continue playing together at the Fortune.[9]

[7] C. W. Wallace, "The Swan Theatre and the Earl of Pembroke's Servants," *Englische Studien* 43 (1911), 345-55; supplemented by William Ingram, *A London Life in the Brazen Age: Francis Langley, 1548-1602*, Cambridge, Mass., 1978, pp. 151-66.

[8] The various agreements, all recorded and witnessed, generally by other players of the company, are conveniently assembled from Henslowe's Diary in Chambers, *The Elizabethan Stage*, II, 151-55.

[9] The agreement is known only from a Chancery suit of 1654, long after the closing of the theaters, when Gunnell's heirs tried to collect. See Leslie

The same managerial purpose to forestall disintegration or desertion is apparent in 1639 in Richard Heton's proposal for a new Queen Henrietta's company patent giving him exceptional powers. One of his "intentions for the rest" has the same binding purpose as Henslowe's agreements of forty years before and Gunnell's bonds of fifteen years before, namely to ensure that Queen Henrietta's men stayed together and remained under his direction at their present theater.[10]

Managers, owners, and players all suffered from this instability of most of the acting troupes of the time, though each group generally thought the other the guilty party. An example of the players blaming the owner for their desertion of his theater is seen in a letter written some time in the winter of 1616-1617 to Edward Alleyn and signed by the seven principal sharers. They had been performing at the Hope theater on the Bankside, a convertible playhouse and bear-baiting arena, and they explain why they had deserted. Their arrangement as to the days on which they should play had been violated, they say, in favor of the bears, and they ask Alleyn's help:

Sir:
I hope you mistake not our removal from the Bankside: we stood the intemperate weather, till more intemperate Mr. Meade thrust us over, taking the day from us which by course was ours; though by the time we can yet claim none, and that power he exacted on us. For the prosecution of our further suit in a house we entreat you to forethink well of the place (though it crave a speedy resolution) lest we make a second fruitless pains. . . .[11]

After the Restoration, Davenant was still trying by agreement in 1660 to keep his players together at the Cockpit. Of

---

Hotson, *The Commonwealth and Restoration Stage*, Cambridge, Mass., 1928, pp. 52-53; and Bentley, *The Jacobean and Caroline Stage*, II, 148-49.

[10] From an unidentified manuscript transcribed by Peter Cunningham in *The Shakespeare Society Papers* 4 (1849), 95-100, reprinted in Bentley, *The Jacobean and Caroline Stage*, II, 684-87.

[11] Greg, ed., *Henslowe Papers*, p. 93. For a discussion, see Bentley, *The Jacobean and Caroline Stage*, I, 200-201 and VI, 207-209.

course many conditions had changed by that time, but managers or owners still had the same problems of holding their players at their theaters.

Though his company attachment often caused trouble for the player, it was also the source of his income and often provided other satisfactions.

To the player who was a sharer, his company, if it was one of the major London ones, gave a certain prestige. In the reign of Elizabeth he wore the badge of the nobleman who was his master—perhaps patron would be the better term, since there is little evidence of any connection with the master's household except for occasional entertainments and even more occasional petitions for privileges or protection in difficult situations. But now and then an extant example does show the influence of an Elizabethan company patron, as when Lord Hunsdon wrote to the Lord Mayor in 1598 requesting that his company be allowed to play at the Cross Keys.[12]

After James came to the throne and the principal London companies were all officially licensed as servants of members of the royal family, the sharers wore the livery of the King or the Queen or the Prince or the Princess and were identifiable on the street as superior to the ordinary apprentice or craftsman or shopkeeper. In a time when court influence was of great value not only in individual transactions but in casual street encounters, not to say assaults and brawls, such advertisement of influencial connections could be of value.

Quarrelling and petty jealousies in performing organizations in all times are notorious, but there is evidence that friendship and trust were not uncommon among the members of London theater troupes. Perhaps the best evidence is to be seen in a few of the extant wills. Of course, most players were too poor to have much to leave and they made no last testament, but quite a number of the extant wills specify remembrances for fellow players, or special confidence in making them executors or trustees. Shakespeare's remembrances

---

[12] See below, pp. 79-80.

to Burbage, Heminges, and Condell, made years after he had retired from London, are well known, but similar bequests to their theatrical associates are made by Thomas Basse, Michael Bowyer, Richard Cowley, John Honeyman, Henry Condell, Thomas Greene, Nicholas Tooley, and especially Augustine Phillips. There are various others. And often fellow players of the company are witnesses to the signature of the testator, suggesting that in several cases they were present at the death-bed.[13]

Most eloquent of this affection for his co-workers in the King's company is the will of Augustine Phillips, made on the 4th of May 1605. The bulk of his estate he divided among his wife and his two daughters, but a surprising number of his colleagues are remembered:

> Item, I give and bequeath unto and amongst the hired men of the company which I am of, which shall be at the time of my decease, the sum of five pounds of lawful money of England to be equally distributed among them.

> Item, I give and bequeath to my fellow [i.e., fellow sharer] William Shakespeare a thirty shilling piece in gold; to my fellow Henry Condell one other thirty shilling piece in gold; to my servant, Christopher Beeston, thirty shillings in gold; to my fellow Lawrence Fletcher, twenty shillings in gold; to my fellow Robert Armin, twenty shillings in gold; to my fellow Richard Cowley, twenty shillings in gold; to my fellow Alexander Cook, twenty shillings in gold; to my fellow Nicholas Tooley, twenty shillings in gold. . . .

[13] The will of each of these players is in print. Thomas Basse: Bentley, *The Jacobean and Caroline State*, II, 631; Michael Bowyer: ibid., II, 635-36; Richard Cowley: *Notes and Queries*, ser. 10, 6 (1906), 368; John Honeyman: Bentley, *The Jacobean and Caroline Stage*, II, 645; Henry Condell: John Payne Collier, *Memoirs of the Principal Actors in the Plays of Shakespeare*, London, 1846, pp. 145-49; Thomas Greene: F. G. Fleay, *A Chronicle History of the London Stage, 1559-1642*, London, 1890, pp. 192-94; Nicholas Tooley: James Boswell, ed., *The Plays and Poems of William Shakespeare . . . By the Late Edmond Malone*, London, 1821, III, 484-89; Augustine Phillips: George Chalmers, *An Apology for Believers in the Shakespeare Papers*, London, 1797, pp. 431-35.

Item, I give to Samuel Gilborne, my late apprentice, the sum of forty shillings, and my mouse-colored velvet hose, and a white taffeta doublet, a black taffeta suit, my purple cloak, sword and dagger, and my bass viol.

Item, I give to James Sands, my apprentice, the sum of forty shillings and a cittern, a bandore, and a lute to be paid and delivered unto him at the expiration of his term of years in his indenture of apprenticehood. . . .

[His wife Anne is made executrix] . . . if the said Anne my wife do at any time marry after my decease that then and from thenceforth she shall cease to be anymore or longer the executrix of this . . . and that then and from thenceforth John Hemings, Richard Burbage, William Slye, and Timothy Whithorne shall be fully and wholly my executors of this my last will and testament as though the said Anne had never been named. And of the execution of this my present testament and last will I ordain and make the said John Hemings, Richard Burbage, William Slye and Timothy Whithorne, overseers of this my present testament and last will and I bequeath unto the said John Hemings, Richard Burbage, and William Slye, to either of them my said overseers for their pains herein to be taken a bowl of silver of the value of five pounds apiece. . . .

One of the two witnesses to the will is Robert Goffe or Gough, who was one of the fellows or sharers in Shakespeare's plays listed in the first Folio. This special remembrance of all the hired men, most of the fellows, and two of the apprentices plus the trust imposed of Heminges, Burbage, and Slye suggest the importance of the company in the life of this player as well as his affection for his associates in the troupe. Of course such affection for colleagues was not universal, but a few of the remaining wills of players show a similar regard for certain of the testator's company associates, though not so many as Augustine Phillips named.

Three of Thomas Heywood's fellow sharers in Queen Anne's

company wrote commendatory verses for his *Apology for Actors* in 1612, and each advertised his company connection by addressing his verses to "To my loving Friend and Fellow, Thomas Heywood" or "To my good Friend and Fellow, Thomas Heywood." There are two or three elegies by players on the deaths of their colleagues, like Thomas Jordan's on the death of Richard Gunnell or William Rowley's elegy on his fellow in Prince Charles's company, Hugh Attwell.

Of course all was not sweetness and light among the players of these dramatic troupes: everyone remembers that Ben Jonson fought a duel with his fellow actor Gabriel Spencer and killed him, in 1598. And the long row between William Bankes and the members and managers of his company in 1635[14] are also examples of the contrary. Yet the many evidences of confidence and affection among fellows of several of the Elizabethan, Jacobean, and Caroline theatrical troupes seem to me to be noteworthy.

We have noticed that in the course of the period twenty or so different troupes played in London, but not, of course, all at the same time. Usually there were four or five companies playing simultaneously in town. There are several allusions to the number of companies playing in competition: the number varies from four to five, but four seems to be the number usually officially recognized.

On 29 March 1615 the Privy Council ordered one of their messengers to bring before them John Heminges, Richard Burbage, Christopher Beeston, Robert Lee, William Rowley, John Newton, Thomas Downton, Humphrey Jeffes, for performing during Lent in spite of the order of the Master of the Revels.[15] These eight players were leading members of four London companies: Heminges and Burbage, the King's Men; Beeston and Lee, Queen Anne's company; Rowley and Newton, the Palsgrave's company; and Thomas Downton and

[14] See below, pp. 41-45.
[15] E. K. Chambers and W. W. Greg, "Dramatic Records from the Privy Council Registers, 1603-1642," *Malone Society Collections* 1, pt. 4 (1911), 372.

Humphrey Jeffes, Prince Charles's (I) company. These four were evidently the officially recognized London companies in 1615.

Four is also the number of companies recognized in 1618 by Sir George Buc, then Master of the Revels. Among his extracts from the lost Office Book of Sir George's successor, Sir Henry Herbert, Edmond Malone copied:

> Of John Heminges, in the name of the four companies for toleration in the holy-days, 44s. January 29, 1618. *"Extracts from the office-book of Sir George Buc.* MSS Herbert"[16]

Other notes made by Edmond Malone and by George Chalmers from now lost manuscripts testify to the number of companies playing in London at a given time. In his *Supplemental Apology for the Believers in the Shakespeare Papers* in 1799 George Chalmers wrote: "When the sceptre of the stage was delivered into his [Henry Herbert's] hands, there appears from the record of his office to have been four established companies of players; exclusive of strangers, who sometimes invaded their territories" (p. 211). Malone wrote in his Variorum edition of Shakespeare, apparently using the same lost manuscript:

> Soon after his [Shakespeare's] death, four of the principal companies, then subsisting, made a union, and were afterwards called The United Companies; but I know not precisely in what this union consisted.[17]

> It appears from the office-book of Sir Henry Herbert, Master of the Revels to King James the First, and the two succeeding kings, that very soon after our poet's [Shakespeare's] death, in the year 1622, there were but five principal companies of comedians in London; the King's Servants, who performed at the Globe and in Blackfriars; the Prince's Servants, who performed then at the Curtain; the Pals-

---

[16] Joseph Quincy Adams, *The Dramatic Records of Sir Henry Herbert, Master of the Revels, 1622-1673*, New Haven, 1917, p. 48.
[17] Boswell, *Plays and Poems*, III, 224.

grave's Servants, who had possession of the Fortune; the
players of the Revels, who acted at the Red Bull, and the
Lady Elizabeth's Servants, or, as they are sometimes de-
nominated, the Queen of Bohemia's players, who performed at the Cockpit in Drury Lane.[18]

These variations between four companies and five companies I interpret as meaning that though Londoners in these
years had their choice among five different companies of players, four of them had special status and certain privileges.
This interpretation is confirmed by two or three occasional
phrases used by the Master in connection with various of his
regulatory actions.

On 12 September 1623 Sir Henry made an entry which
has apparently been garbled in later transcriptions,[19] but only
the straightforward part of his notation concerns us here, ". . .
It was acted at the Red Bull, and licensed without my hand
to it; because they were none of the four companies." Whatever was meant by "the four companies," it is apparent that
five were acting in London in these later years, though one
did not belong to the four officially recognized "United Companies." When Richard Kendall, wardrobe keeper at the Salisbury Court theater, told Thomas Crosfield about the London companies in July 1634, he listed five companies, naming
their theaters and their principal players.[20]

Sir Henry Herbert also said a number of years later that
there were five companies operating in London in his time.
In 1662 when Sir Henry was trying to reassert his old claims
to be Master of the Revels in opposition to Sir William Davenant, he submitted to the Lord Chancellor a list of the fees
he had received from the companies before the wars. One
item reads: "For a share from each company of four companies of players (besides the late King's company) valued at

[18] Ibid., III, 57-59
[19] See Bentley, *The Jacobean and Caroline Stage*, III, 30-32.
[20] Fredrick S. Boas, ed., *The Diary of Thomas Crosfield*, London, 1935, pp.
71-73.

£100 a year, one year with another, besides the usual fees, by the year.[21]

Such a large number of competing London theatrical troupes not only testifies to the appetite for drama of a population of under 300,000 (in the 1590s far less) but it offered greater opportunities for employment to the players. When a London company broke up, there was always a chance that the un-employed player could get a job as a hired man in another London troupe and a greater chance that he could arrange to eke out a living with one of the many companies touring in the provinces. But there is no evidence that touring was ever very profitable, and it was certainly uncomfortable in the mire and the rain.

[21] Adams, *Dramatic Records of Sir Henry Herbert*, p. 121.

CHAPTER III

Sharers

THROUGHOUT THE PERIOD the ranking players in the adult companies were the sharers, so called because their remuneration was not a weekly wage, as in the case of the hired men, or valuable training as in the case of the apprentices, but a share in the receipts for each performance by the company. Other terms for the same status were in common use: "patented member" because only the sharers were named in the royal patents for the companies; "fellow" in the first sense given in the *Oxford English Dictionary*, "One who shares with another in a possession, official dignity, or the performance of any work: a partner, a colleague, or co-worker." "Fellow" is the term commonly used by the leading players in referring to each other. Shakespeare's usage in his will was characteristic. He bequeathed money to buy rings to "my ffellowes John Hemynge, Richard Burbage, & Henry Cundall." The same usage of this title of familiarity and respect is found in the wills of other actors: John Bentley, Alexander Cooke, Thomas Greene, John Heminges, John Honeyman, Simon Jewell, Augustine Phillips, John Shank, and John Underwood.[1]

Not only were the sharers the leading players in the company, but in the eyes of the law and of the regulatory agencies they *were* the company, and all the others in the troupe merely their employees. The extant patents for theatrical companies usually name each of the sharers in the official document, but the minor players, the apprentices, and all the many necessary theatrical functionaries are simply blanketed under the phrase, "and the rest of their associates."[2]

The fact that the sharers were the official company is apparent in other theatrical records. When in 1624 the King's men performed a now lost play called *The Spanish Viceroy* without having had it officially licensed for performance by the Master of the Revels, they were in serious trouble; not only had they violated the law, but they had offended their immediate supervisor; Sir Henry Herbert was very jealous of his prerogative. Sir Henry kept in his records their letter of abject apology:

---

[1] These wills have all been printed. John Bentley's can be found in *Modern Philology* 29 (1931), 111-12; Alexander Cooke's in George Chalmers, *An Apology for the Believers in the Shakespeare Papers*, London, 1797, pp. 447-49; Thomas Greene's in F. G. Fleay, *A Chronicle History of the London Stage, 1559-1642*, London, 1890, pp. 192-94; and John Heminges' in James Boswell, ed., *The Plays and Poems of William Shakespeare . . . By the Late Edmond Malone*, London, 1821, III, 191-96; John Honeyman's in G. E. Bentley, *The Jacobean and Caroline Stage*, 7 vols., Oxford, 1941-1968, II, 645; Simon Jewell's in *Review of English Studies* 25 (1974), 129-30; Augustine Phillips' in Chalmers, *An Apology for Believers in the Shakespeare Papers*, pp. 431-35; John Shank's in Bentley, *The Jacobean and Caroline Stage*, II, 646-48; John Underwood's in John Payne Collier, *Memoirs of the Principal Actors in the Plays of Shakespeare*, London, 1846, pp. 229-32.

[2] E. K. Chambers and W. W. Greg, "Dramatic Records from the Patent Rolls: Company Licences," *Malone Society Collections* I, pt. 3 (1909), 260-83.

. . . we do confess and hereby acknowledge that we have offended, and that it is in your power to punish this offense, and are very sorry for it; and do likewise promise hereby that we will not act any play without your hand or substitute's hereafter, nor do any thing that may prejudice the authority of your office: So hoping that this humble submission of ours may be accepted, we have thereunto set our hands. . . .

The letter is signed by eleven sharers or patented members of the King's company.[3]

In the same way the sharers were the legal Lord Admiral's company in 1598. The debt of the company to Philip Henslowe was acknowledged by the signatures of ten sharers of the company, J. Singer, Thomas Downton, William Bird, Robert Shaw, Richard Jones, Gabriel Spencer, Thomas Towne, Humphry Jeffes, Charles Massey, and Samuel Rowley.[4] Similarly on 20 March 1615/16 the sharers of Prince Charles's (I) company acknowledged to Edward Alleyn and Jacob Meade that they stood indebted to Philip Henslowe, deceased, and Jacob Meade for £400 for loans and "playinge apparell" and they would repay £200 out of the takings from the gallery at the Hope theater, and would continue to play at that theater. Ten sharers signed the agreement.[5]

In Jacobean and Caroline times when the major London companies were all under the sponsorship of some member of the royal family—the Lady Elizabeth, the Duke of York, Prince Charles, as well as the King and Queen—it was ordinarily only the sharers and not the lesser members of the troupe who

[3] Joseph Quincy Adams, *The Dramatic Records of Sir Henry Herbert*, New Haven, 1917, p. 21. Two patented members did not sign, John Heminges and Henry Condell, though they were named first in the new patent for the company issued six months later. I can only conjecture that they had somehow purged themselves of the offense.

[4] R. A. Foakes and R. T. Rickert, eds., *Henslowe's Diary*, Cambridge, 1961, p. 87.

[5] W. W. Greg, ed., *Henslowe Papers*, London, 1907, pp. 90-91.

27

were given the special status of Grooms of the Chamber in Ordinary and who had the liveries and exemption from arrest attached to that status.[6]

The sharers in the theatrical companies of the period 1590 to 1642 are commonly said to have been made up of the most distinguished and popular performers in the troupe excepting, of course, those boys who attained fame while they were still apprentices, like Salmon Pavy, Nicholas Burt, and Richard Robinson. To a certain extent this identification of sharers and superior players is valid. Of course the sharers of different companies included their most popular performers, men like Burbage and Alleyn and Kempe and Tarleton and Field and Thomas Greene and Robert Armin and Richard Perkins and John Shank and Andrew Cane and Joseph Taylor. But a good many sharers never attained any special distinction for their performances. The best-known example is William Shakespeare. Nor were John Heminges and Henry Condell, though of immense value to the company and sharers for a good many years, ever distinguished players, and for more than a decade of their active careers they were certainly inconspicuous in performances, if they were on stage at all.

In other London companies several of the known sharers lacked distinction as actors. Thomas Heywood was a long-time sharer in Worcester-Queen Anne's company though there is no evidence that he ever made much of an impression as an actor, and the same is true of Richard Gunnell and Charles Massey and John Cumber and Christopher Beeston and John Townsend. Sometimes we can tell why these undistinguished players remained sharers: obviously William Shakespeare and Thomas Heywood were valuable to their companies as writers, but certainly a share was not the common way of paying a devoted playwright. There is no evidence that John Fletcher or Philip Massinger or Thomas Dekker or Thomas Middleton

[6] E. K. Chambers, *The Elizabethan Stage*, 4 vols., Oxford, 1923, I, 311-13; and G. E. Bentley, "The Troubles of a Caroline Acting Troupe: Prince Charles's Company," *Huntington Library Quarterly* 41 (1978), 233-35.

or James Shirley (who each wrote almost as many plays for their companies as Shakespeare did for his) were ever sharers. William Rowley was a sharer in the Duke of York-Prince Charles's (I) company, but he was a well-known comedian as well as a writer. Heminges and Beeston and Gunnell were obviously of value as managers or treasurers or business agents, and all of them, like Shakespeare, began as actors.[7]

But there was a financial element involved in becoming a sharer in a dramatic company of the time. Any successful troupe required capital, mostly for costumes, but also for wages for hired men and other theatrical functionaries—wardrobe keepers, stagekeepers, gatherers, musicians, bookkeepers, or prompters—for new plays, for licensing fees, and for travelling expenses, if only to Hampton Court or Greenwich or Windsor or Whitehall. Some of this capital evidently came from sharers. There are a number of indications of this fact, but the most fully known case is that of William Bankes and his experiences in becoming a sharer in Prince Charles's (II) company in the mid-1630s. The details of the affair are known only from a Bill of Complaint brought in the Court of Requests in February 1634/35 by William Bankes, a sharer in Prince Charles's (II) company, against the leaders of that company, the well-known actors Andrew Cane (or Keyne) and Ellis Worth, and from the joint answer of Keyne and Worth.[8] Both parties agree that Bankes paid £100 to become a sharer in the company, and they agree that he was promised that as a sharer he would be made a Groom of the Chamber.

This investment of sharers in the "stock" of the company is alluded to in the affairs of other companies. According to the widow of the prominent player Thomas Greene who died in 1612, he had laid out for the company £37, and at his death the company (Queen Anne's) owed her £80 in payment for

[7] See below, Chapter VI, for a discussion of managers of theatrical troupes in the period.
[8] See Bentley, "The Troubles of a Caroline Acting Troupe," pp. 217-49.

his full share, as was customary with the company.[9] The leading sharers of the same company in a Chancery suit of 1618 had said that when their fellow sharer, Robert Lee, left the organization they agreed to pay him £60 as soon as he returned some of the company property. And in his will of 31 December 1635 John Shank, a sharer and principal comedian of the King's company, admonished his fellows to pay to his widow the £50 which was due "for my share in the stock, books, apparel, and other things according to the old custom and agreement amongst us."[10]

That this sort of deposit by the sharers in the chief company of the time was not unusual is shown by a statement in a Chancery suit of 1655 brought by Theophilus Bird, who about 1640 had become a sharer in the King's company after a career with Queen Henrietta's men, against Thomas Morrison who has married the widow of Bird's old colleague in both companies, Michael Bowyer.[11] Bird says in his Chancery Bill of Complaint that

. . . the said company being at the time of your Orator's said admission thereinto, possessed of a stock consisting of apparel, books [i.e., play mnuscripts], hangings, and other goods of the value of £3,000 and upwards, your Orator at his said admission into the said company disbursed and deposited the sum of £200 towards the said apparel, books, goods, and other things, being £150 at least more than others

[9] See the Answer of Susan Baskervile and William Browne, 23 May 1623 in the Chancery suit of *Worth, Cumber, and Blaney v. Baskervile and Brown*, transcribed in Fleay, *A Chronicle History of the London Stage*, pp. 279-92.

[10] See the will of John Shank, in Bentley, *The Jacobean and Caroline Stage*, II, 646-48.

[11] This Chancery suit was discovered and transcribed by the Wallaces before World War I, but never printed. Without knowledge that the Wallaces had used the documents before him, Leslie Hotson rediscovered and published a few quotations and a reference in *The Commonwealth and Restoration Stage*, Cambridge, Mass., 1928, pp. 31-34 and 315. My quotations come from the full transcriptions in the Wallace Papers in the Huntington Library, San Marino, California.

of the said company had done, and was more than his proportion of the said clothes and stock did amount unto. . . .

In their answer to Bird, the Morrisons disagree, of course,
about the sums of money involved, but in the suits of the
time it is usual for one party to maximize and the other to
minimize cash values and payments. For our present purposes
the more significant point is that there is no disagreement about
the fact that as a new sharer in the major company of the time
Theophilus Bird did deposit a sum of money in the treasury
of the rich and successful King's men, just as William Bankes
had made a deposit with Prince Charles's (II) troupe, one of
the poorer and more struggling theatrical organizations.

That money was involved in becoming a sharer in a London theatrical troupe ought not to be surprising, though it is
seldom considered. Play production had become vastly more
expensive since the early days when four or five men and a
boy trudged the country roads beside a wagon loaded with
theatrical gear. Bird claimed in his Bill of Complaint that the
royal company's stock of apparel, books, hangings, and other
goods was worth £3,000, and though the defendants claim,
naturally, that this sum is too large, it does not seem unreasonable to me. In August 1641 the company claimed exclusive
rights to over sixty *unpublished* plays, and their entire repertory (most of which they tried to control) consisted of 170
identifiable titles.[12] Since many extant documents, such as
Henslowe's accounts, indicate that the costumes cost the companies more than plays, £3,000 does not seem an excessive
evaluation for a long-established troupe which had frequently
to display itself before royalty.

A similar statement about the value of the company stocks
was made fifteen or more years earlier when the King's men,
though rich and powerful, had not yet accumulated the assets
they had in 1640. This estimate comes in a complaint of
Thomas Hobbes, a player who had been a sharer in Prince
Charles's company during the reign of James. When his pa-

[12] See Bentley, *The Jacobean and Caroline Stage*, 1, 65-66 and 108-134.

tron succeeded as Charles I, Hobbes was one of those who became a King's man. For some reason, however, he had apparently not been made a Groom of the Chamber as the others were, and this distressed him. In the notes of Sir Edward Coke for an audience at Whitehall is an item under the head, "King Charles His Servants": "Thomas Hobbes comedian, now left out of the number new sworn, being engaged for the stock debt of their company in £500, desireth to be sworn as the rest are or disengaged.[13] The difference in the sums cited by Hobbes and Bird could be accounted for by the accumulations and inflation of fifteen years, or Bird may have exaggerated somewhat. At any rate each statement is evidence of the great value of the possessions of King Charles's company.

Thus the contribution of capital as well as histrionic ability was a requirement for the sharers in those dramatic companies that entertained the London subjects of Elizabeth, James, and Charles. In at least one known instance, and one suspects in others, the money was more important than the acting ability. In the case of William Bankes, who brought suit against his colleagues of Prince Charles's (II), there is no evidence that he was ever a player of any note at all, but the company of Prince Charles obviously needed his £100. How often this situation was repeated we shall never know; one would guess not infrequently in the minor London companies but less often with the major and more solvent ones.

Even with Henslowe's companies in the early days, the situation did not differ in its essentials. Though Henslowe bought the costumes and the plays, the company had to pay him back. And a new sharer joining after the troupe was well established enjoyed the benefits of the plays, costumes, and hangings already owned, and it was fair enough that he should contribute something for the assets his colleagues had already paid for.

It was customary for this financial stake of a sharer in the

[13] *Historical Manuscripts Commission*, 12th Report Appendix 1 (London, 1888), p. 198.

company to be recognized as part of his estate, and a payment was supposed to be made to him when he left the company or to his wife at his death. About 1613 Charles Massey was trying to borrow money from Philip Henslowe and wrote about his security. He said

> . . . for sir I know you understand that there is the com-position between our company that if any one give over with consent of his fellows, he is to receive three score and ten pounds (Anthony Jeffes hath had so much); if any one die his widow or friends whom he appoints is to receive fifty pounds (Mrs. Pavy and Mrs. Towne hath had the like). . . .[14]

In his will of December 1635, John Shank, a leading sharer in the King's company, desires that his fellow sharers in the company "do not abridge my said wife and executrix in the receiving of what is due unto me and my estate amongst them, as namely fifty pounds for my share in the stocks, books, apparel, and other things according to the old custom and agreement amongst us."[15]

The situation was similar in the company of Prince Charles (II); both plaintiff and defendants agree that George Stutville was paid £30 for his share in the stock when he left the com-pany about the same time.[16] Twenty years earlier the arrange-ment for fellows leaving the company prevailed with Queen Anne's men, a troupe once more prosperous than Prince Charles's men. In the Chancery suit of *Perkins &c. v. Lee* the plaintiffs say that when Robert Lee, one of the sharers, left the organization, he received £60 provided he return the play-books, clothes, and other goods belonging to the company.[17]

Apparently there were exceptions to this custom of return-ing money to widows, at least in Queen Anne's troupe, pos-sibly because of the deterioration in the affairs of those play-

[14] Greg, ed., *Henslowe Papers*, p. 64.
[15] See Bentley, *The Jacobean and Caroline Stage*, II, 647.
[16] See Bentley, "The Troubles of a Caroline Acting Troupe," pp. 217-49.
[17] Wallace Papers.

ers. In a suit in Chancery in 1623, *Ellis Worth and John Blaney v. Susan Baskervile and William Browne*,[18] two well-known sharers in the company, Thomas Heywood and Richard Perkins, testified. Richard Perkins of St. James Clerkenwell aged "44 or thereabouts" testified that

> He knew one John Thayer who was a half sharer in the company of players at the Red Bull who departed this life about 11 years since, and sayeth he did also know Thomas Albanes who was a [?] quarter sharer in the company who died about five or six years agone and this deponent sayeth that he is well assured that neither the wives nor executors or administrators of the said Thayer and Albanes [had] anything allowed of the remainders or survivors of the said company in [?] of the said Thayer and Albanes' shares. And this deponent also saith that he knoweth Thomas Heywood and Francis Walpole who were sharers in the company left the same and yet he saith that neither Heywood, Walpole, nor himself this deponent ever had afterwards any allowance from the said company. Neither doth this deponent know any reason that anything should be demanded in that kind for he saith there was never any agreement made between the company for the allowing to the executors or administrators of such as should die or to such as should depart the company any sum or money whatsoever. . . .
>
> R. Perkins

The testimony of Richard Perkins is corroborated by his fellow sharer, the dramatist Thomas Heywood. Thomas Heywood of the parish of St. James's Clerkenwell aged 49 years or thereabouts told the interrogators:

> That within these 14 or 15 years he hath known one John Thayre who was one half sharer amongst the company of players at the Red Bull and who had bought it with his money and afterwards died and yet there was not one penny or other recompense paid or allowed to the executor or any

[18] London, Public Record Office C 24/500/103.

other in recompense [?] thereof and this deponent saith that he doth also know Richard Perkins and Francis Walpole two of the said company who left the company and had no allowance albeit they were sharers at the time of their departure from the said company. Also he saith that himself this day being a full sharer in the company did depart from them but yet had no allowance of the said company so that this deponent verily believeth that there was no agreement in writing made by the said whole company for the payment of any sum of money if any sharer should die or otherwise depart the company. . . .   Thomas Heywood

This authoritative contradiction in 1623 of the agreement made a decade earlier when Robert Lee left this troupe is puzzling. It may well have been that the rapidly declining fortunes of Queen Anne's men after Beeston left them had made it impossible to continue the old custom. It should be remembered also that the action of which this testimony is a part derived from Susan Baskervile's attempts to force the disintegrated Queen Anne's men to pay her money she claimed they owed her as chief legatee of their former manager, Thomas Greene, who had died eleven years before.

In any case it is apparent that this custom of buying out a sharer's interests was a theater custom, like so many others, which could be forgotten or ignored in times of adversity.

Not only did sharers need to have some capital to contribute, but their obligations to the troupe were not wholly discharged on the stage. Money had to be collected for the company's performances at court. The receipts for such payments were always signed by certain sharers. In the earlier days different sharers seem to have performed this chore. In March 1594/95 the payment for the performance of two plays at court in the previous Christmas season was made to three sharers of the Lord Chamberlain's company, William Kempe, William Shakespeare, and Richard Burbage; in the following year two other fellows of the company, John Heminges and George Bryan, collected. In the subsequent years of Elizabeth's reign

the receipts were signed by Thomas Pope and John Heminges, but for more than thirty years thereafter Heminges, as
manager, was payee.

The collection of fees for royal performances was similar in
the other companies of sufficient distinction to be commanded
to perform at court: fees for the Queen's men were collected
by John Dutton, John Laneham, and Lawrence Dutton; for
the Earl of Nottingham's company by Robert Shaw and
Thomas Downton; for the Lord Admiral's company by Martin Slater and Edward Alleyn, mostly Alleyn.[19]

HALF SHARES

Various allusions in documents of the period establish the fact
that some of the sharers of a theatrical troupe owned only half
a share. No doubt the most familiar of such allusions is the
one in the third act of *Hamlet*. It will be remembered that
after the success of the play scene, Hamlet, in high excitement about the success of the performance he has arranged,
cries to Horatio,

> Would not this, sir. . . .
> get me a fellowship in a cry of players, sir?

And Horatio replies soberly

> Half a share

and Hamlet

> A whole one I.

Philip Henslowe also refers in his Diary to the half shares
of certain players. On the first of June 1595 he loaned to his
improvident and frequently imprisoned nephew, Francis
Henslowe, ". . . In ready money to lay down for his half
share with the company which he doth play withal to be paid

---

[19] Chambers, *The Elizabethan Stage*, IV, 163-67. See Chapter VI below on
managers.

unto me when he doth receive his money which he lent to
my lord Burt or when my assigns doth demand it . . . £9."
The company cannot now be identified, but the transaction
is witnessed by "Wm Smyght player, gorge Attewell, player,
Robard Nycowlles player."

Two and one half years later Henslowe had an accounting
of money received on the half share of Humphry Jeffes, a
Lord Admiral's man for several years. Sir Walter Greg inter-
prets this transaction as an incompleted attempt on the part
of the company to buy back a half share from Jeffes, who is
known to have continued with the company for several years
after this. "A just account of the money which I have received
of Humphry Jeffes' half share beginning the 14 of January
1597 [98] as followeth."[20] There follows a list of seven payments of a few shillings each in the next three months. Then
Henslowe goes on, "This sum was paid back again unto the
company of my Lord Admiral's players the 8th of March 1598
and they shared it amongst them. I say paid back again the
sum of £3."[21] The reason for this attempt is by no means
clear, but it is obvious enough that Humphry Jeffes held a
half share.

In 1623 in their testimony in the suit of *Ellis Worth and John
Blaney v. Susan Baskervile and William Browne* both the experienced players, Richard Perkins and Thomas Heywood, refer
to the half share of Thomas Albanes in the company.[22]

There is even evidence that on occasion a full sharer was
reduced to half a share. In a letter of Richard Jones to Edward
Alleyn, probably of 1591/92, Jones writes that "I am to go
over beyond the seas with Mr. Browne and the company but
not by his means, for he is put to half a share, and to stay
here, for they are all against his going. . . ."[23] The wording
clearly suggests the company's disapproval of Browne but not

[20] W. W. Greg, ed., *Henslowe's Diary*, 2 vols., London, 1904-1908, II, 287.
[21] Foakes and Rickert, eds., *Henslowe's Diary*, pp. 9 and 71.
[22] See the more extended testimony of these witnesses quoted above, pp.
34-35.
[23] Greg, ed., *Henslowe Papers*, p. 33.

why. We can glean only the presumption that it was possible for a troupe to reduce a full sharer to a half sharer.

These scattered pieces of evidence are enough to show that the companies did make use of half sharers and that the public—at least theater audiences—were expected to be aware of the fact.

Why these men had only half shares one can only guess. Neither Francis Henslowe nor Humphry Jeffes much less John Thayer and Thomas Albanes were performers of any distinction, and Horatio's remark to Hamlet is evidently intended to be belittling. I would surmise that these half-share holders had paid only half the entrance fee subscribed by the whole-share holders; certainly the £9 which Philip Henslowe loaned his nephew is much less than any other sharer's fee known. I am aware of no evidence as to how their half-sharer status affected the function of these men in the councils of the company.

There seems to have been a growing tendency in the reigns of James and Charles for the companies to concentrate financial and managerial functions in the hands of one, two, or three sharers. In some troupes this concentration approached the managerial system of the Restoration companies. That development can be treated more conveniently in Chapter VI.

SELECTION OF PLAYS

Another responsibility of the sharers had to do with additions to the repertory. Precisely what the procedure was in the judging of new manuscripts offered for production cannot yet be determined; probably it differed from troupe to troupe and from period to period. Certainly, in the 1590s when fewer actable old plays were available for revival, the players whose purchases were underwritten by Philip Henslowe had to buy more new manuscripts than did the King's men in the 1630s when they already owned all Shakespeare, nearly all Beaumont and Fletcher, and most of Massinger, Middleton, and Jonson.[24]

There is enough evidence to show that the sharers often had to assemble to listen to the reading of a new composition and to pass judgment on it. There are various references to this practice. On 3 December 1597 Henslowe recorded in his diary a payment of twenty shillings to Ben Jonson "upon a book which he showed the plot unto the company. . . ." After several payments to Drayton, Dekker, and Chettle for a play called *The Famous Wars of Henry I and the Prince of Wales*, Henslowe recorded on 13 March 1597/98 that he lent the company "for to spend at the reading of that book" at the Sun in New Fish street, five shillings. On 8 November 1599 Robert Shaw wrote to Henslowe that "we have heard their book and like it" and requested Henslowe to advance £8 to Wilson for it. In May 1602 Henslow recorded in his Diary what he had paid out for wine for the company "when they read the play of Jeffa."[25]

Several years later, in 1613, half a dozen letters from the playwright Robert Daborne refer to this play-reading custom. On 8 May Daborne wrote to Philip Henslowe that the play he was working on would be ready soon, so that when the company finished with "this new play they are now studying" Henslowe would please to "appoint any hour to read to Mr. Allin." Again on the 16th he wrote that he would read some of the new play to Henslowe and Alleyn, "for I am unwilling to read to the general company till all be finished." About a month later he wrote that the company would not have to delay for him because that same week he would deliver in the last word . . . "& will that night they play their new play read this. . . ." In December 1613, Daborne, still wanting money, wrote that the new play he was working on would make "as good a play for your public house as ever was played"

---

[24] See Bentley, *The Jacobean and Caroline Stage*, I, 108-134.

[25] Foakes and Rickert, eds., *Henslowe's Diary*, pp. 85, 88, 201; Greg, ed., *Henslowe Papers*, p. 49.

and that "upon the reading it" the company would have Henslowe pay out for them £20 rather than lose such a fine play. To a letter of 31 December 1613 Daborne adds a postscript "on Monday I will come to you & appoint for the reading the old book & bringing in the new."[26]

One cannot be certain, of course, that this custom of reading a new manuscript to all sharers was universal, but evidently it was common. The chore must have consumed a deal of the time of sharers, especially in the early days when so many more new plays were required than later.

What happened when the sharers listened to the plays must be mostly a matter for conjecture. Surely not every play offered could have had a complete reading before all the patented members; they would have had time for little else. Presumably someone had done a preliminary reading, but who? I have found no answer to this question. There are a few records of the rejection of play manuscripts by the players, but they do not tell us much.[27]

And what happened with play manuscripts submitted by the regular attached dramatists for their companies, like the plays Thomas Heywood wrote for Queen Anne's company or James Shirley for Queen Henrietta's or William Rowley for the Prince's men or Richard Brome for the Salisbury Court players or Shakespeare, Fletcher, Philip Massinger, and James Shirley during their different periods of attachment to the Lord Chamberlain-King's company?[28] Since these playwrights were so intimately associated with the companies of players for which they were writing, the sharers may well have known in advance what was being composed and could even have been consulted about particular scenes or characters or stagings while the new manuscript was in process of composition. For such attached dramatists the usual reading be-

[26] Greg, ed., *Henslowe Papers*, pp. 69-81.

[27] See G. E. Bentley, *The Profession of Dramatist in Shakespeare's Time*, Princeton, 1971, "Rejections," pp. 79-82.

[28] Ibid., *passim*, esp. pp. 30-37.

fore the sharers may have been omitted. Or perhaps it became something more in the nature of a meeting of the ways and means committee than of an assessment committee.

Yet in at least one instance a play written by an attached dramatist for the company to which he was contracted was rejected by the sharers. Richard Brome had signed a contract in 1635, renewed in 1638, with the sharers of Queen Henrietta's company and the owners of the Salisbury Court theater to write plays exclusively for them. Troubles developed, and the ten sharers in Queen Henrietta's company and the owners of the Salisbury Court brought suit in the Court of Requests against Brome. In the usual fashion of lawsuits, the two parties make numerous charges against each other. In his answer Richard Brome says:

> . . . before Easter term 1639 this defendant brought them another new play written all but part of the last scene. But this defendant found that divers of the company did so slight the last-mentioned plays and used such scornful and reproachful speeches concerning this defendant and divers of them did advise the rest of them to stop all weekly payments towards this defendant. . . .[29]

One could wish for more evidence of the deliberations of the sharers before they accepted a proffered manuscript and turned it over to the prompter for annotation and the preparation of sides. And who was in charge of the casting? I cannot answer this question with confidence. Presumably casting was discussed with attached dramatists while their plays were being composed, but many plays written by free-lance dramatists were performed. Surely such dramatists as Henry Shirley, Robert Davenport, Lodowick Carlell, Arthur Wilson, William Berkeley, or Jasper Mayne, who had a play or two produced by the King's men, were not consulted about the casting. One can only speculate that such casting may have

---

[29] See Ann Haaker, "The Plague, the Theatre, and the Poet," *Renaissance Drama*, n.s. 1 (1968), 304.

been done by the manager or leader of the company in consultation with the sharers.[30]

RECRUITMENTS AND DISMISSALS

The sharers of the company must also have had much of the responsibility for recruitment to their ranks and for the dismissal of unsatisfactory members. The number of sharers in a troupe seems to have remained more or less constant at ten or twelve,[31] and commonly a new sharer was acquired only when an old one died, retired, or gave up his fellowship for one in another troupe. But there were exceptions. Will Kempe, who was the most famous comedian of his day and the subject of numerous allusions,[32] left the company apparently in 1599, about the time of his spectacular dance from London to Norwich, one of the most notorious feats of the period. The popular Kempe ceased to be a member of the Lord Chamberlain's company and at that time sold his shares in the new Globe theater, then abuilding, to Shakespeare, Heminges, and Augustine Phillips.[33] There is no evidence that he ever returned to the Lord Chamberlain's company; he seems to have spent some months doing other dancing feats. He was succeeded as principal comedian by Robert Armin, and not long after had become a member of the Earl of Worcester's company, a troupe clearly inferior to the Lord Chamberlain's.

It is odd for an actor as famous as Kempe to leave the lead-

[30] See below, Chapter VI, "Managers."

[31] See T. W. Baldwin, *The Organization and Personnel of the Shakespearean Company*, Princeton, 1927, pp. 46-89. Actually the number of sharers even for the King's company was not quite so rigorously maintained as Baldwin contends, but in general his arguments for a fairly constant group are well taken.

[32] See Edwin Nungezer, *A Dictionary of Actors and of Other Persons Associated with the Public Representation of Plays in England before 1642*, New Haven, 1929, pp. 216-22.

[33] See the suit of *John Witter v. John Heminges and Henry Condell* in the Court of Requests, C. W. Wallace, "Shakespeare and His London Associates," *University of Nebraska Studies* 10 (1910), 54.

ing company of the time; and, so far as we know, it is unparalleled for an actor to go off on solo feats of his own like the dance to Norwich and the alleged dance over the Alps into Italy. Was he dropped because of his long absence? Were the dancing spectacles motivated by a break with the company?

There is no reliable evidence, but the departure of Kempe, one of the principal attractions at the Globe, surely presented a problem to the sharers. The selection of Robert Armin as their new comedian and sharer was obviously a matter of great concern and must have required protracted discussions among the patented members.

A more fully documented disciplinary action by a group of sharers is that of Prince Charles's (II) company against William Bankes. Again the affair is known through a suit in the Court of Requests, *William Bankes v. Andrew Keyne and Ellis Worth* in 1635. Both parties agree that Bankes became a sharer by paying into the "stock of the company" £100. But Bankes complains that he has been assessed for the purchase of costumes, though he asserts that he had been promised exemption from such levies; that he has not been paid his dividends; that he has not been made a Groom of the Chamber as the other sharers were and as he was promised. He claims that all his dealings were with Worth and Keyne hence he makes them defendants in his suit.

A very different story is told in the Answer of Worth and Keyne, which, on analysis, is much more in accord with facts and customary practices.[34] The defendants say that Bankes had introduced himself

> unto these defendants and to the rest of the company of the Prince's players of the private playhouse in Salisbury Court in the bill mentioned (they being in all eleven in number) that he the complainant might enter into the said company the complainant paying into the stock of the said company

[34] See Bentley, "The Troubles of a Caroline Acting Troupe" for both the quotations from the documents of the suit and a discussion of the accuracy of the statements of the two parties.

the sum of one hundred pounds, whereunto these defendants and the rest of the said company assented. And thereupon the complainant did agree to pay to the said company one hundred pounds and to become an actor with the defendants in the said exercise of stage playing and to bear his ratable and proportionable part of the charges of apparel and other necessary charges incident thereunto from time to time and to be conformable to the orders of the said company. And thereupon and not otherwise the said whole company of players of that house (and not the said defendants alone) did agree to and with the complainant that he should have and enjoy his proportionable part and share of such profit and benefit as should accrue and arise unto the said company and that they would employ themselves as actors in the said company.

This answer of Worth and Keyne indicates what from other sources would appear to have been the normal practice, though not elsewhere so explicitly stated. And consideration of Bankes and his money by the eleven sharers of Prince Charles's company was one of the normal extrahistrionic activities of the patented members of a troupe.

But the problems of the sharers with Bankes went far beyond this initial consideration. Further along in their Answer Worth and Keyne deny some of his complaints and explain others. They say that some three weeks before Bankes's complaint he had departed from the company:

And since his departure his share is set apart for him and he may have it if he will rejoin himself to the said company according to the said agreement. But these defendants say that the complainant hath not been conformable to the orders of the said company but hath broken the same orders by his disorderly behavior to the very great prejudice of the said company whereof these defendants doubt not but that they shall be able to make due proof to this honorable court.
. . .

Worth and Keyne say further that if Bankes will come back and behave himself they are ready and willing

> to go with the complainant to speak for him that he might be sworn his Majesty's servant in ordinary, the complainant being at the charge thereof and paying such fees and duties as were to be paid for the same which these defendants have been and are ready to do so as he [Bankes] rejoin himself again to these [sic] company and be conformable thereto. . . .

Bankes did come back, as is proved by the fact that ten months later he and three others were sworn Grooms of the Chamber "to attend the Prince his highness in the quality of player."

This suit in the Court of Requests tells us nothing of what Bankes's offenses had been, but serious they evidently were, and protracted discussions among the sharers must have been required.[35]

The company of Prince Charles was greatly inferior to the King's men at the Blackfriars and the Globe and to Queen Henrietta's troupe at the Phoenix. Those troupes would never, so far as we can tell, have made a full sharer of a man like William Bankes. But the responsibilities of the sharers were similar.

---

[35] The dismissal of a sharer was evidently not too unusual, since it had been explicitly provided for in the contract, probably of 1613, between Henslowe and Meade on the one hand and Nathan Field representing the company (Lady Elizabeth's?) on the other.

> . . . And further that the said Philip Henslowe and Jacob Meade shall and will at all times upon request made by the major part of the sharers of the said company under their hands remove and put out of the said company any of the said company of players if the said Philip Henslowe and Jacob Meade shall find the said request to be just and that there be no hope of conformity in the party complained of. . . . (Greg, ed., *Henslowe Papers*, p. 24)

The fact that the sharers were to take the initiative suggests to me that difficulties with a nonconforming sharer had prompted expulsions in London companies before. This clause is evidently not another example of Henslowe's attempts at dominance.

Finally, there is one method of recruitment of which I know only a single example, but which should be noticed. On the 6th of May 1633, the Lord Chamberlain addressed a warrant to John Lowin and Joseph Taylor, who had been the leaders or managers of the King's company since the death of John Heminges:

> Whereas the late decease, infirmity, and sickness of divers principal actors of His Majesty's company of players hath much decayed and weakened them, so that they are disabled to do His Majesty's service in their quality, unless there be some speedy order taken to supply and furnish them with a convenient number of new actors. His Majesty having taken notice thereof and signified his royal pleasure unto me therein, these are to will and require you and in His Majesty's name straightly to charge, command, and authorize you and either of you to choose receive and take into your company any such actor or actors belonging to any of the licensed companies within and about the city of London as you shall think fit and able to do his Majesty service in that kind. Herein you may not fail. And this shall be your sufficient warrant and discharge in that behalf. Court at Whitehall the 6th of May 1633. To John Lowen and Joseph Taylor, two of the company of his Majesty's players.[36]

The drafting of players was not wholly without precedent, but the earlier example is outside the scope of this work and rather different in character. It is best recounted by Edmund Howes in his continuation of Stowe's *Annales*.

> Comedians and stage-players of former time were very poor and ignorant in respect of these of this time; but being now grown very skillful and exquisite actors for all matters, they were entertained into the service of divers great lords; out of which companies there were twelve of the best chosen,

---

[36] "Dramatic Records: The Lord Chamberlain's Office," *Malone Society Collections* 2, pt. 3 (1931), 361.

46

and, at the request of Sir Francis Walsingham they were sworn the Queen's servants and were allowed wages and liveries as grooms of the chamber. And until this year 1583 the Queen had no players.[37]

The unique order of 6 May 1633 to the leaders of the King's company to draft any London player or players they thought they needed is another example of the dominance of the royal troupe in London theatrical affairs. Probably any player in London would have been happy to be so drafted, for increased income and prestige would normally follow. What was the attitude of the managers of the other London companies whose players were so drafted is another matter.[38]

DUTIES OF SHARERS

What were the regular duties and responsibilities of sharers? So far as I know there is only one extant document that outlines them in detail. This agreement is far from a normal one, but though it stipulates excessive fines, and is an attempt to establish a dictatorship (which soon failed) the duties and responsibilities enumerated can, I think, be taken as normal.

In August 1613 Philip Henslowe joined with Jacob Meade in a builder's contract to transform the Bear Garden into a dual purpose house, namely the Hope theater, for the exhibition of both bear-baiting and playacting. The enterprise did not last long: the first company deserted in about a year, and Henslowe died in two or three years.[39]

As a part of this project an agreement was drawn up with one of the players, Robert Dawes. Presumably there were agreements with other players of the company as well, but no trace of them has been found. The articles between Henslowe

---

[37] Stowe, *Annales*, 1615, p. 697, as quoted in Chambers, *The Elizabethan Stage*, II, 104-105.

[38] See below, Chapter VI, on managers.

[39] See Chambers, *The Elizabethan Stage*, II, 448-71; and Bentley, *The Jacobean and Caroline Stage*, VI, 200-214.

and Meade on the one hand and the player Robert Dawes on the other were clearly designed to establish Henslowe as a theatrical dictator rather in the fashion of the attempt of Richard Heton twenty-five years later. Henslowe failed, and the agreement can scarcely have been wholly typical of most companies. Nevertheless the duties and responsibilities enumerated appear to be those expected of a sharer in a normal London troupe.

The document, now lost, was formerly among Henslowe's papers; it is dated 7 April 1614.[40] I have excerpted these papers, I hope judiciously, because of the number of provisions that apply to the payment of rents or special obligations to Henslowe and Meade and not to the duties and responsibilities that may be taken to be more typical of most sharers.

> [Articles of Agreement,] made concluded and agreed upon and which are to be kept and performed by Robert Dawes of London Gent. unto and with Phillip Henslowe Esquire and Jacob [Meade Waterman] in manner and form following, that is to say
>
> Imprimis. The said Robert Dawes for him his executors and administrators doth covenant promise and grant to and with the said Phillip Henslowe and Jacob Meade their executors administrators and assigns in manner and form following, that is to say that he the said Robert Dawes shall and will play with such company as the said Phillip Henslowe and Jacob Meade shall appoint for and during the time and space of three years from the date hereof for and at the rate of one whole share according to the custom of players; and that he the said Robert Dawes shall and will at all times during the said term duly attend all such rehearsal which shall the night before the rehearsal be given publicly out; and if that he the said Robert Dawes shall at any time fail to come at the hour appointed, then he shall and will pay to the said Phillip Henslowe and Jacob Meade their executors or assigns twelve pence; and if he come not

40 Greg, ed., *Henslowe Papers*, pp. 123-25.

before the said rehearsal is ended then the said Robert Dawes
is contented to pay two shillings; and further that if the
said Robert Dawes shall not every day whereon any play
is or ought to be played be ready apparelled and—to begin
the play at the hour of three of the clock in the afternoon
unless by six of the same company he shall be licensed to
the contrary, that then he the said Robert Dawes shall and
will pay unto the said Phillip and Jacob or their assigns
three [shillings] and if that he the said Robert Dawes happen to be overcome with drink at the time when he [ought
to] play, by the judgment of four of the said company, he
shall and will pay ten shillings, and if he [the said Robert
Dawes] shall [fail to come] during any play having no license or just excuse of sickness he is contended to pay twenty
shillings. . . . and likewise shall and may take and receive
his other moity . . . the moneys received at the galleries
and tiring house due toward the paying to them the said
Phillip Henslowe and Jacob Meade of the sum of one
hundred twenty and four pounds [being the value of the
stock of apparel furnished by the said company by the said
Phillip Henslowe and Jacob Meade] . . . the one part of
him the said Dawes or any other sums . . . to them for any
apparel hereafter newly to be bought by the [said Phillip
Henslowe and Jacob Meade until the said Phillip Henslowe
and Jacob Meade] shall thereby be fully satisfied contented
and paid. And further the said Robert Dawes doth covenant [promise and grant to and with the said Phillip Henslowe and Jacob Meade that if he the said Robert Dawes]
shall at any time after the play is ended depart or go out of
the [house] with any [of their] apparel on his body, or if the
said Robert Dawes [shall carry away any property] belonging to the said company, or shall be consenting [or privy to
any other of the said company going out of the house with
any of their apparel on his or their bodies he the said] Robert Dawes shall and will forfeit and pay unto the said Phillip and Jacob or their administrators or assigns the sum of
forty pounds of lawful [money of England]. . . .

. . . [In testimony] for every such whereof I the said Robert
Dawes have hereunto set my hand and seal this [sev]enth
day of April 1614 in the twelfth year [of the reign of our
sovereign lord &c.]   Robert Dawes

Since this detailed agreement is the only one of its kind that
has been preserved, it is not easy to distinguish those provisions which may be taken as typical from those which are
peculiar to Henslowe and Meade and their attempt to establish an autocracy at the Hope. Dawes's agreement to attach
himself permanently to the Hope and its owners no matter
what troupe occupied the theater was not, so far as one can
tell, usual at the Globe, the Blackfriars, the Red Bull, the
Phoenix, or the Fortune. The sharer's allegiance was ordinarily to his company and not to the theater or its owner. It is
true that in 1624 Richard Gunnell persuaded six sharers of
the Palsgrave's company to sign a bond to continue to play
together at the Fortune, but this was an attempt to preserve
a faltering troupe, not to tie individuals to a theatrical entrepreneur.[41]

The provision about attendance and punctuality at rehearsals I take to be common, though fines for violations in most
companies would be paid not to the owner of the theater but
to the company treasury.[42] Similarly I take the fines for absence, tardiness, or drunkenness at performances to be common, though again the money would ordinarily go not to the
theater owner but to the company.

The responsibility of Dawes as a sharer for the company
debt for supplies and for further purchases of costumes and
properties is a common obligation,[43] but except for those companies financed by Philip Henslowe or Edward Alleyn the
payment of the sharer for his interest in past purchases and

[41] See Bentley, *The Jacobean and Caroline Stage*, 1, 148-49.
[42] The passage in *Histriomastix* (Act IV 1610 quatro), in which Posthaste is
fined one shilling for coming late to rehearsal indicates that the custom was
familiar. The two cases are not, however, precisely parallel since Posthaste
is the poet and not an actor.
[43] See above, pp. 29-32.

for new ones as they were made seems to have been due to the company and not to the theater owner.

The problem of actors making off with costumes or some-times with play scripts is alluded to in other contexts. Perhaps the most revealing is in the agreement between Martin Slater and his company recited in a Chancery Bill of Complaint of 9 February 1608/09.

> It is . . . agreed that all such apparel as is abroad shall be brought in . . . it is further . . . agreed . . . that if at any time hereafter any apparel, books, or any other goods or commodities shall be conveyed or taken away by any of the said parties without the consent and allowance of the said residue of his fellow sharers and the same exceeding the value of two shillings, that then he or they so offending shall forfeit and lose all . . . benefits . . . besides the loss of their places and all other interests which they may claim amongst us. . . .[44]

Although these duties, obligations, and punishments spec-ified for Robert Dawes cannot be demonstrated to be the same as those of all sharers in all companies of the time, it seems to me likely that other established troupes had similar under-standings. The irregularities listed are those which would be troublesome in other Jacobean and Caroline companies, and most of them are referred to in Henslowe's and Alleyn's pa-pers and in various suits of the time, though not elsewhere grouped together and specifying penalties.

SHARERS' INCOMES

As we have seen, the sharers in Elizabethan, Jacobean, and Caroline dramatic companies were not paid wages as the hired

---

[44] *Transactions of the New Shakespeare Society*, Vol. 1887-92, pt. 3, p. 276. In May 1598 Henslowe had bought from this same Martin Slater five plays for the Admiral's men. All five had formerly belonged to the company. Had Slater made off with them when he left the company about a year before? (Foakes and Rickert, eds., *Henslowe's Diary*, pp. 89 and 93.)

men were; they were directors of the organization, and their recompense was a share in the profits.

There is plenty of evidence that the sharers did receive a portion of the take at each performance, but until the reign of Charles I almost no direct and reliable evidence of how much money this might be. Henslowe's Diary shows clearly enough in various entries that sharers were paid from the receipts but not how much per sharer. In a few instances sharers assigned to Henslowe the income from their shares, but only occasionally does the entry record what the sum was or, if a sum is set down, what proportion of the share it constituted. Probably most specific is the record of 1 April 1598, "Received of Gabriel Spencer at several times of his share in the galleries as followeth beginning the 6 of April 1598." There follow the records of five payments, but they were made at irregular intervals of from eight to forty-three days apart and there is no indication as to whether the sums—from four to seven shillings—were Spencer's total share for that day or only the sum he chose to pay to Henslowe.

Well known is Henslowe's entry about the player and poet Ben Jonson.[45]

> Received of Benjamin Jonson's share as
> followeth   1597
>
> Received the 28 of July 1597 . . . 3s 9d

The entry is, however, ambiguous, since "share" could mean either a share in the receipts of the company or a share in the payment for a play or for the revisions in a play. Though there is evidence elsewhere in the Diary that Jonson was a player, there is none that he was ever a sharer.

It would be interesting and useful to know how much a share might be expected to produce in the course of a year. Until the last decade of the period, however, the evidence is too scattered, too contradictory, and too inferential to allow any sound generalizations for all companies. Such slippery

[45] Foakes and Rickert, eds., *Henslowe's Diary*, pp. 67-68 and 52.

evidence is used in Appendix II, "Finance in the Shakespearean Company," of T. W. Baldwin's *The Organization and Personnel of the Shakespearean Company* but even for this best-known
troupe of London players the conclusions seem to me to be
totally unreliable.

The variations in the compensation reaching sharers during
the period 1590-1642 must have been great. First, there are
the variations according to date. The cash rewards available
to a major player in 1591 would fall far short of those available
to sharers in almost any London troupe in 1639 when all had
royal patents and inflation had soared. Again there are large
discrepancies between the receipts of a minor troupe like Prince
Charles's (II) men and those of a major company like the players of King Charles. This discrepancy between the incomes
of fellows of minor and major organizations is due not only
to the comparative receipts of playhouses like the Blackfriars
and the Globe on the one hand and the lowly Red Bull on
the other, but also to the fact that extratheatrical fees such as
those for court performances, guilds, and Inns of Court performances, and individual rewards for participation in guild
and royal pageantry are paid in nearly all recorded examples
to players in the major troupes like the King's men and the
Queen's men. Finally the theater receipts, upon which the
dividends of the sharers depended, fluctuated wildly from
season to season. In plague years of 1593, 1594, 1603, 1604,
1625, 1630, 1631, 1636-37, and 1640 there were no London
gate receipts for significant periods. In 1625 the plague was
so severe and the closing so protracted that all London companies except the King's went bankrupt. The plague of 1636-
37 was less severe but more protracted, and again all London
theaters were closed for months on end.[46] Such fluctuations
compound the difficulties raised by the paucity of evidence of
direct payments.

The most reliable figures on a sharer's annual income derive

[46] See Bentley, *The Jacobean and Caroline Stage*, II, 652-72; and F. P. Wilson,
The Plague in Shakespeare's London, Oxford, 1927.

from a series of petitions to the Lord Chamberlain.[47] These petitions ("The Sharers' Papers") primarily concern the holdings of actors and others in two playhouses, the Blackfriars and the Globe; the figures about acting shares are mentioned only incidentally, but they come from reliable sources. As may be remembered, three leading sharers in the King's company were trying to persuade the Lord Chamberlain to force John Shank, Cuthbert Burbage, Winifred Burbage, and young William Burbage to sell them part of their housekeepers' shares in the Blackfriars and Globe theaters. The three complaining sharers, Robert Benfield, Eyllaerdt Swanston, and Thomas Pollard, assert that

> . . . upon a medium made of the gains of the housekeepers and those of the actors one day with another throughout the year, the petitioners will make it apparent that when some of the housekeepers share the 12 shillings a day at the Globe the actors share not above 3 shillings. And then what those gain that are both actors and housekeepers and have their shares in both your Lordship will easily judge. . . .

To these assertions John Shank, the veteran comedian and longtime sharer in the comapny, replies:

> That whereas the petitioners in their complaint say that they have not means to subsist, it shall by oath (if need be) be made apparent that every one of the three petitioners for his own particular hath gotten and received this year last past of the sum of £180 which, as your suppliant conceiveth is a very sufficient means to satisfy and answer their long and patient expectation, and is more by above the one half than any of them ever got or were capable of elsewhere. . . .

This surprisingly large sum is verified and made slightly more explicit by the three Burbages in their own reply to the Lord Chamberlain, supplementary to John Shank's:

---

[47] "Dramatic Records: The Lord Chamberlain's Office," pp. 362-73.

Then to show your Honor against these sayings that we eat the fruits of their labors, we refer it to your Honor's judgment to consider their profits, which we may safely maintain, for it appeareth by their own accounts for one whole year last past beginning from Whitsun-Monday 1634 to Whitsun-Monday 1635 each of these complainants gained severally as he was a player and no housekeeper £180. Besides Mr. Swanston hath received from the Blackfriars this year as he is there a housekeeper above £30, all which being accounted together may very well keep him from starving.

This large sum of £180 which "might very well keep them from starving" includes, of course, sizable amounts that were each sharers' portion of the "rewards" paid the company for court performances.[48] One hundred eighty pounds is truly a surprising amount for a player to receive; it must be remembered, however, that no other troupe handled anything like the large receipts that came to the King's men.

No comparatively precise and authoritative figures are available for other companies or other times, but one of almost the same date as the reports of John Shanks and the Burbages shows how different the situation was in one of their rival troupes, Prince Charles's (II) men. In the Court of Requests suit of *Bankes v. Worth and Keyne*, Ellis Worth and Andrew Keyne, managers of the company, reply on 18 February 1634/35 to the complaint of William Bankes that he had not received returns that were his right as a sharer.

that the complainant hath been and is allowed such particular share and benefit of the gain and profit gotten at the said playhouse called the Red Bull as was or is due unto him by the agreement made between the company and the complainant in that behalf. And the complainant or his wife did usually attend the sharing of the gains of the said playhouse from time to time at the end of every play and did receive all such moneys as were due the complainant for his

[48] See Bentley, *The Jacobean and Caroline Stage*, I, 97-98.

share together with an allowance of six pence by the day for every day they acted over and above the complainant's share, which did amount to twenty nobles [six shillings and eight pence, or one-third of a pound] per annum or thereabouts . . . these defendants do believe that the complainant or his wife for his use hath received for the complainant's share of the said stage playing about the sum of one hundred pounds with the said six pence per day and five pounds for progress money.

By analyzing this statement and noting that the sum covers a period of two years, it can be deduced that Bankes's income as a sharer was approximately £40 per year. Of course it was to the advantage of Worth and Keyne to exaggerate the payment of the company to the complainant, but even so it is clear that the sharers in Prince Charles's company received far less than the patented members of the King's company at about the same date.[49] It must be remembered that these figures come from late dates when the profitable court performances were far more numerous than in the days of Elizabeth, and when inflation had greatly diminished the value of the Elizabethan pound sterling.

Then there were various additional payments for special occasions for the better companies and for certain individuals—payments at noble houses, at the Inns of Court, or at guild halls. Probably lucrative were performances at great houses, but very few records have been unearthed. The only extensive account so far in print is the one Lawrence Stone made from the papers of the Earl of Cumberland and Lord Clifford.[50] But these records really apply to companies on tour; the houses concerned are so far from the capital that they could not have been visited by a regular London company unless it were touring. Nevertheless, the frequency of the vis-

[49] For the suit and for an analysis of the figures, see Bentley, "The Troubles of a Caroline Acting Troupe," esp. pp. 241-42.

[50] *Malone Society Collections* 5 (1960), 17-28. Also see below, Chapter VII, "London Companies on Tour."

its recorded and the sums paid to the players are suggestive
of what London companies might have received for performances at noble palaces in or near town.

These figures on the income of sharers are most unsatisfy-
ing, except for Prince Charles's (II) men and for the King's
players toward the end of the period, when we can be sure
that prices and payments were much greater than in the 1590s.
During the reigns of Elizabeth and James the evidence is too
spotty and too uncertain for me to hazard estimates of the
usual incomes of sharers in the London companies.

Occasions for Payment of Sharers

There are several references to the occasions when sharers
were paid their dividends, and they seem to indicate roughly
the same methods in different London companies and at different times. To us the method seems oddly primitive and
direct. At the end of each regular performance (except for
court and private performances, when payment was often long
deferred) there seems to have been a simple dividing up of the
cash.

This nightly division of receipts seems to be required in the
mutilated contract (presumably of 1613) between Nathan Field
for the Lady Elizabeth's company and Jacob Meade and Philip
Henslowe. ". . . And they the said Philip Henslowe and Jacob Meade . . . grant and agree that there shall be due account given every night to any one that shall by the company
be appointed thereunto. . . ."[51]

Of course the receipts from the parts of the house reserved
for housekeepers were deducted and the wages for the hired
men would, one would assume, also have been set aside. But
the cash from the players' parts of the theater seem to have
been literally parcelled out on a board or a table.

This custom of payment at the end of every performance
was evidently in vogue by Prince Charles's (II) company in

[51] Greg, ed., *Henslowe Papers*, p. 24.

1635; it is explicitly referred to by Worth and Keyne in their Answer in the suit of Bankes referred to before. These defendants reply to the complaint of Bankes that he had received no money: "And the complainant or his wife did usually attend the sharing of the gains of the said playhouse from time to time at the end of every play and did receive all such moneys as were due the complainant for his share. . . ."[52]

The same systems of dividend payments is indicated in the epilogue for Richard Brome's play, *The English Moor, or the Mock Marriage*, performed by Queen Henrietta's company in 1637, though not published until 1659 in the collection *Five New Plays*. The epilogue, speaking of the dodges to which this author (Brome) refuses to resort, says:

> Now let me be a modest undertaker
> For us the players, the play, and the play-maker
> . . . .
> And all that in defense the Poet can say
> Is that he cannot mend it by a jest
> I'th epilogue exceeding all the rest
> To send you off upon a champing bit,
> More than the scenes afforded of his wit.
> Nor studies he the art to have it said
> He skulks behind the hangings as afraid
> Of a hard censure, or pretend to brag
> Here's all your money again brought in i'th bag
> If you applaud not, when before the word
> 'Twas parcel'd out upon the sharing-board.

This primitive method of handling dividends of sharers seems rather crude for well-organized companies like Queen Henrietta's and for the King's men; one would suppose that Beeston and Heminges could have improved upon it. But I have been able to find references to no other method of paying the sharers their regular dividends.

[52] Bentley, "The Troubles of a Caroline Acting Troupe," p. 241.

SHARERS' EXTRAS

In addition to the payments to the sharers for their regular performances as a full troupe, there are records of payments to individual sharers for participation in the festivities of the London livery companies.

The records of the City guilds have been combed by Jean Robertson and D. J. Gordon in their "A Calendar of Dramatic Records in the Books of the Livery Companies of London, 1485-1640;"[53] but though the feasts and pageants of the guilds often used players, the accounts seldom give names as well as amounts paid.

In 1611 John Lowin, who became a prominent sharer in the King's company, had a large role in the Lord Mayor's pageant, and according to the Goldsmiths' records agreed that "himself should provide a horse and furniture for himself and the horse, and for his paines therein is referred to the consideration of Master Wardens."[54] Lowin was a little different from the others in that he had served an apprenticeship under a goldsmith, but in 1611 he was a King's man. How much the "Master Wardens" decided to pay Lowin for himself, his horse, and its furniture is not recorded.

In the following year the new Lord Mayor was Sir Thomas Swinnerton, Merchant Tailor. In the pageant which his company prepared in his honor, John Lowin's fellow, John Heminges, had an even larger part. The company accounts carry the entry:

> Item paid to Master Heminges and Master Thomas Dekker, the Poet, for the device of the land shows, being a sea chariot drawn by the sea horses, one pageant called Neptune's throne, with seven liberal sciences, one castle called Envy's Castle, one other pageant called Virtue's Throne, and for the printing of the books of the speeches, and for

[53] *Malone Society Collections* 3 (1954).
[54] Ibid., p. 81.

59

the persons and apparel of those that went in them, the sum of . . . £197.0.0[55]

Unfortunately this sum is not itemized, but the opening statement sounds as if Heminges had a principal part in the composition. When the pageant, *Troia-Nova Triumphans*, was printed in 1612, however, only Dekker's name appeared on the title page. Heminges had been employed by the Merchant Tailors several years before in training his apprentice John Rice to deliver a speech at the Merchant Tailors' dinner for royalty.

Much later, in 1639, William Hall of the King's Revels company was paid by the Drapers' Guild for his part in preparing their pageant *Londini Status Pacatus*. The entry reads:

Item paid to William Hall the player for his music and actions in Cheapside the sum of . . . £13.6.8[56]

The very scattering of these records suggests that there may have been other examples of players being paid for their parts in traditional shows. But the only generalization one can make is that it seems likely that various sharers in the major companies made a little money on the side by helping in the pageantry for Lord Mayor's shows and other City occasions.

For the leading companies there were occasional grants of assistance in times of distress, such as those given the King's men near the end of the severe plague of 1603 and again during the plague of 1636-37. In the Revels accounts at the beginning of the reign of James I is the entry:

To Richard Burbage one of his Majesty's comedians upon the Council's warrant dated at Hampton Court 8 February 1603 [/04] for the maintenance and relief of himself and the rest of his company being prohibited to present any plays publicly in or near London by reason of great peril that might grow through the extraordinary concourse and as-

[55] Ibid., p. 85.
[56] Ibid., p. 130.

sembly of people to a new increase of the plague till it shall please God to settle the city in a more perfect health: by way of his Majesty's free gift . . . £30.[57]

In the later protracted plague of 1636-37 King Charles was even more generous. During that plague a warrant was issued on 13 December 1636:

> . . . the King having commanded his servants the players to assemble their company and keep themselves together near the Court, gives them an allowance of £20 per week, which is to be paid to John Lowen and Joseph Taylor, on behalf of their company; such allowance to commence from the 1st November last, to continue during his Majesty's pleasure, and to be taken as of his princely bounty.[58]

Individual members of the King's company also achieved special recognition to which some monetary reward must have been attached. In 1632 Queen Henrietta decided that she and several of her ladies would give a performance of Walter Montague's *The Shepherd's Paradise*. There was much talk about the enterprise both before and after the performance. On 15 September 1632 John Pory wrote to Viscount Scudamore:

> The Queen's Majesty with some of her ladies, and maids of honor is daily practicing upon a Pastoral penned by Mr. Walter Montague. And Taylor the prime actor at the Globe goes every day to teach them action.

Six weeks later the same correspondent wrote Scudamore: ". . . Mr. Taylor, the player, hath also the making of a knight given him for teaching them how to act the Pastoral."[59]

So far as I know this use of a professional player as a coach

---

[57] Peter Cunningham, *Extracts from the Accounts of the Revels at Court in the Reigns of Queen Elizabeth and King James I, from the Original Office Books of the Masters and Yeomen*, Shakespeare Society, vol. 7, London, 1842, p. xxxv.

[58] *Calendar of State Papers, Domestic*, London, 1636-37, p. 228.

[59] Quoted from the Scudamore Papers by J. P. Feils, *Shakespeare Survey* 11 (1958), 109-110.

for amateur performances at court is unique. Considering the social status of Queen Henrietta and the ladies of her court versus that of a professional player, as well as the jealousies usual among court ladies, one marvels at the tact which must have been required of Taylor. His selection for the post is no surprise, for at the time he was probably the most distinguished player in London as well as a manager of the premier company. He must have been rewarded liberally for his services.

Taylor received other court rewards, but too much later to seem related to his coaching activities. In the Lord Chamberlain's Warrant Books under date of 29 September 1639 occurs the entry: "A warrant to swear Mr. Joseph Taylor, yeoman of the Revels to His Majesty in the place of William Hunt, deceased." And six weeks later Taylor's patent confirming him in his new office was copied into the Warrant Books. It is too long and verbose to quote in full, but it provides that Taylor is to have the office for life; he is to receive a fee of six pence a day; he is to receive yearly a royal livery coat "such as the yeoman officers of our household have of us"; and he is "to have and enjoy one sufficient house or mansion as shall hereafter be assigned to the said Joseph Taylor for the sure better and safe keeping of our said vestures, apparels, and Trappers together with all manner of other commodities and advantages to the said offices to be due and accustomed. . . ."[60] In spite of his new position Taylor appears to have remained active in the King's company, receiving payments for court performances with Lowin and Swanston on several occasions.

John Lowin, another prominent sharer of the company and later a co-manager with Taylor, also received an honor and no doubt profits from a court appointment. In the notes by one of the Masters of Requests, Sir John Coke, prepared for his first audience with Charles I on 12 May 1625, occurs the following: "King James's servants . . . John Lowen, porter,

[60] "Dramatic Records: The Lord Chamberlain's Office," pp. 391 and 343-46.

who bought his place, being a player, for £200, to be continued in it. . . . His Majesty's comedians to be sworn again in
ordinary. . . ."[61]

All these extra fees might suggest at first glance that one
way and another the players had a fairly lucrative profession,
but such a conclusion would be very far from the truth. It
should be noted that only five players are named, John Lowin,
Joseph Taylor, John Heminges, John Rice, and William Hall.
There were hundreds of other stage people in London in these
years, none of whom is known to have received any of these
perquisites. It should be further noted that all but one of these
players, William Hall, belonged to the Lord Chamberlain-
King's company. Even the odd, wholly undramatic, payment
of William Shakespeare and Richard Burbage for painting the
shield and devising the motto of the Earl of Rutland for the
anniversary of the accession of James I, though it seems to
have no theatrical connection at all, involved two more fellows
of the King's company.[62] Again the records testify to the overwhelming dominance of the King's company and the fallacy
of taking anything that happened to its members as typical of
the lives of London players.

[61] *Review of English Studies* 1 (1925), 184. From *Historical Manuscripts Commission*, Cowper MSS., p. 194.

[62] See E. K. Chambers, *William Shakespeare: A Study of Facts and Problems*,
2 vols., Oxford, 1930, II, 153. On 31 March 1613, Shakespeare was paid
forty-four shillings for devising the impressa, and Burbage the same for painting it.

CHAPTER IV

Hired Men

"HIRED MEN" is the term commonly used in the reigns of Elizabeth, James, and Charles for those theater people who were not named in the patents and did not share in the profits but were paid weekly wages by the sharers. The term was used by both players and laymen. In the anonymous late Elizabethan play *Histriomastix* one of the soldiers says: "Come on Players, now we are the Sharers, and you the hired men." A leading actor in the King's company, Augustine Phillips, in his will of May 1605 leaves £5 to be distributed amongst "the hired men of the company." In 1623 the actor Richard Baxter testified in a Chancery suit that he had come to the players of the Red Bull "as an hired man to the company." Three sharers of the King's company complained in 1635 that out of the sharers' dividends there is "defrayed all wages to hired men." In 1640 the Master of the Revels issued a special pass to "the

Prince's Players' hired men." And after Parliament's abolition of all theatrical enterprises, the anonymous author of *The Actors' Remonstrance*, 1643/44, a former sharer of some dramatic troupe, complained that "our Hired-men are dispersed, some turned Soldiers and Trumpeters, and others destined to meaner courses or depending on us, whom in courtesy we cannot see want for old acquaintance sake."[1]

The distinction between sharers and hired men or servants or "hirelings" of the players was clearly explained in July 1634 to Thomas Crosfield, a Fellow of Queen's College, Oxford. On the 18th, Crosfield was visited by one of a troupe of touring players whom he calls "The company of Salisbury Court at the further end of Fleet Street against the Conduit." Crosfield noted in his diary what had been explained to him about the London theatrical troupes. After listing nine members of his own company, the informant, Richard Kendall, continued, "These are the chief, whereof seven are called sharers, i.e., such as pay wages to the servants and equally share in the overplus: other servants there are as two clothes keepers, Richard Kendall and Anthony Dover."[2] As Kendall implies, though he mentions only "clothes keepers" or tiremen or wardrobe keepers, the basic distinction is that hired men did not, like the major actors, or sharers, receive a percentage of the profits from the theater, nor did they work for their keep and their training and a fee for their masters as did the boys or apprentices. All hired men, whatever their duties, worked for weekly wages. The distinction is clearly implied in two of the tickets of privilege granted to the hired men of the King's company. On 27 December 1624 the Master of the Revels listed twenty-one names and said that they "are all employed by the King's Majesty's servants in their quality of playing as

---

[1] Several examples of the use of the terms "hired men," "hirelings," or "journeymen" in the nondramatic literature of the time are given in E. K. Chambers, *The Elizabethan Stage*, 4 vols., Oxford, 1967, I, 362n. "Hired man" is, however, the term nearly always used by the players themselves.

[2] G. E. Bentley, *The Jacobean and Caroline Stage*, 7 vols., Oxford, 1941-1968, II, 688-89.

musicians and other necessary attendants. . . ." Thirteen years later a similar document of 1636/37 was issued from the Lord Chamberlain's Office. It protected eleven men from arrest. Part of the sample form reads: "Whereas the bearer hereof Richard Baxter hath been and is employed by His Majesty's Servants the players of the Blackfriars and is of special use unto them both on the stage and otherwise. . . ."[3] In both documents "the King's servants" refers to the sharers of the company, the patented members, the employers of the hired men.

These employees were minor actors, musicians, prompters or book holders, stagekeepers, wardrobe keepers or tiremen, or sometimes gatherers. Of course, any of these functionaries of the playhouse could be called upon to act minor roles in performances, especially in crowd scenes. Usually the performers with few or no lines are not named in extant cast lists, but now and then the surviving play texts, especially prompt manuscripts, reveal what must have been a common practice. In the Folio text of *A Midsummer Night's Dream* in the first scene of the fifth act before the entrance of Bottom and his fellow players is the direction "*Tawyer with a Trumpet before them,*" a line evidently crept in from a prompt manuscript. Tawyer was one of the twenty-one men listed in Sir Henry Herbert's ticket of privilege of 1624 referred to above. In the British Museum manuscript of Thomas Heywood's *The Captives*, a prompt stage direction at V,2 reads, "stagekeepers as a guard." In Glapthorne's *The Lady Mother* the company musicians have an active part. Shakespeare's use of a small group of his company's musicians to take part in the action on the stage is familiar in plays like *Romeo and Juliet* and *Othello*. In the modified version of Marston's *Malcontent*, acted by Shakespeare's company in 1604, the Induction begins with the entrance of Will Sly, "a tireman following him with a stool." The tireman, or wardrobe keeper, has two or three lines.

[3] "Dramatic Records: The Lord Chamberlain's Office," *Malone Society Collections* 2, pt. 3 (1931), 380-81; and Joseph Quincy Adams, *The Dramatic Records of Sir Henry Herbert*, New Haven, 1917, pp. 74-75.

It does not seem likely that the book holder or prompter could often be spared for an acting role during a performance. The "Book-keeper" in the Induction to Jonson's *Bartholomew Fair* performed at the opening of the Hope theater in 1614, may have been the actual book keeper for the Lady Elizabeth's company, but it seems more likely that he was a regular player impersonating the company's book keeper, who would have been busy with his regular duties during the opening scene of a performance.

In their heyday a major company could have a good many of these hired men. On 27 December 1624, the Master of the Revels issued a certificate to protect from arrest, imprisonment, or other molestation the hired men of the King's company; twenty-one men are named. Several can be identified: one is the book keeper; several are musicians; several are little-known players; but six are known as theatrical personnel from this document only. The fact that half a dozen of the names in this certificate are otherwise totally unknown is suggestive. If so many of the men necessary for performances at Blackfriars and the Globe by the richest and most fully documented company of the time are lost in obscurity save for this single record, how many of the "necessary attendants" attached to the twenty or so less prominent London troupes during these fifty-two years have completely disappeared? All signs suggest that there were many more players in London than we can at present identify. Certain parish registers support this assumption.[4] Of these London "players" of whom

---

[4] Most of the parish registers of births, marriages, and burials that are extant either in print or in manuscript are little more than lists of names and dates. In a city like Tudor and Stuart London where so many names are the same it is usually impossible to identify players in these registers. But there are a few sets of parish registers, like those of St. Giles without Cripplegate, St. Botolph's Aldgate, and St. Saviour's Southwark that record the occupation of the father of the christened child and sometimes are even more explicit in a burial register; as when the clerk of St. Botolph's Aldgate recorded in November 1615, "Robert Armin free of the Goldsmiths and a Player was buried the thirteenth day." In these three unusually explicit registers there are more than twenty men called "player" by their parish clerks who are otherwise unknown in any theatrical connection.

we know only that they fathered a child or suffered the loss of a wife or child, it is likely that most were hired men. Of nearly all the sharers we know more, because they are generally named in the required legal patents for their companies, and as superior actors they are more likely to be named in allusions, financial records, or lawsuits. Boy actors were generally too young to sire children or to be named in lawsuits. Hired men probably constituted the largest class of theatrical personnel living in London in Shakespeare's time.

Hired Men Who Were Primarily Players

As the tickets of privilege of 1624 and 1636/37 have shown, there were a good many hired men—certainly in the King's company and presumably in others as well—who were not primarily players. But these musicians, stagekeepers, and other helpers often appeared on the stage, as we have seen in the examples of *The Captives, A Midsummer Night's Dream, The Lady Mother, Romeo and Juliet*, and *Othello*; a good many other examples can be gleaned from the chance printing of prompters' notes in printed texts, and still more from extant prompt manuscripts like that for Massinger's *Believe as You List*.

Is it possible to identify those hired men who were primarily actors and not musicians or wardrobe keepers or tiremen or gatherers or stagekeepers? One source of information is the casts and player lists published in certain quartos and folios and listed in a few manuscript plays. Unhappily there are less than thrity of them and almost never do they give a full cast; eight to twelve players are usually named and a third to half the named roles are unassigned. Of course these unassigned roles are the ones most likely to have been filled by hired men, but the majority of them are too small to require a trained performer.

These casts give good reason for certain conclusions about hired men. They show that, at least in the companies from which we have several sets of assigned roles, the majority of the hired men cannot have been primarily players. We have

68

seen that in December 1624 twenty-one individuals were named hired men of the King's company, yet in the seven casts for productions by this company in the years 1626-1632 (*The Roman Actor, The Deserving Favorite, The Lovers Melancholy, The Picture, The Wild Goose Chase, The Soddered Citizen,* and *The Swisser*) the numbers of hired men assigned roles are four, three, four or five, one, one, three, and one. These figures suggest that of the twenty-one hired men the King's company needed in 1624 to supplement the efforts of the thirteen sharers and the apprentices, not more than five or six of them needed to be primarily actors. The fact that all but three or four of these hired men who were assigned roles in the plays of the King's company became, in later years, sharers in this or some other company indicates that they were indeed players and not tiremen or stagekeepers filling in.

The persons who appeared as hired men in casts or lists (including the Jonson folio lists) of the King's company but who over a period of thirty-five years became sharers in this or some other London troupe were John Duke, Christopher Beeston, John Lowin, Alexander Cooke, William Eccleston, John Underwood, Thomas Pollard, William Penn, John Honeyman, and probably Anthony Smith. These hired men were evidently actors. Players who appeared in more than one King's cast but are not known ever to have become sharers are Patrick, Greville, Vernon, Horne, and Nicholas Underhill. Even though they are not known ever to have reached the top of their profession, I am inclined to think that these particular hired men were players and not wardrobe keepers or musicians filling in.

There is some reason to think that these dispositions of sharers and hired men in the King's company were fairly normal. The five casts for Queen Henrietta's men show similar numbers and dispositions except for a slight increase in the use of hired men: two, three, three, three, four. In Queen Henrietta's casts the hired men who later became sharers in some company are John Young, Christopher Goad, Theophilus Bird or Bourne, and George Stutfield. Hired men in Queen

Henrietta's company who never became, so far as we know, sharers in any London troupe were William Reynolds, William Shakerley, William Wilbraham, John Dobson, Robert Axen, and John Page.

HIRED MEN, NOT PLAYERS

Although, as we have seen, those hired men who were not primarily players did appear occasionally on the stage in performances, their primary activities in the theaters were not histrionic. They played music, or took care of costumes, or swept the stage and moved props, or prepared prompt manuscripts and actors' sides, or collected admissions at the door. Something is known of the activities of all these lesser theatrical folk, though in some classes tantalizingly little. Most frequently mentioned of these nonacting groups are the musicians.

HIRED MEN, MUSICIAN-PLAYERS

The fact that there exist a few instances in which a man is sometimes called musician, sometimes player in one or two parish registers is suggestive that the man concerned was probably a theater musician hence the varied designations. See Francis Hitchins, once player, once drummer in St. Giles Cripplegate registers; Edward Minshaw, gent, player, musician, and again player, St. Saviour's Southwark; Thomas Heywood, St. Saviour's Southwark, 1600-1610 four times player, once musician; Thomas Marbeck, in 1603 a musician in St. Saviour's Southwark records but in Admiral's record of 1602 as a player.[5]

Perhaps these irregularities show that those musicians who played in the theaters were often classified as players, but the answer is not clear. Some of the contradictions may reflect

[5] Bentley, *The Jacobean and Caroline Stage*, II; "Shakespeare's Fellows," *Times Literary Supplement*, 15 November 1928, p. 856.

simple errors made by the parish clerks, or some may indicate changes of profession. It is also possible that in one or two cases different men of the same name may be involved.

In any case, these few examples from parish records are not enough to invalidate the evidence showing that theater musicians, though included in exemptions for hired men, were generally considered a separate group.

MUSICIANS

The extensive use of music in all Tudor and Stuart dramatic productions sometimes surprises modern readers. The vast majority of all extant plays of this period call for vocal or instrumental music, generally both, and there is copious evidence that the music was of a fairly high order. Even in the early sixteenth-century days of the poor touring companies of four to six men and a boy, musical demands are made of the players; even then music was an important part of English dramatic activities. David Bevington points out how common it was in the early sixteenth-century plays:

> In a remarkably high percentage of plays offered for acting, all or nearly all of the actors are required to sing, usually as a group. In *The Longer Thou Livest* all four players are on hand on two separate occasions to sing. . . . The two songs in *New Custom* are each rendered by all four actors in the troupe. *The Tide Tarieth*, with four players, has three songs and each is sung by a quartet. In *Trial of Treasure* all five players join in song. . . . In *Lusty Juventus*, *Like Will to Like*, and *King Darius*, the number of singers equals the number of players, and in *Three Laws* and *Mary Magdalen* all but one of the actors sing.[6]

In the nineties Henslowe was buying musical instruments for his companies as several of his entries show:

[6] David M. Bevington, *From "Mankind" to Marlowe: Growth of Structure in the Popular Drama of Tudor England*, Cambridge, Mass., 1962, p. 98.

> Lent unto Richard Jones the 22nd of December 1598 to buy a bass viol and other instruments for the company . . . 40 shillings
>
> Lent unto Thomas Downton the 13th of July 1599 to buy instruments for the company the sum of . . . 30 shillings
>
> Lent unto the company the 6th of February 1599 to buy a drum when to go into the country . . . 11 shillings 6 pence
>
> Received of Mr. Henslowe this 7th of February 1599 the sum of 22 shillings to buy 2 trumpets . . . 22 shillings
> Robt Shaa[7]

A few years later there is a tribute to London theater music in one of the tales in *Ratsies Ghost*: "I pray you (quoth Ratsey) let me hear your music, for I have often gone to plays more for music sake than for action. . . ."[8]

A similar impression of music in the theaters is recorded in 1617 in a letter of the chaplain of the Venetian Embassy in London:

> The other day, therefore, they determined on taking me to one of the many theatres where plays are performed, and we saw a tragedy, which diverted me very little, especially as I cannot understand a word of English, though some little amusement may be derived from gazing at the very costly dresses of the actors, and from the various interludes of instrumental music, and dancing, and singing. . . .[9]

Years later theater musicians, at least in London's most distinguished playhouse, had a high reputation. Bulstrode Whitelocke wrote a set of memoirs for his children in which

[7] R. A. Foakes and R. T. Rickert, eds., *Henslowe's Diary*, Cambridge, 1961, pp. 102, 122, and 130.

[8] *Ratsies Ghost, or the Second Part of His Mad Pranks and Robberies* (1605), facsimile edition of the Rylands copy, ed. H. B. Charleton, Manchester, 1932, A3.

[9] *Calendar of State Papers, Venetian*, London, 1910, XVI, 67.

he tells something of his life as a young lawyer at the Middle Temple; at that time he made some of the preparations for the notorious *Masque of Peace* presented by the lawyers to the King and Queen. He says:

> I was so conversant with the musicians, and so willing to gain their favor, especially at this time, that I composed an air myself, with the assistance of Mr. Ives, and called it *Whitelocke's Coranto*; which being cried up was first played publicly by the Blackfriars music, who were then esteemed the best of common musicians in London. Whenever I came to that house (as I did sometimes in those days) though not often, to see a play, the musicians would presently play *Whitelocke's Coranto*, and it was so often called for that they would have it played twice or thrice in an afternoon.[10]

Whitelocke implies that the musicians at Blackfriars formed a permanent group and not a temporary collection of musicians. He indicates the same in his accounts for the production of Shirley's *Masque of Peace* when he assigns a chariot each to the Blackfriars music and to the Phoenix musicians (see below).

The same assumption that the Blackfriars music was a permanent unit is seen in an account of events in Barbados after the closing of the theaters.

> As for music and such sounds as please the ear, they wish some supplies may come from *England* both for instruments and voices, to delight that sense, that sometimes when they are tired out with their labor, they may have some refreshment by their ears; and to that end, they had a purpose to send for the music that were wont to play at *Blackfriars*, and to allow them a competent salary, to make them live as happily there, as they had done in *England*. And had not extreme weakness, by a miserable long sickness, made me uncapable of any undertaking, they had employed me in

[10] Charles Burney, *A General History of Music*, New York, 1935, II, 299. From Whitelocke's manuscript.

the business, as the likeliest to prevail with those men, whose persons and qualities were well known to me in *England*.[11]

Probably the musicians were the most distinctive and exclusive group among the hired men of the London dramatic companies—at least in the latter half of the period. Not only were they a unit but certain records suggest that some of these theater orchestras had a certain independent existence. Edmond Malone, who had the original of Herbert's Office Book, now lost, said that "From Sir Henry Herbert's Manuscript I learn, that the musicians belonging to Shakespeare's company were obliged to pay the Master of the Revels an annual fee for a license to play in the theater." And then he quotes from Sir Henry Herbert's manuscript: "For a warrant to the musicians of the King's company this 9th of April, 1627—£1.0.0."[12]

Other records show theater musicians hired as a unit for entertainments at the Inns of Court, or mention their charges for special performances outside the theater. In Bulstrode Whitelocke's account of the preparations for the Inns of Court presentation of Shirley's *Triumph of Peace* in 1633/34 he lists the various floats and chariots in the procession. He says that the second chariot carried the Blackfriars music "John Adson, Ralph Stretch, Henry Field, Ambrose Beeland, Francis Parker, Thomas Hutton, and two boys," and that "the first chariot carried the Phoenix musicians, Jeffrey Collins, Thomas Hunter, John Levasher, Nicholas Underhill, Edward Wright, John Strange, and two boys."[13]

Similarly in 1634 the Drapers' accounts for their Lord Mayor's Show for Sir Henry Garway list: "Item paid to William Hall the player for his music and actions in Cheapside the sum of £13.6.8."[14] Since William Hall was a member of Prince

---

[11] Richard Ligon, *A True and Exact History of the Island of Barbados*, London, 1657, p. 107.

[12] Adams, *Dramatic Records of Sir Henry Herbert*, p. 46.

[13] Andrew J. Sabol, "New Documents on Shirley's Masque, The Triumph of Peace," *Music and Letters* 47 (January 1966), 25-26.

[14] Jean Robertson and D. J. Gordon, "A Calendar of Dramatic Records in

Charles's (II) company at this time presumably his music was provided by musicians belonging to that company.

Indicative of the same custom of theater orchestras playing for fees outside their theaters is a statement of the anonymous player who published *The Actors' Remonstrance or Complaint . . .* in 1643/44; complaining of the sad state of the actors and their employees since Parliament's closing of the theaters:

> Our music that was held so delectable and precious that they scorned to come to a Tavern under twenty shillings salary for two hours, now wander with their instruments under their cloaks, I mean such as have any, into all houses of good fellowship, saluting every room where there is company with *Will you have any music Gentlemen. . . .* [A3^V–A4]

I know of no conclusive evidence of the number of musicians in a theater orchestra during this period, but there is a suggestive repetition of the number six. Whitelocke listed six names as the Blackfriars orchestra he hired and six names of musicians in the Phoenix orchestra. The same number is noted in Henry Glapthorne's play *The Lady Mother*, extant only in manuscript until 1882, but licensed for production 15 October 1635 and performed by the Revels company at the Salisbury Court theater.[15] In Act II Captain Suckett calls for the musicians to help him and when they come in, he says:

> . . . where are they? Let me see how many's of you, 1, 2, 3, 4, 5, 6. Good. Can any of you dance?[16]

In December of 1624 the Master of the Revels issued an exemption from arrest during the time of the Revels for twenty-one men "all employed by the King's Majesty's servants in their quality of playing as musicians and other necessary attendants, and are at all times and hours to be ready with their

---

the Books of the Livery Companies of London, 1485-1640," *Malone Society Collections* 3 (1954), 130.

[15] See Bentley, *The Jacobean and Caroline Stage*, IV, 483-85.

[16] Arthur Brown, ed., *The Lady Mother by Henry Glapthorne*, Malone Society, Oxford, 1958 (1959), ll. 694ff.

best endeavors to do his Majesty's service (during the times of the Revels)." John P. Cutts has succeeded in identifying seven of these men as musicians. Some of the other names are not yet certainly identifiable, and two or three of the musicians may have been on temporary duty for the revels. Nevertheless, the number is suggestively close to the six indicated in the other records noted.[17]

The scene just quoted from *The Lady Mother* is another of the numerous examples which might be cited in which the company musicians were called upon not only to play in their music room before, during, and after the performance, but to be on stage as a part of the action. In this scene the musicians are on for more than fifty lines and the leader has several lines to speak. Shakespeare's use of the company's musicians on stage in *Romeo and Juliet* and *Othello* is familiar to all; numerous examples from other plays might be cited. Clearly it was generally assumed that the musicians were not confined to the music room but were available whenever the playwright and the company wanted a group of instrumentalists in the action on stage.

It has been suggested to me that though there are numerous allusions to musicians playing in theaters and though the majority of the extant plays of the period call for music, it is possible that a regular orchestra may not have been part of every established dramatic company. Some theaters may have simply called in London consorts when the performance of a play required instrumental music.

The passages already quoted seem to me to rule out this expedient for the Blackfriars, the Phoenix, and the Salisbury Court at least in the 1630s. As for the public theaters in the reigns of Elizabeth and James, I cannot prove that musicians were a regular part of every theater staff, but surely the musicians who played an hour's concert before the performance

[17] John P. Cutts, "New Findings with Regard to the 1624 Protection List," *Shakespeare Survey* 19 (1966), 101-107.

at Blackfriars in 1602[18] must have been attached to that theater.

I have encountered no allusions to the summoning to a theater of an unattached group of musicians, but of course I cannot say that it never happened. For the established companies of Jacobean and Caroline London the substitution of occasional musicians on call for a regular attached orchestra would seem to me to have been a very awkward and unreliable expedient.

TRUMPETERS AND DRUMMERS

Of course the group in the music room of Elizabethan, Jacobean, and Caroline theaters did not include the drummers and trumpeters who were in such constant demand. Every theater had to have them, but they seem not to have been included in the term "musicians," at least as it was used in the theaters. The music historian, Sternfeld, points out that "The trumpeters belonged to a special guild and did not play in combination with other instruments.[19]

There must have been a good many trumpeters in London, for they were in constant use not only in all playhouses but for all sorts of state occasions. When the Iron Mongers company produced Dekker's *London's Tempe, or The Field of Happiness* as a Lord Mayor's Show, thirty-six trumpeters were employed, according to James Peller Malcolm; the accounts for Queen Anne's funeral show payments to twenty-eight trumpeters; the accounts of Shirley's *Masque of Peace* record the use of seven pairs of trumpeters.[20]

It is not extraordinary in a society so accustomed to trumpeting that three trumpet calls customarily announced the opening of theater performances. The scores of references to

---

[18] See Chambers, *The Elizabethan Stage*, II, 46-47.

[19] Frederick W. Sternfeld, *"Troilus and Cressida*: Music for the Play," *English Institute Essays* (1952), 121.

[20] James Peller Malcolm, *Londinium Redivivum*, London, 1803-1807, II, 45; H. C. De Lafontaine, *The King's Musicke*, London, 1909, p. 52.

77

this custom are so familiar that it seems unnecessary to cite any. So far as one can find, all theaters, public and private, normally used this announcement system.

But within the performance trumpets and cornets were in regular use too. The stage directions often call for a "flourish" or a "tucket" or a "sennet." Used in moderation these offstage music devices can be extremely effective, even thrilling, as a good modern performance of almost any of Shakespeare's histories and many of his tragedies have shown. But there are Jacobean and Caroline assertions that the more vulgar theaters overused their drums and trumpets.

Shortly after the Company of the Revels moved into the Red Bull theater, a house frequently charged with vulgarity, they announced in the prologue for their comedy *The Two Merry Milkmaids, or the Best Words Wear the Garland,*

> This day we entreat all that are hither come
> To expect no noise of guns, trumpets, nor drum,
> Nor sword and target; but to hear sense and words
> Fitting the matter that the scene affords.
> So that the stage being reform'd and free
> From the loud clamors it was wont to be
> Turmoiled with battles; you I hope will cease
> Your daily tumults, and with us wish peace.
>   [1620 edition]

Years later Edward Howard in his criticism of vulgarity in the Restoration theaters reminded the players,

> . . . but we may remember that the Red Bull writers, with their drums, trumpets, battles, and heroes have had this success formerly, and perhaps have been able to number as many audiences as our theatres. . . .
>   [*Six Days' Adventure*, 1671, A4ᵛ]

However crude the excessive use of trumpeting at the Red Bull may have been, a reading of a large number of Elizabethan, Jacobean, and Caroline plays makes it obvious that trumpets or cornets were called for in many scenes in other

theaters as well. Since the London trumpeters had an organization of their own, it was probably necessary to have one or
two among the hired men of any company. Besides their daily
"three soundings" to announce performances, the trumpeters
were called upon less constantly during most plays—especially Caroline ones—than were musicians in general. Presumably these trumpeters would often have been available for
a single act as "walk-ons" or for other miscellaneous chores.

In the Caroline plays drummers are also less frequently
mentioned in the dialogue or in the stage directions than they
had been in earlier plays. I have found no references to
professional drummers in the theaters. Tarleton, Kempe, and
other comedians are known to have used drums, but drumming was certainly not their primary function. Perhaps odd
players or hired men could take care of the drumming when
necessary.

In the earlier years of the period when the London companies were not so far removed from the old troupes which
spent much of their time touring the provinces, the use of
drums and trumpets to summon audiences in London as in
the country is mentioned. On 8 October 1594, Lord Hunsdon, then Lord Chamberlain and patron of Shakespeare's
company, wrote to the Lord Mayor requesting toleration for
his company of players in the City. His letter reads in part:

> . . . where my now company of players have been accus-
> tomed for the better exercise of their quality and for the
> service of her Majesty if need so require to play this winter
> time within the City at the Cross Keys in Gracious Street.
> These are to require and pray your lordship, the time being
> such as thanks be to God there is now no danger of the
> sickness, to permit and suffer them so to do. The which I
> pray you the rather to do for that they have undertaken to
> me that where heretofore they began not their plays till
> towards four o'clock, they will now begin at two and have
> done between four and five and will not use any drums or
> trumpets at all for the calling of people together and shall

be contributories to the poor of the parish where they play according to their abilities. . . . H. Hunsdon[21]

This use of drums and trumpets to summon crowds to performances in the country is familiar, but I know of no record of the use of drums as summoners for theater crowds in London after 1594. The use of drums in plays is common enough, but not their use as advertising for performances.

PROMPTER OR BOOK HOLDER OR BOOK KEEPER[22]

Though the work of the prompter was obviously important for London companies producing so many different plays each season as did troupes like the Lord Chamberlain-King's men, the Admiral-Palsgrave's men, and Worcester-Queen Anne's men, the evidence for his precise activities is meager and scattered. Much of the job description for this position must be inferential.

It has been suggested to me that the prompter's function in the metropolitan companies may have been carried on from time to time by various fellows of the troupe. Such an arrangement seems to me to be improbable, except possibly in emergencies. When companies produced as many different plays and as many revisions involving as many men and boys as did Elizabethan, Jacobean, and Caroline theater organizations, the prompter's chores must have been so multifarious

---

[21] E. K. Chambers and W. W. Greg, eds., "Dramatic Records of the City of London: The Remembrancia," *Malone Society Collections* 1 (1907), 74.

[22] All three terms were in regular use by theater people as well as the general public in the reigns of Elizabeth, James, and Charles. The prompt book itself was known as "the book" (see W. W. Greg, *Dramatic Documents from the Elizabethan Playhouses*, 2 vols., Oxford, 1931, 1, 192-93). This general usage sometimes produces what seem odd redundancies to modern readers. Greg points out entries in the Stationers' Register: "a booke called the booke of David and Bethsaba," "A booke called the booke of the m'chant of Venyce," "a booke called The booke of Pericles Prynce of Tyre." Obviously the printer was registering a prompt copy with this title either on the manuscript or on a wrapper.

and vital and many of them so nerve-wracking that irregular substitutions would surely have produced chaos.

Though the prompters were, by the very nature of their function, not much in the public eye, they are several times referred to, twice or thrice by name. In a Court of Requests suit of 20 May 1603 concerning affairs at the Boar's Head, Oliver Woodliffe describes Israel Jordane as "of London, Scrivener, belonging unto Browne and his fellow stage-players." Of course this statement is none too specific, but C. J. Sisson thinks that it "suggests that [Jordane] was the scribe and book-keeper of Worcester's men."[23]

Much more specific is the statement made by John Taylor, the Water Poet in *Taylor's Feast*, 1638: "I myself did know one *Thomas Vincent* that was a Book-keeper or prompter at the Globe playhouse near the Bank-end in Maid Lane. . . ." There is no other known reference to Vincent; presumably he worked in the early days of the Globe, since Taylor mentions him in connection with Singer, who was dead before 1612.

As will be noted later, the Master of the Revels mentions Knight as book keeper for the King's men in 1633, but no others are specifically named, though there have been various conjectures.

Plays and essays sometimes mention obvious functions of the prompter which merely indicate the assumption that the audience was aware of his activities. The Character of an Excellent Actor, in the Overbury collection, says:

> He doth not strive to make nature monstrous; she is often seen in the same scene with him, but neither on stilts nor crutches; and for his voice, 'tis not lower than the prompter, nor louder than the foil and Target.[24]

In John Fletcher's *Maid in the Mill* of 1623, after some confusion, Bustofa says, "That's true indeed: they are out of their

---

[23] C. J. Sisson, *The Boar's Head Theatre; An Inn-Yard Theatre of the Elizabethan Age*, London, 1972, p. 73.

[24] W. J. Paylor, ed., *The Overburian Characters to which is added a Wife*, by Sir Thomas Overbury, Oxford, 1936, pp. 76-77.

parts sure, It may be 'tis the Book-holder's fault: I'll go see. *Exit*" (II,2). Similarly in Richard Brome's *Antipodes*, performed by Queen Henrietta's men at the Salisbury Court theater in 1638, a voice "within" says "Dismiss the Court," whereupon Lord Letoy says, "Dismiss the Court: can you not hear the Prompter?" (III,8). In the additions to Thomas Goffe's *The Careless Shepherdess*[25] occur the lines:

Loud Music sounds.
But hist, the Prologue enters. *Landl.* Now it chimes. All in
to the Play, the Peals were rung before.
Pro. Must always I a Hearer only be?

Spark. Thrift.

He being out, is laughed at, by

Spruce. Landl.

Pro. Pox take the Prompter. *Exit*

These samples of references to the prompter show him in functions that might be characteristic of almost any period, but for the years 1590 to 1642 he must have been more indispensable than commonly. Not only were most companies producing scores of new plays, but in the earlier years of the period, 1590-1610, rarely was a play given consecutive performances; in the later years there were seldom more than three consecutive performances. Under such conditions a letter-perfect rendition must have been unheard of, and prompting a constant necessity. Furthermore, as the notes in the few surviving prompt manuscripts show, the prompter had to carry out a good many of the functions of a modern stage manager, seeing that the props were ready to be brought on, boys were ready to sing offstage or on, offstage noises were ready, musicians were in position before they had to come on stage—all this for several different plays each week.

In addition, it must be remembered that rarely in Elizabethan and Jacobean days, and seldom after, could prompter or players have been working from printed pages. The prompter had his full text and the players had their sides. But all were

---

[25] See Bentley, *The Jacobean and Caroline Stage*, IV, 501-505.

in longhand—and in some of the extant examples very poor and messy longhand it was.[26]

Much more of the prompter's time must have been taken up in working on prompt copies and the sides for actors than in prompting at actual performances; so much time in fact that one man could scarcely have written all that a company required, and most theatrical troupes must have been forced to employ scribes for much of the copying. Even if the dramatist's "fair copy" was legible enough for prompting, the entire 2,000 lines or so had to be copied for the actors' sides.[27]

Even after the prompter had a fair copy of the new play, he had a great deal to do before it could be performed. First it had to be licensed for performance by the Master of the Revels. Usually the Master does not say what individual brought in the manuscript, but on one occasion in October 1632 Sir Henry Herbert noted that it was Knight, the book keeper for the King's company, who paid him his £2.0.0 fee for licensing Ben Jonson's *Magnetic Lady*.[28]

Next the prompter had to see that any corrections, deletions, or revisions required by the Master were made in the prompt copy and in the sides of the several players. This chore could be assumed, but we have one record of Sir Henry Herbert's specific orders. In 1633 the King's men revived Beaumont and Fletcher's *The Woman's Prize or The Tamer Tamed*, but much in the play displeased Herbert. He wrote the company prompter:

Mr. Knight,
In many things you have saved me labor; yet where your judgment or pen failed you, I have made bold to use mine. Purge their parts as I have the book. And I hope every

[26] See the facsimiles in the second volume of Greg's *Dramatic Documents from the Elizabethan Playhouses*.

[27] These sides were the most ephemeral sort of theater material; only one is known to have survived from the period, that of Edward Alleyn for the role of Orlando in Greene's *Orlando Furioso*. Greg, *Dramatic Documents from the Elizabethan Playhouses*, I, 176-81. Most of my material on prompters is derived from this book.

[28] Adams, *Dramatic Records of Sir Henry Herbert*, p. 34.

hearer and player will think that I have done God good service, and the quality no wrong; who hath no greater enemies than oaths, profaneness, and public ribaldry, which for the future I do absolutely forbid to be presented unto me in any playbook, as you will answer it at your peril. 21 October 1633.[29]

The Master seems to suggest ("in many things you have saved me labor") that Knight had done some preliminary censoring for him on previous manuscripts; at any rate he flatly orders him to do so in the future. This was another chore for the prompter and one that seems likely to have got him into disagreements with players and dramatists.

But this censorship was by no means the end of the prompter's preproduction chores. He had to add to the dramatist's fair copy, or the scribe's transcription of it, scores of directions for properties and offstage sounds. Dramatists never made such directions sufficiently specific and frequently omitted them entirely. The book keeper usually had to add anticipatory stage directions, warnings for actors to be ready, such as *"Gascoine: and Hubert below: ready to open the trap door for Mr. Taylor"* on folio 18b of the prompt manuscript of Philip Massinger's *Believe as You List*, or in the entrance direction in the plot of *Frederick and Basilea* played by the Admiral's men at the Rose in 1597: "Basilea servant: Black Dick, Dick."

Somebody had to cast the play, and though the major roles were probably set by the players in conference, the many minor roles and their doubling probably had to be worked out by the prompter and he had to remember who had been assigned what walk-on. Hence the names of players appearing in the prompt manuscripts are mostly those of hired men or boys whose assignments in that play could easily be forgotten; names of major actors usually appear only incidentally, as in the case of Joseph Taylor in the quotation from *Believe as You List*.

Another function of the prompter is somewhat problemat-

[29] Ibid., p. 21.

ical, namely the making of a Plot or Plat for each play produced. It is problematical, because there are only seven extant
examples, all of them dating from the first twelve years of our
period. The question is, did the theaters continue to use them
until the closing of 1642? Their obvious usefulness is such
that I am inclined to guess that they were always used, but I
know of no evidence after about 1602. Sir Walter Greg, the
great authority on the subject, says that "Theatrical Plots are
documents giving the skeleton outline of plays, scene by scene,
for use in the theatre."[30] They summarize the entrances and
other nonverbal activities. To quote Sir Walter again, ". . .
we may suppose that these were prepared for the guidance of
actors and others in the playhouse, to remind those concerned
when and in what character they were to appear, what properties were required, and what noises were to be made behind
the scenes."

The prompter would have been the obvious man to make,
or at least to supervise the making of such Plots. They were
essentially aids to him as well as to the players in getting them
on stage at the proper moment and with the proper equipment, a real difficulty when the repertories were so large and
the run of each play so short. It is suggested that the Plot
hung backstage for the consultation of players uncertain about
their entrance cues.

Of course the Jacobean and Caroline use of Plots is speculative, since no example later than 1602 has been discovered,
but then most other records used inside the theaters after
Henslowe have disappeared too. Since a Plot for the play would
have been so helpful to the overworked prompter, I am inclined to think that they were used by the later companies as
by the earlier ones.

All the chores so far outlined involve the work on new plays,
but many productions in the reigns of Elizabeth and James
and probably most of those in the reign of Charles I were
revivals, plays that had been first mounted anywhere from

---

[30] Greg, *Dramatic Documents from the Elizabethan Playhouses*, I, 1, 3.

one to thirty years before. And a good many of these revivals, probably most of those for plays ten or more years old, involved revisions. Henslowe's Diary is full of payments to dramatists for revising or adding to old plays. Many title pages of printed plays advertise such revisions, and prologues often refer to them.[31]

All these revisions required more work, presumably done by the hard-working prompter. Not only did the revisions and deletions have to be added to the prompt copy, but changes in the personnel of the company required adjustments. Even in a troupe so stable as the King's men, boys grew too old or too tall for their old roles, and established actors died and were succeeded by sharers who might be equally competent but talented in different ways. When one notes that the repertory of the King's company in 1641 contained over sixty plays that had never been printed, to say nothing of one hundred or more which had been[32] the task of the book keeper swells to monumental proportions.

SCRIBES

Those hired copyists who accomplished part of the numerous chores of the prompters were not, so far as is known, really players or any organized part of the dramatic companies. One would guess that a number of scribes were given occasional employment, and they must have copied out thousands of pages for the various London troupes. Even Ralph Crane, the best-known of these copyists, says, as noted below, that he had "some" employment by the King's men. Presumably much of the work of these men was the writing out from the prompt manuscript the sides of the players, but the little identifiable copyists' work which has come down consists for the most part of copies of plays made for wealthy patrons.

[31] See the chapter on revisions in G. E. Bentley, *The Profession of Dramatist in Shakespeare's Time*, Princeton, 1971, pp. 235-63.

[32] See Bentley, *The Jacobean and Caroline Stage*, i, 65-66 and 108-134.

The best, almost the only one, of these copyists still identifiable is Ralph Crane, whose career has been studied by Professor F. P. Wilson.[33] Crane himself records that although he
had worked chiefly for lawyers, he had sometimes worked for
the King's company. In his volume of religious verse entitled
The Workes of Mercy, which he published in 1621, he wrote:

> And some employment hath my useful pen
> Had 'mongst those civil, well-deserving men
> That grace the Stage with honor and delight,
> Of whose true honesties I much could write,
> But will compris't (as in a Cask of Gold)
> Under the Kingly Service they do hold.

A number of his transcriptions have been identified. His copy
of Fletcher's *Sir John van Olden Barnavelt* has been used as a
prompt book, but more of his dramatic transcriptions have
been made for private collectors: Middleton's *A Game at Chess*,
the version of Fletcher's *Humorous Lieutenant* entitled *Demetrius
and Enanthe*, and Middleton's *The Witch*. If so much of his
work with the plays of the King's men is identifiable, one is
tempted to think that he may have done more of the lost prompt
books and of the hundreds of lost sides which the King's company had to have.

Anyone who has rummaged through the hundreds of thousands of legal documents of this period in the Public Record
Office has surely been impressed by the great number of
copyists who must have been working in London from 1590
to 1642. How many of them, like Ralph Crane, earned a few
extra shillings by copying plays and sides for the theatrical
companies? And who were they? And were any of the regular
hired men of the theatrical troupes good enough penmen to
be assigned some of the endless copying?[34]

---

[33] F. P. Wilson, "Ralph Crane, Scrivener to the King's Players," *The Library*, 4th ser., 7 (1927), 194-215.

[34] Perhaps we should remember that John Downes, the veteran prompter
in the Restoration theater, says that he did all this copying of sides himself.
Downes says that from 1662 to 1706 he worked for Davenant's company,

WARDROBE KEEPERS OR TIREMEN

The theater records of this period are full of accounts of expenditures for costumes; in fact, one would estimate that the greatest expense of any company of players in the period was the purchase of costumes. The most casual leafing through the pages of Henslowe's Diary is enough to show that he was putting out for his various companies a good deal more money in the purchases of costumes and costume materials than he was paying the dramatists for the plays in which this finery was displayed. These proportions, of course, represented sound economy. If the play turned out to be a complete failure, the money paid the playwright was not recoverable, while the costumes could be used for play after play; even after the fabric had worn out the gold or copper or silver trimming could be used to decorate other costumes in later plays. Color in "Elizabethan" performances came primarily from the gorgeous (and expensive) costumes of the actors. Foreign visitors to London theaters almost always comment on the splendid dresses of the actors.

The large stock of fine clothes which every company required and to which they were constantly adding must have demanded unremitting protection and care, but there are surprisingly few references to company wardrobe keepers or "clothes keepers" or "tiremen."

Henslowe made several payments to tiremen in the late years of Elizabeth but most show little about the duties of these wardrobe keepers. They do buy clothes or materials on order, and some of the entries suggest that the tireman himself was making part of the costumes. On 3 December 1596 Henslowe made an entry, "Delivered unto Stephen the tireman for to

---

"And as Book keeper and Prompter, continu'd so, till October 1706. . . . Writing out all the Parts in each Play; and Attending every Morning the Actors Rehearsals, and their Performances, Afternoons" (*Roscius Anglicanus*, London, 1708, p. A2). Even if this statement is accurate, there was much less copying to be done at Lincoln's Inn Fields, for many of the plays produced were revivals of plays already in print.

deliver unto the company for to buy a headtire and a rebato and other things, £3.10." Henslowe paid the "tyre man" ". . . for money which he laid out to buy taffeta for the play of Cardinal Wolsey . . . 13 d." And on 4 September 1602 he wrote into the company's accounts: "paid unto your tireman for making of William Kemp's suit and the boys'. . . 8s. 8d."

One of Henslowe's regular playwrights for a few years was Wentworth Smith, who is recorded as writing or collaborating in at least fifteen lost plays, first for the Admiral's men and later for the Earl of Worcester's men. Henslowe entered several payments for costumes for one of Smith's plays, *The Two Brothers*, which he sometimes calls *The Three Brothers*; a couple of these entries seem to imply that the tireman not only bought the material but made the costumes himself. In October 1602 he recorded:

> Lent at the appointment of the company unto the tireman to buy say for the play of the 2 brothers to make a witche's gown the sum of . . . 18/

> Paid unto the tireman for making of the devil's suit and "sperethes" [?] and for the witch for the play of the 3 brothers the 23 of October 1602 the sum of . . . 10/9

For another play by Wentworth Smith, the popular *Black Dog of Newgate*, Henslowe paid out for Worcester's men later in the following year:

> Delivered unto the tireman for the company 1602 [i.e., 1602/ 03] to buy 8 yards and a half of black satin at 12/ a yard to make a suit for the 2nd part of the Black Dog the sum of . . . £5.2   15 February[35]

[35] Foakes and Rickert, eds., *Henslowe's Diary*, pp. 50, 180, 215, 218, 219, 224. It is difficult for us to put in perspective these sums paid out by Henslowe and other financial agents, partly because the rate of inflation differed so vastly for different commodities, and partly because we find it incredible that the Elizabethan players spent such fantastic sums for costumes. The £5.2.0 that Henslowe paid the tireman to buy black satin for a costume for the second half of *The Black Dog of Newgate* would have purchased 204 play quartos in the bookstalls that year.

There are, of course, hundreds of other costume entries in the Diary, but most of them indicate the prices of the stuffs purchased rather than particular activities of the tiremen.

The names of three other tiremen (though for a boy company not an adult one) are known from a suit of 1608 discovered by Mark Eccles. Eccles says:

> David Yeomans, a tailor who could not sign his name, testified that Kirkham, Kendall, Hawkins, and "one Gibbyns" had made an inventory of the playhouse apparel and goods when Yeomans was "taken in by the masters of the said playhouse to be tyreman in the room of one Robert Rutson and one Goffe."[36]

During the years 1612-1616 William Freshwater, Merchant Tailor, aged seventy-two in 1620, was evidently a wardrobe keeper for Queen Anne's men at the Red Bull. In the Court of Requests suit brought by John Smith against Christopher Beeston concerning old debts for materials bought for Queen Anne's company, William was called to answer interrogatories in May 1620. He testified that he had himself frequently been sent to Smith to get materials. He said:

> . . . he knoweth it so to be for that he himself being a workman to the said company hath often and diverse times gone to the plaintiff's house sometimes by direction from the said Beeston and sometimes as sent by others of the said company for divers stuffs which they had occasion to use. . . .[37]

In the passage in Crosfield's Diary concerning the information regarding London companies given him by Richard Kendall, partly quoted above (see p. 65) there is an introductory statement. The diary entry, it will be remembered, is dated 18 July 1634:

[36] Mark Eccles, "Martin Peerson and the Blackfriars," *Shakespeare Survey* 11 (1958), 102.

[37] C. W. Wallace, "Three London Theaters of Shakespeare's Time," *University of Nebraska Studies* 9 (1909), 332.

One Richard Kendall about the age of 50 or upwards, belonging to the company of players of Salisbury Court that came to Oxford this year came to see me and related unto me divers particular stories, vizt.

1. Of his particular state and education in his youth at Kirkby Lonsdall where he served his apprenticeship to a tailor, and afterward went to Cambridge where he stayed but little, and then went to London where he became servant to Sir William Slingsby—and now he is one of the two keepers of the wardrobe of the said company.

And the enumeration of the companies ends with the account of Kendall's company at Salisbury Court. The final sentence is:

These are the chief, whereof seven are called sharers, i.e., such as pay wages to the servants and equally share in the overplus: other servants there are as two clothes keepers, Richard Kendall and Anthony Dover.[38]

Two later references to wardrobe keepers or tiremen tell us little about the men or their duties, but they do indicate the public awareness of the position among the hired men of the London troupes. In 1643/44 the anonymous player who wrote *The Actors' Remonstrance* included in his lament about the plight of the theater people since the closing of the theaters: "For our tiremen, and others that belonged formerly to our wardrobe, with the rest, they are out of service: our stock of clothes, such as are not in tribulation for the general use, being sacrificed to moths. . . ."

When John Downes, prompter in the Restoration theater, wrote his *Roscius Anglicanus*, he gave some account of the beginnings of the Restoration theater:

In the year 1659 . . . Mr. Rhodes a bookseller, being Wardrobe keeper formerly (as I am informed) to King Charles

[38] Frederick S. Boas, ed., *The Diary of Thomas Crosfield*, London, 1935, pp. 71-72.

the First's company of comedians in Blackfriars, getting a
license from the then governing State. . . .[39]

The number of these tiremen or wardrobe keepers who were
tailors or had been apprenticed to tailors or who were paid
for making or altering costumes is highly suggestive. Surely a
third-rate company like the one at the Salisbury Court theater
in 1634 did not own enough costumes to require two full-time
tiremen to keep track of them, but if most wardrobe keepers
were tailors making new costumes and repairing old ones, the
number is easily accounted for. In this connection it will be
remembered that when William Bird of the Palsgrave's men
wrote to Edward Alleyn in 1617 about the dishonest John
Russell who had been cheating the company as box holder,
Bird declared Russell would never again be allowed to hold
the box, "Yet, for your sake, he shall have his wages, to be a
necessary attendant on the stage, and if he will pleasure himself and us, to mend our garments when he hath leisure, we'll
pay him for that too. . . ." This offer would seem to imply
that the Palsgrave's men had more mending and altering than
their regular wardrobe keepers could manage.

Some slight suggestion of what the size of the wardrobe of
the Palsgrave's men might have been can be derived from some
miscellaneous papers of Philip Henslowe. The Lord Admiral's men, whose costumes he records, were the direct antecedents of the Palsgrave's and though some of the articles in
their collection of 1592/93 had surely worn out or had been
sold, it can be assumed that the troupe had bought many
others in the subsequent years. Henslowe lists: *"The book of
the Inventory of the goods of my* Lord Admiral's men, *taken the
10 of March in the year* 1598 [i.e., 1598/99]." With the supplementary list dated three days later over 270 items of dress are
included.[40] It can be assumed that the much richer and older

[39] P. C1. For a discussion of men of the name see Bentley, *The Jacobean and
Caroline Stage,* II, 544-46.

[40] W. W. Greg, ed., *Henslowe Papers,* London, 1907, pp. 113-16 and 118-
21.

King's company of the 1620s and 1630s had more costumes than the Palsgrave's of 1592/93.

That a wardrobe keeper could also be a "necessary attendant" or even an actor on the stage is indicated by the Induction that the King's Men had John Webster write for Marston's *Malcontent* probably in 1603 or 1604. It will be recalled that the Induction appearing in the third edition of *The Malcontent* consists of a conversation among five members of the company speaking under their own names, William Sly, Richard Burbage, John Lowin, John Sinklo, Henry Condell, plus the wardrobe keeper. The opening stage direction reads: "*Enter W. Sly, a Tire-man following him with a stool.*" The tireman has only three short speeches (within the capacity of almost any adult) and then presumably returned to his other duties. There would seem to be no reason that wardrobe keepers could not perform similarly in this or other companies, though not in their own characters.

GATHERERS OR BOX-HOLDERS

The most heterogenous group among the hired men was the gatherers; often called the box-holders for the obvious reason that they stood at the doors holding a box to receive admissions. Richard Flecknoe wrote in a melancholy piece which he dated 1652:

> From thence passing on to Blackfriars, and seeing never a playbill on the gate, no coaches on the place, nor doorkeeper at the playhouse door, with his box like a churchwarden, desiring you to remember the poor players. . . .[41]

Thirty years before in the previously noted letter to Edward Alleyn about John Russell, William Bird had said

> There is one John Russell, that by your appointment was made a gatherer with us, but my fellows finding often false to us have many times warned him from taking the box;

[41] Richard Flecknoe, *Miscellania*, London, 1653, 16-16ᵛ.

93

and he as often, with most damnable oaths, hath vowed never to touch. Yet, notwithstanding his execrable oaths, he hath taken the box, and many times most unconsciona- bly gathered, for which we have resolved he shall never more come to the door. . . .[42]

The gatherers were a heterogeneous group in a variety of ways; perhaps most conspicuously in that they were the only ser- vants of the Elizabethan theaters known to have included both men and women. Various references attest to this diversity, most succinctly a passage in the newsbook *Perfect Occurrences* for 5 October 1647, describing a raid on a performance of *A King and No King*: "The Sheriffs of the City of London with their officers went thither, and found a great number of peo- ple; some young Lords and other eminent persons; and the men and women with the boxes (that took monies) fled. . . ."[43]

Perhaps the most specific and accurate record of a female gatherer is to be found in the will of Henry Condell and later of his wife, Elizabeth. In his last testament of 13 December 1627, the veteran sharer of the King's company and house- keeper in both the Globe and the Blackfriars theaters be- queathed to his old servant Elizabeth Wheaton a mourning gown, forty shillings, and ". . . that place of privilege which she now exerciseth and enjoyeth in the houses of the Black- friars, London, and the Globe on the Bankside [for life] if my estate shall so long continue in the premises. . . ." This be- quest was renewed in the will of Condell's widow, Elizabeth, eight years later: "Item. I do give and bequeath unto Eliza- beth Wheaton widow, the gathering place at the Globe during my lease. . . ."[44]

In other theaters besides the Globe and Blackfriars there were women gatherers. On 11 April 1612, the player Robert

[42] Greg, ed., *Henslowe Papers*, pp. 85-86.
[43] Quoted in Leslie Hotson, *The Commonwealth and Restoration Stage*, Cam- bridge, Mass., 1928, p. 26.
[44] See Bentley, *The Jacobean and Caroline Stage*, II, 638-42.

Browne wrote to Edward Alleyn requesting Alleyn's good offices for his friend, an actor named Rose.

> . . . I understand that Mr. Rose is entertained among the Prince's men and means to stay and settle himself in that company and to set up his rest and to do his best endeavors only in that company. . . . In the meantime he hath requested me to be solicitous for him to you (who he knows can strike a greater stroke amongst them than this) as to procure him but a gathering place for his wife, for he hath had many crosses and it will be some comfort and help to them both, and he makes no doubt but she shall so carry herself in that place as they shall think it well bestowed by reason of her upright dealing in that nature. . . .[45]

The same assumption that gatherers were both male and female is made by the anonymous private theater actor who published *The Actors' Remonstrance or Complaint* in 1643. He recites the parlous state of all theater people since Parliament closed all playhouses more than a year before, and continues: "Nay, our very doorkeepers, men and women, most grievously complain that by this cessation they are robbed of the privilege of stealing from us with license. . . .[46]

But the gathering was not invariably done by women or by people of low status in the company. There are allusions to senior sharers holding the box. As early as 1583 the newly formed company of Queen Elizabeth was on tour and played at Norwich. There was a fracas when a local man tried to see the performance at the Red Lion Inn without paying. A scuffle ensued; two sharers left the stage to assist the gatherer; the culprit was chased and eventually stabbed. The important detail for our present purpose is that the cheated box-holder was John Singer, a sharer and one of the founding players of Queen Elizabeth's company.[47]

[45] Greg, ed., *Henslowe Papers*, p. 63.
[46] *The Actors' Remonstrance or Complaint*, London, 1643, p. A3ᵛ.
[47] See G. M. Pinciss, "The Queen's Men, 1583-1592," *Theatre Survey* 11 (May 1970), 51-52.

Another senior player who is known to have "held the box" was Richard Errington, leader of a provincial company. In the autumn of 1627 his company was on tour and playing at Ludlow; again there was an affray, and Errington testified in the ensuing investigation:

> The information of Richard Errington of the city of London, pewterer, aged fifty years or thereabout, deposeth and saith that upon yesterday about ten or eleven of the clock at night, this deponent being one of the company of his Majesty's players who then were acting in the said house, and this deponent taking money at the door. . . .[48]

One must note that these two examples of senior players acting as gatherers both come from provincial records. I am inclined to doubt that sharers ever held the box at a London theater except in some special situation; at least, I know of no record of such activity on the part of a patented member in London.

As one might expect, a recurrent problem the sharers had with their low-paid gatherers was theft. I have found no record of any method of checking the cash in the box against the number of spectators in the house. Presumably the actor Rose had this problem in mind when in recommending his wife as a prospective gatherer, he authorized Robert Browne to assure Edward Alleyn that ". . . he makes no doubt but she shall so carry herself in that place as they [the company] shall think it well bestowed by reason of her upright dealing in that nature. . . ." Alleyn and his company were not so fortunate in their experience with other gatherers, as the previously quoted letter concerning John Russell shows.

Thomas Heywood, who had had a long experience with the problems of the London theaters and their players, wrote an epistle for his *Apology for Actors* in 1612, "To my good Friends and Fellows the City-Actors." He concluded with a

---

[48] John Tucker Murray, *English Dramatic Companies 1558-1642*, 2 vols., London, 1910, II, 326.

96

wish implying what the constant problems of the players were: "So wishing you judicial audiences, honest poets, and true gatherers, I commit you all to the fullness of your best wishes. Yours ever, T. H." It is a little surprising to see a veteran dramatist and company sharer like Heywood put honest gatherers on a par with judicious audiences and fair-dealing playwrights.

The passage in *The Actors' Remonstrance or Complaint* quoted above continues with an example of one of the methods used by gatherers to defraud their employers:

> Nay, our very doorkeepers, men and women, most grievously complain that by this cessation they are robbed of the privilege of stealing from us with license: they cannot now as in King Agamemnon's days seem to scratch their heads where they itch not, and drop shillings and half crown pieces in at their collars.

One hundred years later the problem of preventing theft at the box still plagued the players, according to Judith Milhouse and Robert Hume.[49]

At the outset of this discussion of gatherers, I noted that they were an heterogeneous group. Not only does the evidence show a mixture of men and women, of hired men and sharers, but there are clear indications that a number of them owed their positions at least in part to the housekeepers of the theaters, rather than to the players who were responsible for the recruitment of the other hired men. Clearly Elizabeth Wheaton held her gatherer's place at the pleasure of the Condells as housekeepers at the Globe and Blackfriars. The dishonest John Russell had held the box at the recommendation of Edward Alleyn.

This anomalous situation presumably arises from the usual method of paying theater rents in the time. In all the cases known the players paid their rent not as a set sum delivered

---

[49] See their article "Box Office Reports for Five Operas Mounted by Handel in London, 1732-1734," *Harvard Library Bulletin* 26 (July 1978), 245-66.

to the owners of their playhouses, but as a percentage of the take at certain doors. Therefore the owners or housekeepers had as much interest in the collections of the gatherers as did the sharers themselves. The fact that in some theaters, like the Globe and Blackfriars and at certain periods the Fortune and the Red Bull, there was some overlap between players and the lay investors made no difference so far as gatherers were concerned. Those sharers, such as Greene and Condell and Shakespeare and John Heminges and John Shank, who were also housekeepers, had two cuts of the daily take, one as sharers and one as housekeepers. Several documents make clear references to this arrangement.

In the long wrangling about housekeepers' shares in the Red Bull theater one of the actions is in the Court of Requests. In reciting the early arrangements about the theater, Thomas Woodford says that he

> . . . did by his indenture of lease . . . in the third year of the reign of your Majesty . . . made between the said Aaron Holland of the one part and Thomas Swinnerton of the other party demise and grant a seventh part of the said playhouse and galleries with a gatherers place thereto belonging or appertaining unto the said Thomas Swinnerton for divers years. . . .[50]

In a Chancery suit of 1623 a very clear statement about the arrangements for a gatherer's place is made in the bill of Thomas Woodford:

> . . . To which eighteenth part there was then and still is incident and belonging by the usual custom a gatherer's place whereby in respect of certain orders made by and between the said company [of players and partners and] sharers or owners of the said house for the avoiding of all differences and controversies concerning their daily charge of gatherers there did arise and grow due unto the said eighteenth part three pence profit a day amounting to eight-

[50] Wallace, "Three London Theatres of Shakespeare's Time," p. 304.

een pence a week to be paid daily or at the end every week [to the said] Swinnerton or to such gatherers as he should nominate or appoint during . . . the time of their playing.[51]

In his answer to Woodford in this suit Aaron Holland questions Woodward's right to the eighteenth share, but he agrees that a gatherer's place was attached to it.

The same involvement of the housekeepers with the gatherers is found in the private theaters. In the draft for his patent with the supplementary papers prepared by Richard Heton, manager (apparently ambitious to be dictator) of the Salisbury Court playhouse and of Queen Henrietta's company in September 1639, the following explanatory note is added, apparently for the reassurance of the players:

> The difference betwixt the first Articles and the last.
> The housekeepers enjoy not any one benefit in the last which they had not in the first.
> And they paid only by the first.
> 1. All repairs of the house.
> 2. Half the gathering places. Half to the sweepers of the house, the stagekeepers, to the poor, and for carrying away the soil. . . .[52]

But the gatherers were not all simply appointees of the housekeepers, there were others who were attached to the company and not the housekeepers. One would guess that the housekeepers' appointees watched over the doors from which came the housekeepers' payments and that the company appointees presided over the doors from which came the money for the sharers. Some such division is implied in the statement about the "last articles" set out by Richard Heton.

For those gatherers who were hired men of the company and not representatives of the housekeepers it does not seem likely that gathering could have been a full-time job. What would a gatherer have done after the two or three hours it

---

[51] Hotson, *The Commonwealth and Restoration Stage*, pp. 84-85.
[52] Bentley, *The Jacobean and Caroline Stage*, II, 686-87.

might have taken him to collect admission fees? One would assume that he could be used in crowd scenes after the first or second acts, and there is a little evidence that he was. The members of crowds or small groups—often with no lines at all—are too unimportant to be named by book holders, but at one point in the plot of *Frederick and Basilia* the scribe has written "guard gatherers." And Greg writes that "Finally, the gatherers provide the Soldiers for sc. xviii"[53] The play was performed at Henslowe's Rose theater on 3 June 1597. I would assume that situations like this occurred not infrequently in later plays using "supers," but the evidence is disappointingly slight.

Another record shows that the employment of a gatherer was not necessarily exclusively collecting at the doors. It will be remembered that John Russell had been taken on as a gatherer through his friendship with Edward Alleyn. Again we refer to the letter about Russell. Bird's letter to Alleyn recounts his dishonesty with the box and declares that the members of the company have forbidden him ever to act as a gatherer again ". . . Yet, for your sake, he shall have his wages to be a necessary attendant on the stage, and if he will pleasure himself and us to mend our garments, when he hath leisure, we'll pay him for that too. . . ." An attendant on the stage might have been almost anything, but the company must have had experience with Russell as a tailor to entrust him with the repair of their garments. One would have thought this repair work the responsibility of the wardrobe keeper; perhaps Russell had assisted him before.

As already noted, any use of a gatherer on the stage must have been confined to the latter acts of the play, because his gathering activities would have kept him busy at the doors during the early acts. It is obvious, therefore, that the only conspicuous part for a gatherer, "Bolt, A Doorkeeper" in the Praeludium for Thomas Goffe's *The Careless Shepherdess* when it was performed at the Salisbury Court probably in 1638,

---

[53] Greg, ed., *Dramatic Documents from the Elizabethan Playhouses*, I, 125.

must have been prepared for an actor, not a practicing gatherer. Incidentally, the opening stage direction shows why the gatherers were sometimes called box-holders: "Bolt. *A Doorkeeper, sitting with a box on the side of the Stage.*"

STAGEKEEPERS

What little information we have appears to indicate that the stagekeepers were the most lowly of the hired men. Such duties as we hear about are those of janitors and miscellaneous walk-ons. Most explicit of the passages referring to them is the Induction to Ben Jonson's *Bartholomew Fair* performed by the Lady Elizabeth's men at the opening of Henslowe's Hope theater on 31 October 1614. It will be remembered that this house was a combination theater and bear garden and olfactory allusions in Jonson's Induction indicate that the bears were already in residence.

This induction is, in part, an example of one of Jonson's favorite devices, namely an anticipation of the attacks on his play by putting criticism of it in the mouths of obviously stupid or inconsiderable characters. Here the stupid character selected is the stagekeeper, and this choice indicates Jonson's observation of the popular estimation of stagekeepers.

The Induction on the Stage

Stage-Keeper. Gentlemen, have a little patience, they are e'en upon coming instantly. He that should begin the play, Master *Littlewit,* the *Proctor,* has a stitch new-fallen in his black silk stocking; 'twill be drawn up ere you can tell twenty. . . . But for the whole *Play,* will you have the truth on't? (I am looking, lest the *Poet* hear me, or his man, Master *Brome* behind the Arras) it is like to be a very conceited scurvy one, in plain English. When 't comes to the *Fair* once, you were e'en as good go to *Virginia* for anything there is of *Smithfield.* He has not hit the humors, he does not know 'hem. . . . But these Master-*Poets* they will ha' their own absurd courses; they will be informed of nothing! He has (*sirreverence*) kicked me three or four times about the Tiring-house, I thank him, for but offering to put in with my experience. I'll be judged by you *Gentlemen*, now, but for one conceit of mine! Would not a fine pump upon the Stage ha' done well, for a property now? And a *Punk* set under upon her head, with her stern upward and ha' been soused by my witty young masters o' the *Inns o' Court*? What think you o' this for a show now? He will not hear o' this! I am an ass! I! and yet I kept the stage in Master *Tarleton's* time, I thank my stars. . . .

    Book-holder: Scrivener. To him.

    Book. How now? What rare discourse are you fallen upon? Ha? Ha' you found any familiars here, that you are so free? What's the business?

    Sta. Nothing, but the understanding Gentlemen o' the ground here asked my judgment.

    Book. Your judgment, rascal? for what? Sweeping the stage? or gathering up the broken apples for the bears within? Away rogue. It's come to a fine degree in these *spectacles* when such a youth as you pretend to a judgment.

Not only do the ideas Jonson assigns this stagekeeper suggest his degree of intelligence, but the book holder expresses an equally low opinion of him. The stagekeeper must have been presented as an oldish man since he kept the stage in the time of the famous comedian Tarleton, who died in 1588 and whose great days were thirty to fifty years before the opening of *Bartholomew Fair*. The book keeper's term "youth" is therefore derogatory. His main function alluded to is sweeping the stage and clearing the auditorium of refuse for the bears.

Of course, it is quite probable that this role of the stagekeeper in the Introduction to *Bartholomew Fair* was taken by an actor impersonating the real stagekeeper at the Hope. But even so the lines must be intended to reflect the general duties and the accepted characteristics of this type of hired man.

Another duty of the stagekeeper is indicated in the postscript of a letter of Robert Daborne to Philip Henslowe. They had been corresponding about a play Daborne was writing too slowly while he appealed for more money. The letter was presumably written in August 1613. The postscript reads: "I pray sir let the boy give order this night to the stagekeeper to set up bills against Monday for *Eastward Ho* and on Wednesday the new play."[54] If the stagekeeper set up all the bills himself this was a fairly extensive daily job. How extensive is suggested by a joke John Taylor printed in his *Wit and Mirth*, 1629:

A Quiblet

Master Field the Player riding up Fleet street a great pace, a gentleman called him and asked him what play was played that day. He (being angry to be stayed upon so frivolous a demand) answered, that he might see what play was to be played upon every post. I cry you mercy (said the gentleman) I took you for a post, you rode so fast. [B6ᵛ]

The joke is scarcely hilarious, but the "every post" implies quite a chore of bill-posting.

Other allusions to the work of the stagekeepers show them mostly in the parts of extras for crowd or battle scenes. I have seen nothing which would require much in the way of talent or experience.[55]

Late in the reign of King James the Company of the Revels presented the anonymous play, *The Two Noble Ladies*, at the Red Bull theater. Twice in the prompt manuscript (Egerton 1994) the book holder has made a note for himself that a stagekeeper is to come on, once as a guard and once as a soldier:

"guard Tay: Stage k:" (folio 228 [5]ᵇ)
"Tay. Gib: Stage k:" (folio 233 [10]ᵃ)

54 Greg, ed., *Henslowe Papers*, p. 71.

55 Leslie Hotson's article, "False Faces on Shakespeare's Stage," *Times Literary Supplement*, 16 May 1952, p. 336, is partly about stagekeepers, but it is a great disappointment. It is mostly conjecture. His only solid evidence comes from college plays, and it is surely obvious that the situation of the amateurs in college plays performed in private halls is vastly different from that in commercial theaters.

Evidently the John Russell, friend of Edward Alleyn who as we have seen was too dishonest to be a gatherer, was a stagekeeper, for William Bird wrote Alleyn in his complaint that though Russell was never to be allowed to hold the box again: "yet for your sake he shall have his wages, to be a necessary attendant on the stage."

In the prompt copy for Thomas Heywood's play, *The Captives* (Egerton 1994), which was licensed for performance by the Lady Elizabeth's men on 3 September 1624, the book keeper has jotted in two reminders of two appearances by stagekeepers: "Stage" (folio 61^b) where he appears as a country fellow and again on folio 70^a he has written "stagekeepers as a guard."

In certain types of situations at the inferior theaters the stagekeepers evidently did not bother to change from their blue smocks. In the arrogant prologue to his *Hannibal and Scipio* performed by Queen Henrietta's men at the Phoenix in 1635, Thomas Nabbes boasts of his play:

> 'Tis free
> As ever play was from scurrility.
> Nor need you ladies fear the horrid sight
> And the more horrid noises of target fight
> By the blue-coated Stage-keepers. . . .

The usual stage-sweeping duties of the stagekeepers are referred to in one of the commonwealth newsbooks among the Thomason Tracts (E 745 4) quoted by Howard H. Schless in a letter to the *Times Literary Supplement*.[56] He quotes from a rather jocose piece in *Mercurius Fumigosus*, for 17 June 1654:

> The same day a clear stage
> And from her no favor

Two masculine Women *Fencers*, being to fight a Duel, had chosen them two feminine men for their Seconds; the *stagekeeper* sweeping of the stage, one of the *Women Fencers* un-

[56] 6 June 1952, p. 377.

tiling the house of a Trencher; and throwing it at the other Woman Fencer's head, hit the *Stage Keeper* such a blow on his upper lip, that ever since he runs *open-mouth'd* at all Gamesters that come. . . .

An unusual statement about the stagekeepers and their payment is part of the documents called Heton's Papers of 1639 published from an unnoted source in *Shakespeare Society Papers*. Heton was manager and apparently part-owner of the Salisbury Court theater.[57] His statement about gatherers seems to indicate that in this theater housekeepers and fellows were not assigned the receipts from different doors as at other theaters. Unfortunately he gives nothing specific about what the duties of the stagekeepers were.

> *The difference between the first articles and the last.*
> The housekeepers enjoy not any one benefit in the last which they had not in the first.
> And they paid only by the first.
> 1. All repairs of the house.
> 2. Half the gathering places. Half to the sweepers of the house, the stagekeepers, to the poor, and for carrying away the soil.
> *By the last articles*
> We first allow them a room or two more than they formerly had.
> All that was allowed by the former articles and half the poet's wages which is 10^s a week.

The rest of Heton's document has no bearing that I can see on stagekeepers. Nor do I see why the housekeepers should have paid any part of the stagekeepers' wages; all the other chores mentioned are connected with the upkeep of the building. Perhaps this proposal to pay half the wages of the stagekeepers was a mere bargaining point; it cannot have cost very much.

[57] See Bentley, *The Jacobean and Caroline Stage*, II, 684-87 and VI, 103-107. Heton's statement about the wages of the poet (Richard Brome) is correct.

WAGES

As we have noticed, the hired men of London companies did not hold shares but were paid weekly wages by the company. How much?

To this question there is no answer that will hold for all companies throughout the period in spite of the fact that various books and articles assert that the standard wages of hired men were such and such. Probably the most common of these grossly oversimplified generalizations derives from Stephen Gosson's statement in *The Schoole of Abuse*, 1579: "Overlashing in apparel is so common a fault, that the very hirelings of some of our players, which stand at reversion of 6s by the week, iet under gentlemen's noses in suits of silk . . ." [6]. It should be kept in mind that Gosson was trying to show players to be proud and overweening. I suppose it is possible that in 1579 some hired men regularly received six shillings a week, but I am inclined to doubt it. And at any rate the facts given below show that not many of them did and few received regularly what they were promised.

The available data shows that payments to hired men varied with the company, the date, the success of the season, and the honesty of the sharers or manager. Wages, like most other payments, were affected by the Jacobean inflation. Some hired men are recorded as agreeing to wages of five shillings a week, some to six, some to eight and some to ten. Furthermore, we have reason to believe that not all the hired men in a given company at a given time received the same weekly wage.

Normally the pay came from the sharers of the company. In their petition to the Lord Chamberlain, Benfield, Pollard, and Swanston, sharers of the King's company in 1635, say that ". . . the said actors defray all charges of the house whatsoever (vizt) wages to hired men and boys, music, lights, &c. . . ."[58]

The man one would expect to have recorded most about

[58] *Malone Society Collections* 2, pt. 3 (1931), 365.

such wages is Philip Henslowe. The entries about wages for hired men in Henslowe's Diary are complicated by the fact Henslowe is handling the agreements for the sharers of his companies, but he appears also to be binding certain hired men to himself.[59] These payments show a good deal of inequality in the remuneration of different hired men. On 11 October 1602 Henslowe recorded that he had "Paid unto Underell at the appointment of the company for wages which they owed him the 11 of October 1602 the sum of . . . 10 shillings." In this entry it is clear enough that a hired man of the Admiral's company was being paid by Henslowe who charged the payment to the company, but there is no indication of how many days were covered by the payment.

In a fragment of the Diary now in the British Museum there is a note in the hand of Edward Alleyn:

> Md that this 8th of December 1597 my father Philip Henslowe hired as a covenant servant William Kendall for 2 years after the statute of Westminster with 2 single pence, A to give him for his said service every week of his playing in London 10 shillings and in the country 5 shillings; for the which he covenanteth for the space of those 2 years to be ready at all times to play in the house of the said Philip and in no other during the said term.
>
> > Witness myself the writer
> > of this E Alleyn

This agreement with William Kendall is clearly different in character from the agreement with Underell, in which Henslowe was, as usual, acting for the company and charging his payment to their account. The Kendall agreement is a personal contract between Henslowe and Kendall and there is no indication that the payments were to be charged to the company. Later there were various charges brought by players against Henslowe that he contracted hired men to himself with

---

[59] See the complaint of the Lady Elizabeth's men about 1615. Greg, ed., *Henslowe Papers*, pp. 86ff.

an agreement never to leave his theater and that such agreements were intended to prevent the company from ever taking advantage of a better arrangement with another playhouse. The agreement with Kendall does show, however, that there was a sharp difference between the wages paid hired men when the company was playing in London and when it was playing on tour.

Earlier in the same year another agreement seems to be of the same general character with a notable difference in wage and a further difference that it was sanctioned by principal sharers in the Admiral's company:

> Memorandum that the 27 of July 1597 I hired Thomas Hearne with 2 pence for to serve me 2 years in the quality of playing for five shillings a week for one year and 6 shillings eight pence for the other year which he hath convenanted himself to serve me and not to depart from my company till this 2 years be ended. Witness to this
>
> John Singer
> James Donson [Tunstall]
> Thomas Towne

Another agreement entered in the Diary about the wages of a hired man appears to be still different in that the man is bound neither to Henslowe nor to the company, but to a leading sharer in the company:

> Thomas Downton the 25 of January 1599 did hire as his convenant servant [blank in the original] for 2 years to begin at Shrove Tuesday next & he to give him 8 shillings a week as long as they play and after they lie still one fortnight then to give him half wages. Witness P. H. & Edward Browne & Charles Massey.[60]

These various agreements make it clear enough that in the Lord Admiral's company there was no uniform payment for all hired men. Not only did the pay differ from man to man

---

[60] Foakes and Rickert, eds., *Henslowe's Diary*, pp. 217, 268-69, 238-39, 45.

but it might be altered with varying situations of the company. One contract says full pay in London, half pay on the road; the Thomas Downton contract does not mention half pay on the road, but it does stipulate half pay when "they lie still" for more than two weeks, i.e., when they were inactive because of plague, Lent, royal mourning, or any other form of suppression. Anyone familiar with the history of the theater in the reigns of Elizabeth, James, and Charles knows that these periods of dark theaters were quite frequent, sometimes lasting for months at a time.

This evidence from Henslowe's records shows the rather straitened circumstances of hired men in the last few years of Elizabeth, but they show only what was promised, not what was received. How often and how regularly did these hired men get the pay they had expected? The theater business is always precarious. Audiences are kept away by bad plays, bad weather, bad performances, war scares, riots, rival attractions, epidemics short of full plague visitations, and other hazards. If the company suffered, one can be sure the hired men suffered first. Other records show how much they suffered.

The most detailed statements about payments to hired men by the sharers in a London company come from the witnesses in the Chancery suit of *Ellis Worth and John Blaney v. Susan Baskervile and William Brown* in 1623. Susan, the relict of Thomas Greene (d. 1612), former manager of Queen Anne's company at the Red Bull, and her son William Browne were trying to collect from the remnants of the company money they claimed the players had owed to Thomas Greene and William Browne. A number of witnesses including both hired men and sharers like Thomas Heywood were called to testify about the financial affairs of the company, but relevant here are the statements of hired men about their pay.

Roger Clarke, dwelling in Golding Lane . . . aged 24, testified that he knew all the parties to the suit, and further testified "That he this deponent hath been for the space of these two years or thereabouts an hired servant in the company of players at the Red Bull and saith that when they hired him they agreed to give unto him 6 shillings a week so long as he should continue their hired servant and they did so set it down in their book and he saith that when good store of company came to the plays that the gettings would bear it, he this deponent was paid his 6 shillings a week, but when company failed he was paid after the rate of their gettings which sometimes fell not out for this deponent's part two shillings six pence a week, nor sometimes twelve pence a week neither had he any more pay than the gettings would bear although they agreed with this deponent to give him six shillings a week, and this deponent saith that the said company and all other companies of players in and about London whatsoever they agree to give unto any that they hire to be their servants or men they usually pay them no more than it will fall out to their shares, as company do come to plays, and if company do come in so fast and so many as that the getting will bear it then the said servants as freedmen [?] have the full of that was agreed they should have, or else not. . . ."

Another witness called to testify in this suit was "John King of the parish of St. Sepulchre London, gentleman, aged 48 years or thereabouts." King testified

That for the space of these 30 years past and upwards he hath been a hired servant to the company of sharers of the players of the Red Bull, and saith that when this deponent came first to be entertained in the said house and company the then sharers did agree with him this deponent to give him wages certain by the week, but yet withal they, the said sharers, told this deponent that if at any time it should happen the getting of the said company to be but small and to decrease that then he should not have his whole wages agreed to be paid unto him but to have his part of the loss thereof as well as the said company and to have a part proportionally only to their gettings, which course hath been ever since held and used amongst the said company. And he further saith that he is sure that they nor any of them the said Sharers do ever pass their promise otherwise than as aforesaid. And he saith that if it were otherwise and were a [duty?] and that the whole wages agreed upon ought always to be paid to the said hired men howsoever it happen, then might he this deponent might [sic] recover of the company above £100 for wages agreed upon which hath not been paid this deponent by reason that sometimes the getting of the said company were small. . . .

Still another hired man testified in this suit. He was "Richard Baxter of St. James's Clerkenwell . . . of the age of 30 years or thereabouts." Baxter testified

That at the time when he this defendant came to be entertained of the company of players at the Red Bull in or near Clerkenwell he [?] as an hired man to the company, the same company did offer and agree with him this deponent to give him ten shillings a week certain wages. But this deponent saith that divers times it fell out that the gettings of the company was so small as that at some times they did pay unto the hired men or servants no wages and some times half wages and some times less. And this deponent further saith that at such times as his said wages was not paid or abridged he did reckon the same up from to [sic] time to time hoping at some time or other he had received it of the company, but yet he saith he never could receive the same for he saith that at the time when he this deponent was entertained by the company none of the said company in particular did promise or agree to pay unto him this deponent the 10 shillings a week but only proposed [?] such an offer to him this deponent which he accepted of and in this manner he saith is all the promise that they of the said company or any of them do make unto any that they entertain. . . .[61]

These records show that in both the Admiral's company in Elizabeth's time and in Queen Anne's company in James's reign the wages promised varied from man to man and from

[61] London, Public Record Office C 24/500/103.

five shillings to ten a week. Moreover one Admiral's hired man agreed to have his wages cut 50 percent when the troupe was on the road, and another agreed to a reduced wage for his first year, and a third to a 50 percent cut when the company had to "lie still." Even with such agreed reductions no Henslowe record shows whether these hired men were always paid what they were promised. Given the fluctuating theater conditions in the 1590s and the three explicit statements of Queen Anne's hired men a couple of decades later, one doubts whether their pay was as regular as the agreements specified.

In King James's reign the hired men of Queen Anne's company were also promised wages varying from six to ten shillings per week, but all three agree that they seldom received their full promised wages, and Roger Clark says that no London company regularly paid the full promised wage and that the hired men did not expect it.

Such was the situation of hired men in the London companies of the period. They were not all paid the same wages in the same company. The wages they were promised varied from five shillings to ten a week, and in at least one instance a man was promised an increase the second year. According to the testimony of three hired men in the Chancery suit of *Worth and Blaney v. Baskervile and Browne* even these promised wages were often paid only in part or not at all. Of course not every company in London was as badly off as Queen Anne's men in 1623; some were probably worse off; no doubt the hired men of the prosperous King's company were better off. But there was no uniformity in wages promised and certainly no uniformity in wages paid. As so often one comes back to the constant precariousness of the theater. That men like John King stayed with such a hazardous occupation for thirty years seems as irrational in 1623 as similar conduct by modern players seems today.

CHAPTER V

Apprentices

THE CONVENTION of the Shakespearean theater most difficult for moderns to accept is that of the boy players. These
children and adolescents were assigned all female roles[1] in the
productions of the adult companies and most of the roles of
any sort in the performances of the boy companies. Since
comparatively few moderns have ever seen professionally *trained*
juvenile actors performing any roles except those corresponding to their own age and sex, many are baffled by the imagi-
native feat of picturing an adolescent boy enthralling a sophisticated audience with his performance of Rosalind, Lady
Macbeth, Webster's Duchess, or Ford's Annabella. Yet those
subjects of the early Stuart kings who had opportunities to

---

[1] This assertion that the boy apprentices were assigned *all* female roles in
the plays produced by the troupes of Elizabethan, Jacobean, and Caroline

see both boys and women in female roles were not impressed by the superiority of the actresses. Thomas Coryat, who published in 1611 a widely read book about his travels, said that in the theaters of Venice he had seen women on the stage. It was not, however, the superiority but the adequacy of the actresses that struck him:

> . . . I saw women act, a thing that I never saw before . . . and they performed it with as good a grace, action, gesture, and whatsoever convenient for a Player, as ever I saw any masculine Actor.[2]

Even more explicit in his comparison, and a great deal more experienced in the theater, was John Downes, book keeper and prompter in the Restoration companies of Davenant and of Betterton. Downes says that he was with Davenant at Lincoln's Inn Fields in 1662,

---

London has been questioned now and then by some Shakespearean scholar who thinks an adult player more likely for a certain role such as Lady Macbeth, Old Margaret in *Richard III*, or the witches in *Macbeth*. So far as I know the evidence offered for such assignments has been the individual scholar's conception of the requirements of such a role and his assumption of the inadequacy of any boy to carry it off.

The only evidence I have found of adults in female roles are the assignments of the veteran comedian John Shank to the role of "Petella, their waiting woman. Their servant John Shank" in the 1652 edition of Fletcher's *Wild Goose Chase*, and "A Kitching Maid by M. Anthony F [T]urner" in the 1631 quarto cast for the revival of Heywood's *Fair Maid of the West* Part I by Queen Henrietta's men. (See Appendix, p. 275.)

Petella is given no lines in the text; the Kitchen Maid appears in only one scene (III,1) and has five lines. The assignment of the Kitchen Maid to Turner is an enigma; he is also down for the part of Bashaw Alcade in Part Two, presumably acted at court at the same time. Could he have played the Kitchen Maid in a much earlier performance by the Lady Elizabeth's company to which he had been attached? (G. E. Bentley, *The Jacobean and Caroline Stage*, 7 vols. Oxford, 1941-1968, II, 607-608.) Since Petella in *The Wild Goose Chase* has no speeches at all, Shank must have gagged his lines. I am not impressed by T. W. Baldwin's suggestion (*The Organization and Personnel of the Shakespearean Company*, Princeton, 1927, p. 176) that he was on to supervise the apprentices, but I have no better one.

[2] *Coryat's Crudities*, London, 1611, p. 247.

And as Book-keeper and Prompter, continu'd so, till October 1706. . . . Writing out all the Parts in each Play; and Attending every Morning the Actors Rehearsals, and their Performances in the Afternoons. . . .

And he wrote of Edward Kynaston, the great actor whom he had prompted in many a performance:

Mr. Kynaston Acted *Arthiope*, in the Unfortunate Lovers; The Princess in the *Mad* Lover; *Aglaura; Ismenia*, in the Maid in the Mill; and several other Women's Parts; he being then very Young made a Compleat Female Stage Beauty, performing his Parts so well, especially *Arthiope* and *Aglaura*, being Parts greatly moving Compassion and Pity; that it has since been Disputable among the Judicious, whether any Woman that succeeded him so Sensibly touch'd the Audience as he.[3]

Dramatists as well as theater functionaries reported the effective impersonations of some of the boy actors. Even such an acid social and dramatic critic as Ben Jonson testified. Best known is his epitaph on the boy player Salmon Pavy who had achieved a reputation—"the stage's jewel"—before he died at the age of thirteen in 1602.[4] More explicit evidence of Jonson's satisfaction with the impersonations of the boy actors is written into a passage in his *The Devil Is an Ass*. One of his characters recites a feat achieved by Richard Robinson, a boy actor in the King's company, the troupe for which the play was written:

Merecraft. . . . But where's this lady?
If we could get a witty boy now, Ingine:
That were an excellent crack. I could instruct him.
To the true height. For anything takes this dottrell.

[3] *Roscius Anglicanus*, London, 1708, p. C2.
[4] "cxx Epitaph on S. P. a child of Q. El. Chappel," *The Workes of Beniamin Jonson*, London, 1616. The boy's Christian name was Solomon or Salmon, not Salathiel as given in nearly all nineteenth- and twentieth-century reprints of the epitaph. See *Times Literary Supplement*, 30 May 1942, p. 276.

Ingine. Why, Sir, your best will be one o' the players!
Merecraft. No, there's no trusting them. They'll talk on't,
And tell their Poets.
    Ingine. What if they do? The jest
Will brook the stage. But, there be some of 'em
Are very honest lads. There's Dick Robinson,
A very pretty fellow, and comes often
To a gentleman's chamber, a friend of mine. We had
The merriest supper of it there one night.
The gentleman's landlady invited him
To a Gossip's feast. Now he, sir, brought Dick Robinson,
Dressed like a lawyer's wife amongst 'em all;
(I lent him clothes) but to see him behave it,
And lay the law, and carve, and drink unto 'em,
And then talk bawdy, and send frolics! Oh!
It would have burst your buttons, or not left you
A seam.
    Merecraft. They say he's an ingenious youth.
    Ingine. Oh, sir! And dresses himself the best! Beyond
Forty o' your very Ladies! Did you ne'er see him?
    Merecraft. No, I do seldom see those toys. But think you
That we may have him?
    Ingine. Sir, the young gentleman
I tell you of can command him. Shall I attempt it?

[II,8]

Jonson's exploitation in this play, as in his *Bartholomew Fair*
and *Cynthia's Revels*, of the interest of his audience in the real-
life personalities of some of the players appearing on the stage
before them is a curious device for him. But more to the point
here is the evidence in this passage that the iconoclastic Jonson assumed his audience would acknowledge the complete
credibility of the female impersonations of a well-trained boy
actor such as Richard Robinson.

The tradition of boys appearing in public performances was
an old one in Shakespeare's time: by 1590 all English towns-
men had long been accustomed to their appearance in public

presentations. The municipal pageantry for local celebrations—visits of monarchs, inaugurations of mayors, religious festivals, coronations, royal weddings, and the like—had involved impersonations and frequently dialogue and singing by juvenile performers since at least the thirteenth century.[5] So that when the commercialization of the drama by the professional acting troupes developed in the sixteenth century there was no novelty in the appearance of boys with men in the travelling troupes in the provinces or in the more settled and prestigious companies in the London theaters.

Since these boys were all minors, they were seldom explicitly involved in those financial transactions and the subsequent litigation from which such a large part of our knowledge of the players and the theaters of the time has been derived. This fact helps to account for the smaller proportion of the boy players than of the adults now known. Occasionally totally unknown boys appear in unique records, as in the list of "Boys" in the record of the visit of Lady Elizabeth's company to Coventry in 1615 (see below, pp. 141-42) and the cast for Jordan's *Money Is an Ass*,[6] or the record of the burial of a boy actor of Queen Elizabeth's company in 1591. The parish registers of St. Peter and St. Paul in Aldeburgh carry the entry: "Humphrie Swaine, a Youth, and servant to one of her Majesty's players, was buried the same day (*7 June*) 1591."[7]

Furthermore the period of notoriety for a successful boy player was likely to be three to eight years, whereas adults like Joseph Taylor, Richard Perkins, Christopher Beeston, Richard Tarleton, Robert Benfield, John Heminges, John Lowin, Robert Armin, John Shank, Andrew Cane, and Will Kempe were all before the public for twenty to forty years, and consequently there was time for many more facts, anec-

---

[5] See H. N. Hillebrand, *The Child Actors*, University of Illinois Studies in Language and Literature 11, Champaign, 1926, pp. 9-39.

[6] See Bentley, *The Jacobean and Caroline Stage*, IV, 685-87.

[7] J. C. Coldeway, "Playing Companies at Aldeburgh 1566-1635," *Malone Society Collections* 9 1977 (1971), 22.

dotes, and comments about them to accumulate. Nevertheless a fair amount of information can be gleaned about the usual conditions under which a boy actor worked in London between 1590 and 1642.[8]

These children and adolescents of the theater, like most middle-class boys of their age group in English cities and towns of the sixteenth and seventeenth centuries, were apprenticed to experienced masters to learn their trade. The majority of such London apprentices were training to become good grocers or shoemakers, merchant-tailors, goldsmiths, haberdashers or fishmongers, printers or drapers, and the terms of their apprenticeships were regulated by the organized guilds to which their masters belonged. Thus the grocers regulated the conduct of their members:

> Ordinance at the meeting of 9 May 1595 of the Court of Assistants of the Grocers that no brother take an apprentice less than 8 or 9 years old or for less than eight years unless such apprentice be 21 years of age at least when he enters into his apprenticeship, so that none shall be made free of the company under 24 at the least, under pain of £3.6.8 to be paid for each offence.[9]

Something similar could probably be found in the records of most of the major London guilds. The apprentice system provided the training for future craftsmen and merchants; it provided part of the work force in a printer's shop or a grocer's establishment; and the fee paid by the father or guardian of the new apprentice[10] was a perquisite for the new master.

---

[8] I am confining my attention almost exclusively to the adult companies for several reasons. Most of the available material on the boy companies has been ably set forth by Hillebrand in *The Child Actors*, nos. 1 and 2. For another reason, the well-known boy companies like the Children of St. Paul's and the Children of the Chapel were only semi-professional. How many of them were primarily singers and how many nonmusical children illegally impressed, as indicated in the Clifton-Robinson suit, we have no clear evidence.

[9] Grocers Company, Court of Assistance, July 1591-July 1616, Grocers Company Book, Guildhall Library, London.

[10] When Shakespeare's colleague and friend Henry Condell apprenticed his

It is to be expected that the customary and long-established system of child labor and novice education would be followed by the dramatic companies, and in a general way it seems to have been. But the profession of player was never so well-integrated into the established economic system as that of grocers, goldsmiths, merchant-tailors, or drapers. Confusion has arisen from the assumption that the players were as strict and uniform as the great London companies which could punish irregularities in their own courts (as indicated in the Grocer's Ordinance of 9 May 1595). There was no legally sanctioned players' guild; though apprentices were taken, trained, and exploited by all theatrical companies, there is no evidence of a set age at which boys were taken and none for a uniform duration of their apprenticeship. The assumption that the players conformed strictly to the pattern of the craft guilds has led to a number or erroneous or dubious conclusions in T. W. Baldwin's exhaustive study of Shakespeare's troupe.[11] He contends that a boy actor was normally apprenticed at the age of ten years, that all apprentices served in feminine and juvenile roles for seven years, and that, if the apprentices remained with the company, they "graduated" or first took over major adult roles at the age of twenty-one. Basing his identifications on these assumptions, Baldwin casts most of the major roles in the plays of Shakespeare and of Beaumont and Fletcher, and sets the dates when many boys began to act and when they were "graduated" to adult roles.

Unhappily the evidence, mostly accumulated since Baldwin wrote, contradicts his assumptions in a good many specific instances. Many boy players were not apprenticed at the age

---

son William, aged fourteen, to Edward Pate, haberdasher, for a term of eight years on 9 June 1625, the elder Condell paid a fee of £20. E.A.B. Barnard, *New Links with Shakespeare*, Cambridge, 1930, pp. 37-38.

Similarly, Philip Henslowe in his record of loans and gifts to or in behalf of his nephew John Henslowe in 1596 included, "Laid out for him to Mr. Newman, dyer, when he took him to prentice, the sum of 40 shillings" (R. A. Foakes and R. T. Richert, eds., *Henslowe's Diary*, Cambridge, 1961, p. 230).

[11] Baldwin, *The Organization and Personnel of the Shakespearean Company*.

of ten, and many did not serve a seven-year apprenticeship. According to his own statement in his petition to the Lord Mayor's Court in August 1631, William Trigg, a leading actor of women's roles in the company of King Charles I, had been apprenticed to Shakespeare's friend, John Heminges, on 20 December 1626 for a term of twelve years for "la 'arte d' une Stageplayer."[12] John Wright testified in a Chancery suit in 1654 that he had been apprenticed to Andrew Cane (or de Caine or Keyne), the famous comedian of Prince Charles's (II) company, at the age of fifteen and had performed throughout his apprenticeship.[13] Stephen Hammerton, the unusually popular young actor of the thirties and forties, had "nine years then to come and to be expired" in his apprenticeship in 1629, according to the Bill of Complaint of William Blagrave, manager and part-owner of the King's Revels company.[14] In an indenture dated 14 November 1606, Alice Cooke apprenticed her son Abell to Thomas Kendall "to be one of the said Children of Her Majesty's Revels and to be practised and exercised in the said quality of playing . . . for and during the term of three years next ensuing."[15] The same term of apprenticeship is indicated in an agreement of 10 March 1607/08 between Martin Slater and the shareholders of the Whitefriars theater quoted in a King's Bench suit of 1609.

> Item, it is likwise . . . agreed . . . by and between the said parties that whereas by the general consent of all the whole company, all the children are bound to the said Martin Slater for the term of three years. He the said Martin Slater doth by these presents bind himself to the residue of the

[12] Mayor's Court Book, 7 Charles I, no. 53-M54, London Corporation Records.

[13] London, Public Record Office, C 24/785/55, quoted by C. J. Sisson, "The Red Bull Company," *Shakespeare Survey* 7 (1954), 67.

[14] London, Public Record Office, REQ-2-681 Court of Requests, quoted in G. E. Bentley, "The Salisbury Court Theatre and Its Boy Players," *Huntington Library Quarterly* 40 (1977), 140-41.

[15] King's Bench, *Coram Rege Rolls*, Michaelmas Term, 5 Jas. I m582, quoted in Hillebrand, *The Child Actors*, nos. 1-2, pp. 197-98.

company in the sum of forty pounds sterling that he shall not wrong or injure the residue of the said company in the parting with or putting away any one or more of the young men or lads to any person or persons, or otherwise without the special consent and full agreement of the residue of his fellow sharers, except the term of his or their apprenticeship be fully expired.[16]

Even in the major guilds of London the age of the newly indentured apprentice was not necessarily ten nor the term of his apprenticeship seven years. As already noticed William Condell, son of the actor Henry Condell, was fourteen when his father apprenticed him to an haberdasher for a term of eight years. Robert Armin, who eventually became principal comedian of the King's company and for whom Shakespeare prepared roles in the first half of the reign of King James, had first been apprenticed to a goldsmith. He bound himself to the goldsmith, "Iohn Louyson" in 1581 for eleven years. John Lowin, later one of the leaders of the King's company, also apprenticed himself to a goldsmith, Nicholas Rudyard, "for the terme of eight years beginning at Christmas in Anno 1593."[17] Lowin must have been approximately sixteen or seventeen years old at this time. Arthur Savill was apprenticed to the actor Andrew Cane for a term of eight years when he was fourteen years old.[18]

The only example I know of a stipulated seven-year term of apprenticeship for a young player is the statement of Edward Damport, made when his touring company was called before the authorities at Banbury on 2 May 1633:

. . . Has gone with this company up and down the country playing stage plays these two years last past. His father

[16] Transcribed by James Greenstreet, *New Shakespeare Transactions*, 1887-92, pt. 3, 276.

[17] Goldsmiths' Prentice Books, transcribed in *Malone Society Collections* 3 (1954), 141 and 167.

[18] See below, p. 126.

promised his master, Edward Whiting, that he should serve him seven years.[19]

But in spite of the variations in the age at which boy players were apprenticed and in the term for which they served, there is no doubt that the acting troupes used the apprentice system to train and hold their boy actors. In addition to the quoted references to the age of the boy and the term of his apprenticeship, there are a good many more in which these juvenile players are explicitly called apprentices. A number of these references indicate that in the adult companies like the Lord Chamberlain-King's company, the Admiral's men, Queen Anne's company, and Queen Henrietta's company, the boys were individually attached to specific fellows of the company, not to the organization as a body.

Most explicit is the statement of William Trigg, or Tregg, made in 1631 when he was nineteen or twenty years old, concerning the beginning of his own training. His petition to the Mayor's Court says that on 20 December 1626 he apprenticed himself to John Heminges, free of the Society of Grocers, to learn "la 'arte d' une Stageplayer."[20]

In his well-informed *Historia Histrionica*, James Wright records a good deal of information about the Restoration actors who had had their training before 1642. He characterizes the boys as "apprentices," sometimes giving the name of the sharer to whom the boy was bound. In the dialogue Lovewit prompts Truman to talk about the old times:

> . . . *Hart* and *Clun* were bred up boys at the *Blackfriars*, and acted women's parts. *Hart* was *Robinson's* boy or apprentice. He acted the Duchess in the tragedy of *The Cardinal*, which was the first part that gave him reputation. *Cartwright* and *Wintershall* belonged to the private house in *Salisbury Court*; *Burt* was a boy first under *Shank* at the

[19] *Calendar of State Papers, Domestic*, London, 1633-1634, p. 48.
[20] Mayor's Court Book, 7 Charles I, no. 53-M54, London Corporation Records.

Blackfriars, then under *Beeston* at the *Cockpit*, and *Mohun* and *Shatterell* were in the same condition with him at the last place. There *Burt* used to play the principal women's parts, in particular *Clariana* in *Love's Cruelty*, and at the same time *Mohun* acted *Bellmente*, which part he retained after the Restoration.[21]

The attachment of the boy actor to a particular leading sharer is found much earlier in Henslowe's Diary in 1599 and 1600. On 19 December 1597 Henslowe made an entry of a loan of thirteen shillings he had made to William Bourne of the Admiral's men and noted that the witness to the transaction was "Thomas Downton's bigger boy whom fetched it for him." Apparently Downton had two apprentices at this time. From later records in the Diary it is evident that one of these boys was Thomas Parsons, but whether he was the bigger or the smaller one is not clear.

Delivered unto Thomas Downton's boy Thomas Parsons to buy divers things for the play of the Spencers the 16 of April 1599 the sum of £5.

Lent unto Thomas Downton the 5 of June 1600 to buy a suit for his boy in the play of Cupid and Psyche the sum of £2.[22]

John Rice, one of the players listed by Heminges and Condell in the Shakespeare folio of 1623 as ". . . the Principal Actors in all these Plays" was John Heminges' "boy" when he performed before James I at the Merchant Taylors' dinner for the King. Samuel Gilborne and James Sands were left bequests as his former apprentices by Augustine Phillips in his will of 4 May 1605. Phillips was quite explicit about the legacy to this "my apprentice," James Sands; it was to be paid to him "at the expiration of his term of years in his indenture

[21] James Wright, *Historia Histrionica*, London, 1699, p. B2.
[22] W. W. Greg, ed., *Henslowe's Diary*, 2 vols., London, 1904-1908, I, 73, 104, and 122.

123

of apprenticeship." Richard Burbage had as his apprentice, Nicholas Tooley, who in his will of 3 June 1623 speaks of "my late Master Richard Burbage" and my "late Master Richard Burbage deceased."

This attachment of a boy player to an established sharer rather than to the company as a whole seems to have been standard in the adult companies throughout the period. Indeed, in stage directions and in prompter's manuscripts it is not unusual to have the apprentice identified by his master's name, as Wright says "Robinson's boy or apprentice" rather than the boy's own name.

In the "Plot" for *Frederick and Basilea*, which was performed by the Admiral's men at the Rose in June 1597, an entrance direction in scene 9 reads: "To them Philipo Basilea E. Dutton his boye." In the fragmentary "Plot" for *Troilus and Cressida* as performed by the Admiral's men about 1599, there are two entrances for "m^r Jones his boy." In the "Plot" for *The Battle of Alcazar* acted by the Lord Admiral's Men about 1589 is the entrance direction "ij Pages to attend the moore m^r Allens boy, m^r Townes boy." The "Plot" for *The First Part of Tamar Cam* as acted by the Admiral's Men about 1602 has the entrance direction "To them Tarmia & her 2 sonns: Jack grigerie & Mr. Denygtens little boy" and at another point "Enter Pigmies: gils his boy & little will Barne."[23] Even in casts where several boys are named, one of them may be designated by his master's name, as in the cast for the manuscript play *The Soddered Citizen* performed by the King's men about 1630; though four of the boys are named, the performer of Miniona's servant is called simply "John: Shanks Boy."[24]

A few years later the same system of individual attachment prevailed in Prince Charles's (II) company according to an affidavit made by Henry Gradwell and William Hall, sharers in that troupe. In the Court of Requests suit of Susan Bas-

[23] W. W. Greg, *Dramatic Documents from the Elizabethan Playhouses*, 2 vols., Oxford, 1921, II, pls. III, V, VI^a, VII.

[24] J.H.P. Pafford and W. W. Greg, eds., *The Soddered Citizen*, Malone Society, London, 1936, p. 3.

kervile (mother and principal legatee of the player William
Browne who died in 1634) against John Rhodes and his wife
Anne, these two players testified that Susan Greene *alias* Baskervile had regularly received at the Red Bull playhouse ". . .
seven shillings a week for an apprentice which was likewise
the said Browne's."[25]
One wonders what was the sanction for these apprenticeships since there is not known to have been any officially recognized guild of players. Three records suggest that sometimes the boy was officially apprenticed to an actor who was
a member of one of the London guilds but trained his apprentice to act in his company's plays rather than in the business
of a grocer or a goldsmith. A number of London players and
managers are known to have been free of city companies: Robert
Armin, Andrew Cane, Robert Keysar, and John Lowin were
Goldsmiths; John Heminges was a Grocer; John Shank was a
Weaver; Thomas Downton was a Vintner; Thomas Taylor
was a Pewterer; James Burbage was a Joiner.[26]
Apparently John Heminges used his privileges as a member
of the Grocers Company in apprenticing the boy player, William Trigg, as noted above. It is also suggestive that Robert
Armin, the comedian in Shakespeare's troupe, belatedly took
up his freedom in the Goldsmith's Company in January 1603/
04 after he had been a player for several years and then on 15
July 1608 took James Jones as his apprentice.[27] Similarly Andrew Cane, the comedian and at this time a leader in Prince
Charles's (II) company[28] took the boy Arthur Savill, who played
Quartille in *Holland's Leaguer*, as his apprentice in the Gold-

[25] Court of Requests, Miscellaneous Books, Affidavit Book, Hilary to Trinity Terms 10 and 11 Charles I, vol. 138, transcribed in the Wallace Papers,
Huntington Library, San Marino, California.
[26] Edwin Nungezer, *A Dictionary of Actors and Other Persons Associated with
the Public Representation of Plays in England before 1642*, New Haven, 1929; and
Bentley, *The Jacobean and Caroline Stage*, ii.
[27] See Jane Belfield, "Robert Armin, 'Citizen and Goldsmith of London,' "
Notes and Queries, n.s. 27 (1980), 158-59.
[28] See G. E. Bentley, "The Troubles of a Caroline Acting Troupe: Prince
Charles's Company," *Huntington Library Quarterly* 41 (1978), 217-49.

smith's Company. "I Arthur Savill the son of Cordall Savill of Clerkenwell in the County of Middlesex, gentleman, do put myself apprentice unto Andrew Cane of London Goldsmith for the term of eight years to begin at Midsummer last past."[29] The statement is dated 5 August 1931 and signed "Arthur Savile." Perhaps an extensive investigation of the Apprentice Books of a number of London guilds would reveal other examples of the use by London players of the city companies in which they had rights.

Relations between Apprentices and Sharers

The relationship between apprentice and master was presumably that of teacher and pupil. One extant record shows such a relationship fairly clearly. In 1607 the Merchant Taylors entertained King James, Queen Anne, and Prince Henry at dinner in their Hall. Ben Jonson was paid to write a speech of eighteen verses to welcome the royal guests, and the speech was delivered by the boy player John Rice. The expense accounts for the occasion show the master-apprentice relationship:

> To Mr. Hemminges for his direction of his boy that made the speech to His Majesty 40 shillings and 5 shillings given to John Rice the speaker.   45[s]

The subsequent entry in the accounts is another reminder of the importance of costume in all appearances of actors:

> To John Mr. Swinnerton's man for things for the boy that made the speech, viz. for garters, stockings, shoes, ribbons, and gloves. . . . 13 shillings[30]

The most extensive series of boy player attachments I have encountered is that asserted by John Shank, principal come-

---

[29] William Ingram, "Arthur Savill, Stage Player," *Theatre Notebook* 37 (1983), 21-22.

[30] The Merchant Taylors' Court Books, transcribed in *Malone Society Collections* 3 (1954), 172-73.

dian of the King's company from about 1615 until his death in 1636. The veteran Shank, one of the chief share-holders in both the Globe and the Blackfriars theaters, was involved in the year 1633 in a dispute with his fellow sharers Robert Benfield, Thomas Pollard, and Eyllaerdt Swanston who were trying to force him to sell to them some of his lucrative playhouse shares. When the controversy was brought before the Lord Chamberlain, the aggrieved Shank recited his faithful services to the company:

> . . . the complainants [i.e., Benfield, Pollard, and Swanston] would violently take from your petitioner the said parts [i.e., his shares in the Globe and Blackfriars theaters] who hath still of his own purse supplied the company for the service of His Majesty with boys, as Thomas Pollard, John Thompson deceased (for whom he paid £40) your suppliant having paid for his part of £200 for other boys since his coming to the company, John Honiman, Thomas Holcomb, and divers others and at this maintains three more for the said service.[31]

The statements of an angry old man (he died the next year, still aggrieved, according to his will) reveal clearly enough his feelings that his great services were not properly appreciated, and that the three young upstarts were trying to push him out of his just rewards. In such a mood not only would the old man be prone to exaggeration but his statements about the seven and more boy players are not so precise as one could wish. He seems to say that both Thomas Pollard and John Thompson were apprenticed to him—"hath still of his own purse supplied the company for the services of His Majesty with boys such as Thomas Pollard, John Thompson"—and that Thompson's apprenticeship was bought from some other master (who could have been an actor of another company or

---

[31] Lord Chamberlain's Warrant Books, transcribed in *Malone Society Collections* 2, pt. 3 (1931), 369.

a member of some guild).[32] Shank omits to say that the company probably paid him seven shillings a week or more for
the services of his trainees, as William Browne, and later
Browne's mother Susan Baskervile were being paid at about
this time for the services of Browne's apprentice. Or as the
Lord Admiral's men thirty-five years earlier were paying
Henslowe three shillings a week for his boy James Bristow,
whom Henslowe had bought from the player William Augustine for £8.[33]

Shank's further statement that he had "paid his part of £200"
since his coming to the company (a period of approximately
twenty years) for "John Honiman, Thomas Holcomb, and
divers others" seems to apply to unnamed boys whose purchase price had been shared by all the patented members but
who had not been especially attached to Shank.

The final assertion that "at this time maintains three more
for the said service" is more ambiguous. "Maintains" should
mean that these three boys lived with him and he housed and
fed them. But Shank does not say that he "supplied them" as
he says he did Pollard and Thompson, nor how much they
cost him as he did for the expensive John Thompson. Furthermore, three boys seems a large number for one patented
member in 1635 when there were about eleven other sharers
in the organization. Certainly the three boys Shank "maintained" did not constitute the entire apprentice group in 1635.
Some of the King's men's plays of the 1630s required more,
even with doubling. One of the very few extant casts with
assigned parts is that of Clavell's *The Soddered Citizen* of about
1630 which was never printed until the twentieth century,
but the manuscript gives a very complete cast. It requires at
least four apprentices. Women's roles are assigned to John
Thompson, to "Will:Trigg" and to "John:Shank's Boy," and

---

[32] As Christopher Babham says he bought out the apprenticeship of the
boy Stephen Hammerton from William Perry, a Draper. London, Public
Record Office, REQ-681, quoted in Bentley, "The Salisbury Court Theatre
and Its Boy Players," pp. 129-49.

[33] Greg, ed., *Henslowe's Diary*, I, 131, 134, and 203.

a juvenile role "Fewtricks, his boy" to Alexander Goffe.[34] Furthermore, it would have been folly for a rich company like the King's to have had no boys in reserve or in preliminary training. To account for the number Shank "maintained" I can only conjecture, rather lamely, that Shank was running a boarding house for two or three apprentices of fellow sharers who were unable to take a boy into their households—widowers? bachelors? wittol cuckolds?

This personal attachment of boys in training to senior players of the company, and the residence of each boy in his master's household, could be expected to produce juvenile resentment, for the boy was involved in a student-teacher and a father-son situation combined. No doubt such resentment often did exist, but I have found little evidence of it. On the other hand there are several extant examples of bonds of affection produced not only between apprentice and master but sometimes between the boy and other members of his master's household as well. The wills of several players testify to such a happy relationship.

Augustine Phillips, who had been a leading member of the Lord Chamberlain-King's company for a decade, died in May 1605. His will reveals ties of affection and trust with various of his colleagues in the company, including seven sharers, "to my fellows William Shakespeare, . . . Henry Condell . . ."; other sharers, John Heminges, Richard Burbage, and William Sly are made executors in the event of the death or remarriage of Phillips' wife Anne. Another member of the company, his brother-in-law, Robert Goffe, was a witness to the will, and £5 are left to be distributed among "the hired men" of the company. But more to the point here are the legacies to two of his apprentices:

> Item, I give to Samuel Gilborne, my late apprentice, the sum of forty shillings, and my mouse-colored velvet hose,

---

[34] See Pafford and Greg, eds., *The Soddered Citizen*, p. 3; and Bentley, *The Jacobean and Caroline Stage*, III, 162-65.

and a white taffeta doublet, a black taffeta suit, my purple cloak, sword, and dagger, and my bass viol.

Item, I give to James Sands, my apprentice, the sum of forty shillings, and a cittern, a bandore, and a lute to be paid and delivered unto him at the expiration of his term of years in his indenture of apprenticehood.[35]

Another member of the King's company, Thomas Pope, made his will on 13 February 1603/04 with a similar bequest: "Item, I give and bequeath to Robert Gough and John Edmans all my wearing apparel, and all my arms, to be equally divided between them."[36] Though Pope does not specifically identify Gough and Edmans as his apprentices, it is likely that they were, or had been. Both are fairly well known actors, both were the right age to have been his apprentices, both lived in Pope's parish, St. Saviour's Southwark, and it is notable that the legacies are similar to those which Augustine Phillips thought appropriate for *his* apprentice a year later.

An adult player who indicated a good deal of trust for the master of his apprentice days was Alexander Cooke, also a member of the King's company and known to have had roles in plays of Jonson, Shakespeare, and Beaumont and Fletcher. At the time he made his will in May 1614, Cooke had several small children whose baptisms are recorded in the registers of St. Saviour's Southwark. He was evidently worried about the future of these children. After ordering the payment of legacies to three of them, he continues:

. . . all which sums of money I do entreat my Master Hemings, Mr. Cundell, and Mr. Francis Caper (for God's cause) to take into their hands, and see it safely put into Grocers' Hall, for the use and bringing up of my poor orphans.[37]

[35] George Chalmers, *An Apology for the Believers in the Shakespeare Papers*, London, 1797, pp. 431-35.

[36] John Payne Collier, *Memoirs of the Principal Actors in the Plays of Shakespeare*, London, 1846, pp. 125-28.

[37] Chalmers, *An Apology for the Believers in the Shakespeare Papers*, pp. 447-49.

It may be further evidence of his trust in his former master that Cooke asked for the money to be deposited in the Hall of the Grocers, the company of which his master, Heminges, was a member.

A decade later another member of the King's company, Nicholas Tooley, made a will showing not only his affection for his deceased master, Richard Burbage, but continued close ties to various members of the Burbage family as well as to that other veteran leader of the Lord Chamberlain-King's company, Henry Condell. The will was dated 3 June 1623. Tooley specified:

Item, I do give unto Mrs. Burbage, the wife of my good friend Mr. Cuthbert Burbage in whose house I do now lodge, as a remembrance of my love in respect of her motherly care over me the sum of ten pounds over and besides such sums of moneys as I shall owe unto her at my decease. Item, I do give unto her daughter Elizabeth Burbage alias Maxey the sum of ten pounds to be paid over unto her own proper hands therewithal to buy her such things as she shall think most meet to wear in remembrance of me. And my will is that an acquitance under her only hand and seal shall be a sufficient discharge in law to my executors for payment thereof to all intents purposes and constructions and as fully as if her pretended husband should make and seal the same with her. Item, I give to Alice Walker, the sister of my late Master Richard Burbage deceased, the sum of ten pounds to be paid unto her own proper hands. . . . Item, I give unto Sara Burbage, the daughter of my late Master Richard Burbage, deceased that sum of twenty and nine pounds and thirteen shillings which is owing unto me by Richard Robinson to be recovered, detained, and disposed of by my executors hereunder named until her marriage or age of twenty and one years which shall first and next happen without any allowance to be made of use otherwise than as they in their discretion shall think meet to allow unto her. Item, I give unto Mrs. Condell the sum

of ten pounds. . . . All the rest and residue of all and sin-
gular my goods chattels, leases, money debts and personal
estate whatsoever and wheresoever (my debts legacies and
funeral charges discharged) I do fully and wholly give and
bequeath unto my aforenamed loving friends Cuthbert Burbage and Henry Condell to be equally divided between them
part and part alike. And I do make, name, and constitute
the said Cuthbert Burbage and Henry Condell the executors of this my last will and testament. . . .[38]

John Heminges, the veteran manager of the King's company
and co-editor of the Shakespeare folio, evidently cherished his
relationship with his former apprentice John Rice, whose actions he had directed when the boy made a speech before the
King at Merchant Taylor's Hall in 1607. After several years
as a sharer in the King's company Rice had left the stage.
Heminges, in his will of 9 October 1630, left twenty shillings
for a remembrance to "John Rice, Clerke of S^t. Saviours in
Southwarke," and he indicated his confidence in the man by
making "my loving friends M^r. Burbage and M^r. Rice" his
overseers for his considerable estate.[39]

A different kind of example of affectionate relations between an apprentice and his master's family is found in a letter preserved among the Henslowe and Alleyn papers at Dulwich College. This undated letter, written in Edward Alleyn's
hand, was dictated to him by his apprentice John Pyk (or Pig)
when the company was on tour, perhaps in 1593. The jocular
tone of the letter to Mrs. Alleyn and the domestic incidents
alluded to suggest that the boy had been living in a happy
family situation.

Mistress:
   Your honest, ancient, and loving servant Pig hath his
humble commendations to you and to my good Master

[38] Prerogative Court of Canterbury, Byrd 83, transcribed in Bentley, *The
Jacobean and Caroline Stage*, II, 649-50.
[39] James Boswell, ed., *The Plays and Poems of William Shakespeare . . . By the
Late Edmund Malone*, London, 1821, III, 191-96.

Henslowe and Mistress and to my mistress' sister Bess for all her hard dealing with me I send her hearty commendations, hoping to be beholding to her again for the opening of the cupboard. And to my neighbor, Doll, for calling me up in a morning, and to my wife Sarah for making clean my shoes, and to that old gentleman, Monsieur Pearl, that even fought with me for the block in the chimney corner. And though you all look for the ready return of my proper person yet I swear to you by the faith of a fustian king never to return till Fortune us bring with a joyful meeting to lovely London.

I cease, your petty, pretty, pratling, parling pig.

By me John Pyk

Mistress, I pray you keep this that my master may see it, for I got one to write it, Mr. Downton, and my master knows not of it.

[addressed]

To his loving Mistress Alleyn on the Bankside over against the Clink.[40]

This evidence of the affection of certain apprentices for their masters and even for other members of the sharer's family are simply what has been preserved. I cannot believe for a moment that there were no resentful or rebellious apprentices in the London professional troupes. Some boys must have proved unteachable and some families uncongenial. Among the scores of sharers in London theatrical companies it is likely enough that there were players who were unsympathetic and even cruel. But the wills and letters cited are enough to demonstrate that the apprentices to the London players were not all the unhappy victims of child labor conditions.

[40] W. W. Greg, ed., *Henslowe Papers*, London, 1907, p. 41. That young Pyk (or Pig) was a favorite is suggested by another record in the Henslowe-Alleyn collection at Dulwich. In Philip Henslowe's inventory of the costumes of the Admiral's men in March 1598 there are eighty-odd items. The name of the actor for whom the costume was purchased is mentioned only five times: William Sly once, John Pyg four times. Foakes and Rickert, eds. *Henslowe's Diary*, pp. 317-23.

A different and rather obscure relationship is the ownership of a boy player and the receipt of the payments for him by a master who was not himself an actor. The clearest example of this is Philip Henslowe and his boy James Bristow. On 18 December 1597 Henslowe noted in his diary: "Bought my boy James Bristow of William Augusten [a player] the 18 of December 1597 for £8." Several times later he records payment to him by the company for this boy at the rate of three shillings per week. Evidently Henslowe himself was not training the boy as other players were; possibly this was just another of Henslowe's obscure sidelines.

RECRUITMENT

Unhappily the evidence concerning methods of recruiting these apprentices for the adult companies is too obscure to allow one to speak with assurance of any normal procedure. It has sometimes been assumed that most of the men who became sharers and hired men in the adult London troupes had had early training in the boy companies. This assumption has no doubt been encouraged by one of the few explicit references to London theatrical affairs that Shakespeare allowed himself to make in his plays. When questioning Rosencrantz about the boy company that has pushed the players visiting Elsinor out of their theater in town, Shakespeare makes Hamlet say:

> What, are they children? Who maintains 'em? How are they escoted? Will they pursue the quality no longer than they can sing? Will they not say afterwards, if they should grow themselves to common players—as it is most like, if their means are no better—their writers do them wrong, to make them exclaim against their own succession?
>
> [Folio text, II, 2]

This statement might be taken to indicate that it was usual for the children of the boy companies to move on into troupes of adult players. Possibly such was the case, but however logical such a program may seem, we do not have the names of enough boy players who appear later in adult London troupes to allow generalizations. I can find only about thirty or thirty-five—like Nathan Field, Theophilus Bird, and Stephen Hammerton—who can be identified first as boy actors and later as members of adult troupes in the metropolis. This number seems very small when we recall that we have records of on toward 1,000 professional players in England in the years 1590-1642.

There are records of a few other methods of recruitment. One is playfully alluded to by Ben Jonson after he had had more than twenty years of experience with adult London companies, especially the Lord Chamberlain-King's men. In his *Masque of Christmas*, an entertainment which was presented at court in 1616, he alludes to a situation that cannot have been uncommon, else it would have missed its comic appeal. In the entertainment "Venus, *a deafe Tire-woman*" forces her way in so that she can see the performance of her son Cupid. To the spectators she boasts about the boy:

> Aye, forsooth, he'll say his part, I warrant him, as well as ere a Play boy of 'em all: I could ha' had money enough for him, and I would ha' been tempted, and ha' let him out by the week to the King's players. Master *Burbage* has been about and about with me; and so has old Mr. *Heminges* too; they ha' need of him. . . .

Of course this is fictional dialogue, but it was written by a man who knew a great deal about the London commercial theater situation, the company involved, and methods used. Burbage is known to have had apprentices and Heminges was the manager of the company in question. The dialogue would have lost most of its effect if the recruitment method asserted had been unheard of at the time.

A number of years later this same practice of boys being sought from their parents for apprenticeship in the theater is alluded to by William Prynne. Of course the attitude of Prynne is quite different from that of Ben Jonson's deaf tirewoman, but the Puritan propagandist could record facts whatever his bias. In *Histrio-Mastix. The Players' Scourge* or *Actors' Tragedy*, 1633, he laments:

> Pity it is to consider how many ingenuous witty, comely youths, devoted to God in baptism, to whom they owe themselves, their services; are oft times by their graceless parents, even wholly consecrated to the Stage (the Devil's Chapel as the Fathers phrase it) where they are trained up in the School of Vice, the Play-house (as if their natures were not prone enough to sin, unless they had the help of art to back them) to the vary excess of all effeminancy, to act those womanish, whorish parts which Pagans would even blush to personate. [Z2-Z2ᵛ pp. 171-72]

Still other recruitments are referred to by the players themselves. In the year 1635 the Sharers' Papers of Cuthbert and Winifred Burbage, brother and widow of Richard Burbage, recite certain facts in the history of the company:

> . . . The father of us Cuthbert and Richard Burbage was the first builder of Playhouses and was himself in his younger years a player . . . and to ourselves we joined those deserving men, Shakespeare, Heminges, Condell, Phillips and others, partners in the profits of that they call the house.
> . . .
> . . . Now for the Blackfriars, that is our inheritance, our father purchased it at extreme rates and made it into a playhouse with great charge and trouble, which after was leased out to one Evans that first set up the boys commonly called the Queen's Majesty's Children of the Chapel. In process of time, the boys growing up to be men which were Underwood, Field, Ostler, & were taken to strengthen the King's service and the more to strengthen the service, the boys daily wearing out, it was considered that house would be as fit for ourselves, and so purchased the lease remaining from Evans with our money and placed men players, which were Heminges, Condell, Shakespeare & . . . these new men [i.e., Benfield, Pollard, and Swanston who were petitioning to be given some of the Burbage shares in the two

houses] that were never bred from children in the King's service. . . .[41]

That the King's men were interested in acquiring the services of some of the boys of the Queen's Chapel when the Blackfriars was taken over is likely enough. However, at the time of this petition, 1635, the Burbages were recollecting events a quarter of a century in the past and the three men they name had been dead twenty-one, sixteen, and eleven years. Ostler, Field, and Underwood had indeed been boys in the Chapel company as is shown in the cast lists for Jonson's *Poetaster*, *Cynthia's Revels*, and *Epicoene* and they had all eventually become players in the King's company, but such biographical evidence as we have makes it doubtful that as boys these three came directly to King James's company in 1608 or 1609. It may be that the company took in several juveniles when they purchased the Blackfriars, but these three are the only former Chapel boys who are known eventually to have become sharers in the King's men.

So far as I know the only formal plan for acquiring boy actors for a major adult company is that revealed in a suit in the Court of Requests in the year 1632, *Christopher Babham v. Richard Gunnell*. Richard Gunnell was a well-known theatrical personality—player, theatrical manager, theater builder, and dramatist, or at least play doctor.[42] In 1629 he joined with William Blagrave, Deputy Master of the Revels, in building the Salisbury Court theater. Christopher Babham is a slightly known figure who was an investor in the Salisbury Court and its boy company. In his Bill of Complaint, 22 October 1632, Babham recites the arrangements at the beginning of the new enterprise:

That whereas one Richard Gunnell and William Blagrave, gentlemen, did join together as partners in share to erect and build a new stage playhouse in or near Dorset Court

[41] "Dramatic Records: The Lord Chamberlain's Office," *Malone Society Collections* 2, pt. 3 (1931), 370-71. For a discussion of the context, see Bentley, *The Jacobean and Caroline Stage*, I, 43-47.

[42] See Bentley, *The Jacobean and Caroline Stage*, II, 454-58.

in the parish of St. Bridget alias Brides, London, as also to train and bring up certain boys in the quality of playing with intent to be a supply of able actors to your Majesty's servants of Blackfriars when there should be occasion, and in the mean time for the solace of your Royal Majesty, when you should please to see them, as also for the recreation of your loving subjects. . . .

This assertion about a Restoration type of training school for young players is most surprising, and one might be inclined to doubt that the new troupe was formed for any such purpose, but Babham's opponent in the lawsuit confirms this statement in his reply to the charges. Gunnell's answer says:

> . . . this defendant and William Blagrave gentleman did join together as partners in share to erect and build a new Stage playhouse . . . as also to train and bring up certain boys in the quality of playing not only with intent to be a supply of able actors to his Majesty's servants of the Black Friars when there should be occasion as by the said bill of complaint is suggested but the solace of his Royal Majesty when his Majesty should please to see them and also for the recreation of his Majesty's subjects.[43]

The existence of such a training school had been totally unsuspected, but these hostile antagonists agree that there had certainly been such an organization. A little more about the enterprise is revealed further along in the documents of the suit. Of course the principal bone of contention between the two parties was, as usual, monies paid or unpaid, but the charges and countercharges of plaintiff and defendant reveal a little more about this curious troupe of boys.

The new venture began at a bad time, for in 1630 there was a plague closing of thirty weeks[44] and the proprietors got very little return on their investment in theater building, costumes, fittings, plays, and the maintenance of the boys. Gunnell had

[43] Bentley, "The Salisbury Court Theatre and Its Boy Players," p. 137.
[44] See Bentley, *The Jacobean and Caroline Stage*, II, 657-58.

to sell his holdings to Babham for £550. But Babham had the same problems as Gunnell had had before him, and did not make all his payments on time; he claims the properties were in worse condition than he had been led to believe. Hence the suit.

Babham in his explanation of the reasons for his delays in paying his installments recounts the number and the sad state of the boys after the plague had forced them to be idle for so many weeks:

> . . . the boys were delivered to your subject in far worse plight than he hoped, for amongst fourteen of them there was not found seven shirts, and but five sheets and a half to lodge them in, their apparel so ragged and so altogether unprovided of fitting necessaries that being in the time of pestilence it might have endangered your subject's life that was constrained to look over and provide a supply to their wants. Diverse of them were likewise sick, and one of them died occasioned by an ill diet, some of them being forced to steal, others to beg for want of sustenance. . . .

In his answer Gunnell, predictably, denies that the boys were in any such serious plight as Babham asserts, but he does agree that there were fourteen boys and adds that in order to avoid infection he had hired a house in Hackney to which he had moved his family and all fourteen boy players.

Both the agreement of the litigants and the large number of boys cited by each of them seem good evidence that the new enterprise was indeed intended to be in part some sort of training school. But the venture must have failed, for thirty weeks of plague-enforced idleness and all the initial expenses of a new company were surely too much for any new organization to withstand. And we know that in December of 1631 this new company of boys, apparently called the King's Revels company, though the name is never used in the lawsuits, was out of the Salisbury Court theater, and the new troupe of Prince Charles's (II) men was in. In the Signet Office Doquet Book is the entry dated December 1631: "A license unto Andrew Kayne and others by the name of servants of the Prince to exercise and practice all manner of plays in their new playhouse in Salusbury Court. . . ."[45] The presence of the new company in the Salisbury Court theater makes it evident that the training school was out, though there is a little somewhat contradictory evidence that the company of boys may have struggled on in the provinces.[46] Surely they could no longer have been seriously training boys for the King's company.

Was this Gunnell-Blagrave attempt to develop a training school for boy actors at the new Salisbury Court theater the first of its kind? That theater had influential connections, since both the Master of the Revels and the Deputy Master had a stake in it.[47] I suspect that this enterprise so helpfully outlined in the Court of Request suit of *Christopher Babham v. Richard Gunnell* was not without antecedent or successor, for in the theater-mad London of these years there was a constant demand for new boy players. The statement of Cuthbert Burbage in his petition to the Lord Chamberlain outlining the past of the King's company, "the boys daily wearing out" must have applied equally to all the scores of dramatic companies, London and provincial. Unhappily I can find no hard evidence of other such training companies, but I have come to suspect two fairly well known troupes, one earlier than the Blagrave-Gunnell venture and one later: the Lady Elizabeth's company and the King and Queen's Young company, or Beeston's Boys.

The Lady Elizabeth's company which was formed as an ordinary London troupe in 1611 evidently fell on hard times and in the next several years is found mostly in the provinces.

---

[45] Ibid., I, 302-303 for further evidence.

[46] See the account of the King's Revels company in ibid., I, 283-301. Of course, this chapter was written thirty or forty years before anyone but the Wallaces knew of *Babham v. Gunnell*; nevertheless, I blush to read my clumsy attempt to reconcile the contradictory evidence then available.

[47] See ibid., VI, 86-115.

Sir Edmund Chambers quotes from *Coventry Papers from Corporation MSS* published in the *Warwickshire Antiquarian Magazine*:

> One of the Company of the lady Elizabethe's players came to this Cittie the 27th of March and said to Thos: Barrowes Clothworker these words. vizt you are such people in this Toune so peevishe that you would have your throats cutt and that you were well served you would be fatched up with pursevaunts.
>
> Witness hereof   THOMAS BARROWES.
>
> The names of the players names named in the patent the lady Elizabethes players bearinge Date the xxxj[th] of May. Anno undecimo Jacobi [1613].

John Townesend }	Sworn officers & none other named
Josephe Moore }	in the patent.

William Perry
Robert Fintrye
George Bosgrove
Thomas Suell
James Jones
Charles Martyn   } Boyes.
Hughe Haughton
James Kneller
John Hunt
Edward
Raphe
Walter Barrett
5 Horses in their Company.[48]

This entry in the Coventry records is quite unusual. The town clerk says explicitly that only Moore and Townsend were named in the patent. Both are known as Lady Elizabeth's men from a number of other records, largely provincial. Patents usually named six to twelve chartered members. Next, the

---

[48] E. K. Chambers, "Elizabethan Stage Gleanings," *Review of English Studies* 1 (1925), 182-83.

number of boys is excessive; twelve boys are more than any play would demand, and we are reminded of the fourteen boys Babham and Gunnell agree were in the training company of the King's Revels sixteen years later. This Lady Elizabeth's company does not seem to be the ordinary poor travelling troupe as they were supporting five horses. Of course, this evidence is quite inadequate to indicate that the troupe at Coventry was a training organization like the one Blagrave was organizing for the Salisbury Court in 1629, but I think it might be worth further investigation.

The other troupe about which I am tempted to speculate is the King and Queen's Young Company or Beeston's boys, 1637 to 1641 or '42. The Master of the Revels seems to have been involved in the organization of this company, as he had been in the Blagrave-Gunnell company. He says the troupe was formed at the King's command. It has been assumed that the resultant organization was an old-fashioned boy company.

But when the company offended the authorities, the Council called before it five men, all known adult actors, surely too many adults for an ordinary boy troupe. Furthermore when a ticket of privilege was issued for the Young company at the Cockpit on 10 August 1639, most—possibly all—of the players named were adults. Moreover when Christopher Beeston died he was succeeded by his son, William. William Beeston was sworn "his Majesty's Servant in Ordinary in the Quality and under the Title of Governor and Instructor of the King and Queen's young company of actors." Why Instructor?

In May 1640 William Beeston was jailed for presenting an unknown play with political allusions to the King's journey to the North. William Davenant was appointed six or seven weeks later to succeed young Beeston. Davenant's patent authorized him

> to take into his government and care the said company of players, to govern, order, and dispose of them for action

and presentments, and all their affairs in the said house as in his discretion shall seem best to conduce to his Majesty's service in that Quality. . . .[49]

This license to "govern" is unusual in patents for players and again suggests an abnormal company.

Then there is the odd statement written by the professional dramatist, Richard Brome, for the epilogue of his play *The Court Beggar* performed in 1639 or 1640 and printed in his *Five New Plays*, 1653.

There's wit in that now. But this small Poet vents none but his own, and his by whose care and directions this stage is govern'd, who has for many years both in his father's days, and since directed poets to write and players to speak till he trained up these youths here to what they are now. I some of 'em from before they were able to say a grace of two lines long to have more parts in their pates than would fill so many Dry-fats. And to be serious with you, if after all this by the venomous practice of some who study nothing more than his destruction, he should fail us, both poets and players would be at loss in reputation.[50]

A further hint that the Beestons' enterprise at the Phoenix or Cockpit in Drury Lane had had some special instructional character is to be found in a Chancery suit, *Beeston v. Rolleston*, brought in 1651. The issue was the control of the Phoenix where there had been a certain amount of surreptitious playing since the Parliamentary prohibition, and to which Rolleston had secured the reversion from the ground landlord. In his bill in Chancery William Beeston says that after an agreement with Rolleston on 2 January 1650/51 he had

[49] See the *Malone Society Collections* 2, pt. 3 (1931), 395. For the context see Bentley, *The Jacobean and Caroline Stage*, I, 324-36.

[50] For the confusion about the environment and dating of this play and the allusions of this quotation, see Bentley, *The Jacobean and Caroline Stage*, III, 61-65.

entered upon the premises and laid out near two hundred pounds about the repairing and fitting the same for [his] occasions. And after that [he] took prentices and covenant servants to instruct them in the quality of acting and fitting them for the stage, for which the said premises were so repaired and amended, to his great charge and damage. . . .[51]

William Beeston's statement that he "took prentices and covenant servants to instruct them in the quality of acting and fitting them for the stage" seems to imply the continuation of the sort of enterprise Richard Brome had spoken of in the epilogue to *The Court Beggar* a decade before.

The sum of these several hints is certainly not conclusive proof that Beeston's Boys or the King and Queen's Young company was a training school for boy players as the troupe at the Salisbury Court theater had been planned to be. But the various documents appear to me to indicate at least that the organization of the Beestons at the Phoenix from 1637 to 1642 was something more than we had previously thought. The words "training," "instructor," and "governor" are used with abnormal frequency in these documents.

But even if there were additional training companies for boy actors besides the one organized by Blagrave and Gunnell in 1629, they were certainly insufficient to provide all the boy players needed for the numerous dramatic companies. The search for likely juveniles must have been unending. The number of boy players required must have been a good deal greater than those needed for the metropolitan troupes.

No doubt many of the boys went into the provincial troupes of whose personnel very little is known. We are prone to think that all professional players worked in the well-known London organizations. It is easy to forget how many road companies were touring the provinces in the years 1590-1642—far more than in London. Miss Alice B. Hamilton said recently that she had found notices of more than fifty different dra-

[51] Leslie Hotson, *The Commonwealth and Restoration Stage*, Cambridge, Mass., 1928, pp. 94-98.

matic companies in the records of Leicester alone during the sixteenth and seventeenth centuries.[52] Three quarters of a century ago in a rather superficial survey of touring companies in the provinces J. T. Murray found local records of the visits of more than 130 different acting troupes in 78 provincial towns from St. Ives to Aberdeen. Though many of these companies surely were short-lived, others evidently were not; they must have involved hundreds of players, and a good many of them must have come from London and not a few could have had juvenile training in London theatrical troupes. Not all boy actors can have been as talented as Nathan Field, Salmon Pavy, and Stephen Hammerton. If no London company had anything to offer the boy player after his voice had changed, the many provincial companies might offer employment, even if not a very good living.

All in all the fact is inescapable that hundreds of boy players must have been performing in London and in the provinces during the years 1590-1642, but the precise ways in which most of them came to their profession or later advanced from feminine to adult roles can at present be only conjectured from pitifully few examples.

WAGES

The remuneration for the boy players who were essential to every dramatic company of the period was food, lodging, training in the profession, and presumably clothes as indicated in *Babham v. Gunnell* above. I have found no record to suggest that any boy ever received cash from his company. He had been bought, in the instances we know, from his master in one of the regular guilds, or from his parents or guardians. The fees paid each week by the company for his services went to the master and not to the boy.[53] Thus Henslowe's

[52] *Records of Early English Drama*, Toronto, 1979, I, 18.

[53] Apparently there were occasional exceptions to the retention of all payments by the master. When the Merchant Taylors' Company entertained the King, Queen, and Prince at dinner in June 1607, the boy actor of the King's

records show that the wages of the boy, James Bristow, whom he had bought from the player William Augusten for £8 on 18 December 1597, were three shillings per week in August 1600. They were paid by the company (greatly in arrears) to Henslowe because he owned the boy.[54]

By 1635 the rate of pay for apprentices like everything else had increased, as is shown in the papers of a suit in that year. William Browne, a sharer in the Red Bull company, died in November 1634. His mother and executrix Susan Greene-Browne-Baskervile brought an action against the company for money due her deceased son. In May 1635, two members of the company, Henry Gradwell and William Hall, testified that among other sums the company had paid Mrs. Baskervile was "seven shillings a week for an apprentice which was likewise the said Browne's."[55]

Spotty as the surviving information about recruiting, attachments, and wages of the boy players may be, it shows something of their position in the theatrical milieu of these years. Though the function of these apprentices was obviously important in the production of great plays like *As You Like It*, *A Woman Killed with Kindness*, and *The Maid's Tragedy*, they were completely subordinate and dependent in the organization of the London professional troupes.

---

company, John Rice, delivered a speech to the royal guests. The Merchant Taylors' records show that the boy's master, John Heminges, was paid forty shillings for coaching his apprentice in the speech, and the boy Rice himself was paid five shillings. One hopes that Heminges did not confiscate the five shillings (*Malone Society Collections* 3 [1954], 172).

[54] Foakes and Rickert, eds., *Henslowe's Diary*, pp. 118, 164, 167, 241.

[55] Court of Requests, Miscellaneous Books, Affidavit Book, Hilary to Trinity Terms 10 and 11 Charles I, vol. 138, transcribed in the Wallace Papers.

CHAPTER VI

Managers

THE COMPLEXITY of the affairs in which Elizabethan, Jacobean, and Caroline repertory companies were necessarily involved required that some one or two players be in charge, at least to the extent of authorizing the purchase of new costumes and costume materials; paying for new plays by free-lance dramatists; getting scripts approved by the Master of the Revels, paying him for licenses for the theater and for occasional privileges, like playing during parts of Lent; paying the company's regular contributions to the poor of the parish, assessing fines against sharers or hired men for infringement of company regulations; calling rehearsals; collecting fees for court and private performances; supervising the preparation and distribution of playbills;[1] and perhaps for paying the hired

[1] The importance of playbills in the economy of the theatrical troupes of the time is indicated in the agreement between Thomas Greene and Martin

men. The extensive financial dealings of the Lord Chamberlain-King's company would have been chaos if all ten or twelve sharers had tried to perform these functions collectively.

On the other hand there is no reason to think that the earlier players' representatives whom I have, perhaps inaccurately, called "managers" usually had anything like the power over their companies later exercised by Davenant, Killigrew, or Garrick. Moreover, such power as these earlier "managers" did exercise appears to have varied a good deal from company to company and from the rather chaotic days of the 1590s to the more strictly organized times of the 1630s.

The familiar need for some sort of professional supervision even in amateur civic productions has been demonstrated by new evidence of their use discovered by Professor Coldewey. Early in the sixteenth century several towns near London—

Slater recited in *Greene v. Slater* in the Court of Common Pleas in 1607. Greene was presumably at this time manager of Queen Anne's company at the Red Bull; Slater, a sworn member of the company, had apparently been touring under the name of Queen Anne's company but with few, if any, of her patented members in his troupe. After the payment to him of £12 by Greene and the other named sharers in Queen Anne's company, Slater agreed that ". . . Although he be sworn one of Her Majesty's players yet in respect and consideration of the sum of £12 to him by them paid he the said Martin Slater shall forbear and be restrained from setting up any bills for playing or playing as in the name of Her Majesty's servants. . . ." And later in the document the point is repeated that neither Slater nor any other by his appointment will "set up or publish any plays or playbills . . . in the name of Her Majesty's players unless he the said Martin shall then have in his company to play with him five other of the said Her Majesty's servants . . ." (Court of Common Pleas, Mich 5 Jas I Roll 1789 MMCXIIII, as transcribed in the Wallace Papers, Huntington Library, San Marino, California).

The abuse in which Slater agrees not to indulge was apparently common. Some sharer in a London company would procure an exemplification of the company's patent, recruit a group of second-rate players, and tour the provinces posing as the authentic London company. Greene and his fellows bribe Slater to desist from this practice. However, the abuse in general continued, not only by Slater but by other London players. The Lord Chamberlain attempted to stop it in 1616 by an order sent to all provincial officials and naming several of the culprits, including Slater (see J. T. Murray, *English Dramatic Companies 1558-1642*, 2 vols., London, 1910, II, 343-44).

Chelmsford, Maldon, Heybridge and Lydd—repeatedly paid men from the metropolis, often called "property players," to supervise and to furnish materials for local dramatic productions. The payments were not small, and a few of the records show the services of the imported "property player" to have been extensive.[2]

In the professional touring troupes of the sixteenth century there seems always to have been a leading player and there are suggestions that he made arrangements and did a certain amount of directing, but the evidence is sparse and not very helpful.[3]

For the period after 1590 the man most often called a manager by modern writers is Philip Henslowe. But this is an error; he was not really a manager, though it seems that he was trying to become one when the Lady Elizabeth's men were tenants at his Hope theater in the years 1614-1615. Henslowe was essentially a theater owner and financier whose extant theatrical records are more extensive than those of any other man of his time. He certainly had many dealings with players, dramatists, tailors, fencers, upholsterers, Revels officials, carpenters, acrobats, and mercers. He laid out the money involved in transactions for the players, but he did so at the direction (usually recorded) of some sharer in the company. Like any financier or "angel" he had an influence on the actions of the companies playing at his theaters. His true function and the misconception that he was an early manager have been most thoroughly discussed by Bernard Beckerman.[4]

[2] See John C. Coldewey, "The Digby Plays and the Chelmsford Records," *Research Opportunities in Renaissance Drama* 17 (1975), 103-121; and his "That Enterprising Property Player: Semi-Professional Drama in Sixteenth-Century England," *Theatre Notebook* 31 (1977), 5-12.

[3] See David Bevington, *From "Mankind" to Marlowe*, Cambridge, Mass., 1962, *passim*; and the scenes with the travelling players in *Hamlet* and *Sir Thomas More*.

[4] "Philip Henslowe" in Joseph W. Donohue, ed., *The Theatrical Manager in Britain and America*, Princeton, 1972, pp. 19-62. Though Beckerman shows clearly that Henslowe was not a manager during the period of the Diary, he goes on to show, mostly from the later letters published in the *Henslowe Papers*

Who were the "managers" for the London professional troupes from 1590 to 1642? And what did they do? The answers to these questions must be less complete and definitive than one would wish, but there is quite a lot of scattered material bearing upon the subject.

The clearest and best defined function of "managers" in these years was dealing with officials—collecting fees for court performances, collecting cloth allowances for liveries for the royal companies, dealing with the Master of the Revels when the company had offended or wanted a new play licensed for performance. But there were others as we shall see.

A dozen or more of these "managers" or company representatives or leaders can be identified in eight or ten different companies during the fifty-two years of playing between 1590 and 1642. But in the first two decades, except for the entries in Henslowe's Diary, the evidence is so scattered and incomplete that one cannot build up a very useful picture of what these earlier managers did. It is likely, of course, that they carried out most of the chores which Heminges and Beeston are known to have undertaken later, but too little of the evidence is extant.

It is fairly clear that Edward Alleyn was performing managerial functions for the Admiral's and the Palsgrave's men in these early years and that he was followed by Edward Juby. It is also clear that Thomas Greene was doing the same for Queen Anne's men in the first decade of the reign of King James, and that the dramatist and clown, William Rowley, functioned as manager for the Duke of York-Prince Charles's company before he became one of the King's men. But the managers most frequently cited are John Heminges in his activities for the King's company, and Christopher Beeston successively for Queen Anne's men, the Lady Elizabeth's men,

---

(ed. W. W. Greg, London, 1907), that Henslowe appears to have been trying to develop real managerial powers over the companies at his theater, the Hope—first the Lady Elizabeth's men and then Prince Charles's—but he antagonized the companies, and there is no evidence that he established himself with the Master of the Revels or the Lord Chamberlain.

Queen Henrietta's company, and the King and Queen's Young company.

JOHN HEMINGES

The most fully documented of the managerial careers of the period is that of John Heminges, whose recorded activities on behalf of the Lord Chamberlain-King's company are numerous. From 1596 to 1630 he was always the sharer who received payment for plays performed before the court by the company. On occasions he was joined by another sharer: twice by Thomas Pope, once by George Bryan, once by Richard Cowley, and once by Augustine Phillips, but generally his name appears alone.

About fifty such payments to Heminges for court performances are recorded, reaching a total of well over £3,000.[5] If he was so consistently the receiver of payments by the Lord Treasurer's office, he probably received the payments for other restricted performances by the company at noblemen's houses, at the Inns of Court (like the performance of *The Comedy of Errors* at Gray's Inn in 1594 or *Twelfth Night* at the Middle Temple in 1602 or *Sir John Oldcastle* before the Lord Chamberlain and the Dutch Ambassador in 1600), or at entertainments for City companies.

Heminges was also the receiver of the cloth for the liveries of the fellows of the company—at least so far as the records show; most of the earlier records have been lost, but from 1619 to his death only Heminges is recorded as the recipient of the biennial allowances for the patented members of the company.[6] On various occasions Heminges, sometimes with another sharer, was used as the official representative of his

[5] David Cook and F. P. Wilson, "Dramatic Records in the Declared Accounts of the Treasurer of the Chamber, 1558-1642," *Malone Society Collections* 6 (1962), 29-81. This large sum is several times what it cost to build a new theater in Heminges' time.

[6] G. E. Bentley, *The Jacobean and Caroline Stage*, 7 vols., Oxford, 1941-1968, I, 90.

company. In 1615 when eight players representing the four London companies were called before the Privy Council to answer for playing during Lent, Heminges and Burbage were called to represent the King's men.[7]

Heminges' dealings with the Master of the Revels show him in another capacity as the representative of his company in whom, by implication, the Master had confidence. On 19 August 1623, Sir Henry Herbert noted that he had allowed

> For the King's players. An old play called *Winter's Tale*, formerly allowed of by Sir George Bucke and likewise by me on Mr. Heminges his word that there was nothing profane added or reformed, though the allowed book was missing; and therefore I returned it without a fee, this 19 of August 1623.

Heminges was also the man who paid fees to the Master of the Revels on behalf of the company. Sir Henry recorded on 20 March 1626/27 "From Mr. Heminges for this Lent allowance £2.0.0." Seven or eight years earlier Heminges had paid a fee to the Master for all four companies, "Of John Heminges in the name of the four companies for toleration in the holy days, 44s. January 29, 1618[/19]." Perhaps the most marked example of Heminges' standing with the Master is found in an Office Book entry of April 1627. Since there was no national copyright law, the publication of the Shakespeare Folio of 1623 had made the texts of these plays available to all acting troupes. On at least one occasion Heminges took care of this competition problem for the company. Sir Henry noted: "[Received] from Mr. Heminges in the company's name to forbid the playing of Shakespeare's plays to the Red Bull company, this 11 of April 1627—£5.0.0." A year before Heminges had handled some unknown situation for the King's men as shown in another entry of Herbert's on 7 July 1626: "[Received] from Mr. Heminges for a courtesy done him about

---

[7] E. K. Chambers, *The Elizabethan Stage*, 4 vols., Oxford, 1967, IV, 342. From the Minutes of the Privy Council.

their Black Friars house—£3.0.0."[8] Edmond Malone noted in Herbert's manuscript, from which he quoted extracts, that

> Heminges, however, it appears from Sir Henry Herbert's manuscript, took some concern in the management of the theatre, and used to present Sir Henry, as Master of the Revels, with his New Years' gift for three or four years afterwards. . . .[9]

Proper cultivation of the right officials was evidently one of a manager's contributions to the welfare of his company. We shall find Christopher Beeston making similar gestures.

The records of the Lord Chamberlain also show official assumptions that Heminges was the responsible agent in the affairs of the King's company and its members. When, in November 1628, a Henry Jenkins petitioned for permission to sue Richard Sharpe (a sharer in the company) for debt, the Lord Chamberlain replied, "I desire Mr. Heminges to satisfy the petitioner out of the first moneys accruing to Richard Sharpe either for his share or dividend, &c.[10] Another record from the office of the Lord Chamberlain presumably shows Heminges handling company affairs. On 14 December 1628 the Lord Chamberlain issued a warrant for the arrest "of Ambrose Beeland and Henry Wilson, Fiddlers, at the complaint of Mr. Heminges."[11] Since both these "Fiddlers" were musicians for the King's men it is likely that Heminges was acting for the company.

Certain other records suggest Heminges functioning for the company but are less explicit than the foregoing. There is an assertion in a Court of Request suit of 1619 that the company

[8] Joseph Quincy Adams, ed., *The Dramatic Records of Sir Henry Herbert, Master of the Revels, 1623-1673*, New Haven, 1917, pp. 25, 48, and 62n.

[9] Edmond Malone, *An Inquiry into the Authenticity of Certain Miscellaneous Papers and Legal Instruments* . . . , London, 1796, p. 251n.

[10] Lord Chamberlain's Petition Book, London, Public Record Office, 5/183, p. 43.

[11] Allardyce Nicoll and Eleanor Boswell, eds., "Dramatic Records, The Lord Chamberlain's Office," *Malone Society Collections* 2, pt. 3 (1931), 348.

had built a house for him on the grounds of the Globe. For a good many years before this, Heminges had lived in the parish of St. Mary Aldermanbury. At least twelve of his children were christened or buried there and he had held a number of parish offices. But after 1619 he appears no more in the records of that parish, except for the entry of his own burial. In the replication of John Witter dated 10 May 1619, to the reply of Heminges and Condell, Witter says:

> And the said defendant Heminges hath adjoining there unto [i.e., the Globe theater] . . . a fair house new builded to his own use for which he payeth but twenty shillings yearly in all at the most. . . .[12]

The building of this house for Heminges was presumably connected with his managerial duties for the company. His residence there would account for his appearance in the token books of St. Saviour's, Southwark, the parish of the Globe.[13]

Finally there are a couple of occasional verses alluding to Heminges as a well-known figure. Since he certainly had less fame as an actor than a number of his fellows, I can account for his mention only on the assumption that he was familiar as an agent or "manager" for the company. The less significant of the two is the ballad on the burning of the first Globe during a performance of *Henry VIII* in 1613. In the five verses Burbage, "the fool" (presumably Robert Armin) and "Henry Condy" are mentioned. The fifth stanza ends,

> Then with swollen eyes like drunken Flemings
> Distressed stood old stuttering Heminges.[14]

Though four sharers in the company are mentioned, Heminges seems to be given a special proprietary position. One

---

[12] C. W. Wallace, "Shakespeare and His London Associates," *University of Nebraska Studies* 10 (1910), 332.

[13] Bentley, *The Jacobean and Caroline Stage*, II, 467.

[14] First printed in *The Gentleman's Magazine* in 1816 and later published by J. O. Halliwell-Phillipps, *Outlines of the Life of Shakespeare*, 2 vols., London, 1907, I, 311. I do not fully trust the authenticity of these verses.

could wish to have more confidence in the contemporary origin of this ballad.

More significant is the epigram attributed to John Donne in a manuscript formerly in the library at Burley-on-the-Hill. Probably it was not written by Donne, but it is contemporary and the role given Heminges in the last couplet is quite fitting for the "manager" of the King's company.

Epi: B: Jo:
Tell me who can when a player dies
    In which of his shapes again he shall rise?
What need he stand at the Judgment throne
    Who hath a heaven and a hell of his own?
Then fear not Burbage, heaven's angry rod
    When thy fellows are angels and old Heminges
        is God.[15]

The choice of Burbage as a player in this epigram is easily accounted for, since he was the most famous London player alive at the time, but Heminges had little or no contemporary reputation as an impressive actor. If, however, he was manager of the King's company to which Burbage belonged, the reason for his selection by the poet for the position of final judgment is obvious. If the epigram had been written by any other lyric poet of the time, the selection of Heminges might have been fortuitous, but Ben Jonson certainly knew more about the inner workings of the dramatic companies of the time than most of his contemporary writers.

Since he was for so long a sharer in the Lord Chamberlain-King's company, more of the activities of John Heminges are recorded than of any of the others to whom I have attributed managership. So far as I can tell these activities were more or less typical of the office in the time.

[15] H.J.C. Grierson, ed., *The Poems of John Donne*, 2 vols., Oxford, 1912, I, 443. "Epi." stands for Epigram, not Epitaph. Hereford and Simpson reprint the epigram in the section of their volume called "Poems Ascribed to Jonson," *Ben Jonson*, 11 vols., Oxford, 1947, VIII, 439.

CHRISTOPHER BEESTON

Christopher Beeston, alias Hutchinson, left more records of his managerial activities than any other player of the period except John Heminges. His career differed in that he functioned for several different companies at different times, and in the fact that during most of his managerial years, i.e., 1612-1638, he was a theater owner, not just one of a group of housekeeping sharers like Heminges, Burbage, Shakespeare, and Condell.

Early in his career Beeston performed with the Lord Chamberlain's company; Ben Jonson listed him, along with Shakespeare, Condell, Burbage, Heminges, and six others as one of the comedians who created a role in *Every Man in His Humor* in 1598. But by 1602 he was one of the Earl of Worcester's men who became Queen Anne's players the next year; in their patent of 1609 he is named second to Thomas Greene, their leader at that time. In 1612 Thomas Greene died and in his will made Beeston one of the three overseers of the disposition of his considerable estate.[16] Beeston at this time succeeded Greene as leader of Queen Anne's company. The fact of his management is clearly stated by his fellows Ellis Worth, John Cumber, and John Blaney in their bill in Chancery against Susan Baskervile, widow of Thomas Greene. Susan had sued them for debts she claimed the company had owed her husband at the time of his death and which the company had made subsequent agreements to pay but had defaulted. The three players say in their Chancery Bill of 1623

And whereas your orators and the rest of their fellows at that time [i.e., Queen Anne's company] and long before and since did put the managing of their whole businesses and affairs belonging unto them jointly, as they were players, in trust unto Christopher Hutchinson alias Beeston, of

[16] F. G. Fleay, *A Chronicle History of the London Stage, 1559-1642*, London, 1890, pp. 192-94. From the transcript of James Greenstreet.

London, gentleman, who was then one of your orators' fellows. . . .[17]

Another lawsuit concerning the affairs of Beeston and Queen Anne's company, this time in the Court of Requests, shows Beeston buying and authorizing the buying of costume materials for the company. The suit, which was brought in 1619, concerns old debts which John Smith says that Beeston, along with his fellows Ellis Worth, Richard Perkins, and John Cumber, bought for the company. As usual, plaintiff and defendants deny most of each others' allegations, but the Bill and Answers, and the depositions of witnesses, make several statements that show some of Beeston's activities and frequently hint at his slipperiness. Smith says that he, between 27 June 1612 and 23 February 1616/17

> . . . at the earnest request and entreaty of one Christopher Beeston [did] deliver or cause to be delivered unto him the said Christopher Beeston and his assigns and at his request and by his direction unto and for the use of the company of players at the Red Bull . . . divers tinsel stuffs and other stuff for their use in playing. . . .

Three of Queen Anne's men who had been made parties to the suit, Ellis Worth, Richard Perkins, and John Cumber, chose to submit Answers separate from Beeston's. They say that with Beeston they were members of Queen Anne's company and had set forth divers plays and comedies at the Red Bull, and they continue that

> . . . for the better ordering and setting forth of which said plays and comedies there required divers officers and that every one of the said actors should take upon them some place and charge and for that the provision of the furniture and apparel was a place of greatest charge and trust and must of necessity fall upon a thriving man and one that was of ability and means, it was agreed by and between the said

[17] Ibid., p. 274.

157

company of actors in manner and form following: that is to say that the said Christopher Beeston in the Bill of Complaint named should defalk out of the collections and gatherings which were made continually whensoever any play was acted, a certain sum of money as a common stock towards the buying and defraying of the charges of the furniture and apparel aforesaid. And that the said Christopher Beeston should buy all the furniture, apparel, and other necessaries. . . . And that the said Christopher Beeston should with the said common stock so collected pay for the said commodities by him hereafter to be bought or otherwise that the said commodities should stand upon the sole and proper account and head of the said Beeston and that no other of the company should be troubled or employed in this business or should pay or stand charged or liable for any commodities so by the said Christopher Beeston to be bought but that the said Christopher Beeston should discharge and free the company and pay all such moneys as should arise by reason thereof . . . and upon this agreement the said Christopher Beeston did undertake this charge and trust and hath for the space of seven or eight years continually when there was any play deducted and defalked divers great sums of money out of the collections and gatherings aforesaid. . . .

Beeston's own Answer to the Bill of Complaint of John Smith, separate from those of Worth, Perkins, and Cumber, is mostly simple denials except for the statement that after Queen Anne's decease (March 1618/19) he had entered the service of Prince Charles.

On 5 May 1620 depositions of several witnesses were taken in the suit. One of them, William Freshwater, merchant tailor, aged seventy-two, gave testimony that verifies the observation that Beeston was buying costume materials for the company in 1612, the year of Thomas Greene's death. Freshwater says that about 1612 he bought materials and requested that

. . . If any the company or workmen belonging to the players at the Red Bull . . . did come of those stuffs he had
bought of the complainant or of any more or other stuff for
the use of the said company that he the complainant should
deliver them from time to time which he the said Beeston
the defendant then promised to see discharged and paid for.
. . .

Freshwater further testified that the orders for the stuffs were
made in Beeston's name, that Freshwater himself was a work-
man and had often gone to the Red Bull. He says that Smith
often refused to hand over the materials without some token
from Beeston. Another witness, Japhathe Weale, haberdasher, deposed that he had seen Beeston examine Smith's
account books in 1618 and acknowledge receipt of the materials. Still another witness, John King, identified here and in
a later suit as a hired man of the company, testified that he
knew it to be true that Smith would not deliver any materials
to any member of the company "except they brought a token
from the defendant, Beeston." King further testified that he
knew the company gave an allowance to Beeston to purchase
materials, ". . . and saieth that the said company did allow
him the said Beeston, one-half of the profit that came of the
galleries towards the satisfying of the complainant's debt which
he received weekly. . . ." King goes on that Smith delivered
materials to Beeston for eight or nine years, but that the company began to break up about three years before [i.e., 1617]
"and at the separation of the said company the said Beeston
did take and carry away all the apparel that was then amongst
the said company and converted them to his own use. . . ."[18]

The various documents of this suit suggest that Christopher
Beeston was a rather slippery character, but the point of interest at the moment is that as manager and "a thriving man
and one that was of ability and means" he bought costume

[18] C. W. Wallace, "Three London Theatres of Shakespeare's Time," *University of Nebraska Studies* 9 (1909), 318, 321-22, 331, 332, 333-34.

materials for the company and was reimbursed by half the profits from the galleries, paid weekly.

The fact that Beeston "at the separating of the said company" in 1617 is alleged to have carried off the costumes is surely not unconnected with the fact that he was at that time building the Phoenix theater, often called the Cockpit in Drury Lane, a house that was his own property and at which he managed, sequentially, several companies of players until his death in October 1638.[19]

Near, or perhaps attached to, his new theater, Beeston appears to have had a residence, as Heminges had at the Globe. After the London apprentices raided and partially destroyed Beeston's new Phoenix on Shrove Tuesday 1616/17, several of them were charged in the Middlesex Special Session of Oyer and Terminer with defacing "the dwelling house of Christopher Beeston."[20]

Since the documents of the Chancery suit of the players against Susan Baskervile show clearly that buying materials for the company was part of Beeston's duties as manager or leader of Queen Anne's troupe, one would assume that he continued this practice with later companies that played in his own theater, when he was even more "a thriving man and one that was of ability and means." Whether other managers or leaders had the same responsibility of buying for their companies, the evidence is too meager to prove, but one would assume that they did.

Beeston's managerial activities after he was established in the Cockpit were as extensive as those of Heminges for a more distinguished and more publicized company, for Beeston was both landlord and manager. Some of the later evidence suggests that he ruled with a high hand over the companies playing at the Phoenix.

His activities for each company at his theater are attested by various records between 1611 and 1638. Like Heminges, Beeston was usually the man who received payment when his

---

[19] See Bentley, *The Jacobean and Caroline Stage*, VI, 47-77.
[20] Ibid., p. 56.

companies performed at court, but fewer payments were recorded. No troupe of the time had anything like the prestige of the King's company or played so often before royalty.

Beeston was also like Heminges in receiving the livery allowances for Queen Henrietta's company so long as they performed at his playhouse. But here his position is not so clear: the warrants for two of the allowances seem to be lost, one names no recipient, and once William Allen signed the receipt.

The managerial position of Christopher Beeston is indicated by the Master of the Revels in 1622. At the time Sir Henry took over his new office, he made a list of the London companies of players and their theaters. When Edmond Malone saw Herbert's manuscript in the eighteenth century, part of the leaf with these lists had already "mouldered away," but three entries remained, one of which was: "The chief of them at the Phoenix. Christopher Beeston, Joseph Moore. . . ."[21] Beeston's position is similarly recorded twelve years later when Queen Henrietta's company was performing at his theater. Thomas Crosfield, the Fellow of Queen's College, Oxford mentioned before, took notes on the facts about London dramatic troupes told him by one of the wardrobe keepers for a visiting London company. Part of his account reads: "2. The Queen's servants at the Phoenix in Drury Lane. Their master Mr. Beeston. . . ."[22]

Just as Heminges ordinarily represented the King's men in their dealings with the Master of the Revels, so Beeston acted for his companies at the Phoenix. His function and his standing with Sir Henry show up most clearly in two entries of the early thirties. The first concerns difficulties about a comedy of James Shirley, the company's attached dramatist at this time.

18 Nov. 1632. In the play of *The Ball*, written by Sherley, and acted by the Queen's players, there were divers personated so naturally, both of lords and others of the court,

---

[21] Adams, ed., *The Dramatic Records of Sir Henry Herbert*, pp. 62-63.
[22] Bentley, *The Jacobean and Caroline Stage*, II, 688.

that I took it ill, and would have forbidden the play, but that Beeston promised many things which I found fault withal should be left out and that he would not suffer it to be done by the poet any more, who deserves to be punished; and the first that offends in this kind, of poets or players, shall be sure of public punishment.

Another entry of Herbert's only nine months later shows Beeston in a transaction reflecting relations with the Master not unlike those of John Heminges:

> Received of Beeston for an old play called *Hymen's Holiday*, newly revived at their house, being a play given unto him for my use, this 15 Aug. 1633, £3.0.0.
> Received of him for some alterations in it £1.0.0.[23]

Again like Heminges, Christopher Beeston took pains to cultivate the Master of the Revels for the benefit of his companies, and, no doubt, of himself as well. The exact date of this entry was not copied by Malone when he had the now lost manuscript in his hands but presumably it was about 1633. Herbert wrote: "Meeting with him [Beeston] at the old exchange, he gave my wife a pair of gloves, that cost him at least twenty shillings." Another record of Sir Henry's is perhaps less reliable since it was made after the Restoration when he was struggling to reassert his old authority as Master of the Revels and was probably overstating his case, but the item nonetheless does show Beeston's position. In December of 1660 Herbert made a series of notes for his arguments for the reinstatement of his old privileges: "To prove that Mr. Beeston paid me £60 per annum besides usual fees and allowances for Court plays."[24] Whether or not the large fee of £60 was exaggerated, the item is clear enough in its assertion of Beeston's position.

After Queen Henrietta's men left (or were forced out of) the Phoenix, Beeston's position as manager of the new com-

---

[23] Adams, ed., *The Dramatic Records of Sir Henry Herbert*, pp. 19 and 35.
[24] Ibid., pp. 67 and 101.

pany becomes even clearer. The new troupe was called the King and Queen's Young company or Their Majesties' Servants. In spite of its name and various references, it was not an old-fashioned boy company but involved several adults.[25] In origin the company was more official than most, for the Lord Chamberlain issued a warrant on 21 February 1636/37: "A Warrant to swear Mr. Christopher Beeston his Majesty's servant in the place of Governor of the new Company of the King and Queen's boys."[26] And three days later the Master of the Revels noted in his Office Book, "Mr. Beeston was commanded to make a company of boys, and begin to play at the Cockpit with them same day."[27]

Another testimony to his command at the Phoenix or Cockpit in Drury Lane is an order sent on 10 June 1637 to the Masters and Wardens of the Stationers' Company by the Lord Chamberlain. His Lordship observed that he had been told that certain London printers were proposing to print plays belonging to the players but which had been stolen or gotten from them by indirect means. He therefore ordered the Masters and Wardens that if any such plays were brought to Stationers Hall that the publishers be forbidden to print without

> some certificate in writing under the hands of John Lowin and Joseph Taylor for the King's Servants [John Heminges had died in 1630] and of Christopher Beeston for the King's and Queen's Young company or of such other persons as shall from time to time have the direction of those companies. . . .[28]

Other documents demonstrating Christopher Beeston's activities as manager of the companies at the Phoenix from 1617 to his death in 1638 might be cited, but these are enough to

[25] See Bentley, *The Jacobean and Caroline Stage*, I, 324n.

[26] Nicoll and Boswell, eds., "Dramatic Records, The Lord Chamberlain's Office," p. 382.

[27] Adams, ed., *The Dramatic Records of Sir Henry Herbert*, p. 66.

[28] Nicoll and Boswell, eds., "Dramatic Records, The Lord Chamberlain's Office," pp. 384-85.

show what he did. His activities were obviously similar to those of John Heminges for the King's men at the Blackfriars and the Globe, except that as owner of the theater Beeston's powers seem greater than those of Heminges. The charges brought against Beeston by John Smith and by Queen Anne's men and his dealings with Queen Henrietta's company during the plague of 1636-37[29] also show that powerful as he was, he was not the generally trusted representative that Heminges was.

THOMAS GREENE

There is a reasonable amount of evidence that before Christopher Beeston took over as manager of Queen Anne's company at the Red Bull his predecessor in management was the comic actor, Thomas Greene, who was so successful in the part of Bubble in Cooke's play *The City Gallant* that the piece was published in 1614 as *Greene's Tu Quoque or The City Gallant*. For the second issue of this play an Epistle to the Reader was written by Thomas Heywood, Greene's fellow sharer and principal dramatist for the company.

> As for Master Green, all that I will speak of him (and that without flattery) is this (if I were worthy to censure), there was not an actor of his nature, in his time, of better ability in performance of what he undertook, more applaudent by the audience, of greater grace at the court, or of more general love in the city: and so with this brief character of his memory I commit him to his rest.

These qualities would be very useful in the manager of a company, especially the rather unexpected "greater grace at the court," and there is evidence that Greene was the manager, at least for the last eight or ten years before his death. His name heads the list of sharers in the draft patent for the company probably in 1603 or 1604. He is also named first in

---

[29] See Bentley, *The Jacobean and Caroline Stage*, i, 236-39.

the company's patent dated 15 April 1609 in the Patent Rolls. In a Chancery suit of 16 June 1623 his widow and executrix (Greene died in 1612) says that:

> . . . the said Thomas Greene deceased . . . was a fellow actor or player of and in the company of actors or players of the late queen's majesty, Queen Anne . . . and was one of the principal and chief persons of the said company, and a full adventurer, storer, and sharer of in and amongst them. . . .[30]

Half a dozen times early in the reign of James, Greene was the recipient of payments for plays given at court by Queen Anne's company. In the first few years of the reign John Duke was usually payee, but from 1608-1612, it was Thomas Greene.

Greene is also seen acting for the company in an agreement made with Martin Slater in 1607, partly transcribed above. The agreement provides that Slater will not set up any bills, or play in London or in the country as the Queen's company unless he has with him five of the sharers of Queen Anne's troupe. Though eight other members of the company are mentioned, the agreement is with Greene and the papers are docketed *"Thos. Greene v. Martin Slater."*[31]

More conclusive evidence of his managership is the testimony given by Thomas Heywood, the dramatist and sharer in Queen Anne's company. In the Chancery suit of 1623 *Ellis Worth and John Blaney v. Susan Baskervile and William Browne*, Heywood was called as a witness. He testified:

> . . . there was no cause for the defendant Susan to pretend any debt to be due to her said husband Greene at his death by the said company for this deponent saith that the said Thomas Greene had in his life time for divers years the taking and receiving of the profits of the half galleries for

[30] James Greenstreet's transcription, *Transactions of the New Shakespeare Society*, 1880-86, pt. 3, ser. 1, p. 499.

[31] Transcript of an entry on Roll 1789 of the Court of Common Pleas, transcribed in the Wallace Papers.

the said company and whether he ever gave account thereof or no to the company this depondent saith he certainly knoweth not, but verily believeth that the said company was not any way indebted unto the said Thomas Greene at the time of his death, but that he was rather indebted to the said company. . . .[32]

This testimony of Thomas Heywood, who had been a fellow of the company for years, seems clear enough; it is corroborated by the testimony of his fellow, Richard Perkins, another well-known player whose performance in *The White Devil* had been praised by John Webster. Perkins said in his testimony as a witness in the same suit that he too thought that the company had owed nothing to Susan's husband since,

Thomas Greene had for certain years the receiving of the profits of the half galleries at the Red Bull for the company, and he saith that to his remembrance he did never know or hear that the said Greene did account to the said company at any time for the same. . . .

The agreement of these two prominent sharers seems to me to leave little doubt that Thomas Greene was acting as manager of Queen Anne's men before Christopher Beeston took over after his death. The arrangement to which both Heywood and Perkins refer, for Greene to take the profits of the half galleries, sounds like a sensible device for supplying the manager with funds for purchases and payments, but I know of no reference to such a specific plan in any other company. In fact I have seen no reference to show how other companies kept their managers supplied with funds.

OTHER MANAGERS

So far as we can tell now, John Heminges and Christopher Beeston were the longest lasting and the most fully recorded of the company managers of the period. There is ample evi-

[32] London, Public Record Office, C 24/500/103.

dence, however, that there were others; indeed, enough evidence to suggest that every company of the time probably had a manager. Perhaps a few examples of the managerial activities of certain of the players for other companies will show how common this type of organization was.

The most inclusive statement implying that each London company had a manager or chief is the one referred to before that Richard Kendall, one of the two wardrobe keepers at the Salisbury Court theater, made to Thomas Crosfield on 18 July 1634 when his company was playing at Oxford. Crosfield numbered the stories which Kendall told him. The one of principal interest here is "5. Of the several companies of players in London which are in number 5." Under this rubric Kendall listed the companies, obviously in order of importance.

> 1. The King's company at the
> private house of Blackfriars: The masters
> or chief whereof are ⎰ Mr. Tailor
> ⎱ Mr. Lowin.

These two prominent sharers in Shakespeare's old company succeeded to Heminges' duties; in fact in his last receipt of payment for court performances in 1630, their names were joined with his. After Heminges' death in that year, Lowin and Taylor always signed for the court payments, often joined by another old sharer, Eyllaerdt Swanston. Unlike Heminges, they were prominent actors as well as managers. When the Queen gave to the company the costumes that had been made for her spectacular performance of *The Faithful Shepherdess* in 1633/34, it was Taylor to whom she presented them. These two new managers also generally received the company livery allowances and dealt with Herbert for the company as Heminges had done.

The next item in Kendall's report of London theatrical affairs is: "2. The Queen's servants at the Phoenix in Drury Lane. Their master Mr. Beeston. . . ." Enough of Beeston's activities have already been recounted.

After the Queen's men under Beeston comes, "3. The Prince's Servants at the Red Bull in St. John street, the chief Mr. Cane a Goldsmith, Mr. Worth Mr. Smith £2,000." It is not clear what the £2,000 means, but we shall hear more later about Andrew Cane, or Keyne or de Caine. It is true that he was a member of the Goldsmith's Company and after the closing of the theaters seems to have returned to his old trade, but in 1634 he had been a player for at least twelve years.

After the report on Prince Charles's company in Thomas Crosfield's notes comes, "4. The Fortune in Golden Lane, the chief Mr. William Cartwright, Edward Armestead, John Buckle, John Kirke." William Cartwright was an old-timer in the theater, having appeared in Henslowe's Diary as early as 1598. He was a friend of Edward Alleyn, and his picture hangs in the gallery at Dulwich College. He is often confused with his son and namesake who continued as a prominent player into the Restoration. Kendall's assertion that William Cartwright was managing the company at the Fortune in 1634 is verified by an entry in the Office Book of the Master of the Revels showing that two years later William Cartwright Senior was performing one of the duties we have seen being discharged by Heminges and Beeston.

> Received of old Cartwright for allowing the [Fortune] company to add scenes to an old play and to give it out for a new one, this 12th of May, 1636 . . . £1.0.0.[33]

The last and fullest account among Crosfield's notes is the one Kendall gave of his own troupe:

> 5. The Company of Salisbury Court at the further end of Fleet street against the Conduit: The chief wereof are 1. Mr. Gunnell a Papist. 2. Mr. John Young. 3. Edward Gibbs a fencer. 4. Timothy Reed. 5. Christopher Goad. 6. Sam. Thompson. 7. Mr Staffield [Stutville]. 8. John Robinson. 9. Curtis Greville. These are the chief whereof 7 are called

---

[33] Adams, ed., *The Dramatic Records of Sir Henry Herbert*, p. 37.

sharers, i.e., such as pay wages to the servants and equally
share in the overplus: other servants there are as two Close
keepers ⎧ Richard
⎨ Kendall &c
⎩ Anthony
⎩ Dover[34]

Before Gunnell became manager of the Salisbury Court theater he had had a career as a Palsgrave's and then as a Prince's
man at the Fortune theater in which he had an interest. The
first indication of his managerial functions known to me is a
bond which six of the Palsgrave's men signed to him in 1624
agreeing to continue to play together at the Fortune and post-
ing a forfeit.[35]

About a year later Gunnell is found dealing with the Master of the Revels much as Heminges and Beeston did. At times,
it is not clear how regularly, theaters were allowed to offer
miscellaneous entertainment during Lent when they were
supposed to be closed. In Lent of 1624/25 Sir Henry Herbert
recorded payments from Gunnell for such privileges: "From
Mr. Gunnell, in the name of the dancers of the ropes for Lent
this 15 March, 1624. £1.0.0." Four days later the Office Book
records a further payment for Lenten entertainment. "From
Mr. Gunnel to allow of a Masque for the dancers of the ropes
this 19 March, 1624. £2.0.0.[36]

In 1629 Gunnell, in partnership with William Blagrave,
Deputy Master of the Revels, built the Salisbury Court theater in which he managed a company intended as a training

[34] Frederick S. Boas, ed., *The Diary of Thomas Crosfield*, London, 1935, pp.
72-73, quoted in Bentley, *The Jacobean and Caroline Stage*, II, 688-89.

[35] A Chancery suit of 1654, *Andrew de Caine v. William Wintersall and Wife
Margaret*, discovered by Leslie Hotson and transcribed in *The Commonwealth
and Restoration Stage*, Cambridge, Mass., 1928, p. 52.

[36] The first entry is from Adams' collection, *The Dramatic Records of Sir
Henry Herbert*, p. 48. The second Adams overlooked. It is taken from his
source, Boswell's edition of Malone's *Plays and Poems of William Shakespeare*,
London, 1821, III, 66.

school for boy actors for the King's men at Blackfriars.[37] This troupe was succeeded at Gunnell's Salisbury Court by Prince Charles's (II) company, the troupe that Richard Kendall lists. About three months after Kendall visited Thomas Crosfield, Richard Gunnell died.

The managers who succeeded Christopher Beeston at the Phoenix or Cockpit in Drury Lane are very explicitly named. Six or seven months after his father's death William Beeston was officially appointed. In the Lord Chamberlain's Warrant Books is the entry:

> A warrant to swear Mr. William Beeston His Majesty's servant in ordinary in the quality and under the title of Governor and Instructor of the King's and Queen's young company of actors. A certificate also for him.[38]

A couple of years later he and two other adult members of this company were jailed for acting a play without license, and the playwright William Davenant replaced him by the Lord Chamberlain's order. This was a very unusual procedure, for there is no indication that the company had anything to do with the appointment; Davenant was a dramatist and an aspiring courtier; there is no evidence that he was ever a player. The warrant of the Earl of Pembroke and Montgomery is also more elaborate than most such:

> Whereas in the playhouse or theatre commonly called the Cockpit in Drury Lane, there are a company of players or actors authorized by me (as Lord Chamberlain to His Majesty) to play or act under the title of the King's or Queen's Servants and that by reason of some disorders lately amongst them committed they are disabled in their service and quality. These are therefore to signify that by the same authority I do authorize and appoint William Davenant, gentle-

[37] G. E. Bentley, "The Salisbury Court Theatre and Its Boy Players," *Huntington Library Quarterly* 40 (1977), 129-49.

[38] Nicoll and Boswell, eds., "Dramatic Records: The Lord Chamberlain's Office," p. 389.

man, one of Her Majesty's servants, in me and my name
to take into his government and care the said company of
players to govern, order, and dispose of them for action and
presentments, and all their affairs in the said house as in
his discretion shall seem best to conduce to His Majesty's
service in that quality. And I do hereby enjoin and command them all and every of them that are so authorized to
play in the said house under the privilege of His or Her
Majesty's servants; and everyone belonging as prentices or
servants to those actors to play under the said privilege that
they obey the said Mr. Davenant and follow his orders and
directions as they will answer the contrary. Which power
or privilege he is to continue and enjoy during that lease
which Mrs. Elizabeth Beeston alias Hutchinson hath or
doth hold in the said playhouse. Provided he be still ac-
countable to me for his care and well ordering the said company. Given under my hand and seal this 27th of June 1640.

P. & M.[39]

This order seems to make Davenant more of a dictator than
a manager; such powers must have been good training for his
later Restoration career. But the duration of Davenant's gov-
ernorship was short. In the following year there is an establishment list of the Servants of the Chamber. Under the section "Revels" appears, "Governor of the Cockpit Players,
William Beeston."[40]

Managerial problems of another London troupe of about
the same time are aired in a previously noted lawsuit in the
Court of Requests brought by William Bankes against Andrew
Cane (Keyne, de Caine) and Ellis Worth in February 1634/
35. This suit and its implications have been discussed more
thoroughly elsewhere[41] but one or two of its points concerning managership may be helpful here. Worth and Cane were

[39] Ibid., p. 395.
[40] Ibid., p. 326.
[41] G. E. Bentley, "The Troubles of a Caroline Acting Troupe: Prince
Charles's Company," *Huntington Library Quarterly* 41 (1978), 217-49.

joint managers of Prince Charles's company at the Red Bull in St. John's Street, as Kendall had told Crosfield in July 1634. This suit concerns affairs of the company beginning two years before, when they were playing at the Salisbury Court before moving to the Red Bull. Banks, who had become a sharer in the company by paying £100.0.0 into the company treasury, calls Worth and Cane "Wardens" of the company, and at another point "Stewards" for the troupe. Worth and Cane deny that they were "Wardens," but they say nothing about "Stewards." In any case the suit makes it clear that they acted as managers and assessed sharers for moneys they had spent for costumes and furnishings, as Beeston had done for Queen Anne's men twenty years before. The suit shows that Banks was disciplined for irresponsible conduct, though it is not clear whether all the sharers or only Worth and Cane were responsible for his suspension.

Finally, something must be said about the managership of Richard Heton, a slightly known figure at the Salisbury Court theater in the last years of Caroline playing. Nothing certain is known of the earlier activities of this man who first appears officially when, like other managers, he collected fees for three court performances given by the Salisbury Court players in October 1635 and February 1635/36. The dates suggest that he may have succeeded Richard Gunnell who had been buried from the parish church of the Salisbury Court, St. Bride's Fleetstreet, on 7 October 1634.[42]

In the Court of Requests is a suit docketed *Heton v. Brome*, brought in February 1639/40 but dealing with events covering earlier years; it concerns Brome's contract as attached dramatist for Queen Henrietta's company at the Salisbury Court.[43]

[42] The manuscript registers of St. Bride's, Fleetstreet, now deposited in the Guildhall Library, London.
[43] The suit was discovered and transcribed by C. W. Wallace some seventy years ago, but never published by him except for a few hints and a sentence or so. It was printed from the Wallace Papers, now in the Huntington Library, by Ann Haaker, "The Plague, the Theater, and the Poet," *Renaissance Drama*, n.s. 1 (1968), 283-306.

Actually the suit is not so much concerned with the familiar activities of a company manager; its primary importance is its revelation of the obligations of an attached dramatist to the company for which he has contracted to write exclusively, as Brome had done.[44] Though the suit in the Court of Requests was brought in the name of the sharers in the company, Richard Heton's name heads the list, and the papers of the suit are docketed *Heton v. Brome*, an indication that Heton was manager of the company at the time the suit was brought.

Much more revealing of Heton and his activities as manager of Queen Henrietta's company in its last years at the Salisbury Court are certain curious documents discovered by Peter Cunningham and published by him more than a century ago without discussion or any hint as to their source.[45] The first of the Heton documents Cunningham found he headed "The following 'Instructions' are endorsed 'Mr. Heton's Papers.' " They reveal the astonishing powers Richard Heton was hoping to exercise over the company some time after an event of March 1639 which Heton alludes to in his justification of his proposals. The document reads in part:

> That the patent for electing Her Majesty's company of comedians be granted only to myself [in contrast to all known company patents for adult companies of the reigns of James and early in the reign of Charles, which were granted to the sharers of the company] that I may always have a company in readiness at Salisbury Court for Her Majesty's service, and that if all or any of the company go away from Salisbury Court to play at any other playhouse already built or hereafter to be built, they from thenceforth to cease to be Her Majesty's servants, and only the company remain-

---

[44] For a full discussion of this relationship, see G. E. Bentley, *The Profession of Dramatist in Shakespeare's Time*, Princeton, 1971, especially Chapter IV, "The Dramatist and the Acting Company" and Chapter VI, "The Dramatists' Contractual Obligations."

[45] *Shakespeare Society Papers* 4 (1849) 95-100. His documents are reprinted in full in Bentley, *The Jacobean and Caroline Stage*, II, 684-87.

ing there to have that honor and title. Myself to be sole governor of the company. The company to enter into articles with me to continue there for seven years upon the same conditions they have had for a year and half last past, and such as refuse, to be removed and others placed in their rooms; for if they should continue at liberty as they now are and have power to take Her Majesty's service along with them, they would make use of our house but until they could provide another upon better terms and then leave us as in one year and half of their being here they have many times threatened when they might not exact any new impositions upon the housekeepers at their pleasure. . . .

The second document is endorsed, "Heton's draft of his patent." This draft patent generally conforms to the standard formal patents which are extant for previous companies except for the lines that read:

. . . Now know ye that we [that is, the King, in whose name all patents were issued] of our especial grace, certain knowledge and mere motion, have licensed and authorize and by these our letters patent do license and authorize our said servant Richard Heton or his assigns from time to time and at all times hereafter to select, order, direct, set up, and govern a company of comedians in the said private house in Dorset House yard for the service of our dear consort the Queen and there to exercise their quality of playing. . . .

The third section of the Heton Papers as published by Peter Cunningham seems to be more or less a series of jottings or reminders, part of which only reinforce or elaborate those claims for dictatorial powers in the first two documents. The first is headed "My Intention for the rest."

That such of the company as will not be ordered and governed by me as of their governor, or shall not by the Master of His Majesty's Revels and myself be thought fit comedians for Her Majesty's service, I may have power to discharge from the company, and with the advice of the Master of the Revels to put new ones in their places. . . .

There is no clear evidence that Heton achieved these powers but it is difficult to imagine a man like Heminges even aspiring to them in his dealings with the King's men.

Finally there is a series of notes which Cunningham introduces as "The short memorandum subjoined was found with the preceding documents" endorsed, "Instructions Touching Salisbury Court Playhouse, 14 September, 1639." These memoranda concern not Heton's powers and privileges as manager of Queen Henrietta's company, but a new set of arrangements, payments, and privileges between the company and the housekeepers of the theater. Though interesting they are not strictly relevant here. Two of them are, however, partly verifiable from other sources and thus tend to lend credence to Cunningham's mysterious documents.

In comparing the advantages to the players in the new contract of the company with the housekeepers as compared with the last, Heton says that in the new they get everything they had before plus "Half the Poets wages which is 10 shillings a week." We know from the summary of Richard Brome's contract as attached poet for the theater that he received twenty shillings a week.[46] Another verifiable sum is the one Heton cited in his next item of advantage to the players, "Half the licensing of every new play which half is also 20 shillings." Sir Henry Herbert's Office Book shows that for the last several years he had indeed been charging the companies £2.0.0 for the licensing of each new play.

These powers that Richard Heton was trying to establish are much more like those which had been granted to William Davenant when he took over from William Beeston than they are like those we have seen John Heminges exercising for the King's company. Indeed, they suggest the authority of Restoration managers more than that of the Elizabethan, Jaco-

---

[46] See the *Heton v. Brome* suit in Haaker, "The Plague, the Theater, and the Poet."

bean, and early Caroline company leaders and agents. There is no evidence I have seen which indicates that this shift of power from the sharers to the manager was taking place at the Globe and Blackfriars as it was at the Phoenix and Salisbury Court. Indeed, the system evolved in the reign of Elizabeth and formalized by Shakespeare, Burbage, Heminges, Condell and the others seems to have changed very little, though the company grew in size, wealth, and prestige, during the half century of its existence.

The foregoing potpourri of examples makes it clear enough, I think, that normally each troupe of players during the period selected someone, most often a senior sharer, to handle the company's official and financial affairs. Obviously the powers of these managers varied widely from company to company, and for several troupes they increased as the Civil Wars approached. The evidence shows that the differences between the Caroline dramatic organizations and the Restoration ones was rather less than has been commonly supposed.

CHAPTER VII

London Companies on Tour

THE HISTORY of English players on tour is much too extensive and too complex to be fully discussed in its entirety in any single chapter or even any single volume. During the period 1590-1642 there were scores of companies on the road at different times, not only in the British Isles, but on the Continent as well.[1]

The majority of these touring troupes were not London companies, but peripatetic provincial organizations. Therefore most of the town and great house records concern troupes of players that seldom or never played in the London theaters. Nevertheless, so far as one can tell, the conditions they met on their tours were essentially the same as those encountered by the Lord Admiral's men. This chapter is intended primar-

[1] See J. T. Murray, *English Dramatic Companies 1558-1642*, 2 vols., London, 1910, II; and A. Cohn, *Shakespeare in Germany in the Sixteenth and Seventeenth*

ily to show what conditions were common, not the particular tours of the London troupes. Fuller, but still incomplete and inadequate notes on the tours of particular major companies, are to be found in the second volume of *The Elizabethan Stage* and the first volume of *The Jacobean and Caroline Stage*.[2]

In spite of the fact that so many of the records do concern provincial organizations, the metropolitan players did go on the road often enough. In earlier years this touring had been taken for granted. In a signed letter of the Earl of Leicester's players to their patron in 1572 asking for a license, the custom is stated clearly. The license is to be used, ". . . to certify that we are your household servants when we shall have occasion to travel amongst our friends as we do usually once a year, and as other noblemen's players do and have done in times past. . . ."[3]

The London companies also toured in plague times, or during London inhibitions, or when some other situation made business in town particularly bad. Such was the situation of

---

Centuries, London, 1865. In the many years since these two books were published numerous articles and monographs have recorded visits of English players unknown to these major scholars, and more records are appearing yearly as the archives of more and more British and Continental towns are thoroughly searched for dramatic records.

Murray's book is the most compendious on the subject, but it is none too satisfactory. A large part of the records he notes are taken from nineteenth-century town histories and not from the original documents, and he missed a number of records. For instance, Giles Dawson ("Records of Plays and Players in Kent," *Malone Society Collections* 7 [1965]) worked on the manuscript records of thirteen towns in Kent alone and found notations of 2,000 payments to visiting entertainers between 1450 and 1642, many not to be found in Murray in any form. It is certain that the examination (which is constantly going on) of original town documents and great house muniment rooms in other counties in England will unearth many more payments to touring entertainers.

[2] E. K. Chambers, *The Elizabethan Stage*, 4 vols., Oxford, 1923; G. E. Bentley, *The Jacobean and Caroline Stage*, 7 vols., Oxford, 1941-1968.

[3] *Malone Society Collections* 1 (1911), 348-49. From the manuscripts of the Marquis of Bath at Longleat.

the travelling players in *Hamlet*. Hence some discussion of touring is essential for an understanding of the professional life of a London player in Shakespeare's time.

For the major London companies, touring was nearly always an unpleasant and comparatively unprofitable expedient to compensate for London misfortunes, and as the metropolitan companies became more prosperous they resorted to the road less frequently than they had in the reign of Elizabeth and in the early years of James. But though these troupes made fewer road trips in the later years, they knew that touring could never be entirely abandoned. This fact is illustrated by Richard Heton's draft patent as late as 1638 or 1639. His proposals show not only that he knew Queen Henrietta's company might have to travel, but he also noted some of the customary settings for provincial performances.

There is no evidence that Heton's proposed patent was ever issued officially but his proposals are illuminating:

. . . And the said comedies, tragedies, histories, pastorals, masques, interludes, morals, stage plays, and such like to show act and exercise to their best profit and commodity as well within their aforesaid playhouse in Dorset House yard, as in any city, university, town, or borough of our said realms and dominions, there to sojourn and abide, if at any time they with their company and associates (whom our said servant Richard Heton shall think fit to select) shall have occasion (by reason of sickness in London or otherwise) to travel, to exercise publicly to their best profit, commodity, and advantage their aforesaid comedies tragedies &c. at all time or times (the time of divine service only excepted) before or after supper within any town halls, guildhalls, moothalls, schoolhouses, or any other convenient places whatsoever. And the same comedies, tragedies, &c. with the times they are to be acted, to proclaim in such places as aforesaid with drums, trumpets, and by public bills, if they think fit, notwithstanding any statute, act, proclamation, provision, restraint or matter whatsoever to the contrary.[4]

Richard Heton was an arrogant man, and he was proposing for himself and his company more rights and privileges than any is known to have secured. Note particularly the "notwithstanding" clause at the close. Many towns specifically forbade several of the privileges he is proposing. Nevertheless, his proposals show what other troupes would have found desirable, and most of which they did, now and then, succeed in getting. But the norm, as we shall see, fell far short of Heton's demands.

The provincial records of the visits of London companies are usually inadequate, seldom naming any plays or more than one of the players present; frequently the name of the visiting company is omitted. Even the fuller records can be misleading, for the account of a visit by the Lady Elizabeth's company, for instance, may refer to a secondary provincial troupe using an exemplification of the London license, or even be a wholly fraudulent document. The provincial records were set down as accounts of moneys paid out; the clerks show on interest in theatrical history.

Shakespeare expresses the usual attitude toward metropolitan companies on tour when he makes Hamlet ask Rosencrantz about the troupe newly arrived at Elsinore:

What players are they?
Ros. Even those you were wont to take such delight in, the tragedians of the city.
Ham. How chances it they travel? Their residence, both in reputation and profit, was better both ways.

About the same time Ben Jonson was also articulating the standard observation about touring players. In scene four of

---

[4] The document was found by Peter Cunningham and published in the *Shakespeare Society Papers* 4 (1849), 95-100, without any indication as to where he found it. There is a convenient complete transcription in Bentley, *The Jacobean and Caroline Stage*, ii, 685-86.

the third act of *Poetaster*, the player, Histrio, is being told how fine a playwright Crispinus is. Tucca says:

> If he pen for thee once, thou shalt not need to travel, with thy pumps full of gravel any more, after a blind jade and a hamper; and stalk upon boards and barrel heads, to an old cracked trumpet. [167-70]

The same attitude toward metropolitan companies on the road is voiced thirty years later by Donald Lupton in his *London and the Country Carbonadoed and Quartered into Several Characters*, 1632. In his Character twenty "Play-houses" he writes:

> Sometimes they [the players] fly into the country; but 'tis a suspicion that they are either poor or want clothes, or else company, or a new play; or do as some wandering sermonists, make one sermon travel and serve twenty churches. [G1ᵛ]

These sneers at touring companies are justifiable for the most part, and especially as applied to the scores of provincial companies. Yet only Heton has mentioned the most frequent cause that drove major London troupes to take to the road, namely the plague. This virulent and usually fatal disease was really endemic in London until the Great Fire destroyed most of the rats in 1666. But there were several years in Shakespeare's era when the death rate was appallingly high: 1593, 1603, 1610, 1625, 1636-37. In these years many of the richer Londoners fled the city, all the theaters were closed, bearbaiting was suppressed, and fairs were cancelled.

The Lord Mayor and Council of London always knew that crowds spread the disease, and in the earlier days there were constant petitions to the Privy Council to close the playhouses. But some time in the nineties there seems to have been an agreement that when the parish clerks reported a total of thirty or more plague deaths per week in the combined parishes of London, then the theaters would be closed. This number is recorded in the draft license for Queen Anne's company of about 1604.

. . . And the said Comedies, Tragedies, Histories, Inter-ludes, Morals, Pastorals, Stage plays and such like to show and exercise publicly when the infection of the plague shall decrease to the number of thirty weekly within our city of London and the liberties thereof. . . .[5]

This regulation explains the point in the passage in Middle-ton's *Your Five Gallants*, probably acted in 1607 and published in 1608,

'tis e'en as uncertain as playing, now up now down, for if the Bill rise to above thirty, here's no place for players. . . .[6]

But not long after, the danger limit was raised to forty. A character in Lodowick Barry's *Ram Alley* acted about 1608 and published in 1611, says, "I dwindle . . . as a new player at a plague bill certified forty. . . ." And this number is verified in the patent for the King's company issued in 1619.

It is easy to see how great was the terror of the citizens which led to such restrictions when it is noted that in the single week ending 4 August 1625, for instance, 3,659 Lon-doners died of the plague. Hundreds of infected houses were marked with the sign "Lord have mercy upon us." And many bodies were dumped unceremoniously and uncoffined into open pits.[7] No Londoner in Elizabethan, Jacobean, or Caroline au-diences would have had any trouble understanding the pre-dicament of Friar John recounted in the second scene of the last act of *Romeo and Juliet*:

> Going to find a barefoot brother out,
> One of our order, to associate me
> Here in this city visiting the sick,
> And finding him, the searchers of the town,
> Suspecting that we both were in a house

---

[5] *Malone Society Collections* 1, pt. 3 (1910), 266.
[6] 1608 quarto F2ᵛ.
[7] See F. P. Wilson, *The Plague in Shakespeare's London*, Oxford, 1927, *passim*.

Where the infectious pestilence did reign,
Seal'd up the doors, and would not let us forth,
So that my speed to Mantua was stay'd.

Such catastrophes drove all metropolitan companies out of London and into the provinces to avoid starvation. Every London player expected to go on the road sooner or later, and of course the provincial companies were nearly always travelling. The reception they met varied with the town and the prejudices of the authorities in charge at the moment.

Hundreds of entries in the records of towns all over England attest the varying receptions of the touring troupes. Often they were not allowed to perform at all, though they were generally given a gratuity in deference to their master. In the accounts of the Chamberlain at Leicester in 1594-95 is the entry: "Item. Given to the Lord Morley's players who were not suffered to play . . . 5s."[8] In the Southampton records is the item dated 18 October [1592]: ". . . to the Earl of Worcester's players for that they should not play . . . £1.0.0" (398).

The discomforts of touring as noted by Jonson in *Poetaster* are less serious than the hazards mentioned by the players of Lord Strange in a petition to the Privy Council of uncertain date (1591-1594):

. . . For as much (right honorable) our company is great and thereby our charges intolerable in travelling the country, and the continuance thereof will be a mean to bring us to division and separation whereby we shall not only be undone but also unready to serve her majesty when it shall please her highness to command us. . . .[9]

These complaints in the petition are obviously from the sharers of the company, but the hired men had equally good rea-

[8] Murray, *English Dramatic Companies*, II, 306. Hereafter when only page numbers are given for provincial records, a reference to this volume is to be understood.

[9] R. A. Foakes and R. T. Rickert, *Henslowe's Diary*, Cambridge, 1961, pp. 283-84.

sons to dread touring. Henslowe's contract with the hired man, William Kendall, in 1597 specified that ". . . He to give him for his said service every week of his playing in London 10 shillings and in the country 5s. . . ."[10] Even worse was the touring situation of Robert Houghton, who testified in his examination in 1633 at Banbury that he

> Came to this company the Thursday before Easter last and played his part in stage plays at Sir William Spencer's [and] at Keinton two or three days this week. Received nothing but meat and drink from them.[11]

NUMBER OF PLAYERS IN COMPANIES ON TOUR

It is reasonable to expect that companies on tour would consist of fewer players than they had when settled in London, and various documents indicate that this was the case. When the Master of the Revels on 9 April 1624 licensed the touring company led by William Perry, he specified a group "not exceeding the number of twenty." The Master of the Revels made a similar stipulation when he licensed on 28 November 1634 a touring group led by William Daniel. The license was copied by the clerk when the company visited Norwich 3 September 1635.

> A Patent under the hand and seal of Sir Henry Herbert Master of the Revels bearing date the 28th of November 1634 made to . . . and the rest of their company not exceeding the number of fifteen persons.[12]

Among the thousands of records of provincial visits one would hope to have found quite a few that noted how many men and boys made up the roster of the visitors. But, as noted before, the town records are financial accounts and the clerks were interested in the amount of money put out; numbers or names are set down, as a rule, only when the visit led to a

---

[10] Ibid., pp. 268-69.
[11] *Calendar of State Papers, Domestic,* London, 1633-34, p. 49.
[12] Murray, *English Dramatic Companies,* II, 273 and 357.

disturbance or a crime. Most of the records of numbers come from great house account books, possibly because the numbers suggested the cost of bedding and feeding.

The earliest of the accounts to give numbers is fictional, but set down by a man with extensive theatrical experience. In his *News from Hell*, 1606, Thomas Dekker wrote a list of expenses for Charon in his ferrying business:

> Item. Lent to a company of country players, being nine in number, one sharer and the rest journeymen that with strolling were brought to death's door 13d. upon their stock of apparel, to pay for their boat hire because they would try if they could be suffered to play in the Devil's name.
> . . .   [H-H^v]

A similar, though indefinite number is implied for a touring group of Queen Anne's men. In a lawsuit of 1607 there is quoted an agreement between Thomas Greene, manager of Queen Anne's company at the Red Bull, and Martin Slater, leader of a touring group. It is agreed that Slater

> shall forbear and refrain from setting up any bills for playing as in the name of Her Majesty's servants unless he the said Martin has gotten into his company to play five others of Her Majesty's players. . . .[13]

Of course the five would be sharers in the company; with Slater they would make six, but hired men and boys would be required as well and Slater's touring Queen Anne's troupe would presumably consist of ten to twelve.

Lord Derby's men who visited Chatsworth in 1611 consisted of "xiiij Players" and were paid £3 on the 5th of June for playing two plays, one after dinner and one after supper.[14] The next year when Derby's men visited the Earl of Cum-

---

[13] Transcript of an entry on Roll 1789 of the Court of Common Pleas, transcribed in the Wallace Papers in the Huntington Library, San Marino, California.

[14] Lawrence Stone, "Companies of Players Entertained by the Earl of Cumberland and Lord Clifford, 1607-39," *Malone Society Collections* 5 (1960), 21.

berland's establishment at Londesborough they carried thirteen players and played four plays. They were paid £4 on 26 March 1612. Later in the same year the Lady Elizabeth's company with sixteen players also came to Londesborough and on the nineteenth of July were paid forty shillings for performing one play "after supper." In 1619 the same castle was visited by fifteen players "who belonged to the late Queen," i.e., Queen Anne who had died four months before. On the 14th of July they were paid thirteen shillings, four pence though they did not play.

One of the more explicit records in these accounts from the books of the Earl of Cumberland and Lord Clifford is the one accompanying the payment of £5 on 11 February 1619/20.

> Item. Given this day in reward to a company of players in number fourteen by his Lordship's appointment, the same being the King's players, the sum of five pounds, which players stayed here at Londesborough from Tuesday till Friday and played 5 plays. So paid them which was my Lord's reward . . . £5[15]

A larger number of players was carried by the Lady Elizabeth's company when they visited Plymouth in 1618/19, no day or month given.

> Item. Given to the Lady Elizabeth's players being 20 persons which had the King's hand for playing as well by night as by day . . . £3.6.

In 1636, when the long plague of 1636-37 was only in its second month, the number of players in the provincial company of John Costine is given at Manchester in 3 July.

> To John Costine, a player with 10 in his company to avoid the town & not to play these dangerous times . . . 00.06.08[16]

There are about a half a dozen other records of provincial visits in which the clerk sets down the number of players in

[15] Ibid., pp. 21, 23, 24.
[16] Murray, *English Dramatic Companies*, II, 385 and 331.

the touring company, all of them within the limits of the numbers cited here, though some are records of London companies and others of companies not known to have had London seasons. All these numbers indicate a reduction in the size of the London troupes when they took to the road. For comparison we can note that the only full rosters for a London company are those from the combined patent list and hired men list of the King's company in 1624 and 1625; these two lists total thirty-five names without the boys.[17] Accordingly the average touring troupe would appear to have been less than half the size of the London King's company at the time of the death of King James.

Several caveats about these figures should be noted. 1) The date of the King's lists is later than most of the provincial notices; 2) the King's company was more prosperous than any other and therefore probably larger; 3) the provincial notices that record the number of players is far less than 1 percent of the total provincial notices reported. There is a further caveat to be noted in two other provincial notices that are abnormal. The first is the list of twenty-eight names of players set down in the Mayor's Court Books at Norwich on 10 March 1634/35. No company is named and the actors were denied permission to play. I think this is a list of players of two different companies that were in Norwich at the same time.[18] The other abnormal list is one reported by Sir Edmund Chambers[19] from an article in the *Warwickshire Antiquarian Magazine*. The entry notes the misdemeanor of "One of the Company of the Lady Elizabethe's players" who came to town on 27 March 1615. Though the entry says it lists the names in the patent of 31 May 1613, it records fourteen names but states that John Townsend and Joseph Moore were "Sworn officers none other named in the patent." The list, therefore, must record those present at Coventry in 1615. This entry has a further distinction in that the twelve names following Townsend and Moore

---

[17] See Bentley, *The Jacobean and Caroline Stage*, 1, 15-18 and 80-81.
[18] Ibid., 1, 283-89.
[19] "Coventry Papers from Corporation MSS.," *Warwickshire Antiquarian Magazine*, pt. 7 (1873), 406, in *Review of English Studies* 1 (1925), 182-84.

are bracketed and labeled "Boyes" and that the entry closes with the statement "5 Horses in their Company." Though the total number of players is similar to the number given in other provincial records, the number of named boys is unique. I am also baffled by the notation of five horses, a notation that suggests more affluence than one associates with companies on tour.

Such evidence as we have, then, suggests that the complement of a London company on the road was not more than half their metropolitan roster. How many of these men were players and how many musicians and other stage functionaries, the evidence does not show. I would guess that most of them were players, some of them performing chores they would disdain in London.

REPERTORIES OF TOURING COMPANIES

When the London companies found it necessary to take to the road they presumably reduced their repertories as well as their personnel. It would have been foolhardy to cart all their manuscripts about the country, and many plays that had been produced on the stage of the Globe or Rose or Fortune would have been more difficult to mount in the temporary playing places in provincial towns. Though the records from Chatsworth and Londesborough quoted above show touring companies performing two, four, and five plays, only one account I know of states just how many plays a London troupe was carrying. When the Salisbury Court players visited Oxford in July 1634, one of the company told Thomas Crosfield, a Fellow of Queen's, that "They came furnished with 14 plays."[20] What part of the repertory of this troupe fourteen plays was cannot be ascertained, but it was less than one-fifth of those owned by Queen Henrietta's men at this time and about one-twelfth those owned by the King's men.[21]

[20] F. S. Boas, *The Diary of Thomas Crosfield*, London, 1935, p. 73.
[21] Bentley, *The Jacobean and Caroline Stage*, I, 250-59 and 108-134.

PROCEDURES ON TOWN VISITS

When a touring company reached a selected town they first went to the local authorities to get permission to play. Scores of the provincial notices gathered by Professor Murray indicate this procedure by beginning "This day. . . ." Thus at Norwich on 7 June 1617 the clerk made the entry "This day Henry Sebeck showed forth to this court a patent . . ." or a year later "This day John Townsend brought a license. . . ."[22]

The custom was a good deal older than these two notices, as is shown in an account published by R. Willis, who says he was seventy-five years old when his book was printed in 1639.

> Upon a Stage-play which I saw
> when I was a child
>
> In the city of *Gloucester* the manner is (as I think it is in other like corporations) that when players of interludes come to town, they first attend the Mayor to inform him what nobleman's servants they are, and so to get license for their public playing. . . .[23]

This permission to play in the town was sometimes granted, though when denied the players were often given a "reward" presumably out of respect for their patron. Sometimes the reasons for denial were given and sometimes not. The statement in the Mayors' Court Books at Norwich on 28 June 1622 gives no reason:

> The company of players of the late Queen Anne came this day and desired to have leave to play according to a patent under the King's privy signet dated ultimo Octobris Anno xv°. And they are forbidden so to do. And there is allowed to them as a gratuity xl[s].

[22] Murray, *English Dramatic Companies*, II, 344.
[23] *Mount Tabor or Private Exercises of a Penitent Sinner . . . Also Certain Occasional Observations*, London, 1639, p. 110.

Sometimes permission was refused without reason and in words that suggest hostility. Such is an entry in the Receivers' Account Book at Plymouth in 1616 or 1617: "Item given to two companies of players which were not suffered to play, to rid them out of town xxxˢ."[24] The hostility occasionally produced even more severe restrictions. On 20 September 1594 the Chamberlain's accounts at King's Lynn note:

> Also at this day it is agreed, by Master Mayor, Master Newelect, and the common council that there shall not hereafter be any plays suffered to be played in this hall called Trinity hall nor the hall called St. George's hall.

Twenty years later on 14 October 1616 the Mayor and Aldermen of King's Lynn went much further in their hostility to players:

> At this day it was agreed that a letter shall be written by Master Mayor and the Aldermen to the Lord Chancellor of England, and the town's High Steward to entreat that he will be a means that all the companies of players which yearly resort to this town may not be suffered here to use playing, notwithstanding their grants and patents made unto them.[25]

But though hostility was sometimes involved in the refusal of permission to play, there were often sound reasons for denying permission; probably the most common was fear of plague infection. At Worcester in 1631 the King's company was dismissed for this reason. "Given to the King's players by Mr. Mayor's direction to prevent their playing in this city for fear of infection . . . 13s. 4d."[26] In the Chamberlain's Accounts at Gloucester the plague is specifically mentioned (as in many other entries in other towns). The entry is not precisely dated but falls in the year between 29 September 1636

[24] Murray, *English Dramatic Companies*, II, 346 and 384.
[25] David Galloway and John Wason, "Records of Plays and Players in Norfolk and Suffolk, 1330-1642," *Malone Society Collections* 11 (1981), 70.
[26] Murray, *English Dramatic Companies*, II, 410.

and 29 September 1637: "Item paid unto William Daniel one of the King's Revels because he should not play being in the contagious time by order of the Justices . . . £1.6.8"[27] Earlier during the terrible plague of 1603 the Chamberlain's accounts of King's Lynn carry under date of 22 July the entry:

> xx[s] allowed to Mr. Mayor for ii companies of players. Paid out of the hall here to Mr. Mayor that he bestowed of the Earl of Huntington and the Lord Evers their players to keep them from playing here this dangerous time.[28]

Other infectious diseases are occasionally mentioned as the reason for the prohibition. In the Gravesend Corporation Minutes for the year 1635-36 is the entry:

> November 25. Paid to the players, for not playing in the town by the appointment of Mr. Mayor and the Court by reason of the Small Pox . . . 00.05.00[29]

Now and then a very unusual reason for denying playing permission is recorded: at Canterbury in the year 1602-03 there is the entry in the Chamberlain's accounts:

> Item paid to Thomas Downton, one of the Lord Admiral's players for a gift bestowed upon him and his company being so appointed by Mr. Mayor and the Aldermen because it was thought fit they should not play at all in regard that our late Queen was then either sick or dead as they supposed.   xxx[s][30]

Such reasons for refusing a company permission to play are understandable enough in any time, but in a number of towns there was administrative distrust of theatrical performances for more particular Elizabethan and Jacobean reasons. The Mayor and his officers were responsible for maintaining their

[27] Ibid., II, 285.
[28] Galloway and Wason, "Records of Plays and Players in Norfolk and Suffolk," p. 69.
[29] Dawson, "Records of Plays and Players in Kent," p. 81.
[30] Ibid., p. 18.

own dignity and keeping the peace in their town. A few of the local records state this problem clearly enough, as in the Chester records under date of 20 October 1615:

> Moreover at the same Assembly consideration was had of the common bruit & scandal which this city hath of late incurred & sustained by admitting of stage players to act their obscene and unlawful plays or tragedies in the common hall of this city thereby converting the same being appointed & ordained for the judicial hearing & determining of criminal offences, and for the solemn meetings & concourse of this house into a stage for players & a receptacle for idle persons; & considering likewise the many disorders which by reason of plays acted in the night do often times happen & fall out to the discredit of the government of this city & to the great disturbance of quiet & well-disposed people & being further informed that men's servants & apprentices neglecting their master's business do resort to inn houses to behold such plays & there many times wastefully spend their master's goods. For avoiding of all which inconveniences it is ordered that from henceforth no stage players upon any pretence or color whatsoever shall be admitted or licensed to set up any stage in the said common hall or to act any tragedy or comedy or any other play, by what name soever they shall term it, in the said hall or any other place within this city or the liberties thereof in the night time or after vi of the clock in the evening.[31]

The Chester fathers were severe in their condemnations, but less explicit records from other towns show a similar uneasiness. In the Burgmote Books at Canterbury is the statement under date of 12 August 1634:

> Also at this Court it is ordered that Master Mayor shall be allowed & paid to him by Master Chamberlain 20 shillings which he gave to certain players which came to this city to

---

[31] Murray, *English Dramatic Companies*, II, 235.

play having commission in that behalf, to the end to avoid disorders and night walking which might come thereby.[32]

It is not difficult to understand the worries of the Court in a provincial town with no street lights of any kind and only a set of often ignorant citizens for amateur policing.

An example of what the town authorities at Canterbury were fearing is to be found in the records of a hearing at Ludlow in November 1627.

1627. Nov. 22. The information of Richard Errington, of the city of London, pewterer, aged fifty years or thereabout, deposeth and sayeth that upon yesterday, about ten or eleven of the clock at night, this deponent, being one of the company of His Majesty's players who then were acting in the said house, & this deponent taking money at the door, he saw certain persons in number five or six, whom this deponent doubting to have been drinking, thinking that they would have offered to this deponent wrong, this deponent took his money out the box and put it in his hand. Then the said persons began to brabble among themselves & thereupon one other of the players came unto the door & demanded what the cause of the noise was. Thereupon one of the persons whom this deponent hearing his name since to be Powell, drew a rapier & ran at this deponent, and this deponent putting off the thrust, closed in with him & took hold of his arm. Whereupon one of the sergeants, William Baker, being called to search of the said house to keep the peace, the foresaid persons fell upon the said Baker & most beastly abused him. And this deponent caused one of his servants, who had a link lighted in his hands, to go forth of the door to give light unto the sergeant & to know who abused him. But one of the said company, whose name as this deponent is since informed is Henry Wilding, forced

32 Ibid., II, 234.

the said servant back again, & gave him sound blows, asking him, "Keep indoors; what is this to thee?"[33]

This testimony is corroborated by the man who brought out the link, John Hill. Such affrays were associated, not without reason, with the visits of players and one can understand how the simplest solution might seem to be to keep the players out of town.

PROVINCIAL PLAYING PLACES

The town hall was doubtless one of the most convenient playing places for the players when they were on the road, but there was often opposition to such use of an official and more or less ceremonial hall. Galloway and Wasson found a record of 17 June 1614 of legal action to be taken at Ipswich if the players got to perform in the moot hall:

> It is agreed at this assembly that it shall not be lawful from henceforth for the Bailiff of this town for the time being or any of them to give any allowance to any players that shall resort to this town to play nor give leave to any such players to play in the moot hall at any time. And if the Bailiffs of this town or any of them should do contrary to this agreement that then the said bailiffs or such of them that shall hereafter give any such allowance or leave to play in the moot hall shall forfeit for every such offence every of them xx[s][34]

But of course towns differed and administrations differed. While some administrations were clearly hostile others were not simply permissive but cordial. Naturally the hope of the touring company was that first they would be allowed to pre-

---

[33] Ibid., II, 326. A very full record of a more bloody affray was recorded in Norwich in 1583. It occurred when Queen Elizabeth's company was playing in the yard of the Red Lion in St. Stephen's in June of that year. See David Galloway's transcription in *The Elizabethan Theatre* 7 (1980), 103-110.

[34] "Records of Plays and Players in Norfolk and Suffolk," p. 184.

sent a play for the Mayor. R. Willis, whose account of his childhood attendance at a play in Gloucester is quoted above, testifies to this custom, probably early in Elizabeth's reign:

> . . . and if the Mayor likes the actors or would show respect to their lord and master, he appoints them to play their first play before himself and the Aldermen and Common Council of the city; and that is called the Mayor's play, where everyone that will comes in without money, the Mayor giving the players a reward he thinks fit to show respect unto them. At such a play my father took me with him and made me stand between his legs as he sat upon one of the benches where we saw and heard very well. . . .

A record of the reward given for the Mayor's play was found by Giles Dawson in the Chamberlain's records of Canterbury for the year 1599-1600: "To the Lord Admiral's players in reward for a play which they played before Mr. Mayor and many of his friends in the Court hall and so ordered by Mr. Mayor and the Aldermen under their hands . . . 40s"[35]

Sometimes the courtesies shown the players went beyond the Mayor's play and a cash reward. At Ludlow there are two entries in the accounts of July 1590:

> Item, to the Queen's Majesty's players 10s. Item, unto them a quart of white wine and sugar at their departing 12d.[36]

At Canterbury in the year 1608-1609 the company of Queen Anne was shown a similar courtesy:

> Item given to Queen's Majesty's players by Mr. Mayor and the Aldermen's consent 20s. Mr. Mayor and the company with him being at the play by them made at the Checker and also spent then in beer and biscuits 8d 20s 8d.[37]

[35] Dawson, "Records of Plays and Players in Kent," p. 18.
[36] Murray, *English Dramatic Companies*, II, 325.
[37] Dawson, "Records of Plays and Players in Kent," p. 19.

Thus when the touring players were fortunate they performed their first play in a town before the Mayor and preferably in the town hall, though sometimes elsewhere, as at Canterbury where Queen Anne's men acted before the mayor and aldermen at the Checkers Inn. The players, of course, hoped to be granted permission to present regular commercial performances elsewhere in the town after they had entertained the mayor and his guests. Often they did, but only a few of the town accounts tell where. The Checker Inn at Canterbury, to which the mayor took his guests, was presumably also used for commercial performances. Two other accounts show inns, the obvious places, being used by the players as theaters for popular audiences. At Norwich on 7 June 1583 the Mayor's Court Books record that after ten of the Earl of Worcester's company had been refused permission to play but given a reward of 26s 8d "for their Lord and master his sake" the players nevertheless "did play in their host his house."

Several years later, also at Norwich, the clerk noted on 17 June 1601, that:

> Whereas my Lord of Hertford's players were suitors to have leave to play at the sign of the White Horse in Tomeland, but for this day it is ordered that no players or plays be made or used in the said house either now or hereafter.[38]

This same inn was used in 1624 by the Lady Elizabeth's players in defiance of a prohibition. The report of their action was entered in the Mayor's Court Books at Norwich on 26 April 1624:

> This day Wakefield, having brought to Master Mayor a note which he found fastened upon the gate of the house of Thomas Marcon, being the sign of the White Horse near Tomeland in Norwich wherein was written these words, 'Here within this place at one of the clock shall be acted an

---

[38] Murray, *English Dramatic Companies*, II, 336 and 338. Earlier Queen Elizabeth's company had performed at the Red Lion Inn. See n. 33 above.

excellent new comedy called *The Spanish Contract* by the Princess' Servants. Vivat Rex.'[39]

The players got into a good deal of trouble for their defiance of the mayor's order, and the leaders of the troupe named in their papers, John Townsend, Alexander Foster, Joseph Moore, and Francis Wambus were called to task and Wambus was committed. Such troubles were not too uncommon. The unique feature of this record is the copy of the playbill. It is the only copy known from the time, though records of the existence of playbills are common enough.

The most explicit information about the use of an inn by a company of touring players comes from the frequently mentioned diary of Thomas Crosfield. In his notes, which he took on his conversations with a member of the Salisbury Court company of players in July 1634, are set down a number of facts about this touring company and the circumstances of their playing in Oxford. The last few lines of Crosfield's report of his conversation read:

> They came furnished with 14 plays. And lodged at the King's Arms where Franklin hath about 3 pounds a day while they stay. i.e., for every play 4 nobles besides the benefit of seats.

Franklin was the owner of the King's Arms, and other entries in the diary show that he customarily had plays at the King's Arms, at least at the time of the Act at the University.[40] How typical the financial arrangement was one cannot say, since it is the only one known. But the arrangement had something in common with the rent agreements at various London theaters, and one might guess that something of the sort prevailed in other provincial inns used by London companies on tour. One might also guess that the landlord placed his "seats" in the galleries around his inn yard, at least that would accord with some of the rent agreements in London.

[39] Murray, *English Dramatic Companies*, II, 348.
[40] Boas, *Diary of Thomas Crosfield*, pp. 73 and xxv-xxvi.

It is not surprising to find inns used as playing places in the provinces since many of the London inns had been so used. Before 1590 London companies had performed in town at the Bell Inn, the Bel Savage, the Bull, the Cross Keys, and at the Red Lion. After 1590 there were still performances at the Cross Keys, the Bull, and the Boar's Head. With so much London experience of the suitability of inns as playhouses the touring companies would naturally seek inns as playing places for their performances when they were on the road.

But inns and the town hall were not the only provincial theaters. It is much more surprising to find records of churches being used for play performances in the provinces, yet two accounts have survived which show that one company had intended to perform in a church and another actually did so.

In the records of the town of Syston, near Leicester, is the item: "1602. Paid to Lord Morden's players because they should not play in the church . . . 12d." A decade earlier Lord Beauchamp's players had actually used the church, though not with permission. On 10 June 1590 in the Mayors' Court Books at Norwich is the entry:

> This day John Mufford, one of the Lord Beauchamp's players being forbidden by Mr. Mayor to play within the liberties of this city and in respect thereof gave them among them xx^s and yet notwithstanding they did set up bills to provoke men to come to their play and did play in XXe church. Therefore the said John Mufford is committed to prison.[41]

Unusual local records about a playing place are found in the churchwardens' accounts for Sherborne in the County of Dorset.[42] Here several entries show the players paying rent to local officials rather than receiving gratuities. There are half

---

[41] Murray, *English Dramatic Companies*, II, 402 and 336.

[42] A. D. Mills, "A Corpus Christi Play and Other Dramatic Activities in Sixteenth-Century Sherborne, Dorset," *Malone Society Collections* 9 1977 (1971), 13-15.

a dozen such entries between 1589 and 1603, such as one in 1598: "of the Queen's Majesty's players for the use of the church house . . . 2/"; and another in 1603: "of certain players for the use of the church house . . . 4/6." Other items in these accounts show the church house being rented to amateurs.

Another provincial playing place, though not mentioned in town records, is cited in other documents as a familiar temporary theater. In Heton's proposed patent for Queen Henrietta's company, he specifies that the company, when on tour, be allowed to play "at all time or times (the time of divine service only excepted) before or after supper within any town halls, guildhalls, moothalls, schoolhouses, or any other convenient places whatsoever. . . ." Heton might be suspected of asking unprecedented privileges, but schoolhouses are mentioned also in the official players' pass issued by the Lord Chamberlain for the King's company in May 1636:

> . . . His Majesty is graciously pleased that they shall as well before his Majesty's setting forth on his main progress as in all that time & after till they shall have occasion to return homewards, have all freedom & liberty to repair unto all towns corporate, mercat[ory] towns & other where they shall think fit & there in their Common Halls, moot halls, schoolhouses or other convenient rooms act plays comedies & interludes without any let hinderance or molestation whatsoever (behaving themselves civilly). Wherein it is his Majesty's pleasure and he doth expect that in all places where they come they be treated & entertained with such due respect & courtesy as may become his Majesty's loyal & loving subjects towards his servants. . . .[43]

One would think that the schoolhouses in most provincial towns would not afford a hall large enough to accommodate a profitable audience, but it is notable that both these records include them though they do not mention the more suitable

[43] From the Lord Chamberlain's Warrant Books, *Malone Society Collections* 2, pt. 3 (1931), 378-79.

inns. Presumably these documents, intended for the town authorities, mention only those halls over which the town fathers had control.

The most surprising, indeed unique, playing place for the touring troupes is recorded at Bristol. Kathleen M. D. Barker had found in records at Bristol and elsewhere references to a theater in Wine street used sometimes by travelling players.[44] The most illuminating of the several records comes from the will of Nicholas Wolffe, Cutler, dated 2 June 1614. Wolffe stipulates that the annuities he has provided are to be paid forever,

> . . . provided always . . . that all the annuities and yearly rents before mentioned and limited to be paid out of my said playhouse shall continue due and payable so long only as the same playhouse shall continue as a playhouse that such players as do resort to the said city or inhabit within the same do usually play there and may be permitted and suffered quietly to play there and no longer.

Among provincial towns only Bristol, so far as presently discovered records reveal, had such a theater in the period 1590-1642. Presumably it was a boon to players on the road, and one would expect further allusions to it to turn up. That Wolffe had experienced or feared municipal interference with his playhouse is implied in his words "may be permitted and suffered quietly."

ROUTES AND DURATION OF PROVINCIAL TOURS

There is very little reliable evidence of the route a London company took when it had to travel. Not only are the transcriptions of local records grossly incomplete, but such records as have been printed usually ignore the title of the com-

[44] Kathleen Barker, "An Early Seventeenth-Century Provincial Playhouse," *Theatre Notebook* 29 (1975), 81-84. See also Mark C. Pilkinton, "The Playhouse in Wine Street, Bristol," *Theatre Notebook* 37 (1983), 14-21 for additional records.

pany, and when a company name is mentioned it is sometimes inaccurate. Now and then the King's name on the license is taken for the name of the company; sometimes the London company named is not really the London troupe. The prevalence of such touring subsidiaries is indicated in an order sent out by the Lord Chamberlain in 1617. This document was brought to Norwich by Joseph Moore of the Lady Elizabeth's company. The Lord Chamberlain's order read in part:

> Whereas Thomas Swinnerton and Martin Slaughter being two of the Queen's Majesty's company of players, having separated themselves from their said company, have each of them taken forth a several exemplification or duplicate of his Majesty's letters patent granted to the whole company and by virtue thereof they severally in two companies with vagabonds and suchlike idle persons have and do use and exercise the quality of playing in diverse places of this realm to the great abuse and wrong of his Majesty's subjects. . . . And whereas William Perry having likewise gotten a warrant whereby he and a certain company of idle persons with him do travel and play under the name and title of the Children of his Majesty's Revels. . . . And whereas also Gilbert Reason one of the Prince his Highness players having likewise separated himself from his company hath also taken forth another exemplification or duplicate of the patent granted to that company and lives in the same kind and abuse. And likewise one Charles Marshal, Humphry Jeffes, and William Parr: three of Prince Palatine's company of players having also taken forth an exemplification or duplicate of the patent granted to the said company and by virtue thereof live after the like kind and abuse. . . .[45]

Obviously the local authorities could not tell for sure whether the company visiting them was the true London troupe or not, so that any two records of visits of Queen Anne's company do not necessarily refer to the same group.

[45] Murray, *English Dramatic Companies*, II, 343-44.

Such situations make it impossible to trace with any assurance the route of any London company on the road. The most reliable evidence I can find about the tour of a London company comes from a series of letters between Edward Alleyn on tour and his family in London. There are six letters which run from May to September in the year of the severe plague of 1593.[46] Alleyn, though a Lord Admiral's man, was on tour with Lord Strange's company. The principal subject of the letters is fear of the plague, precautions to be taken against it, and friends who have been victims.

Alleyn's first letter in the series is dated "from Chelmsford the 2 of May 1593." The second letter is written to Alleyn by Philip Henslowe "from London the 5 of July 1593," in which he says, ". . . I pray you likewise do my commendations unto all the rest of your fellows and I pray God to send you all that good health that we have as yet at London. . . ."

The third letter is written by Alleyn from Bristol to his wife in London on 1 August. He says

> . . . if you send any more letters, send to me by the carriers of Shrewsbury or to West Chester or to York to be kept till my Lord Strange's players come. And thus sweetheart with my hearty commendations I cease from Bristol this Wednesday after St James his day being ready to begin the play of Harry of Cornwall. . . . We shall not come home till All Hallows Tide. . . .

The fourth letter is written by Henslowe to Alleyn, apparently in August 1593 with news about the family of another touring player, ". . . Robert Brown's wife in Shoreditch and all her children and household be dead and her doors shut up. . . ."

The fifth letter from Henslowe to Alleyn, dated 14 August 1593, comments on an event of the tour:

> . . . very glad to hear of your good health which we pray God to continue long to his will and pleasure for we heard

[46] Foakes and Rickert, eds., *Henslowe's Diary*, pp. 274-81.

that you were very sick at Bath and that one of your fellows
were fain to play your part for you which was no little grief
unto us to hear, but thanks be to God for amendment for
we feared it much because we had no letter from you when
the other wives had letters sent. . . . & I pray you son
commend me heartily to all the rest of your fellows in general for I grow poor for lack of them. . . .

The final letter in the series was written on 28 September
from Henslowe to Alleyn:

. . . It hath pleased the Lord to visit me round about and
almost all my neighbors dead of the plague, and not my
house free for my two wenches have had the plague, and
yet thanks be to God liveth and are well. . . . and as for
my lord a Pembroke's which you desire to know where
they be they are all at home and have been this five or six
weeks for they cannot save their charges with travel as I
hear and were fain to pawn their apparel for their charge.
. . .

These letters show that Lord Strange's men had started their
tour before May the 2nd, and Alleyn says in his letter of
August 1st that "we shall not be home till All Hallows Tide."
Thus the tour was expected to last for at least six months.
Since 1593 was a bad plague year, the tour may have lasted
longer than most, but the plagues of 1603, 1610, 1625, and
1636-37 were at least as bad.

Since the earliest letter is sent from Chelmsford, near London, that stop may have been an early one. The other letters
show that from Bath and Bristol the company expected to go
on to Shrewsbury, West Chester, and York, covering a large
area. Presumably Strange's men were having more success
than Henslowe reported for Pembroke's company.

The lines quoted are eloquent of the fear of the plague by
all the correspondents; the passages deleted as irrelevant for
the tour are largely concerned with plague fears and plague
precautions.

SUMMARY

Incomplete and inaccurate as these town records are, they do show the astonishing multiplicity of theatrical productions in England during the reigns of Elizabeth, James, and Charles. Murray alone lists more than one hundred companies on tour and Stone and Dawson add several others. The London companies played under the same conditions as the others though they seem to have commanded somewhat more respect from local authorities.

The extent and duration of the tours of the Londoners cannot be ascertained except in the case of Lord Strange's company in 1593. But in the periods of long plague closing when the theaters were often closed for months[47] the companies must have toured until they lost too much money as Pembroke's men did in 1593.[48]

One would guess that such bankruptcy from touring was not unusual, but the only other example I know is the suggestion of impending bankruptcy in the petition of Lord Strange's men quoted above.

On arriving at a town the first act of the touring players was to call on the local authorities to get permission to play, first, if possible, before the mayor and his guests in the town hall, later before the general populace for entrance fees. Often permission to play at all was denied, for a variety of reasons, or no reason, though usually some cash gift was made to the prohibited players.

[47] See Bentley, *The Jacobean and Caroline Stage*, II, 652-72.
[48] I know of only one recorded exception to the plague touring rule. During the visitation of 1636-37 an apparently unique grant was made to the King's company:

The King having commanded servants the players to assemble their company and keep themselves together near the Court, gives them an allowance of £20 per week, which is to be paid to John Lowin and Joseph Taylor, on behalf of their company; such allowance to commence from the first of November last, to continue during his Majesty's pleasure, and to be taken as of his princely bounty. [*Calendar of State Papers, Domestic*, London, 1636-37, p. 228.]

When a London company concluded that it would be forced to tour, one of the first steps would have been to select the personnel of the travelling group and the repertory to be carried. The number of touring players seems to have varied from ten to twenty, but I have found no evidence as to the principle of selection. One would guess that sharers had first choice, since their professional income would have been reduced to nothing while the theaters were closed. Some boys and hired men presumably were included, but certainly not all of them. The repertory taken would have been a selection from the plays owned; the only number of plays known to have been taken was fourteen, but this number may have been larger than most since the company was playing at Oxford.

Such were the conditions encountered by the London dramatic companies when they decided they had to take to the road to escape London prohibitions. There is little evidence that the local authorities received the travellers with enthusiasm, except perhaps in some of the great houses and castles. But though indications of hostility can be found, the records do not show it to have been so pervasive as Puritan comments imply. General hostility is not compatible with the great numbers of provincial visits recorded. Travel in sixteenth- and seventeenth-century England was not comfortable even for royalty, and for the metropolitan players it can scarcely have been profitable. But touring was an inescapable part of the life of London players.

CHAPTER VIII

Casting

THE CASTING of plays by the professional companies of London in the years 1590-1642 was a simpler process than it usually is in the twentieth century. In the first place, all these troupes were repertory companies, hence the available players were fixed as to numbers and familiar as to talents and limitations. In the second place a high proportion of the plays produced were prepared by a dramatist with the specific company in mind, so that he could develop at least his principal characters with some consideration for the talents of the fellows of the company. This phenomenon of the custom-made play of course characterized the work of all attached dramatists while they were committed to write for their particular companies[1]—dramatists like Heywood, Fletcher, Massinger,

[1] See G. E. Bentley, *The Profession of Dramatist in Shakespeare's Time*, Princeton, 1971, pp. 30-37.

Shakespeare, Shirley, and Brome. In Elizabeth's time this knowledge of the producing company also guided many of the horde of playwrights paid by Philip Henslowe to write plays for the Admiral's and for Worcester's men. The many recorded instances in which Henslowe made down payments or installment payments to various playwrights show that the writer knew as he worked what company was expected to produce his play.[2]

These facts made anything in the nature of tryouts unnecessary and made it unlikely that a play written for the company would include major roles unsuited to the abilities of permanent members of that troupe. There is one sort of exception to this rule pointed out in Heywood's popular play *The Rape of Lucrece*. At the end of the 1608 edition is a Note to the Reader: ". . . we have inserted these few songs, which were added by the stranger that lately acted *Valerius* his part, in the form following." Two songs follow. Essentially the same note appears in the editions of 1609, 1614, 1630, 1638. There is a rather unconvincing attempt to identify this stranger in Allan Holaday's edition of the play.[3] So far as one can tell from the available evidence, however, this use of a player from outside the company was unusual.

But not all plays produced by London troupes had been written for them. More difficult casting problems could arise when a piece originally written for some other company had to be staged. In 1603 or 1604 the King's men (possibly when they were still the Lord Chamberlain's company) appropriated Marston's *Malcontent*, written shortly before for a boy company. In this instance Shakespeare's company made rather extensive changes in the text, as can be seen by a comparison of the first two quartos with the third. The new version is one-third again as long; it has an induction in which Sly, Bur-

---

[2] See, for example, partial payments made in 1597, 1598, and 1599 to Chettle, Haughton, Dekker, Jonson, Drayton, and Hathaway. R. A. Foakes and R. T. Rickert, eds., *Henslowe's Diary*, Cambridge, 1961, pp. 63, 64, 65, 73, 85, 88, 89, 99, and 123.

[3] *Illinois Studies in Language and Literature*, vol. 34, no. 3 (1950), pp. 16-19.

bage, Lowin, Sinklo, and Condell take part under their own names, and they reveal the fact that Burbage is to take the role of Malvole. Perhaps the most significant change is the addition of a comic character to the play, Passarello. This addition is not an insignificant one, for Passarello's role, with the other lines added to support him, runs to 257 lines, almost as many as the Fool has in the nearly contemporary *King Lear*. George Hunter has made the brilliant suggestion that the company had these lines added in order to exhibit Robert Armin, the new comedian of the troupe.[4]

Similar, though surely much less drastic, changes must have been required when William Cartwright's *The Royal Slave*, written to be performed by the undergraduates at Christ Church, Oxford, was, by order of the King, presented by the King's company at court on 12 January 1636/37.[5]

These plays were single examples, but casting problems must have been encountered when sizable chunks of the repertory of one company were transferred to another. Such a large transfer took place when Christopher Beeston added a good part of the repertory of the Lady Elizabeth's company to that of Queen Henrietta's men.[6]

Still another cause for casting adjustments arose when a London troupe revived a play which, though written for them, had been first cast thirty years or more before. Examples are *Othello, the Moor of Venice* presented by the King's men at court on 6 December 1636 and *Every Man in His Humour* shown before the King on 17 February 1630/31. All the original actors in each play were either dead, retired, or too old for their original roles at the time of the Caroline performances before royalty.

A few plays have printed statements in the quartos about

---

4 John Marston, *The Malcontent*, ed. George K. Hunter, London, 1975, pp. xlvii-xlix.

5 See G. E. Bentley, *The Jacobean and Caroline Stage*, 7 vols., Oxford, 1941-1968, III, 134-41.

6 Ibid., I, 218-22 and 250-59.

casting changes. One of the most explicit is to be found in the 1633 edition, the first, of Marlowe's *Jew of Malta*. This play had been frequently acted in Henslowe's theaters in the early 1590s, and of course Edward Alleyn had become famous in the leading role. For the 1633 performance Thomas Heywood wrote a dedication and two prologues and two epilogues, presumably at the request of the manager of Queen Henrietta's company, his friend Christopher Beeston. One prologue is explicit about the casting of a revival.

The Prologue to the Stage at
the Cockpit

	We know not how our play may pass this stage,
(Marlowe)	But by the best of poets* in that age
	The Malta Jew had being, and was made;
(Alleyn)	And he then by the best of actors* played.
	In *Hero and Leander* one did gain
	A lasting memory; in *Tamburlaine*,
	This Jew, with others many, th' other won
	The attribute of peerless, being a man
	Whom we may rank with (doing no one wrong)
	Proteus for shapes and Roscius for a tongue,
	So could he speak, so vary. Nor is't hate
(Perkins)	To merit in him* who doth personate
	Our Jew this day, nor is it his ambition
	To exceed, or equal, being of condition
	More modest; this is all that he intends
	(And that too at the urgence of some friends):
	To prove his best, and if none here gainsay it,
	The part he hath studied, and intends to play it.

Richard Perkins was the leading actor in Queen Henrietta's and an old friend of Heywood's.

The recasting necessitated by the passage of time is similarly recorded in the prologue which the King's men commissioned for their revival of *Bussy d'Ambois*. These lines appear in the 1641 (third) quarto of the play.

> . . . FIELD is gone,
> Whose action first did give it name, and one
> Who came the nearest to him, is denied
> By his gray beard to show the height and pride
> Of D'AMBOIS' youth and bravery; yet to hold
> Our title still a-foot, and not grow cold
> By giving it o'er, a third man with his best
> Of care and pains defends our interest;
> As RICHARD he was liked, nor do we fear
> In personating D'AMBOIS he'll appear
> To faint, or go less, so your free consent,
> As heretofore, give him encouragement.

Apparently this "third man" was Eyllaerdt Swanston, for Edmund Gayton says in his *Pleasant Notes upon Don Quixote*, 1654,

> . . . for he was instantly metamorphosed into the statliest, gravest, and commanding soul, that ever eye beheld. *Taylor* acting *Arbaces* or *Swanston D'Amboys* were shadows to him.
>
> [E1, p. 25]

A very few plays are printed in editions that record numerous cast changes in a revival. The 1623 quarto of Webster's *Duchess of Malfi* prints a cast for the performance of the play by the King's company. Such printed casts are extremely rare, and this one is rarer still because it records certain changes in the casting since the first performance, probably nine or ten years before, by the same troupe. This cast names fifteen different members of the organization, but six of them occur in pairs and numbered:

> Ferdinand, 1 *R. Burbidge*, 2 *I. Taylor*.
> Cardinall, 1 H. *Cundaile*. 2 *R. Robinson*
> Antonio, 1 *W. Ostler*. 2 *R. Benfield*.

Since Burbage died in 1619 and Ostler in 1614, and since Condell had ceased to act, the players numbered 2 must have replaced those numbered 1 in a revival between 1619 and 1623.

These general conditions of casting can be supplemented

and extended by a consideration of the comparatively few remaining printed casts and manuscript prompt copies and "Plots." It must be borne in mind that such lists have been preserved for only a tiny fraction of the plays of the period known at least by title, about 1,500,[7] that several of them are mere lists of players with no assignment of roles, and that several of the lists or casts are of dubious authority or are irrelevant for the London professional companies.

There are several types of such lists or casts: "Plots," folio lists, quarto lists, casts in manuscript, casts of questionable authority, and casts of amateurs.

Earliest and most irregular are the seven "Plots" prepared for plays—six of them lost—produced in the last dozen years of Elizabeth's reign. The basic work on these peculiar and difficult documents has been done by Sir Walter Greg in his *Dramatic Documents*. He defines and then explains:

> Theatrical Plots are documents giving the skeleton outline of plays, scene by scene, for use in the theatre, a small group of which has survived from the last twelve years or so of Elizabeth's reign. . . . It is clear to us now that there was nothing exceptional about the plays for which Plots were required. Although we are without external information on the point we may suppose that these were prepared for the guidance of actors and others in the playhouse, to remind those concerned when and in what character they were to appear, what properties were required, and what noises were to be made behind the scenes. The necessity for some such guide would be evident in a repertory theatre, and we may feel assured that the Plot was exhibited in a place convenient for ready reference during performance. There seems, indeed, every probability that documents similar in general character to those we possess were usual, if not universal, in Elizabethan playhouses. . . .[8]

[7] See Bentley, *The Profession of Dramatist in Shakespeare's Time*, p. 199.

[8] W. W. Greg, ed., *Dramatic Documents from the Elizabethan Playhouses*, 2 vols., Oxford, 1931, I, 2 and 3-4.

There are seven of these Plots extant, most of them mutilated, and one or two in fragments so small as to be almost useless except to indicate that they had been similar in character to the others. They have all been so fully and expertly analyzed by Sir Walter Greg that detailed treatment here would be supererogation; I simply summarize parts of Greg's work.

The Plot for *The Dead Man's Fortune* seems to have been prepared for the Admiral's men about 1590. The second Plot, that for *2 Seven Deadly Sins*, appears to have been prepared for a revival by Lord Strange's men also about 1590. The third Plot is for *Frederick and Basilea*, a play performed as new by the Admiral's men at the Rose 3 June 1597. The fourth is the Plot for *Fortune's Tennis*, a mere collection of fragments but preserving enough names to make clear that it was prepared for performance by the Admiral's men, conjecturally about 1597-98. The fifth Plot is another fragment, but a larger one, for the production of *Troilus and Cressida* by the Admiral's men probably in 1599. The sixth Plot, that for *The Battle of Alcazar*, was prepared for a revival by the Admiral's men, probably late in 1598 or early in 1599. Sir Walter says of it, "This Plot, in spite of its mutilated condition, really affords the key to the whole series, since it is the only one for which there is extant a text of the play enabling us to examine its construction in some detail."[9] The seventh Plot was prepared for a revival of the first part of *Tamar Cam* by the Admiral's men in 1602. The original manuscript has disappeared and Sir Walter has had to work from a transcript of the original made by George Stevens and printed in 1803.

In his *Dramatic Documents* Greg has written a section on "General Characteristics" of these Plots. He says:

> In its most fundamental aspect a Plot consists of the record of the successive entrances of the characters of a play, with some record expressed or implied, and varying much in completeness, of the corresponding exits. This is essential, but almost all examples exhibit in varying degrees two other

[9] Ibid., I, 145.

features: namely some record of properties and other requirements of the stage, and some record of the actors assigned for the individual parts.[10]

Since only one Plot, that for *The Battle of Alcazar*, was prepared for a play which is still extant, one can only guess the importance of roles in most of these Plots from the number of scenes in which the character appears and sometimes from a general knowledge of the story.

Nevertheless these Plots do offer grounds for a few observations. The superior status of the sharers is attested by the common but not invariable use of "Mr." with their names. Sharers are generally assigned what appear to be the major roles, though Richard Allen was given the role of Frederick and the prologue and the epilogue in *Frederick and Basilea*.

Somewhat surprising is the large number of performers identified in the fullest of the Plots: twenty-four are named in *The Battle of Alcazar* and twenty-nine in *Tamar Cam I*. A number of these players are unknown or only slightly known from other records and several may have been gatherers or attendants. In the Plot for *Frederick and Basilea* unnamed "Attendants" and "Gatherers" are assigned minor roles.

Perhaps most conspicuous is the amount of doubling in several of these Plots. Many players have an extra role or two, and in *Frederick and Basilea* Thomas Hunt has five, and "black Dick" has five. In *The Battle of Alcazar* the majority of the actors named have more than one role, and Mr. Charles has three, W. Kendall has four, and George Somerset has five. In *Tamar Cam I* Towne has three, "Mr. Sam" three, Dick Jubie seven, W. Cartwright five, and Thomas Marbeck at least eight.

The second class of casts or player lists is that found in the seventeenth-century collected editions of the plays of Jonson, Shakespeare, and Beaumont and Fletcher, specifically in the Jonson folio of 1616, the Shakespeare folio of 1623, and the second Beaumont and Fletcher folio of 1679. For the purpose of identifying roles the least helpful of these is the list pub-

[10] Ibid., I, 73.

lished by John Heminges and Henry Condell in their collection of the plays of Shakespeare. It is headed "The Names of the Principall Actors in all these Playes." The twenty-six names which follow are simply Heminges' and Condell's acknowledgment of the contributions of their fellows who had brought Shakespeare's plays to life on the stage. All of them had been sharers in the company at one time or another, but the plays they performed in, or the dates of the contributions, do not appear. Some of these players, like Augustine Phillips, died about the middle of Shakespeare's career, or like Will Kempe left the company at about that time. Others, like John Lowin, Robert Armin, and John Shank had not joined the company until half the plays had been produced. Others, like Nathan Field, were babes in arms when Shakespeare wrote his earliest plays; still others, like Joseph Taylor, could have performed only in revivals since he did not join the King's company until after Shakespeare's death in 1616. No doubt they all did perform in the plays of the company's chief dramatist, but at various times, and in one or two instances only in revivals. All of these men eventually became sharers in the company, and this fact is apparently the basis of Heminges' and Condell's selection of names for their list. The First Folio is very much a company document, edited and dedicated by the manager of the company and his longtime associate. They have listed only twenty-six names; obviously many more players would have been required to stage the thirty-six plays printed in the folio. Clearly most, if not all, the hired men and boys required for productions at The Theatre, the Globe, and Blackfriars have been omitted. The list is not inclusive, but is a roll of the principal members of the Lord Chamberlain-King's whom Heminges and Condell chose to honor.

More helpful than the Shakespeare folio single list of the "Principall Actors in all these Playes" are the groups of players whose names Ben Jonson printed with each of the nine plays included in his "Works" in 1616. Unlike Heminges and Condell, he attached each list to a particular play and gave the date of production. Jonson, the most meticulous and perhaps the most arrogant dramatist of his time, is also the first English playwright to acknowledge the cooperation of the players by naming some of them with every play. Appended to each comedy or tragedy is a list of players like that which accompanies the piece that was given pride of place, *Every Man in His Humor*:

This Comœdie was first
Acted, in the yeere
1598.
By the then L. Chamberlayne
his Seruants.
The principall Comœdians were.

Will. Shakespeare.	Ric. Bvrbadge.
Avg. Philips.	Joh. Hemings.
Hen. Condel.	Tho. Pope.
Will. Slye.	Chr. Beeston.
Will. Kempe.	Joh. Dvke.

With the allowance of the Master of Revells.

Each of the six following comedies and two tragedies has a similar list. Three of the comedies, produced by boy companies, have lists of six or eight boys each. The other plays were all produced by the Lord Chamberlain-King's company and each is accompanied by a list of six, eight, or ten players. This company is sufficiently well known for us to tell roughly what Jonson's principle was in naming players. Most of these players—in the case of *Every Man out of His Humor* all of them—were sharers in the company at the time the play was produced. In the *Every Man in* list the first eight were sharers; Beeston and Duke were only hired men, and as such were properly placed last in the list. Jonson ignored the apprentices required for the roles of Dame Kitely, Mrs. Bridget, and Tib. Though there is no indication which parts in the play were taken by Beeston and Duke, it is likely that they played minor characters, perhaps doubling two or three.

For *Every Man out of His Humor*, acted the following year by the same company, Jonson listed only six players; all six were sharers. For the company's performance of *Sejanus* in 1603, eight players are named, six of whom were sharers at the time. The other two, John Lowin and Alexander Cooke, became sharers later, but in 1603 they were apparently only hired men. There are no clues to their roles.

For *Volpone*, acted two years later in 1605, Jonson named only six performers, including Lowin and Cooke again, but by 1605 they may have become sharers. For *The Alchemist* of 1610 the playwright listed ten King's men, eight of whom were sharers. The other two, John Underwood and William Eccleston, were apparently still hired men in 1610, though they both became sharers later. The *Catiline* list of 1611 is the same as that of *The Alchemist* of the previous year, except that the boy Richard Robinson appears instead of the sharer Robert Armin. Obviously there was no comic role for Armin in this tragedy. It is interesting that Jonson chose to name the boy Robinson, since he had excluded all performers of women's roles from his other lists for this company. Was Robinson notably effective? Jonson singled him out for special praise as a female impersonator in the text of *The Devil Is an Ass* performed by the company five years later.

According to this catalogue, then, Jonson thought that when he collected for posterity those plays he deemed worthy of him[11] he also thought it worthwhile to let posterity know the names of the players who created these roles on the stage, but not *which* roles, nor *all* the performers. About 80 percent of those named were sharers; only one boy was named and six hired men, two of them twice. All these hired men were evidently promising actors, for all of them later became sharers in this or in other companies. The lists also indicate that major roles in Jonson's plays were seldom, if ever, taken by hired

---

[11] It should be remembered that Jonson was being selective. Several of his dramatic compositions, written before *Catiline* and *The Alchemist*, were omitted: *A Tale of a Tub, The Case is Altered, Richard Crookback, Hot Anger Soon Cooled, Robert II, King of Scots, The Page of Plymouth, The Isle of Dogs,* and probably others, since he told Drummond of Hawthornden in 1618/19 that half of his comedies were not in print.

men, though some of the hired men named were evidently talented enough to be made, at a later date, sharers in the King's company.

The third folio with lists of players is the Beaumont and Fletcher second folio of 1679. Since at the date of publication Beaumont had been dead for sixty-three years and Fletcher for fifty-four, it is unlikely that either had anything to do with the lists.

In the first Beaumont and Fletcher folio of 1647, none of the thirty-four plays and a masque had been accompanied by any list of players, though the dedication was signed by the ten patented members or sharers of the King's company still available five years after the closing of the theaters. The second folio adds eighteeen plays not printed in the folio of 1647 because they had previously appeared in quartos, making a total of fifty-two plays and a masque. Twenty-five of these plays are accompanied by short lists of players, presumably those of the first performance. All but two of the twenty-five lists are attached to plays belonging to the King's company. Most of these lists name eight actors, but one names four, two name five, three name six, and two name seven. Never are roles assigned.

These lists in the second Beaumont and Fletcher folio are not very helpful. In the first place their authenticity is questionable; no one knows who made them or when, whereas the Shakespeare list was made by John Heminges and Henry Condell, two of the most knowledgeable theater men of their time, and both had acted in the plays of their friend Shakespeare. The Jonson lists were made by one of the most experienced and certainly the most meticulous playwright in London. The lists in these two folios may not tell us all we want to know, but what they do tell can be relied upon.

Not only is the authenticity of the 1679 lists uncertain, but none is dated; some seem to be for revivals, so that sometimes one cannot tell whether a given player in a list was a hired man or a sharer at the time represented by the list. It appears that most of those named were sharers at the time, and there are more names of apprentices than in the Shakespeare and Jonson lists—as one might expect considering the greater prominence of women's roles in the Beaumont and Fletcher plays.

These plays were so frequently revived that their owners, the King's company, withheld most of them from publication for many years, and therefore (in the usual absence of reliable external evidence) the date of first performance for most of them can be only guessed. Indeed, for most of the plays with actor lists the dates currently assigned for first performances depend upon the biographical facts in the careers of the players named, on the shaky assumption that these lists represent first productions. This assumption is a dubious one, since we do not know when or by whom these casts were set down. Several of the men named are known to have been first hired men and later sharers. Their status at the time the list was made is therefore probably unascertainable.

So much for the information about roles and status to be derived from these folio lists of nearly two hundred names (involving a good many duplications). They look very promising at first glance, but further investigation proves them disappointing. More can be learned from the casts or lists in a few quarto editions of Jacobean and Caroline plays.

Before the Restoration of Charles II, quarto editions of English plays very rarely printed casts or even lists of the players. There are only fifteen or sixteen such quartos among the 800 or more plays printed before 1660.[12] They all come from the second half of the period, and for some reason more than half of them were published in the years 1629, 1630,

[12] There are a few quartos that name one or two actors, usually on the title page or in a prologue or preface. These men were, as one would expect, leading players like Edward Alleyn, Will Kempe, Richard Perkins, or Thomas Greene, whose names might be relied upon to attract attention and therefore to sell books. Of course no player ever achieved such distinction while he was still a hired man. Now and then a player gets mentioned in the dialogue, as when Jonson flatters Burbage and Nathan Field in *Bartholomew Fair* or Richard Robinson in *The Devil Is an Ass*.

1631, and 1632. It should be no surprise that the majority of these printed casts and lists come from the productions of King Charles's company or Queen Henrietta's. These helpful quartos are:

Middleton, *The Inner-Temple Masque*, 1619, Prince Charles I
Webster, *The Duchess of Malfi*, 1623, King's
Massinger, *The Roman Actor*, 1626, King's
Ford, *The Lovers' Melancholy*, 1629, King's
Carlell, *The Deserving Favorite*, 1629, King's
Shirley, *The Wedding*, 1629, Queen Henrietta's
Massinger, *The Renegado*, 1630, Queen Henrietta's
Massinger, *The Picture*, 1630, King's
Heywood, *The Fair Maid of the West*, I, 1631, Queen Henrietta's
Heywood, *The Fair Maid of the West*, II, 1631, Queen Henrietta's
Marmion, *Holland's Leaguer*, 1632, Prince Charles II
Nabbes, *Hannibal and Scipio*, 1637, Queen Henrietta's
Richards, *Tragedy of Messalina*, 1640, King's Revels
Fletcher, *The Wild Goose Chase*, 1652, King's
Davenport, *King John and Matilda*, 1655, Queen Henrietta's
Jordan, *Money is an Ass*, 1668, King's Revels

In addition to these casts in printed quartos there are four others for plays first acted in the reigns of James or Charles but not printed until the nineteenth and twentieth centuries. They are:

Fletcher and Massinger, *Sir John Van Olden Barnavelt*, BM. MS. Add. 18653, acted 1619, King's
Clavell, *The Soddered Citizen*, privately owned, acted c. 1630?, King's
Massinger, *Believe as You List*, BM. MS. Egerton 2828, acted 1631, King's
Wilson, *The Swisser*, BM. MS. Add. 36759, acted 1631, King's

The Swisser and *The Soddered Citizen* manuscripts have formal casts prefixed to the texts of the plays. The *Sir John Van Olden Barnavelt* and the *Believe as You List* manuscripts are prompt copies. For the latter an unusually full, though not complete, cast can be pieced out from the prompter's notes.[13] These quarto and manuscript lists of performers are set out in full with some analysis in the Appendix.

Nearly all these casts or lists are fuller than any in the three folios, and all but two or three assign most of the major roles in the play. Unfortunately these plays which we can cast with some assurance constitute less than 2.5 percent of the plays surviving from our period, to say nothing of the hundreds of lost plays. And about half of them were produced by the King's men, the wealthiest and largest troupe, presumably better equipped to cast their plays effectively than organizations like the Palsgrave's company, Queen Anne's company, or the Duke of York's company, to say nothing of the minor troupes of Queen Elizabeth's reign. We cannot be certain, of course, that the practices revealed by the casts of the King's company and of Queen Henrietta's company are equally characteristic of their competitors at the Red Bull, the Fortune, or the Hope; nor is there any assurance that the casting of these plays, produced in the years 1619 to 1642, is an accurate reflection of the normal distribution of roles in the years 1590-1618. Players, however, are notoriously conservative in their methods, and it is rather likely that production customs of the earlier period did not differ radically from those of the later. One has to remember, of course, that troupes like King Charles's company and Queen Henrietta's men had a good deal more money and other resources than the troupes of the nineties like the Lord Admiral's men or Lord Strange's.

---

[13] Since this study is concerned with professionals, I am eliminating from consideration the several casts for amateur productions, most of them Oxford or Cambridge college plays like *Zelotypus*, *Melanthe*, *Ignoramus*, *Loiola*, *The Rival Friends*, or *Valetudinarian*, or school plays like *Apollo Shroving*, performed by schoolboys at Hadleigh in Suffolk, or amateur country house productions like those of Mildmay Fane, Earl of Westmorland.

CASTING GENERALIZATIONS

From these printed and manuscript casts and lists a few general conclusions may be drawn.

1) The overriding importance of the sharers in each company is unmistakable. The list of "Principall Actors" in the Shakespeare folio names sharers only; the condensed casts given by Ben Jonson in his "Works" of 1616 name sharers forty-one times, hired men ten times, an apprentice once; the actor lists in the second Beaumont and Fletcher folio, though of uncertain authority and doubtful date, appear to give the same predominance of sharers, but the lists of this folio of 1679 record more names of apprentices than do the Shakespeare and Jonson collections.

In the casts of the printed quartos and formal manuscripts the dominance of sharers is again shown. The major adult roles are given to sharers: at least 123 of all roles cast, though roughly one-third of all the parts in these plays have no performers assigned.

2) The names of the sharers listed in these casts exhibit another phenomenon: no extant cast assigns roles to *all* the players known to have been sharers at the date of first performance of the play.[14] For the King's company the casts of the 1630s average about seven fellows, whereas their royal patent of 24 June 1625 had named thirteen and their livery list of 6 May 1629, fourteen. By 1631 Heminges and Condell were dead, and several of the plays had no major comic role for John Shank, but even so there were always at least three or four sharers not assigned. What did they do? Minor unassigned roles with doubling problems are a possibility, but surely not a very extensive one, since the company was paying twenty-one hired men according to the list of those protected on 26 December 1624.[15] Did the unnamed sharers have some sort of supervising functions?

3) These same quarto and formal manuscript casts name

---

[14] *The Battle of Alcazar* seems to be an exception to this generalization.
[15] See Bentley, *The Jacobean and Caroline Stage*, I, 15-16.

hired men about fifty-two times and apprentices about sixty-five times. The hired men and apprentice counts are somewhat less assured than those of the sharers because of the uncertain status of the named performer in a few instances, and the uncertain identity in some instances when only nicknames are used. These rough figures suggest that the apprentices were more conspicuous on the stage than the hired men were; and this in spite of the fact that such records as we have indicate that the major companies enrolled a good many more hired men than apprentices. The conclusion, as suggested in Chapter IV, seems to be that hired men contributed more to the London troupes as stagekeepers, prompters, wardrobe keepers, gatherers, musicians, and walk-ons than they did as identifiable performers.

A further indication that apprentices were generally more conspicuous on stage than hired men is to be seen in the assignment of leading roles. Richard Allen, who played Frederick and presented the prologue and the epilogue in *Frederick and Basilea*, is the only hired man I can find playing a lead, but even in this play "Dick (Dutton's Boy)" appears as Basilea in eleven scenes.

Shakespeare's plays, though not cast, show prominent roles written for the apprentices in the company. Boys have the lead in *The Merchant of Venice, As You Like It, All's Well that Ends Well*, and *Cymbeline*. Often Shakespeare planned the second role for a boy, as in *The Comedy of Errors, Romeo and Juliet, Henry VI, Part I, Twelfth Night, The Merry Wives of Windsor, Measure for Measure, Macbeth, Antony and Cleopatra*. In twelve of the plays of Shakespeare the third role was prepared for a boy.[16]

As one might have expected, leading roles are given to boy actors in many of the plays of Beaumont and Fletcher. The longest role in the play was prepared for a boy player in *The*

[16] The line counts are conveniently set out in T. W. Baldwin's *The Organization and Personnel of the Shakespearean Company*, Princeton, 1927, between pp. 226 and 227.

Knight of Malta, *The Humorous Lieutenant*, *The Laws of Candy*, *The Pilgrim*, and *A Wife for a Month*. The second longest role went to an apprentice in *The Captain*, *A Very Woman*, *The Lovers' Progress*, *Thierry and Theodoret*, *The Pilgrim*, *The Double Marriage*, and *Love's Pilgrimage*. Even in plays whose lines have not been counted one calls to mind the prominence of roles for the boys in *The Duchess of Malfi*, *The Fair Maid of the West*, *The Roaring Girl*, *'Tis Pity She's a Whore*, and *The Northern Lass*.

4) A certain amount of typecasting is suggested by these folio, quarto, and formal manuscript lists. Most obvious is the specialization of the comedians. Their general popularity during the reigns of Elizabeth, James, and Charles is attested in the multiplicity of popular allusions to them—more than to other players except for the stars like Alleyn, Burbage, and possibly Joseph Taylor, and to the managers like Heminges and Beeston. See the allusions to Tarleton, Kempe, Thomas Greene, William Rowley, Armyn, Shank, William Robbins, and Timothy Reade.[17] The customary casting of these men in comic roles is indicated not only by the many allusions to them and by their assignments such as Greene to Bubble in *Greene's Tu Quoque*; Rowley to Plumporridge in *The Inner Temple Masque*, the fat clown in *All's Lost by Lust*,[18] the Fat Bishop in *A Game at Chess*; Shank to Hilario in *The Picture*, Hodge in *The Soddered Citizen*, Sir Roger in *The Scornful Lady*; and William Robbins to Carazie in *The Renegado*, Rawbone in *The Wedding*, and Clem in *The Fair Maid of the West*.

Equally indicative of the specialization of the comedians is the omission of the names of such popular players from the casts of plays without prominent comic roles. We have already noted the absence of Robert Armin's name from the Jonson folio list of players for the tragedy of *Catiline*, though

---

[17] Consult under their names in Edwin Nungezer, *A Dictionary of Actors and Other Persons Associated with the Public Representation of Plays in England before 1642*, New Haven, 1929; and Bentley, *The Jacobean and Caroline Stage*, II.

[18] Though there is no cast for this play, Rowley's performance is recorded in the dramatis personnae as "*Iaques*, a simple clownish Gentleman, his sonne, personated by the Poet."

he was listed as a player in the almost contemporary *Alchemist*. Though John Shank had a reputation as a comedian and was a prominent fellow of the King's company and a part-owner of their two theaters, his name does not appear in the casts or lists for their plays omitting his specialty, *Sir John van Olden Barnavelt*, *The Deserving Favorite*, *The Swisser*, or *Believe as You List*. One odd appearance of John Shank's name is in the full cast for *The Wild Goose Chase* where he is assigned the role of "PETELLA their waiting-woman Their Servant Mr. Shanck." But there are no lines for Petella in the play. I can only conjecture that Shank gagged his lines, but this is a feeble guess since there seems to be little scope for Petella in this comedy.

A similar practice is indicated in the casts for Queen Henrietta's company. Their principal comedian, William Robbins, is listed as playing the comic roles of Carazie in *The Renegado*, Rawbone in *The Wedding*, and Clem in *The Fair Maid of the West*; but in *King John and Matilda* and *Hannibal and Scipio* which are without important comic roles his name does not appear.

Typecasting for comedians is also suggested but not demonstrated by the change in type of comic roles which Shakespeare wrote for the Lord Chamberlain's company while the buffoon and dancer, Will Kempe, was a fellow of the troupe—Costard, Dromio, Launce, Bottom, Shallow, Dogberry—to the new type of singing court fool which he wrote after Kempe's departure and his replacement by Robert Armin—Touchstone, Feste, the Fool in *King Lear*. Professor Ringler's ingenious argument that Armin played Edgar in *King Lear* and that the Fool was played by a boy[19] is interesting but not convincing. Such casting would seem to me to violate not only the normal practices of the professional players but the whole tradition of the Court Fool which is emphasized in the tragedy by the coxcomb and by the frequent references to it.

[19] "Shakespeare and His Actors: Some Remarks on *King Lear*," *Proceedings of the Comparative Literature Symposium*, vol. 12, ed. Wendell M. Aycock, Lubbock, Texas, 1981, pp. 183-94.

There are further suggestions of at least periodic typecasting in the frequently noted appearance in three of Shakespeare's comedies of the late nineties of paired heroines of contrasted stature and contrasted temperaments—Helena and Hermia, Beatrice and Hero, Celia and Rosalind. Since there are no clues yet discovered to the identities of the boys for whom the roles were written, or even any assurance that two particular boys were playing together for several years, this suggestion must be taken as speculative though attractive.

Somewhat similar is Baldwin Maxwell's contention that the "hungry knave" characters in the Beaumont and Fletcher folio plays were written for John Shank. The roles are Corporal Judas in *Bonduca*, Geta in *The Prophetess*, Mallfort in *The Lover's Progress*, Lazarello in *Love's Cure*, Onus in *The Queen of Corinth*, and Penurio in *Women Pleased*. The excessive leanness of each of these characters is pointedly remarked upon in the text of the play.[20] All seem to have been written while Shank was a fellow.

These examples from the plays of Shakespeare and of Fletcher are not quite the same as the others in that they suggest an attached dramatist or poet-in-ordinary writing roles for particular players in his company, not the company's regular assignment of roles according to the specialties of its fellows and apprentices.[21]

Another sort of evidence of typecasting, at least for one man for a short period, is to be seen in a series of contemporary allusions to Stephen Hammerton during the last few years before the closing of the theaters. The most comprehensive of these allusions is the one made by Wright in his *Historia Histrionica*.

---

[20] Baldwin Maxwell, "The Hungry Knave in the Beaumont and Fletcher Plays," *Philological Quarterly* 5 (1926), 299-305.

[21] The classic attempt to cast all the Shakespearean plays and a number of others performed by the Lord Chamberlain-King's company is that of Baldwin, *The Organization and Personnel of the Shakespearean Company*. While there are many valuable suggestions in this book, a good many of Baldwin's conclusions seem to me to go far beyond his evidence.

. . . at the same time *Amyntor* was Play'd by *Stephen Hammerton* (who was at first a most noted and beautiful Woman Actor, but afterwards he acted with equal Grace and Applause, a Young Lover's Part). . . .[22]

The statement about the apprenticeship of Hammerton is verified, at least so far as the dates are concerned, by statements in a suit in the Court of Requests in 1632.[23] Hammerton's apprenticeship would have expired in or about 1638 shortly before the references to him in the young lovers' roles.

Hammerton as a juvenile lead, almost a matinée idol, is attested by a few epilogue allusions in plays of the King's men after the "noted and beautiful Woman Actor" had become an adult. In the epilogue to Shirley's *The Doubtful Heir* the Captain questions the gentlemen in the audience about the play they have just seen:

. . . now, pray tell
How did the action please ye? was it well?
How did king Stephen do, and tother Prince?

Since the king in the play is named Ferdinand, Stephen must mean the actor, Stephen Hammerton.

The same sort of implication about this actor is to be found in the epilogue to John Suckling's comedy for the King's men, *The Goblins*. The speaker inquires about the reception of the play:

The women—Oh, if Stephen *should be kill'd!*
Or miss the lady, how the plot is spill'd.

Since there is no Stephen in the play, Hammerton must have played Orsabrin.

Of the same sort, though even more flattering to young Hammerton, are two passages in the epilogue for Thomas Killigrew's *The Parson's Wedding*, a Blackfriars play of about

[22] See Bentley, *The Jacobean and Caroline Stage*, II, Appendix, p. 693.
[23] See G. E. Bentley, "The Salisbury Court Theatre and Its Boy Players," *Huntington Library Quarterly* 40 (1977), 129-49.

1640.[24] At the end of the play, the Captain, about to speak the epilogue, puts off Lady Love-all with, "Think on't, *Stephen* is as handsome, when the Play is done, as Mr. Wild was in the Scene." And a little later the Captain concludes the play with

> What say you, Gentlemen, will you lend your hands to join them; the Match you see is made; if you refuse, *Stephen* misses the Wench, and then you cannot justly blame the Poet. For you know they say, that alone is enough to spoil the Play.

Even several years after the closing of the theaters the popularity of Stephen Hammerton in romantic roles was still remembered. In his verses for the Beaumont and Fletcher folio of 1647 Henry Harington wrote:

> *Ladies cannot say*
> *Though* Stephen *miscarri'd that so did the play.*

These miscellaneous examples do show that at various periods in its history the King's company, at least, assigned certain roles to particular players who had developed specialties. It appears to me notable that most of the roles cited here were written by attached dramatists of the company—Shakespeare, Fletcher, and James Shirley. Before making any valid statements about typecasting as a general practice, even in the King's company, one would need information about many more of the role assignments even in these cited plays. Still more essential would be casting information about the scores of plays produced by the company but written by unattached playwrights like Barnaby Barnes, George Wilkins, Tourneur, Middleton, Henry Shirley, Richard Brome, Lodowick Carlell, William Davenant, John Ford, Ben Jonson, and the several anonymous plays in the repertory list of 1641.[25]

On the basis of the evidence now available one can only say

[24] See Bentley, *The Jacobean and Caroline Stage*, IV, 701-705.
[25] See ibid., I, 65-66 and 108-134.

that typecasting seems to have been common for leading comedians. Beyond this there is evidence that for short periods in the Lord Chamberlain-King's company certain specialties like the hungry knave, the handsome young lover, the paired heroines seem to have been exploited by attached dramatists of the company. I have found no evidence of a consistent practice of typecasting for all plays. Certainly the major role in the best-known plays cannot have been typecast, and typecasting cannot have been the controlling principle in the preparation of plays or in the selection of sharers for the King's company or for Queen Henrietta's.

DOUBLING

For the professional players doubling had been a normal feature of casting for generations before Shakespeare came to London. Indeed, doubling was a euphemism: common enough was tripling and quadrupling and even quintupling as shown by the printed casts of Tudor interludes and by a few of the later Plots and prompt manuscripts. Versatility was certainly required of all professional players, men and boys, sharers, hired men, and apprentices.

David Bevington has collected the many examples of Tudor plays written to be performed by touring companies, of limited size, several published with casting charts on the title pages, and he has shown brilliantly how the plays were constructed to facilitate such doubling. He shows how this principle of construction was dominant through the time to Marlowe.[26]

The practice of constructing commercial plays to allow for doubling was still important after Marlowe, even when the acting troupes had grown much larger than six men and a boy. Shakespeare was careful to observe it, as has been demonstrated for his earlier plays.[27] One might have assumed that

[26] David Bevington, *From "Mankind" to Marlowe*, Cambridge, Mass., 1962.
[27] William A. Ringler, Jr., "The Number of Actors in Shakespeare's Early Plays," in *The Seventeenth Century Stage*, ed. G. E. Bentley, Chicago and London, 1968, pp. 110-34.

the doubling was less extensive in Jacobean and Caroline times when the companies were larger and richer than the sixteenth-century strollers had been, but evidently this was not the case. The 1607 quarto of *The Fair Maid of the Exchange* presents a rather elaborate doubling chart; the 1610 quarto of *Mucedorus* carries a chart showing how "Ten persons may easily play it"; and the 1631 prompt manuscript of Massinger's *Believe as You List*, performed by the largest and richest of the Caroline London companies, shows the most complex doubling of all.

Audiences were fully aware of this practice as occasional comments show. In the Induction for Marston's *Antonio and Mellida* Alberto says to Piero "the necessity of the play forceth me to act two parts." In his *Histrio-Mastix* (1633, L1^v, p. 262) William Prynne says that "lascivious love songs" are sung on the stage: "between each several action; both to supply that chasm or vacant interim, which the tiring-house takes up, in changing the actors' robes to fit them for some other part in the ensuing scene. . . ." In Richard Brome's comedy, *The Antipodes*, performed, according to the statement on the title page of the quarto of 1640, by Queen Henrietta's company in 1638, there is a dialogue between Barbara and Blaze in the fourth scene of the fifth act (K3-K3^v).

> *Bar.* O *Tony.*
> I did not see thee act ith' play. *Bla.* O, but
> I did though *Bab*, two Mutes. . . .
> A Mute is one that acteth speakingly,
> And yet says nothing. I did two of them.
> The Sage Man-midwife, and the Basket-maker.

Proper doubling is occasionally noted in published texts. The cast printed in the quarto of Thomas Nabbes' *Hannibal and Scipio* shows William Sherlock in the roles of Maharball and Prusias; Hugh Clark playing Nuntias and Syphax; Robert Axen, Bomilcar and Gisgon. These examples are merely indications that doubling was well known; they are never full casts, for they leave six to twenty roles unassigned.

Far more illuminating than such literary publications or manuscripts intended for patrons are the papers prepared for

use in the theaters where the purpose was aid in the performances, not exploitation of readers. Very enlightening about
the custom of doubling are the seven "Plots" which have been
enumerated and defined above. Though none of these Plots
lists a formal dramatis personae with assigned roles, all of
them give the names of actors, including sharers, hired men,
and boys. Doubling is required of most of these players, usually of the hired men but often sharers as well. In the Plot for
the revival of *The Seven Deadly Sins* II, apparently as revived
by the Lord Strange's men at the Curtain, probably in 1590,
twenty names of performers are recorded, several only nicknames or Christian names, and therefore not always certainly
identifiable, but the evidence of doubling is overwhelming.
Most of the major roles are unassigned, but three sharers are
named, two with a single role, one with a simple double.
Though Richard Burbage (then about seventeen years old) has
only two roles, Richard Cowley was assigned eight parts, John
Duke six, Robert Pallant six, and J. Holland five. The boys,
never given their full names, had only one or two roles apiece.[28]

Though the manuscript of the Plot for *The Battle of Alcazar*
is only a fragment with some pieces missing, it has the advantage of being the only Plot for which a text of the play is also
available, though the printed text is for an abridged version.
Greg thinks the Plot represents a revival of 1598 or 1599 certainly by the Admiral's men. This Plot names ten sharers
(each designated "Mr.") though two of the known sharers are
omitted, seven or eight hired men, and apparently seven boys,
though nicknames may cover some duplication, and the actor
of one female role is omitted. According to this Plot the majority of the players, even the sharers, had more than one role
to play, though for the major characters the second role, if
any, was a slight one. Edward Alleyn, Thomas Doughten,
and Thomas Towne appear not to have doubled at all. The
number of roles assigned each player is smaller than in *The*

[28] Greg, ed., *Dramatic Documents from the Elizabethan Playhouses*, I, 105-122
and II, unpaged.

Seven Deadly Sins II, but "Mr. Sam." has six parts to play, and George Somerset five.

The most intricate doubling is recorded in the prompt manuscript for Philip Massinger's *Believe as You List*, performed by the King's company in 1631. In this very full prompt book twenty-nine roles are assignable from the book keeper's notes, but the players for nineteen other roles are unrecorded in this manuscript; eighteen players of the company are assigned roles but at least eight others known to have been associated with the King's company at about this time fail to appear.[29] Eight of the assignments are to sharers in the company, nine to performers who were probably hired men. Though there are at least seven roles for apprentices in the play, none is assigned by name, though a prompter's note at line 1970 reads: "Harry: Wilson: & Boy ready for the song at ye Arras:" Although the leading sharers like Joseph Taylor, Eyllaerdt Swanston, John Lowin, Richard Robinson, and Robert Benfield have single parts, other sharers like Thomas Pollard, William Penn, and Thomas Hobbes are required to double. But the most surprising feature of the casting for *Believe as You List* is not the number of roles entrusted to individual players; *Tamar Cam I* and *The Battle of Alcazar* both require certain actors to impersonate more characters. But in Massinger's play the same character is sometimes divided between two or even three players.

Such evidence shows that doubling was basic in the casting of Elizabethan, Jacobean, and Caroline troupes, that it could be at least as intricate in the King's company in 1631 as it had been in the Admiral's in 1589, and that less doubling was required of sharers and apprentices than of hired men.

Though only the prompt manuscript of *Believe as You List* shows a single role being performed by two or three different players, it seems likely that expedients resorted to by the

[29] C. J. Sisson, ed., *Believe as You List by Philip Massinger*, Malone Society, Oxford, 1927, pp. xxxi-xxxiv. Of course several of the unnamed players probably took some of the nineteen roles not assigned in the manuscript.

dominant King's men in 1631 would also have been used by poorer and smaller troupes. As Sisson points out, roles so divided can have conveyed little individuality in the performance. It should be noted, however, that such shifting of actors would have been easier in large-cast historic plays using togas and robes than in comedies with contemporary English settings. Comedies of this sort are more usual in late Jacobean and Caroline times than they had been in Elizabethan. Moreover the comedies of Jonson, Middleton, Shirley, and Brome tend to use twenty to twenty-five characters as opposed to the forty-nine of *Believe as You List*.

After the consideration of so much scattered material bearing upon casting, it is chastening to note that the great majority of the evidence which has been found comes from the Lord Admiral's company, the King's company, and Queen Henrietta's men, while very little has been found concerning the more than a dozen other troupes playing in London during the period. Moreover, the evidence is bunched chronologically, coming mostly from plays performed 1589-1602 and 1626-1642. We can only assume that practices of unnoted companies and practices during the unrepresented periods would conform. Perhaps these assumptions are not too hazardous, since the three troupes represented are the major ones, and since the practices apparent in the King's company's prompt manuscript for *Believe as You List* in 1631 do not seem to differ much from those observed in the Plot the Lord Admiral's men had prepared for their performance of *The Battle of Alcazar* in 1598 or 1599.

All the evidence testifies to the dominant importance of the sharers who are almost always given the leading roles. But it is equally notable that very seldom in the extant lists are roles assigned to *all* the men known to have been sharers at the time of performance.

Another feature of performances made apparent in these lists is the comparative prominence of the apprentices; usually two or three of the boys have more lines than any of the hired men. In a few plays, such as *The Merchant of Venice, As You*

Like It, *All's Well that Ends Well*, and *Cymbeline*, and several of the plays of Beaumont and Fletcher, the leading role has been prepared for a boy.

Typecasting, which has been postulated by several theater historians, is exhibited to only a limited extent in these lists. Comic roles regularly go to recognized comedians. Also, there seem to be periods of the exploitation of certain actors in roles fitted to them, like the "hungry knave" to John Shank in certain Beaumont and Fletcher plays, and the young lover roles in the years 1638 to 1641 to Stephen Hammerton. But the habitual selection of new sharers to carry on a standard "line" as claimed by Baldwin for the Lord Chamberlain-King's company is not confirmed by these casts and lists. Baldwin's detailed fitting of all the leading characters in the plays of Shakespeare and of Beaumont and Fletcher involves far too much speculation, dubious dating, age approximation, and details of a player's complexion and coloring to be trusted as far as he carries it.[30]

[30] Baldwin, *The Organization and Personnel of the Shakespearean Company*, pp. 198-283.

CHAPTER IX

Conclusions

IN THE YEARS between 1590 and 2 September 1642 when the Lords and Commons issued their order that "publike Stage-Playes shall cease, and be forborne" the profession of player flourished in England as never before and seldom since.[1] Though most of the one thousand and more known professional players in England were poor men frequently without London employment, the status of the profession improved in these years and a few of the players accumulated respectable estates as shown by their wills and by occasional allusions. In 1619 Edward Alleyn founded the College of God's Gift at Dulwich. Sir Richard Baker, a contemporary, said of Alleyn's action: "This man may be an example, who having gotten his wealth by stage playing converted it to this pious

[1] . . . annual earnings of actors and actresses are adversely affected by the frequent periods of unemployment experienced by many. According to

2 3 4

use, not without a kind of reputation to the Society of Players."[2] Similarly Ralph Crane wrote in 1621 that his pen had had employment

> . . . mongst those civil, well deserving men
> That grace the stage with profit and delight.

The rise of the London players from their obsolete classification in the category of rogues and vagabonds, to which their enemies still liked to consign them, is also illustrated by the more elaborate publication of their plays in handsome volumes like the Jonson folio of 1616 and the Shakespeare folio of 1623, by their official patents as companies of players under the patronage of members of the royal family, by their livery, by the appointment of most of the sharers as Grooms of the Chamber in ordinary, by their increasingly frequent appearances in command performances at court, and by the appointment of some of them to particular court posts, such as the appointment of John Lowin to be King's Porter and by the royal patent issued in 1639 to Joseph Taylor creating him Yeoman of the Revels to His Majesty.

The organization of these professional troupes was guild-like, with the sharers, generally named in the company patent as the legally responsible members, at the top. They shared the receipts from certain parts of the theater after every performance, and they shared the fees for court performances which eventually became considerable. In the year March 1638 to January 1638/39 the court performance fees for the King's players amounted to £300. In this company several sharers—

---

data obtained by the Actors' Equity Association (which represents actors who work on the stage) and the Screen Actors Guild, between two-thirds and three-quarters of their members earned $2,500 or less a year from acting jobs in 1978, and less than 5 percent earned over $25,000 from such work. [*Occupational Outlook Handbook*, 1980-81 ed., U.S. Department of Labor Bureau of Statistics, March 1980, Bulletin 2075, p. 458.]
See also William J. Baumol and William Gordon Bowen, *Performing Arts, the Economic Dilemma: A Study of Problems Common to the Theater, Opera, Music, and Dance*, New York, 1966.

[2] Richard Baker, *A Chronicle of the Kings of England*, London, 1684, p. 423.

Burbage, Shakespeare, Heminges, Condell, Shank, Taylor, Lowin, Ostler, Underwood, Kempe, Phillips, and Pope—also at different times owned shares in the company's two theaters and thereby received a second cut of the daily receipts. This sharers' ownership of the company playhouse was not common, however. It should also be remembered that this troupe of King James and King Charles was the most prosperous one known.

The group of sharers of a troupe selected new patented members, sometimes from other companies, sometimes from the ranks of their own hired men. These new sharers had to pay an entrance fee to cover their part in the company store of costumes and play manuscripts and toward new purchases and new fees and other expenses. This payment for a share is referred to several times, but the total sum is seldom mentioned. In February 1634/35, William Bankes said that he had paid £100 to become a sharer in the company of Prince Charles (II) in the early thirties, and William Bird or Bourne says that he paid £200 to become a sharer in the King's company in about 1640. Some companies, possibly most, had an agreement to return at least part of this fee if the sharer left the company and returned all its property then in his possession. At least some companies acknowledged an obligation to pay back a portion of his entrance fee to the widow of a deceased member.

Sharers selected, or ratified the selection, of new plays. They appear also to have ratified decisions to fine or to dismiss transgressing members. Sharers took most of the principal roles in the plays for which we have casts or lists. But these lists almost never show every sharer assigned to a role.

Employed by the sharers were the hired men: stagekeepers, prompters or book holders, wardrobe keepers or tiremen, musicians, gatherers, and minor players. The number of these hired men in a company increased with increasing prosperity during the period, and it must have varied from the poorest to the richest companies, but we know that on 27 December 1624 the Master of the Revels issued a protection from arrest for twenty-one hired men of King James's company. It is clear that the majority of these men were not primarily players, but most of them could be called upon to appear on the stage in minor roles in plays with large casts. The sharers paid these dependents two to ten shillings a week in prosperous periods. In hard times these hired men took what they could get— sometimes nothing.

Boy players for the female and juvenile roles were apprenticed for varying periods to individual sharers, not to the company; they received board, room, clothing, and professional training, but no wages.

The method of training these boys is not clear. A few of them, but not many, had been in the early boy companies but apparently most of those so trained were no longer juveniles when they transferred. In 1629 Richard Gunnell and William Blagrave were licensed to "train and bring up certain boys in the quality of playing with the intent to be a supply of able actors to your Majesty's servants of Blackfriars." There is some suggestion that the Lady Elizabeth's company in its later days may have had some such function, and there is a similar suggestion for Beeston's Boys. At best these organizations could not have prepared all of the boys needed in the several London troupes of players. Most of the training must have been supervised by the individual sharer to whom the boy was apprenticed.

Within the playing company, notably in the troupe of the Lord Chamberlain-King's men, there is evidence of cordial, even affectionate, relationships, particularly among sharers and between apprentices and their masters, as shown in several wills. Of course there are also examples of discord as in the charges and countercharges at the breakup of organizations, and in the quarrel between John Shank and his fellows Benfield, Pollard, and Swanston over shares in the Globe and Blackfriars theaters.

In the play written for the London companies there are normally fewer roles for the boys than for the adults—usually four to six boys were required though it seems to have been common for some of them to double. Though it was usual for the longest and most difficult roles in the plays of the period to be written for sharers, there are a number of testimonials to the effectiveness of certain boys and in several familiar plays the longest role or the second longest was prepared for an apprentice.

It would seem logical that many of these boy players should eventually have become sharers, but the extant records do not show so many of these logical progressions as one would have expected. The clear examples are Nathan Field, Richard Perkins, John Underwood, William Ostler, Nicholas Tooley, Richard Sharpe, Thomas Holcomb, John Honeyman, John Rice, Theophilus Bird, Hugh Clark, and Nicholas Burt.

The business affairs of these London companies were complex, and they required responsible supervision. Hundreds of costumes had to be ordered and paid for; theater rents had to be paid; plays had to be commissioned, paid for, licensed, and fees paid to the Master of the Revels not only for licenses but for various privileges; court and other private performances had to be arranged and payments collected; transportation to palaces and great houses had to be provided; liveries had to be received and distributed; hired men had to be employed and paid; new properties had to be collected; rehearsals and other meetings of the company had to be scheduled; provincial tours had to be arranged and financed; playbills had to be printed and distributed. The number, complexity, and interdependence of these chores were such that they could not have been divided among six to eighteen sharers without producing chaos. Clearly the administrative affairs of a London company had to be concentrated in the hands of one or two men.

The extant records make it clear that most—probably all—troupes had such an administrator. We should call him an actor-manager since for all but two of these known functionaries (Richard Heton and William Davenant) we have records of their activities as players, but the term actor-manager seems not to have been used for them before 1642. Various designations are found in different records: steward, chief, warden, governor, leader, master.

The most clearly defined of these administrators is John Heminges acting for the Lord Chamberlain-King's company, and succeeded after 1630 by Joseph Taylor and John Lowin; Christopher Beeston, acting for first Queen Anne's company, then for the Lady Elizabeth's, then for Queen Henrietta's, and finally for the King and Queen's Young company or Beeston's Boys; Edward Alleyn for the Admiral's and the Palsgrave's.

Other managers not so fully identified are Thomas Greene acting before Beeston for Queen Anne's men; William Rowley for Prince Charles's (I) men; Richard Gunnell for the Palsgrave's men and later for the Salisbury Court players; William Davenant for a short period for Beeston's Boys, preceded and followed by William Beeston; Ellis Worth and the comedian Andrew Cane for Prince Charles's (II) company at the Salisbury Court and the Red Bull theaters in the thirties; William Cartwright, Senior, in succession to Richard Gunnell at the Fortune theater; and finally Richard Heton for Queen Henrietta's men during their last years.

Though the greatest profit and prestige for all players was to be found in London, circumstances forced every company to go on the road at various times. The commonest cause for such travels was the plague which led to closing orders for the theaters at least fourteen times during the years 1590-1642. Such restraints varied in length according to the death rate, from a few weeks to eighteen months. The playhouses were also closed for periods of mourning for Queen Elizabeth, Queen Anne, and King James, and for varying periods during Lent. Sometimes prohibitions resulted from the exploitation by the players of censorable material, and at other times scanty London audiences prompted travel.

Of course there were scores of provincial troupes on the road at all times; the general appetite for play performances during these years seems insatiable. Such provincial companies provided competition for the touring London troupes not because they played in the same town at the same time but because a very recent visit from provincials made the mayor and council reluctant to grant playing permission to the Londoners.

When the sharers of a London company decided that they must travel, they had to select a reduced repertory and a reduced number of players. Though there are many hundreds of town records of players' visits, disappointingly few of them record the number of players travelling and only one the exact number of plays they carried. From 1590 to 1607, no numbers are mentioned in the reported town records. Between 1607 and 1637 nine accounts give the number of players in the visiting troupe as from nine to twenty.

As to repertories, one account says that four plays were presented by the Lord Derby's men at Londesborough in 1612; another that the King's company performed five plays before the Earl of Cumberland in 1619/20. But the only account known which specifies exactly how many play books were being carried by a touring company is the statement of Richard Kendall at Oxford in 1634. He says that his company, the King's Revels of Salisbury Court theater, was carrying fourteen plays.

When the personnel and the repertory had been selected presumably the gear (costumes and properties) had to be collected, transportation arrangements made, and an itinerary determined. Unfortunately I have no evidence at all about these steps except for a few stray references to horses, wagons, and hampers.

Once on the road and in a selected locality, the leaders of the troupe had to call on local officials to identify themselves and to request permission to perform. The response to their request varied widely from town to town and from year to year: sometimes permission was denied because of hostility; sometimes it was refused for fear of epidemics; sometimes because of apprehension of local disorders which now and then accompanied performances, especially at night. When permission to perform their plays was refused the players were usually given a gratuity out of respect for their royal or noble patron.

If their reception was cordial the players hoped to begin their visit with a performance called "the Mayor's play" before the council and their guests in a civic building. But several communities, though allowing public performances, forbade the use of the town hall. For other performances a convenient place had to be secured. The preferred auditorium seems to have been an inn like the Checkers Inn at Canterbury, or the White Horse or the Red Lion at Norwich, or the King's Arms at Oxford, but other provincial playing places are mentioned, such as common halls, moot halls, schoolhouses, even churches, and at least one provincial playhouse.

When .the London companies cast their plays the assignments were normally restricted to those sharers, hired men, and apprentices belonging to the troupe at the time. Such cramping restrictions in casting were alleviated by the fact that many plays (perhaps most of those prepared for the major companies) were written with a particular organization and its personnel in mind. Such anticipation always, during the time of their contract, characterized the work of attached dramatists or poets-in-ordinary, like Heywood, Fletcher, Massinger, Shakespeare, Shirley, William Rowley, and Richard Brome. Even for many unattached playwrights such anticipation was common. *Henslowe's Diary* and his correspondence are replete with records of payments made to dramatists before a play was begun or during the course of its composition.

The sources of our knowledge of casting are very few compared with the large number of plays performed by the London companies during the period. They are seven extant Plots or production synopses of action, a few prompt books, three collections: the Jonson folio of 1616, the Shakespeare folio of 1623, and the Beaumont and Fletcher folio of 1679. In addition there are a few formal manuscripts with incomplete casts and sixteen or seventeen quartos with printed casts, never complete assignments of parts, and all of them after 1618, most of them from 1629 to 1632.

The collective evidence of these casts, lists, and notes make it clear that major roles were generally assigned to sharers; less important parts were given to hired men. The plays of the period in general, cast or uncast, make it clear that boys would have been more conspicuous on the stage than the hired men. In a few plays the longest role was a boy's, but though these roles are conspicuous—Portia, Rosalind, Helena, Imogen, and perhaps a score of others—they are found in a small minority of the 600 or 700 play texts surviving from the period.

Typecasting, though apparent in a number of instances, does not seem to have been the dominant practice among the London companies of the period. Leading comic roles do appear to have gone regularly to the known comedian among the sharers—Kempe, Armin, Shank, Greene, Robbins, Rowley, Cane, Reade. A few other specialities can be observed for limited periods, as the romantic juvenile for Stephen Hammerton in plays of the King's men in the last four or five years before the Civil Wars. Perhaps a few other roles were written for a specific cadaverous player or a notoriously bulky sharer or an unusually talented singing boy, but the regular preparation by attached dramatists of type roles for type actors is not suggested by the available evidence.

One feature of casting among the dramatic companies of the time does appear to have been universal—doubling. Of course this practice had been common among the players for more than a century, as Bevington's *"Mankind" to Marlowe* shows, and it is not yet completely extinct. But the lists, casts, prompt books, and Plots extant for the period 1590-1642 show that all the companies represented must have taken doubling for granted. Not only do the prompt books and Plots show most players assuming more than one role, but several actors were required to represent four or five or even eight different characters. One prompt book shows instances of one role divided among two or three players. Individualization among minor characters, especially in the large-cast historical plays, cannot have been expected.

The profession of player in these years, though too glamorous to please the moralists and the Puritan preachers, was strenuous and uncertain. It was really profitable for only a few, and most of those few were sharers in the Lord Chamberlain-King's company.

APPENDIX

Casts and Lists of Players

THE CASTS set out for reference in this appendix are those found in printed quartos and formal manuscripts; they are the most full, precise, and authentic casts that have come down to us. Here they are organized according to the producing company: Prince Charles's (I), one; King's, ten; Queen Henrietta's, six; Prince Charles's (II), one; King's Revels, two.

PRINCE CHARLES'S (I) COMPANY

The first cast to be printed in a quarto, that for *The Inner Temple Masque, Or Masque of Heroes*, 1619, is, of course, an abnormal piece for professional players since, as a masque, it required far fewer spoken lines than plays and fewer characters. As the title shows, the masque was put on by the lawyers of the Inner Temple; the dancers, always most conspicuous in a masque, were members of the Inner Temple, and the Templars were the producers. The professional players hired to speak Middleton's lines were:

The Parts	*The Speakers*
D. Almanacke.	Ios. Taylor.
Plumporridge.	W. Rowley.
A Fasting-day.	I. Newton.
New-yeere.	H. Atwell.
Time.	W. Carpenter.
Harmonie	A Boy.

The first four players were sharers in the acting troupe of Prince Charles; Joseph Taylor, the leading performer with the longest role in the masque, was later to become a star performer in the King's company. William Rowley, the dramatist, is assigned his usual part of the fat clown. The only hired man listed is William Carpenter who, as *Time*, had only twelve lines to speak. Perhaps the part was too insignificant for a sharer; or possibly Carpenter was especially good in the role of old men, as Ben Jonson said Salmon Pavy was. Very little is known about Carpenter as an actor but apparently later, before the death of King James, he became a sharer in the company. The boy who played *Harmonie* had no speaking lines, but he sang three important songs. Presumably he was an apprentice in Prince Charles's troupe, since he is listed with the others of the company.

The King's Company

The Duchess of Malfi

The next cast to be printed was that for the 1623 quarto of John Webster's *Duchess of Malfi* as acted by the King's company in 1613 or 1614 with certain cast changes indicated for a revival after 1619. Webster himself must have had something to do with the publication of the play since he signed the dedication, and since the quarto prints commendatory verses by Thomas Middleton, William Rowley, and John Ford; such verses were ordinarily solicited by the author himself. One would assume, therefore, that Webster also recorded the cast, or at least approved of it.

The Actors Names.

Bosola, *I. Lowin.*

Ferdinand, 1 *R. Burbidge,*
2 *I. Taylor.*

Cardinall, 1 *H. Cundaile.*
2 *R. Robinson.*

Antonio, 1 *W. Ostler.*
2 *R. Benfield.*

Delio, *I. Vnderwood.*

Forobosco, *N. Towley.*

Malateste

The Marquesse of Pescara,
I. Rice.

Siluio, *T. Pollard*

The seuerall mad-men N. Towley,
I. Vnderwood, &c.

The Dutchesse, *R. Sharpe.*

The Cardinals Mis. *I. Tomson.*

The Doctor, ⎫
Cariola, ⎬ *R. Pallant*
Court Officers. ⎭

Three Young Children.

Two Pilgrims

Though this cast is gratifyingly full, there are certain difficulties about it. The numbers before the actors of the roles Ferdinand, the Cardinal, and Antonio seem to mean that Burbage, Condell, and Ostler created the roles and Taylor, Robinson, and Benfield replaced them in a revival. Since Ostler died late in 1614 and Richard Burbage early in 1619, the opening performance must have taken place before the end of 1614 and the revival between 1619 and the publication date of 1623. But it is difficult to believe that the original performers of all the other roles were still playing them between 1619 and 1623 after an interval of five or more years, especially the three boys Richard Sharpe, John Thompson, and Robert Pallant. Since John Thompson played a female role in *The Swisser* in 1631 it seems unlikely that he could have played the Cardinal's mistress seventeen years before. Furthermore, the bracket enclosing the roles of the Doctor, Cariola, and Court Officers is certainly wrong; Robert Pallant could not have played all six roles. The officers and the Doctor are adult roles and Cariola a boy's role; moreover Cariola and the four officers, all with speeches, appear in the same scene, III, 2. One can only guess that the bracket is a printer's error, that Robert Pallant played only Cariola, and that the roles of the Doctor and the four officers are unassigned. It also seems likely that the cast printed in the 1623 quarto is the cast for the revival, and only Burbage, Condell, and Ostler are singled out for their memorable creation of the roles in the first performance.

If this is correct, the cast for the revival was made up of six sharers, one hired man, Thomas Pollard, and four boys. The unassigned roles of the Doctor, the four officers, and Malateste were presumably also taken by hired men.

As usual, a large number of roles are unassigned or not even mentioned. Besides those named but unassigned, the production required servants, guards, executioners, attendants, ladies-in-waiting, an Old Woman, and Antonio's son. Such omissions are usual in the extant casts. These roles would have required several hired men and boys, and the parts would pretty surely have been doubled or even tripled.

The Roman Actor

Massinger's *The Roman Actor* was licensed for performance by the King's company on 11 October 1626 and published in 1629 in an elaborate quarto with a dedication, six sets of commendatory verses (one by the leading player, Joseph Taylor), and a cast.

The persons presented.	The principall Actors.
Domitianus Caesar	Iohn Lowin.
Paris the Tragædian.	Ioseph Taylor.
Parthenius a free-man of *Caesars*.	Richard Sharpe.
Ælius, Lamia, and *Stephanos*.	Thomas Pollard.
Iunius Rusticus.	Robert Benfield.
Aretinus Clemens, Caesars spie.	Eyllardt Swanstone.
Æsopus a Player.	Richard Robinson.

Philagus a rich Miser.	Anthony Smith.
Palphurius Sura, a Senator.	William Pattricke.
Latinus a Player.	Cvrtise Grevill.
3. Tribunes.	
2. Lictors.	George Vernon.
	Iames Horne
Domitia the wife of *Ælius Lamia*.	Iohn Tompson.
Domitilla cosin germane to *Cæsar*.	Iohn Hvnnieman.
Iulia Titus Daughter.	William Trigge.
Cænis, Vespatians Concubine.	Alexander Govgh.

To begin with, the error in lineation must be noted; Vernon and Horne, neither of whom was a boy in 1626, have slipped down among the creators of the female characters. Obviously they should be opposite the Lictors and Tribunes. It could well be that these two hired men handled all the Lictors and Tribunes needed in the play, for the Lictors appear in Act I only and the Tribunes in Act V only. The first Tribune has 90 to 100 lines, but the second only 4 or 5 lines in two scenes; the third Tribune had only 3 lines in one scene; his lines could have been handled by a stagekeeper, or even cut.

The division of the roles in *The Roman Actor* among the different classes of players is similar to that of the other plays of the King's men with casts: eight sharers, four hired men, and four boys. The roles assigned to these hired men, William Patrick, Curtis Greville, George Vernon, and James Horne, are not all negligible. The first Tribune, presumably played by George Vernon, though it could have been James Horne, has nearly 100 lines, and Greville's Latinus about 60.

The Deserving Favorite

The 1629 quarto of *The Deserving Favorite*, written by the courtier-huntsman and amateur dramatist, Lodowick Carlell, is said on the title page to have been acted first before the King, by the King's men, and later by them at Blackfriars.

This is a reversal of the usual order. The date of performance is uncertain; one can be sure only that the piece was performed not later than 1629, and probably not before 1625 when Smith was still a member of another acting company. The cast given is:

THE NAMES OF THE ACTORS.

M^r. Benfield, *the King*.
M^r. Taylor, *the Duke*.
M^r. Lewin, *Iacomo*.
M^r. Sharpe, *Lysander*.

M^r. Swanstone, *the Count Vtrante*.

M^r. Robinson, *Count Orsinio, and Hermite*.

M^r. Smith, *Gerard*.

Women.
Iohn Honiman, *Clarinda*.
Iohn Tomson, *Cleonarda*.
Edward Horton, *Mariana*.
Iaspero, Bernardo, Seruants, Huntsmen, &c.

This small cast of six or seven sharers (all properly designated as M^r. if Smith was already a sharer) and three boys is not enough to produce the play. Carlell has omitted from his cast three named servants, a messenger, two unnamed but numbered servants, an "Executioner" and "Attendants." None of these characters has any significant number of lines and all are of inferior rank, perhaps therefore not worthy of note by the aristocratic Carlell. Probably three or four hired men could have handled them all, but there is no evidence.

The Lovers' Melancholy

The next recorded cast was printed in the 1629 quarto of Ford's tragedy *The Lovers' Melancholy*, which had been licensed for performance by King Charles's company in November 1628. Though the front matter gives a list of players longer than most, there is no assignment of roles.

The names of such as acted.

Iohn Lowin.	Richard Sharpe.
Ioseph Taylor.	Thomas Pollard.
Robert Benfield.	William Penn.
Iohn Shanck.	Cvrteise Grivill.
Eylyardt Swanston.	George Vernon.
Anthony Smith.	Richard Baxter.

Iohn Tomson.
Iohn Honyman.
Iames Horne.
William Trigg.
Alexander Govgh.

This list has some puzzling aspects: it is longer than most; it names seventeen players, though there are only sixteen named roles in the play; in the usual separation of men and boys, it names five players for the four female roles, including the waiting maid; James Horne was not a boy but a hired man who had received livery for King James's funeral procession four years before and had taken an adult role in *The Roman Actor* two years before. Eight or nine of the adult players were sharers in the King's company: Lowin, Taylor, Benfield, Shank, Swanston, Pollard, Penn, and Sharpe; the status of Anthony Smith in the company at this time is not clear. The hired men listed are Greville, Vernon, Baxter, Horne, and possibly Smith. There are four boys, John Thompson, John Honeyman, William Trigg (who had been apprenticed to John Heminges only the year before), and Alexander Gough.

The number of hired men in this cast is high; it suggests that in 1628 at least four and possibly five of the wage-earning assistants were competent actors, though none attained later prominence.

The Picture

Philip Massinger's tragicomedy, *The Picture*, was licensed for performance by the King's company in June 1629 and published in quarto with a cast and a set of commendatory verses by Thomas Jay in 1630. Jay commends Massinger's modesty in admitting his inferiority to Jonson and Beaumont; it is suggestive of contemporary reputations that Jay does not mention the company's most devoted dramatist, William Shakespeare. The cast reads:

Dramatis personæ.	The Actors names.
Ladislaus King of Hungarie.	*Robert Benfield.*
Eubulus an old Counsaylor.	*Iohn Lewin.*
Ferdinand Generall of the army.	*Richard Sharpe.*
Mathias a knight of *Bohemia.*	*Ioseph Taylor.*
Vbaldo, 2. wild courtiers.	*Thomas Pollard.*
Ricardo,	*Eylardt Swanstone.*
Hilario seruant to *Sophia.*	*Iohn Shanucke.*
Iulio Baptista a great scholler.	*William Pen.*
Honoria the Queene.	*John Tomson.*
Acanthe a maid of honor.	*Alexander Goffe.*
Sophia wife to *Mathias.*	*Iohn Hunnieman.*
Corisca, Sophias woman.	*William Trigge.*

6. Masquers
6. seruants to the Queene
Attendants

According to this list the performance in 1629 used seven sharers, Benfield, Lowin, Sharpe, Taylor, Pollard, Swanston, and Shank; probably one hired man, William Penn; and four apprentices, John Thompson, Alexander Gough, John Honeyman, and William Trigg. But the unassigned roles indicate that at least six more, even assuming extensive doubling, were required. Two of the masquers were boys, one of whom sang and one played the lute. Several of the servants have a few lines to speak, and there is a Poet who is not mentioned at all in the dramatis personae. More than six additional performers must have been needed. Two of them had to be boys with some musical ability. More hired men than William Penn were surely needed even if several of the roles like the messenger and certain of the attendants and servants to the Queen were doubled.

The Wild Goose Chase

The most descriptive of the printed casts for plays of the King's company is that for Fletcher's comedy *The Wild Goose Chase*. The records show that this play was popular[1] and partly for this reason it was not printed for about thirty years after first production. The circumstances of printing throw light on the cast. When Humphry Moseley published the first Beaumont and Fletcher folio in 1647, he claimed to print all the Beaumont and Fletcher plays that had not been published before, but he admitted that there was one play, which in spite of diligent search, he could not find, *The Wild Goose Chase*. Five years later he published an elaborate folio edition of this single play in a size convenient for insertion into the 1647 collection. The title page says that the play was being printed for the "private Benefit" of John Lowin and Joseph Taylor "By a Person of Honour," and Lowin and Taylor wrote an elegiac dedication for the book.

The comedy was probably first produced in 1621 since there is a record of a court performance in the Christmas season of that year. But the cast printed in the 1652 edition is impossible for 1621; Swanston and Penn had not yet joined the company in that year, and Stephen Hammerton had not yet been apprenticed as a boy actor.[2]

The cast is probably that for a revival in the winter of 1632. But the honorific "Mr." was conventionally used then for sharers, and certainly the boy actor of Oriana was not a sharer at that time. A little analysis shows that "A Person of Honour" was using the term for all the players of the company

[1] See G. E. Bentley, *The Jacobean and Caroline Stage*, 7 vols., Oxford, 1941-1968, III, 425-30.
[2] Ibid., and G. E. Bentley, "The Salisbury Court Theatre and Its Boy Players," *Huntington Library Quarterly* 40 (1977), 139-44.

who had become sharers before the closing of the theaters; Hammerton and Honeyman had, and Trigg and Gough had not.

DRAMMATIS PERSONÆ

DE-GARD, A Noble stayd Gentleman that being newly lighted from his Travells, assists his sister *Oriana* in her chase of *Mirabell* the *Wild-Goose*.

Acted by Mr. *Robert Benfield.*

LA-CASTRE, the Indulgent Father to *Mirabell*.

Acted by Mr. *Richard Robinson.*

MIRABELL, the *Wild-Goose*, a Travayl'd Monsieur, and great defyer of all Ladies in the way of Marriage, otherwise their much loose servant, at last caught by the despis'd *Oriana*.

Incomparably Acted by Mr. *Joseph Taylor.*

PINAC, his fellow Traveller, of a lively spirit, and servant to the no lesse sprightly *Lillia-Bianca*.

Admirably well Acted by Mr. *Thomas Pollard.*

BELLEUR, Companion to both, of a stout blunt humor, in love with *Rosalura*.

Most naturally Acted by Mr. *John Lowin.*

NANTOLET, Father to *Rosalura* and *Lillia-Bianca*.

Acted by Mr. *William Penn.*

LUGIER, the rough and confident Tutor to the Ladies, and chiefe Engine to intrap the *Wild-Goose*.

Acted by Mr. *Hilliard Swanston.*

ORIANA, the faire betroth'd of *Mirabell*, and wittie follower of the *Chase*.

Acted by Mr. *Steph. Hammerton.*

ROSALURA   the Aërie Daugh-
LILLIA-BIANCA ters of *Nantolet*.

William Trigg.
Sander Gough.

PETELLA, their waiting-woman. Their Servant Mr. *Shanck*.

MARIANA, an English Courtezan.

A Young FACTOR, by Mr. *John Hony-man*.

PAGE.
SERVANTS.
SINGING-BOY.
TWO MERCHANTS.
PRIEST.
FOURE WOMEN.

With the interpretation that the cast dates from 1632 but that the use of "Mr." dates from after 1642, it becomes clear that the profitable revival at Blackfriars in the winter of 1632[3] was performed by twelve named players, eight of whom were sharers at that time, Benfield, Robinson, Taylor, Pollard, Lowin, Penn, Swanston, and Shank. One of the named actors, John Honeyman, was then still in the status of hired man, though he later became a sharer. Three of the players were apprentices, Hammerton, Trigg, and Gough.

Quite a number of additional players would have been needed for the twelve roles not assigned in the printed cast; seven of these parts needed boy actors, Mariana, the Singing Boy, the Four Women, and the Page. Actually the play has two apprentices' roles not listed at all in the dramatis personae, the Post Boy in I, i, and the boy who introduces Mariana in III, i. Without doubling, the juvenile and female roles would have required twelve boy actors; even with doubling it would appear that seven or eight must have been required. Possibly at this time the King's company could draw extra boys from the King's Revels company which had been organized in 1629 to train boy actors for the use of the King's company.[4] The servants, the two merchants, and the Priest would presumably have been assigned to hired men.

The most curious feature of the printed cast is the assignment of the role of Petella, the waiting woman, to John Shank, the leading comedian of the company who had been an actor for at least twenty-two years and had had a son born in 1610. It is even more curious that this well-known patented member

[3] Bentley, *The Jacobean and Caroline Stage*, VI, 22-23.
[4] See *Huntington Library Quarterly* 40 (1977), 137-39.

of the King's company should be assigned a role for which there are no lines in the printed text. Presumably Shank gagged lines, as comedians are known to have done. But there are no scenes that seem to give much scope for Petella, and Shank's assignment here is curious.

CASTS IN MANUSCRIPT: KING'S MEN'S

Among the plays of the repertory of the King's company never published in the seventeenth century but still extant in manuscript, there are four that have casts or extensive prompter's notes from which casts can be assembled. They are Fletcher and Massinger's *Sir John van Olden Barnavelt* performed by the company in August 1619; Clavell's *The Soddered Citizen*, probably produced about 1629 or 1630; Arthur Wilson's *The Swisser*, acted at Blackfriars in 1631; and Philip Massinger's *Believe as You List* also performed in 1631.

The character of these manuscripts leaves no doubt that the casts are authentic.

Sir John van Olden Barnavelt

The earliest extant prompt manuscript of the King's company is Fletcher and Massinger's *Sir John van Olden Barnavelt*, never printed until the late nineteenth century but preserved in British Museum MS. Add. 18653. Though the play was written by prominent dramatists attached to the most prominent company, they had the temerity to deal with contemporary religious and political affairs in Holland, and some aspects of this treatment the Master of the Revels, then Sir George Buc, found objectionable. Though the censored material was deleted from the manuscript and the play was performed, publishers may have been wary of it. The manuscript was written out by Ralph Crane, who several times worked for the King's men; there are many prompter's notes.

The play can be securely dated in August 1619, so that it

is earlier than all but one of the printed casts, but by only a few years.[5] As is usual in prompt copies, this manuscript shows the bookholder's concern with minor players and doubled roles, properties, entrances and exits, not with the major characters who would have been sharers. The largest roles in the play are those of Barnavelt, the Prince of Orange, Leidenberch, Vandort, Bredero, and Modesbargen, each of whom has more than 100 lines, but none of the performers of these roles are indicated by the prompter. For the other fifteen or so roles, ten players are named, though generally by abbreviations not always easily expanded. Two of the ten are sharers, Richard Robinson, possibly John Rice and Robert Goffe, and as usual all three of the sharers are given honorific, "M^r." None of these sharers is assigned a major role and at first glance their mention is puzzling. But a little analysis makes their appearance somewhat less abnormal. "Mr Gough" appears only once, and then apparently as an attendant on Leidenberg, surely too small a role for the complete assignment for a sharer. But his name has been crossed out, so that his function in the play, if any, is unknown. "Mr Rob." and "Mr Rice" appear several times as captains, but since the captains are never named, the prompter was presumably trying to keep them straight. Robinson also doubled as an ambassador, and Rice as a servant.

A somewhat unusual feature of this prompt manuscript is the naming of three of the apprentices: Thomas Holcomb, who played the Provost's wife; "G. Lowen," who played Barnavelt's daughter and who is known from this record only; and "Nick," probably Nicholas Underhill,[6] who was assigned the role of Barnavelt's wife. Why the prompter, contrary to the normal practice, needed to be reminded about all the boys in named roles, I do not know.

The other four players identified in these prompt notes are

---

[5] See Bentley, *The Jacobean and Caroline Stage*, III, 415-17.
[6] See ibid., II, 516.

somewhat uncertain because of the use of abbreviations, nick-names, and initials. "Mr Bir" who brings in a chair may have been George Birch; "migh," "mighel" who played a captain, a soldier, and a huntsman cannot be identified; "T.p.," "Tho. po." who played Holderus and a servant was evidently Thomas Pollard; "R.T." who played a messenger, an officer, a servant, and a huntsman cannot be identified.

Obviously the prompt manuscript of *Sir John van Olden Barnavelt* is much less helpful in understanding casting customs than that of *Believe as You List.*

In the manuscript there is no dramatis personae and no cast. Those given here were compiled by Dr. Wilhelmina Frijlinck for her edition of the play (Amsterdam, 1922), page clx.

The Soddered Citizen

About the same time as they put on Massinger's *Picture* the King's men produced John Clavell's piece *The Soddered Citizen.* Until 1936 this play was known only from Humphry Moseley's two entries in the Stationers Register in 1653 and 1660. Both entries were misleading because both gave the wrong author and one was two different plays entered as title and subtitle. The manuscript turned up nearly three hundred years later and was edited by John Henry Pyle Pafford for the Malone Society.

Clavell was an amateur, a gentleman who had turned highway robber, was captured, convicted, and pardoned by the King. Like a good many modern criminals he exploited his notoriety and published in 1628 a long poem entitled *A Recantation of an ill led life, Or a discouerie of the High-way Law.* The King's men also exploited his notoriety by producing his poor play with a prologue alluding to the author's highway career. The comedy, probably produced in 1629 or 1630[7] carries in the manuscript a cast of King's men.

[7] Ibid., III, 161-65.

THE PERSONS	(AND)	ACTOURS
S^r. Wittworth	A younge gent' of qualitie	Richard Sharpe & Prologue & Epilogue
Makewell	A Doc: of Phisicke	Robert Benfield
Vndermyne	A wealthy Cittizen	John Lowen
Miniona	his Daughter	John Thompson
Modestina	his Orphant	Will: Trigge
Sly	his Servant	John Honyman
Mountayne	A Goldsmith	Curtoys Grivell
Brainsicke	A deboyst young gent' & a Prisoner	Tho: Pollard
ffewtricks	his Boye	Allex: Goffe
Clutch	his Keeper	Anthony Smith
Shackle	his other Keeper	Nich: Vnderhill
Hodge	A countrey fellowe	John Shanke
Birdlyme	A Scrivener	Brain: disguis'd
Brayde	A Haberd: of small ware	Shac: disguis'd
Querpo	A decayde gent'	Clut: disguis'd
A Mayde	Ser: to Miniona	John: Shanks Boy
A Maide	Ser: to Modestina	Mute &c.
	3. Creditors	
	2. Commissioners	
	1. Sollicitor	
	Servants	
	and Mutes	

The thirteen players listed by Clavell are in proportions similar to those in several other casts: six sharers, Sharpe, Benfield, Lowin, Pollard, Smith, and Shank; three hired men, Greville, Honeyman, and Underhill; and four apprentices, Thompson, Trigg, Gough, and the unnamed apprentice of John Shank. At least seven other roles are cited plus an unspecified number of servants and Mutes. In II, 6 there are six servants, all of whom speak; in IV, 2 there are three servants, as well as seven masquers whom Clavell presumably designated as

"Mutes." A certain amount of doubling would have been possible, but in IV, 2 the three servants and the seven masquers are all on stage at the same time. Probably this play would have required the use of a few of the nonacting personnel as well as two or three unnamed hired men.

It is interesting that Clavell wanted to name the player who delivered the prologue and the epilogue. In extant casts this identification is rare, though sometimes the name of the speaker is printed with the text of the prologue or epilogue; more often the character in the play who delivered the epilogue can be deduced from what he says of himself and the play.

The Swisser

Another amateur play acted by the King's men about this time was Arthur Wilson's, *The Swisser*.[8] The piece was never printed in its own time, though listed more than once in the Stationers Register. It remained in manuscript in the British Museum (MS. Add. 36759) until Professor Albert Feuillerat edited it in 1904.

The title page of the manuscript, in the author's hand, reads

THE SWISSER
ACTED
AT THE BLACKFRIARS

1631

The following page of the manuscript lists the cast of King's men:

THE SCÆNE
Lombardie

PERSONS	ACTORS
THE KING OF THE LOMBARDS	*Sharpe.*
ARIOLDUS, a nobleman retir'd	*Taylor.*

[8] Ibid., v, 1267-74.

ANDRUCHO, A Swisser otherwise Count ARIBERT banisht	*Lowin.*
TIMENTES, A fearefull Generall	*Pollard.*
ANTHARIS } Two old noble men CLEPHIS } Mortall Enemies	*{ Benfield { Penn.*
ALCIDONUS, Sonne to ANTHARIS	*Swanston.*
ASPRANDUS } Two Gentlemen ISEAS }	*{ Smith. { Greuill.*
PANOPIA The KINGS sister	*Tomson.*
EURINIA, A Captiue	*Goffe.*
SELINA, Daughter to CLEPHIS	*Trigg.*

1 Gentleman.   4 Souldiers.

1 Gentlewoman.   2 Seruants.

Guard.

As one might have expected from its date—a year or two after *The Soddered Citizen*—this cast is quite similar to that for Clavell's play. The Wilson piece used eight sharers, Sharpe, Taylor, Lowin, Pollard, Benfield, Penn, Swanston, and Anthony Smith; one hired man, Greville; and three apprentices, John Thompson, Alexander Gough, and William Trigg, compared to Clavell's six sharers, three hired men, and four boys. Like *The Soddered Citizen, The Swisser* also listed about ten unnamed characters, but most of them appear in only one scene. Again like Clavell's play *The Swisser* also has a song by an unlisted boy. Since the singing boy also appears in Fletcher's *The Wild Goose Chase* revived about the time the others were first produced, it would seem that Blackfriars had a popular boy singer at this time.

Believe as You List

Much more complete casting and more complex doubling is found in Philip Massinger's holograph manuscript with prompter's corrections and additions for his King's men's play *Believe as You List*, licensed for performance by the Master of

the Revels on 7 May 1631. This prompt copy was meticu-
lously edited for the Malone Society by Charles J. Sisson in
1927.

This important document is so extensively annotated that
the majority of the performers in the production can be identified. The dramatis personae is unusually large for a major
company in the 1630s. At least forty-four characters are indicated even allowing for only one Roman soldier; players can
be assigned for twenty-nine of these roles, thus giving the
largest number of cast assignments we have, even though about
nineteen roles are unassigned. More hired men than usual are
named, though, as in most prompt manuscripts, the names of
fewer principal actors, since an experienced prompter would
not need to remind himself of their identity. Indeed, the names
of six of the seven sharers who can be cast are not in any stage
direction of the prompter. They come from a list of needed
properties jotted down after the epilogue, e.g., "Act: 5: A
Letter for Mr Benfield," "2 letters for Mr Lowen." Examination of the events in the acts cited shows what roles were
taken by Robert Benfield, John Lowin, Eyllaerdt Swanston,
Thomas Pollard, Joseph Taylor, and Richard Robinson.

Professor Sisson, who prepared the excellent edition of the
play, worked out most of the cast from the author's manuscript and the prompter's notes. At the end of his introduction
Sisson printed the following deduced cast, eighteen names if
we count "Boy."

LIST OF CHARACTERS AND CAST
in order of appearance.

ANTIOCHUS king of Lower Asia.   Joseph Taylor.
   a Stoic Philosopher

CHRYSALUS ⎫
SYRUS   ⎬ bondmen of   Elyard Swanston.
GETA   ⎭ Antiochus.

BERECINTHIUS, a Flamen of Cy-   Thomas Pollard.
   bele.

first Merchant ⎫
second Merchant ⎬ former subjects
third Merchant ⎭ of Antiochus.

TITUS FLAMINIUS, Roman Envoy
to Carthage.

CALISTUS ⎫ Freemen of
DEMETRIUS ⎭ Flaminius.

John Honyman.
William Penn.
Curtis Greville.
John Lowin.

⎧ (1)Richard Baxter.
⎪ (2)Thomas Hobbes.
⎨ (1)William Pattrick.
⎪ (2)Francis Balls.
⎩ (3)'Rowland' (Rowland
Dowle?)

AMILCAR, Prince of Carthage.
HANNO
ASDRUBAL   Senators of Carthage.
CARTHALO
Carthaginian Officers

⎧ "Rowland"
⎨ William Mago
⎩ "Nick" (Nicholas Burt?)

LENTULUS, Roman Envoy to Carthage in place of Flaminius.

Richard Robinson

TITUS, a spy in the service of
Flaminius.

Richard Baxter

PRUSIAS, King of Bithynia.
The Queen of Bithynia.
PHILOXENUS, chief counsellor to
Prusias.
Attendants on Prusias.

⎧ 'Rowland'
⎨ William Mago
⎪ Francis Balls
⎩ 'Nick'

a Lady in attendance on the Queen.
Bithynian Guard
A. METELLUS, Roman Proconsul
in Asia.
SEMPRONIUS, a Roman Centurion
under Metellus.
a Jailor at Callipolis.

William Penn

265

[a Lute Player] within	Henry Wilson
[a Singer]	'Boy'
a Courtesan from Corinth.	
a Jailor's assistant.	'Rowland'
MARCELLUS, Roman Proconsul in Sicily.	Robert Benfield
Attendants upon Marcellus.	{ 'Rowland' Francis Balls 'Nick' Richard Baxter
CORNELIA, wife to Marcellus	
a Moorish Woman, servant to Cornelia.	
a Roman Captain under Marcellus.	William Pattrick
Roman Soldiers.	

The roles which are assigned to no players are ones to which the prompter gives no clue, though several of them are more than bit parts. Amilcar, Prusias, A. Metellus, Sempronius, the Courtesan, and Cornelia each have more than fifty lines to speak.

In addition to the players required for the eighteen or nineteen unassigned roles, two more hired men, probably not actors, are noted as being required for an off-stage function. A stage direction entered by the prompter in IV, 1 reads "*Gascoine: & Hubert below: ready to open the Trap doore for Mr Taylor.*" William Gascoigne was one of the twenty-one men "all imployed by the Kinges Maiesties servants in their quallity of playinge as Musitions and other necessary attendants" in the list of the Master of the Revels dated seven years before, 27 December 1624. Hubert is known only from this prompter's note.

Obviously *Believe as You List* has more characters than the other plays with casts of the King's company during these years. Moreover, the prompter's attention to minor roles gives us a good deal more information about casting plays than the other lists afford.

The seven sharers named here and there by the prompter, Joseph Taylor, Eyllaerdt Swanston, William Penn, Thomas Pollard, John Lowin, Richard Robinson, and Robert Benfield comprise over half of the known patented members in 1631. It seems not unlikely that the roles of Amilcar, A. Metellus, Sempronius, and Prusias were taken by sharers, though there could well have been doubling, as there certainly was among the hired men.

No apprentices are named for the five female roles or for the boy who sang to the accompaniment of Henry Wilson's lute in IV, 2. It is possible that the singer was a musician rather than a boy actor. Doubling among the boys would have been easy, since the Queen of Bithynia and her lady appear only in the third act, the Courtesan only in the fourth act, and Cornelia and her woman only in Act V.

The ten hired men named in this prompt manuscript comprise the largest number identifiable for any play of the period. Evidently not all of them were players. Henry Wilson was a musician attached to the company, and the boy singer may have been one too. The only task assigned to Gascoigne and Hubert was the opening of the trapdoor, a feat which would surely have been assigned to stagekeepers. The other hired men, John Honeyman (recently a boy actor but not yet a sharer), Thomas Hobbes, (possibly a sharer), Curtis Greville, Richard Baxter, William Patrick, Francis Balls, Rowland Dowle [?], William Mago, Nicholas Burt [?] are all known from other documents as players.

One of the most distinctive features of the performance of *Believe as You List* in 1631, as revealed by the prompter's notes, is the intricacy of the doubling. Professor Sisson's careful analysis, though long, is worth quoting.

There can be little doubt that Demetrius is acted by Balls at l. 830, and not by 'Rowland,' who is clearly shown at l.

732 as a Carthaginian officer. This character is thus represented, at different stages, by no less than three actors, and Calistus by two. The confusion in later representations of 'officers' is almost insoluble. But it seems clear that after l. 2556 Baxter ceases to be the officer of Flaminius, whether under the name of Titus (as A. conceives him) or of Demetrius (as M. continues this character eliminated by A.), and becomes an officer of Marcellus at l. 2632. He receives orders from Marcellus as 'servant' l. 2711, is described by Antiochus as servant of Marcellus, l. 2712, and enters in this capacity at l. 2716. Flaminius is reasonably left servantless in this scene of his disgrace. One may fairly conjecture that the missing indication at l. 2861 would show Baxter (or possibly 'Rowland') as the Guard who hales him off to prison, in either case a pretty reversal of function on the part of the actor. These arrangements are all very significant of the want of individuality in such minor parts, even considerable speaking parts, as are those of Calistus and Demetrius. It may be observed that Pattrick and Rowland play Demetrius when he is to speak, and Balls when he has a silent part. Hobbes acts Calistus, ll. 829 sqq., a silent part, and continues it, now a speaking part, in the following scene, ll. 1185 sqq., when Baxter is required for the long-continued part of Titus, ll. 1257 sqq., into which Demetrius seems to be merged by A.

The principal parts are taken by actors who were well-known members of the King's company. Among others available for parts, to which A. gives no clue, were Richard Sharpe, Anthony Smith, John Shanke, George Vernon, James Horne, and for women's parts John Tomson, Alexander Gough, William Triggs, to judge from the casts given in Quartos of plays written by Massinger for the King's company, dated 1629 and 1630. Little is known of Baxter and Mago, and nothing of 'Rowland,' Balls, and 'Nick,' or the lute-player 'Harry Wilson.' . . . 'Rowland' is probably Rowland Dowle, who figures in the list of servants of the King's players granted privileges in 1636. 'Nick' was probably Nicholas Burt, who served under Shanke with the King's men . . . 'Harry Willson' is probably another member of the family of musicians, of whom Nicholas Wilson and the 'Iacke Wilson' mentioned in the quarto of *Much Ado about Nothing* (1600) are recorded. . . .

It must be remembered that the doubling indicated in this quotation still leaves more than thirteen roles unaccounted for. And the number thirteen still allows for only one Roman soldier when more were surely needed. Sisson names eight unassigned players known to have been in the company at the time *Believe as You List* was being prepared for production. Obviously the unassigned roles must have required even more doubling. There can be no doubt that the practice was characteristic of performances throughout the period 1590-1642. What William Ringler has shown so clearly was the custom in Shakespeare's plays of the 1590s,[9] the prompt manuscript of *Believe as You List* shows was still characteristic of the same company thirty to forty years later when it was much richer and thoroughly established as the dominant troupe in the city.

Queen Henrietta's Company

The casts so far considered—except the first for *The Inner Temple Masque*—all come from the same company, the troupe of greatest prestige and greatest wealth in the time. In the reign of Charles I, from which most of the extant casts derive, the second ranking company was that of Queen Henrietta Maria, a troupe which was formed in 1625 or 1626 and acted with success at Christopher Beeston's Phoenix theater in Drury Lane until the owner-manager ousted them during the long plague closing of 1636-37.

The six extant casts for this company were published between 1629 and 1655. Written first was Massinger's *Renegado*, printed in 1630 with a cast that dates from 1625 or 1626,

[9] "The Number of Actors in Shakespeare's Early Plays," in *The Seventeenth Century Stage*, ed. G. E. Bentley, Chicago and London, 1968, pp. 110-34.

though the play must have been written a year or two before for the predecessors of the Queen's men at the Phoenix, the Lady Elizabeth's men; James Shirley's *The Wedding*, acted probably in 1626 and printed in 1629; Thomas Heywood's *The Fair Maid of the West*, Part I, probably written before 1610 for another company but revived by Queen Henrietta's men about 1626 with their cast and published in 1631; *The Fair Maid of the West*, Part II, probably first acted about 1629 and published with Part I in 1631; Robert Davenport's *King John and Matilda*, acted some time between 1628 and 1634 but not issued from the press until 1655; and finally Thomas Nabbes's *Hannibal and Scipio*, acted in 1635 and published in 1637.

These casts of Queen Henrietta's men are similar to those for the King's company, and it is noteworthy that the majority of them come from plays first published in the same years as those plays of the King's company which were printed with casts.

The Renegado

The dramatis personae for Philip Massinger's comedy, *The Renegado*, assigned nine named roles to nine players, two of whom were apprentices, Edward Rogers and Theophilus Borne or Bird. Unfortunately the adult players named in these Queen's men's casts are much more difficult to classify as sharers or hired men than those for the King's. The original patent for the Queen's men (which probably named the sharers) has not yet been discovered, and the six extant records of livery allowances made to members of the company do not name the sharers but only a manager or a leading actor who is to receive livery for himself and twelve or thirteen "his fellowes." But the extant evidence suggests that the sharers in the *Renegado* cast were John Blaney, John Sumner, Michael Bowyer, William Allen, and William Robbins. Robbins was a popular comedian who is known to have played comic roles in at least five of this company's plays, *The Renegado*, *The Wedding*, *The Fair Maid of the West* I and II, and *The Changeling*.

The hired men in the cast were William Reynolds and William Shakerley. It is notable that the nine assigned roles are described, but the ten or twelve unassigned roles are not. Though Turk 1 and Turk 2 have a few lines to speak, Turk 3 and the sailors are walk-ons. Some could be doubled.

Dramatis Personæ	The Actors names.
ASAMBEG, *Viceroy* of Tunis.	Iohn Blanye.
MVSTAPHA, *Basha* of Aleppo.	Iohn Sumner.
VITELLI, *A Gentleman of* Venice *disguis'd.*	Michael Bowier.
FRANCISCO, *A Jesuite.*	William Reignalds.
ANTHONIO GRIMALDI, *the* Renegado.	William Allen.
CARAZIE, *an Eunuch.*	William Robins.
GAZET, *seruant to* Vitelli.	Edward Shakerley.
AGA.	
CAPIAGA.	
MASTER.	
BOTESWAINE.	
SAYLORS.	
IAILOR.	
3. TVRKES.	
DONVSA, *neece to* Amvrath.	Edward Rogers.
PAVLINA, *Sister to* Vitelli.	Theo. Bourne.
MANTO, *seruant to* Donusa.	

The Wedding

James Shirley's comedy, *The Wedding*, is more fully cast than Massinger's play; fourteen players are named as compared with nine for *The Renegado*. Seven of the named actors were sharers: Richard Perkins, Michael Bowyer, John Sumner, William Robbins, William Sherlock, Anthony Turner, and William Allen; three were hired men, William Wilbraham, John Young, and John Dobson, who is known as an actor from this record only. Somewhat exceptionally, all four boy actors for the female roles are named: Hugh Clark, John Page, Edward Rogers, and Timothy Reade. In this play the unassigned roles number less than half those for *The Renegado*. Only one of them, the Surgeon, has as many as twenty-five lines and though most of the others speak a few lines, their scenes are so few and so scattered that these unassigned roles could easily be doubled.

William Robbins has a comic role again, a rather substantial part of nearly 200 lines. Robbins also speaks the epilogue, and in character. This assignment and its nature suggest that he had already begun to achieve a reputation, that he could rely upon a favorable reception, and that he was able to cajole an audience effectively.

The Actors Names.

Sir *Iohn Belfare*.	*Richard Perkins*.
Beauford, a passionate louer of *Gratiana*.	*Michael Bowyer*.
Marwood, friend to *Beauford*,	*Iohn Sumpner*.
Rawbone, a thin Citizen.	*William Robins*.
Lodam, a fat Gentleman,	*William Sherlock*.
Iustice *Landby*.	*Anthony Turner*.
Captaine *Landby*.	*William Allin*.
Isaac, Sir *Iohns* man.	*William Wilbraham*.
Hauer, a young Gentleman, louer of mistresse *Iane*.	*Iohn Yong*.
Camelion, *Rawbones* man,	*Iohn Dobson*.
Physician Surgeon	
Keeper Seruants.	

Gratiana, Sir *Iohns* Daughter.	*Hugh Clarke*
Iane, Iustice *Landbyes* daughter,	*Iohn Page*.
Millicent, *Cardona's* daughter,	*Edward Rogers*
Cardona,	*Tymothy Read*.

The Fair Maid of the West, I and II

The casts for the two parts of Thomas Heywood's *The Fair Maid of the West, or A Girl Worth Gold* are somewhat confusing at first glance. Part I and Part II were published together in 1631, when Part I was more than twenty years old, though Part II, obviously a sequel, appears to have been first produced only a year or so before publication.[10] The fact that both title pages boast of a court performance suggests that they were acted together, a suggestion apparently confirmed by the fact that there is no epilogue for Part I and no prologue for Part II, but only a prologue addressed to the court before Part I and an epilogue obviously to the court for Part II.

The fairly full cast (ten actors) before Part I must be that for the revival with Part II, for the players named are the familiar members of Queen Henrietta's company, a troupe which was not organized until fifteen or more years after Part I first appeared, but which inherited a number of the plays written (as this one was) for the old Queen Anne's troupe. The five actors named in the dramatis personae for Part II must be those who had no recorded roles in Part I or whose parts were changed for Part II.

The cast for Part I names ten players for the twenty-seven named roles, in addition to "Petitioners, Mutes, personated." It is noteworthy that Christopher Goad is assigned two roles, one of the few instances in which doubling is specified in a printed cast.

Since Part I and Part II appear to have been acted together, it is probably best to consider them as one cast. Thus we have altogether ten actors named for Part I, Michael Bowyer, Richard Perkins, Hugh Clark, Christopher Goad, William Sherlock, William Robbins[on], Anthony F[T]urner, Robert Axell, William Allen, William Wilbraham; and for Part II five actors named, Theophilus Borne or Bird, Anthony Turner, John Sumner, Robert Axell, and Christopher Goad. But three of the five also appear in Part I though in different roles, so that we have a cast for the double feature of twelve Queen Henrietta's men. Seven of them were sharers at the time, Michael Bowyer, Richard Perkins, William Sherlock, William

---

[10] See Bentley, *The Jacobean and Caroline Stage*, IV, 568-71.

Robbins, Anthony Turner, William Allen, and John Sumner; three were hired men, Christopher Goad, Robert Axen (or Axell), and William Wilbraham; two—Theophilus Borne and Hugh Clark—were apprentices.

But in Part I there are about seventeen unassigned roles. In Part II there are about ten, but they ought not to be added together. In the first place, it is not absolutely certain whether the unassigned roles in Part II were simply played by the actors who had taken them in Part I or whether they were thought not worth recording. In the second place, all the extras available for Part I were also available for Part II if Part I and Part II were presented together.

There are two or three oddities about these two casts for *The Fair Maid of the West*. In the dramatis personae for Part I six of the ten named players are given the honorific "M^r": Bowyer, Perkins, Robbins[on], F[T]urner, Allen, and Wilbraham. In most of the various theatrical documents of the time this title, when it is used, designates a sharer; in such documents those actors not given the title were usualy hired men or boys. But here Wilbraham is called "M^r" though I can find no other evidence that he was ever a sharer in this company, while Sherlock is not so honored here though other documents show that he *was* a sharer. I can only suggest an error, though I am unhappy to question old documents to cover my own ignorance.

Another oddity is the assignment of "A kitching Maid" to Anthony Turner. Why should a sharer have played a female role? And since the character appears in only one scene and speaks only five lines, why should the actor be mentioned at all?

Another minor puzzle: since Wilbraham played Bashaw Alcade in Part I, why was the role given to Turner in Part II? In neither part does the role of Bashaw Alcade amount to much.

Again, the ordering of the characters is highly abnormal. The men's roles are not separated from the boys' roles in the usual manner, nor are the characters listed in roughly the order of importance. The lineation in the quarto dramatis personae is very odd. One wonders what sort of a manuscript the printer had, and who listed these roles.

The Fair Maid of the West
Part I

Two Sea Captains.
Mr. Caroll, *A Gentleman.*
Mr. Spencer. *By* Mr. Michael Bowyer.
Captain Goodlack, Spencers *friend*; by Mr. Rich. Perkins.
Two Vintners boyes.
Besse Bridges, *The fair Maid of the west*; by Hugh Clark.
Mr. Forest, *a Gentleman; by* Christoph. Goad.
Mr. Ruffman, *a swaggering Gentleman; by* William Shearlock.
Clem, *a drawer of wine under* Besse Bridges; *by* Mr. William Robinson.
Three Saylers. A Surgeon.

A kitching Maid; by Mr. Anthony Furner.
The Maior of Foy, *an Alderman, and a servant.*
A Spanish Cap. by C. Goad.
An English Merchant; by Rob. Axell.
Mullisheg, K. of Fesse, by Mr. Will. Allen.
Bashaw Alcade; by Mr. Wilbraham.
Bashaw Ioffer.
Two Spanish Captains.
A French Merchant.
An Italian Merchant.
A Chorus.
The Earl of Essex going to Cales: *the Maior of* Plimoth, *with Petitioners, Mutes, personated.*

The Fair Maid of the West
Part II
Dramatis Personae

Toota, *Queen of* Fesse, *and wife of* Mullisheg. By Theophilus Bourne.
Bashaw Ioffer.
Ruffman.
Clem, *the Clown.*
Mullisheg, *King of* Fesse
Bashaw Alcade. *By* Mr. Anthonie Turner.

A Guard.
A Negro.
A Chorus.
A Captain of the Bandetti.
The D. of Florence, *with followers.* By Mr. Joh. Somner.
The Duke of Mantua. By Rob. Axall.

Mr. Spencer.	*The D. of Farara. By* Chris-
Capt. Goodlacke.	toph. Goad.
Forset.	*An English Merchant.*
Besse Bridges.	*Two Florentine lords.*
A Porter of the kings gate.	Pedro Venture, *Generall at*
A Lieutenant of Moors.	*Sea for the D. of Florence.*

King John and Matilda

Robert Davenport's historical tragedy, *King John and Matilda*, can be dated only not earlier than about 1628, since Hugh Clark had had a boy's role in 1626, and since the list of "the Actors that first Acted it on the Stage" includes the names of Christopher Goad and John Young who are known to have been no longer members of Queen Henrietta's company in July 1634, not later than early 1634. I think, however, it belongs late in that six-year period, since Hugh Clark who played the large and demanding role of Bess Bridges in *A Fair Maid of the West* in 1626 must have had time to become not only an adult but a sharer in the company.

This quarto has certain affinities with the handsome folio edition of John Fletcher's *The Wild Goose Chase* published three years earlier in 1652 with a cast of King's men. As the Fletcher comedy was published for the "private Benefit" of the actors John Lowin and Joseph Taylor, this one was "Printed for *Andrew Pennycuicke.*" As Lowin and Taylor signed the dedication of *The Wild Goose Chase*, so Pennycuicke signed the epistle to the Earl of Lindsey in *King John and Matilda* in which he says "*my selfe being the last that that* [sic] *acted Matilda in it.*" Moreover, the cast printed for the Davenport play singles out for praise Richard Perkins and William Sherlock as that for *The Wild Goose Chase* had singled out Joseph Taylor, Thomas Pollard, and John Lowin.

The cast itself is somewhat odd and perhaps not entirely trustworthy. No apprentices are named for the female roles of Queen Isabel, Matilda, Ladies of honor, and Lady Abbess. All ten players named are given the title "M." generally reserved for sharers. But it is unusual for sharers to have taken all the leading roles with none carried by hired men. Furthermore, if Robert Axen ["Iackson"], Christopher Goad, and John Young were ever sharers in Queen Henrietta's company this is the only evidence of it. Both Goad and Young were members of a lesser company by July 1634. Pennycuicke does not appear to have been infallibly honest,[11] and I suspect that Axen, Goad, and Young were really hired men when they played in *King John and Matilda*.

"Other Lords and Gentlemen, Attendants on the *King*" would include three characters named in the text but not in the cast, Richmond, Winchester and Mowbray, who have ten to sixty-five lines each, and a child called merely "Boy" in the text who has about fifty lines. All in all the cast Pennycuicke presents with his edition seems rather careless and one wonders how much to rely upon it.

There is a big scene in the fifth act which would seem to require several extra "Barrons" and four or six "Virgins" to carry Matilda's hearse. This act also has "The Song in Parts" which would require at least two singers in addition to musicians for the "Hoboyes" and "Flutes" who play for the procession.

The Names of the Persons in the Play,
And of the Actors that first Acted it on the
Stage, and often before their *Majesties*.

King *John*.	M. *Bowyer*.
Fitzwater,	M. *Perkins*, ⎰ Whose action gave Grace to the Play.
Old Lord *Bruce*,	M. *Turner*.
Young *Bruce*,	M. *Sumner*.
Chester,	M. *Iackson*.
Oxford,	M. *Goat*.
Leister.	M. *Young*.
Hubert,	M. *Clarke*.
Pandolph,	M. *Allen*.

[11] See ibid., ΙΙ, 524-25, and Rudolph Kirk, ed., *Philip Massinger's The City Madam*, Princeton, 1934, pp. 9-15.

Brand,   M. *Shirelock*, who performed
excellently well.

Other Lords and
  Gentlemen, At-
  tendants on the
King.

           Queen *Isabel.*
           Matilda.
           Ladies of honour.
           Lady *Abbesse.*

Hannibal and Scipio

The last Queen Henrietta's men's cast which has been pre-
served in a quarto is that for Thomas Nabbes's historical tragedy, *Hannibal and Scipio*, "Acted in the yeare 1635. by the
Queenes Majesties Servants, at their Private house in *Drury
Lane*" according to the 1637 title page. The cast names seven
sharers, William Sherlock, John Sumner, William Allen, Hugh
Clark, Anthony Turner, Michael Bowyer, and Richard Per-
kins; four hired men, George Stutville, Robert Axen, John
Page, and Theophilus Bird; and one apprentice, Ezekiel Fenn.
Four of the players named in the cast, two sharers and two
hired men, are given double roles: Sherlock played Maharball
and Prusias, Clark played Nuntius and Syphax, Stutfield played
Soldier and Bostar, and Axen played Bomicar and Gisgon.
The amount of doubling is not unusual, but it is uncommon
for so much to be indicated in the cast of principal players.
Another oddity is the single boy named, Ezekiel Fenn, who
played Sophonisba.

    This play uses a large number of characters, notably four
female roles plus "Ladies" in addition to Ezekiel Fenn's role
of Sophonisba. There are four adult roles not in the cast plus
Soldiers and "A full Senate." Obviously *Hannibal and Scipio*
required a good deal of doubling in addition to the eight roles
listed as doubled in the cast. The Soldiers, Attendants, and
the Senators do not speak; evidently they are the "Mutes"

who need not have been players at all. As in *King John and Matilda*, there is vocal music, a song with a chorus in Act I, Act II, and Act IV. Apparently Queen Henrietta's men could rely on their musicians in 1635.

The speaking persons.

Maharball.	By *William Shurlock.*
Himulco.	By *John Sumner.*
Souldier.	By *George Slutfield.*
A Lady.	
Hannibal	By *William Allen.*
2. other Ladies.	
Nuntius.	By *Hugh Clerke.*
Bomilcar.	By *Robert Axen.*
Syphax.	By *Hugh Clerke.*
Piston.	By *Anthony Turner.*
Crates.	
Messenger.	
Scipio.	By *Michael Bowyer.*
Lelius.	By *Iohn Page.*
Sophonisba.	By *Ezekiel Fenn.*
Massanissa	By *Theophilus Bird.*
Hanno.	By *Richard Perkins.*
Gisgon.	By *Robert Axen.*
Bostar.	By *George Stutfield.*
Lucius.	
A young Lady.	
Prusias.	By *William Shurlock.*

Mutes.

Ladies.   Souldiers.
Attendants.   Senators.

PRINCE CHARLES'S (II) COMPANY

Holland's Leaguer

This troupe was much less important than the King's company or Queen Henrietta's men and much less is known of it;

for most of its members our information is less secure than for their more established competitors. Only one of their casts is known, that for the performance of Shakerley Marmion's *Holland's Leaguer* produced at the Salisbury Court theater in December 1631 shortly after the company had been licensed.

Probably the most unusual feature of this cast is the large number of apprentices. One wonders if some of the boys had been held over from the previous tenants of the Salisbury Court theater (the speaker of the prologue says that Prince Charles's company was "New planted in this soile"). The previous occupants of the theater had been the King's Revels company, a kind of training school to provide apprentices for the King's company. A lawsuit in the Court of Requests in 1632 carries the statement that the King's Revels was organized,

> . . . to train and bring up certain boys in the quality of playing not only with intent to be a supply of able actors to his Majesty's servants of the Black Friars when there should be occasion as by the said bill of complaint is suggested but the solace of his Royal Majesty when his Majesty should please to see them and also for the recreation of his Majesty's loving subjects.

At one time this King's Revels troupe consisted of at least fourteen boy actors. Possibly some of them had been left at the Salisbury Court theater when Prince Charles's (II) company moved in.[12]

Dramatis Personae

Philautus, a Lord inamored of himselfe.	William Browne.
Ardelio, his parasite.	Ellis Worth.
Trimalchio, a humorous gallant.	Andrew Keyne.
Agurtes, an Impostor.	Mathew Smith.
Autolicus, his disciple.	Iames Sneller.
Capritio, a young Novice.	Henry Gradwell.
Miscellanio, his Tutor.	Thomas Bond.

[12] See the *Huntington Library Quarterly* 40 (1977), 129-49.

Snarle, } *friends to Philautus* *Fidelio.* }	Richard Fowler. Edward May.
Ieffery, tenant to Philautus	Robert Huyt.

Triphœna, wife to Philautus.	Robert Stratford.
Faustina, sister to Philautus.	Richard Godwin.
Millecent, daughter to Agurtes.	Iohn Wright.
Margery her maid.	Richard Fouch.
Quartilla, Gentlewoman to Tripœna.	Arthur Savill.
Bawd.	Samuell Mannery.
2 Whores. Pander. Officers.	

The cast for Marmion's play is fuller than most, sixteen players. The first eight, Browne, Worth, Keyne, Smith, Sneller, Gradwell, Bond, Fowler, were presumably sharers at this time, since all appeared in the list of Prince's players made Grooms of the Chamber five months later. The next two in the list, Edward May and Robert "Huyt," were probably hired men, since they do not appear in the list of Grooms. The last six players were assigned female roles and were presumably apprentices, though none had appeared in theatrical records before, and only Wright and Mannery later. The two whores for whom no actors are named, could be doubled by two of the boys listed, as could "Boy," who appears in I, 5.

Andrew Keyne (Cane) who had a reputation as a comedian and who was one of the leaders of the troupe has a rather long comic role, nearly 400 lines.

THE KING'S REVELS COMPANY

Another company with a single certain London cast is the one called the King's Revels, or sometimes the Children of the Revels. It is now known that the company was established in 1629 to train boy players for the premier royal troupe, King Charles's company, and that in 1630 there were at least fourteen boys attached to the Children of the Revels.[13] But the

---

[13] See ibid.

character of the company obviously changed, for in July 1634, when they visited Oxford, there were at least eleven adults in the organization.[14] It is to this later period that *The Tragedy of Messallina* must belong.

The Tragedy of Messallina, The Roman Empress

The *Messallina* cast, published in the quarto of 1640, presumably the one for the first performance of the play, must date after 18 July 1634, when William Cartwright, Sr., was a member of another company, and before 12 May 1636, when all theaters were closed by plague to remain so about eighteen months; besides, the boy performer of the role of Messallina had a son christened in November 1637.[15]

Since the extant records of this company are scanty, one cannot be too sure about the status of the individual members of the cast, but it would appear that the first four named were sharers, William Cartwright, Sr., Christopher Goad, John Robinson, and Samuel Thompson. The fifth and sixth men in the cast, Richard Johnson and William Hall, were hired men, and Barrett, Jordan, and Morris were apprentices.

Even with extensive doubling, however, it would seem next to impossible for a second-rate company like the King's Revels to stage this play in its printed form. Besides the roles cast, there are over thirty other characters (most of whom speak), dances, processions, and spectacles, including Messallina and Silius appearing aloft in a cloud and then descending as in a masque. Surely the play must have been cut for this company. Indeed, after the duet by two spirits near the end of the fifth act, appears this comment in a stage direction: "*After this song (which was left out of the Play in regard there was none could sing in Parts). . . .*" Since this play is such an amateur composition obviously brought to the press by the author, it is not unlikely that other parts of the play were cut for the performance.

---

[14] See Bentley, *The Jacobean and Caroline Stage*, II, 688-89.
[15] See ibid., V, 1002-1004 and II, 359.

The Actors Names.

Claudius Emperour—*Will. Cartwright Sen.*
Silius chiefe Favorite
 to the Empresse.   *Christopher Goad.*
Saufellus chiefe of Counsell
 to *Silius* and *Messallina*   *Iohn Robinson*
Valens)
Proculus) Of the same faction and favorites.
Menester an actor and Favorite)
 compel'd by the Empresse.) *Sam. Tomson.*
Montanus a Knight in *Rome*)
 defence vertuously inclined.) *Rich. Iohnson.*
Mela Seneca's Brother—*Will. Hall.*
Virgilianus and)
Calphurnianus) Senators of *Messallinas* Faction.
Sulpitius of the same Faction.
Narcissus)
Pollas) Minnions to the Emperour of his faction.
Calistus)
Evodius a Souldier.

Messallina Empresse—*Iohn Barret.*
Lepida mother to *Messallina*—*Tho. Iordan.*
Sylana wife to *Silius*—*Mathias Morris.*
Vibidia matron of the Vestalls.
Calphurnia a Curtizan.
Hem and *Stitch*, two Panders.
Three murdered *Roman* Dames.
Manutius and *Folio*, Servants to *Lepida.*
Three Spirits.
Two severall Antimasques of Spirits and Bachinalls.

Money Is an Ass

Another play with which the King's Revels company seems to have been associated, though the evidence is incomplete, is Thomas Jordan's *Money Is an Ass.* The first 1668 issue calls the piece "A Comedy, As it hath been Acted with good Applause." But no name of either company or theater is to be found on the title page.

Most of what is known of this comedy comes from the front matter of the two issues of the play, the second of which is also dated 1668, but is entitled *Wealth Outwitted, or Money Is an Ass*.

In the second issue is Jordan's dedicatory epistle with the lines:

> This Play was writ by *Me* & pleas'd the Stage,
> When I was not full fifteen Years of Age.

The prologue "Spoken by Night" makes assertions which seem to show that all the players were boys:

> *Tis new, Ime sure, nere Acted, There's none know it*
> *We never had more Tutor then the Poet.*
> *Since it is thus, Let us harsh censures 'scape.*
> *Had every Actor been some others Ape,*
> *Seen his part Plaid before him, you might say,*
> *We had been Children, not to Act the Play;*
> ....
> *We are but Eight in Number, therefore he,*
> *That drew this piece, being confin'd not free*
> *Could not so well declare himself as when*
> *He shall confine, his Persons to his Pen.*
> *Accept of this, next time, we shall prepare*
> *To feast your Senses with more curious fare.*

All of this is somewhat confusing, especially since Jordan is known to have been a rather slippery character. Of the eight boys named in the cast two are otherwise unknown, but six of them are included in a list of players copied into the town records at Norwich on 10 March 1634/35, and a good many of these Norwich players appear elsewhere in connection with the King's Revels company. I can only conjecture that while Jordan was a boy actor in the King's Revels company "he wrote a play which the adult actors allowed the boys to present entirely on their own, probably under private auspices, since the performance took place at night."[16]

Though Jordan's play is poor stuff, he showed far greater dramatic economy than did Nathanael Richards in *Messallina*. Jordan assigned one character to each player and had to rely on extras for only Silver and Hammerhead and their wives. These characters appear only in Act IV, scene 3; they have only six or seven lines among them, and they never appear again. But none of the eight named actors could have played the roles since all eight appear in this scene. The four tiny roles would have been no strain for the most inexperienced boy actors.

The Actors Names.

Captain Penniless.	*Tho. Jordain.*
Mr. Featherbrain.	*Wal. Williams.*
Clutch.	*Tho. Loveday.*
Money.	*Tho. Lovel.*
Credit.	*Nich. Lowe.*
Callumney.	*Tho. Sandes.*
Felixina.	*Amb. Matchit.*
Feminia.	*Wil. Cherrington.*

The Wasp, or Subject's Precedent

A third play which has been associated, with some show of plausibility, with the King's Revels Company is a manuscript of the otherwise unknown piece, *The Wasp*. Though the manuscript bears no ascription to company or theater, it is a prompt manuscript with a few inserted names which suggest the King's Revels troupe.

The existence of this manuscript play in the Alnwick Castle collection had been known to several scholars, but its details were not generally available until the appearance in 1976 of the edition of the late Professor J. W. Lever for the Malone Society. Besides the usual prompt manuscript modifications,

[16] See ibid., IV, 678-81 and 685-87.

additional stage directions, property warnings, and notes, the names of six players appear: "Iorden, Barot, Morris, Ellis, Ambros, Noble." Lever identifies all but the last (who does not appear elsewhere): Thomas Jordan, John Barrett, Mathias Morris, Ellis Bedowe, and Ambrose Matchit. The first three had taken women's roles in the King's Revels' performance of Richards' *Messallina*; Bedowe and Matchit are also associated with the King's Revels company. In *The Wasp* manuscript all six actors named have minor adult roles, except "Ambros," who as the young son of Archibald ("filius") has fifty-five or sixty lines.

The King's Revels company, in which all the named players except "Noble" had appeared, was founded in 1629 as a group to train boy actors for the King's company.[17] The troupe is not well known, and the manuscript of *The Wasp* adds little to our knowledge of its management and casting practices. Apparently five of the six actors named were hired men, one was a boy, and none were sharers.

CASTS DUBIOUS OR UNCERTAIN

There are a certain number of casts that do not have the authenticity of those printed above, but that may have some value for occasional consultation. Most of them are manuscript additions or annotations of early editions; the difficulty is that there is usually no evidence as to who wrote the annotations. Was it one of the players? Was it a spectator who had witnessed an early performance? Was it someone drawing on his memories of what his father or grandfather had told him? Was it a guesser? Was it a nineteenth- or twentieth-century reader or scholar exhibiting his ingenuity? Or was it a well-informed forger, like Collier? Or even James Orchard Halliwell-Phillipps who, though certainly a vandal and apparently a thief, has not, I think, been demonstrated a forger?

---

[17] See "The Salisbury Court Theatre and Its Boy Players," pp. 129-49.

Philaster, or Love Lies a Bleeding

The prolific nineteenth-century scholar, James Orchard Halliwell-Phillipps, developed a crude and destructive predecessor of the useful photocopying machine. He kept his notes by cutting pages from sixteenth- and seventeenth-century books and manuscripts and pasting them into his properly classified scrapbooks, even going so far, in one instance I remember, as to cut out the Induction to *Bartholomew Fair* from four different copies of the Jonson folio in order to have it handily classified under four heads in four different scrapbooks.

In one of these scrapbooks, of which there are more than one hundred in the Folger Shakespeare Library, there is pasted signature A3 of the 1634 quarto of Beaumont and Fletcher's *Philaster*. This popular play, first acted by the King's men about 1609 but kept in active repertory by the company for over thirty years, was printed in 1620, 1622, 1628, 1634, 1639, 1652, [1663], 1679, and 1687. It was from a copy of the fourth quarto that Halliwell-Phillipps clipped for his scrapbook the page in which the players' names have been added in manuscript.

This cast as transcribed by David George in his article in *Theatre Notebook*[18] is as follows:

The King.	Benfield
PHILASTER, heire to the Crowne.	Ey Clarke
PHARAMOND, Prince of Spaine.	Pollard
DION, a Lord.	Lowin
CLEREMONT, ⎱	Pen
	Noble Gentlemen his Associates.
THRASALINE, ⎰	Bird
ARETHVSA, the Kings daughter.	Wat

[18] "Early Cast Lists for two Beaumont and Fletcher Plays," *Theatre Notebook* 28 (1974), 9.

GALLATEA, a wise mod-   White
est Lady attending
the Princesse.
MEGRA, A Lascivious   Thomas
Lady.
and old Wanton Lady,
or croane.
Another Lady attending
the Princesse.
EVPHRASIA, Daughter of   Charles
Dion but disguised
like a Page called *Bel-*
lario.
An old Captaine.   Patrick
Fiue Citizens:
A Countrey fellow.   Patricke
Two Woodmen.
The Kings Guard and
Traine.

Expanding the names, one finds that the King is asserted
to have been played by Robert Benfield, Philaster by Hugh
Clark, Pharamond by Thomas Pollard, Dion by John Lowin,
Claremont by William Penn, and Thrasaline by Theophilus
Bird. All six of these players are known to have been sharers
in the King's company 1640-1642. The parts of an old Captaine and a Countrey Fellow are said to have been doubled
by William Patrick known to have been a hired man in the
company at least as late as January 1636/37. The four roles
assigned to apprentices were Arethusa to Walter Clun, and
the page called Bellario to Charles Hart, both of whom are
said by Wright to have been "bred up Boys at the *Blackfriars*;
and Acted Women's Parts," though there is no extant contemporary evidence of their attachment to the King's company.
The other two boys are less certain. Gallatea is said to have
been played by White [?] and Megra by Thomas, but no apprentices with such names can be assigned to King Charles's
company at present. Several boy players of the period are

possibilities, but none can be associated with the company. This fact is not necessarily a contradiction of the authenticity of this cast, for certainly the King's men had more apprentice actors than we can name now.

In sum, this cast seems a likely one for a performance of *Philaster* by the King's company in 1641, 1642, or 1643, but its authenticity cannot be assumed.

The Maid's Tragedy

This exceedingly popular play of Beaumont and Fletcher's was printed at least ten times in the seventeenth century, though the first edition did not appear until eight years or more after the first performance. In the Folger Shakespeare Library is a copy of the quarto of 1630 (the third) in which there appears to have been at some time a manuscript cast. On the verso of the title page in this edition appears a dramatis personae under the head SPEAKERS. Unfortunately the Folger copy has been very heavily cropped at some time, so that the players' names which had been written in front of, not behind, the characters' names, have been mostly trimmed away. In an article in *Theatre Notebook*[19] David George has transcribed the dramatis personae with what remains of the casting and has expanded these remains to assign players of the King's company in about 1630 to certain roles.

[Benfiel]d	King
[Tay]lor	Amintor
[Grev]ill	Diphilus
S[hank]	Diagoras
E[dward] C[ollins]	Antiphila
S[harp]	Night

The evidence for these identifications seems to me much too slight to give them any standing. One would have to assume an annotator who used a most eccentric system of abbrevia-

[19] David George, "Pre-1642 Cast-Lists and a New One for 'The Maid's Tragedy,'" *Theatre Notebook* 31 (1977), 22-27.

tions; too many of his abbreviated names, seven of thirteen, even Mr. George cannot assign to any known member of King Charles's company; the fact that the names appear in the 1630 quarto is no evidence for any particular date; they might have been intended for a performance of 1650 or 1680. Furthermore we have no evidence that the original annotations were intended for members of the King's company at all. They could have been made for some amateur performance in the country, like those of Mildmay Fane at Apthorpe, or those which Arthur Wilson says took place with some regularity at Draiton and Chartley.[20]

All things considered, this copy of *The Maid's Tragedy* at the Folger has not really yielded any information about the casting of their plays by the King's company.

The Shoemakers' Holiday

In *The Shakespeare Society's Papers* is an article signed "Dramaticus" and dated 7th November 1848, which gives an alleged cast of about 1600 for Dekker's play.[21]

"Dramaticus" begins by asserting that Robert Wilson collaborated with Dekker in the play, and continues:

My reason for stating that Robert Wilson, as well as Thomas Dekker, was engaged upon "The Shoemakers' Holiday" is, that a friend of mine, who really does not know the value of it, but who, at the same time, is unwilling to part with it, has a copy (in a tattered condition, I am sorry to say) with the names of the two dramatists at the end of the preliminary address. The names are not printed, but they have been added in manuscript in a hand-writing coeval, I think, with the date of publication, but, at all events, very little posterior to it; moreover, (and this is quite as curious, though, perhaps, not quite as important) with the names of the actors against all the principal parts, as they were sus-

[20] See Bentley, *The Jacobean and Caroline Stage*, ii, 292-99 and v, 1267-69.
[21] *Shakespeare Society Papers* 40, (1849), 110-22.

tained when the comedy was first brought out. These are not made to precede the play in a regular list of the *dramatis personae*, as has been usual since the Restoration, but they are inserted in the margin as the piece proceeds, and as the different performers enter. . . . I have extracted the names of the characters, and I have placed after them, in the intelligible fashion of a modern play-bill, the names of the different actors, showing precisely the parts they filled.

King of England	Jones.
Nobleman, his attendant	H. Jeffes.
Earl of Lincoln	Rowley.
Lord Mayor of London	Shawe.
Rowland Lacy	Massy.
Simon Eyre, Shoemaker	Dowton.
Hodge, his foreman	Singer
Firke, his man	Wilson
Ralph, a soldier	Jewby.
Hammond, a city merchant	Towne.
Warner, his friend	Flower.
Scott, friend to the Lord Mayor	Price.
Askew, friend to Lacy	A. Jeffes.
Dodger, the Earl of Lincoln's man	Jones.
Lovell, an officer	Day.
Dame Eyre	Birde.
Jane, wife to Ralphe	H. Jeffes.
Rose, daughter to the Lord mayor	Dowton's boy, Ned.
Sibill, servant to Rose	Alleine.

To various historians and bibliographers (Fleay, Chambers, Greg), these additions in "a hand-writing coeval, I think, with the date of publication" have smelled fishy and there are several touches in the style of John Payne Collier, the most adept literary forger of his time and an active member of the Shakespeare Society. Sure enough, about a century later the copy "in a tattered condition" turned up in the Houghton Library at Harvard. On the title page is the autograph of J. Payne

Collier and inserted into the volume is a sheet of paper in Collier's own hand with the list of actors, though in a different order from the one he used in his article.[22] Collier knew a great deal about Elizabethan plays and stage history, and the cast he invented is not an impossible one. Unfortunately its only authority is Collier's active and scheming imagination.

Volpone and The Alchemist

Other manuscript casts in printed plays have been reported by James A. Riddell.[23] In a copy of the Jonson Folio of 1616, once owned by Robert Browning, there are manuscript assignments in what appears to be a seventeenth-century hand of nine roles in *Volpone*, two in *The Silent Woman*, nine in *The Alchemist*. The two assigned in *The Silent Woman* are Sir Amorous to Hugh Attawell and Morose to Will. Barksted. These are too few to mean much in a study of casting.

In *Volpone* and *The Alchemist* the majority of the leading roles are assigned to the principal players of the King's company as follows:

	Volpone		*The Alchemist*
Volpone	*Richard Burbadge*	Subtle	*Richard Burbadge*
Mosca	*Henry Condell*	Face	*Nat: Feild*
Voltore	*Nath: Feild*	Dol. Common	*Richard Birch*
Corbaccio	*John Hemings*	Dapper	*John Vnderwood*
Corvino	*Nich: Tooly*	Drugger	
Avocatori		Love-Wit	*Bentley*
Notario		Epicure Mammon	*John Lowin*

---

[22] Fredson Bowers, "Thomas Dekker, Robert Wilson, and *The Shoemaker's Holiday*," *Modern Language Notes* 64 (1949), 517-19.

[23] "Some Actors in Ben Jonson's Plays," *Shakespeare Studies* 5 (1969), 285-98.

Nano		Surley	*Hen: Condell*
Castrone		Tribulation	
Grege		Ananias	*Nich: Tooly*
Politique- Would-Bee	*John Lowin*	Kastrill	*Will: Eglestone*
Peregrine	*Goffe*	Da. Pliant	
Bonario	*John Vnderwood*	Neighbours.	
Fine Madame Would-bee	*Richard Birch*	Officers.	
Celia		Mutes.	
Commandadori			
Mercatori			
Androgyno			
Servitore			
Women			

In the light of our knowledge of the personnel of the Shakespearean company these castings for *Volpone* and *The Alchemist* are all plausible except for "Bently" in the role of Love-Wit. As Dr. Riddell points out, no actor named Bently is known in the reign of James I or Charles I. A member of Queen Elizabeth's company, John Bentley, seems to have been fairly well known in the early 1580s, but he died in 1585.[24] Riddell conjectures that "Bently" is a lapse for "Benfield" who appears in a number of casts of the company and had become a sharer by 1619. The role of Love-Wit is not unlike others Benfield assumed later but his participation in this performance can be only a guess.

If the two casts are genuine and accurate except for the lapse of *"Bently"* they must date before 16 March 1618/19 when Richard Burbage was buried and after 1615 or 1616 when Nathan Field joined the company. In this period of about three years Burbage, Condell, Field, Heminges, Tooley, Lowin, Goffe (Robert) and Underwood of the *Volpone* cast

[24] See Edwin Nungezer, *A Dictionary of Actors and of Other Persons Associated with the Public Representation of Plays in England before 1642*, New Haven, 1929, pp. 44-45.

were sharers in the company. The player *"Richard Birch,"* an apprentice, presumably, who took the female roles of Doll Common and "Fine Madam Would-bee" is found in no other record of this or of any other company. A *George* Birch was a member of the company in the 1620s but he does not seem likely to have been an apprentice 1616-1619 since he was married to Richard Cowley's daughter in January 1618/19. Conceivably a young adult could have played the hoyden Doll or the virago Madam Would-bee, but the name "Richard" is used twice. It seems to me more likely that the roles in this performance of *Volpone* were taken by eight sharers and an hitherto unknown boy, Richard Birch, for there had to be a good many more boy actors than we know by name now.

The cast for *The Alchemist* is very similar to the one for *Volpone*: eight sharers and a boy. John Heminges and Robert Goffe are omitted; *"Bently"* and William Eccleston are added. If *"Bently"* was meant for Benfield, we again have eight sharers and a boy. It is notable that no hired men are in either cast.[25]

It seems a plausible conclusion that these two casts derive from revivals of the two Jonson plays by their owner, the King's company, some time between 1615 and January 1618/19. The fact that the book in which the notes are written was not published until 1616 does not necessarily mean that the performance noted took place after that date; the writer might simply have remembered a performance he had seen a year or so before he wrote.

But there is no evidence of the identity or trustworthiness of the writer.

Amateur Casts

A number of casts for the productions of plays by amateurs are extant for the period 1590-1642, some in print and some

[25] See Bentley, *The Jacobean and Caroline Stage*, II, under each player's name.

in manuscript. Obviously they are of no value for an understanding of the profession of player in the time. Most of them come from productions at the colleges of Oxford or Cambridge; one or two from schools; and a few from amateur performances at great houses or even at court.

Index

INDEX

Chatsworth, 185, 188
charters, *see* patents
Chelmsford, 202, 203
Cherrington, William, 285
Chester, 192
Chettle, Henry, *see* Drayton, Michael
churches as playhouses, 198, 241
churchwardens, 11
City Gallant, The, see Cooke, John
Clark, Hugh, 229, 238, 271, 272, 273, 274, 275, 276, 277, 278, 279, 287, 288
Clarke, Roger, 109, 112
Clavell, John, *The Soddered Citizen,* 69, 124, 128, 219, 220, 223, 258, 260-62, 263
Clifford, Lord, 56
Clink, 7
Clun, Walter, 122, 287, 288
coaching, 61-62, 126, 167, 284
Cockpit theater, 8, 17, 23, 123, 142, 160, 170, 171, 209
Cohn, A., *Shakespeare in Germany in the Sixteenth and Seventeenth Centuries,* London, 1865, 177-78n
Coldeway, J. C., 117n, 149n
Collier, John Payne, 286, 291-92; ed., *The Alleyn Papers,* London, 1843, 5n; *Memoirs of the Principal Actors in the Plays of Shakespeare,* London, 1846, 5n, 19n, 26n, 130n
Collins, Edward, 289
Collins, Jeffrey, 74
comedians, 60, 79, 102, 223-24, 233, 242, 257, 272, 281
Comedy of Errors, The, see Shakespeare, William
commendatory verses, 7, 248, 250, 254
Condell, Elizabeth, 94
Condell, Henry, 5, 11, 15, 19, 25, 27n, 28, 42n, 93, 94, 98, 118-19n,

121, 123, 129, 130, 131, 136, 154, 156, 176, 208, 210, 214, 215, 217, 221, 236, 249, 250, 292, 293
contracts, 7
Cook, David, and F. P. Wilson, 151n
Cooke, Abell, 120
Cooke, Alexander, 19, 26, 69, 130, 216
Cooke, John, *The City Gallant,* 164
correspondence, 7
Coryat, Thomas, 114, 114n
Costine, John, 186
costumes, 5, 20, 29, 30, 32, 43-44, 49, 50, 51, 60, 88-93, 101, 106, 116, 123, 126, 129, 130, 133n, 157, 158, 159, 160, 172, 181, 203, 236, 238, 240
Court Beggar, The, see Brome, Richard
court fool, 224
Court of Requests, xiii, 16, 29, 41, 43, 45, 55-56, 81, 90, 98, 124, 127, 140, 153, 157, 171, 172, 226, 280
court performances, 9, 35, 53, 55, 56, 62, 150, 151, 161, 162, 164, 165, 167, 172, 208, 235, 238, 255, 273
Coventry, 117, 141-42, 187
Cowley, Richard, 19, 151, 230, 294
Crane, Ralph, 11, 86-87, 235, 258; *Works of Mercy,* 11, 87
Crosfield, Thomas, 23, 65, 90-91, 161, 167, 170, 188, 197. *See also* Boas, Fredrick S.
Cross Keys theater, 7, 18, 79, 198
Cumber, John, 28, 156, 157
Cunningham, Peter, 17n, 61n, 173, 173n, 174, 175
Curtain theater, 7, 15, 22, 230
Cutts, John P., 76n
Cymbeline, see Shakespeare, William
Cynthia's Revels, see Jonson, Ben

301

Library of Congress Cataloging in Publication Data

Bentley, Gerald Eades, 1901-
The profession of player in Shakespeare's time, 1590-1642.

Includes bibliographical references and index.
1. Theater—England—History. 2. Actors—England. I. Title.
PN2589.B46   1984   792'.028'0942   83-43059
ISBN 0-691-06596-9

Gerald Eades Bentley is Murray Professor of English Emeritus
at Princeton University and author of the seven-volume
Jacobean and Caroline Stage (Clarendon Press), *Shakespeare
and Jonson* (Chicago), and other works.